OTHER A T
THE SCARE

MW00685722

1. *The A to Z of Buddhism* by Charles S. Prebish, 2001. *Out of Print. See No. 124.*
2. *The A to Z of Catholicism* by William J. Collinge, 2001.
3. *The A to Z of Hinduism* by Bruce M. Sullivan, 2001.
4. *The A to Z of Islam* by Ludwig W. Adamec, 2002. *Out of Print. See No. 123.*
5. *The A to Z of Slavery and Abolition* by Martin A. Klein, 2002.
6. *Terrorism: Assassins to Zealots* by Sean Kendall Anderson and Stephen Sloan, 2003.
7. *The A to Z of the Korean War* by Paul M. Edwards, 2005.
8. *The A to Z of the Cold War* by Joseph Smith and Simon Davis, 2005.
9. *The A to Z of the Vietnam War* by Edwin E. Moise, 2005.
10. *The A to Z of Science Fiction Literature* by Brian Stableford, 2005.
11. *The A to Z of the Holocaust* by Jack R. Fischel, 2005.
12. *The A to Z of Washington, D.C.* by Robert Benedetto, Jane Donovan, and Kathleen DuVall, 2005.
13. *The A to Z of Taoism* by Julian F. Pas, 2006.
14. *The A to Z of the Renaissance* by Charles G. Nauert, 2006.
15. *The A to Z of Shinto* by Stuart D. B. Picken, 2006.
16. *The A to Z of Byzantium* by John H. Rosser, 2006.
17. *The A to Z of the Civil War* by Terry L. Jones, 2006.
18. *The A to Z of the Friends (Quakers)* by Margery Post Abbott, Mary Ellen Chijioke, Pink Dandelion, and John William Oliver Jr., 2006.
19. *The A to Z of Feminism* by Janet K. Boles and Diane Long Hoeveler, 2006.
20. *The A to Z of New Religious Movements* by George D. Chryssides, 2006.
21. *The A to Z of Multinational Peacekeeping* by Terry M. Mays, 2006.
22. *The A to Z of Lutheranism* by Günther Gassmann with Duane H. Larson and Mark W. Oldenburg, 2007.
23. *The A to Z of the French Revolution* by Paul R. Hanson, 2007.
24. *The A to Z of the Persian Gulf War 1990–1991* by Clayton R. Newell, 2007.
25. *The A to Z of Revolutionary America* by Terry M. Mays, 2007.
26. *The A to Z of the Olympic Movement* by Bill Mallon with Ian Buchanan, 2007.
27. *The A to Z of the Discovery and Exploration of Australia* by Alan Day, 2009.
28. *The A to Z of the United Nations* by Jacques Fomerand, 2009.
29. *The A to Z of the "Dirty Wars"* by David Kohut, Olga Vilella, and Beatrice Julian, 2009.
30. *The A to Z of the Vikings* by Katherine Holman, 2009.
31. *The A to Z from the Great War to the Great Depression* by Neil A. Wynn, 2009.
32. *The A to Z of the Crusades* by Corliss K. Slack, 2009.
33. *The A to Z of New Age Movements* by Michael York, 2009.
34. *The A to Z of Unitarian Universalism* by Mark W. Harris, 2009.
35. *The A to Z of the Kurds* by Michael M. Gunter, 2009.
36. *The A to Z of Utopianism* by James M. Morris and Andrea L. Kross, 2009.
37. *The A to Z of the Civil War and Reconstruction* by William L. Richter, 2009.

224. *The A to Z of Contemporary Germany* by Derek Lewis with Ulrike Zitzlsperger, 2010.
225. *The A to Z of the Contemporary United Kingdom* by Kenneth J. Panton and Keith A. Cowlard, 2010.
226. *The A to Z of Denmark* by Alastair H. Thomas, 2010.
227. *The A to Z of France* by Gino Raymond, 2010.
228. *The A to Z of Georgia* by Alexander Mikaberidze, 2010.
229. *The A to Z of Iceland* by Gudmundur Halfdanarson, 2010.
230. *The A to Z of Latvia* by Andrejs Plakans, 2010.
231. *The A to Z of Modern Italy* by Mark F. Gilbert and K. Robert Nilsson, 2010.
232. *The A to Z of Moldova* by Andrei Brezianu and Vlad Spânu, 2010.
233. *The A to Z of the Netherlands* by Joop W. Koopmans and Arend H. Huussen Jr., 2010.
234. *The A to Z of Norway* by Jan Sjåvik, 2010.
235. *The A to Z of the Republic of Macedonia* by Dimitar Bechev, 2010.
236. *The A to Z of Slovakia* by Stanislav J. Kirschbaum, 2010.
237. *The A to Z of Slovenia* by Leopoldina Plut-Pregelj and Carole Rogel, 2010.
238. *The A to Z of Spain* by Angel Smith, 2010.
239. *The A to Z of Sweden* by Irene Scobbie, 2010.
240. *The A to Z of Turkey* by Metin Heper and Nur Bilge Criss, 2010.
241. *The A to Z of Ukraine* by Zenon E. Kohut, Bohdan Y. Nebesio, and Myroslav Yurkevich, 2010.
242. *The A to Z of Mexico* by Marvin Alisky, 2010.
243. *The A to Z of U.S. Diplomacy from World War I through World War II* by Martin Folly and Niall Palmer, 2010.
244. *The A to Z of Spanish Cinema* by Alberto Mira, 2010.
245. *The A to Z of the Reformation and Counter-Reformation* by Michael Mullett, 2010.

The A to Z of Modern Italy

Mark F. Gilbert
K. Robert Nilsson

The A to Z Guide Series, No. 231

The Scarecrow Press, Inc.
Lanham • Toronto • Plymouth, UK
2010

Published by Scarecrow Press, Inc.
A wholly owned subsidiary of
The Rowman & Littlefield Publishing Group, Inc.
4501 Forbes Boulevard, Suite 200, Lanham, Maryland 20706
http://www.scarecrowpress.com

Estover Road, Plymouth PL6 7PY, United Kingdom

British Library Cataloguing in Publication Information Available

Library of Congress Cataloging-in-Publication Data

The hardback version of this book was cataloged by the Library of Congress
as follows:

Gilbert, Mark, 1961–
    Historical dictionary of modern Italy / Mark F. Gilbert, K. Robert Nilsson. —
2nd ed.
        p. cm. — (Historical dictionaries of Europe ; no. 58)
    Includes bibliographical references.
    1. Italy–History–1870–1914–Dictionaries. 2. Italy–History–20th century–
Dictionaries. I. Nilsson, K. Robert, 1927– II. Title.
    DG555.G53 2007
    945.003–dc22   2007004309

First edition by Mark F. Gilbert and K. Robert Nilsson, European Historical
Dictionaries, No. 34, Scarecrow Press, Lanham, Md., 1999, ISBN 0-8108-3584-3.
This book is the paperback edition of *Historical Dictionary of Modern Italy:
Second Edition.*

ISBN 978-0-8108-7210-3 (pbk. : alk. paper)

∞™ The paper used in this publication meets the minimum requirements of
American National Standard for Information Sciences—Permanence of
Paper for Printed Library Materials, ANSI/NISO Z39.48-1992.
Printed in the United States of America

In memory of Bob Nilsson

Contents

Editor's Foreword

Although Italy is one of the oldest countries in Europe, rooted as it is in Etruscan civilization, Magna Graecia, and the Roman Empire, it is also a new country in the sense that it was only united under Piedmont in 1861. Yet, differences persist between the more prosperous North and the far poorer South, and regionalism remains strong. Moreover, Italy's progress has been far from smooth or exempt from turmoil, most notably during the Fascist regime and World War II, and gradually muted but serious conflicts between right and left have plagued it ever since. Despite its efforts, the postwar regime has been unable to overcome all the tensions and thoroughly modernize the state, although its economy has fared well enough until recently and its society has changed remarkably. Moreover, Italian leaders have taken the country into all the European ventures from the very start, and Italy plays an important role in the European Union.

So much has happened in Italy since unification that there seems to be no end to what might be surveyed in this volume. It has therefore focused on certain prominent individuals, basic institutions, crucial events and fundamental features needed to understand modern Italy. Of course, it also sheds light on the occasionally larger than life persons who have emerged and shaped its course. Along with history and politics, the dictionary includes entries on economics, society, and culture. The context for all this is provided in an introduction, and the chronology traces the many twists and turns in greater detail. The lists of acronyms, kings, presidents, and prime ministers are useful references. And the selective bibliography is a good starting place for readers who want to know more.

As some have noticed, changes in Italy are not only theatrical, they sometimes almost verge on soap opera, as in the previous government, so it is harder than elsewhere to keep up with events. This makes the

xvi • EDITOR'S FOREWORD

second edition of the *Historical Dictionary of Modern Italy* particularly welcome. The first edition was written by K. Robert Nilsson and Mark F. Gilbert. The former, who was professor emeritus at Dickinson College, sadly passed away shortly after publication of the first edition, and so the work on this second edition was undertaken by Professor Gilbert alone. He has taught Italian politics and history at Dickinson College, the University of Bath in England, and the Johns Hopkins School of Advanced International Studies in Bologna and teaches contemporary European history at the University of Trento, Italy. He has written extensively on Italian politics, including *The Italian Revolution: The End of Politics Italian Style?* This experience has certainly benefited the second edition, which is not only updated but considerably expanded.

Jon Woronoff
Series Editor

Acknowledgments

The first edition of this book was begun by Bob Nilsson and myself in 1996 when I was assistant professor of political science at Dickinson College and Bob was professor emeritus in the same discipline at the college. Bob and his wife Judy were great friends to my wife and me during our time in the United States and before that during Bob's last year as director of Dickinson College's European Studies program in Bologna. Bob and I collaborated on the first edition for three years. In editing and extending this second edition, I realized just how much Bob knew about a huge range of topics in Italian life, language, and society. An expert on post-1945 party politics, he had nevertheless contributed to a large number of the cultural and social entries in the dictionary, and most of his original contribution remains in this second edition. Bob died shortly after the publication of the first edition of this book, and Dickinson College renamed its Bologna Center in his honor. It was a worthy tribute to an outstanding teacher and remarkable man who knew Italy as very few foreigners can claim to do.

I would like to thank Jon Woronoff for his considerable patience and his help with the editing of this book, and Susan McEachern of Rowman & Littlefield for authorizing the use of the map, which was originally published in the second (2004) edition of *Europe Today*, edited by Ronald Tiersky. The first edition of this dictionary was prepared by Vickie Kuhn of the Political Science Department at Dickinson College; her fine work made preparing this second edition all the easier.

Between 1997 and 2002, I taught modern Italian history and Italian language in the Department of European Studies at the University of Bath. Writing the first edition of this book helped me enormously in the preparation of my lectures. I made many friends at Bath, and my particular regards go to the Italian section of the department, namely Jacqui Andall, Anna Cento Bull, Adalgisa Giorgio, and Ernest Hampson, for having made my years at Bath so enjoyable and worthwhile. This book would have been very different had I not worked among such knowledgeable and enthusiastic colleagues.

My wife, Luciana, is the root source of my interest in Italy. She and Francisco have put up with me as usual while I passed long hours in the office ensuring that I had "bolded" the right words and cross-referenced correctly.

The book contains much new material (there are more than 70 new entries, and dozens of former entries have been expanded or significantly revised). I hope it will be a useful source of information for people who wish to know more about this undeniably fascinating country.

Acronyms and Abbreviations

ACI	Azione Cattolica Italiana (Catholic Action)
AGCI	Associazione Generale delle Cooperative Italiane (General Association of Italian Cooperatives)
AGIP	Azienda Generale Italiana Petroli (Italian General Petroleum Agency)
AN	Alleanza Nazionale (National Alliance)
BR	Brigate Rosse (Red Brigades)
CCD	Centro Cristiano Democratico (Christian Democratic Center)
CDL	Casa delle Libertà (House of Freedoms)
CDU	Cristiani Democratici Uniti (United Christian Democrats)
CERN	Conseil Européen pour la Recerche Nucléare (European Center for Nuclear Research)
CGIL	Confederazione Generale Italiana del Lavoro (Italian General Confederation of Labor)
CIA	Central Intelligence Agency
CIPE	Comitato Interministeriale per la Programmazione Economica (Interministerial Committee for Economic Planning)
CISL	Confederazione Italiana Sindacati Lavoratori (Italian Confederation of Workers' Unions)
CISNAL	Confederazione Italiana Sindacati Nazionali Lavoratori (Italian Confederation of National Workers' Unions)
CLN	Comitati di Liberazione Nazionale (National Liberation Committees)
COBAS	Comitati di Base (Base [membership] Committees)
COREL	Comitato per la Riforma Elettorale (Committee for Electoral Reform)

CSM	Consiglio Superiore della Magistratura (High Council of the Magistracy)
DC	Democrazia Cristiana (Christian Democracy Party)
DE	Democrazia europea (European Democracy Party)
DL	Democrazia e Libertà (Democracy and Liberty Party)
DN	Destra Nazionale (National Right)
DNA	Direzione Nazionale Antimafia (National Antimafia Agency)
DS	Democratici di Sinistra (Democrats of the Left)
ECSC	European Coal and Steel Community
EEC	European Economic Community
EMS	European Monetary System
ENEA	Ente per le Nuove Tecnologie, l'Energia e l'Ambiente (Research Council for New Technology, Energy and the Environment)
ENEL	Ente Nazionale per l'Energia Elettrica (National Electricity Agency)
ENI	Ente Nazionale Idrocarburi (National Hydrocarbons Agency)
EU	European Union
EUR	Esposizione Universale di Roma (Rome Universal Exhibition)
FGCI	Federazione Giovanile Comunista Italiana (Italian Communist Youth Federation)
FIAT	Fabbrica Italiana Automobili Torino (Italian Automobile Factory: Turin)
FUCI	Federazione Universitaria Cattolici Italiana (Catholic University Graduates' Movement of Italy)
GAP	Gruppi armati pattriotici (Patriotic Action Groups)
GDF	Guardia di Finanza (Financial Police)
GDP	Gross Domestic Product
GL	Giustizia e Libertà (Justice and Liberty)
GNP	Gross National Product
GUF	Gioventù Universitaria Fascista (Fascist University Youth)
IMF	International Monetary Fund
IRI	Istituto per la Ricostruzione Industriale (Institute for Industrial Reconstruction)

ISTAT	Istituto Centrale di Statistica (Italian Central Statistical Agency)
LIT	Lire Italiane (Italian Lire)
LN	Lega Nord (Northern League)
LUISS	Libera Università Internazionale per gli Studi Sociali (Free University for the Social Sciences)
MLD	Movimento di Liberazione della Donna (Women's Liberation Movement)
MSI-DN	Movimento Sociale Italiano-Destra Nazionale (Italian Social Movement-National Right)
MUP	Movimento d'Unità Proletaria (Movement of Proletarian Unity)
MVSN	Milizia Volontario di Sicurezza Nazionale (Voluntary Militia of National Security)
NATO	North Atlantic Treaty Organization
OAS	Organisation Armée Secrete (Secret Army Organization)
OEEC	Organization for European Economic Cooperation
ONB	Organizzazione Nazionale Balilla (National Balilla)
OVRA	Opera Volontaria per la Repressione Antifascista (uncertain) (Volunteer Organization for the Repression of Antifascism)
PATT	Partito Autonomia Trentino-Tirolese (Party for the Autonomy of the Trentino-Tirolese)
PCI	Partito Comunista Italiano (Italian Communist Party)
PdA	Partito d'Azione (Action Party)
PdCI	Partito dei Comunisti Italiani (Party of Italian Communists)
PDS	Partito Democratico della Sinistra (Democratic Party of the Left)
PLI	Partito Liberale Italiano (Italian Liberal Party)
PLO	Palestine Liberation Organization
PNF	Partito Nazionale Fascista (National Fascist Party)
PPI	Partito Popolare Italiano (Italian Popular Party)
PR	Partito Radicale (Radical Party)
PRC	Partito di Rifondazione Comunista (Communist Refoundation Party)
PRI	Partito Repubblicana Italiano (Italian Republican Party)

PSDI	Partito Socialista Democratico Italiano (Italian Socialist Democratic Party)
PSI	Partito Socialista Italiano (Italian Socialist Party)
PSIUP	Partito Socialista Italiano d'Unità Proletaria (Italian Socialist Party of Proletarian Unity)
PSLI	Partito Socialista dei Lavoratori Italiani (Italian Socialist Workers' Party)
PSRI	Partito Socialista Riformista Italiano (Italian Reformist Socialist Party)
PSU	Partito Socialista Unificato (Unified Socialist Party)
RAI	Radio Autodiffusione Italiana (State Broadcasting Service)
RSI	Repubblica Sociale Italiana (Italian Social Republic)
SEA	Single European Act
SVP	Süd Tirol Volkspartei (South Tyrol People's Party)
TAR	Tribunale Amministrativo Regionale (Regional Administrative Tribunal)
TUPS	Testo Unico di Pubblica Sicurezza (Consolidated Public Security Law)
UC	Unione di Centro (Center Union)
UDC	Unione dei Democratici Cristiani e Democratici del Centro (Union of Democratic Christians and the Center)
UDN	Unione Democratica Nazionale (National Democratic Union)
UDS	Unione Democratica Socialista (Democratic Socialist Union)
UIL	Unione Italiana del Lavoro (Italian Union of Labor)
UN	United Nations
UQ	Fronte dell'Uomo Qualunque/The Common Man's Front
USSR	Union of Soviet Socialist Republics

Chronology

1797 Constitution of the Cisalpine Republic with the tricolor flag. Venice is absorbed by Austria.

1802 Cisalpine Republic becomes the Italian Republic, with Milan as its capital.

1804 Adoption of the Napoleonic Code Civil of 1803.

1805 Napoleon I crowns himself King of Italy in Milan.

1815 Congress of Vienna restores absolute rule in Italian peninsula.

1820 Middle class revolution in Naples and popular uprising in Palermo. Neapolitan troops invade Sicily. Five thousand die in street battles in September.

1821 Austrian troops crush the revolt in Naples. Ferdinand I restored to the throne. Revolution in Turin; Charles Albert concedes a Constitution, but then reneges.

1822 Congress of Verona.

1827 First edition of Manzoni's *The Betrothed*.

1831 Revolts in Central Italy against papal rule. Austrian intervention. Mazzini founds Giovine Italia.

1833 Mazzinian conspiracy against the Kingdom of Piedmont-Sardinia discovered. Mazzini condemned to death in absentia.

1834 Mazzinian uprisings in Genoa and Savoy thwarted.

1835 Cholera epidemic. More than 50,000 die over next two years.

1839 First railway between Naples and Portici.

1843 Publication of Gioberti's *On the Moral and Civil Primacy of the Italians*.

1846 Election of Pius IX, the "Liberal Pope."

1848 Revolutions in Palermo, Naples, and Turin. Constitutional monarchy introduced in Turin. Revolts against Austrian rule in Venice and Milan. War between Piedmont and Austria; Austrian victory at Custoza. Civil and political rights granted to Jews in Piedmont-Sardinia.

1849 Roman Republic proclaimed. War declared between Piedmont and Austria. Charles Albert abdicates after defeat at Novara. Victor Emmanuel II becomes king. Austria and France restore papal authority.

1851 First performance of Verdi's *Rigoletto*.

1852 Cavour becomes premier in Piedmont.

1855 Piedmontese troops participate in the war in Crimea. New outbreak of cholera.

1858 An Italian nationalist, Felice Orsini, attempts to kill Napoleon III of France. Cavour signs the pact of Plombières with Napoleon and secures French aid against Austria.

1859 War between Franco–Sardinian alliance and Austria leads to the peace of Villafranca (July). Cavour resigns. Bologna, Tuscany, Modena, and Parma reject papal rule and appeal to be united with Piedmont.

1860 Cavour returns to power in Turin. Garibaldi's "Thousand" sail to the aid of a revolt in Palermo. Garibaldi establishes dictatorship in Sicily and invades the mainland. Cavour annexes central and southern Italy. **October 26:** Garibaldi yields his conquests to Victor Emmanuel II.

1861 Victor Emmanuel II crowned *Re d'Italia* in March. Catholic Church boycotts elections. Cavour dies in June.

1862 An attempt by Garibaldi to liberate Rome is thwarted by the Italian army. Garibaldi himself is wounded.

1865 Florence becomes capital of Italy.

1866 Italy allies with Prussia and makes war on Austria. Italy defeated at Custoza and Lissa. After Prussian victory at Sadowa, Italy, gains Venetia, but not the Trentino, despite Garibaldi's victories there.

1867 Garibaldi defeated at the battle of Mentana. Rome remains in papal hands. Cholera epidemic kills thousands.

1868 Grist tax introduced by Quintino Sella.

1869 Death of Carlo Cattaneo, republican and democrat.

1870 Rome is occupied by Italian troops in September after the defeat of Napoleon III in the Franco–Prussian War. Only Vatican city left to the pope.

1871 Law regulating relations between the pope and the Italian state introduced. Verdi's *Aida* performed for the first time.

1872 Death of Giuseppe Mazzini.

1876 Agostino Depretis becomes prime minister, promises social and electoral reforms and the abolition of the grist tax—the "parliamentary revolution."

1878 Death of Victor Emmanuel II and Pius IX. Replaced by King Humbert I and Leo XIII. In November, an anarchist attempts to kill Humbert, who is saved by the bravery of his prime minister, Benedetto Cairoli.

1879 First telephones introduced in Italy.

1882 Death of Giuseppe Garibaldi. Italy joins the Triple Alliance. Depretis gives birth to *trasformismo* by persuading rightist deputies led by Marco Minghetti to join his government. Electoral law extends the vote from 600,000 electors to over 2,000,000, but this is still less than 7 percent of the population.

1884 Cholera epidemic kills thousands, especially in Naples.

1885 Italian colonialism begins with the occupation of territories along the banks of the Red Sea.

1886 First child labor law.

1887   Five hundred Italian troops massacred at Dogali in Ethiopia. Depretis dies in July; in August Francesco Crispi becomes premier.

1889   Treaty of Uccialli with Menelik of Ethiopia. Italian colonial gains recognized.

1890   Death penalty abolished.

1891   Publication of the encyclical *Rerum Novarum*.

1892   The Italian Workers' Party, forerunner of the Partito Socialista Italiano/Italian Socialist Party (PSI), founded in August.

1893   Banca Romana scandal brings down Giovanni Giolitti.

1894   Sicilian peasants' uprising suppressed by Francesco Crispi.

1896   Renewed war between Italy and Ethiopia ends in the disaster of Adowa in March. Crispi's second government collapses. Showing of the first Italian film, *The Arrival of the Train at Milan Station*.

1897   Conservative leader Giorgio Sidney Sonnino proposes increased executive power for the king and a reduction in the power of Parliament.

1898   Italian soccer championship begins. Year of bread riots throughout Italy. At least 80 and possibly as many as 300 workers are killed in Milan by government troops. PSI leader Filippo Turati arrested.

1900   King Humbert I assassinated at Monza by an Italian anarchist from Paterson, New Jersey. Victor Emmanuel III is crowned in July.

1901   Zanardelli cabinet formed in February; takes the side of labor in agricultural and industrial disputes. PSI deputies support the government in Parliament. Record year for strikes.

1903   Death of Pope Leo XIII and of Giuseppe Zanardelli, who is replaced by Giovanni Giolitti.

1904   PSI's revolutionary wing wins control of the party. First general strike in September. Year of violent labor discontent.

1906   First centralized trade union, the General Confederation of Work, formed in Milan. Camillo Golgi and Giosue Carducci win the Nobel prizes for medicine and literature.

1908 A massive earthquake in December takes tens of thousands of lives in Sicily and Calabria. Messina and Reggio Calabria are devastated.

1909 Marinetti publishes the futurist manifesto in Paris. First Giro d'Italia bicycle race. Guglielmo Marconi wins the Nobel Prize in Physics.

1911 Italy declares war on Turkey and occupies Libya. Benito Mussolini leads violent strikes against the war; Italian atrocities against the civilian population cause an international outcry.

1912 Universal male suffrage introduced in May. Treaty of peace signed with Turkey in October after lengthy talks. The PSI expels its "ministerialist" wing and takes an increasingly revolutionary line.

1913 Record year for strikes and immigration to the United States. Gentiloni pact signed between moderate Liberals and the Catholic Electoral Union.

1914 Antonio Salandra becomes premier. One hundred thousand troops are needed to quell riots in northern Italy led by Mussolini. Italy remains neutral after the outbreak of war.

1915 Italy promises to enter the war on the side of Britain and France in April. War declared on Austria in May; on Turkey in August.

1916 Italy declares war on Germany in August after victory in the battle of Gorizia.

1917 Women lead strikes and protests against the war in the spring. Pope Benedict XV appeals for an end to the "useless slaughter." Disaster of Caporetto in October. Italian army suffers huge losses of men and material. Vittorio Emmanuel Orlando becomes premier.

1918 Italian victory in the battle of Piave restores the territory lost the previous year.

1919 Foundation of the Catholic Partito Popolare Italiano/Italian Popular Party (PPI) and Mussolini's Movimento dei fasci italiani, soon to be known as the Partito Nazionale Fascista/National Fascist Party (PNF) and its members, Fascists. Electoral law introduces proportional representation. Italy is "robbed" of the territorial gains it expected by the Treaty of Saint-Germain. Gabriele D'Annunzio, with the tacit support of the Italian government, seizes Fiume on September 12.

1920 Strikes throughout the country; labor movement splits among communists, moderate trade unionists, and the PSI. Giolitti returns to power and in November signs Treaty of Rapallo, which resolves the border question with Yugoslavia. Italian troops expel D'Annunzio from Fiume in December.

1921 Formation of the Partito Comunista Italiano/Italian Communist Party (PCI). Victory for the PSI and the PPI in national elections held in May. Thirty-five Fascists elected with Giolitti's backing. Ivanoe Bonomi forms new government. Major banking crisis.

1922 Death of Pope Benedict XV and Giovanni Verga, novelist. Bonomi and Facta governments collapse in the face of Fascist lawlessness. Mussolini becomes premier after unopposed March on Rome.

1923 Fascist power consolidated. Gentile reform of education; Acerbo electoral law introduced. Mussolini bombards and occupies Corfu.

1924 Fiume becomes Italian. Fascist victory in elections. Opposition parties, despite intimidation, obtain 35 percent of the vote. Giacomo Matteotti is murdered by a Fascist squad, provoking the opposition parties to boycott Parliament. First radio broadcasts.

1925 Mussolini takes personal responsibility for all the crimes committed by the Fascists in 1924, including the murder of Matteotti. Manifesto of Fascist intellectuals published; Croce publishes counter-manifesto. Antifascist newspaper *Non Mollare* founded in Florence.

1926 Three attempts on Mussolini's life lead to suspension of leading antifascist newspapers and passage of laws abolishing all opposition parties, establishing special tribunals for political cases, and confiscating the possessions of antifascist exiles.

1927 Organization of the OVRA (secret police). Independent trade unions dissolved. Campaign to increase the birthrate begins. Grazia Deledda wins the Nobel Prize in Literature.

1928 New electoral law. Citizens are given the choice of voting for or against an approved slate of 400 fascist candidates. Introduction of an official textbook in schools.

1929 Signature of the Lateran pacts guaranteeing a degree of church autonomy from the regime. Plebiscite held under the new electoral laws produces a 98.4 percent majority for the Fascist slate of candidates. Giustizia e Libertà/Justice and Liberty (GL), an antifascist organization, founded in Paris. Italian Academy founded in Rome; Benedetto Croce refuses to join.

1932 "Exhibition of the Ten Years of Fascist Revolution" in Rome. Italy wins the second-highest number of medals in the Los Angeles Olympics.

1933 Creation of the Institution for Industrial Reconstruction (IRI) to coordinate state investment in industry. In 1934, establishes dominant position in the banking sector.

1934 Law on corporations passed. Second plebiscite gives the Fascist list a majority of 99.84 percent, in a poll characterized by lower absenteeism. The Italian soccer team wins the world cup (a feat they repeat four years later). After an attempted Nazi coup in Austria, Mussolini mobilizes troops in support of the Austrian government. Luigi Pirandello, a noted supporter of the regime, wins the Nobel Prize in Literature.

1935 France gives Italy a free hand in Ethiopia, and in October Italian troops begin occupying the country. Italy is condemned by the League of Nations and limited sanctions are applied.

1936 Addis Ababa occupied by Italy in May. "Italian East Africa" is formed (comprising Somaliland, Ethiopia, and Eritrea), and King Victor Emmanuel III takes the title of emperor. In October foreign minister Galeazzo Ciano signs a protocol committing Italy and Germany to conduct a joint campaign against Bolshevism and to sustain Franco in the Spanish Civil War (Axis). Large Italian expeditionary force is sent to Spain.

1937 Death of Communist leader Antonio Gramsci. Carlo and Nello Rosselli, the organizers of GL, are murdered in France. All sexual relations between Africans and Italians are banned. Mussolini meets Hitler in Munich. In December, Italy leaves the League of Nations.

1938   Adolf Hitler makes official visit to Italy in May, shortly after occupying Austria with Italian support. Mussolini mediates between Britain and France, and Germany, at Munich. So-called third wave of the Fascist revolution begins; racial laws against Jews are introduced in November. Enrico Fermi wins the Nobel Prize in Physics. Fermi leaves for the United States rather than return to Italy.

1939   Parliament is abolished and replaced by a Chamber of Fascists and a Chamber of Corporations. "Pact of Steel" signed with Germany in May. Italy, however, refuses to enter the war in September, pleading military unpreparedness.

1940   Italy declares war on France and Britain in June. Angered by Hitler's refusal to allow Italy a place at the armistice talks with France, Mussolini invades Greece in October, but Italian forces are swiftly defeated. One hundred twenty thousand Italians are captured by the British in North Africa.

1941   The war in North Africa causes large casualties among Italian troops; Mussolini sends a contingent of over 60,000 troops to Russia to help the German war effort. War declared on the United States on December 11.

1942   German and Italian forces drive the British back in North Africa but are decisively beaten at the battle of El Alamein. Eight Italian divisions are annihilated. Huge losses are also counted on the Russian front. The Action Party and Christian Democracy Party are formed.

1943   FIAT workers strike for "bread and peace" in March. Italo-German forces surrender in Tunisia. Sicily is invaded by Anglo-American troops in July. On July 25, the Fascist Grand Council deposes Mussolini. Marshal Badoglio becomes premier. Mussolini is arrested but is later liberated by the Germans. On 8 September, Italy surrenders to the Allies. German troops occupy Rome; 4,500 Italian soldiers are massacred by the Germans on the Greek island of Cephalonia. Mussolini establishes the Italian Social Republic at Salò on Lake Garda.

1944 Five former members of the Fascist Grand Council, including Ciano, are condemned to death by the Salò Republic at Verona in January. The Gestapo murders 335 political prisoners in Rome as a reprisal for a partisan attack. King Victor Emmanuel III is persuaded to make his son, Humbert, Lieutenant-General of the Realm, clearing the way for the formation of a government that includes the PCI and the Democrazia Cristiana/Christian Democracy Party (DC) in June. The PSI and the Action Party, the other main resistance forces, remain uncommitted.

1945 The workers of northern Italy rise in rebellion in Genoa, Milan, and Turin. Mussolini is captured by partisans and shot on 28 April. His body, and the corpses of other Fascist officials, are exposed to public vilification in Milan's Piazza Loreto. Some 15,000 suspected Fascists are executed during the spring. In June, partisan leader Ferruccio Parri is appointed prime minister of a leftist coalition. He is replaced by Alcide De Gasperi (DC) in December after a cabinet crisis.

1946 In May, Victor Emmanuel III abdicates shortly before the referendum on the monarchy on June 2 and the election of a Constituent Assembly. By a narrow margin, Italy votes for a republic in its first ever free election by universal suffrage. The DC emerges as the largest party, with 35 percent of the vote. Enrico De Nicola is appointed provisional head of state.

1947 **May:** De Gasperi forms a government without the participation of the PSI or the PCI. Italy loses its colonies and control over Trieste by the terms of the treaty of peace signed at Paris in February. **December 22:** The text of the new Constitution is approved by the Assembly. After receiving the presidential signature, it comes into force on January 1, 1948. **End of December:** Victor Emmanuel III dies in exile in Egypt.

1948 DC wins 48 percent of the vote in April elections. De Gasperi forms a cabinet that includes the small center parties. Luigi Einaudi of the Partito Liberale Italiano/Italian Liberal Party (PLI) is elected first president of the republic. In July an attempt is made to assassinate PCI leader Palmiro Togliatti. In response, riots break out in northern Italy. First showings of De Sica's *The Bicycle Thief*, Visconti's *The Earth Trembles*, and Rossellini's *Germany, Year Zero*.

1949   Italy joins North Atlantic Treaty Organization (NATO). Huge protests in southern Italy for land reform.

1950   Peasants occupy uncultivated land throughout southern Italy. A limited agricultural reform follows by the end of the year. Southern Development Fund created. The writer Cesare Pavese commits suicide.

1951   Great Britain, France, and the United States propose that Italy be recognized as a full-fledged democracy in September. Italy begins process of moral rehabilitation.

1952   Italy joins the European Coal and Steel Community (ECSC). Bicycle racer Fausto Coppi wins the Tour de France. The following year, he becomes world champion. Benedetto Croce dies in November.

1953   A "Swindle Law" is enacted, which changes electoral rules to give the winning coalition a "prize" in seats. In general elections held in June, the DC and its allies obtain less than 50 percent of the vote and the law is thus not applied.

1954   Alcide De Gasperi dies. Television broadcasts begin. Italy takes over administration of the former American and British zones of Trieste.

1955   Election of Giovanni Gronchi as president of the republic in April. The FIAT 600—the first popular Italian automobile—rolls off the assembly lines in Turin. Start of the "economic miracle." Italy admitted to membership of the United Nations (UN).

1956   A narrowly proportional form of election law is adopted in March. Constitutional Court instituted. The alliance between the PCI and the PSI weakens. Hundreds of intellectuals desert the PCI after the party backs Soviet oppression of the Hungarian revolution.

1957   **March:** Treaty of Rome establishing the European Economic Community (EEC) signed. Italy becomes one of the six founder members. **September:** Death of the antifascist historian and political thinker Gaetano Salvemini.

1958   DC wins uneventful elections. Amintore Fanfani becomes prime minister. Pope Pius XII dies and is replaced by the liberal Pope John XXIII.

1959 Publication of Tomasi Di Lampedusa's *The Leopard* and first showing of Fellini's *La Dolce Vita*. Salvatore Quasimodo wins the Nobel Prize in Literature. Peak year for migration from the South to the booming cities of Lombardy and Piedmont.

1960 Femando Tambroni forms a government with the support of the neofascist Movimento Sociale Italiano/Italian Social Movement (MSI). Riots break out throughout Italy, and Fernando Tambroni is replaced by Fanfani as premier. Rome hosts the Olympics; Italy is fourth in the medals table with 13 golds.

1962 Fanfani forms a government that enjoys the parliamentary neutrality of the PSI. Antonio Segni becomes president of the republic.

1963 Defeat in the elections for the DC, which recedes to just 38 percent. The PLI doubles its share of the vote, while the PCI obtains 25 percent for the first time. **October:** Almost 2,000 people die in Belluno and Udine after the collapse of a dam. **December:** Aldo Moro forms a government that includes four PSI ministers.

1964 Moro government enters into a lengthy crisis, but eventually reforms. During the crisis General Giovanni De Lorenzo, head of the *carabinieri* and former chief of the secret services, distributes to select police and army officials a plan for a coup d'etat by the armed forces. Palmiro Togliatti dies in August. Failing health forces Segni to resign from the presidency. He is replaced by Giuseppe Saragat in December.

1966 Worst flooding of the century swamps Florence, Siena, and Venice. Volunteers from all over the world help save the cities' art treasures. The PSI and the Partito Socialista Democratico Italiano/ Italian Socialist Democrat Party (PSDI) form a short-lived unified socialist party.

1967 Student sit-ins preface a long decade of tumult in the universities and factories. First pornographic movies and magazines appear.

1968 Student riots throughout Italy. In Sicily, an earthquake kills 300 people in January. Adultery is decriminalized. The PCI condemns the Soviet suppression of the Prague Spring.

1969 **December:** A bomb kills 17 and wounds nearly 90 in Milan's Piazza Fontana. Beginning of the so-called strategy of tension by mysterious neofascist groups.

1970 Enabling legislation passed instituting a regional tier of government and authorizing referendums. Divorce legalized in December. A group of ultrarightists led by Prince Junio Valerio Borghese occupy the Ministry of the Interior briefly in December.

1971 Giovanni Leone becomes president of the republic in December on the twenty-third ballot.

1972 Giulio Andreotti forms the first of his seven governments in January. After elections in May, in which the MSI gains ground, Andreotti forms a second administration. Censorship laws are loosened; an explosion of hard-core pornography ensues.

1973 Neofascist lawlessness and speculation against the lira bring down the Andreotti government. The Pinochet coup in Chile prompts PCI leader Enrico Berlinguer to ponder a "historic compromise" with the DC in September.

1974 Italy votes by an unexpectedly large margin to retain the new divorce law in a May referendum. The Italicus, a train running between Rome and Munich, is blown up by terrorists. Twelve people are killed. **November:** Vittorio De Sica dies.

1975 Eugenio Montale wins the Nobel prize for literature. The writer and film director Pierpaolo Pasolini is murdered.

1976 High-ranking Italian politicians are accused of having received huge sums from the U.S. aerospace company Lockheed. One thousand people are killed in an earthquake in Udine. A general election is held in June in a feverish climate prompted by the possibility that the PCI will "overtake" the DC and form a government. In the event, the DC remains at nearly 39 percent and the PCI gets just over 34 percent. The DC is left without a majority, but the PCI permits Andreotti to form an administration and to govern. A Communist, Pietro Ingrao, becomes Speaker of the Chamber of Deputies.

1977 The Red Brigades, extreme left terrorist cells, commit dozens of attacks on judges, journalists, policemen, and politicians. Right-wing and ultraleft groups clash in Rome; the armed forces have to be used to quell student riots in Bologna. **June:** Roberto Rossellini dies.

1978   Aldo Moro is kidnapped and, after 55 days of imprisonment, is murdered by the Red Brigades. Giovanni Leone is forced to resign from the presidency after the question of his involvement in the Lockheed affair and other financial scandals become publicly debated. He is replaced by Alessandro Pertini. A moderate abortion law is passed. John Paul I dies only a month after assuming the papacy; a Polish bishop, Karol Wojtyla, becomes the first non-Italian pope since the sixteenth century.

1979   All cooperation ends between the DC and the PCI. In the ensuing elections, the PCI falls back to 30 percent of the vote. Italy enters the European Monetary System (EMS), and American nuclear missiles are installed in NATO bases in Italy. Partito Repubblicana Italiano/Italian Republican Party (PRI) leader Ugo La Malfa, one of postwar Italy's most respected politicians, dies.

1980   **June:** An Italian airliner crashes into the sea off the island of Ustica (Palermo). Eighty people are killed. The Libyan air force and NATO are both suspected of shooting the plane down. **August:** A huge bomb devastates Bologna railway station, killing 85 people and wounding over 200. Neofascist terrorists are blamed. **October:** Southern Italy is shaken by an enormous earthquake that leaves 6,000 dead and hundreds of thousands homeless. Deaths of two of the PCI's historic leaders, Giorgio Amendola and Luigi Longo.

1981   John Paul II is seriously wounded by a would-be assassin in Rome. The Propaganda Due masonic lodge is discovered; 900 high-ranking Italian businessmen, army officers, journalists, and politicians are implicated in planning to transform Italian institutions by secretive means. In May voters reject both a Catholic attempt to abolish the abortion law and a radical attempt to make the law more liberal in a national referendum. Giovanni Spadolini (PRI) becomes the first non-DC premier in the republic's history at the head of a five-party coalition that includes the PSI of Bettino Craxi.

1982   The DC elects Ciriaco De Mita as party leader. Spadolini's administration comes to an end in August after Craxi engineers a political crisis. Two prominent antimafia fighters, PCI deputy Pio La Torre and General Carlo Alberto Dalla Chiesa, are killed by organized crime in Sicily. The Italian national soccer team wins the world cup for the third time.

1983 Thirty-two life sentences are given to the killers of Aldo Moro. In June, national elections result in a massive defeat for the DC, which sinks to less than 33 percent of the vote. Bettino Craxi becomes premier in August. Andreotti is accused of being the mastermind behind the P2.

1984 During the campaign for the elections to the European Parliament, PCI leader Enrico Berlinguer dies of a stroke. Two million people attend the funeral. The PCI overtakes the DC in the Euro-poll, obtaining over 33 percent of the vote. Bettino Craxi and the church agree to revisions of the Lateran pacts, which end Catholicism's status as the official religion of the state.

1985 A referendum against a law passed by the Craxi government to end automatic cost-of-living increases is defeated. In June, Francesco Cossiga is elected president of the Republic. *Achille Lauro* crisis roils Italian–American relations but boosts Craxi's standing with public opinion and the Arab world. Deaths of two of postwar Italy's most eminent novelists, Italo Calvino and Elsa Morante.

1986 The so-called maxitrial of over 400 alleged mafiosi takes place in Palermo. After two years of hearings, life sentences are meted out to almost the entire leadership of Cosa Nostra, including the boss of bosses, Michele "the pope" Greco. Tensions between the DC and the PSI cause the downfall of Craxi's first government in June after nearly three years in power—a postwar record. Craxi forms a second cabinet in August on the understanding that he will give way to a DC premier in March 1987.

1987 Craxi reneges on his promise to resign, causing the most difficult and drawn-out government crisis of the 1980s. In June, elections are held to resolve the issue. The PSI does well, advancing to 14 percent, and the PCI's share drops again. Giovanni Goria (DC) becomes premier at the head of a hapless administration that is sabotaged mercilessly by the PSI. A referendum held in November abolishes Italy's nuclear power program. The writer Primo Levi commits suicide in April.

1988 Ciriaco De Mita replaces Goria, becoming premier in April. Italy is paralyzed by wildcat strikes called by unofficial trade unions in the transport sector. Death in May of Giorgio Almirante, historic leader of Italian neofascism.

1989 The DC removes De Mita from the party leadership, replacing him with Arnaldo Forlani. In July, De Mita is replaced as prime minister by Andreotti. The end of communism in Eastern Europe provokes vast changes in the PCI. Its leader, Achille Occhetto, announces his intention to transform the party into a formation "new even in name." Death of the Sicilian novelist and political activist Leonardo Sciascia in November.

1990 Parliament whitewashes a report revealing that there was widespread electoral fraud in Naples in the 1987 elections. Sixty-seven percent of a special conference of the PCI back Occhetto's decision to create a new party. In October, Occhetto announces that the new party will be called the Partito Democratico della Sinistra/Democratic Party of the Left (PDS). Regional elections reveal the local strength of the Lombard League. A secret network of underground anticommunist armed cells known as "Gladio" is discovered. Death in February of Alessandro Pertini, Italy's most loved president and wartime hero. Italy plays host to the soccer world cup.

1991 Italian airmen and ships participate in the Gulf War. The PCI's Twentieth Party Congress votes in February to change the party's name. A faction leaves to form the Partito di Rifondazione Comunista/Communist Refoundation Party (PRC). Autonomist movements unite to form the Lega Nord/Northern League (LN). President Cossiga uses presidential powers to block investigation of his role in the creation of "Gladio" and attacks Italy's institutions in an endless series of public outbursts. A referendum on electoral reform passes by a huge majority in June against the wishes of the party hierarchies. Tens of thousands of Albanian boat people attempt to migrate to Italy.

1992 Treaty of Maastricht signed in February. General elections in April end in a historic defeat for the DC and a triumph for the LN. President Cossiga resigns, provoking a major political crisis. After the mafia kills prosecutor Giovanni Falcone, Parliament elects Oscar Luigi Scalfaro (DC) to the presidency. The "Clean Hands" corruption investigation begins; hundreds of DC and PSI politicians, including Craxi, are implicated by the end of the year. In September the lira collapses and the new government of Giuliano Amato (PSI) is forced to take emergency measures to save the country from financial crisis.

1993 The Amato government collapses under the weight of the corruption investigations and public demands for change after a second referendum on electoral reform in April. The governor of the Bank of Italy, Carlo Azeglio Ciampi, is appointed premier. The LN achieves a massive victory in local elections held in June. In December, political leaders of all parties publicly admit to huge corruption in the trial of a Milanese businessman; investigations begin into the mafia links of several prominent politicians, notably Giulio Andreotti, who is eventually charged with ordering the murder of a journalist, Mino Pecorelli, in 1979. Death, in November, of Federico Fellini.

1994 Victory, in elections held under new majoritarian rules, of the media entrepreneur Silvio Berlusconi. Together with the LN and the neofascist Alleanza Nazionale/National Alliance (AN), Berlusconi forms a government in May. Berlusconi's government lasts until December, when the LN votes against the government in a vote of confidence. By December, Berlusconi, too, is indicted.

1995 The most tormented government crisis even of postwar Italian history is resolved by the appointment in January of Lamberto Dini, an economist and banker, at the head of a government of unelected technocrats. Dini is supported in Parliament by the LN, the PDS, and the remnants of the DC, who have retaken the name of the PPI. The polemics aroused by Dini's appointment cause the lira to plummet against the mark and lead to worries about Italy's political stability. Romano Prodi, a Bologna economics professor, forms a center-left coalition with the support of the PDS. The Olive Tree Coalition (Ulivo), as it is known, rapidly wins public support.

1996 Prodi wins national elections held in April, but his government is dependent on the PRC for a majority in Parliament. The new government is forced to make harsh economic decisions to meet the deadlines laid down for monetary union by the Maastricht treaty. A bicameral commission on constitutional reform is announced. In September the LN, flush with victory because of its strong showing in the general elections, proclaims that it will work for the Constitution of an independent republic of Padania.

1997 **March:** Italy agrees to head a multinational UN force to assist in ensuring humanitarian aid to Albania. Over 16,000 refugees flee that country to land in nearby southern Italy. **April:** Administrative elections in many Italian cities see the PRC gain while other major parties, both in the Olive Tree Coalition and in the opposition, fare poorly. **October:** The PRC protests deep budget cuts in pensions and health care by threatening to withdraw its support of the government.

1998 Italy qualifies to convert to the euro in May. However, the bicameral commission on constitutional reform collapses in June and the Olive Tree Coalition government falls on a vote of confidence on October 9. Massimo D'Alema becomes prime minister of a new center-left government at the end of October. The new government is immediately plunged into a diplomatic crisis when Abdullah Ocalen, leader of the Kurdish guerrilla movement in Turkey, surrenders to Italian authorities. Ocalen is wanted in both Germany and Turkey and faces the death penalty in the latter. He is extradited to Turkey in January 1999. Earlier in the year, in February, a low-flying U.S. jet cuts the cable of a ski gondola in the Trentino town of Cavalese, killing 20 tourists and provoking widespread indignation. In party politics, the Democratici di Sinistra/Democrats of the Left (DS) supersede the PDS on 13 February 1998; AN, meanwhile, holds a major conference in Verona to continue its shift toward a postfascist ideological identity. In July, Berlusconi is sentenced to two years and nine months' imprisonment, pending appeal, on four charges of corrupting tax officers. Berlusconi's sentence evokes international discussion of the "Berlusconi Problem" and the normality of Italian democracy. Berlusconi is acquitted in May 2000 of one of the charges and the court finds extenuating circumstances for the others.

1999 On 1 January 1999, the exchange rates of the 11 participating currencies are fixed and the euro becomes a financial reality. Romano Prodi creates the Democrats for the Ulivo, a new political formation, in February and polemicizes with the DS and the PPI. He leaves Italian politics in June to become president of the European Commission. The D'Alema government vacillates over the NATO bombing of Kosovo and Yugoslavia, first condemning, then supporting, the raids. The government's other major decision of the year is the privatization of ENEL, the state electricity company, in which the state retains a 51 percent stake. D'Alema resigns in December to reshuffle his government. This is the first government crisis managed by President Carlo Azeglio Ciampi, who is elected on 13 May, with broad bipartisan support. Roberto Benigni's *La Vita è bella*, a daring tragicomic film about Italian Jews in Auschwitz, wins three Oscars, including best picture, in March.

2000 The pope opens the Jubilee year in Rome. The culmination will be a huge open-air mass in Rome on 19 August attended by more than 2,000,000 young people from all over the world. In politics, the year is dominated by the creation in February of the Casa delle Libertà/House of Freedoms (CDL) by Silvio Berlusconi, which links together Forza Italia, the LN, AN, and two centrist parties in a right-of-center coalition. The new coalition achieves a substantial victory in the regional elections of April 2000, taking over 60 percent of the vote in Lombardy. D'Alema's government falls after the vote, and D'Alema is replaced by Giuliano Amato. In October, Francesco Rutelli, the youthful mayor of Rome, is nevertheless preferred to Amato as the Olive Tree Coalition's candidate for the premiership in the 2001 general elections. On the sporting front, Italy reaches the final of the European football championship, losing 2–1 to France on 2 July, and finishes an excellent seventh in the medals table of the Sydney Olympics in September, winning 13 gold medals. The disgraced former premier Bettino Craxi dies in Tunisia in January.

2001 Striking victory for Silvio Berlusconi's CDL in general elections in May despite an international press outcry against the Milanese businessman, whom *The Economist* denounces as "unfit to govern Italy." The center-right parties take nearly 50 percent of the popular vote and Forza Italia, Berlusconi's own party, obtains 29.4 percent (10.9 million votes), easily the highest total of any single party. The new government immediately has to deal with a major crisis: In July an estimated 9,000 anarchists and no-global activists cause massive street violence in Genoa during the G8 summit. One demonstrator is killed by police gunfire, 180 people are injured, and tens of millions of euros of damage is done to the city center. On 22 July, a police blitz in a Genoa hostel housing no-global demonstrators provokes polemic after dozens of innocent protesters are savagely beaten by policemen. On 8 October, a collision between two aircraft at Milan's Linate airport causes 118 deaths and a major investigation into airport security. In foreign policy, Italy approves U.S. military action in Afghanistan on 9 October with a bipartisan motion of Parliament. Parliament also approves Italian participation in the peacekeeping force in the following month. Death in July of Indro Montanelli, famous journalist and writer and outspoken critic of Silvio Berlusconi.

2002 Euro notes circulate from 1 January. Lira notes disappear from circulation on 28 February. The introduction of the euro is accompanied by a lengthy polemic about shopkeepers exploiting the monetary changeover to raise prices. In politics, the year starts badly for Berlusconi's coalition when Renato Ruggieri resigns as foreign minister on 5 January in protest of the euroskeptical attitudes of the government. Berlusconi takes over the ministerial portfolio and acts as his own foreign minister until November, when he is replaced by Franco Frattini. The government's aggressive rhetoric against the judiciary, and its attempts to favor the prime minister by decriminalizing offences of which Berlusconi himself is accused, provokes a backlash in civil society. Milanese judge Francesco Saverio Borrelli invites the judiciary to "resist, resist, resist" against political pressures on 15 January. In February, the so-called girotondo movement is launched by film director Nanni Moretti and other leading intellectuals. On 24 March, the small parties of the center-left, including the PPI, consolidate into a single party called Democrazia e Libertà/Democracy and Liberty Party (DL). Francesco Rutelli is the first party leader. On 14 September, approximately one million people protest against the government's abuse of the law-making process to serve political ends.

The year is also characterized by personal tragedies. On 7 March, more than 50 would-be immigrants are killed when their boat capsizes near the island of Lampedusa. Thirty-seven die in similar circumstances on September 15. On 19 March, left-wing terrorists inspired by the Red Brigades kill a Bologna University teacher and government consultant, Marco Biagi. The killers are later arrested after a train shootout in which a policeman is killed. A trade unionist called Massimo D'Antona had previously been killed by the same gang of terrorists, in May 1999. On 31 October, 27 children and their teacher are killed in Molise when a primary school collapses during an earthquake.

2003   The year opens with intense political protests over the war in Iraq. Over a million antiwar activists march through Rome on 15 February. The Berlusconi government nevertheless approves the use of NATO bases in Italy by U.S. jets and on 15 April votes to take part in a peacekeeping exercise in Iraq; 3,000 Italian troops are eventually sent at the end of the conflict to serve in southern Iraq. On 12 November, 19 Italian soldiers and 8 Iraqis are killed by a suicide bomber at the Italian mission headquarters in Nassirya. Italy's European policy falls into disarray after Berlusconi opens the Italian presidency of the European Union (EU) in July by insulting a German deputy of the European Parliament. Following further anti-German remarks made by government ministers, Chancellor Gerhard Schröder is forced to cancel a planned vacation in Italy. Italy's presidency fails to get EU-wide approval of the constitutional treaty proposed by a constitutional convention in July 2003.

Domestic politics is dominated by the conflict between the courts and the political class. On 29 April, Cesare Previti, Berlusconi's longtime close advisor, is condemned to 11 years' imprisonment for corruption. Giulio Andreotti's decade-long legal battle against charges of murder and association with the mafia is ended by an unequivocal acquittal on the first charge and a somewhat less ringing vote of confidence on the second. At the end of the year, Parmalat, a foodstuffs multinational, collapses amid Enron-like allegations of fraud, false accounting, and illegal disposal of assets. Death, on 24 January, of FIAT boss Gianni Agnelli. Luciano Berio, a daunting contemporary composer, dies in May.

2004   On 5 May, Berlusconi's government reaches its 1060th day, the longest administration in republican Italy's history. In June, however, European elections are won by the center-left opposition, and Forza Italia's share of the vote falls to just 21 percent. The cause of the government's lack of popularity is Italy's economic malaise. Low growth, rising public debt, and worries about competitiveness characterize political discourse in 2004. On July 3, Giulio Tremonti, "superminister" for economic affairs, resigns and is replaced by Domenico Siniscalco. The year is dominated by political turbulence within the CDL, and at the end of the year Berlusconi is obliged to bring one of his principal critics, Marco Follini, the secretary of the Unione dei democratici cristiani e di centro/Union of Christian Democrats and the Center (UDC), into the government as deputy prime minister. The year is also marked by the abolition of compulsory military service starting 1 January 2005 and, on 29 October, by the signature of the EU constitutional treaty in Rome. Norberto Bobbio, a leading philosopher, dies on 9 January. Umberto Bossi, the leader of the LN, is hospitalized for six months after a heart attack. Bossi's absence from politics slows passage of the CDL's sweeping proposed reform of the Constitution, which is the centerpiece of its domestic agenda but is regarded with hostility by the UDC.

2005   On 10 February, Romano Prodi, now free of his commitments in Brussels, presents the Unione, a new electoral alliance between the Olive Tree Coalition and the PRC. The new alliance enjoys quick successes. In April, it inflicts a crushing defeat on the CDL in the regional elections. The center-right wins only Lombardy and Venetia; the other 13 regions without a special statute vote for the center-left. The defeat weakens Berlusconi's political position. He resigns on 20 April and presents a reshuffled administration on 27 April. The new government is plagued by political turmoil: In October, the same month that Romano Prodi wins a "primary" to become the Union's official leader, Marco Follini declares Berlusconi unsuitable to be prime minister. Further political tension is caused by the publication of illicit recordings of telephone conversations that appear to show that the governor of the Bank of Italy, Antonio Fazio, had intervened behind the scenes to prevent a Dutch bank from taking over Antonveneto, a small northern Italian bank. Fazio is forced to resign in December, but in the meantime the affair arouses considerable international criticism.

In November, the government enacts a constitutional reform empowering the president of the Council of Ministers, creating a Senate of the Regions, and transferring exclusive competence to the regions for matters concerning health care, the police, and education. It is the most sweeping reform to the 1948 Constitution in the history of the Republic. The new law is to be subject to ratification by a confirmatory referendum. In December, the government also passes a new electoral law restoring proportional representation. The death on 2 April of John Paul II causes widespread public mourning.

2006   The first four months of the year are dominated by the electoral campaign, in which Silvio Berlusconi, whose defeat was taken for granted at the onset, leads the CDL to near-victory. After the poll on 9–10 April, only 24,000 votes separate the two coalitions in the elections to the Chamber of Deputies, with both sides getting approximately 19 million votes. In the Senate elections, the CDL actually gets more votes than the Union, but obtains fewer seats. The Union, however, is reliant on the votes of the life senators for a majority. The new Parliament chooses Giorgio Napolitano to succeed Carlo Azeglio Ciampi on 10 May. On 17 May, Romano Prodi presents his new government, which survives a vote of confidence in the Senate by a narrow margin. At the end of June, the CDL's constitutional law is heavily defeated in the confirmatory referendum: 62 percent vote against. On 9 July, Italy wins the World Cup for the fourth time, beating Germany in the semifinal and France in the final. In August 2006, Italy takes a leading role in the decision to send an EU peacekeeping force to Lebanon to police the ceasefire between Hizbullah and Israel. Over 2,000 Italian troops are committed. Italy pledges itself to take command of the mission in February 2007.

Introduction

Italy is a country that exercises a hold on the imagination of people all over the world. Its long history has left an inexhaustible treasure chest of cultural achievement: There is hardly a town in Italy that does not repay a visit. Great historic cities such as Rome, Florence, and Venice are among the most sought-after destinations in the world for tourists and art lovers. Italy's natural beauty and cuisine are rightly renowned.

But Italy's history and politics are also a source of endless fascination. Modern Italy has consistently been a political laboratory for the rest of Europe. In the 19th century, Italian patriotism was of crucial importance in the struggle against the absolute governments reintroduced after the Congress of Vienna in 1814–1815. The subsequent transformation of this patriotic feeling, which was celebrated by the great British historian G. M. Trevelyan in his trilogy of books on Giuseppe Garibaldi, into a jingoistic form of nationalism and imperialism, is less well known but equally significant in historical terms. Italy's parliamentary democracy struggled against the powerful ideological forces unleashed by the country's poverty and its political class's ambitions until 1922, when Fascism came to power. After the fall of Fascism during World War II, Italy became a model of rapid economic development, though its politics has never been less than contentious and its democracy has remained a troubled one.

This book is an attempt to introduce the key personalities, events, social developments, and cultural achievements of Italy since the beginning of the 19th century, when Italy first began to emerge as something more than a geographical entity and national feeling began to grow.

LAND AND PEOPLE

The long boot-shaped peninsula of Italy separates the Mediterranean basin into western and eastern halves. In addition, the largest islands in the Mediterranean Sea, Sicily and Sardinia, are both part of Italian territory. Italy is just over 300,000 square kilometers (115,830 square miles) in size and some 1,500 kilometers (938 miles) in length. It has some 7,600 kilometers (4,722 miles) of coastline. The country's northernmost cities, Aosta and Bolzano, are in the heart of the Alps; Sicily, by contrast, is just a ferry ride away from North Africa. In all there are 12 degrees of latitude between the southernmost tip of Sicily and the frontiers with France, Switzerland, and Austria. Italy's geographical coordinates are N 42° 50, E 12° 50.

The North has a continental climate, with occasional extremes of heat, humidity, and cold; the South is more typically Mediterranean in temperature, with scorching heat in the summer and mostly mild winters. Daytime summer temperatures are 33–35°C in the North, 38–42°C in the South. In the winter, by contrast, southern towns such as Palermo or Naples rarely drop below freezing point and may even enjoy temperatures of 10–15°C, while the Po River valley endures long weeks of subzero weather and dense fog. The South is very dry; indeed, water shortages are becoming a political problem of some importance.

Almost all the country is mountainous. In Sicily there are peaks exceeding 3,000 meters (9,847 feet), including Mount Etna, one of the world's highest active volcanoes. The Apennines run for 745 miles like the shinbone of the Italian boot through Umbria, the Marches, Abruzzi, Molise, and Campania. The highest peaks are in the western Alps: Monte Rosa is over 4,600 meters (15,203 feet) in height and Monte Bianco (Mont Blanc), Europe's highest mountain, is 4,810 meters (15,755 feet). The highest points in the eastern Alps are to be found in the Trentino and in Alto Adige. These are Ortles, at 3,905 meters (12,812 feet), and Gran Zebrù (in German, Königsspitze), at 3,857 meters (12,654 feet). The Alps are populated by several linguistic minorities of some importance. Ladini are to be found in large numbers in Friuli, Trentino, and Alto Adige; German speakers are a large majority of the people that inhabit Alto Adige, or Süd Tirol. French speakers dwell in the Valle d'Aosta.

The only lowland areas are the fertile flood valley of the Po River, Italy's longest river at 652 kilometers (405 miles), and the heel of the Italian boot, Apulia. Many of Italy's largest industrial cities (Turin, Milan, Brescia, Bologna, Padua) are concentrated in the Po River valley, while Apulia boasts some of Italy's most important ports: Bari, Taranto, and Brindisi.

The mountainous terrain ensures that population density is very high in the flatter, more accessible parts of the country and along the coast. Big cities such as Milan, Genoa, Rome, and Naples all have densities of over 2,000 people per square kilometer, and almost all of the country, including some of the most mountainous areas, has more than 200 inhabitants per square kilometer. Only the sun-scorched, barren uplands of Sardinia, southern Italy, and Sicily are sparsely inhabited. Even the Alps are dotted with villages and thriving small commercial centers.

In addition to the Po, other important rivers are the Adige, which flows from the Alps to the Adriatic sea and is some 410 kilometers (255 miles) in length, and the Tiber (Tevere), which is also just over 400 kilometers in length. There are several important lakes, of which the largest is the pistol-shaped Lake Garda, which is 370 square kilometers (143 square miles) in area. Lake Garda is shared by the regions of Venetia, Lombardy, and the autonomous province of Trentino. Other important lakes are Lake Bolsena in Latium and Lakes Maggiore and Como on the Lombardy–Switzerland border.

Italy is divided into 20 regions and 103 provinces (*see* REGIONALISM). The largest region in population is Lombardy, which has nearly 9.5 million inhabitants, 16 percent of the nation's total population. The largest region in area is Sicily, with a surface area of 25,700 square kilometers (9,925 square miles).

HISTORICAL DEVELOPMENT

A visitor to Italy today, observing the busy commercial success that pervades almost the entire peninsula, might be excused for thinking that the country had enjoyed a long history of Swiss-like political stability, economic development, social cohesion, and peace. In fact, Poland aside, no other European nation has been so constantly ravaged by war and invasion as Italy. The peninsula has been an enticing prize for the dominant European power of every epoch since the final collapse of Rome in AD 476. Beginning with the Lombards, who swept through all of northern and central Italy after AD 568 and gradually established (by the standards of the time) a well-administered, though loosely organized, state that increasingly coveted the wealthy but less politically cohesive South, Italy has absorbed waves of foreign invasion that have left their traces in the cultural and political DNA of the peninsula's inhabitants.

At the risk of over-generalizing, it has been broadly true that the accidents of geography and history ensured that the North has been influenced by northern Europe, and in particular the civilizations of France and Germany, while the South has been dominated by Mediterranean powers. The South, as a consequence, has known a more absolutist tradition of rule, while the cities of the North were freer to develop their own forms of rule. The Holy Roman Empire, to which northern Italy nominally belonged after AD 773, when the Lombards were defeated by Charlemagne, was not able to exercise its authority in the peninsula after Charlemagne's death in AD 814, and political power in northern Italy devolved on local noblemen and churchmen. The North's primary form of organization became the city-state: small, with a politically active aristocracy and a sometimes turbulent populace. These cities were hardly models of good government. They were riven by bloody factional strife and interfamily warfare, but they were economically dynamic, and possessed—to use, anachronistically, the language of modern-day political science—a conscious political identity. This enabled them to unite against an outside aggressor: Between 1152 and 1176, the efforts of Frederick Barbarossa to restore the Holy Roman Empire's authority in northern Italy were defeated by a league of northern Italian cities, the Lega Lombarda.

In the South, by contrast, the Arabs, who occupied Sicily and much of southern Italy in AD 827, turned Palermo into one of the most prosperous and technologically advanced cities in the world in the ninth century. They were supplanted in the 11th century by the Normans, who established a highly centralized form of government that brooked no opposition.

The last attempt to unify the peninsula before the 19th century took place at the beginning of the 13th century when Frederick Barbarossa's grandson, Frederick II, who had inherited the throne of Sicily from the Normans, endeavored to restore imperial authority over both the papacy and the city-states. Italy was ravaged by a civil war between the supporters of the empire (the Ghibellines) and the pope (Guelfs). After 30 years of constant fighting, the country was left prostrated but disunited upon Frederick's death in 1250. Frederick's successors continued the struggle, but the papacy was aided by the French king of Anjou, who made southern Italy part of the Angevin empire in 1266. By the beginning of the 14th century, Italy lacked any central authority whatever: Neither the papacy, the Angevins, nor the Holy Roman Empire was strong enough to impose order on the peninsula, which broke down into perpetual and internecine warfare. In 1316, the papal curia was removed to Avignon in southern France, removing the one symbol of authority in central Italy, which soon degenerated into anarchy and baronial feuding.

Consolidation took place in the 14th century, which saw the rise of several native Italian principalities or republics to positions of power within the peninsula. Under the leadership of the Visconti family, Milan established itself as the dominant force in the North and Center of the country. Its main rivals were Venice, which enjoyed stable aristocratic government, a growing empire in Dalmatia, and domination over the northeast of the peninsula, and Florence, which overran nearly all of modern-day Tuscany. All three of these states eclipsed the Angevins, whose hold on southern Italy was somewhat tenuous, and who were replaced as rulers by the expansionist Kingdom of Aragon in the 15th century. The three great Italian states of northern and central Italy were the envy of Europe from 1300 onward. They were the most populous and wealthy societies of their day, with an advanced industrial base, sophisticated banking systems, and sublime levels of artistic achievement. The Renaissance, the revival of classical learning, was of course a Europe-wide phenomenon, but its home was in Italy, where the wealth of the noble families enabled artistic patronage on a grand scale. The 14th and 15th centuries were the age of Petrarch, Boccaccio, Michelangelo, Raphael, and Benvenuto Cellini; before them had come the towering genius of Dante, the poet whose writings mark the transition between the ancient world and the modern.

Renaissance Italy, despite the creation in 1454 of an "Italian League" among Milan, Venice, Florence, the papacy, and the Kingdom of Naples, was plagued by continual warfare. At the end of the 15th century Italy was invaded by Charles VIII of France, who was followed by the Spanish and the forces of the revived Holy Roman Empire. Italy became a battleground for the powers. This was the age of Niccolo Machiavelli, the Florentine diplomat whose willingness to accept the ruthless laws of *Realpolitik* still shocks, but who saw clearly that the wealth and artistic glory of the Italian states counted for nothing in the absence of military preparedness, social discipline, and political unity. Machiavelli's classic,

Il Principe (*The Prince*), was published in 1519, the same year that Charles of Ghent took the imperial title. By dynastic chance, Charles already possessed the crowns of Spain, Austria, and Burgundy, and thus controlled all of continental Europe from the Polish border to Spain—except Italy, which split the vast empire in half, and France, with whom he fought several bloody wars throughout his reign. France's hold on Lombardy was ended after the battle of Pavia in 1525, and in 1530 Charles conquered Florence. Charles annexed Milan for Spain; placed Florence in the hands of the Medici family; established the dukedoms of Savoy, Ferrara, Mantua, Urbino, Modena, and Parma; left Lucca, Venice, and Genoa as aristocratic republics; allowed papal control over much of central Italy; and ruled Naples and the South through a viceroy. In the following decades, Venice, the one Italian state to retain some status as a European power, saw its empire in the eastern Mediterranean nibbled away by the rising power of the Ottoman Turks.

Italy thus entered a long period of domination by the Spanish crown, and the parts of the peninsula that were most directly ruled by Spain were drawn into the Spanish state's decline and eventual fall. Southern Italy, in particular, was bled dry by the need to subsidize the gargantuan edifice of the Spanish court and was deeply influenced politically by the corruption and feudalism of Spanish rule. Italy became one of the chief prizes for the powers of Europe in the War of the Spanish Succession (1701–1713). The main beneficiary of the war, in Italian terms, was Austria, which annexed Lombardy in 1707 and added Mantua and the mainland South in 1714, with Sicily passing briefly under the control of the Dukedom of Savoy, which also expanded its influence in Piedmont. Savoy, a hereditary duchy enjoying great autonomy from the Holy Roman Empire, which had been governing a tract of territory on both sides of the Alps since the Middle Ages, exchanged Sicily for Sardinia in 1720. The new Kingdom of Sardinia, and its capital, Turin, became an established power within the peninsula. The map of Italy was redrawn twice more before 1748. Austria's gains were reduced later in the same century after the short War of the Polish Succession (1733–1735), when Charles Bourbon of Spain became king of the Two Sicilies and reunited Naples with Sicily. In 1748, the peace of Aix-la-Chapelle, which brought to an end the War of the Austrian Succession, saw the Bourbons extend their influence, while Modena fell into Austrian hands. Between 1748 and 1796 the Italian peninsula was at peace; astonishingly, this was the longest period without major war since the fall of the Roman Empire.

In 1796, Napoleon invaded Italy at the head of the French revolutionary army, ending the Venetian Republic's long independent history and driving the Savoys from Turin; he returned again in 1800 to reestablish French dominion. Like the Lombards, Franks, Arabs, Normans, Angevins, Aragonese, French, Spanish, and Austrians before him, he drew and redrew the political map of the peninsula with scant regard for the wishes of its inhabitants (see NAPOLEONIC ITALY). In so doing, however, he created the Kingdom of Italy in 1805. Naples was added the following year, with only Sicily remaining outside French rule. Napoleon undertook an ambitious period of modernization: A unified civil code was introduced, the power of the clergy was reduced, and internal customs duties were abolished. Many of these reforms were only partially implemented, but an important principle had at least been established. Italy, finally, was being treated as something more than a geographic expression: It had begun the process of becoming a state.

MODERN ITALY

The starting point in the story of modern Italy is the Congress of Vienna (1814–1815), at which the great powers of Europe—notably Austria—put the lid of absolutist rule on the cauldron of Italian national and liberal sentiment brought to a boil by the French Revolution and the Napoleonic conquests in Italy. Four main powers dominated the peninsula after the treaty: Austria, which regained sovereignty over Venice and Lombardy and exercised decisive influence over the nominally independent duchies of Tuscany, Modena, Parma, and Lucca; the Kingdom of Sardinia, comprising modern-day Sardinia, Liguria, Piedmont, Aosta, and Nice, which was restored to the House of Savoy; Naples, which was restored to Ferdinand IV of Bourbon and which swiftly annexed Sicily to create the Kingdom of the Two Sicilies; and the Papal States, consisting of modern-day Emilia-Romagna, Lazio, and the Marches, which was directly ruled by the pope. The areas closest to the Austrian border (Trento and Friuli) were absorbed into Austria itself. All told, the Congress of Vienna left nearly five million Italians under direct Austrian rule.

The first half of the 19th century was marked by uprisings against absolute rule in Naples and Turin. Spurred on by the *carbonari,* secret societies of progressive young noblemen, soldiers, professionals, and students, liberal revolutions broke out in Naples in 1820, Piedmont in 1821, and the Papal States in 1831. The goal of the revolutionaries—a Constitution, similar to the one adopted in Spain in 1812, which compelled the crown to share executive power with a parliament elected by the wealthier classes—seems modest in retrospect, but it was bitterly resisted by the arch-conservative chief minister of the Austrian Empire throughout this period, Klemens von Metternich, who feared that the contagion of liberal ideas would spread to his own realm. Forceful Austrian intervention soon quelled all three uprisings, but the fact that the monarchies and duchies of Italy relied on a foreign power for their continued existence inevitably led to the struggle against absolute rule transforming itself into a nationalist one. By 1848, the "year of revolutions," nationalist feeling was widespread among the Italian middle and upper classes. One of the leading nationalists, the former priest Vincenzo Gioberti, became prime minister of Sardinia after King Charles Albert, under popular pressure, granted constitutional rule; another, the republican Giuseppe Mazzini, became part of the committee of "dictators" that ruled Rome after a popular uprising had driven out the pope. All of Italy from Venice to Palermo was incandescent with revolutionary activity in 1848–1849 (*see* REVOLUTIONS OF 1848).

THE RISORGIMENTO

The revolutions of 1848 nevertheless met the same fate as their predecessors. Austrian troops crushed uprisings in Lombardy and Venetia; French soldiers restored the pope's authority in Rome; and the Sardinian army, which supported the rebels in Milan and Venice, proved woefully unable to match the Austrians on the battlefield and was defeated at the battles of Custoza and Novara. The rising star of Sardinian politics, Count Camillo Benso di Cavour, drew the conclusion that nationalist fervor was not by itself enough to ensure the expulsion of Austria from the peninsula: Diplomacy and economic modernization were of greater importance. Cavour became premier of the Kingdom of Piedmont-Sardinia in 1852 and swiftly began building railways, opening protected markets to foreign competition, and strengthening the military. In foreign policy, he cultivated Britain and France, sending a contingent of Bersaglieri to the Crimean War in 1855, thereby winning a seat at the subsequent peace conference in Paris. In 1858, at Plombières, Cavour struck a cynical secret bargain with Emperor Napoleon III of France, under the terms of which he would surrender Nice and Savoy to France in exchange for guaranteed French assistance in a defensive war with Austria. At the same conference, it was foreseen that all of northern Italy would be annexed by Sardinia, that a French prince would rule over a central Italian state, and that Naples would be ruled by a figure acceptable to the French. The three kingdoms would be organized in a loose Italian federation, with the pope as the nominal head. Cavour's conception of a united Italy, in short, recognized the necessity for a foreign and papal role and was principally directed at extending the Savoyard Kingdom of Piedmont-Sardinia's own power and ridding the peninsula of the Austrians.

In the event, almost all of Italy was unified by October 1860, and King Victor Emmanuel II of Sardinia was crowned "*Re d'Italia*" in March 1861. In other words, Cavour obtained more for the throne of Sardinia than he had originally intended. Historians have been divided over how far his diplomatic skills were responsible for this striking success. Cavour can take credit for forcing the Austrians' hand and tricking them into war in April 1859 and for having prepared the Sardinian army to the point where it was able to provide vital support to its French allies in the summer of 1859. But both national feeling and sheer chance played an undeniably important role. Without such incidental factors as the incompetence of Austrian diplomacy, the vainglory of Napoleon III, and the military genius of the "hero of two worlds," Giuseppe Garibaldi, unification might have been postponed for several decades. National feeling led to the peoples of central Italy rising in support of Cavour after the outbreak of war with Austria and to their eventual annexation by Piedmont-Sardinia in the spring of 1860—although Cavour handled masterfully the diplomatic tensions caused by this move. Hostility to feudalism enabled Garibaldi to lead successful revolutions in Sicily and the rest of the South in the spring and summer of 1860 and might have led to Italian unification taking a more radical turn had Cavour not risked international displeasure by invading the Papal States and marching on Garibaldi's headquarters in Naples in October 1860.

Garibaldi himself contributed immensely to Cavour's success by placing his nationalist principles ahead of his republican and socialist sympathies and surrendering his conquests in southern Italy to Victor Emmanuel without bloodshed. Unification, in other words, was the outcome of a complex combination of human, diplomatic, and political factors. It remains true, however, that without Cavour's instinctive grasp of the principles of *Realpolitik*, events might well have taken a vastly different turn. The Piedmontese statesman is the only Italian leader of the last two centuries who can stand comparison with such great figures in modern European history as Bismarck, Gladstone, Masaryk, Churchill, De Gaulle, and Adenauer.

LIBERAL ITALY

The Italy that emerged in March 1861 was essentially Piedmont-Sardinia writ large. The capital of the new state was Turin, the Statuto Albertino (the Constitution of 1848) was adopted in toto for the new kingdom, and almost all of the dominant political figures were Piedmontese. The North was by far the richest part of the country and the only one that was industrialized. Many of Italy's subsequent problems can be traced to the lopsided balance of power within the new state. Southern Italy, in particular, was undeniably neglected by the northern power brokers in industry and politics and was left to stagnate—with the complicity of its own ruling class of landlords and aristocrats—as a semifeudal backwater.

In addition to immense economic difficulties, the new Italian state had to complete the process of unification. Venetia, Trentino, and Trieste remained under Austrian control in 1861, and the pope's authority in Rome was protected by a French expeditionary force that had no difficulty in crushing an attempt by Garibaldi and a small army of patriots to seize the city at the battle of Mentana in 1867. The questions of Venetia and Rome were resolved by astuteness. In 1866, Italy allied with Prussia against Austria and, despite a poor military performance, was rewarded with Venetia after the war. In 1870, the defeat of Napoleon III at the hands of Bismarck allowed Italy to march troops into Rome. Papal possessions were reduced in size to the walls of the Vatican, and for the next 50 years, church–state relations were extremely tense. The

Church suspended all diplomatic relations with the Italian state, did its best to have Italy ostracized by Catholic nations such as France, and banned Catholics from taking part in Italian political life. Only in 1913, when the rise of socialism alarmed the Vatican hierarchy, was this ban relaxed.

Italian socialism arose in particularly intransigent form because the Italian state failed, in the 30 years following unification, to provide elementary social justice. Newly unified Italy was "liberal" in the sense that it could boast parliamentary institutions, but it was not in any way democratic. Unlike Britain, where the suffrage was extended to almost all the adult male population by 1884, and where trade unions were granted significant opportunities to organize manual workers, Italian governments were reluctant to concede basic political rights to the working class. From 1876 onward, after the "parliamentary revolution" brought Agostino Depretis to power, Italy was governed by the so-called parliamentary left, but Depretis, despite many promises, failed to widen the suffrage in any significant way. An electoral law extending the suffrage from 600,000 voters to just over 2,000,000 was passed against stiff parliamentary opposition in 1882, but this was still less than 7 percent of the adult population. Having passed this law, Depretis rid himself of his more radical parliamentary supporters by appealing to the conservative opposition to "transform themselves" into a force of government (*see TRASFORMISMO*). Only in 1912, long after comparable European states, was universal male suffrage conceded, and the first election under these rules was held in 1913.

A similarly narrow-minded view prevailed in the political class's attitude toward socialism and trade unionism. Depretis's successors (he died in 1887)—even former radicals such as Garibaldi's onetime secretary, Francesco Crispi—took a harsh line with the nascent movements of the working class and peasants. Crispi used the regular army to crush a peasant revolt in Sicily in 1893–1894, and in 1898, a government that included prominent moderates suppressed bread riots in Milan with implacable zeal. Hundreds of striking workers were killed by troops commanded by General Bava Beccaris. Repression made no difference to the growth of the workers' movements. Social conditions, including blatantly unjust systems of land tenure, made inevitable their appearance on the political scene. A greater show of tolerance, and a less ruthless defense of the propertied class's privileges, might have led the

Partito Socialista Italiano/Italian Socialist Party (PSI), which was founded in 1892, to develop into a moderate "labor" force on the British model. Its founder, Filippo Turati, was a pragmatic figure who warned against violent revolution, and other early Socialists were willing to co-operate with relative progressives such as the several-times premier, Giovanni Giolitti, to win concrete social and political reforms. Instead, the PSI embraced both dogmatic Marxism and the violent syndicalism espoused by the French theorist Georges Sorel. By 1912, the PSI had developed an intransigence of its own. Its new voice was Benito Mussolini, who would soon quarrel with the PSI over the issue of intervention in the Great War, but who relished the turbulent mass politics offered by the labor movement.

IMPERIALISM AND WAR

Readiness to experiment with the politics of violence was growing on the political right too. Italy's colonial adventures, which began with Depretis in the mid-1880s, and continued under Crispi in the 1890s, failed to leave Italy with an adequate place in the sun and, on two occasions—at Dogali in 1887 and Adowa in 1896—ended in military setbacks at the hands of Ethiopian tribesmen. By the first decade of the 20th century, nationalist theorists (including some socialists) were claiming that Italy was a "proletarian" nation that had been robbed of its birthright by rapacious powers such as Britain and France. This resentful mood led directly to a short war with Turkey that ended with Italy occupying the Dodecanese Islands, including Rhodes, and most of modern-day Libya. These gains were confirmed by the Treaty of Lausanne in October 1912. Such a minor war (only 3,000 Italians were killed) was hardly sufficient for the more headstrong members of the nationalist intelligentsia, or for "futurist" thinkers such as Filippo Tommaso Marinetti, whose *Futurist Manifesto* (1909) described war as the world's only "true hygiene."

The desire for war at all costs was a decisive force in pushing Italy into war on the side of the Entente in May 1915, although a majority of the Italian people were opposed to intervention and Italy was bound by treaty to Austria and Germany. Italy had followed a pro-German foreign policy since 1882, when it joined the Triple Alliance. The Triple Alliance, which gave Italy an Austro-German military guarantee in the event of an aggressive French war, made perfect sense in strategic terms, but it was unpopular with a vocal section of Italian public opinion, the so-called *irredentisti*, who resented the fact that no effort was being made to recapture the "unredeemed" territories of Trento and Trieste. After the outbreak of war in August 1914, Italy's leaders saw the opportunity to bargain for a return of the Italian-speaking parts of the Austrian Empire. Italy argued that it deserved compensation for entering the war, and a cynical auction took place between the two warring blocs of powers, with Austria eventually offering a generous territorial settlement in exchange for Italy's at least remaining neutral. Giolitti famously wrote that the Central Powers had offered *parecchio* (a large amount) and favored neutrality. The Entente offered more, however. The Treaty of London, secretly signed in April 1915, promised to satisfy Italy's imperial dreams in the eastern Mediterranean. Huge, intimidating public demonstrations were held by the nationalists during what was called the "radiant May," and a climate of support for intervention was created. On 24 May 1915, Italian troops invaded Austrian-held territory near Trieste.

World War I was an unmitigated disaster for Italy. Italian troops suffered hundreds of thousands of casualties vainly trying to push the Austro-German forces back across the Isonzo River near Trieste and out of their impregnable strongholds in the Trentino and Venetian Mountains. No fewer than 11 Italian offensives took place on the Isonzo front before mounting losses and plummeting morale brought the Italians to an exhausted halt. In October 1917, an Austro-German counterattack at Caporetto made short work of the demoralized Italians, who fell back to the Piave River, almost at Venice, suffering huge losses in men and materials. Here, fighting with immense bravery, the army narrowly succeeded in holding the line. When the Austrian Empire collapsed in 1918, Italy reoccupied the territories lost in October 1917, but the defeat of Caporetto left an indelible scar on the national consciousness.

World War I brought Italy fewer compensations in terms of territory or prestige than its leader had expected. Needing to placate Woodrow Wilson's desire to construct a new Europe on the principles of self-determination, Britain and France reneged on the Treaty of London, and Italy's dreams of establishing a colonial empire in the eastern Mediterranean were dashed. Italy's representative, Premier

Vittorio Emanuele Orlando, briefly walked out of the peace conference at Paris in 1919, but this show of petulance was to no avail. By
the terms of the Treaty of Saint-Germain, Italy was grudgingly given
a frontier with Austria at the Brenner Pass (thus absorbing German-
speaking Bolzano), and Trieste came under Italian rule. Fiume (Rijeka), a city on the Dalmatian coast with a substantial Italian population, was given to the new Kingdom of Yugoslavia, a decision the
nationalists regarded as an affront to Italy's dignity. With the tacit
consent of the Italian government, the poet Gabriele D'Annunzio, a
war hero, led a column of bravos to Fiume and established his own
petty dictatorship until a new Italian government, headed—for the
last time—by Giolitti, finally plucked up the courage in 1921 to drive
D'Annunzio and his legionnaires out.

D'Annunzio's action at Fiume was symbolic of the violence and
the contempt for the rule of law that was by now endemic in Italian
politics. The years 1920–1922 are known in Italy as the "red biennial." They were years in which the PSI, which had been severely
censured during the latter years of the war for its hostility to the
conflict, celebrated its victory in the elections held in 1919 by taking
to the streets and pressing the workers' economic demands. Street
clashes between the PSI and the so-called Fasci di combattimento,
formed by Mussolini after the war, became commonplace, and the
Italian state eventually degenerated into anarchy. Several figures, including the world-renowned philosopher Benedetto Croce, actually
welcomed Mussolini's accession to power in October 1922 as a way
of restoring the fundamental condition for a free society—law and
order—to the political scene (*see* MARCH ON ROME). But this
judgment failed to recognize that the Fascists were the principal organizers of the violence that was disfiguring Italian political life.
Croce later argued in his *Storia d'Italia 1870–1915* that Fascism had
"nothing to do" with the course of Italian history since the Risorgimento. For him, Fascism was simply a form of political gangsterism.
A much younger contemporary (who died of a beating inflicted upon
him by a Fascist squad), Piero Gobetti, saw things differently. He
said in his book *La rivoluzione liberale* (*The Liberal Revolution*,
1925) that "Fascism is the autobiography of a nation." The point is
still being debated among Italians.

FASCISM

Mussolini was the effective head of state from October 1922 to July 1943. King Victor Emmanuel III, whose refusal to sign an order to take emergency measures against Mussolini's illegality eased the Fascist movement's path to power, acquiesced in every step in the creation in Italy of *lo stato totalitario*—the totalitarian state. In 1924, after a Fascist squad kidnapped and killed an opposition deputy, Giacomo Matteotti, the king failed to side with the democratic forces, which boycotted Parliament in protest. The king's silence, and the democrats' own reluctance to act unconstitutionally, probably saved Mussolini's career from an ignominious end. In 1925–1926, all opposition to Fascism was outlawed, and Mussolini became Duce, and by 1930 a new legal, electoral, and institutional structure—the so-called corporate state—had been erected to reflect the principles of Fascist ideology. The state's presence in the daily life of the population was never as pervasive as in Nazi Germany or the Soviet bloc, nor were individual liberties ever entirely wiped out, but the intellectual rejection of liberal principles of constitutional government was as great as in Germany and Russia. The only nonfascist institution that exercised some limited degree of independence from the regime was the Catholic Church. The Lateran pacts, signed by Mussolini and Pope Pius XI in 1929, ended the long period of hostility between church and state and established Catholicism as the official state religion.

Mussolini was brought down by his decision to ally Italy with Nazi Germany. This move, which was accompanied by the introduction of racial laws against Italy's Jewish community, constrained Mussolini to follow the German dictator on military adventures for which Italy was little prepared, and which eventually exposed the vaunted Fascist state for the hollow shell it was. Despite Mussolini's defiance of the League of Nations during Italy's 1935 invasion of Ethiopia and Italy's involvement in the Spanish Civil War, Mussolini could have joined forces with Britain and France as late as 1939. Blinded by Germany's power, by his own antidemocratic ideology, or perhaps just by vainglory, the Fascist dictator decided that Italy should sign the "Pact of Steel" with Hitler instead. Italy burned its bridges with the Allies by invading France in June 1940, and in 1941 invaded Greece, where its army was humiliated and had to be rescued by German troops. In North Africa, British and Commonwealth soldiers made short work of Italian forces whenever they were not stiffened by the presence of German troops, and Italy's colonial empire in Africa swiftly fell under British control.

By 1943, Italy's situation had become desperate. The Allies — including, after December 1941, the United States — invaded Sicily in June 1943, provoking the final crisis of the Fascist state. During the night of 24–25 July 1943, the Fascist Grand Council, the cabinet of the Fascist movement, passed a vote of no confidence in Mussolini's leadership. The king, shifting with the political wind, signed a warrant for the Duce's arrest and appointed Marshal Pietro Badoglio, the general who had led the war in Ethiopia, to be the country's new leader. Italy officially surrendered on 8 September 1943, whereupon Badoglio and the king fled to the Allied-occupied South, but surrender did not bring an end to conflict. For two years, Italy was once again a battlefield as the Allies inched their way up the peninsula against stiff German opposition. The North, meanwhile, was the setting for a brutal civil war between the mostly communist and socialist partisans and the squads of the newly constituted Italian Social Republic, which Mussolini, who had been spirited from jail by the Germans, presided over from Salò on the banks of Lake Garda. Thousands died in this internecine conflict. The Nazis also committed some of the worst atrocities of the war on Italian soil (*see* RESISTANCE; SALÒ, REPUBLIC OF). Mussolini's own death, after the victory of the Allies in Europe, was itself an atrocity. Fleeing in disguise with his mistress and a handful of faithful followers, he was captured by partisans near the Swiss border. He and his followers were summarily executed and their bodies were strung up by the feet in Milan's Piazza Loreto, where they were vilified by the crowds. The leaders of postwar Italy had, above all else, to take into account the seething hatred that could endorse such a barbaric act. Hundreds of acts of murder and violence were committed in the first months after liberation: Italy might very well have lapsed into a nationwide civil war had it not been blessed with political leadership of an exceptionally high caliber.

THE FIRST REPUBLIC

This leadership was provided by the men who headed the two most coherent and representative political formations to emerge during the wartime years: Alcide De Gasperi, the leader of the Democrazia Cristiana/Christian Democracy Party (DC), and Palmiro Togliatti, of the Partito Comunista Italiano/Italian Communist Party (PCI). Togliatti, who had spent the Fascist years and the war as a leading functionary of the Comintern in Moscow, returned from exile in the autumn of 1943 and set the party's face against the revolutionary strategy that many Italian workers would have preferred. The PCI participated in the Allied-backed governments formed in wartime and then cooperated fully with the postwar governments headed by Ferruccio Parri, a partisan hero of radical political sympathies, and De Gasperi, who became premier for the first time in December 1945. De Gasperi steered the country to the momentous elections of June 2, 1946, with great skill, and Italy voted to abolish the monarchy and elect a Constituent Assembly of delegates. In the elections, De Gasperi's DC emerged as the largest party, with 35 percent of the vote, although the PSI and the PCI, the two next largest parties, jointly polled more votes than the DC. The assembly thus elected drew up a complex Constitution that reflected socialist principles (Article 1 states that "Italy is a Republic founded on labor"), and established a parliamentary form of government that jealously guarded against the possibility of a powerful executive branch. Together with the proliferation of political parties caused by the adoption of a strongly proportional electoral system, this constitutional bias in favor of the legislative branch of government has been the chief reason for the notorious instability of Italian governments throughout the postwar period: Italy has had more than 60 since the implementation of the Constitution on January 1, 1948.

While the Constitution was in preparation, De Gasperi purged his cabinet (allegedly at the behest of the United States) of the PCI and the PSI. The April 1948 elections, held at the height of the postwar clash between the United States and the USSR, were marked by overt attempts by both superpowers to influence the political struggle in Italy. The DC took 48 percent of the vote and gained an actual majority of seats in Parliament, while the PCI replaced the PSI as the party of choice for the organized working class. De Gasperi, however, was astute enough to realize that the elections had not given the DC a free hand. He governed with the assistance of the "lay" (i.e., non-Catholic) center parties and introduced such important acts of social justice as the land reform of 1950. In foreign policy, he steered Italy back into the international community, brokering Italian membership in the North Atlantic Treaty Organization (NATO) and becoming one of the founding fathers of the movement for European unification. By the time of his death in 1954, the Italian economy was on the brink of a surge of sustained growth known as the "economic miracle" and a rising tide of unprecedented prosperity that eased many of the country's social tensions. De Gasperi's was an immense achievement, but one he could not have managed without the PCI's studied moderation. The immediate postwar period established the DC and the PCI as the two central forces in newly democratic Italy, a state of affairs that did not break down until the 1990s.

The "economic miracle" is the lasting achievement of Christian Democracy. Whatever the sins of the men who followed Alcide De Gasperi—and there were many—it is impossible to deny that under the DC, Italy became richer and more prosperous than at any other time in its history. Yet the DC also presided over social changes that accompanied the reduced dependence on the traditional agricultural economy, including the secularization of Italian society. Even changes of which the DC disapproved came irresistibly to pass: For example, divorce was introduced in 1970; obscenity restrictions were lifted; the universities were opened to the masses; a limited abortion act was passed in 1978 and defended, in its turn, by a popular vote in 1981; and the Catholic Church's status as the official religion of the state was ended in 1984 (*see* REFERENDUMS). The DC presided over this transformation in conventional mores and standards with some discomfort, occasional distress, and much flexibility of doctrine.

The same doctrinal flexibility enabled the DC to cooperate with the PSI during the 1960s and to survive a wave of industrial and social unrest in the early 1970s by forging a "historic compromise" with the far-sighted reformist leader of the PCI, Enrico Berlinguer (*see COMPROMESSO STORICO*; OPENING TO THE LEFT). The so-called government of national solidarity (1976–1979) was an unnatural marriage of convenience, but it did at least defend Italian democracy from the attacks of the most merciless European terrorist movement of the 1970s, the Brigate Rosse/Red Brigades. Hundreds of judges, politicians, policemen, and civil servants were killed, wounded, kidnapped, or kneecapped by the terrorists in these years, the most famous victim being Aldo Moro, a five-time DC prime minister and the architect of the DC's collaboration with the PCI.

ECONOMY

The post-1945 prosperity of Italy is a crucial development in the country's history and a source of great national pride. Resource-poor Italy industrialized later and less thoroughly than any other country in Western Europe. Although the period 1861–1914 saw high economic growth, investment in infrastructure (especially railways), and the emergence of a substantial but overprotected industrial sector, Italy still lagged behind other major countries in every index of well-being. Employment remained primarily agricultural, and rural Italy was characterized by a backward system of land ownership (*see LATIFONDI*). The grinding poverty bred by near-feudal forms of land ownership was the main cause of the high migration rates of the prewar years (*see* POPULATION). An agricultural economy of this kind was not suited for the efforts required by modern war. The national debt increased sevenfold in the decade 1910–1920, as the Italian state struggled to meet the costs of a long, intensive war. In 1919–1920 the lira collapsed under the strain of the government's deficit spending, passing from LIT 13 to the U.S. dollar to nearly LIT 30 in a single year. Since Italy imported almost all its primary materials and was even a large net importer of food, this devaluation unleashed inflationary pressures within the economy and squeezed the standard of living of the ordinary wage earners, who had already been hard hit by increased taxation during the war. Adding to the difficulties of the economy was the problem of rapidly increasing unemployment, as the factories that had been churning out war materials were suddenly compelled to adjust to a peacetime economy in a near-bankrupt country. The Italian state's first experiment in public ownership of a manufacturing concern came in 1919 when the government intervened to save Ansaldo, a shipyard and armaments manufacturer based in Genoa.

One of Mussolini's initial attractions for Italy's most eminent financiers and economists was that he promised to discipline government spending and to follow classical laissez-faire doctrines to get the economy back on its feet. Fascism presided over the stabilization of the economy. Totalitarian ideology played a part in this process, but sheer necessity also forced the dictatorship's hand. The Italian economy was devastated by the Great Depression of 1929–1932, when unemployment levels reached 25 percent and industrial output dropped by almost a third. Lack of demand brought hundreds of major industrial companies and banks to their knees, and Mussolini was compelled to create, in 1933, the public holding company that would eventually grow to be one of Europe's largest employers of labor—the Istituto per la Ricostruzione Industriale/Institute for Industrial Reconstruction (IRI).

It is a measure of Mussolini's vainglory and lack of judgment that he involved economically battered Italy in ambitious foreign policy adventures and the alliance with Germany. In 1938, Italy's industrial capacity had just about recovered its 1929 levels of production, which were themselves hardly higher than the levels reached prior to 1915. In other words, he repeated the error of the Italian nationalists during World War I by waging modern war with a still backward economy. By the end of the conflict, war-blasted Italy's industrial production was only a quarter of prewar levels. In 1946, Italy had the highest illiteracy rate, lowest rate of industrialization, worst infrastructure, lowest per capita income, and least efficient agriculture of any Western European country except fascist Spain and Portugal. All these problems, moreover, were particularly acute in the South.

Economic development in the South accordingly became a priority in the postwar period. Italian governments pumped money into the Cassa per il Mezzogiorno—the Southern Italian Development Fund—to improve infrastructure, build an industrial base, and modernize communications. By the 1970s, southern Italians enjoyed approximately the same purchasing power (though not income per capita) as northern Italians, although the Mezzogiorno's economy was unhealthily dependent on prestige projects by state-owned companies, and hundreds of thousands of southerners had headed to the booming factories of Lombardy and Piedmont in the 1960s. This move reinforced a long historical process. Lombardy's population grew by 141 percent in the century between 1871 and 1971, while the population of the nation as a whole grew by approximately 90 percent.

Yet the economic unity of North and South, a century after political unification, proved to be a fleeting achievement. In textiles, optics, machine-tools, ceramics, furniture, and agricultural products, Italy's northernmost regions have enjoyed a second economic miracle since the early 1980s. The main Turin to Venice highway across the Paduan plain is accompanied by an almost unbroken row of new factories, warehouses, and retail outlets. Businesses in this region form "clusters" of producers who know one another well, place orders among themselves, and trust one another to deliver high-quality goods on time. Add an obsession with design and traditional standards of craftsmanship, and the recipe for northern Italy's success is not hard to decipher. The North is now richer in per capita income than much of northern Europe (and, indeed, large parts of the United States). By all the indicators of personal wealth (car ownership per capita, ownership of consumer goods, personal savings rates), Italy now ranks alongside wealthy countries like Germany, the Netherlands, and Great Britain.

With this unprecedented affluence have come profound changes in personal behavior and the composition of society. The birthrate, at just 1.3 children per adult woman, is among the lowest in Europe, despite the fact that strongly Catholic Italy has the lowest divorce rate and number of births outside marriage of any industrialized country. This figure reflects both the fact that the modernization of the economy has led many working women to postpone both marriage and childbirth and a widespread desire among Italians to maximize their potential for consumption by not having children. The lower birthrate and the booming economy have meant that for the first time in its history Italy has become an importer of people. Migrants from the countries of the North African shore, Albania, former Yugoslavia, and Eastern Europe have begun to arrive in large numbers (*see* IMMIGRATION). For Albanians, in particular, Italy is regarded as a promised land offering fabulous riches. These new migrants have not always been made welcome, a fact that shames the many Italians who remember the overt discrimination and ethnic stereotyping endured by Italian migrants to Switzerland and Germany in the 1950s. The best estimate is that there are today between 2.3 and 3 million people of foreign origin in Italy, by no means all of them refugees from poverty.

The Mezzogiorno, despite encouraging recent signs of growing entrepreneurship, has not shared in Italy's economic prosperity. Per capita income in the poorest southern provinces (Agrigento and Caltanisetta in Sicily, Cosenza and Catanzaro in Calabria) is half the figure reached by the richest provinces of the North (*see* ECONOMY; PIANURA

PADANA; SOUTHERN ITALY). It is hardly an exaggeration to say that the Italian peninsula today harbors one economy that matches Germany and another that is barely more productive than Portugal, and arguably less prepared than Portugal for the challenges globalization will inevitably bring in the coming decades. The most telling statistic is unemployment: Levels of joblessness rose sharply in southern Italy in the late 1980s and 1990s and today average well over 20 percent of the working population in such badly hit regions as Sardinia, Sicily, Calabria, and Campania. In the North, by contrast, unemployment has averaged 6 percent or less over the last decade, and there are some cities (Treviso, the home of the Benetton clothing group, being the classic example) where the vigor of local industry is such that it requires an influx of outside labor every year to keep the factories going.

The politicians had no answer to this regional disparity in economic performance or for the social pathologies—notably the revival of the mafia—that were generated as a consequence. Instead of dealing with the structural problems of the southern economy, which would have meant a painful period of retrenchment, the DC and PSI-dominated five-party coalition that controlled Italy between 1981 and 1991 preferred to throw money at the South's malaise, increasing wasteful subsidies, keeping open unproductive plants, doling out absurdly generous pensions and benefits, and giving local (often mafia-controlled) politicians unsupervised access to the public till (*see PENTAPARTITO*). Such policies led to the Mezzogiorno's economy becoming assisted—that is, one that cannot stand on its own—and caused a surge in gang warfare as the criminal clans of southern Italy fought for a share of the influx of public money in state investment and for the relief for the effects of the 1980 earthquake.

THE POLITICAL CRISIS SINCE THE 1990s

The failure of Italy's politicians to take structural measures to render the Mezzogiorno more economically competitive reflected the nature of the DC's essentially distributive vision of politics. By the 1980s the DC had been in uninterrupted power for over 40 years and had presided over the creation of one of the most dirigiste economies in the noncommunist world. Inevitably the state-owned industries and banks were gradually absorbed into the patronage networks of the parties of government, which used them as a combination of employment agency and private bank rather than as commercial undertakings. The state railways, the postal service, and the publicly owned banks were all characterized by inefficiency and the regular need for infusions from the national treasury. The possession of a party card, as opposed to managerial competence, was a sine qua non for a career in the state-run industries. Party-appointed placemen dominated the national television service, turning its news programs into propaganda for the DC and its socialist allies. *Lottizzazione*, to give patronage its Italian name, was taken for granted in the universities, the health service, the highway authorities, the schools, the law, and the civil service.

Such a system could only endure so long as the parties of government did not exceed the limits of financial prudence. In the 1980s, as the DC and the PSI struggled for power within the five-party coalition, they failed to respect this elementary rule of systemic self-preservation. Public spending ballooned faster than a sharp increase in taxes, infrastructure was neglected, and those projects that were initiated were manifestly conditioned by corruption. In 1990, the national debt exceeded 100 percent of the Gross Domestic Product (GDP)—up from a relatively healthy 60 percent in 1980—imposing a crushing burden in interest repayments.

Italy was increasingly being governed in a way that recalled Latin American countries like Colombia or Mexico at the same moment that its most prosperous regions were emulating Germany, Switzerland, and the rich economies of northern Europe. Such a contrast was bound to provoke a political reaction, and at the end of the 1980s the reaction duly came. The rapid rise of the Lega Nord/Northern League, a populist mass movement preaching the dismantling of the unified Italian state, was, in retrospect, a natural development, although it took both the political class and academic observers by surprise. In the 1992 general elections, the Lega took 9 percent of the national vote and 17 percent of the votes in the North, inflicting a great defeat on the DC, which slipped under 30 percent for the first time in 50 years.

The rise of the Lega was only one of the major changes in the Italian political system at the beginning of the decade. Of equal importance were the transformation, between November 1989 and February 1991, of the PCI into a democratic socialist party, and the growing popular movement for electoral reform, which led to changes in the electoral law that were bitterly opposed by the political elite in June 1991. Italy's leaders seem to have underestimated the force of the reformist wind in Italian society. Indeed, the disappearance of the communists seemingly convinced them that their hold on power was unassailable. They could not have made a greater error. After their shocking defeat in the 1992 elections, the DC and the PSI were swept from power by the judiciary, popular fury, and the financial markets. The lira was devastated in the summer of 1992, collapsing against the German mark and the French franc, and Italy came perilously close to a loss of international confidence. The most stringent austerity measures in postwar Italian history were introduced, and, in short order, the political system erected by the DC crumbled ignominiously. Thousands of politicians, including almost all the most senior figures in the DC and the PSI, were indicted on corruption charges, or charges of association with the mafia, by prosecutors finally free of political interference. Italy was forced to face the fact that for the third time in its history as an independent state, it had fallen victim to a profound crisis of regime.

Ever since 1992–1993, Italians have been engaged in a debate over the new state that might replace the First Republic. The debate has been both fierce and inconclusive. Despite the rise of new political forces, such as Forza Italia, a party founded and led by the media entrepreneur Silvio Berlusconi, and the center-left Olive Tree Coalition, headed by the current premier, the former academic and president of the European Commission, Romano Prodi, no new vision of Italy's future has caught the public imagination. It is perhaps for this reason that Italians tend to be ardent supporters of the European Union (EU). They arguably find in the process of European integration a sense of identification with a bold project that they are denied in national politics.

One hundred and forty years after unification, Italy finds itself in a position analogous to the one inherited in 1861 by the new Kingdom of Italy. Then, as now, the nation's leaders had to repair devastated public finances. Then, as now, Italy faced the challenge of holding together two separate social and economic realities within the same country. Then, as now, Italy had to establish itself as a force that counted within the community of European nations. Contemporary Italy's politicians might do well to take a leaf from the book of solutions employed by the statesmen who led post-Risorgimento Italy. The virtues of public austerity, political courage, personal probity, and skillful diplomacy practiced by the *destra storica* ("historic Right") during the governments of Luigi Federico Menabrea, Giovanni Lanza, and Marco Minghetti (1868–1876) have proven to be the exception rather than the rule in Italian history, but they remain valid guides for a country that has been all too prone to succumb to rhetoric, all-encompassing solutions, and cynical political horse-trading. This brief period is often passed over by historians giving a synoptic account of modern Italian history (a convention that we have followed ourselves in this introduction), but the achievements of Italy's governments in that period are unquestionable. At the cost of widespread peasant riots against the so-called grist tax on milled grain, the historic right's austerity measures saved the nascent Italian state from bankruptcy and allowed Italy to take its place on the European stage. For a few brief years, Italy had what it has ever since struggled to find—a political class that subordinated its personal and class interests to the national interest.

The Dictionary

– A –

ACCADEMIA D'ITALIA (Italian Academy). The Fascist regime's aspirations to renew Italy's status in **literature** and learning found expression in 1926 with the foundation of the Accademia D'Italia. The academy consisted of 60 eminent thinkers, divided into four distinct categories: the moral and historical sciences; literature; the physical, natural, and mathematical sciences; and the arts. The first 30 members were named in a royal decree, while the remainder were chosen by Mussolini himself from a list of names proposed by the academicians. From 1929 to 1944, the academy was housed in La Farnesina, the 15th-century palace in **Rome** that today houses Italy's foreign ministry. In 1939, the number of members was expanded to 80. These salaried academicians meant that Italy, no less than France, would have its guardians of the nation's intellectual and artistic life.

The academy's mission officially was to "coordinate the intellectual movement in Italy," but it had little success in this regard. From the historian's point of view, it is interesting to note just how many leading Italian intellectuals were willing to lend their names to an institution that had an obvious propaganda purpose. Its president between 1930 and 1937 was **Guglielmo Marconi**, the inventor of the wireless; **Gabriele D'Annunzio** succeeded him. Other intellectuals who either heard the siren call of fascist ideology or were seduced by the extremely generous stipends offered by the institution included the physicist **Enrico Fermi**, the dramatist **Luigi Pirandello**, the poet **Filippo Tommaso Marinetti**, and the philosopher **Giovanni Gentile**, who became president of the institution in 1944 and transferred its seat to **Florence**.

ACERBO, GIACOMO (1888–1969). First elected to **Parliament** in 1919 as a nationalist, Giacomo Acerbo soon switched to **Benito Mussolini**'s **Partito Nazionale Fascista**/National Fascist Party (PNF). In July 1921, he signed the so-called pact of pacification with the **Partito Socialista Italiano**/Italian Socialist Party (PSI) on behalf of the Fascist movement. In November 1922, he entered Mussolini's first cabinet as undersecretary in the prime minister's office. In this role, he was responsible for the notorious Acerbo Law of 1923, which guaranteed electoral victory for the Fascists and their allies in the elections of January 1924 by giving bonus seats to the party with a plurality.

Acerbo was one of the leading Fascist officials tainted with the political responsibility for the murder of **Giacomo Matteotti** in 1924. He resigned his post, becoming deputy speaker of the Chamber of Deputies, although he returned to government office in the 1930s as minister for agriculture, and as minister for finance in the last years of the regime. On 25 July 1943, he was one of the members of the **Fascist Grand Council** who voted to revoke Mussolini's power to conduct the war. Regarded by the Fascist faithful as a traitor (he was condemned to death in the **Republic of Salò**), he was hardly looked upon with favor by Italian democrats. During the government of **Ivanoe Bonomi**, he was arrested and sentenced to 30 years' imprisonment. After the war, however, he was soon amnestied. Acerbo, who by profession was an agricultural economist, returned to university teaching. He died in **Rome** in 1969. *See also* ELECTORAL LAWS.

ACHILLE LAURO. An Italian cruise ship named after a prominent right-wing politician from **Naples**, the *Achille Lauro* became famous in October 1985 when members of a splinter group from the Palestine Liberation Organization (PLO) took control of the vessel while it was en route to Port Said, Egypt, and terrorized its 500 passengers and crew. Sensitive to its relations with the Arab states, Italy tried to achieve a diplomatic solution to the crisis. With Egyptian cooperation, it was agreed that the terrorists would surrender in exchange for safe conduct to the Yugoslav capital of Belgrade. The only proviso was that no violent acts punishable by Italian law had been committed aboard the ship. When it became clear that an American tourist had, in fact, been killed, both the United States and the Italian governments wanted Egypt to allow extradition of the four perpetrators for trial. While en route to Yugoslavia, an Egyptian airliner carrying the Palestinians was forced by two U.S. jets to land at Sigonella in Sicily. President Ronald Reagan demanded the extradition of the terrorists; Egypt demanded that they be set free. Caught on the horns of a dilemma, Italian premier **Bettino Craxi** chose to placate Arab opinion. It was decided that there was insufficient evidence to hold the terrorists and they were allowed to leave for Belgrade.

An internal political crisis followed. The pro-American **Partito Repubblicano Italiano**/Italian Republican Party (PRI) temporarily resigned from the government and the Craxi administration was forced to submit to a parliamentary vote of confidence. Craxi defended his actions vigorously. In a speech to the Chamber of Deputies, he criticized U.S. over-eagerness to apply military solutions to diplomatic problems and defended the Palestinian struggle for autonomy. The *Achille Lauro* incident was a watershed in Italian–American relations, since it illustrated that the geopolitical realities of Italy's position in the Mediterranean were potentially of equal or even greater importance for the country's foreign policy as the American alliance. *See also* FOREIGN POLICY.

ACTION PARTY. *See* PARTITO D'AZIONE (PdA).

ALBANIA. During **World War I**, Italy offered hospitality to the provisional Albanian government in Durazzo (Durres), an Albanian port city over which Italy had established a de facto protectorate. Austria seized the city in February 1916. Control over Albania's inhospitable mountains was hotly contested by Austrian and Italian forces until the war's end.

By 1926, the mutual assistance Treaty of Tirana ensured that Albania had become, in effect, an Italian protectorate: The banking system and much of its commercial life were already operating under Italian auspices and financing. Within a year, the prime minister was crowned as Zog I. In 1931, large Italian loans under Italian supervision put most of Albania's economy under effective Italian control while purporting to modernize an abysmally poor and undeveloped country. The Italian response to a brief attempt by Zog to loosen Italy's hold was to send the Italian fleet to browbeat him into submitting to even greater Italian influence over Albania's army, schools, and economy. By the mid-1930s, most officers in the Albanian army were Italian.

Germany's 1938 Anschluss with Austria and subsequent annexation of Czechoslovakia prompted **Benito Mussolini** to consider redressing the Balkan imbalance by directly annexing Albania. Italy's sudden invasion in April 1939 forced Zog to leave for Greece, while a new Albanian Constituent Assembly asked for union with Italy, a request to which King **Victor Emmanuel III** readily acceded.

In the following year, the virtual dismemberment of Romania by the Soviet occupation of (formerly Russian) parts of Romania and by cessions of other territories to Hungary and Bulgaria led Mussolini to ask Greece for the right to use Greek bases in the event of hostilities. When the request was refused, Italy invaded Greece from Albania on 28 October 1940.

Within a month, the Greeks had not only repelled the Italians but had occupied a quarter of Albania and taken nearly 30,000 Italian prisoners, obliging Germany to send 50,000 troops to Italy's assistance. Together with British defeats of Italian forces in Africa, this resulted in Italian prestige plummeting, and Mussolini's hopes of waging a **parallel war** in the Mediterranean independently of Germany were dashed. Hereafter Italy was to be the subordinate partner in a relationship that continued to cost Germany manpower and matériel.

When the postwar isolation of a rigidly Stalinist Albania came to an end in the late 1980s, thousands sought to leave. They naturally turned to the closest European nation. An overnight ferry ride was all that separated them from entry into the European Community and to the wealth of Western opportunities. Italy suddenly found itself having to deal with boatloads of illegal, undocumented Albanian immigrants seeking refuge from deprivation. Police wearing surgical gloves herded the new arrivals into soccer stadiums and loaded them on buses to be shipped to northern cities and to **Rome**, where, they were told, they would be provided with work permits and helped to find housing and employment. However, stunned Albanians were then put on other buses and sent to airports for flights back to Tirana. Thereafter, they were reluctant to accept at face value any Italian official assurances.

Beginning in early March 1997, the disintegration of the Albanian state led Italy to begin evacuating Italian and European nationals. On 14 April 1997, Italy accepted the United Nations Security Council invitation to lead a coalition of forces from France, Greece, Hungary, Rumania, and Spain to protect humanitarian-aid deliveries. *See also* IMMIGRATION.

ALBERTINI, LUIGI (1871–1941). The founder of modern Italian journalism, Luigi Albertini was a native of the province of Ancona. After working in London on *The Times*, he began his career at the *Corriere della Sera* in 1896, and within four years he had become editor. A journalistic innovator, Albertini was a staunch critic of **Giovanni Giolitti** and a warm supporter of constitutional conservatives such as **Sidney Sonnino** and **Antonio Salandra**. The *Corriere* backed Italy's entrance into **World War I** in 1915; as the voice of Italian patriotism, the paper became one of the best-selling dailies in Europe, with sales of over one million copies every day.

Albertini's political influence waned after the rise of **Benito Mussolini**. The *Corriere* opposed the **March on Rome** in the name of constitutional legality, and following the murder of the Socialist leader **Giacomo Matteotti** in June 1924 openly supported the liberals and democrats who boycotted Parliament to protest Mussolini's conduct. Mussolini, as soon as he was able, returned the favor by depriving Albertini of his editorship in 1925. Albertini, who had been made a senator in 1914, conducted a dignified policy of parliamentary opposition to the Fascist regime until his death in 1941. His three-volume *Origins of the War of 1914*, published posthumously in 1942–1943 and translated into English in the early 1950s, is widely regarded as one of the greatest of all works of diplomatic history. *See also* AVENTINE SECESSION; PRESS.

ALLEANZA NAZIONALE/National Alliance (AN). The heir to the neofascist **Movimento Sociale Italiano**/Italian Social Movement (MSI), the AN has established itself as the third-largest party in Italy. The AN was created by the party secretary of the MSI, **Gianfranco Fini**, in January 1994, when he persuaded a handful of former **Democrazia Cristiana**/Christian Democracy Party (DC) conservatives to add a gloss of relative moderation to the MSI. Fini then allied the neofascists with **Silvio Berlusconi** during the March 1994 electoral campaign. The MSI-AN obtained 13.5 percent of the vote—by far the best postwar performance of the Italian far right. In **Rome**, and other parts of southern Italy, the MSI-AN's share of the vote reached 25 percent. The MSI-AN subsequently took a prominent part in Berlusconi's government, a fact that drew intense criticism from French statesmen such as Jacques Delors and François Mitterrand.

In January 1995, following the collapse of Berlusconi's administration, the MSI officially renamed itself the AN. The party also abandoned—in theory, at any rate—its attachment to the corporatist economic principles traditionally espoused by fascism, and embraced the rhetoric of free market reforms and a smaller state. Fini additionally reassessed and criticized the MSI's historical legacy, in particular its long-standing defense of Mussolini's **Salò** republic. Stung by this rethinking (but not rejection) of the party's fascist past, a handful of extremists, led by **Giuseppe "Pino" Rauti**, left to form an openly fascist movement. Since 1995, Fini has intensified this process of self-criticism by visiting Israel and by openly condemning the 1938 **racial laws** against Italy's Jews.

Since the late 1990s, the AN has been a sometimes frustrated junior partner in the **Casa delle Libertà**/House of Freedoms (CDL), Berlusconi's right-wing coalition. Fini himself has emerged as one of the politicians most trusted by the Italian public. The AN roughly maintained its share of the vote in the elections of 1996, 2001, and 2006, consistently obtaining around 12 percent of the vote, but it has not, as many expected, overtaken Berlusconi's **Forza Italia** to become the largest right-wing party in Italy. Fini's unarguable skills as a political communicator cannot wholly disguise the party's somewhat unsavory origins. *See also* ALMIRANTE, GIORGIO; ELECTORAL LAWS.

ALMIRANTE, GIORGIO (1914–1988). The historic leader of the **Movimento Sociale Italiano** /Italian Social Movement (MSI), Almirante was an unapologetic defender of the **Republic of Salò** who nevertheless managed to bring the neofascist movement in Italy a degree of respectability. He was born in Salsamaggiore in the province of Parma in 1914. During the final years of the war he took part in the brutal civil war waged between the partisans and **Benito Mussolini**'s dying regime, as an officer in one of the republic's most notorious militia units, the *Decima mas*. After the war, he was elected one of the MSI's six deputies in the **Constituent Assembly**. Almirante was elected leader of the MSI in 1947, but in the 1950s and 1960s, the MSI's relatively moderate wing, headed by Arturo Michelini, won control. Almirante was not prepared to compromise with the **Democrazia Cristiana**/Christian Democracy Party (DC), or to turn the MSI into a party that worked within the political system. As much as any communist, he rejected the institutions and economic system of capitalist democracy. As late as 1968, Almirante, despite his age, led neofascist hooligans in a street battle at the faculty of law at the University of **Rome**.

Despite such adventures, Almirante was reelected leader of the MSI in June 1969 upon the death of Michelini. He followed a more realistic policy of integrating the MSI into the political system and openly accepted democratic procedures, but successfully managed to retain the party's attachment to the principles of fascist ideology. He showed skill at exploiting the preoccupations of the "silent majority" alarmed by the anarchistic state of the nation's factories and universities, and linked the party with the monarchists to form the so-called National Right coalition in the elections of 1972, winning over 8 percent of the national vote. Almirante's strategy became known as **"fascism** in a double-breasted suit," a phrase that captured his willingness to jettison the more obvious symbols of fascism, without rejecting its substance. At the same time, however, he was unable (or unwilling) to distance the MSI from the numerous far-right subversive organizations that spread terror in Italy in the early 1970s, and consequently he never managed to complete fascism's transformation to respectability. The MSI's vote declined steadily after 1972. Almirante shrewdly picked **Gianfranco Fini** as his heir apparent shortly before his death in Rome in 1988. Without Almirante's strategic vision, the wholesale modernization of Italian neofascism put into effect by Fini since the early 1990s would have been impossible, but his legacy is an ambiguous one. Unlike Fini, Almirante never dreamed of apologizing for the brutalities and excesses of the Fascist dictatorship or for the death squads of Salò.

ALPS. The northern parts of Lombardy and Piedmont, and the whole of Trentino-Alto Adige and Valle d'Aosta, are home to some of the highest mountains in Europe and to some of the most spectacular scenery. The highest peak in the western Alps is Monte Bianco (Mont Blanc) at 4,810 meters (15,788 feet), but several other mountains top 4,000 meters (12,800 feet). In the eastern Alps, the highest point is the Ortles group (3,905 meters or 12,812 feet), which is on the border between Lombardy and the Trentino. The eastern Alps are dominated by two mountain chains of breathtaking natural beauty, the Brenta and the Dolomites. Tourists come from all over the world to see the effect of the sunset on the pinkish Dolomite rocks of Val Gardena (Alto Adige) and Val di Fassa (Trentino). The Alpine regions are also famous for their lakes and for the many elegant and expensive resorts that dot their shores. The three largest lakes are Lake Maggiore (Lombardy), Lake Como (Lombardy), and Lake Garda (Lombardy–Trentino–Venetia), but there are literally hundreds of smaller ones.

Culturally, the Alpine regions are sharply distinct from the rest of Italy. There are three main non-Italian ethnic groups: the French dialect–speaking Aostans (100,000 strong), the German speakers from Alto Adige (over 200,000), and the Ladino speakers in the Trentino and Alto Adige (approximately 30,000). But even in the nominally Italian parts of Lombardy, Piedmont, and Trentino the people speak strong dialects that are extremely difficult or even impossible for other Italians to understand. It is not an exaggeration to say that practically every valley speaks its own language.

These cultural and linguistic differences from the rest of Italy have been recognized politically. Trentino-Alto Adige and the Valle d'Aosta are special autonomous regions that—together with Sicily, Sardinia, and Friuli-Venezia Giulia—enjoy greater decisional power than most of the rest of Italy's regional governments. Three political forces represent the local minorities: the Union Valdotaine, the **Süd Tirol Volkspartei**/South Tyrol People's Party (SVP), and the Partito Autonomista Trentino-Tirolese/Party for the Autonomy of Trentino Tirolese (PATT). To this list should be added the **Lega Nord**/Northern League (LN), which began its meteoric flight in the valleys of northern Lombardy and whose stronghold remains the rural valleys of the Lombard provinces of Sondrio, Bergamo, and Varese.

Tourism—mostly German, although large numbers of visitors are increasingly coming from states in central and eastern Europe—is the mainstay of the Alpine region's economy. The resorts of Courmayeur, Sestriere, Madonna di Campiglio, Val Gardena, and Cortina d'Ampezzo offer some of the best skiing in the world. High-quality wine (especially in Trentino and Alto Adige), fruit growing, dairy farming, forestry and wood products, and the production of winter sports equipment are also major sources of income.

Overall, the Alpine regions have the highest standard of living in Italy. The province of Bolzano is one of the 10 wealthiest areas in the European Union (EU), with an income per capita of 159 percent of the EU average (Eurostat, 18 May 2006). The Valle d'Aosta's per capita income is 133 percent of the same average; the Trentino is at 129 percent. Trento, Bolzano, Sondrio, and other Alpine towns are regularly rated among the most livable places in Italy. *See also* DIALECTS; MINORITIES; REGIONALISM.

AMATO, GIULIANO (1938–). The only leading member of the **Partito Socialista Italiano**/Italian Socialist Party (PSI) to emerge unscathed from the corruption scandals of 1992–1993, Giuliano Amato is an academic lawyer and political theorist by profession; indeed, he is widely regarded as one of Italy's most able constitutionalists and intellectuals.

Elected to **Parliament** in 1983, Amato passed to high ministerial office during the government of **Giovanni Goria**, becoming both vice premier and minister of the treasury. He continued as treasury minister under **Ciriaco De Mita**. In June 1992, Amato was chosen to head a government that would prove to be the most troubled administration of contemporary Italian history. Within weeks of taking office, the lira collapsed dramatically, the parties forming his majority had become targets for the judiciary, the **mafia** had murdered a famous prosecuting attorney, and Amato had to enact the largest act of budgetary belt-tightening since **World War II**—nearly 90 trillion lire (at the time, U.S. $60 billion) of new taxes and spending cuts. His government, which was rocked by regular ministerial resignations as the corruption investigations crept higher and higher up the political ladder, eventually fell apart in April 1993, after the referendums on political and electoral reforms. Amato, however, was personally untouched by the scandals.

In 1995, Amato became the head of the Italian antitrust authority, a role of some importance since his tenure in the job coincided with a wave of privatizations by the Italian state. In 2000–2001, he briefly headed a second government, but his spell in office was obstructed by the litigious character of his majority. Somewhat to his chagrin, Amato was passed over as the center-left **Olive Tree Coalition's** candidate for premier in the May 2001 general elections. Amato subsequently became vice president of the "convention" charged with drawing up a Constitution for the European Union (EU). Amato is a likely future **president of the Republic**. He is certainly one of the few senior politicians in Italy with a clean past, substantial ministerial experience, high intellect, and international reputation. *See also* CURRENCY.

AMENDOLA, GIORGIO (1907–1980). The son of **Giovanni Amendola**, he enrolled in the **Partito Comunista Italiano**/Italian Communist Party (PCI) in his native **Naples** in 1929. Two years later, he embarked secretly for Paris to participate in the organizational work of the PCI in the French capital. On one of his secret repatriations, he was arrested and tried by the Special Tribunal (for political crimes). His sentence was reduced—after an amnesty for the 10th anniversary of the advent of the regime—to five years of *confino*. He was given two more years for having organized protests among the other prisoners. In 1937, he accepted PCI orders to return to France to take charge of party publications.

When he reentered Italy in 1943, it was to assume responsibilities as the party's leading expert on the South and as one of the directors of party clandestine activities. After 8 September 1943, he represented the PCI on the Military Council of the **Comitati di Liberazione Nazionale**/National Liberation Committees (CLN). In that capacity, he was one of the organizers of the Via Rasella partisan bombing of a German guards' vehicle, an event that led to the Fosse Ardeatine killings. From **Rome** he went to **Milan**, where he narrowly escaped arrest, then on to **Turin**, where he was one of the three directors leading what had become a popular insurrection.

In the 1945 government of **Ferruccio Parri**, he was undersecretary to the Council Presidency, a post he retained in the first government of **Alcide De Gasperi** until July 1946. He served in the **Constituent Assembly** and on the Central Committee of the PCI as well as in the newly elected Parliament, to which he was regularly reelected. In 1976, he was also chosen for membership in the European Parliament.

By the time of the 11th Party Congress in 1966, Amendola had moved to the relative right within the Central Committee, closer to **Giorgio Napolitano**, **Enrico Berlinguer**, and **Luigi Longo**. Amendola even proposed reunification with the **Partito Socialista Italiano**/Italian Socialist party (PSI). Such a union, if victorious, would have permitted the pursuit of policies of full employment and increased public spending on pensions, schools, hospitals, and housing. Amendola was a vigorous critic of the 1968 student revolts and of the far-left movements that emerged from them. Amendola died in Rome in June 1980. *See also* RESISTANCE.

AMENDOLA, GIOVANNI (1882–1926). Born in **Naples** on 15 April 1882, Amendola was to become the leader of the **Aventine Secession**. This talented liberal deputy and one-time cabinet minister suffered beatings by Fascist thugs on 26 December 1923, and again in 1925 (at Montecatini) at the hands of Carlo Scorza, a Fascist who was to become secretary of the **Partito Nazionale Fascista**/National Fascist Party (PNF) in 1943. While serving in the government of **Luigi Facta** as minister for colonial affairs, Amendola had been one of the three who persuaded the prime minister to prepare for royal signature a decree of martial law to stop the **March on Rome**. Facta's repeated failure to persuade the king and the latter's refusal to sign cleared the way for the call to Rome of **Benito Mussolini** to form a government.

Amendola's final parliamentary address, listing the wrongs committed in **Fascism**'s name, was repeatedly interrupted by Mussolini and the blackshirts. In the violence-ridden elections of 1924, Amendola founded and led the Unione Democratica Nazionale/National Democratic Union (UDN) (the constitutional opposition), only 14 of whose candidates were elected. After the Matteotti slaying, many deputies from the **Partito Comunista Italiano**/Italian Communist Party (PCI) and the **Partito Popolare Italiano**/Italian People's Party (PPI) withdrew from Parliament and retired to the Aventine Hill. Their leader, Amendola, was convinced that King **Victor Emmanuel III** would act against Mussolini once the Fascist leader was implicated in the kidnapping and murder of a parliamentary deputy. However, far from provoking the hoped-for public reaction, this move showed itself to be completely ineffective. The king clearly disliked the prospect of having socialists in government more than he did the rule of Fascism to which, after all, he was closely tied by virtue of his past support.

Amendola had been an editorialist for **Bologna**'s daily newspaper, *Resto del Carlino* (1912–1914), and had supported the war in **Libya** as well as intervention in **World War I**. From the *Carlino*, he went to the more prestigious *Corriere della Sera* of **Milan**, where he served between 1914 and 1920, opposing the Balkan expansionism of foreign minister **Sidney Sonnino**. In 1922, he founded—and was editor of—*Il Mondo* of Rome. His impassioned antifascist editorials, especially after the Matteotti crime, were among the most telling and probably explain Fascist motives in the several beatings administered to him. He also signed **Benedetto Croce**'s *Manifesto degli Intellettuali*.

Amendola became one of the so-called *fuorusciti*, the antifascist expatriates. Their number grew and included—in addition to Amendola—**Francesco Nitti**, **Carlo Sforza**, **Luigi Sturzo**, **Gaetano Salvemini**, **Piero Gobetti**, **Claudio Treves**, **Pietro Nenni**, and **Filippo Turati**. Amendola died in Cannes, France, on 7 April 1926. In 1950, his ashes were removed to his native Naples. *See also SQUADRISMO.*

ANDREOTTI, GIULIO (1919–). The personification of the Italian postwar political elite, Giulio Andreotti must be regarded as both a statesman of international reputation and a deeply ambiguous political figure. Born in **Rome**, Andreotti became a force in the nascent **Democrazia Cristiana**/Christian Democracy Party (DC) while president of Federazione Universitaria Cattolici Italiana/Catholic University Graduates' Movement of Italy (FUCI) during the war. A protégé of both **Alcide De Gasperi** (whose private secretary he became) and Giovanni Battista Montini, the future Pope Paul VI. Andreotti founded the DC's daily newspaper, *Il Popolo* (*The People*), and was elected to the **Constituent Assembly** in 1946. His first major ministerial job came in 1954, when he was appointed minister of the interior by **Amintore Fanfani**. For the next 40 years, he was an ever-present figure in Italy's shifting cabinets, usually holding posts of great sensitivity, such as defense, the interior ministry, or foreign affairs. By the late 1960s, Andreotti was the leader of the right-wing faction within the DC and the chief point of reference for both the Americans and the Vatican.

Andreotti first became prime minister in 1972, at the head of a short-lived center-right coalition with the **Partito Liberale Italiano/** Italian Liberal party (PLI). Unlike other key figures in the Italian defense establishment, he survived a bribery scandal in the mid-1970s when the American aerospace company Lockheed was accused of paying off leading DC politicians, and, in 1976, he was the logical choice as prime minister when the DC and the **Partito Comunista Italiano/**Italian Communist Party (PCI) chose to form a government of national solidarity after the inconclusive elections of that year. Like his mentor De Gasperi, Andreotti offered the United States a guarantee that the growing communist presence in Italian political life would not deflect Italy's pro-Western stance in foreign affairs. The government of national solidarity lasted until 1978, by which time Andreotti had skillfully succeeded in implicating the PCI in most of his government's most unpopular decisions. The kidnapping and murder of **Aldo Moro** in March–May 1978 caused immense public criticism of Andreotti, who was accused of doing too little to save Moro's life; wildly, it was alleged that Andreotti and his American sponsors were happy to see the back of Moro, who was the architect of the policy of greater cooperation between the DC and the PCI.

Scandal continued to dog Andreotti in the early 1980s, when he was accused of being the mastermind behind the subversive **Propaganda Due** Masonic lodge and of being the political protector of a shady financier, Michele Sindona, who died in prison in 1987 after drinking poisoned coffee. Andreotti escaped unscathed from both scandals and served as foreign minister throughout most of the 1980s. In July 1989, after an internal power struggle within the DC, Andreotti became prime minister once more, at the head of an administration in which the DC effectively shared power with the **Partito Socialista Italiano/**Italian Socialist Party (PSI) of **Bettino Craxi**. He remained as prime minister until June 1992. In all, Andreotti headed seven governments.

The famously witty Andreotti once said, in near-defiance of the dictum that "all power corrupts, but absolute power corrupts absolutely," that "power wears out those who do not have it." Many Italians believe that Andreotti has been corrupted by his half-century hold on the highest positions of the Italian state. In the spring of 1993, he was accused of being the Sicilian **mafia**'s political godfather by several former criminals who had decided to cooperate with the authorities. One *pentito* (state's witness) even claimed that he saw Andreotti exchange a kiss of greeting with Toto Riina, the mass murderer who emerged as boss of bosses in the mafia in the early 1980s. Even more sensationally, Andreotti was accused of having ordered the homicide of a well-known Roman journalist, Rino Pecorelli, in 1979, in order to obstruct the publication of a major investigation into his financial dealings.

Andreotti, after a lengthy investigation and trial, was eventually found guilty by a popular jury of the murder of Pecorelli in 2002 and sentenced to 24 years' imprisonment, but the conviction was overturned upon appeal in October 2003. He was found not guilty of colluding with the mafia in the 1980s, although with the caveat that the court found that he *had* used the mafia's influence to strengthen his political position in Sicily prior to the emergence of the bloodier form of criminality represented by Riina. Conveniently, the statute of limitations had run out for these offences. Despite this somewhat equivocal verdict, Andreotti has retained his place as a life senator, is an urbane presence on TV talk shows, and in 2006 was even proposed as a possible president of the Senate. *See also COMPROMESSO STORICO*; *PENTAPARTITO*.

ANTONIONI, MICHELANGELO (1912–). Postwar Italy's most intellectually challenging film director, Michelangelo Antonioni was born in Ferrara. His career in the cinema began in the 1940s, when he was an editor of *Cinema*, the film magazine directed by **Benito Mussolini**'s son Vittorio. Antonioni was soon dismissed for political reasons. During the German occupation, Antonioni joined the **Partito d'Azione** and took an active role in the **resistance**.

Antonioni's early films were documentaries. His first feature film was *Cronaca di un amore* (*Chronicle of an Affair*, 1950), but his first real success was the internationally acclaimed *Le amiche* (*The Girlfriends*, 1955), which won the Silver Lion award at the Venice festival. Antonioni's masterpiece, however, is probably the 1960 film

L'Avventura (*The Adventure*), which won the Special Jury prize at the Cannes film festival. *L'Avventura* was followed in short order by two other classics, *La Notte* (*Night*, 1961) and *L'Eclisse* (*The Eclipse*, 1962). In these films, Antonioni's almost painfully austere direction reaches its peak. Alienation has seldom been portrayed this deftly by any artist, although Antonioni is careful, in all three films, to offer a counterpoint character, played in every case by the talented actress Monica Vitti, who retains normal human feelings of warmth, spontaneity, and friendship.

In the late 1960s, Antonioni directed two major English-language films. *Blow Up* (1966) was a sardonic look at the "swinging sixties"; *Zabriskie Point* (1970) was a big-budget movie that somewhat didactically condemned the materialistic emptiness of modern Californian life. Antonioni has made few films since 1970, although *The Passenger* (1975) won critical acclaim. In 1994, Hollywood recognized the work of this most uncommercial of directors with an Oscar for lifetime achievement.

ARDITI. Sometimes drawn from the ranks of long-term prisoners whose sentences were reduced for undertaking hazardous wartime duty, infantry assault units (shock troops) of *arditi d'assalto* were highly effective on the Austrian front in **World War I**. Their distinctive uniform consisted of a black fez on which appeared a skull and crossbones carrying a dagger between its teeth, and a black shirt bearing the slogan "Me ne frego!" (I don't give a damn!). The mythology surrounding the Arditi appealed to the Fascists, who adopted the Arditi's black shirt and their anthem, "Giovinezza." *See also SQUADRISMO.*

AVENTINE SECESSION. The Aventine secession was a boycott of **Parliament** in June 1924 that paradoxically left **Benito Mussolini** with a solid Fascist majority in the Parliament elected in the violence-ridden 1924 general elections. The secession was a response to the kidnapping and murder of **Giacomo Matteotti**, who had bravely condemned Fascist illegality from the Parliament's benches. The nonfascist opposition almost to a man retired "to the Aventine," one of the seven hills of Rome to which members of the plebeian party had withdrawn (in 123 BC) in their struggle with the Roman aristocratic party. The Aventinians from the **Partito Comunista Italiano**/Italian Communist Party (PCI) returned to the Parliament in November 1924. In January 1926, the *popolari* of the **Partito Popolare Italiano**/Italian People's Party (PPI), on instructions from their party congress, also returned. But Mussolini insisted that they should acknowledge that the Fascist revolution was an accomplished fact. The Aventinians refused, and the Chamber, with a clear Fascist majority, voted to expel all 123 Aventine deputies. This left a handful of liberals who had not joined the Aventine Secession in an otherwise totally Fascist Chamber of Deputies. For the next several years, this Parliament passed laws that formalized the dictatorship of the Fascist Party and the state.

AXIS, ROME-BERLIN. The Axis was a pact signed in Berlin on 24 October 1936 between the Italian foreign minister, **Galeazzo Ciano**, and his German counterpart, Konstantin von Neurath. The Axis was a symbolic break by the Fascist regime, after its successful war against **Ethiopia**, from its position of equidistance between Nazi Germany and the imperialist powers (Great Britain and France). The pact was not just symbolic, however. The two countries pledged to collaborate in the struggle against communism, to back Francisco Franco in the **Spanish Civil War**, and to resolve tensions between them over Austria. **Benito Mussolini** did not, in fact, oppose the unification of Austria with Germany in March 1938, reversing his previous policy.

Despite signing the pact with Germany, Italy continued to play a double game. On 2 January 1937, Italy signed a "gentlemen's agreement" with Britain guaranteeing the status quo in the Mediterranean, and as late as April 1938, in the so-called Easter accords, held discussions with Britain and subsequently with France. The overall trend in Italian policy was marked, however. In November 1937, Italy joined Germany and Japan in the anticommunist pact that the other two nations had established in November 1936 and on 11 November 1937 abandoned the League of Nations. Adolf Hitler visited **Rome**, amid scenes of great pomp and ceremony, in May 1938. Mussolini backed Germany during the crisis over the German-speaking territories of Czechoslovakia in September 1938 and acted as an honest broker between Germany and Britain and France at Munich on 30

September 1938. Mussolini's return to Italy from Munich was greeted by cheering crowds, who proclaimed him the "defender of peace."

During the winter of 1938–1939, Mussolini decided that the future definitely lay with Germany. Following Nazi Germany's absorption of the remainder of Czechoslovakia in March 1939 and Italy's own invasion of Albania in April 1939, the regime took the decisive step of signing the "Pact of Steel" with Germany on 22 May 1939. By this treaty, Italy committed itself to joining with Germany in any conflict (not only a defensive war) in which its partner was involved and not to advance a separate offer of an armistice or peace without its partner's consent. Italy almost immediately breached the Pact of Steel by evading its obligation to declare war on Britain and France in September 1939. *See also* FOREIGN POLICY.

AZIONE CATTOLICA ITALIANA/Catholic Action (ACI). Founded in January 1908 to coordinate the new social organizations that had been established after the publication of the papal encyclical *Il fermo proposito* in 1905, Catholic Action is the evangelical arm of the **Vatican** in Italian society. Its major development came in the 1920s, during the pontificate of Pius XI. Anxious to avoid a clash with **Benito Mussolini**, Pius abandoned the **Partito Popolare Italiano**/Popular Party (PPI) to its fate and relied almost entirely on the ACI to promote Christian values. It did so via four main institutions: the Federation of Italian Catholic Men, the Society of Catholic Youth, the Catholic University Federation, and the Catholic Women's Union of Italy. For the most part, these organizations cooperated with the Fascist state's initiatives, but the youth organizations, the Boy Scouts in particular, clashed with the totalitarian objectives of the state.

One of Pius's principal goals during the negotiations that led to the signing of the **Lateran pacts** in 1929 was the preservation of the Church's right to educate young people. Although Pius succeeded in this goal, the proliferation of ACI activities, in particular the publication of specialist publications for the family and **women**, and the use of church halls for meetings, film shows, and cultural activities, inevitably brought the ACI into conflict with the authorities. In June 1931, all Catholic youth associations were forbidden by law. Pius responded with the encyclical *Non abbiamo bisogno*, which criticized certain aspects of Fascist ideology as being incompatible with Christianity. Despite this stand on principle, both Pius XI and his successor, Pius XII, were subsequently obliged to tighten ecclesiastical control over the movement.

With the return to democracy, there was a huge proliferation of specialist Catholic associations (for doctors, university and school teachers, jurists, chemists, even artists), and an impressive increase in the ACI's membership from the already imposing figure of 2.5 million in 1943 to over 3.3 million by 1959. In these years, the ACI—particularly under the leadership of Luigi Gedda (1952–1959)—became one of the Church's weapons in the ideological battle waged by Pius XII against the **Partito Comunista Italiano**/Italian Communist Party (PCI). When Pope John XXIII ascended to the Holy See in 1958, the ACI's semipolitical role became less accentuated. The theological innovations of the second Vatican Council (1962–1965) emphasized the essentially religious function of Church-sponsored organizations. This reduction in what may reasonably be termed its propaganda role, and the increasing secularization of society, caused ACI membership to fall sharply in the 1970s and 1980s, but Catholic associations still penetrate every sphere of Italian life and have a formative effect on the lives of many Italians even today. *See also* CATHOLICISM; PAPACY.

– B –

BADOGLIO, PIETRO (1871–1956). Despite a lengthy military career, Pietro Badoglio is chiefly remembered today for negotiating Italy's surrender in September 1943. Badoglio's early battle honors were earned during Italy's colonial wars. During **World War I**, he was quickly promoted to the rank of general. He commanded an army corps at the battle of **Caporetto**, but even though the Austrian breakthrough occurred in his sector, he escaped blame, emerging as second in command to General **Armando Diaz**. After the war, he was appointed to the Senate in 1919 and served as ambassador to Brazil between 1923 and 1925 before becoming chief of the General Staff. Between 1929 and 1934, he was governor of Italy's colonies in

Libya, where he suppressed the local nationalist movement with some brutality. The same willingness to use massive force was seen during the war in **Ethiopia** in 1935–1936. Badoglio, in command of the invading Italian forces, used poison gas and indiscriminate bombing to smash the under-equipped troops of Emperor Haile Selassie. Badoglio's reward was to be made duke of Addis Ababa and viceroy of the new colony. In 1940, Badoglio was reappointed chief of the General Staff and also chaired the committee responsible for organizing Italy's efforts to achieve autarky. Badoglio, who was a reactionary and a monarchist rather than a convinced Fascist, resigned when the Italian expeditionary force was humiliatingly defeated in Greece in 1941.

On 25 July 1943, King **Victor Emmanuel III** turned to Badoglio to replace **Benito Mussolini** after the Fascist leader's destitution of power by the **Fascist Grand Council**. In a radio address, Badoglio warned that Italy would remain in the war and that he would repress any attempts to disturb public order. During the next five days, troops fired upon antiwar protesters throughout Italy, killing and wounding several hundred people. On 27 July, all political parties were outlawed and the Fascist Grand Council, Special Tribunal, and Chamber of Fasci and Corporations were all eliminated, while the Fascist militia was incorporated into the army. Italy's drastically worsening military and economic situation, however, constrained Badoglio to surrender to the Allies on 3 September 1943. News of the surrender was officially communicated on 8 September, and the following day, Badoglio, the king, and selected courtiers fled from **Rome** for the safety of Brindisi, already occupied by the Allies. There, they established a governmental seat.

Badoglio's first government endured until April 1944. It declared war on Germany in October 1943, but was unable to persuade even moderate opponents of **Fascism** to join its ranks while it continued to be so closely associated with the king. When this problem was resolved by the appointment of Prince Umberto as lieutenant of the realm, Badoglio was able to form a second cabinet that included **Partito Comunista Italiano**/Italian Communist Party (PCI) leaders **Palmiro Togliatti** and Fausto Gullo. The administration, however, lasted little more than a month. Following the liberation of Rome, it was replaced on 18 June 1944, by a government that was more representative of Italian democratic opinion. Badoglio retired into private life and spent the next 10 years writing his memoirs and defending his military and political reputation. He died in his native Grazzano Monferrato (Piedmont) in 1956. *See also* SALÒ, REPUBLIC OF.

BALBO, CESARE (1789–1853). One of the most prominent Piedmontese liberals, Balbo published in 1844 a hard-headed essay entitled *Delle speranze d'Italia* (*The Hopes of Italy*), which laid down a pragmatic policy for national unification that had immense influence on the political elite of Piedmont-Sardinia. Briefly, Balbo argued that all plans for the future of Italy were subordinate to ridding Italy of Austria, and that this desirable goal could only be achieved by the army of the Kingdom of Piedmont-Sardinia, not by popular insurrection. No democrat, Balbo's vision for Italy was a federation of constitutional monarchies guided by Piedmont. In 1847, together with **Camillo Benso di Cavour**, Balbo founded the influential moderate newspaper, *Risorgimento*.

In March 1848, Balbo, who had played a prominent role in drawing up the so-called **Statuto Albertino**, became the first constitutional prime minister of Piedmont-Sardinia, an appointment that was confirmed by the first-ever free elections in Italy on 27 April 1848. His tenure as premier was brief. Following Piedmont's defeat at Custozza in July 1848, Balbo's government resigned. He died in his native **Turin** in 1853. *See also* CATTANEO, CARLO.

BALBO, ITALO (1896–1940). Born in Quartesana, Ferrara (Emilia-Romagna), to a family of schoolteachers, at the age of 14 Balbo was one of the irredentists who volunteered to conquer the Albanian coast in order to make the Adriatic an Italian lake. At 17, he led a group of bicyclists on the road from Ferrara in the thick of the 1914 events of "red week" clad in his Garibaldine red shirt and ready to proclaim a socialist republic in Emilia-Romagna. His subsequent service in **World War I** (he became a lieutenant in the *Alpini*) and his nationalism, spirit of adventure, and natural combativeness equipped him well for his postwar activities as an organizer and leader of Fascist squads in the Po Valley. Prior to the **March on Rome**, some regarded him as a potential rival to **Benito Mussolini** to head the **Partito Nazionale Fascista**/National Fascist Party (PNF).

Balbo was put in charge of the militia after Mussolini came to power but had to resign after the murder of **Giacomo Matteotti**. In 1926, he headed a movement to depose the king in favor of a Fascist republic but was thwarted by General **Pietro Badoglio**. As minister of aviation between 1929 and 1933, he personally led an Italian seaplane-group (he was an enthusiastic pilot) called, grandiloquently, an "armada," on transatlantic formation flights to Chicago and Brazil.

Mussolini was so irritated by Balbo's popularity that he made him governor of **Libya** in order to remove him from the seat of power in **Rome** and from any temptation to challenge the Duce himself. Despite his dissent from the alliance with Nazi Germany, he was put in command of Italian forces in North Africa in 1940, when he was accidentally shot down by Italian antiaircraft fire over Tobruk. He was probably the only Fascist hierarch who was unintimidated by Mussolini. *See also* QUADRUMVIRATE; *SQUADRISMO.*

BANCA D'ITALIA. Created in 1893 in the wake of the **Banca Romana** financial scandal by the fusion of three substantial banks, the Banca d'Italia has played a crucial role in Italy's economic and political development. Until 1926, the Bank had to share the emission of currency with two other banks, the Bank of **Naples** and the Bank of **Sicily**, but in that year its exclusive right both to issue banknotes and to act as regulator of the banking system was affirmed. Following a banking crisis brought on by the dire economic conditions of the early 1930s, in March 1936, the Bank's legal autonomy was established and its regulatory powers were broadened. After **World War II**, the bank, putting into practice the constitutional protection of savings guaranteed by article 47 of the **Constitution** of 1948, conducted a rigorous anti-inflation policy that formed the basis of the **economic miracle** of the 1950s and 1960s. In the 1970s and 1980s, the Bank was freed from the obligation to buy surplus treasury bonds and gained considerable autonomy to set interest rates.

The governor of the Bank of Italy is a major figure in Italian society, and several of them have combined banking with subsequent political careers. **Luigi Einaudi** was governor before he became **president of the Republic** in 1948; **Carlo Azeglio Ciampi** was governor from 1979 to 1993 and left only to become first premier, then treasury minister, and finally president. Tommaso Padoa-Schioppa, treasury minister in the government formed by **Romano Prodi** in 2006, is a former high official of the Bank of Italy; so were **Lamberto Dini** and **Guido Carli**.

The governor of the Bank is a lifetime appointment and is thus theoretically free from political pressures. In 2005, this arrangement was shown to have its drawbacks when the then governor, Antonio Fazio, was accused of having improperly favored an Italian bank that was trying to ward off a takeover bid by a Dutch rival. Fazio clung to his post until the scandal forced him to resign. The Bank had previously been the only major Italian institution untouched by the malaise in public life and had enjoyed an international reputation for both technical competence and probity. *See also* ECONOMY; EUROPEAN INTEGRATION.

BANCA ROMANA. The largest financial and political scandal of liberal Italy occurred in 1893–1894 as a consequence of the failure of the Banca Romana, which was one of six banks authorized to issue currency notes. A secret auditors' report in 1889 accused the bank of numerous breaches of the law and found the bank to be technically insolvent. The government, anxious not to cause panic in the market, did not act on the report. In December 1892, however, it was leaked to an opposition member of Parliament. The then prime minister, **Giovanni Giolitti**, was forced to form an impartial committee of inquiry that confirmed the calamitous state of the bank's books. The scandal widened in 1893 when it became clear that many politicians and newspapers had been bribed by the bank for silence and support. Giolitti introduced a banking reform law in August 1893 that reduced the number of banks authorized to print notes to just three and that intensified state controls over the emission of money. This action did not prevent a run on the banks at the end of the year and did not save Giolitti from being the most illustrious political victim of the scandal. In November 1893, a parliamentary inquiry found Giolitti guilty of negligence. The inquiry could find no proof that Giolitti had been bribed, but this suspicion obviously hung over the prime minister. Giolitti was forced to resign.

In 1894, the scandal spread further when documents provided by Giolitti proved that his political rival, **Francesco Crispi**, together with members of his family, had been beneficiaries of substantial undisclosed "loans" from the Banca Romana. When this fact was revealed by a five-man parliamentary committee of inquiry on 15 December 1894, Crispi responded by suspending a parliamentary sitting that intended to debate his involvement in the scandal. Fearing arrest, Giolitti left Italy for Berlin, where he remained until February 1895. Crispi, meanwhile, kept Parliament closed until May 1895, when he called, and won, fresh national elections thanks to a large vote in his favor in southern Italy. In December 1895, Giolitti was finally absolved of any wrongdoing by the Chamber of Deputies. Crispi's large parliamentary majority, and growing public boredom, enabled the prime minister to cut his losses by burying the whole affair.

BANFI, ANTONIO (1886–1957). Banfi has been one of the most influential thinkers of this century within the Italian academy. A philosopher of science who increasingly turned his attention to social theory, his thought departs from the central discovery of "modern" (i.e., post-Galileo) astronomy: that humanity is not the center of the universe or the reason for its existence. In his most famous book, *L'uomo copernicano* (*Copernican Man*, 1950), Banfi argues that this fact compels humankind to resolve the human dilemma by using our faculty of "critical reason" (instead of blind faith in man's metaphysical destiny) to create a free and progressive regime on earth. After 1945, Banfi increasingly identified "critical reason" with Marxism, which he seemingly regarded as a master science that superseded all other forms of social explanation. Banfi was also the author of a number of works on the life and thought of Galileo Galilei and many works on pedagogy. Between 1940 and 1949, he edited the groundbreaking academic review *Studi filosofici* (*Philosophical Studies*). In 1957, he died in his native **Milan**, where he had taught throughout his career.

BASSANI, GIORGIO (1916–2000). Along with **Primo Levi**, Giorgio Bassani is probably the finest postwar writer produced by Italy's small Jewish community. Born in **Bologna** in 1916, Bassani was raised in the Po Valley city of Ferrara, which provides the backdrop for his most important works. He was an active member of the **resistance** during the war and was jailed for his antifascist activities. He has written many books, but the most widely remembered are

Cinque storie ferraresi (*Tales of Ferrara*, 1956) and *Il giardino dei Finzi-Contini* (*The Garden of the Finzi-Continis*, 1964), the poignant tale of a Jewish-Italian family that was transformed into an Oscar-winning film by **Vittorio De Sica**. Together with **Tommaso Di Lampedusa**'s *Il Gattopardo* (*The Leopard*, 1959), which Bassani was instrumental in getting published, *Il giardino dei Finzi-Contini* broke the neorealist monopoly in Italian arts and letters, and signaled a greater interest among Italian writers in introspection, fine writing, and traditional settings. Bassani was a founding member and early president of *Italia Nostra*, an association committed to the preservation of Italy's heritage. He died in **Rome** in April 2000. *See also* LITERATURE; RACIAL LAWS.

BASSO, LELIO (1903–1978). An uncompromising socialist, Lelio Basso was both one of the historic leaders of the **Partito Socialista Italiano**/Italian Socialist Party (PSI) and a stern critic of its policies in the 1960s. Born in the province of Savona (Liguria), Basso joined the PSI while a student and wrote for or edited several of the principal literary and ideological journals of the Italian left, including **Piero Gobetti**'s famous *Rivoluzione liberale* (*Liberal Revolution*). In 1928, he was arrested and confined on the isle of Ponza (Campania) for three years. Upon release, he was kept under strict surveillance, and in March 1940 he served six months' internment in a camp near Perugia.

In January 1943, Basso, who had always been one of the most outspoken voices of the PSI's "maximalist" wing, instituted a new party, the Movimento d'Unita Proletaria/Movement of Proletarian Unity (MUP). In August of the same year, the MUP merged with the by now almost moribund PSI, and the new party became the Partito Socialista Italiano d'Unità Proletaria/Italian Socialist Party of Proletarian Unity (PSIUP). The party program contained many echoes of Basso's belief that the Italian socialist movement should struggle for a socialist revolution, not parliamentary democracy. He was soon criticizing the timidity of the party leadership, and in November 1943 he gave up his membership.

After returning to the fold in May 1944, Basso became the PSIUP's chief organizer in northern Italy, successfully nurturing the party's clandestine networks in the factories of Lombardy and Piedmont. In April 1945, he was one of the leaders of the Milanese insurrection against the Germans. His courageous clandestine work was rewarded in July 1945 when he became the vice secretary of the party.

Basso was elected to the **Constituent Assembly** in June 1946 and took a prominent role in its work. In January 1947, he became party leader at the stormy **Rome** congress of the PSIUP, which saw the party's moderates, led by **Giuseppe Saragat**, leave the party. During Basso's tenure as leader, the newly renamed PSI identified itself closely with the **Partito Comunista Italiano**/Italian Communist Party (PCI)—even to the extent of condoning the February 1948 coup in Czechoslovakia, but the strategy proved an electoral disaster. Basso was replaced as party leader in July 1948 after the triumph at the polls of the **Democrazia Cristiana**/Christian Democracy Party (DC).

Basso never yielded in his revolutionary beliefs. He opposed any arrangement with the DC, and in 1963, when **Aldo Moro** formed the first DC-PSI administration, Basso was one of 24 PSI deputies who broke ranks to found a new Marxist party that defiantly took the name of the PSIUP. In the late 1960s, Basso participated in the Russell War Crimes Tribunal on American atrocities in Vietnam. He died in **Rome** in 1978. *See also* NENNI, PIETRO.

BATTISTI, CESARE (1875–1916). Martyr, socialist, and soldier, Cesare Battisti was born in Trento (then still part of Austria) in 1875. He studied at universities in both Austria and Italy, where he came into contact with the liberal socialist ideas of **Gaetano Salvemini**. In 1895, Battisti founded *La Rivista popolare trentina* (*The Trentino Popular Review*) to propagate socialist doctrines and the right of self-determination for Austria's Italian-speaking minority. In 1904, his activities earned him a prison term in Innsbruck jail. During **World War I**, Battisti abandoned his lifelong pacifism. The war seemed to him to be a golden opportunity both to liberate the Trentino and to bring about the collapse of the Austro-Hungarian Empire, which he believed would be a prelude to the creation of a European federation of democratic socialist states. Battisti enrolled in the Italian army and served bravely as a junior officer. He was captured by the Austrians in July 1916, tried as a traitor, and hanged at Trento. **Filippo Turati**

eulogized him as "a socialist in principle and in action" in a speech to the Chamber of Deputies in December 1916. In Trento, his memory is revered—several of the city's streets and squares are named after him and a monument consecrated to his name overlooks the city from a mountaintop. *See also* REGIONALISM.

BECCARIA, CESARE (1738–1794). Born in **Milan**, Beccaria studied jurisprudence at Pavia until 1758 and was drawn into an illuminist circle whose members published, between 1764 and 1766, the journal *Caffe*. In this setting, the young jurist wrote *Dei delitti e delle pene* (*Of Crimes and Punishment*, 1764). By arguing that prevention is more useful than repression or punishment, he launched the movement to seek individualized punishments in criminal law and to let the punishment fit the crime. For the first time, the possibility was considered that wrongdoers might be rehabilitated with humane treatment. After translation into virtually every European language (the French edition bore a commentary by Voltaire), these ideas spread to the entire Western world and—with the eventual adoption of the civil law in Africa, Asia, South America, and the Middle East—to the rest of the world as well. Frederick the Great of Prussia, Empress Catherine of Russia, and Pietro Leopoldo of Tuscany vied to incorporate Beccaria's ideas into programs of judicial reform. Speedy trials, elimination of torture and of the death penalty, and equality of treatment and of punishment regardless of social class trace their origins to Beccaria. His book is probably the single most influential work on Western criminal (penal) procedure. The principles that only legislators (not judges) can make laws and that punishment can flow only from illegal acts (*nullum crimen sine lege; nullum poena sine lege*) stem from Beccaria. Having rejected offers of a post in St. Petersburg, he accepted a teaching appointment from the Austrian government. It took him to Brera in December 1768, where his course on David Hume became the basis for his *Elementi di economia pubblica* (*Elements of Political Economy*).

So impressed was the Hapsburg government that he was offered, and accepted, nomination to Austria's Supreme Economic Council (1771), simultaneously beginning his life as a bureaucrat and ending his extraordinary creativity. His daughter Giulia (born in 1762 of his union with his first wife, who died in 1774) was to become the mother of **Alessandro Manzoni**.

BERIO, LUCIANO (1925–2003). One of the most important contemporary composers, Luciano Berio was born in the province of Imperia (Liguria). His father was an accomplished musician, and Berio's early training was at home. He completed his studies at **Milan** conservatory, where he graduated in composition and orchestral conducting in 1950, and in the United States. In the late 1950s, Berio emerged at the forefront of efforts to modernize the classical canon by integrating electronic sounds into his orchestral pieces. He edited an academic journal of avant-garde music, *Incontri musicali* (*Musical Encounters*), and collaborated with the noted novelist **Italo Calvino** and the poet Edouardo Sanguineti. In the 1960s and 1970s, Berio taught composition in some of the most prestigious conservatories in the world, including the Juilliard School in New York, as well as Harvard and Columbia Universities. He also met the soloist Cathy Berberian, his first wife, who became the "voice" for some of his most complex and challenging works. In addition to electronic music, Berio is noted for having infused the classical form with themes from Japanese and Indian music, for his interest in folk music and rock, and for his creation of musical collages that quote from other composers. His most famous works are probably *Sinfonia* (1968), *Folk Songs* (first version, 1964; second version, 1973), and *Coro* (*Choir*, 1976). Berio died in **Rome** in May 2003.

BERLINGUER, ENRICO (1922–1984). Born in **Sardinia** to a family of minor aristocrats, Berlinguer joined the **Partito Comunista Italiano**/Italian Communist Party (PCI) at 21 and became active in the local youth section and in antifascist activity. At the end of 1944, he was called to **Rome** to serve on the national secretariat of the party's youth movement. He worked constantly within the party in various capacities. He was elected a deputy in 1968, was elected vice secretary to serve with **Luigi Longo** in the next year and, in 1972, became general secretary of the party, a position that he held for 12 years until his death.

Berlinguer is remembered for three main reasons. First, applying to party policy the strictures of both **Antonio Gramsci** and **Palmiro**

Togliatti, he advanced "polycentrism" and the notion of each country finding its own road to socialism. After Nikita Khrushchev's "Secret Speech" (criticizing Stalin and Stalinism) at the 20th Congress of the Soviet Communist Party in 1956 and the Hungarian uprising of the same year, the PCI seemed destined to continue losing adherents. Nonetheless, party leaders such as Luigi Longo and, in his turn, Berlinguer, displayed a combative spirit in criticizing the Soviet Union for its actions in Czechoslovakia, in promising to retain Italy's membership in the **North Atlantic Treaty Organization (NATO)**, and in backing away from ideological dependence on the USSR. This willingness to distance the PCI from the USSR came to be called "Eurocommunism," although neither the French nor the Portuguese communist parties ever criticized Moscow as bluntly as did Berlinguer or his Spanish counterpart Santiago Carillo. In 1981, after Poland's General Wojciech Jaruzelski had suppressed the independent trade union, Solidarity, Berlinguer remarked that the "propulsive force" of the Soviet revolution had run its course.

Second, Berlinguer advanced the *compromesso storico* (historic compromise). Preoccupied by the events in Chile, where a military coup d'état had overturned a Marxist government, Berlinguer argued that the PCI must never make a similar mistake in Italy. When the PCI came within a few percentage points of overtaking the **Democrazia Cristiana**/Christian Democracy (DC) in the 1976 elections, Berlinguer agreed to the formation of a government of national solidarity by the DC to which the PCI gave parliamentary support. Berlinguer thought the position of the PCI in 1976 was quite different from that of the **Partito Socialista Italiano**/Italian Socialist party (PSI) in 1963: the left was stronger in every way and a cautious alliance with the DC could be expected to lead to genuine structural change in Italian society and state. He was to be disappointed. The modesty of the results seemingly validated **Pietro Ingrao**'s warning that the PCI risked having to choose between confrontations with the state (which they could only lose) and being co-opted by the system (which would mean the end of the PCI as a revolutionary force). But the PCI did help steer Italy through the political and economic upheavals of the 1970s, showing great sense of the state.

Third, Berlinguer is associated with the concept of austerity, which makes him almost unique in postwar Italian political history. Together with Luciano Lama, then head of the Confederazione Generale Italiana del Lavoro/Italian General Confederation of Labor (CGIL), Berlinguer bent his efforts to persuading Italian workers to salvage capitalism by accepting a policy of relative austerity and wage restraint in exchange for greater investment in the South and among youth. He also repeatedly raised the "moral question," regarding personal probity among the political elite as a central issue for successful democratic institutions.

Upon his death in June 1984, even the pope eulogized Berlinguer as an honorable man convinced of the rightness of his principles. Millions of people, including many noncommunists, turned out for his funeral. *See also* ANDREOTTI, GIULIO; BRIGATE ROSSE (BR); MORO, ALDO; TRADE UNIONS.

BERLUSCONI, SILVIO (1936–). A Milanese businessman who created Italy's first nationwide private television (TV) network, Silvio Berlusconi has led **Forza Italia** since its genesis in 1993 and is one of the democratic world's most controversial politicians.

Berlusconi made his first fortune in real estate dealings in the late 1960s and early 1970s. In 1977, he acquired his first **media** holding, a share in **Indro Montanelli**'s anticommunist newspaper *Il Giornale Nuovo*. End of the 1970s, he launched his first private TV company. By 1980, his flagship company, Canale 5, went on the air—the first private TV network to have a national audience. In subsequent years, Berlusconi added two more private TV companies, Italia 1 and Rete 4, to his empire. This growing presence in the media sector was judged to be illegal by the courts in 1984; briefly, Berlusconi's TV channels were taken off the air. His close personal and political links with the then prime minister, **Bettino Craxi**, proved their worth, however. The Craxi government passed a decree law in October 1984, swiftly baptized the "Berlusconi Law," which retroactively legalized Berlusconi's activities.

In the mid- and late 1980s, Berlusconi added the AC Milan soccer team and the giant Mondadori publishing corporation to his holdings. He also established a near-monopoly over the production and sale of TV advertising, and started (less successful) TV companies in France and Spain. By 1990, he was the owner of one of the largest private companies in the world. In August 1990, the passage of a toothless law regulating media ownership appeared to have consolidated his dominance of the Italian private media for good. Berlusconi was forced to sell his stake in *Il Giornale* to his brother Paolo, but the right of a private entrepreneur to own three national television networks was protected by the new law.

The collapse of the Italian political system and Craxi's disgrace represented a threat to Berlusconi. He could be sure that a leftist government would attempt to break his monopoly on the media market. This appears to be one of the main reasons why, in December 1993, with a marketing blitz that recalled the launch of a new soap powder rather than a political party, Berlusconi founded Forza Italia and nominated himself as a potential prime minister. Skillfully allying himself with the **Lega Nord**/Northern League (LN) in northern Italy and with the **Alleanza Nazionale**/National Alliance (AN) in the South, Berlusconi's right-wing coalition, the Polo della libertà, won an astonishing victory in elections to the Chamber of Deputies in March 1994. Less than four months after its launch, Forza Italia became Italy's largest political party.

Berlusconi has been the leader of Italy's political right ever since. His first government lasted only eight months (May–December 1994), and his coalition was narrowly defeated in the general elections of April 1996, but in the late 1990s he constructed the **Casa delle Libertà**/House of Freedoms (CDL) and led this coalition to a striking victory in the general elections of May 2001. Berlusconi became prime minister and governed for a full parliamentary term until April 2006, a feat previously managed in the postwar period only by **Alcide De Gasperi** (1948–1953).

Berlusconi's time in politics has been marred by problems with the law and by the inherent conflict of interest in his dual role as media entrepreneur and politician. For these reasons, the authoritative periodical *The Economist* described him as "unfit to lead Italy" prior to the 2001 elections. During his political career, Berlusconi has been investigated for a dozen different offenses, including drug trafficking, links with the **mafia**, perjury, corruption of judges, bribery of politicians, and, most commonly, fraudulent accounting. Some of these allegations were clearly false: No evidence was found to back the drugs charges and the accusations of mafia connections were not substantiated. Other charges were seemingly true. Berlusconi has been found guilty of bribing Bettino Craxi of fraudulent accounting, and of having given false testimony about his membership in the subversive **Propaganda Due** masonic lodge. Amnesties and recognition, by the legal authorities, of "extenuating circumstances" have alone kept him out of prison; he also used his coalition's substantial parliamentary majority between 2001 and 2006 to pass legislation retrospectively decriminalizing the law on fraudulent accounting and to obtain for himself a temporary amnesty from prosecution. Berlusconi remains under investigation for tax fraud, corrupting a British tax lawyer, and violations of Spanish antimonopoly legislation. Berlusconi's former lawyer and close advisor, Cesare Previti, was finally convicted in 2005, after a 10-year legal marathon, of bribing a judge on Berlusconi's behalf.

Berlusconi's premiership was also controversial for his unorthodox personal diplomacy. In June 2003, he opened the six-month Italian presidency of the European Union (EU) with a long harangue against a socialist deputy of the European Parliament who had heckled his speech: Berlusconi likened the deputy to a concentration-camp commandant, causing a furor across Europe. Berlusconi also vaunted his supposedly warm personal friendships with President George W. Bush and with Russian premier Vladimir Putin and, in pursuit of these friendships, followed a much less Eurocentric foreign policy than any of his predecessors as premier.

Under Berlusconi's leadership, Italy's public finances, after a decade of slow improvement, began to worsen again. Berlusconi's five-year government saw low economic growth and tepid increases in state revenue. Public spending, by contrast, increased. Italy's sovereign debt rating was cut in 2004 and again in October 2006 by leading international ratings agencies.

Despite these policy failings, Berlusconi remains a formidable communicator and a shrewd political operator. During the 2006 election campaign, his energetic, populist style unquestionably won votes for Forza Italia, which scored 23 percent and retained its position as Italy's largest party by a substantial margin. There is no doubt that a large segment of the Italian electorate identifies with Berlusconi and is disposed to forgive both his political errors and his somewhat shady past. *See also* EUROPEAN INTEGRATION; MANI PULITE; PRESS.

BERSAGLIERI. Organized in 1846 by General **Alfonso La Marmora Ferrero** as part of the army of the Kingdom of Piedmont-Sardinia, these assault infantry were praised by Anglo-French general officers for their performance in the Crimean War, contributing much from the point of view of Piedmont-Sardinia's military prestige.

Two particulars mark the *Bersaglieri*: their means of locomotion and their uniform. A light infantry, their march-step is a trot enabling them to cover great distances in short order and requiring that all be in excellent physical condition. Even their (brass) instruments are played at a trot. In both 20th-century world wars, they were issued sturdy, collapsible—hence, portable—bicycles that further enhanced their mobility. Second, their uniforms set them apart from the rest of the Italian army, an important factor in the morale of any armed force. La Marmora's original uniform was black with a high collar; that has given way to the standard-issue brown of other Italian troops. However, there remains of the original uniform the headgear, a flat-brimmed patent leather hat kept cocked at a jaunty angle over the right ear by a thick leather chin strap. To the low, round crown is affixed a cluster of shiny black and green feathers cascading over the right shoulder. In both **World War I** and **World War II**, as well as in United Nations (UN) missions in Lebanon, Somalia, Bosnia, and **Albania**, a smaller cluster of feathers adorned the steel helmets of these troops.

BERTINOTTI, FAUSTO (1940–). A trade unionist and political activist from **Milan**, Fausto Bertinotti was elected president of the Chamber of Deputies in April 2006. Bertinotti's early political training was in the **Partito Socialista Italiano**/Italian Socialist Party (PSI), where he was a militant in the "maximalist" faction of the party headed by **Riccardo Lombardi**. Bertinotti left the PSI, however, in 1964, as a protest against its decision to join the government and eventually, in 1972, joined the **Partito Comunista Italiano/** Italian Communist Party (PCI). He was by this time an important figure in the trade union movement. In 1980, Bertinotti, as regional secretary of the Confederazione Generale Italiana del Lavoro/Italian General Confederation of Labor (CGIL) in Piedmont, was deeply involved in the 35-day occupation of the **FIAT** car plant. Bertinotti subsequently became an official at national level in the CGIL.

Bertinotti opposed the decision to transform the PCI into the **Partito Democratico della Sinistra**/Democratic Party of the Left (PDS) after the fall of communism, although he did not initially join the breakaway **Partito di Rifondazione Comunista**/Communist Refoundation Party (PRC). He joined the PRC only in September 1993, but by January 1994 he was already party secretary. Bertinotti remained secretary until May 2006, being reelected four times.

Bertinotti made an electoral pact with the **Olive Tree Coalition**, headed by **Romano Prodi**, during the 1996 elections. He opposed many of the government's policies, however, and the PRC eventually brought the Prodi government down in a confidence vote in October 1998. Bertinotti's action provoked a split in the PRC and a strong faction, led by the party's founder, **Armando Cossutta**, left the party and continued to support a center-left government formed by **Massimo D'Alema**. Bertinotti's PRC cultivated a strong anticapitalist, antiglobalization, anti-American line and today unquestionably ranks among the most left-wing parties in Europe. The 2001 general elections, however, showed that the PRC would underperform in electoral terms in the absence of an electoral accord with the rest of the left. The PRC was an important component of the "Union," the winning coalition in the 2006 elections. In October 2005, Bertinotti challenged Prodi for the leadership of the coalition in nationwide primaries and obtained a respectable 15 percent of the vote. *See also* TRADE UNIONS.

BERTOLUCCI, BERNARDO (1940–). The son of a literary critic and poet, Bertolucci's own first book of poems won the prestigious Viareggio prize in 1962. In the same year, he directed his first feature film. Two years later, his first critically acclaimed movie, *Prima della rivoluzione (Before the Revolution*, 1964), which tells the story of a young aristocrat who flirts with revolutionary politics before settling down into a conventional marriage, won the Prix Max Ophuls at Cannes.

In 1968, Bertolucci joined the **Partito Comunista Italiano**/Italian Communist Party (PCI), which was the prelude to an extraordinary burst of creativity at the beginning of the 1970s. *La strategia del ragno (The Spider's Stratagem*, 1970) and *Il conformista (The Conformist*, 1971) won Bertolucci international acclaim. The latter film, which describes a tormented young fascist intellectual coming to terms with his homosexuality, was a spectacular critical success. The film received an Oscar nomination and won the National Film Critics' award.

In 1972, Bertolucci's fame turned to notoriety after the production of *L'ultimo tango a Parigi* (*The Last Tango in Paris*, 1972). Its graphic sex scenes caused the film to be banned in Italy, and Bertolucci was deprived of his vote for five years. Critical opinion on the film's merits continues to be divided, with some regarding the film as a watershed for the cinematic art, others as embarrassingly overblown and pretentious. Bertolucci's real masterpiece is arguably the 1976 five-hour epic *1900*, which was shot in his native Po River valley with an international cast that included Burt Lancaster, Robert De Niro, Gerard Depardieu, and Donald Sutherland. A violent, squalid, heroic panorama of Italian life and politics from 1900 to 1945, the film contains some of the most moving—and most disturbing—images ever portrayed on film.

In recent years, Bertolucci has moved into the commercial mainstream. The *Last Emperor* (1987), shot on location in China, was an epic film of glorious beauty that told the tale of Pu Yi, the last emperor of China, who survived Japanese invasion and the cultural revolution to end his life as a gardener in Beijing. The film won several Academy Awards, including best picture. *See also* CINEMA.

BIANCHI, MICHELE (1883–1930). Born in Belmonte Calabro (Calabria), Bianchi came to be known as a firebrand syndicalist (and interventionist regarding **World War I**) in the heady days of organizing the field workers in the Po Valley. When he tossed in his lot with **Benito Mussolini** at the first Fascist rally at Piazza San Sepolcro in **Milan**, he retained the reputation for fanatical devotion to his syndicalist principles. He was chosen for membership on the first central committee of the **Partito Nazionale Fascista**/National Fascist Party (PNF), of which he became the first secretary general. His relations with other Fascist leaders, were often strained, however. It was apparently Bianchi, as party secretary, who urged the **March on Rome** on an indecisive Mussolini. During the Fascist coup in October 1922, Bianchi telephoned **Rome** pretending to be the prefect of Perugia reporting that only surrender to the Fascists could avert serious bloodletting. Prime Minister **Luigi Facta** took this seriously and finally began the process of organizing resistance to **Fascism**, publicizing a decree requesting emergency powers that resulted in the immediate dissolution of some Fascist bands. The king refused to countersign the decree, however, thereby ensuring the victory of Mussolini. Before his sudden death in 1930 Bianchi became a PNF parliamentary deputy and, in 1929, minister for public works, a position he used to Calabria's advantage. *See also* FASCIST GRAND COUNCIL; QUADRUMVIRATE.

BISSOLATI, LEONIDA (1857–1920). A voice for moderate social democracy in early twentieth-century Italy, Leonida Bissolati studied at Pavia and **Bologna** universities before becoming a lawyer and local politician in his native city of Cremona (Lombardy). Elected to Parliament as a Socialist in 1895, he became the editor of the daily newspaper of the **Partito Socialista Italiano**/Italian Socialist Party (PSI), *Avanti!* His willingness to cooperate with relatively progressive liberals such as **Giovanni Giolitti** won him the reputation of being a "ministerialist" with the PSI's left wing. By 1910, Bissolati was diverging even from his fellow moderate **Filippo Turati**. Unlike Turati, who regarded reformism as a necessary tactical step on the road to the establishment of a socialist state, Bissolati became increasingly convinced that the introduction of such reforms as universal male suffrage should be themselves the objective of the socialist movement. Bissolati was consulted in 1911 on the occasion of the formation of Giolitti's new government, and although he refused any ministerial post, he had committed (in the eyes of PSI militants) the grave error of negotiating with the bourgeois state. Bissolati supported Giolitti's colonial war in **Libya** in 1912. This was the final straw for the party's "maximalist" wing, which expelled him from the party. Together with **Ivanoe Bonomi**, he formed a reform socialist party, but the new movement did not attract the mass membership he expected from the northern trade unions.

Bissolati was one of the warmest supporters on the Italian center-left of Italian intervention on the side of the Allies in 1915. Despite his relatively advanced age, Bissolati volunteered for the army and served at the front as a sergeant in the *Alpini*. He was wounded twice and received the Silver Medal for gallantry in combat. In June 1916, he became minister without portfolio and later, after the disaster at **Caporetto**, served as a minister under **Vittorio Emanuele Orlando**.

Although Bissolati was inclined to blame the antipatriotic and pacifist activities of the PSI for the poor showing of the Italian troops, it would be wrong to regard his wartime ministerial experience as one in which he finally renounced his former ideals. In 1918–1919, he fought a stern political battle for the renunciation by Italy of its territorial gains in Dalmatia and the Tyrol. His argument that occupying these territories undermined the principle of national self-determination made no impression on the Italian nationalists, who made Bissolati one of their favorite targets. Bissolati died in **Rome** in May 1920, despised and distrusted by both the nationalist right and the PSI.

BLASETTI, ALESSANDRO (1900–1987). The most interesting film director of the Fascist period, Alessandro Blasetti is widely regarded as a precursor of **neorealism**. His first major movie, *1860*, which was made in 1934, is considered by many critics to be his masterpiece. A nationalistic portrayal of **Giuseppe Garibaldi**'s expedition to **Sicily**, it has a number of deftly handled battle scenes and, anticipating later directors such as **Roberto Rossellini** and **Luchino Visconti**, uses ordinary people rather than actors in several speaking roles. The final scene of the film, which the director cut after the war, was set in **Mussolini**'s **Rome**. The following year, Blasetti produced a more overtly Fascist film, La *vecchia guardia* (*The Old Guard*, 1935), which celebrated *squadrismo* and the **March on Rome**. In 1941, he directed *La corona di ferro* (*The Iron Crown*), a mystical fairy tale with elaborate, costly sets and a more ambiguously profascist message. In 1942, Blasetti abruptly shifted away from big-budget epics and made a simple drama about a traveling salesman who meets an unmarried pregnant girl and urges her family to show compassion for her, *Quattro passi fra le nuvole* (*A Stroll in the Clouds*, 1942), an important milestone in the Italian **cinema**'s path to the classic neorealist works of the late 1940s. Blasetti's post-1945 output was vast, but of generally lower quality, though an exception to this judgment might be made for his 1957 feature *Amore e chiacchiere* (*Love and Chatter*). Blasetti died in Rome in February 1987.

BLOCCO NAZIONALE. The general elections of November 1919 weakened the hold on power of Italy's traditional governing parties by rewarding the **Partito Socialista Italiano**/Italian Socialist Party (PSI) and the **Partito Popolare Italiano**/Italian People's Party (PPI) with a substantial share of the vote. Accordingly, in May 1921, **Giovanni Giolitti** tried to reestablish his parliamentary majority by forming a great coalition of liberals, conservatives, nationalists, reformist socialists, and **Benito Mussolini**'s Fascists to confront the two mass parties. As a political maneuver, the creation of this so-called national bloc was a success: The coalition obtained 275 seats in the Chamber of Deputies, compared to the 122 won by the PSI, the 107 won by the PPI, and the 16 of the newly constituted (in 1921) **Partito Comunista Italiano**/Italian Communist Party (PCI). The chief consequence of Giolitti's move, however, was to give legitimacy to Mussolini's Fascists, who had been humiliated at the polls in 1919 but now emerged with 35 seats.

BOBBIO, NORBERTO (1909–2004). Born and raised in **Turin**, Norberto Bobbio was a professor of political and legal philosophy at the University of Turin from 1948 to 1979 and was made a life senator in 1985. Bobbio was born into an upper-class, pro-Fascist family, and it was only when he reached university that he began to make the acquaintance of a formidable group of intellectuals and critics of the regime. His friends included such luminaries as **Cesare Pavese**, **Carlo Levi**, the future publisher Giulio Einaudi, and the journalist Vittorio Foa. Bobbio had a somewhat ambiguous relationship with **Fascism**. As he very honestly admitted in his 1997 autobiography, he was willing to write servile letters to the minister for the universities protesting his commitment to the Fascist cause; on the other hand, he and his closest friends were strong critics of the theory and practice of the Fascist state and were identified as troublemakers by the police.

Bobbio's life was changed by the war and by the **resistance** movement to Fascism. He was a member of the **Partito d'Azione**/Action Party (PdA) and took part in clandestine activities in Turin during the war. Bobbio believed that the resistance was a moral turning point for Italy, and he was always passionately committed to the democracy that emerged in 1948. He was scathing about the student revolutionaries of the 1960s, who claimed that postwar Italy had constructed an oppressive antidemocratic regime, although he did sympathize with many of their criticisms of the Italian university system.

Bobbio's early academic work was in the philosophy of law, and he holds an important place among contemporary scholars of this field. He was also an expert interpreter of Thomas Hobbes and edited *De Cive* for an Italian audience in 1948. The nature of the political conflict in Italy, however, meant that he was forced to debate concrete political questions with communist thinkers. A secular democrat and a liberal, he persisted in defining dialogue as a corrective to the limitless nature of human folly and exaggeration. In his view, dialogue is the only route to democracy. Two famous books, *Politica e cultura (Politics and Culture*, 1950) and *Quale socialismo? (Which Socialism?* 1976) were the result of Bobbio's attempts to keep open dialogue with the **Partito Comunista Italiano**/Italian Communist Party (PCI).

By the beginning of the 1970s, he had become a supporter of the **Partito Socialista Italiano**/Italian Socialist Party (PSI), regarding it as a force that had moved away from the orthodox Marxism of the PCI and toward cooperation with the left of the **Democrazia Cristiana/** Christian Democracy (DC) in pursuit of a new progressivism. Yet he was never a PSI "loyalist." He was one of the few socialists who openly criticized **Bettino Craxi** in the 1980s.

Bobbio wrote a number of important works of political philosophy while in "retirement." His thoughts on the future of democracy, on just war theory, and on human rights were all translated into English (as well as numerous other European languages). His book *Destra e sinistra (Left and Right*, 1996) was actually a best-seller in Italy and elsewhere in Europe—an unusual fate for an academic book in any field, let alone in one as challenging as political philosophy. In 1992, Bobbio was spoken of as a potential candidate for **president of the Republic**; to his relief, the proposal came to nothing. When this heir to the liberal-socialist tradition of **Piero Gobetti**, **Gaetano Salvemini**, and **Carlo Rosselli** died in January 2004, he enjoyed growing international fame as one of the key European political thinkers and intellectuals of the postwar period.

BOCCIONI, UMBERTO (1882–1916). The most important **futurist** painter and sculptor, and the most subtle theoretician of the futurist movement, Umberto Boccioni left his native Reggio Calabria before he was 20 years old to live in **Rome** and Paris, where he was greatly influenced by the work of Georges Seurat. Upon returning to Italy, he was one of the founders of the futurist movement: his *Tumult in the Gallery* (1909) was the first major work produced by a futurist artist. Boccioni's paintings, with their emphasis on urban, industrial themes, and their remarkable ability to capture movement, faithfully reflect the ideas of the "Manifesto of Futurist Painters," published in 1910, which Boccioni cowrote with Carlo Carrà, Luigi Russolo, and Giacomo Balla. *The City Awakes*, painted in 1910 and currently housed in the Museum of Modern Art in New York, is arguably the finest example of his early work. Boccioni also published a "Manifesto of Futurist Sculptors" in 1912 and produced a number of powerful bronzes that attempt to portray the human form in the context of its environment.

Boccioni's style became increasingly abstract after 1911 and was greatly influenced by cubism. *Dynamism of a Human Body* (1913), in which no obvious figure is visible, is a good example of his later work. He fought in **World War I** and died, tragically young, in 1916 in Verona after a heavy fall from a horse. *See also* MARINETTI, FILIPPO TOMMASO.

BOLOGNA. Modern Bologna shows abundant signs of its Etruscan origins, its Roman past, and its wealth in the Middle Ages. Its long-lasting sense of civic engagement has been used to explain the remarkable "workability" and efficiency of this provincial and regional capital. Papal for three centuries, part of Napoleon's Cisalpine Republic (1796–1814), followed by a period under Austrian rule, it is known chiefly for its university, the oldest in the Western world, having been founded in 1088. It is also known for its small-scale industry, its political energy, and its delicious cuisine.

From 1945 onward, this city of nearly 400,000 has been mostly governed by the left. Until 2000, both its mayor and a city council plurality were drawn from the **Partito Comunista Italiano**/Italian Communist Party (PCI). Innovative governance has made it a showcase city. For example, a housing plan, begun in 1970, expropriated (with compensation) and rebuilt war-damaged properties of the inner city. Preference in rentals was given to pensioners, students, and tenant cooperatives. Thus, while retaining a mix of citizens in the heart of the city, Bologna's center escaped being gentrified or converted to warehouses.

The imagination brought by the local PCI to metropolitan problems is further illustrated by the system of *quartieri* or neighborhoods. Each of these decentralized units has a meeting hall, a health center, and a records section. Identity cards, citizenship papers, wedding certificates and licenses, birth and death certificates, tax status, and residency records can all be procured from one's *quartiere*; in some, by computer. Eighteen were created in the original 1960 legislation; they have since been consolidated into nine of these minicity halls. Each serves as a meeting place where residents meet to discuss measures under consideration by the city council. Thus, before any initiative is taken, all affected neighborhoods will have had an opportunity to judge its impact. Closing redundant schools or modifying traffic patterns is thoroughly debated before action is taken.

But all is not bliss in Bologna, the "fat and the learned," as it is called. Its political energies have sometimes been violent. During the German occupation, the Gothic Line that ran just south of the city was often at the center of partisan warfare. After protracted battles at several of the portals between partisans and the German garrison, the city was liberated on 25 April 1945, by the Polish Expeditionary Forces attached to the British Eighth Army. The local **Comitato di Liberazione Nazionale**/National Liberation Committee (CLN) had already established a de facto city administration.

The 1960s and 1970s were the years of maximum student activism, in Bologna as elsewhere. On 11 March 1977, a meeting held in the university's Anatomy Hall by a group of militant Catholics calling themselves Comunione e Liberazione (Communion and Liberation) was set upon by student Maoists. Clashes between these groups raged in the university area and surrounding streets. Finally, the Carabinieri were called in by the rector. One student, a known militant of **Lotta Continua**, was killed. The ensuing rioting brought tanks and armored personnel carriers into the university district. Student activists saw the PCI as part of the bourgeois establishment and condemned it as unfit to represent any hope of revolutionary change. Such views nourished the **Brigate Rosse**/Red Brigades (BR) and also produced a terrible response from the political right. On 2 August

1980, hundreds were injured and 85 people were killed when a bomb, thought to be planted by fascist terrorists, exploded in the second-class waiting room of Bologna's railroad station. *See also* RESISTANCE; STRATEGIA DELLA TENSIONE.

BOMBACCI, NICOLA (1879–1945). One of the leading figures of the Fascist regime, Nicola Bombacci began his career as a political activist in the **Partito Socialista Italiano**/Italian Socialist Party (PSI). He was one of the leaders of the party's "maximalist" wing and won notoriety after the revolution in Russia in 1917 by appealing to Italians to follow the Bolshevik example. In 1918, he was arrested and condemned to over two years' imprisonment for antiwar activities but was soon released and was elected to Parliament in 1919. In 1921, he was among the founders of the **Partito Comunista Italiano**/ Italian Communist Party (PCI), but was expelled in 1924 and drew ever closer to his former PSI comrade, **Benito Mussolini**. From 1927 onward, Bombacci was an open Fascist, playing an important role as the regime's spokesman to the working class. He remained faithful to Mussolini even after the dictator's fall in July 1943 and became one of the most influential figures in the **Republic of Salò**. Together with Mussolini, Bombacci drew up the so-called Manifesto of Verona, which outlined a confused program that incorporated socialist ideals such as the nationalization of public services with anti-Semitic rhetoric. He was with Mussolini in the desperate flight to Dongo near the Swiss border in April 1945 and shared the dictator's gruesome end.

BONINO, EMMA (1948–). An internationally respected activist for human rights and a successful politician, Emma Bonino was born in Bra (Piedmont) and educated at **Milan**'s Bocconi University. Her political career began in the abortion rights movement in the 1970s. Bonino was first elected to Parliament for the **Partito Radicale/** Radical Party (PR) in 1976 and to the European Parliament in 1979. Bonino has campaigned for many causes during her career, including the rights of individuals oppressed by communist states such as China, the abolition of the death penalty, **women**'s rights in third world countries such as Afghanistan (where she was arrested by the Taliban in 1997), and highly controversial causes such as the liberalization of drugs. She was a strong supporter, on humans rights grounds, of the **North Atlantic Treaty Organization**'s (NATO) intervention in Kosovo in 1998; a position that was controversial with the strong pacifist component of the human rights movement in Italy.

Bonino, in fact, is no bleeding-heart liberal. Her economic ideas are definitely conservative. She is an advocate of liberalization, deregulation, tax cuts and other measures to increase competitiveness in the more cosseted parts of Italy's economy. Politically, Bonino has emerged from the huge shadow thrown by **Marco Pannella**. She was nominated by the first government of **Silvio Berlusconi** to be member of the European Commission. Bonino was given authority over a mixed bag of responsibilities, including fishing policy and consumer protection, as well as human rights, but was widely regarded as an outstanding success in the job. In June 1999, the "Bonino list" obtained 8.5 percent of the votes in the European elections, the highest vote ever obtained by the PR and testimony to Bonino's personal popularity.

In recent years, Bonino has been a prominent international campaigner against female genital mutilation and an active participant in Italian political life. In 2006, she led the PR into an alliance with the Democratic Socialists called the "Rose in the Fist." The alliance was unsuccessful (obtaining less than 3 percent of the vote), and this failure at the polls may have prevented her from becoming foreign minister. Bonino was nevertheless appointed to the government by **Romano Prodi** and currently serves as minister for European affairs and foreign trade.

BONOMI, IVANOE (1873–1951). Born in Mantua (Lombardy), Ivanoe Bonomi was one of the most important early theorists of the nascent **Partito Socialista Italiano**/Italian Socialist Party (PSI). He contributed to **Filippo Turati**'s influential magazine, *Critica sociale*, from 1895 onward, briefly edited the party newspaper *Avanti!*, and in 1907 published a controversial book, *Le vie nuove del socialismo* (*The New Roads of Socialism*), in which he argued that the workers' movement needed to reject Marxist dogma and concentrate on winning social reforms by adhering to British-style laborism—a position that found little support in the increasingly revolutionary PSI. Bonomi, who was elected to **Parliament** in 1909, was expelled from the PSI in 1912 along with others of the party's moderates. Together with **Leonida Bissolati**, Bonomi founded the Partito Socialista Riformista Italiano/Italian Reformist Socialist Party (PSRI), but it never obtained a mass following.

Bonomi supported the war and saw combat as a junior officer. In 1916, he became minister for public works in the government of **Paolo Boselli** and later became minister of war. Bonomi was himself prime minister between July 1921 and February 1922. His attitude toward the growing Fascist threat was somewhat equivocal. During the elections of May 1921, he joined **Giovanni Giolitti** as a candidate for the **blocco nazionale**. As prime minister, he did little to obstruct the outrages committed by the Fascist squads.

During the Fascist epoch, Bonomi eked out a precarious living as a writer of history books, the most important of which, *La politica italiana da Porta Pia a Vittorio Veneto* (*Italian Politics from Porto Pia to Vittorio Veneto*, 1943), later became a widely used school textbook. In June 1944 he returned to political activity as the figurehead premier of the provisional government containing all the leading democratic forces in Allied-controlled Italy. His popularity with the British enabled him to survive a government crisis in November–December 1944, but after the end of the conflict in May 1945, the partisans of northern Italy would not accept his continuation in office. When he resigned, his place was taken by **Ferruccio Parri** of the **Partito d'Azione**/Action Party (PdA).

Bonomi fought the June 1946 elections in the company of **Benedetto Croce**, **Vittorio Emanuele Orlando**, and **Francesco Nitti** as the leader of the Unione Democratica Nazionale/National Democratic Union (UDN), but these remnants of prefascist Italy fared poorly at the polls, obtaining less than 7 percent of the vote. One last institutional burden awaited him: a member of the new Italian Senate by right, he was elected by his fellow senators to be president of the first elected Senate in Italian history in May 1948 and remained in that position until his death in 1951. *See also* BADOGLIO, PIETRO; SALÒ, REPUBLIC OF.

BORDIGA, AMADEO (1889–1970). Twentieth-century Italy's most prominent Trotskyite, Amadeo Bordiga was an engineer from Naples who played a prominent role in the "maximalist" wing of the **Partito Socialista Italiano**/Italian Socialist Party (PSI). In 1919, Bordiga supported the party's entry into the Third International on Soviet terms, even though Vladimir Ilyich Lenin had insisted that the PSI could only become a member if it called itself a "communist" party and if it expelled such notorious moderates as **Filippo Turati**. When the PSI hesitated to bow to Lenin's demands at a special conference of the party in January 1921, Bordiga, together with **Antonio Gramsci**, left the PSI and founded the **Partito Comunista Italiano**/Italian Communist Party (PCI). Bordiga's ideological position was clear. In the words of the motion adopted by the PCI's Second Congress in March 1922, the choice was "either Communism or **Fascism**." No alliance with the bourgeois parties (in practice, all other parties) was possible, only armed resistance to the Fascists under the direction of the PCI (even though Bordiga must have been aware that the PCI lacked the military strength to assume this role).

After the "maximalist" wing of the PSI finally expelled Turati in October 1922, Bordiga's intransigence on this point caused the PCI itself to split. Some communists, at Soviet urging, rejoined the PSI, which was readmitted to the Third International, and others, led by Bordiga, refused. This fanatical adherence to party dogma demoralized the entire Italian left and unquestionably weakened the working class's response to Fascism.

Bordiga was arrested and tried for "conspiracy against the state" in 1923, but remarkably managed to convince the magistrates of his innocence. Within the PCI, his position weakened as the Stalinist wing of the party gained strength. In 1926, at the PCI's Third Congress in Lyon, he lost the party leadership to Gramsci and was eventually expelled. After a period of internal exile, he was allowed to resume the engineering profession by the authorities in 1930. Bordiga dedicated himself to his work and took no further part in leftist politics, although in his old age he did write a two-volume history of Italian communism's left wing. At the time of his death in 1970, he had become a cult figure for the PCI's young critics in the student and workers' movements.

BOSELLI, PAOLO (1838–1932). Born in the Ligurian city of Savona, Paolo Boselli was elected to Parliament for the first time in 1870. An academic lawyer, Boselli held a series of second-rank ministerial posts between 1888 and 1906. In June 1916, Boselli, who had been a strong supporter of Italian intervention in **World War I**, was called upon to replace **Antonio Salandra** as prime minister after initial Austrian successes had led to the fall of the town of Asiago. He formed a cabinet that contained representatives from all the political parties except the **Partito Socialista Italiano**/Italian Socialist Party (PSI). Boselli, however, proved to be an inadequate choice as prime minister. His inexperience in military and foreign affairs, lack of a personal political base, and advanced age all hindered his ability to control either the authoritarian commander of the Italian forces, General **Luigi Cadorna**, or the unruly members of his majority. His government fell after the disaster of **Caporetto** in October 1917 emphasized the dramatic failings of the Italian war effort.

Boselli became a nationalist and a fascist after the war, although he held no further political office. He died in **Rome** in 1932.

BOSSI, UMBERTO (1943–). The charismatic leader of the **Lega Nord/** Northern League (LN), Umberto Bossi was born into a working-class family in Varese (Lombardy). He was a dance-band guitarist, handyman, hospital orderly, and part-time medical student before he found in political activity his true vocation. A chance meeting in 1979 with Bruno Salvadori, the leading ideologue of the autonomist Union Valdotaine (claiming to speak for the Aosta region of northwest Italy), gave Bossi a taste for the autonomist brand of politics. In 1982, Bossi founded the Lega Lombarda/Lombard League and shrewdly gave this new movement a populist program (recommending, for instance, a "Lombards first" policy in public administration). He soon revealed a genius for political propaganda. A string of electoral victories followed, and in February 1991, Bossi successfully united all the autonomist parties in northern Italy into a single party under the leadership of the LN. His goal in this period was to break the mold of Italian politics and compel what he disparagingly calls the "Roman parties" to transform Italy's highly centralized state into a federal republic based on three "macroregions": the North, the Center, and the South.

When the political system seemed to collapse in 1992–1993, Bossi briefly emerged as a power broker at a national level. The LN briefly became the most widely supported party in the country, with huge levels of support in the North. Much of the LN's electorate was stolen from it, however, by the creation of **Silvio Berlusconi**'s **Forza Italia**. Bossi cooperated with Berlusconi initially; in December 1994, he brought down Berlusconi's first government, provoking a five-year breach between the two men.

Nevertheless, Bossi seems to have succeeded in establishing the LN as the party of choice for a substantial segment of the northern electorate (especially those who live in the Alpine regions of Lombardy, Venetia, and Friuli). In September 1996, following the LN's outstanding performance in the April 1996 elections, Bossi proclaimed the foundation of the independent republic of "Padania" (the Po River valley) in northern Italy. Showing his usual flair for publicity, he embarked on a symbolic voyage down the Po to carry a flask of "sacred" water from the river's source to the sea at Venice.

Bossi changed the LN's line in 1999 and made peace with Silvio Berlusconi to form the **Casa delle Libertà**/House of Freedoms (CDL). He became minister for constitutional reform in 2001. Prodded by Bossi, the House of Freedoms proposed a major constitutional revision whose centerpiece was "devolution" of significant powers to the regional governments.

Bossi leads the LN as if it were a cult or sect rather than a political party. There is no doubt that he is venerated by the LN's members and exercises a deep personal authority over them. In 2004, Bossi was stricken by illness and came close to death. None of the other leaders of the LN has emerged as a worthy substitute.

For all his antics, and his sometimes unsavory rhetoric, Bossi is the colorful expression of a genuine mood of disquiet and frustration with central government among the small-scale entrepreneurs of the Paduan Plain. *See also* PIANURA PADANA; REGIONALISM.

BOTTAI, GIUSEPPE (1895–1959). One of the leading Fascist intellectuals, Giuseppe Bottai fought as a volunteer during **World War I**, rising to the rank of captain. After the war, he was one of the original founders of the *fasci di combattimento*, organizing the Fascist squads in his native Lazio. Nevertheless, he was widely regarded as one of the few genuine intellectuals among the hierarchs of the **Partito Nazionale Fascista**/National Fascist Party (PNF). Editor of *Critica Fascista*, the moderation of his position on many issues and genuine openness to debate won him a relatively liberal reputation among the regime's opponents. It also caused him trouble with **Benito Mussolini**. His opposition to the PNF's increasing identification with the state almost caused his expulsion from party activity after Mussolini cracked down on internal dissent in October 1925.

Despite his aversion to the party state, Bottai held a number of important governmental posts in the 1920s and 1930s. Between 1926 and 1932, he was the most enthusiastic exponent of **corporatism** as an ideology and, as minister for the corporations, was entrusted with turning theory into practice. He became governor of **Rome** in 1936 and minister for education between 1936 and 1943. In this last post he enforced the **racial laws** and was also responsible for imposing on all schoolchildren compulsory membership in the regime's paramilitary **youth movements**. On the other hand, his *Carta della scuola* (School Charter), because it opened public schools to workers, was widely praised among Fascist dissidents on the left.

Between 1940 and 1943, Bottai published *Primato*, which seemingly sought to rescue Italian **literature** and culture from purely propagandistic uses. Its pages included essays by Fascist left dissidents, distinguished antifascists, and regime apologists.

When war broke out in 1939, Bottai—who had already expressed private doubts over the desirability of the alliance with Germany—was one of many prominent figures who opposed Italy's participation. Together with some of the old prewar liberal politicians, he began to draw close to the crown in the hope of inspiring in **Victor Emmanuel III** some initiative that might withdraw Italy from the war. On 25 July 1943, Bottai was among the 19 members of the **Fascist Grand Council** who voted to deprive Mussolini of his powers. For this "crime," he was condemned to death in absentia by the **Republic of Salò**. In 1944, he fled Italy to North Africa, where he joined the French Foreign Legion. In 1945, he was sentenced to life imprisonment by the High Court of Justice, but he was amnestied in 1947 without having served a single day in prison. Bottai died in Rome in January 1959. *See also SQUADRISMO.*

BRIGATE ROSSE/Red Brigades (BR). A terrorist movement whose leadership, especially in the early years, was drawn largely from radical Catholic elements of the sociology faculty at the University of Trento, the BR waged a ruthless war against the Italian state from

1971 onward. The Red Brigades set as their goal the embarrassment of the **Partito Comunista Italiano**/Italian Communist Party (PCI) by provoking the state into such repressive actions as to oblige all those who thought themselves revolutionaries to choose between acting on revolutionary rhetoric on the one hand or, on the other, sustaining the dominance of an allegedly oppressive, bourgeois state. Their methods were violent: "kneecapping" and on occasion, kidnappings and assassinations. Their targets were initially those on the relative left end of the political spectrum who advocated or symbolized the collaboration between the reformist center parties or factions and parties of revolutionary tradition. Journalists, jurists, academics, and trade unionists were all attacked, and the responsibility was always accepted—indeed, proclaimed—by the leadership of the Red Brigades.

The BR's boldest move was the kidnapping on 16 March 1978 of **Aldo Moro**. The meticulous planning of the daylight attack on the protective vehicles that preceded and followed Moro's automobile— his entire five-man police bodyguard was killed—enabled Moro's kidnappers to whisk him into hiding before a **police** response could be organized. In fact, as subsequent investigation eventually revealed, his hiding place was always in central Rome rendering police searches and road checks futile. After 55 days in captivity, and apparently following bitter quarrels as to his fate among the Brigades' leadership, Moro was murdered and his body left in the trunk of a small automobile parked—symbolically—midway between PCI national offices and the national headquarters of the **Democrazia Cristiana**/Christian Democracy (DC) in **Rome**.

One line of response urged from some quarters was the enactment of measures expanding police powers and diminishing civil rights. This was not the method chosen by the Italian political leadership. Partly because the principal parties were divided between those ready to treat the BR as a legitimate interlocutor—the **Partito Socialista Italiano**/Italian Socialist Party (PSI)—and those who refused to contemplate such a course of action, no repressive measures were initiated. The inaction of the government and its avowed determination not to violate constitutional rights denied the BR the provocation that they sought, and their own increasingly random violence gradually lost them most sympathy in public opinion. Clever police work—

coordinated by **Carlo Alberto Dalla Chiesa**—also contributed to the BR's decline. In January 1983, Aldo Moro's killers—including the BR's chief strategist, Mario Moretti—were condemned to life sentences in Rome after a nine-month trial. Nevertheless, as late as April 1988, a BR cell was responsible for the murder of Professor Roberto Ruffilli, a close advisor to the then premier, **Ciriaco De Mita**, who was one of the leading advocates within the DC of Aldo Moro's philosophy of compromise with the PCI.

When U.S. General James Lee Dozier was kidnapped and held prisoner by the Red Brigade for 40 days between December 1981 and February 1982, his hiding place was uncovered by a combination of good police work and luck. The police organized a textbook raid on the apartment and freed the general unharmed, without a shot having been fired, taking several prisoners and uncovering incriminating documents that helped equip the Italian judiciary to incarcerate much of the top leadership of the BR.

The BR inspired several imitators, the most violent of which was a group called *Prima linea* ("Frontline"). This group's most notorious member was Marco Donat Cattin, the son of a DC cabinet minister, who eventually gave evidence at the 1983 trial of his former comrades. In recent years, cells inspired by the myth of the BR have renewed the terrorist struggle. In March 2002, one such group (five of whose members have since been sentenced to life imprisonment) murdered Marco Biagi, a Bologna academic lawyer whose only sin was proposing the partial liberalization of Italy's very rigid labor laws.

BROSIO, MANLIO (1897–1980). Born in **Turin**, Brosio was a wartime partisan and, during the latter stages of the war, became leader of the **Partito Liberale Italiano**/Italian Liberal Party (PLI), taking part in the second **Ivanoe Bonomi** administration as minister without portfolio and as vice premier under **Ferruccio Parri** after the end of the conflict. The PLI bore substantial responsibility for the crisis that brought down Parri's short-lived administration in November 1945, but any hopes Brosio might have had of acceding to the premiership were dashed by the emergence of **Alcide De Gasperi**. Brosio was minister for defense in the first postwar cabinet to be headed by the leader of the **Democrazia Cristiana**/Christian Democracy (DC).

An antimonarchist in a largely royalist party, Brosio joined the **Partito Repubblicano Italiano**/Italian Republican Party (PRI) in 1946, but gave up active politics for diplomacy in 1947. He was successively Italian ambassador to Moscow, London, Washington, and Paris. In 1964, he became secretary general of the **North Atlantic Treaty Organization (NATO)**, the first Italian to hold this post (the only other Italian so honored is Sergio Balzanino, in 1994–1995). In 1972, he returned to politics, being elected to the Senate for the PLI. He died in his native Turin in 1980.

BUONARROTI, FILIPPO MICHELE (1761–1837). Conspirator, republican, and agitator, Filippo Buonarroti was a disciple of Jean Jacques Rousseau and an early communist. Born in Pisa, he became a French citizen during the revolution and was sent to Italy as a secret agent. After the fall of Maximilien Robespierre, he took part in Babeuf's unsuccessful "conspiracy of equals" against the Directory and was forced to flee to Geneva. After the return of absolutism to Italy, he organized a secret society called the "Sublime Perfect Masters," a neomasonic organization with elaborate rituals and hierarchy, whose task was to coordinate revolutionary activity in Italy. In fact, despite his tireless work for the cause, Buonarroti never obtained a serious following among the underground sects. The monarchism of the *Carboneria* was antithetical to him, although he exerted more influence than **Giuseppe Mazzini** among its sects. Buonarroti was a republican, like Mazzini, but his political philosophy was inspired by a Robespierrean vision of the need for a dictatorship of the enlightened that was at odds with Mazzini's more democratic goals. He broke with Mazzini in 1834. Buonarroti was the author of an important treatise on politics, *La conspiration pour l'égalité, dite de Babeuf* (*The Conspiracy for Equality, as Told by Babeuf*, 1828), in which he reflected upon the impact of the French Revolution on European politics since 1789. He died in Paris in September 1837.

BUTTIGLIONE, ROCCO (1948–). Born in the Adriatic resort of Gallipoli (Apulia), Buttiglione initiated his career as a political philosopher under the conservative Catholic scholar Augusto De

Noce. He is the author of numerous widely translated books and articles on Marxism and Catholic political thought and was personally and intellectually close to Pope John Paul II, Karol Wojtyla.

In March 1994, Buttiglione entered politics and was elected to Parliament as a deputy for the reborn **Partito Popolare Italiano**/Italian People's Party (PPI). Almost immediately, at the end of July 1994, he became party leader. Although a conservative, Buttiglione surprisingly sought to achieve good relations with the **Partito Democratico della Sinistra**/Democratic Party of the Left (PDS) and, in December 1994, joined with the PDS and the **Lega Nord**/Northern League (LN) to defeat the government of **Silvio Berlusconi** in a parliamentary vote of no confidence. Buttiglione strongly supported President Scalfaro's subsequent decision to establish a government of technocrats headed by **Lamberto Dini**.

In the spring of 1995, however, Buttiglione switched sides and proposed joining the right-wing alliance of **Forza Italia**, the Centro Cristiano Democratico/Christian Democratic Center (CCD), and the **Alleanza Nazionale/**National Alliance (AN). The PPI's majority, preferring the alliance with the PDS, strongly opposed this tactic and succeeded in passing a vote of no confidence in Buttiglione's leadership in March 1995. Buttiglione launched a new centrist party, the Cristiani Democratici Uniti/United Christian Democrats (CDU) in July 1995, which eventually merged with the CCD to form the **Unione dei Democratici Cristiani e di Centro**/ Union of Christian Democrats and of the Center (UDC). This party has retained the legal right to make use of the shield and cross emblem of the old **Democrazia Cristiana**/Christian Democracy (DC).

Buttiglione has remained a leading figure in the UDC and was minister for Europe in the government formed by Silvio Berlusconi in May 2001. In the summer of 2004, Buttiglione was proposed by the Italian government as European Union (EU) commissioner for justice and home affairs. Buttiglione's outspoken conservative views on the EU's social agenda (he is strongly opposed, for instance, to gay marriage) led to a major polemic over his nomination from homosexual and feminist groups, and the justice committee of the European Parliament eventually voted in October 2004 to reject his name.

– C –

CADORNA, LUIGI (1850–1928). Born in Verbania (Piedmont), Luigi Cadorna was commander in chief of Italian forces on the Isonzo River from May 1915 to November 1917, when he was replaced by General **Armando Diaz** after the disastrous battle of **Caporetto**. Only Allied reinforcements and a stiffened Italian resistance at the Piave River averted disaster. Determined counterattacks culminated in Austria suing for peace.

The Italian Commission of Inquiry on the Caporetto disaster, which reported in 1919, assigned much of the responsibility to Cadorna for having used his position to undermine the prestige of rivals among other senior officers rather than in properly caring for his troops. Certainly, he was a harsh disciplinarian who had no qualms about executing troops for insubordination or other infractions of the military code. Cadorna egregiously attributed the losses at Caporetto to his men's cowardice. He became field marshal in 1924.

CAIROLI, BENEDETTO (1825–1889). The eldest son of a family of patriots, Benedetto Cairoli's four brothers all died fighting for Italian unification. Benedetto himself was one of the "Thousand" who sailed with **Giuseppe Garibaldi** to **Sicily** in 1860. He was elected to **Parliament** in 1861, but returned to the battlefield to fight for the liberation of **Rome** in 1867. Romantic and quixotic, he could not match the political acumen of **Francesco Crispi** or **Agostino Depretis**. He nevertheless became prime minister three times between March 1878 and May 1881. Cairoli's governments were largely composed of politicians from northern Italy (he himself was from Pavia) and came to ignominious ends. His first government collapsed following an assassination attempt on King Umberto, the second as a result of the French occupation of Tunis. Cairoli was opposed to Depretis's style of government and allied with Crispi, **Zanardelli**, **Nicotera**, and Alfredo Baccarini to form the so-called Pentarchy, which led the parliamentary opposition to Depretis. Cairoli died in **Naples** at the villa of King Umberto in August 1889.

CALAMANDREI, PIERO (1889–1956). One of 20th-century Italy's leading liberal intellectuals, Piero Calamandrei was also a respected jurist and a prominent opponent of **Fascism**. Born in **Florence**, Calamandrei postponed his career as a professor of law to serve as a volunteer during **World War I**. He was an active antifascist from the very beginning of the regime. Together with Ernesto Rossi, **Gaetano Salvemini**, and **Carlo and Nello Rosselli**, he was one of the founders of an antifascist circle of intellectuals in Florence that the Fascist squads brutally suppressed in December 1924; he signed **Benedetto Croce's** 1925 manifesto of antifascist intellectuals. In the 1940s, he honorably resigned his university chair rather than write a letter publicly proclaiming his loyalty to **Benito Mussolini**.

In 1942, Calamandrei was one of the founders of the **Partito d'Azione**/Action Party (PdA). He was elected to the **Constituent Assembly** in 1946 and became one of the principal authors of the **Constitution** of 1948. In 1948, he was elected to **Parliament** as a member of the **Partito Socialista Democratico Italiano**/Italian Social Democratic Party (PSDI), although he later strongly disagreed with his party's support for the **North Atlantic Treaty Organization (NATO)** and its increasing closeness to the **Democrazia Cristiana**/Christian Democracy (DC). Unlike many in the PSDI, Calamandrei believed that democratic socialists could find intellectual common ground with the **Partito Comunista Italiano**/Italian Communist Party (PCI) both within Italy and without, and to this end he founded the intellectual review *Il Ponte* (*The Bridge*) in 1945. Ever since then, this magazine has been one of the most important forums for intellectual debate on the Italian left. Calamandrei died in Florence in 1956.

CALCIO. Catholicism is only the formal religion of Italy; *calcio* (association football or soccer) is the religion that inspires most fervor. It is impossible to have a full understanding of Italian social life in this century without knowing something about this hugely popular sport.

Soccer was imported from England in the late 1880s and took organized form in the early 1890s. The first soccer club was formed in 1893 in **Genoa**, and the first soccer championship, won by Genoa, took place in May 1898. The early championships were organized on a knockout basis, but after **World War I** the soccer clubs were placed into the system of leagues that is common for most professional sports in Europe. Today, the premier league, Serie A, consists of 20 leading clubs that play one another twice (once at home, once away) in a season that lasts from September to the end of May. The championship-winning club is the one that has amassed most points at the end of the season; clubs earn three points for a win and one point for a tie. The three clubs that earn the fewest points in the season are relegated to Serie B and are replaced by the three clubs who do best in the junior championship. There is also a semiprofessional Serie C, which is organized into northern and southern divisions, and a long array of amateur leagues at regional, provincial, and municipal levels.

The biggest clubs—Juventus (which plays in **Turin**), AC Milan, *Internazionale* of Milan, and AC Roma—are among the wealthiest sporting businesses in the world. Games between the top teams are watched by as many as 80,000 people and by enormous TV audiences all over the globe. Many of the leading players from Germany, France, South America, and Africa play in Italy, and the top stars earn salaries that match those of basketball or baseball players in the United States. Soccer has not been exempt from the malaise in Italian public life, however. In 2006, a major match-fixing scandal hit several top teams, including Juventus, which was demoted to Serie B after a judicial investigation.

Italy and Brazil are the most successful nations in international soccer competition. Italy's most famous clubs have won numerous trans-European and intercontinental club championships, and the *nazionale*, or national team, has won the World Cup on four occasions (1934, 1938, 1982, 2006) and been losing finalist twice (1970, 1994). In 1990, Italy hosted the World Cup, putting on a spectacular show in colossal state-of-the-art stadiums especially built for the event. Italian soccer has historically been characterized by a heavy reliance on defensive, tactical play designed to frustrate opposition teams, but in recent years clubs have adopted a more adventurous, attacking style.

CALOGERO, GUIDO (1904–1986). A prominent philosopher who took an active political role, Calogero was born in **Rome**, where he took his degree in 1925 with a thesis on Aristotle's logic. Calogero became one of the leading Italian interpreters of the philosophy of the ancients, especially Aristotle, of his time. His first *maestro* was the Fascist philosopher **Giovanni Gentile**, and Calogero contributed many articles to Gentile's ambitious *Encyclopaedia*. Calogero obtained a university lectureship in 1927, when he was just 23 years old, and taught at the **Universities** of Rome and **Florence** before becoming professor of philosophy at Pisa in 1935.

Unlike his mentor Gentile, Calogero was a convinced antifascist from the late 1920s onward. In the late 1930s, together with a Tuscan intellectual, Aldo Capitini, Calogero developed liberal-socialist ideas and, on his own account, published a famous collection of lectures called *La scuola dell'uomo* (*The School of Man*). Such writings made Calogero an influential figure among the antifascist thinkers of Tuscany and were a key influence on the evolution of the ideas of the **Partito d'Azione**/Action Party (PdA). Calogero subsequently became a prominent member of the PdA, from 1943 to its dissolution in 1948. However, his antifascist activities led to his being arrested, deprived of his university chair, and condemned to two spells of imprisonment during the war.

After the war, Calogero had a varied political and journalistic career on the political left. He was one of the founders of the **Partito Radicale**/Radical Party (PR) in 1955; in the 1960s, he supported, together with **Norberto Bobbio**, the creation of the Partito Socialista Unificato/Unified Socialist Party (PSU). He remained an important figure in academic philosophy in both Italy and abroad. His teachings and political writings won him many disciples, the most prominent being **Carlo Azeglio Ciampi**. Bobbio called Calogero "the youngest of my masters" in an article written in 2001. Calogero died in Rome in 1986.

CALVINO, ITALO (1923–1985). The son of two expatriate Italian university botanists, Calvino was born in Havana, Cuba, although his parents returned to Italy in 1925. Calvino began his university studies in the same field as his parents in 1941, but the war intervened. Calvino was called up by the **Republic of Salò**, but rather than serve he went into hiding. In 1944, he joined the **Partito Comunista Italiano**/Italian Communist Party (PCI) and took part in intensive partisan fighting. As for so many Italians, this was an experience that shaped the rest of his life.

After the war, Calvino returned to the university, this time to study literature, and worked for the PCI and the publishing house Einaudi. His first political articles were published by the magazine *Il Politecnico*, and, in 1946, he completed his first novel, *Il sentiero dei nidi di ragno* (*The Path to the Nest of Spiders*), a work in the neorealist idiom that described the partisan struggle through the eyes of a child. It was the first novel in what would prove to be an extremely prolific career as a writer, critic, translator, and social theorist. Unlike his close friends **Cesare Pavese** and **Elio Vittorini**, Calvino evolved into a writer of *favole* (fables). *Fiabe italiane* (*Italian Fables*, 1956) and *Marcovaldo* (1963) are perhaps the high points of his literary output.

Calvino also showed notable political independence. In 1956, he broke with the PCI after the party condoned the Soviet Union's brutal suppression of the Hungarian workers' movement. While he never renounced his progressive sympathies, Calvino himself admitted that he became more detached from politics after 1956. This did not stop him, however, from joining in the intense debate over communism in the literary magazines of the Italian left or from being an outspoken opponent of the Vietnam War. By the 1970s, Calvino had become an internationally recognized writer, especially in France, which awarded him the *Légion d'honneur* in 1981, and in the United States, where he was invited to conferences and to give lectures. Calvino was preparing to give the Norton lectures on poetry at Harvard University when he died of a stroke in September 1985. He would have been the first Italian to perform this most prestigious of academic tasks.

CANOVA, ANTONIO (1757–1822). Born in the province of Treviso, in the foothills of the **Alps**, Antonio Canova is the greatest genius of the neoclassicist movement in sculpture. He hailed from a family of stone masons. The patronage of a wealthy local family enabled Canova to pursue his studies at the academy for fine arts in **Venice**. In 1780, he produced *Daedalus and Icarus*, his first famous work.

Canova was given a three-year scholarship by the Venetian authorities to study in **Rome**. He swiftly produced a series of masterpieces that compelled his contemporaries to regard him as being on a par with such great masters of the Italian tradition of monumental art as Bernini and Michelangelo. In 1787, he completed his monument to Pope Clement XIV, which established his reputation as one of the finest sculptors in Italy. In 1793, he produced *Cupid and Psyche*, a work that procured him the offer of becoming court sculptor in Saint Petersburg. Canova, however, chose to remain in Italy, although he traveled widely and was well-known throughout Europe.

Canova produced many great works between 1798 and his death in 1822. His *Perseus with the Head of Medusa* (probably 1800) was placed, by papal decree, in a special room of the **Vatican** hitherto reserved for the finest works of the Renaissance. His best-known work, however, is probably *The Three Graces*, a depiction of the three daughters of Zeus, who are said to represent Joy, Charm, and Beauty. Two versions exist. The earliest version was sent to the court of the tsar and is still to be found in the Hermitage museum in Saint Petersburg. The second was commissioned in 1813 by the Duke of Bedford for his home at Woburn Abbey in England. The sculpture shows the three nudes clustered together, heads touching, enjoying a shared confidence in an atmosphere of slightly bashful eroticism.

Canova was charged in 1815 with negotiating the return of art treasures looted by Napoleon during his conquest of the Italian peninsula. He carried out this delicate task with some skill and received as a reward the title of Marquis of Ischia and an annual pension of 3,000 crowns. Canova spent much of his by now considerable wealth on his own tomb in his native village of Possengo. He died in **Venice** in October 1822.

CAPORETTO, BATTLE OF. A small town near what is today the Italian–Slovenian border, Caporetto was the scene of the greatest defeat in Italian military history. Following the failure of the Italian army's 11th offensive on the Isonzo River in August 1917, the Austro-German high command launched a major counteroffensive. German assistance to Austria was not matched by the British and French until the situation became desperate. On the first day (24 October 1917), the Austro-German forces swiftly recovered the few kilometers that the Italians had taken over the preceding two and a half years of fighting. The Italian line broke at Caporetto and was routed, stopping only at the Piave River—almost at **Venice**—where the new line held. Fortunately for Italy, not only did the Austro-

German forces outrun their supplies, but Britain and France sent reinforcements in early November. Losses at Caporetto were extremely high. More than 10,000 Italian troops had been killed, 30,000 wounded, and 293,000 captured. A measure of morale is provided by the desertion of some 300,000 soldiers. *See also* TRIESTE; WORLD WAR I.

CARABINIERI. *See* POLICE.

CARBONERIA. Secret societies of middle- and upper-class supporters of constitutional government and Italian unification, the *carboneria* (literally, "coal-burners") sprang up in **Naples** and southern Italy during the Napoleonic occupation, spreading in the subsequent two decades to Spain, France, and northern Italy. There they came into contact with similar associations, such as the *Federati* of Lombardy, and were infiltrated by the more radical followers of **Filippo Buonarroti**. Like the Freemasons, the *carboneria* were distinguished by a complex series of rituals, passwords, and emblems; were structured into a rigid hierarchy of grades of initiation; and were bound to absolute secrecy about their activities.

The *carboneria* were agents of revolution in the insurrections of Naples, Piedmont, and Lombardy in 1820–1821, and of hundreds of other revolutionary acts throughout the peninsula in the 1820s and 1830s. As such, they were the subject of bitter persecution from the authorities and from rival reactionary sects such as the *calderari* in the Kingdom of the Two Sicilies. The limits of the *carboneria* as a revolutionary organization were exposed by the failure of uprisings in central Italy in 1830–1831. Limited by their own secrecy and rituals to select categories of mostly wealthy students, soldiers, and professionals, the *carboneria* were able to establish provisional governments in Modena, Parma, and **Bologna**, but then lacked the numbers or coordination to fend off the Austrian troops that moved quickly to the aid of the pope. The *carboneria* were thereafter eclipsed by **Giuseppe Mazzini**'s *Giovine Italia*, which was much less elitist and ritualistic in its composition and behavior, and by the liberal reformers of the so-called neoguelphist movement such as **Cesare Balbo** and **Vincenzo Gioberti**.

CARDUCCI, GIOSUE (1835–1907). A poet who led Italian letters back to the classical tradition and away from the romanticism of **Giacomo Leopardi**, Carducci was born in Lucca (Tuscany) but spent almost all of his working life as a professor of rhetoric at **Bologna** University. In 1901, Carducci republished his life's work in a six-volume edition. The poems that have best withstood the test of time were published between 1861 and 1887. The most famous, perhaps, is "A Satana" ("Hymn to Satan," 1862), in which he vaunted atheism and rationalism at the expense of all transcendental philosophies, German idealism, as much as traditional **Catholicism**, although he was a fierce anticlerical. In 1876, he was elected to **Parliament** as a republican but never took his seat. In his latter years, however, his views became less intransigent and radical and became tinged with nationalism and a sense of Italian cultural superiority (he supported, for instance, Italy's colonial wars). By the 1890s, he was a popular national institution. Nominated to the Senate in 1900, in 1906, he, together with **Camillo Golgi**, who won the prize for medicine the same year, became the first Italian to win the Nobel prize. When he died in Bologna the following year, his funeral was attended by huge crowds. *See also* LITERATURE.

CARLI, GUIDO (1914–1993). Born in Brescia (Lombardy), Carli worked for the International Monetary Fund (IMF) between 1947 and 1950 before becoming a member of the controlling committee of the European Payments Union. In 1957–1958, he held the post of minister for foreign trade. In 1960, Carli was appointed governor of the **Banca d'Italia**, a position he held until 1975. In 1976, he became president of **Confindustria**, the association of Italian manufacturers.

Carli's political career began in 1983 when he was elected as an independent, but with the support of the **Democrazia Cristiana/** Christian Democracy (DC), to the Senate. He was reelected in 1987. Carli served as minister of the treasury in **Giulio Andreotti**'s sixth and seventh governments (1989–1992). From this office, he did his best to protest against the growing national debt and to argue for the austerity that was anathema to the parties of government. Carli, however, was just one of three economics ministers and had no control over the departments of budget and finance. In effect, his reputation and international standing were being used as a fig leaf to cover the fiscal and monetary laxity of the parties of government. He died in Spoleto in 1993. In commemoration, the following year the Libera Università internazionale degli studi sociali/Free University for the Social Sciences (LUISS), a private university of very high quality in **Rome**, renamed itself in his honor. Carli had been president of LUISS from 1978 to his death. *See also* ECONOMY; *PENTA-PARTITO*.

CARNERA, PRIMO (1906–1967). Born in Sequala, in Friuli, Primo Carnera was heavyweight champion of the world in the 1930s and a symbol of Fascist athletic prowess. A huge man (he was six feet seven inches in height and weighed 270 pounds; he weighed 17 pounds at birth), Carnera initially wanted to be a carpenter. When he was 18, he moved to live with relatives in France, where he worked as a circus strongman. He was taken up by a professional coach, Paul Journée, and a somewhat unscrupulous manager, Léon See, and began his professional boxing career in 1928. Nicknamed the "ambling Alp" and the "good giant," in all he fought 108 bouts between 1928 and 1946, winning 88 (70 by knockout) and losing 15.

Carnera won the world championship in June 1933 when he defeated the American boxer Jack Sharkey. In October of the same year, he defended the title against the Spanish champion Paulino Uzcudun before a huge crowd in **Rome**. Carnera became a hero in the Fascist press and his image was widely used for propaganda purposes. The following year, however, he lost his title to Max Baer in a hard-fought match. In 1935, Carnera, who had always been carefully protected by his managers, rashly fought a young Joe Louis and was battered. Although he continued to fight on, he was never again a top-rank boxer. Carnera's humiliation at the hands of a black boxer discomfited the Fascist state at a moment when racial themes were beginning to appear in the regime's propaganda.

Carnera turned to wrestling in his late career and also made a number of appearances in films, including **Alessandro Blasetti**'s *La Corona di ferro*. Carnera was also the subject of a 1956 film starring Humphrey Bogart that insinuated that many of his fights had been fixed by the mob. Professional boxing was a dirty business then as now, and Carnera's managers, notably See, had many dubious connections, but there seems little reason to suspect that Carnera was anything less than one of the best boxers of his generation. He died in his native Friuli in June 1967.

CARRISTI. In the argot of political journalism, the *carristi* are those who endorsed the use by the Soviet Union of armored vehicles (*carri armati*) to put down the Hungarian uprisings of October 1956, or who advocated a rigid pro-Soviet line toward Czechoslovak attempts at reform under Dubcek—in short, the most Stalinist elements of the former **Partito Comunista Italiano**/Italian Communist Party (PCI). The term was also applied to "Kabulisti" (those who applauded Soviet intervention in Afghanistan). Within the PCI, the *carristi* were in the majority in 1956, when the 8th Congress of the PCI in December 1956 backed the Soviet Union's action despite fierce internal dissension and the walkout of many leading intellectuals, most notably the historian Furio Diaz and **Antonio Giolitti**. In August 1968, by contrast, the PCI officially denounced Soviet repression in Prague, calling it "an unjust decision" that could not be "reconciled with the principle that each communist party and every socialist state has a right to autonomy and independence." There were, nevertheless, many hardliners within the party who disapproved of the increasing criticism leveled at the USSR by the PCI's leaders, especially **Enrico Berlinguer**, in the 1970s.

CARUSO, ENRICO (1873–1921). The "great Caruso" was one of the most famous opera tenors of all time. Like Placido Domingo or Luciano Pavarotti today, he also reached a wide public: His recording in 1902 of Leoncavallo's *Vesti la giubba* was the first gramophone record to sell one million copies.

Caruso was born in **Naples** to a desperately poor working-class family and began singing in the choir of the local parish priest, Padre Giuseppe Bronzetti. He paid for singing lessons by working alongside his father as a mechanic. Caruso began his public career in Naples in 1894, although his break came in 1897 when auditioning for a performance of *La Bohème* in Leghorn before the great composer **Giacomo Puccini**, who allegedly asked, "Who sent you to me? God himself?" Between then and 1903 he performed all over Italy, in Argentina, and in Russia. In 1903, he began a lengthy professional relationship with the New York Metropolitan Opera that lasted until his untimely death from pleurisy in 1921. In all, Caruso appeared more than 600 times on the New York stage in almost 40 productions.

Caruso's repertoire ranged across the classics of contemporary Italian opera to Mozart and to popular Neapolitan folk songs. The one Italian folk song everyone knows, "O sole mio," was made internationally famous through Caruso's recording of it.

CASA DELLE LIBERTÀ/House of Freedoms (CDL). The electoral alliance formed by **Silvio Berlusconi** prior to the 2001 general elections, the CDL unifies the principal parties of the political right. These are **Forza Italia**, the **Alleanza Nazionale**/National Alliance (AN), the **Unione dei Democratici Cristiani e di Centro**/Union of Christian Democrats and the Center (UDC), and the **Lega Nord**/Northern League (LN). A number of other small center-right parties are also represented: The **Partito Repubblicano Italiano**/Republican Party (PRI), with its long history, but nowadays negligible public support, is the most significant of these. Forza Italia is by far the largest party in terms of popular support: It has consistently obtained over 25 percent of the popular vote since Berlusconi entered politics in 1994. The parties of the CDL formed a government, under Berlusconi's leadership, in May 2001 and governed until it was narrowly defeated in the elections of April 2006. The government, despite its large parliamentary majority, was somewhat unstable, with the rifts between the UDC and the League being particularly ferocious. The centerpiece of the CDL's program, a major revision of the **Constitution**, was finally approved after five years of wrangling within the coalition, but was then rejected in a **referendum** in June 2006. *See also* BOSSI, UMBERTO; CASINI, PIERFERDINANDO; FINI, GIANFRANCO.

CASINI, PIERFERDINANDO (1955–). The **Bologna**-born Casini is the most likely heir to **Silvio Berlusconi** on the center-right of Italian politics. Casini was the personal assistant of **Arnaldo Forlani** and quickly emerged in the 1980s as one of the few new faces that the **Democrazia Cristiana**/Christian Democracy (DC) could offer. He was elected to **Parliament** in 1983; by 1987, aged little more than 30, was already a member of the national steering committee of the DC.

When the DC sank during the corruption investigations of the early 1990s, Casini, who had been untouched by scandal, emerged as a potential leader on the right. He was the moving spirit behind the formation of a new party, the Centro Cristiano Democratico/Christian Democratic Center (CCD), which allied itself with Berlusconi in the elections of 1994 and 1996. The CCD kept the DC's memory alive and acted as a magnet for other Christian Democrats. In 2002 three Christian Democrat parties merged to form the **Unione dei Democratici Cristiani e di Centro**/Union of Christian Democrats and the Center (UDC), of which Casini became the leader.

In 2001, Casini was elected president of the Chamber of Deputies following the electoral victory of the **Casa delle Libertà**/House of Freedoms (CDL). Casini greatly added to his reputation for statesmanship between 2001 and 2006 by subtly distancing himself from the controversial figure of Berlusconi, while remaining firmly in the camp of the center-right. The UDC performed very well in the 2006 general elections, doubling its vote relative to 2001 and gaining many votes at the expense of **Forza Italia**. Casini is currently a parliamentary deputy.

CASSA PER IL MEZZOGIORNO (Southern Development Fund).
The creation of the Cassa per il Mezzogiorno was the outcome of growing unrest in **southern Italy** over rural poverty, and together with the land reform of 1950 was an attempt to raise living standards for the South. Under the land reform, idle farmlands were expropriated and distributed among farm workers. In areas ridden by malaria for centuries, over 2,000,000 acres were apportioned among 45,000 families in the first dozen years of the reform. The Cassa also paid up to 20 percent of the costs incurred by municipalities that built enterprise zones for small and medium industries in depressed areas of fewer than 200,000 inhabitants.

The Cassa was to be accountable to **Parliament** through a minister without portfolio (elevated to cabinet rank in 1965 as minister for the Mezzogiorno). Projects were approved by the Comitato Interministeriale per la Programmazione Economica/Interministerial Committee for Economic Planning (CIPE), giving rise to additional rivalries, tensions, and delays. Moreover, the local agencies established to coordinate infrastructure investments and land allocations and to administer the state's largesse became fiefdoms of local political leaders, who were often accused of waste, favoritism, and inflated administrative overhead.

The early Cassa was guided by three coherent goals in dealing with the gap between North and South. The first objective was to address the land-tenure problem by a system of expropriation (paying the owners with 30-year, interest-bearing bonds) and redistribution among those who actually worked the land. Most continued to reside in their home village.

The second phase was the building of the infrastructure needed not only for industrialization but to enhance the productivity of southern agriculture. This meant all-weather roadways, irrigation, flood control, electrification, modern port facilities, improved railways (most south of **Rome** were single track), and quality control in storage and processing facilities, together with such essential social overhead expenditures as schools, clinics, and public housing.

The third stage meant luring the assignees from the mountain villages, which they had shown themselves reluctant to leave. The Cassa not only built houses on the assigned plots but made moving into them a condition of retaining assigned land. They also built community centers comprising a church, a meeting hall, a clinic, and a pharmacy (not always staffed), and—in most cases—an elementary school. Yet people remained attached to their villages despite the relative absence of amenities of any sort. New, isolated, lowland houses, therefore, often were used as toolsheds by those who trudged daily between hilltop villages and newly acquired land.

Efforts were also made to encourage southern entrepreneurs and small industry. Industrial parks were set aside from expropriated lands and subdivision lots sold at subsidized prices with mortgage payments deferred. Local youth with no prospects beyond duplicating their fathers' lives were recruited into industrial training programs paid for by the Cassa, **FIAT**, and other private-sector firms, both domestic and foreign. Many previously unemployed individuals—both male and female (in a setting where **women** were still expected to stay at home with the children)—were introduced to factory discipline and to a totally new role for women outside the home. Of the many women who became the family's chief breadwinner, few were willing to continue playing the subordinate role to which tradition had accustomed them.

Locating a few large industries in the South—"cathedrals in the desert" as northern journalists dubbed them—produced cement factories (a necessary initial step for the building trades), oil refineries and petrochemical plants, vastly improved port facilities to ship both imported crude oil and the refined product, fertilizer plants, the Taranto steel mills of Italsider, asphalted highways, improved railways and airports, as well as the aforementioned infrastructure in elementary schools and modest housing.

Recent statistics, however, indicate how unsuccessful these efforts have been in closing the North–South gap. Southern Italians enjoy today a far higher standard of living and level of consumption than was conceivable just one generation ago. However, it is equally true that life in the North and Center has improved even more rapidly, thus widening the separation of the country's regions. That conditions might have been worse without the efforts of the Southern Development Fund is not an easily testable proposition. What is clear is that many southerners continue to feel that life has not been fair to them. Per capita incomes in the richest cities of north-central Italy average around €25,000–€30,000, while the poorest cities of the South average about €15,000. The former is 40 percent over the national average; the latter, 40 percent below that average. It is too soon to say whether the 1986 devolution of the Cassa's functions to regional and local institutions will have the desired effect. *See also* COOPERATIVES; LAND REFORM; *LATIFONDI*.

CATHOLIC ACTION. *See* AZIONE CATTOLICA ITALIANA (ACI).

CATHOLICISM. There can be few countries in which the influence of organized religion is as pervasive as Italy, and although Italians have adopted modern patterns of social behavior (the use of contraception, **divorce**, and abortion) disapproved of by the Church, most Italians still describe themselves as practicing Catholics. Almost all children are baptized and confirmed, and the number of nonreligious funerals is negligible. This is true even in the "red," former communist regions such as Tuscany and Emilia-Romagna. The Church follows "Roman" rites everywhere except **Milan**, where rites initiated by

Saint Ambrose are followed, and two small dioceses in Apulia, where the Byzantine rites traditional for the area's Albanian minority are celebrated.

The Church is organized hierarchically, with the pope, who is also bishop of **Rome**, as the spiritual and effective head of the Church in Italy, as well as of the Church worldwide. Beneath the pope are nine cardinals (who have the right to vote in the papal conclave), over 20 archbishops, approximately 250 bishops, and about 34,000 parish priests—approximately one for every 1,200 inhabitants. Nearly 5,000 young Italian men are studying for the priesthood—far fewer than in the early decades of this century, but still higher than in the 1970s and 1980s, when there was an authentic crisis of vocation. In addition, there are about 125,000 nuns in the various orders. All told, there are about 200,000 "religious figures" in Italy.

The Catholic Church is an active promoter of social and youth associations through the various organizations coordinated by **Azione Cattolica Italiana**/Catholic Action (ACI). More than four million people are members of one Catholic association or another. Seven percent of Italian schoolchildren go to the 1,600 Catholic schools; parish priests provide religious instruction in state schools; and nuns are frequently employed in preschool care, nursing, old people's homes, and charitable foundations for drug and alcohol addicts. Italians may give 8 euro for every 1,000 that they pay in taxation to help religious organizations in their charitable activities.

Other religious faiths are growing in strength, however, not least because of **immigration** from North Africa. As a result of immigration, there are approximately 500,000 Muslims resident in Italy. Italy's Jewish community numbers about 35,000. Protestant churches of all denominations have about 200,000 members. In recent years, Buddhism has excited an increasing interest among young Italians. *See also* LATERAN PACTS; PAPACY.

CATTANEO, CARLO (1801–1869). Milanese by birth, Carlo Cattaneo was both an independent-minded scholar and a political activist of great integrity. Between 1835 and 1844 he edited *Il Politecnico*, a review specializing in the scientific analysis of social questions, and achieved European-wide fame for his pioneering work in the social sciences. Although he had never participated in any of the secret revolutionary societies, he emerged as one of the leaders of the revolt against Austrian rule in **Milan** in 1848. When the Austrians defeated Piedmont-**Sardinia** at Custoza, he was obliged to flee to Paris. There, he wrote, in French, *L'insurrection de Milan en 1848* (*The Milan Insurrection of 1848*), a book that was sternly critical of King **Charles Albert**'s conduct of the war.

Cattaneo, in fact, was an unabashed republican, federalist, and democrat who was deeply suspicious of the unification of Italy as a constitutional monarchy. He was opposed to Piedmontese annexation of **Sicily** and **Naples** in 1861 (breaking with **Giuseppe Garibaldi** over this issue), and in 1867, on being elected to Parliament, he refused to swear an oath of loyalty to the crown and was thus unable to take part in the assembly's work. He spent most of his last years at Castagnola, near Lugano in Switzerland, as a somewhat disdainful critic of the new Italian state. Over five years, 1859–1864, he brought out a second series of *Il Politecnico*. He died in Castagnola in 1869. In recent years, Cattaneo's life and work have enjoyed a revival: Italy's foremost institute of research in the social sciences is named after him, and the **Lega Nord** claims him as a distinguished pioneer of federalist doctrine in Italy.

CAVALLOTTI, FELICE (1842–1898). A picturesque figure much given to duels with his political rivals, Felice Cavallotti nevertheless played an important political role in liberal Italy. A radical, a democrat, and a republican, Cavallotti took part in **Giuseppe Garibaldi**'s expedition to **Sicily** in 1860 when he was barely an adolescent. After a career as a poet, playwright, and editor—in his native **Milan**—of the leading radical daily of the time, *Il Gazzettino rosa* (*The Pink Gazette*), he entered **Parliament** in 1873 and soon became one of the leading critics of **Agostino Depretis**'s reluctance to carry out social reforms. In 1879, he and Garibaldi founded the Lega della democrazia/League for Democracy. As leader of that body, he fought a fruitless battle for universal male suffrage, repression of the clergy, decentralization of the state administration, and improvements in public hygiene (he worked as a volunteer in **Naples** in 1884 when the city was stricken by cholera). He was a prominent figure in the irredentist movement and took an active role in the protests against Austrian rule in **Trieste** and, more generally, was strongly critical of the Italian government's link with Germany and Austria in the **Triple Alliance**. In 1886, he became leader of the radical party in Parliament. By then, he was Garibaldi's heir apparent in the public imagination, and he campaigned against political corruption and took an active part in the parliamentary investigation into the **Banca Romana** scandal. In June 1895, in the wake of the scandal, he published an open letter addressed to "the honest people of all parties" that contained a richly documented account of the corruption of the then prime minister, **Francesco Crispi**. Rather than debate Cavallotti's accusations in the Chamber of Deputies, Crispi and his supporters voted to close Parliament for six months.

In the 1890s, Cavallotti and the Radicals united with the Republicans to press for social reforms of a more explicitly socialist character, but Cavallotti never quite arrived at an open endorsement of the nascent workers' movement. Cavallotti was killed in his 32nd duel in 1898 by a fellow parliamentary deputy, Ferruccio Macola.

CAVOUR, CAMILLO BENSO DI (1810–1861). The younger son of a noble family from **Turin**, Cavour entered politics by way of journalism. In 1847, he founded *Il Risorgimento*, a liberal journal that pressed for the establishment of a constitutional **monarchy**. Philosophically, Cavour was influenced by English utilitarianism, especially Bentham, and the classical economists (Adam Smith, David Riccardo, John Stuart Mill). But an even greater influence was the French philosopher and statesman Alexis de Tocqueville. Like de Tocqueville, Cavour was an aristocratic liberal, convinced of the need for wider political participation but acutely aware of the dangers of the coming democratic age.

Cavour favored Piedmontese intervention in the Lombardy uprising against Austrian rule in 1848; in 1849, he was elected to the first constitutionally elected **Parliament** in Turin. His ministerial career began almost immediately; long interested in modern techniques of scientific farming, he became minister for agriculture in 1850. He was promoted to the finance ministry the following year. Cavour became prime minister of the kingdom of Piedmont-**Sardinia** in 1852. His sojourn in office was characterized by the far-reaching modernization of the economy and society. Faithful to his liberal principles, Cavour slashed tariffs and encouraged foreign investment, multiplying annual exports to the rest of Europe fourfold by the end of the 1850s, although the benefits of this increased economic activity went mostly to the propertied classes, not to the urban poor. At the cost of perilously indebting the state, Cavour also initiated many public works to raise the standard of infrastructure to European levels and modernized the organizational structure and military preparedness of the army.

Cavour's spell as prime minister was also characterized by an attack on the privileges of the Church. In part to placate the anticlerical Left who were supporting him in Parliament, in 1855 Cavour introduced a law abolishing the contemplative orders of monks (i.e., those who did not fulfill a teaching function or perform good works). The passage of the *legge sui frati* was one of the most strenuous challenges to Cavour's authority of his entire ministry, and thereafter he followed a more conciliatory policy toward the Church, proclaiming his belief in a "free church in a free state."

Cavour's foreign policy initially aimed less at Italian unification than at extending Sardinia's authority over the whole of northern Italy. The failure of the Sardinian army to drive Austria out of the North in 1848–1849, however, had convinced Cavour that Sardinia would only be able to expand its territorial possessions in Italy with the help of Britain and France. To ingratiate himself with the two liberal European powers, Cavour agreed to send a corps of soldiers to the Crimea in 1854, a move that secured him no concrete territorial advantage but did enable him to raise the Italian question, in the teeth of fervent Austrian opposition, at the subsequent Paris peace conference in February–March 1856. Cavour's chosen ally was Napoleon III of France, against whom an assassination attempt was made by an Italian nationalist in January 1858. Cavour used the attack as a means of emphasizing the relative moderation of Sardinia, and in July 1858, he signed the pact of Plombières with Napoleon. By this agreement, Cavour ceded Nice and Savoy to France and conceded that **southern Italy** and the central Italian states would be placed under the control of rulers favorable to France in exchange for a French guarantee of military assistance in the event of an Austrian war on Piedmont-Sardinia. Piedmont-Sardinia would add Lombardy and Venetia to its possessions after a victorious war.

This cynical deal was nullified by events once Austria had declared war on Piedmont in April 1859. Pro-Piedmontese insurrections broke out in Tuscany, Modena, and the Papal States (Cavour's agents had been at work), and Napoleon, seeing his own hopes of territorial gains in Italy evaporating, did his best to repair the damage by abandoning the war against Austria and reneging on the pact of Plombières. The peace of Villafranca (July 1859) left Austria still in command of Venetia, and Cavour, who was no favorite of King **Victor Emmanuel II**, was forced to resign. Moody by nature, Cavour contemplated suicide after this disaster for his strategy.

He was out of office for a mere six months. The duchies of central Italy were determined to unify with Piedmont, and Cavour was called back to office to negotiate their annexation with Napoleon III. While Cavour was dexterously completing this task, radical nationalists, led by **Giuseppe Garibaldi**, were contemplating less diplomatic methods of completing Italian unification. Cavour was initially skeptical of Garibaldi's expedition to **Sicily** in the spring of 1860, but once the redshirts had seized power in **Palermo** and crossed into southern Italy, Cavour was quick both to take advantage of the collapse of the Kingdom of the Two Sicilies and to prevent the contagion of nationalist and democratic ideas from spreading. Piedmontese troops invaded the Papal States in September 1860, and at Teano on 26 October 1860, Garibaldi surrendered his conquests to **Victor Emmanuel II**. Cavour's subtle *Realpolitik* had been successful beyond his own intentions: Piedmont-Sardinia had effectively digested most of the rest of Italy, with the consent of the great European powers.

Cavour became the first prime minister of the new Kingdom of Italy in March 1861. In June 1861, years of overeating and excessive drinking caught up with the Piedmontese statesman, and he died without warning at the still relatively young age of 51. Italy was left to face the challenge of completing its reunification without the services of the one 19th-century Italian statesman of comparable stature to Otto von Bismarck, William Gladstone, or Klemens von Metternich. *See also* MAZZINI, GIUSEPPE; REVOLUTIONS OF 1848; RISORGIMENTO.

CHARLES ALBERT (Carlo Alberto) (1798–1849). Heir to the throne of the kingdom of Piedmont-**Sardinia**, Charles Albert vacillated between absolutism and liberal constitutionalism for most of his adulthood. He was born in **Turin** in October 1798 and was forced to take political responsibility at an early age when King Victor Emmanuel I appointed him regent during the March 1821 insurrection in Piedmont. Charles Albert first tried to placate the insurgents by embracing the idea of a constitutional monarchy, but then reneged, joining the camp of his uncle, Charles Felice, who crushed the insurrection and restored absolute rule. Charles Albert, in order to give proof of his faith in absolutism to the Congress of Verona (1822), served and fought as a common soldier in the French army that invaded and defeated the Spanish constitutionalists in 1823.

He became king of Piedmont-Sardinia in 1831. **Giuseppe Mazzini** greeted his accession to the throne by writing Charles Albert an open letter appealing to the new king to take the lead in the struggle for national independence. He responded by stamping out Mazzini's *Giovine Italia* movement, a policy that led to a farcical attempted coup by Mazzini's supporters in 1834. In other respects, however, Charles Albert was more liberal: He abandoned mercantilism, built railways, ended feudalism, and reorganized the army.

In the mid-1840s, responding to the liberalism of Pope Pius IX, who had instituted notable judicial, social, and political reforms in the Papal States, Charles Albert veered toward the creation of a constitutional monarchy. The **Statuto Albertino**, adopted in March 1848, acted as the basic law of Italy until the ratification of the Republican Constitution in 1948. Piedmont-Sardinia consequently escaped the upheaval of revolution in 1848, which, in Italy, led to popular insurrections against the Austrians in **Bologna** and **Milan**, as well as the creation of a republic in **Venice**.

In April 1848, Charles Albert declared war on Austria. The Piedmontese army was defeated at Custoza on 25 July, and in August he was constrained to make peace and allow the Austrians to retake Milan. The war, however, was not over. Incited by a nationalist Parliament and public opinion, Charles Albert attacked once more in March 1849. The Piedmontese were crushed by the Austrians at Novara on 23 March, and he abdicated the throne in favor of his son, **Victor Emmanuel II**. He left for exile in Portugal, where he died just four months later.

CENTRAL ITALY. The core of central Italy is Tuscany, with its spectacular scenery and the famous historical centers of **Florence** (the region's largest city), Pisa, Volterra (a major center of the pre-Roman Etrurians), and Siena. The other regions are Umbria (whose largest cities are the splendid cathedral hill towns of Assisi, Orvieto, Perugia, and Urbino), the Marches (Pesaro, Ancona), the northernmost part of Latium, and the Abruzzi, whose largest cities are Aquila and Pescara. The tiny independent republic of San Marino is also to be found between Umbria and Romagna.

Tourism is a mainstay of the local economy: Florence, Siena, and the Isle of Elba are among the most sought-after destinations in the world. The region also boasts a flourishing wine industry (Chianti and Montepulciano) and substantial numbers of small enterprises specializing in high-quality craft products. Marble from the province of Massa Carrara is reputed to be the finest in the world, and quarrying and working marble is an important source of income. Nevertheless, the region does not have the same industrial dynamism that characterizes Venetia, Lombardy, or Emilia-Romagna, and per capita incomes, although over the European average, are lower than in northern Italy. According to recent European Union figures, Latium, which is boosted by the presence of well-paid public functionaries in **Rome**, enjoys a standard of living that is 124 percent of the European Union (EU) average; the figure for Tuscany is just under 120 percent.

Politically, the area is mostly "red." Tuscany and Umbria in particular are bastions of the **Democratici di Sinistra** /Democrats of the Left (DS) and were formerly strongholds of the **Partito Comunista Italiano**/Italian Communist Party (PCI). Over 60 percent of the electorate in Tuscan cities, such as Florence, Siena, and the port city of Leghorn (Livorno) voted for the center-left coalition led by **Romano Prodi** in the April 2006 elections. The DS was easily the single largest party. In Umbria, support for the left was only slightly lower. The Abruzzi, by contrast, was a former fiefdom of the **Democrazia Cristiana**/Christian Democracy Party (DC). Both northern Latium and the Abruzzi voted only narrowly in favor of Prodi's coalition in 2006.

The region's terrain is dominated by the Apennines mountain chain, whose highest point is Gran Sasso (Abruzzi) at 2,914 meters (9,565 feet). The Gran Sasso was the site of the fortress in which **Benito Mussolini** was briefly imprisoned in 1943 before his rescue by German parachute troops. *See also* ALPS; PIANURA PADANA; REGIONALISM.

CHRISTIAN DEMOCRACY. *See* DEMOCRAZIA CRISTIANA (DC).

CIAMPI, CARLO AZEGLIO (1920–). A lifelong public servant, the Tuscan Ciampi became governor of the **Banca d'Italia** in 1979, an appointment that enabled him to warn publicly against the budgetary irresponsibility of the **Bettino Craxi** and **Giulio Andreotti** governments of the 1980s. In April 1993, following the collapse of the government headed by **Giuliano Amato**, Ciampi was President **Oscar Luigi Scalfaro**'s choice to head an interim administration that would pass a new electoral law and restore calm and international confidence.

The first nonparliamentarian ever to be made premier, Ciampi formed a government that included several former Communists in ministerial posts, as well as members of the **Democrazia Cristiana/** Christian Democracy Party (DC) and **Partito Socialista Italiano/** Italian Socialist Party (PSI) who had been untainted by the scandals that had brought the Amato administration down. This government fell apart even before its ministers had had the chance to take the oath of office when the refusal of the Chamber of Deputies to allow a judicial investigation into the private affairs of Bettino Craxi led to a walk-out by the **Partito Democratico della Sinistra/**Democratic Party of the Left (PDS). Ciampi replaced the PDS's nominees with nonpartisan technocrats and governed as ably as the circumstances permitted until the election of March 1994.

In 1995, Ciampi became president of the European Commission's advisory group on competitiveness, but he was swiftly recalled to Italian politics by **Romano Prodi**. In May 1996, he was made the treasury and budget minister in the new center-left administration. Ciampi's prestige proved vital in this role; there is little doubt that Italy would not have qualified for membership of the Euro in 1999 without him. Ciampi's personal authority was decisive in imposing rigid measures to get Italy's public finances in better shape and in convincing the European Commission and the other member states of the European Union (EU) to relax the rules to allow Italy to participate. Like **Alcide De Gasperi**, **Antonio Segni**, and **Emilio Colombo** before him, Ciampi has been awarded the Charlemagne prize for services to European unity.

Ciampi was the natural choice in May 1999 to succeed **Oscar Luigi Scalfaro** as **president of the Republic** and was elected, on the first ballot, by a substantial bipartisan majority. Despite the political tensions arising during the often turbulent 2001–2006 government presided over by **Silvio Berlusconi**, with whom Ciampi often found himself in personal disagreement, Ciampi's presidency was a great popular success. In May 2006, politicians on both the right and the left even mooted the possibility that he should be reelected for a second seven-year term as president. Ciampi modestly turned down the offer, however, and is today senator for life in the Italian **Parliament**. *See also* CURRENCY; EUROPEAN INTEGRATION.

CIANO, GALEAZZO (1903–1944). The son of one of **Benito Mussolini**'s intimate advisors, Galeazzo Ciano married Edda, the only daughter of the Duce and his favorite child. His fortunes in party and government circles quickly rose. By 1936, he had been made a count as well as foreign secretary, a post that he retained until February 1943. In some interpretations, while the war in **Ethiopia** was meant to assuage the wounds remaining from Italy's 1896 humiliation at Adowa, the "crusade" in Spain to assist Franco was desired by Count Ciano and his circle of younger Fascists similarly to prove their mettle.

In the **Fascist Grand Council** meeting of 25 July 1943, Ciano was among those supporting the resolution to put the armed forces under royal control, thereby ending Mussolini's role. Significantly, neither the police nor the militia intervened to prevent this coup, and **Fascism**'s founder was imprisoned at Gran Sasso. After Mussolini's liberation by German paratroopers and subsequent installation at **Salò**, the Duce had Ciano and a dozen others arrested, tried, and executed by a firing squad, prompting Winston Churchill's comment that his admiration for Mussolini had grown the moment that "he had his son-in-law shot."

Perhaps Ciano's major contribution to posterity was the diary that he kept beginning in 1936. Parts had been secreted away by Edda, who made them available to publishers after the war. Their account of Ciano's steadily growing doubts about Mussolini's mental stability have proved an important source for historians.

CINEMA. Few countries can boast a cinematic history as rich as Italy's. The first kinetographs appeared at the end of the 19th century, and techniques developed rapidly. By the eve of **World War I** director Giovanni Pastrone was producing such innovative epics as *Cabiria* (1914) and *Gli ultimi giorni di Pompeii* (*The Last Days of Pompeii*, 1913), which won a worldwide public and are still regarded as masterpieces of the early cinema. In the 1920s and 1930s, the Italians struggled to match Hollywood as the big-budget movies made possible by the American film industry's superior financing made inroads into the Italian domestic market. The number of domestic films distributed in Italy dropped from over 200 in 1920 to less than a dozen a year by the end of the decade.

This decline had a political dimension. In **Mussolini**'s Italy, the domination of foreign films was seen both as a symptom of the failure of Fascist policies of economic autarky and a relatively uncontrolled source of information about the rest of the world. Consequently, film production was centralized in 1935 in a single government-owned company, and the Italian government built "Hollywood on the Tiber"—the Cinecittà film complex near **Rome**. Influential film magazines such as *Nero e Bianco* (*Black and White*) and *Cinema* (the latter edited by Mussolini's son, Vittorio) were started. By 1942, nearly 100 films were being produced every year. Although many of these films were propagandistic in tone, several were outstanding works of art. **Alessandro Blasetti**'s ambiguous fairytale *La corona di ferro* (*The Iron Crown*, 1941) and the romantic comedies of Mario Camerini were highly successful in technical, artistic, and box office terms. Even some of the propaganda movies—Blasetti's *La vecchia guardia* (*The Old Guard*, 1935), Augusto Bianco's haunting *Lo squadrone bianco* (*The White Squadron*, 1936)—reached high artistic levels.

After the war, **neorealist** directors such as **Roberto Rossellini**, **Luchino Visconti**, **Vittorio De Sica**, and **Michelangelo Antonioni** made films hailed by critics everywhere. Yet the average Italian did not watch their grimly beautiful depictions of working-class and peasant life. In the 1950s and 1960s, Italians watched instead *la commedia all'Italiana* and a whole new generation of actors, many of whom (Claudia Cardinale, Sophia Loren, Gina Lollobrigida, Vittorio Gassman, Marcello Mastroianni, Ugo Tognazzi) went on to achieve fame outside Italy. They also watched that unique Italian invention, the "spaghetti Western" of **Sergio Leone** and, by the early 1970s, experimented with pornography in films.

The relentless competition provided by Hollywood has arguably been resisted more successfully in Italy than anywhere else in Europe except France, although American films do dominate the box office. Hit comedies still tend to star Italian actors and have Italian settings. Moreover, in the 1980s and 1990s, a new wave of Italian directors made watchable, artistically successful films. Some of these films have even been successfully exported to the United States — Giuseppe Tornatore's *Cinema paradiso* (*Paradise Cinema*, 1991), the Anglo-Italian coproduction *Il postino* (*The Postman*, 1995), and Roberto Benigni's Oscar-winning *La vita è bella* (*Life Is Beautiful*, 1999) being particularly good examples. The Italian cinema's resilience should not surprise anyone; there is a deep love for the cinema and its greatest artists in Italy. When the director **Federico Fellini** died in November 1993, there were several days of what amounted to unofficial national mourning. A similar emotional outpouring greeted the death, in December 1996, of Marcello Mastroianni. *See also* MORETTI, NANNI; ROSI, FRANCESCO; TOTÒ.

COBAS. The Comitati di Base/Grassroots Committees began as organizers of wildcat protests — particularly among highly skilled unionists (teachers, airline pilots, railway locomotive engineers) — against the leveling of wages achieved by negotiators from the official **trade unions**. The *appiattimento* (flattening) of incomes was the result of seeking to raise the earnings of those at the lowest levels and was therefore abhorrent to those whose skills were, in their view, inadequately rewarded and whose incentives for accepting greater supervisory responsibilities were undercut by the perceived meagerness of income increments.

Beginning in the 1980s, the COBAS initiated work stoppages to protest settlements reached by union federation negotiators. They insisted that the years of training and or formal education needed for their work entitled them to a larger share of any increments. To trade unionists, the COBAS's position perfectly illustrates "corporativism," that is, the readiness of the members of a particular economic sector to use their numerical strength and/or strategic position to seek advantages for their own category without regard to the general interests of the working class or of the society as a whole.

The roots of the COBAS, however, are also to be found in the Confederazione Generale Italiana del Lavoro/Italian General Confederation of Labor (CGIL) of the late 1960s. Young workers unused to trade union discipline sometimes regarded union moderation in negotiations as a betrayal. At the Pirelli tire plant in 1969, a compromise settlement resulted in the organization of a Comitato Unitario di Base/United Base Committee (CUB). This workers' council attracted adherents from all skill levels by denouncing both the CGIL and the **Partito Comunista Italiano/**Italian Communist Party (PCI) as "soft on management."

COLLODI, CARLO (pseud. Carlo Lorenzini, 1826–1890). Collodi was born in **Florence**. By profession a journalist, and a very successful one, he was also an ardent nationalist who fought as a volunteer in the wars of national liberation of 1848 and 1859. Collodi's claim to fame rests, however, not on his journalism, or his place in the annals of the **Risorgimento**, but on his skill as a writer of children's stories. In particular, in 1881, he published in the magazine *Il Giornale per Bambini* the first episode of what subsequently became *Le avventure di Pinocchio* (*The Adventures of Pinocchio*). The story of how Pinocchio was carved from a magical piece of wood by the childless carpenter Geppetto, becomes a living puppet with a mind of his own who disobeys both his father and the voice of conscience, and has many terrible adventures but is eventually transformed into a real boy by his courage and love for Geppetto is one of the most famous of all children's tales. The moral of Collodi's tale was that children should be obedient, hardworking, truthful, and studious if they wanted to grow up as decent individuals. But the story also features policemen who arrest the innocent while letting the bad go free, and a society in which children's **education** is neglected (Pinocchio learns to write with a twig and blackberry juice instead of pen and ink). In *Pinocchio*, Collodi was also satirizing the absence of the Italian state as a moral force able to help its citizens choose the right path in life.

Collodi died in Florence in 1890 after publishing several other children's stories. *See also* LITERATURE.

COLOMBO, EMILIO (1920–). Born in the deep south of Potenza in Basilicata, Colombo went from militance in **Azione Cattolica Italiana (ACI)**/Catholic Action to candidacy in the **Democrazia Cristiana**/Christian Democracy Party (DC) while still in his twenties. He was one of the youngest delegates to the **Constituent Assembly** in June 1946. On election to the **Parliament** on the DC list, he served in the first governments of **Alcide De Gasperi** as undersecretary for agriculture. Over the next 10 years, he dominated the agriculture ministry, eventually becoming minister, and played an important role in the modernization of Italy's rural regions.

In **Amintore Fanfani**'s first government, he was minister of foreign trade. He continued in that post in the governments of **Antonio Segni**, **Fernando Tambroni**, and Fanfani II and IV while also becoming a member of the DC National Council. He became minister of the treasury in the 1960s, serving in the governments headed by **Giovanni Leone** and **Aldo Moro**. He was to hold the treasury post longer than anyone in the history of the republic.

For two years (1970–1972), he was **president of the Council of Ministers**. He gained foreign policy experience by being minister for United Nations (UN) relations in **Giulio Andreotti**'s first government in 1972. In addition to constant reelection from Potenza-Matera, he was elected to the European Parliament in 1976, a body that he eventually served as president.

Colombo's service as foreign minister in the government of **Arnaldo Forlani** in 1980 was a precursor to his appointment to the same post in the two governments of **Giovanni Spadolini** (1981–1983) and the fifth Fanfani government. During the Spadolini governments, he launched, together with his German counterpart, Hans-Dietrich Genscher, a major initiative to revitalize the European Community's institutions and policies. The initiative led to the "solemn declaration" of Stuttgart in June 1983 that restored momentum to a Community that was, at that moment, riven with dissent over the budget contributions of its member states. Colombo was the third Italian politician (after De Gasperi and Segni) to be given the Charlemagne award by the European Parliament for his contributions to **European integration**.

Colombo's priestlike demeanor belied his shrewdness in using Italian state aid for the benefit of his Basilicata political constituency. One of the few Italian politicians who has been both a successful national powerbroker and a respected international figure, Colombo continues to play an active role in politics, as life senator.

COMITATI DI LIBERAZIONE NAZIONALE/National Liberation Committees (CLN). On 9 September 1943, representatives of the major antifascist parties formed a clandestine Committee of National Liberation in **Rome**. Regional and local committees were formed subsequently; in northern Italy, a separate committee, the CLN-Alta Italia, operating secretly in **Milan**, was formed. The **Partito d'Azione**/Action Party (PdA), the **Democrazia Cristiana**/Christian Democracy (DC), the **Partito Liberale Italiano/** Italian Liberal Party (PLI), the followers of **Ivanoe Bonomi**, and the two Marxist parties, the **Partito Socialista Italiano**/Italian Socialist Party (PSI) and the **Partito Comunista Italiano**/Italian Communist Party (PCI), despite their strong ideological disputes, agreed to make national liberation their primary objective. The PCI emphasized this priority. When **Palmiro Togliatti** returned from the USSR (in spring 1944), he insisted—in the *svolta di Salerno* (the Salerno about-turn)—on postponing political questions until after the war. In the meantime, his party was ready to cooperate with and even take part in a transitional government under **Pietro Badoglio**. Defeating the forces of Germany and their Fascist allies was what mattered most.

In June 1944, the king, without abdicating, turned over his powers to Crown Prince Humbert, styling him Lieutenant-General of the Realm. Badoglio resigned, and Ivanoe Bonomi formed a provisional government of all six CLN parties in liberated Rome. The CLN and the CLN-AI continued with the task of organizing and authorizing partisan activity against the Germans and **Benito Mussolini**'s followers. *See also* RESISTANCE.

COMMUNIST PARTY (PCI). *See* PARTITO COMUNISTA ITALIANO (PCI).

COMMUNIST REFOUNDATION. *See* PARTITO DI RIFON-
DAZIONE COMUNISTA.

COMPROMESSO STORICO. The genesis of the *compromesso storico*
(historic compromise) was three articles published by **Enrico
Berlinguer** in *Rinascita* (*Rebirth*), the weekly journal of political
strategy and theory of the **Partito Comunista Italiano/**Italian Communist Party (PCI) in October 1973. Berlinguer argued that the PCI,
which, at that moment, hoped to overtake the **Democrazia Cris-
tiana/**Christian Democracy Party (DC) and become Italy's largest
party, should avoid above all else the civil disorders and American intervention that the turmoil the socialist experiment of Salvador Al-
lende had provoked in Chile. He defined a program that would spur
social change without antagonizing "vast strata of the middle-
classes" or undercutting the efficiency of the economy. Berlinguer
recommended that the party seek out "every possible convergence
and understanding among popular forces" by working toward the
transformation of Italian society in collaboration with the DC and
the **Partito Socialista Italiano** /Italian Socialist Party (PSI)—a grand
coalition of political forces that together would have the support of
75–80 percent of the electorate. The "Left alternative" of a PCI-PSI
coalition, Berlinguer argued, would have had the effect "of splitting
the popular masses, liquidating de facto our encounter with Catholic
[social] forces, moving the DC toward the right, thus isolating and
defeating the left, and therefore, in the final analysis, bringing about
the defeat of the cause of democracy and its development in our
country."

There were four main implications of Berlinguer's argument. He
was rejecting "proletarian internationalism" and the demand that national communist parties should accept subordination to the Soviet
party. Each country had to find its own path to socialism. Second, his
proposals were a rejection, in advanced industrial countries at any
rate, of the doctrinal notion of a "dictatorship of the proletariat."
Third, they embodied a perception of the class struggle as resolvable
by a broadening of the consensus rather than by revolution. And finally, they implied acceptance of economic, ideological, and social
pluralism as a prerequisite to building a socialist democracy based on
an interclass consensus wide enough to overwhelm any opposition.

By implication, this doctrinal change of course meant persuading non-Marxist Catholics and diffident, anticommunist socialists to accept a common program without, at the same time, alienating the communist mass membership.

Berlinguer's ideological innovations were encouraged by the DC leader **Aldo Moro**, and they underpinned the PCI's decision to give its parliamentary support to the "government of national solidarity" formed by **Giulio Andreotti** after the 1976 general elections. They were also responsible for the February 1978 decision by the leaders of the principal **trade unions** to advocate an unpopular program of wage restraint, increased profitability, and increased returns on investments in order to attack unemployment, inflation, and the southern question. This decision may well have saved Italian big business from collapse. Eventually, however, the party's position opened such a gap between the PCI leadership and the union leaders, on the one hand, and the rank and file, on the other, that the PCI had to withdraw its benevolent support of the Andreotti government, leading to the elections of June 1979, in which the PCI's support fell back from its 1976 high.

The *compromesso storico* thus ended in political failure. Ideologically, however, Berlinguer had worked a change that outlasted his death in 1984. The PCI had determined that it intended to stabilize Italian capitalism and render it more efficient and socially just, rather than fight it tooth and claw. This newfound emphasis on gradual change, of course, was resisted by many party members—particularly the older Stalinists—for they recognized that it meant a definitive abandonment of the party's traditional Leninist goals. *See also* COSSUTTA, ARMANDO.

CONCORDAT. *See* LATERAN PACTS.

CONFINDUSTRIA. The Italian employers' federation, Confindustria is one of the largest and best-organized lobby groups for private industry in the world. Confindustria was born in May 1910 and initially had its headquarters in **Turin**. It moved to **Rome** in 1919, but in its early years it was dominated by industrialists from the "industrial triangle" encompassing **Milan**, Turin, and **Genoa**. Confindustria was somewhat equivocal about the rise of **Fascism**. On the one hand, the association welcomed the fact that the strikes and violence of the "red biennio" of 1920–1922 had been stopped. On the other hand, Confindustria publicly criticized the violence of the Fascist squads and only recognized the official Fascist trade union in 1925. The Fascist state bailed out numerous substantial enterprises during the economic crisis of the 1930s, and its autarchic economic policies allowed some of Confindustria's members to enjoy monopoly pickings. However, private enterprise could not but chafe at the totalitarian ideology and semitotalitarian reality of the Fascist state.

In the postwar period the association was dominated by its president, Angelo Costa (in 1945–1955 and again in 1966–1970), a Genoese industrialist who supported a policy of negotiation with the **trade unions** and of liberalization of the market despite the opposition of some of the association's members in heavily protected industries. Confindustria backed Italy's entrance into the European Economic Community (EEC) with the treaties of Rome 1957. During the 1960s and 1970s the association was obliged to reform itself to take into account the growing numbers of new members from small and medium-sized industries in the northeast and south. Even today, the association is to some extent divided by the split between its large industrial firms, with their cross-holdings and links to the closed world of Italian private banking, and the more entrepreneurial and assertive small companies that have provided Italy with so much of its recent economic success.

In the late 1960s and 1970s, Confindustria had to deal with the tense industrial relations of the time. For the most part, it appeased the militant unions by signing an accord indexing salaries to inflation in 1975 and accepting the introduction of some of the most restrictive labor laws in the world. Only the steady (at times, not so steady) devaluation of the lira enabled industry to maintain its competitiveness, but until **FIAT** broke a car workers' strike in 1980, there was little or no sign of the employers' willingness to stand up to the unions. Since the 1980s, however, the employers have become more assertive in their calls for reform. Confindustria has been demanding since the early 1990s that the government get the public finances in order, lower employment taxes, and liberalize the economy. Confindustria recognizes that the inefficiency of the Italian state is acting as a brake on business competitiveness. Since Italy converted to the euro in

1999, thus ending its reliance on devaluation, its competitiveness has declined sharply in comparison with Germany and France, its nearest continental rivals.

A number of important individuals have headed Confindustria in its century-long history. Giovanni Agnelli served as president between 1974 and 1976; he was replaced by **Guido Carli**. The current president is Luca Cordero di Montezemolo, a former assistant to **Enzo Ferrari** who became president of Ferrari and then of FIAT. *See also* ECONOMY; EUROPEAN INTEGRATION.

CONFINO. This was one of several ways of dealing with those guilty of political or conspiratorial offenses during the Fascist regime, introduced in the *Testo Unico di Pubblica Sicurezza* (TUPS) in 1931. The Consolidated Text of the Public Security Law asserted that a person convicted of "conspiracy to commit a crime" or of acts compromising the security of the state might, as an alternative to incarceration, be ordered to leave his own city or town to take up residence in an assigned locality (*residenza obbligata*) where he would be free to move about, seek employment, and generally live a normal life so long as he reported in person to the local **police** at specified intervals. This practice is still in use today, particularly for those accused of associating with known *mafiosi*. Especially under **Fascism**, however, use was also made of "internal exile" or obligatory residence under police supervision in a place so remote and often so little populated as to be a virtual free-range prison. One was sent "to the border" or *al confine*, the very edges of the nation. The writer **Carlo Levi** described his experience of forced residence in a famous postwar novel, *Cristo si è fermato a Eboli (Christ Stopped at Eboli)*. Other prominent antifascists were sent into exile on such isolated islands as Lipari and Ventotene.

CONSTITUENT ASSEMBLY. When World War II ended, the form of government and the role of the **monarchy** itself were major issues to be decided by the Italian people. After a lengthy delay during which Italy was governed by provisional governments headed by **Ferruccio Parri** and (from December 1945) **Alcide De Gasperi**, the resolution of these questions was left to the Constituent Assembly elected on 2

June 1946. The election was Italy's first ever free election by universal suffrage.

The election provided a balanced outcome. The **Democrazia Cristiana**/Christian Democracy Party (DC) was easily the largest party, with 207 delegates (35.2 percent of the vote). The DC's success was offset, however, by the strong showing of the parties of the left. The Partito Socialista Italiano d'Unita Proletaria/Italian Socialist Party of Proletarian Unity (PSIUP) took 115 seats (20.7 percent), and the **Partito Comunista Italiano**/Italian Communist Party (PCI) obtained 104 seats and 19 percent of the vote. Right-wing parties represented were the **Partito Liberale Italiano**/Italian Liberal Party (PLI), (41 seats, 6.8 percent) and Fronte dell'Uomo Qualunque/The Common Man's Front (UQ), which received 5.3 percent of the vote and took 30 seats. Republicans, Monarchists, and the **Partito d'Azione**/Action Party (PdA) were also represented.

On the same day, Italians voted to end the monarchy by a margin of 54.2 percent to 45.8 (12.72 million votes to 10.72 million). The North and Center of Italy were strongly in favor of a republic; the South equally strongly for the king, with 80 percent of voters supporting the monarchy in **Naples**. Since the Republic had not secured a majority of all votes cast (only of valid votes), King Humbert II initially refused to accept the result. De Gasperi stood firm, however, and Humbert was forced into exile.

At the end of June 1946, the Constituent Assembly elected **Enrico De Nicola** provisional head of the Italian Republic. Alcide De Gasperi, who was the leader of the largest of the parties, was asked to form a new government that included members of the DC, the PCI, and the Partito Repulblicano Italiano/Republican Party (PRI). *See also* COMITATI DI LIBERAZIONE NAZIONALE (CLN); CONSTITUTION VICTOR EMMANUEL III.

CONSTITUTION. Italy's Constitution was drafted by the **Constituent Assembly** between July 1946 and December 1947. It became law on 1 January 1948. It has proved to be a remarkably durable document that has been little amended.

The Constitution was a compromise between the two principal parties of the left, the **Partito Socialista Italiano**/Italian Socialist Party (PSI) and the **Partito Comunista Italiano**/Italian Communist Party (PCI) with the **Democrazia Cristiana**/Christian Democracy (DC). The

DC allowed the Constitution to contain articles whose values reflected the progressive social goals of the leftist parties in return for an article (art. 7) that constitutionalized the **Lateran pacts** and for institutions that imposed strong checks and balances on the power of the majority in the Chamber of Deputies.

Thus, key articles of the first half of the Constitution recognize the role of the working class in Italy (art. 1 proclaims that "Italy is a Republic founded upon labor") and the right to strike. Concentrations of economic power are limited while emphasis is put on the need for land reform. Other social rights include "obligatory and free" **education** for eight years; article 34 states that even those who lack financial means "have a right to reach the highest possible level of studies." Every worker is entitled to pay reflective of the "quality and quantity" of his or her work but in any case, "adequate to ensure for himself and his family a free and dignified existence." He or she is also entitled to a day off per week, a right that may not be renounced. Female workers have "the same rights and, in the same job, the same pay as the male worker." Moreover, working conditions must allow that the woman's "essential familial function be fulfilled and assure to the mother and child special and adequate protection." The Constitution was a major breakthrough for the equality of **women** in Italy.

The secretary of the PCI, **Palmiro Togliatti**, was convinced that the social transformation of Italy would be brought about incrementally through the electoral strength of the PCI and its allies. In 1948, a workers' republic by parliamentary means did not seem entirely out of the question. In the event, however, a 1948 judgment of the Court of Cassation ruled that the progressive aspirations of the Constitution were merely "programmatic" and need not be actuated immediately. This judgment ensured that many of the Constitution's provisions remained a dead letter.

The institutions of the Italian Republic were arranged to ensure that strong government was impossible. Executive power is diluted by ensuring that neither the **president of the Republic** nor the **president of the Council of Ministers** (prime minister) can set the government agenda and exercise independent power. For the legislature, the principle of perfect bicameralism was followed. This means that the government must command a majority in both chambers and that both the Senate and the Chamber of Deputies must pass all legislation for it to become law. The Constitution also provided for the possibility of popular abrogative **referendums** to cancel laws regarded as unjust by a strong current of public opinion. Legislation enabling referendums was passed only in the 1970s, but since then Italy has been one of the democracies that has made most use of the referendum instrument.

The Constitution also abolished the death penalty except in times of war and repudiated war as an instrument of resolving international disputes. One result of this has been that all commitments of troops that are not on missions explicitly sanctioned by the United Nations (and even some that are) are the source of huge political controversy. *See also*: ELECTORAL LAWS; PARLIAMENT.

COOPERATIVES. Italian cooperatives trace their origins to the Mutual Aid Societies formed by rural workers seeking unity of action to get the highest prices for the labor they sold and lower prices for what they bought. By 1886, the *Lega delle Cooperative* (League of Cooperatives) had been formed. It proved the basis for the **Partito Socialista Italiano/**Italian Socialist Party (PSI). Undermined by the Fascist regime, cooperatives were restored by the **Comitati di Liberazione Nazionale/**National Liberation Committees (CLN). In the negotiations that culminated in the new republican **Constitution** of 1948, they were given specific standing in Article 45.

A half-century later more than 100,000 cooperatives have over 7,000,000 members and constitute a huge and important part of the Italian **economy**. The largest federations of cooperatives were closely affiliated with political parties: the Lega with the **Partito Comunista Italiano/**Italian Communist Party (PCI) and the PSI; the Conicoop (Cooperative Confederation) with the **Democrazia Cristiana/**Christian Democracy (DC); and the *Associazione Generale delle Cooperative Italiane/*General Association of Italian Cooperatives (AGCI) with the lay parties of the center. In the 1880s more than three-fourths of the cooperatives were located in the northern regions, 14 percent in Italy's center, and 0.5 percent in the South. A century later, of nearly 16,000 co-ops in the Lega, 44 percent were in the North, 24 percent in the Center, and 32 percent in the South, traditionally diffident regarding cooperative efforts.

The Lega ranks fourth in annual turnover among Italian enterprises and includes one of the largest insurance companies in Italy (UNIPOL), as well as venture capital (Fincooper) and both merchant banking and commercial banking. Producers' cooperatives operate in areas as varied as agriculture, fishing, construction, metalworking, printing, and stone masonry. Service cooperatives range from office cleaning, waste disposal, and building maintenance to transport (trucking, taxis, commuter aircraft, and buses), while professional services can be sought from cooperatives of engineers, architects, doctors, caterers, tax consultants, labor consultants, accountants, and marketing researchers. Consumers' cooperatives also operate large supermarket chains.

Italian law allows 10 persons to seek financing for a cooperative. If all the members are between 18 and 25 years of age, they are entitled to receive additional help from regional authorities. State subsidies are available for the first three years. Other benefits include an easing of the social security burden and preferential treatment in bidding for public contracts.

COPPI, FAUSTO (1919–1960). In the view of many experts, Fausto Coppi was the greatest cyclist of all time; nobody would deny that he was the most spectacular. His willingness to break from the main group in lengthy, solitary *fughe* of tens, even hundreds of kilometers, made him a byword for stamina and courage. His duels with another great Italian cyclist, Gino Bartali, are one of the greatest chapters in the history of the sport. The fact that Coppi was associated with the left, while Bartali was a devout Catholic, only added spice to their rivalry.

In a career spanning 17 years (1939–1956), Coppi won 128 races, including the Tour de France twice, the **Giro d'Italia** five times, and the World Road championship in 1953 by over six minutes from the second-place finisher—a performance that many regard, even today, as the finest ever seen in a one-day race. He smashed the one-hour distance record in 1942. Had his career not been interrupted for four years by the war, there seems no doubt that this imposing list of victories would be even longer.

Coppi's life, however, is also important for nonsporting reasons. In September 1954, he caused a national scandal when the police, applying to the letter Italy's laws against adultery, arrested his married lover, the actress Giulia Occhini. In 1955, Occhini was sentenced to three months' imprisonment for abandoning her husband's home and Coppi was sentenced to two months. The sentences were conditional only, so neither actually spent time behind bars, but the affair highlighted the Italian state's readiness to interfere in the private lives of its citizens. The adultery laws were later repealed in 1969. Coppi died on 2 January 1960, in his native Alessandria (Piedmont), of malaria contracted during a holiday in Africa.

CORFU. The island of Corfu, which was a territory contested by Italy and Greece, was the setting for **Benito Mussolini**'s first act of disobedience to international opinion and to the will of the League of Nations. The crisis began in August 1923 when an Italian military mission charged with delimiting the border between Greece and Albania was fired upon near Giannina in Greece. The commander of the mission, General Enrico Tellini, and three others were killed. Without consulting the League of Nations, a furious Mussolini sent an ultimatum to Greece requesting a formal apology, an indemnity of 50 million lire, and a rapid inquiry to find the guilty and punish them with death. The Greek government, which denied responsibility for the incident, declined. The Italian navy bombarded and occupied Corfu on 31 August 1923.

Greece appealed to the League of Nations, and on 3 September 1923, the League condemned Italy's action. Mussolini threatened to withdraw from the organization but subsequently backed down when a conference of ambassadors from the other major European powers accepted that Italy's claim to an indemnity was legitimate. Italian troops evacuated Corfu at the end of September 1923. An international commission of inquiry proved unable to identify the perpetrators of Tellini's murder. The Corfu incident, while trivial in itself, illustrated Mussolini's impatience with the new forms of international governance and his ambitions to extend Italy's power in the Mediterranean. *See also* ETHIOPIA; FASCISM; FOREIGN POLICY.

CORPORATISM. Corporatism was perhaps the most original idea to emerge from **Fascism**. Essentially, it was meant to include institutional devices for controlling all instruments of production—both management and labor—in the interests of an assertive national policy of autarchy, that is, the organization of the economy so as to reduce or eliminate dependence on foreign sources of supply. Management and labor were to be organized—economic sector by economic sector—into guildlike units, membership in which was to be compulsory for the practitioners of a trade or the manufacturers of a given product. These "corporations" were recognized by the state and given a representational monopoly within their respective categories in exchange for observing certain state controls on the choice of leaders and the articulation of demands.

The Ministry of Corporations—headed by **Benito Mussolini** himself—required that all members of unions be "of good moral character" (i.e., loyal to Fascism) and that only those syndicates recognized by the Confederazione Italiana Sindacati Nazionali Lavoratori/Italian Confederation of National Workers' Unions **(CISNAL)** were to take part in corporatism's activities. Catholic and Socialist **trade unions** were hence effectively excluded: Only contracts signed by Fascist unions would have legal effect. Territorial organizations of employees in a particular sector formed labor syndicates, and the employers (of 10 percent of the workforce) formed federations of employers' associations, on provincial, regional, and national levels. Labor tribunals were organized as sections in each of the 16 Courts of Appeal to hear disputes left unresolved by conciliation. Their chief criterion was ostensibly national welfare rather than either the interests of labor or capital. Strikes and lockouts were prohibited. At the national level, these territorial federations were to generate "corporations" that were to increase productivity within their sectors. This was to be syndicalism as administered by the omnipotent state through its National Council of Corporations made up entirely of Mussolini appointees and chaired by the secretary-general of the Fascist Party.

Although first implemented by the Fascists, corporatist doctrine was not entirely original. Its most important doctrinal antecedent was to be found in the papal encyclical *Rerum Novarum* (1891), which was antiliberal, antibourgeois, and supportive of the rights of the unorganized worker. State corporatism was introduced to the world almost simultaneously with the Great Depression.

CORRADINI, ENRICO (1865–1931). The founder and editor of the influential Florentine periodical *Il Regno* between 1903 and 1905, Enrico Corradini was one of the most widely read journalists and intellectuals in prefascist Italy. An ardent nationalist and implacably antisocialist, Corradini was as responsible as any Italian for diffusing the philosophy of power worship, hypernationalism, and contempt for parliamentary procedure that proved a fertile breeding ground for **Fascism**. Borrowing the language of his socialist adversaries, Corradini advanced the idea that Italy was a "proletarian nation," robbed of its rightful role and position in world affairs by plutocratic nations such as Britain and, above all, France. Through this lens, imperialism became a substitute for socialism, an alchemic experience that would forge Italy as a strong, unified state and would solve the economic difficulties of the Mezzogiorno by providing a dignified outlet for emigration.

In 1910, Corradini was one of the founders of the Italian nationalist movement and became editor of its newspaper, *L'Idea nazionale* (*The National Idea*). His was one of the loudest voices raised in support of intervention in May 1915, and he was one of **Giovanni Giolitti**'s most contemptuous critics during and after the war. Corradini supported the fusion of the nationalist movement with the Fascist Party in 1923 and served as a minister under **Mussolini** in 1928. He died in **Rome** in 1931. *See also* PRESS.

COSSIGA, FRANCESCO (1928–). Born in the Sardinian province of Sassari, Francesco Cossiga was active in the **Democrazia Cristiana**/Christian Democracy Party (DC) from his early teens, and, in 1958, he was elected to the Chamber of Deputies. Cossiga's political career has been characterized by controversy. In 1964, he was the go-between during secret negotiations between his political patron, President **Antonio Segni**, and General Giovanni De Lorenzo, then head of the Italian Secret Service, who was later accused of plotting to overthrow the state. As a junior minister for defense in the late 1960s, Cossiga participated in the establishment of the so-called **Gladio** networks: secret groups of "patriots" who were supposed to organize and lead resistance to an eventual Soviet invasion of Italy. Many believe, however, that the real purpose of Gladio was to subvert a legitimately elected communist government in Italy; it has also been alleged that there was a link between Gladio and right-wing terrorism.

Cossiga was given the important task of combating the **Brigate Rosse/**Red Brigades (BR) in 1976. His tenure as minister of the interior was generally successful until the March 1978 kidnapping and May 1978 murder of **Aldo Moro**. Police incompetence during the Moro affair inspired conspiracy theorists to suggest that Italy's right-wing establishment and its allies in the U.S. Central Intelligence Agency (CIA) were content to see Moro, the architect of the *compromesso storico* with the **Partito Comunista Italiano/**Italian Communist Party (PCI), perish at the hands of his terrorist captors. In Cossiga's defense, it should be stressed that the BR's price for Moro's life—political recognition—was regarded as an unacceptable demand by all the principal political parties except the **Partito Socialista Italiano/**Italian Socialist Party (PSI).

Cossiga resigned after Moro's death. In September 1979, President **Alessandro Pertini** asked him to form a government, which lasted for a year. In 1983, Cossiga moved from the Chamber of Deputies to the Senate and was immediately elected to the presidency of the upper chamber. In 1985, he became the eighth man to be elected **president of the Republic**. Just 57 years old, he was (and still is) the youngest man ever to hold the office.

In the first five years of his presidency, Cossiga behaved with grave dignity; his deft handling of the 1987 government crisis was praised even by his political opponents. After the public disclosure of the Gladio networks in the fall of 1990, however, Cossiga took a more outspoken line: His *esternazioni* ("outbursts") became famous. He also provoked a constitutional crisis by availing himself of his formal power to chair the Consiglio Superiore della Magistratura/ High Council of the Magistracy (CSM), the governing body of the Italian legal profession, and then using that position to block judicial investigations into Gladio. Cossiga's antics were at least partly motivated by impatience at the inadequacies of the political system. He said in July 1991 that there was an "authentic and remarkable contradiction" between Italy's extraordinary postwar economic success and the miserable failure of its political institutions and parties. Disgusted by the behavior of the government parties, Cossiga resigned on 25 April 1992, with three months of his mandate still to run.

Since 1992, Cossiga has continued to play a maverick political role. In October 1998, when **Romano Prodi** was defeated in a confidence vote, Cossiga saved the **Olive Tree** government from dissolution when several of his allies crossed the floor of **Parliament** to form a new majority. *See also* SOLO PLAN.

COSSUTTA, ARMANDO (1926–). A card-carrying member of the Partito dei Comunisti Italiani/Party of Italian Communists (PCI) and a partisan when he was just 17 years old, Cossutta has never wavered in his communist faith. Imprisoned in the latter stages of the war, he rose in the hierarchy of the PCI by dint of becoming a contributor to both *L'Unità* and *Rinascita* (respectively, the daily newspaper and theoretical weekly of the PCI) and a tireless party worker in his native **Milan**. In 1966, he was invited to join the national secretariat in **Rome**. Within 10 years, he was put in charge of coordination with regional and other autonomous areas, a position that he held until 1983. During that period, he was elected simultaneously to the Chamber of Deputies and to the Italian Senate on the PCI list in six elections, beginning in 1972. In each case, he opted for accepting the Senate seat.

Within the party, his was the voice of a shrinking minority of **carristi**. In the 1983 congress and in that of 1986, he was in the forefront of those who dissented from the party's move away from its traditional acceptance of the Soviet model. Continuing in his losing battle in favor of Stalinist orthodoxy, Cossutta fought **Achille Occhetto**'s attempts to replace the PCI with a new progressive party every step of the way. Cossutta was the preferred Italian point of reference for the Soviet leadership and was one of the few Western politicians to welcome the attempted coup by Soviet hardliners against Mikhail Gorbachev in August 1991.

The PCI's February 1991 decision to abandon its communist identity prompted Cossutta to depart and form a new movement, the **Partito di Rifondazione Comunista**/Communist Refoundation Party (PRC). Cossutta was elected its first secretary at its initial congress in January 1992 and, as **Fausto Bertinotti**'s star waxed, subsequently became president of the PRC. In 1998, Cossuta dissented from the PRC's decision to overthrow the government of **Romano Prodi** and became one of the founding members of a new political formation, the Comunisti d'Italia/Communists of Italy (PDCI).

CRAXI, BENEDETTO (Bettino) (1934–2000). Born in **Milan**, Craxi's early political career was in local government. The protégé of Italian socialism's historic leader, **Pietro Nenni**, he was elected to the national executive committee of the **Partito Socialista Italiano/** Italian Socialist Party (PSI) in 1965 and three years later was elected to the Chamber of Deputies. In 1976, he took the place of Francesco De Martino as party leader after the PSI's poor performance in the elections of that year.

As party leader, he initially followed an opportunistic line trying to undercut the **Partito Comunista Italiano/**Italian Communist Party's (PCI) support among the organized working class by espousing far-left policies. He was the only politician to favor negotiating with the **Brigate Rosse/Red Brigades** (BR) during the kidnapping of **Aldo Moro** in 1978. After the 1979 general elections, President **Alessandro Pertini** gave Craxi the burden of trying to form a coalition government, but Democrazia Cristiana/Christian Democracy (DC) opposition blocked this move.

Despite the DC's hostility, Craxi realized that the 1979 elections had left the PSI as the fulcrum of the political system because the DC could not continue to govern without the PSI's parliamentary support. At the PSI's congress in April 1981, Craxi pragmatically transformed its platform along centrist, social democratic lines, and launched his own candidacy for the prime ministership with American-style attention to the publicization of his personality and image. Initially disappointed in his objectives (the first non-DC prime minister was **Giovanni Spadolini** of the **Partito Repubblicano Italiano**/Italian Republican Party (PRI) in June 1981), Craxi finally became premier in August 1983, at the head of a five-party coalition, the so-called *pentapartito*.

Craxi governed until April 1987, winning an inflated reputation for decisive leadership both in Italy and abroad. By standing up to the **trade unions** and the PCI when they tried to restore, via **referendum**, a law ensuring automatic cost-of-living pay increases, he weakened the power of organized labor. And although he was a strong supporter of the **North Atlantic Treaty Organization (NATO)** and respected by the Ronald Reagan administration, Craxi did not hesitate to reject American demands for the surrender of the Arab terrorists who murdered an American citizen on the Italian cruise liner, the *Achille Lauro*, in 1985.

Despite these achievements, Craxi's premiership represented the beginning of the end for the Italian party system. Determined both to overtake the PCI and to rival the DC, the PSI plunged both hands into the pork barrel while in government. Italy's economic boom in the 1980s was largely due to the Italian state's generosity as the PSI and the DC competed to outspend one another, with apparent disregard for Italy's public finances. By 1990 Italy's national debt stood at 100 percent of GDP, and the country was risking bankruptcy.

For two years after the end of his premiership, Craxi engaged in a bitter struggle for power with the leader of the DC, **Ciriaco De Mita**. Craxi essentially won this political battle. The DC replaced De Mita with **Arnaldo Forlani** in February 1989, and the PSI was given a large number of important (and patronage-rich) ministries in the July 1989 government formed by **Giulio Andreotti**. Craxi, Andreotti, and Forlani governed as a triumvirate until April 1992. These years saw the end of all fiscal restraint in Italian government and were the high tide of corruption among the Italian political elite.

After December 1992, Craxi became the target of dozens of corruption inquiries. He was eventually found guilty in four separate trials and was condemned to long prison sentences. From 1994 onward, however, he resided—in defiance of a court order for his return to Italy—in his luxurious villa in Hammamet, Tunisia. Craxi died in Tunisia in January 2000. Remarkably, a number of leading Italian politicians, notably **Silvio Berlusconi**, have portrayed Craxi as a victim of judicial persecution. *See also* BOBBIO, NORBERTO; GORIA, GIOVANNI; MANI PULITE.

CRISPI, FRANCESCO (1819–1901). Almost alone of the major figures who created the Italian state, Francesco Crispi was a southerner, from Agrigento in **Sicily**. He took an active role in the **Palermo** uprising in 1848 and was subject to political persecution both in Sicily and then in Piedmont (to which he had escaped in 1849) as a consequence of his republican ideals. A Mazzinian, Crispi was forced to live in exile until 1860, when he returned to Italy to organize the voyage of **Giuseppe Garibaldi**'s "Thousand" redshirts to Sicily. It was Crispi, on 11 May 1860, who proclaimed Garibaldi's dictatorship over Sicily.

Crispi became a parliamentary deputy in 1861. In 1864, he broke with the republicans by declaring himself willing to accept the **monarchy**. His anticlericalism and pro-Garibaldi sentiments, however, ensured the continuation of his radical reputation, although his overweening ambition and violent temperament won him few friends. Following the victory of the constitutional left in 1876, Crispi became first president of the Chamber of Deputies, then minister of the interior. However, he was forced to resign from the latter post within three months, after he was charged with bigamy. He was later acquitted on a technicality.

A scandal of this magnitude might have been expected to kill Crispi's career. Crispi, however, became the leading backbench critic of **Agostino Depretis**'s policy of *trasformismo*. Nevertheless, when Depretis offered him the post of minister of the interior in 1887, Crispi's lust for high office proved too strong. After Depretis's death in July 1887, Crispi finally reached the top of the greasy pole and became prime minister, a post that he held until February 1891. Crispi, anticipating **Benito Mussolini**, also occupied the posts of foreign minister and interior. As prime minister, he followed a policy of close collaboration with Germany (Crispi had first met Bismarck in the 1870s and was a warm admirer of the German statesman) and of overt hostility to the Catholic Church. Relations between the Church and the Italian government became so bad during Crispi's premiership that Pope Leo XIII thought seriously of abandoning **Rome**.

Crispi's second government (December 1893 and March 1896) was characterized by grandiose imperial ambitions, rising social tensions, and the violent repression of the Sicilian peasants' uprising in 1896. From December 1894 to May 1895, Crispi suspended **Parliament** rather than allow it to vote on a motion condemning his involvement in the **Banca Romana** scandal. Despite this undemocratic behavior, Crispi won a landslide victory in the eventual general elections. However, Crispi had been politically damaged as a consequence of having antagonized and alarmed every other important figure of the day. The calamitous defeat of the Italian expeditionary force in **Ethiopia** at Adowa in 1896 brought his career to an ignominious end. He died in **Naples** in 1901. *See also* CATHOLICISM;

CAVALLOTTI, FELICE; D'ANNUNZIO, GABRIELE; RISORGI-
MENTO.

CROCE, BENEDETTO (1866–1952). One of the greatest philosophers in modern Italian history, and arguably one of the greatest
philosophers of history of this century, Benedetto Croce also became
a symbol of the intellectual resistance to **Fascism**.

He was born in the province of Aquila (Abruzzi). When he was just
17, both parents and his sister died in an **earthquake**, and he was
obliged to move to **Rome**, where he lived with his uncle, the economist and cabinet minister Silvio Spaventa. While in Rome, he began
studying law, but soon became distracted by the lectures of the Marxist philosopher **Antonio Labriola**. Croce's first major book was an
original critique of Marxism, *Materialismo storico ed economia
marxista* (*Historical Materialism and Marxist Economics*), but
Marxism soon came to seem a rudimentary and inadequate form of
historical explanation for Croce. Of far greater interest were G. W. F.
Hegel and Giambattista Vico (whose current intellectual standing as
one of the most important philosophers of the 18th century owes
much to Croce's rediscovery of his work). Between 1902 and 1909
Croce, in the words of the title of his most famous book in this period, explained "what is alive and what is dead in the thought of
Hegel."

During the same period, Croce founded and edited the intellectual
review *La Critica*. Together with his collaborator, **Giovanni Gentile**,
Croce carried on an intellectual battle in the pages of his journal
against both the growing irrationalism of the younger thinkers and
the waning influence of positivism and Marxism. Later, after Gentile
himself had espoused Fascism, Croce combated his former colleague's apologetics for **Benito Mussolini** in *La Critica*. The review
was published continually from 1903 to 1944. Even Mussolini dared
not totally silence Croce's voice.

Croce was a neutralist in 1915. During the war years, he became
increasingly interested in the theory of historiography. After a brief
spell as minister for education in 1920, Croce turned to actually writing political history. It was through the medium of narrative history
that Croce made arguably his most effective protests against Fascism.

Croce's *Storia d'Italia, 1871–1915* (*History of Italy, 1871–1915*) and his *Storia d'Europa nel secolo decimonono* (*History of Europe in the 19th Century*) snubbed the pretensions of Fascism to be a new phase in Italian and European history. In elegant, erudite prose, Croce made the case for the liberal state and parliamentary institutions and exalted the "religion of liberty." Croce was directly active in opposing the regime after the murder of **Giacomo Matteotti** in 1924. He countered Gentile's 1925 attempt to rally intellectual opinion to the Fascist cause with a counter-manifesto signed by the cream of Italy's liberal intelligentsia, opposed the **Lateran pacts** in a famous Senate speech, and refused all intellectual collaboration with the regime. He was, for instance, almost the only prominent Italian intellectual who refused to contribute to Gentile's *Enciclopedia italiana*. Unsurprisingly, the Fascists made life difficult for him. From the mid-1930s, Croce lived under virtual house arrest.

Croce lent his name and reputation to the **Partito Liberale Italiano/** Italian Liberal Party (PLI) after September 1943. He took part in the wartime cabinets of **Pietro Badoglio** and **Ivanoe Bonomi** and was elected to the **Constituent Assembly** in June 1946. But direct political activity was never his forte. In 1947, he retired from politics to found the Institute for Italian Historical Studies. He died in 1952 in **Naples**, where he had lived almost continuously since 1886.

CURRENCY. The former Italian unit of currency was the lira (lire in the plural form). Its origins lie in the monetary reforms of Charlemagne, undertaken between 793 and 794. Twenty *soldi* or 240 *denari* constituted a *lira*. By the 13th century, there were Lombard lire, Venetian lire, Genoese lire, Florentine lire, and others, the value of each determined by the precious-metal content of the coins.

The first lire used throughout Italy were coined in the *Regno Italico*, which was established by Napoleon in 1806. The bimetallic lira of united Italy was introduced on 24 August 1862, and its value was established as 4.5 grams of silver or 0.293 grams of gold. At the same time, six banks were authorized to print paper currency. The Papal states (Latium, Emilia-Romagna, Marches, Umbria) did not begin to use the lira until 1866. In 1926, the **Banca d'Italia** was given a monopoly on the printing of paper currency.

World War I, in Italy as elsewhere, brought wild inflation that ruined many bourgeois families, small landowners, and those living on rents. By 1920, the lira was valued at one-fifth of its 1914 level. The ruination of the old bourgeoisie was accompanied by the creation of "new rich," black-marketeers, and arms manufacturers particularly. Exchange controls that had been established in 1918 by agreement with Great Britain, France, and the United States had run their one-year course and duly expired; the result was the further collapse of the lira's value on international markets. Whereas in 1914, $100 would purchase 518 lire, the same $100 bought 2,857 lire in 1920. Because Italy depended on imports of many foodstuffs, especially wheat, and industrial energy sources, such as coal and oil, the effect on the cost of living was devastating.

Benito Mussolini, ever sensitive to matters of prestige, saw the falling lira as an affront to national honor. Ignoring the advice of those economic counselors who foresaw that an overvalued lira would have a deflationary effect, he apparently thought that what mattered was public enthusiasm, and he coined the slogan *quota novanta*, suggesting thereby that no rate of exchange below 90 lire to the British pound would be tolerated (in 1925, it had been near 145). In December 1927, the Duce decreed that the exchange rate with the pound sterling should be 92.46, which had the predictable effect of making Italian goods prohibitively expensive to foreign buyers.

As an occupied country after **World War II**, Italy found its currency pegged to the U.S. dollar at a rate of $1 for 630 lire. Italy became a member of the International Monetary Fund (IMF) in 1960, and the exchange rate stabilized at 625 lire to the dollar until 1973, when the floating exchange rate was begun worldwide. The lira, suffering the effects of high domestic inflation, declined against the dollar and other European currencies throughout the 1970s. Membership in the European Monetary System (EMS) brought relative currency stability until September 1992, when the lira, buffeted by waves of speculative selling, crashed against the German mark and other European currencies. The lira remained Italy's currency until January 1, 1999, when Italy qualified to use the euro. Lira notes were replaced by euro notes on 1 January 2002. *See also* ECONOMY; EUROPEAN INTEGRATION.

– D –

D'ALEMA, MASSIMO (1949–). Massimo D'Alema has been a leading national figure in Italian politics since the summer of 1994. D'Alema's early career was spent in the party organization of the former **Partito Comunista Italiano**/Italian Communist Party (PCI), first as head of the party's youth federation, then as a member of the party secretariat, then as a parliamentary deputy, and as managing director of *L'Unità*, the PCI's daily newspaper, between 1988 and 1990. As deputy leader of the PCI during the traumatic years 1989–1991, when the PCI experienced a profound identity crisis following the collapse of communism in Eastern Europe, D'Alema played a crucial role in the party's transformation into the **Partito Democratico della Sinistra** /Democratic Party of the Left (PDS).

When D'Alema took over as leader of the PDS from **Achille Occhetto** in 1994, many regarded him as an uninspired choice who would reflect the wishes of the party bureaucracy. It has instead become clear that D'Alema is one of the few contemporary Italian politicians with vision. As the title of a book of his speeches proclaimed, he envisages Italy becoming "a normal country." He interprets this as meaning that Italy must develop constitutional arrangements in which the government has the power to implement its policies without being held hostage by minority parties in **Parliament**, in which there is a genuine social market economy without the deformations of patronage politics, and in which there is alternation in power between a center-left party and a center-right party.

D'Alema's support was crucial both for the formation of the **Olive Tree Coalition** in 1995 and also for the broadening of the PDS in 1998 to create the **Democratici di Sinistra**/Democrats of the Left (DS), of which he became president. In 1997, D'Alema chaired an important bicameral commission of Parliament that had the task of rewriting the **Constitution** of 1948. The bicameral commission drew up a draft constitution after months of political wrangling, but then failed when **Silvio Berlusconi** ceased to cooperate in the process. D'Alema was widely criticized on the left for his willingness to negotiate with Berlusconi. Despite this setback, D'Alema replaced **Romano Prodi** as prime minister in October 1998 and headed two litigious governments between then and the spring of 2000. In May

2006, after being talked of as a candidate for **president of the Republic**, he became foreign minister in the newly elected center-left government.

DALLA CHIESA, CARLO ALBERTO (1920–1982). A general in the *Carabinieri*, Carlo Alberto Dalla Chiesa served the Italian state with great bravery against two deadly internal enemies: the terrorists of the **Brigate Rosse**/Red Brigades (BR), and the Sicilian **mafia**.

Born in the province of Cuneo (Piedmont), Dalla Chiesa joined the *Carabinieri* in 1942. Most of his career was spent combating illegality in Campania and **Sicily**, although in 1968 he was placed in charge of relief efforts after the tragic **earthquake** in **Palermo**. In the early 1970s, he returned to Piedmont at a time of great political activism and violence in the factories of **Turin**. His success in combating terrorism in Piedmont led to his appointment as the national coordinator of antiterrorist activity following the tragic kidnapping and death of **Aldo Moro**. Much of the Italian state's success in tracking down and defeating the menace of the BR can be attributed to Dalla Chiesa's persistence and skill.

In December 1981, Dalla Chiesa became vice-commander of the *Carabinieri*; a few months later, following the murder by the mafia of Pio La Torre, a deputy of the **Partito Comunista Italiano**/Italian Communist Party (PCI), he was sent to Palermo to direct the Italian state's efforts to restore legality and order in Sicily. His tenure of the job was short-lived; in September 1982, Dalla Chiesa and his young second wife were ambushed and killed. Dalla Chiesa's death caused a heated debate in Italy. In two passionate and detailed books, Dalla Chiesa's university professor son, Nando, has argued the thesis that his father was assassinated by the crime bosses with the knowledge of senior politicians within the **Democrazia Cristiana**/Christian Democracy Party (DC). *See also* POLICE.

D'ANNUNZIO, GABRIELE (1863–1938). Poet, adventurer, and novelist, Gabriele D'Annunzio is one of the most flamboyant personalities in modern Italian history. Born in Pescara in 1863, he published his first collection of verse, *Primo vere* (1879), when he was just 16 years old. In the 1880s, he became a celebrity thanks to a series of critically acclaimed novels, of which *Il Piacere* (*Pleasure*, 1888) is perhaps the most widely read today; collections of decadent, sensual verse (*Canto Novo* in 1882 being the most significant); and a well-deserved reputation for *don giovannismo*. An ardent nationalist, his verse voiced the patriotic and imperialist sentiments of the era of **Francesco Crispi**; in 1897, D'Annunzio was elected to **Parliament** as a representative of the extreme right. Within three years, however, D'Annunzio, inspired by the socialists' physical bravery in pursuit of their cause, had swung to the extreme left. Whether on the right or the left, certain themes are constant in his copious political writings: irrationalism, detestation of the masses, francophilia and anglophobia, contempt for the processes of bourgeois parliamentary democracy, and a fascination with war and violence.

D'Annunzio was naturally a partisan of Italian intervention in **World War I**, in which he fought with great bravery as a volunteer pilot in the Italian air force, losing an eye in combat. It is claimed that he once flew a biplane over Vienna in order to drop from the sky pages of his poetry. When the war was over, he led an attempt by enraged Italian nationalists to defy the Treaty of Versailles (which had granted the city of **Fiume** (Rijeka) in present-day Croatia to the newly formed Yugoslavia, not to Italy). With the tacit support of many influential figures in Italian politics, D'Annunzio established his own little city-state in Fiume and ruled as duce for a year until the government of **Giovanni Giolitti**, at the end of 1920, compelled the poet and his "legionnaires" to abandon the city by shelling and by the deployment of regular army troops.

D'Annunzio plainly had much in common with **Benito Mussolini**, but his relations with the Fascist leader were marked by acute rivalry. For several months in 1922, D'Annunzio's splendid villa on the shores of Lake Garda became a meeting place for antifascists of all political persuasions, who regarded the poet as a figure around whom national reconciliation might be possible. The **March on Rome**, however, put an end to D'Annunzio's hopes of emerging as a national leader. D'Annunzio did not add his voice to **Benedetto Croce**'s dignified and courageous opposition to the Fascist state. Like the playwright **Luigi Pirandello**, the poet made his peace with the new regime and even accepted, shortly before his death, the presidency of the **Accademia d'Italia**. *See also* FOREIGN POLICY; LITERATURE; MONTALE, EUGENIO.

D'AZEGLIO, MASSIMO TAPARELLI (1798–1866). The fourth son of a prominent nobleman who was the legate of the Sardinian throne at the court of Pope Pius VII, Massimo D'Azeglio initially followed a literary and artistic career. He studied painting in **Florence** and **Milan**, where he met and married Giulia, the daughter of the novelist **Alessandro Manzoni**. D'Azeglio himself dabbled in **literature**. In 1833, he published *Ettore Fieramosca*, a novel of no lasting literary value, whose ardently nationalist and anti-Austrian content nevertheless make it an important historical document.

In 1845, with the encouragement of his cousin **Cesare Balbo**, D'Azeglio made a tour of the Papal States (Tuscany, Emilia-Romagna, the Marches). Upon his return, he wrote a celebrated exposé of the misgovernment prevailing in the regions under the Church's control, *Degli ultimi casi di Romagna* (*On the Recent Incidents in Romagna*, 1846), which established him as a national political figure.

D'Azeglio was a moderate and a constitutionalist. After the disasters of the war of 1848–1849 (in which he fought and was wounded), he became prime minister of Piedmont-**Sardinia** and negotiated the peace agreement with the Austrians. D'Azeglio remained as prime minister until 1852, when he was replaced by **Camillo Benso di Cavour**. Thereafter he held no office, but was a trusted counselor to King **Victor Emmanuel II**. During the second war with Austria in 1859, he was an active publicist on behalf of the Italian cause. The extension of Piedmontese authority to **southern Italy** left him perplexed, however. He was convinced that no good could come of fusion with **Naples**. He died in **Turin** in 1866. Today, he is chiefly remembered for his aphorism about the **Risorgimento**: "We have made Italy: now we must make the Italians."

DE BONO, EMILIO (1866–1944). Born in the province of **Milan** (Lombardy), De Bono was a monarchist and conservative who acted as a conduit between **Benito Mussolini** and the **monarchy**. In 1912, he had been chief of the General Staff in **Libya**. In **World War I**, he served in **Albania** and on the Austrian front. After the war, he joined the **Partito Nazionale Fascista**/National Fascist Party (PNF) and helped organize the Fascist militia. Once in power, Mussolini made him chief of police in **Rome**, but when the murder of **Giacomo Matteotti** by Fascist thugs led to a public outcry, De Bono resigned from the post. In 1929, he became minister for colonial affairs and, in 1935, high commissioner for East Africa. In 1936, De Bono was put in command of ground forces in the war in **Ethiopia** despite his age (he was nearly 70). He was subsequently promoted to the rank of marshal in order to clear the way for **Pietro Badoglio**, who concluded operations in six months. De Bono was among those who voted to deprive Mussolini of his powers at the fateful meeting of the **Fascist Grand Council** on 24–25 July 1943, and was thus among those executed by firing squad on the Duce's orders in January 1944 at Verona. *See also* GRANDI, DINO; MARCH ON ROME; QUADRUMVIRATE; *SQUADRISMO.*

DE CHIRICO, GIORGIO (1888–1978). Born in Greece, De Chirico is one of the most enigmatic painters of the 20th century. After an early cubist period, he was influenced by the futurist painter Carlo Carrà. Together with Carrà, De Chirico gave birth to the so-called metaphysical school of art, which—by emphasizing stillness, emptiness, natural light, and the hyperrealistic depiction of objects— deliberately contradicted the frenzied celebration of motion that characterized futurist painting.

De Chirico's best work is unforgettable once seen; his figures are like a tailor's dummies—eyeless, mouthless, and disquieting. His street scenes are as different from the crowded thoroughfares and kinetically charged piazzas portrayed by **Umberto Boccioni** as can be imagined. De Chirico painted the porticoed squares of desolate villages baking under a blue Mediterranean sky, with large areas of murky shadow and houses whose large windows look out blankly on to the street. The few human figures are solitary individuals, engaged in aimless tasks, and usually draped in shadow. Both dadaism and surrealism, and much of the best Fascist architecture, owed a great deal to De Chirico's work.

De Chirico's artistic production from the late 1920s onward is considered to have declined in originality and quality. He died in **Rome** in 1978. *See also* FUTURISM; PIACENTINI, MARCELLO.

DE FELICE, RENZO (1929–1996). A controversial historian who wrote a monumental seven-volume work on the life and times of **Benito Mussolini**, Renzo De Felice was born in Rieti (Latium). As a young historian, he was a member of the **Partito Comunista Ital-iano**/Italian Communist Party (PCI), but broke with the PCI, along with many other Italian intellectuals, after the leadership of the party justified the oppression, in 1956, by Soviet tanks of the Hungarian revolution against communist rule. De Felice taught for many years at La Sapienza University in **Rome**.

De Felice's claim to fame is that he broke a number of taboos regarding **Fascism**. When he began publishing the fruits of his researches on Mussolini in the 1960s, the prevailing consensus was that Fascism was a right-wing movement, like Nazism, that had been unpopular with the Italians and that had been largely overthrown through the efforts of the Italians themselves. De Felice revised this picture in ways that many intellectuals found difficult to accept. The first volume of his life of Mussolini insisted upon the socialist roots of Fascist ideology; other volumes drew a sharp distinction between Fascism and Nazism, emphasized that Fascism maintained a revolutionary appeal and—perhaps most controversial of all—contended that many Italians supported the regime almost until its end and that the years 1929–1936, in particular, had been the "years of consensus." Especially after De Felice published an outspoken interview with the American historian Michael Ledeen in 1975, these findings aroused lively polemic, and De Felice often had to face noisy demonstrations during his lectures and ostracism from his colleagues.

De Felice took a number of provocative positions during the last years of his life—he notably spoke slightingly of the wartime **resistance**—and by the time of his death in Rome in 1996 he was widely regarded almost as an apologist for Mussolini.

DE GASPERI, ALCIDE (1881–1954). Born in the Trentino while that province was still Austrian, De Gasperi studied in Vienna and was elected to the Austrian Parliament as a representative of the Italian-speaking minority in 1911. Despite his irredentist views, he was allowed to travel to **Rome** in 1915 when he was introduced to **Sidney Sonnino**, then Italy's foreign minister. When, at the war's end, the "unredeemed territories" formerly under Austrian jurisdiction were annexed by Italy, he took part in the founding of the **Partito Popolare Italiano**/Italian People's Party (PPI) and became a member of its national council. He was elected to Italy's **Parliament** in 1921. In

October 1922, in opposition to the PPI's leader, **Luigi Sturzo**, he successfully recommended that the PPI should take part in **Benito Mussolini**'s new government. He replaced Sturzo as leader of the PPI, but the increasingly dictatorial tendencies of Mussolini led him to oppose the regime. De Gasperi was one of the leaders of the **Aventine Secession** after the murder of **Giacomo Matteotti**. He was arrested and served a brief prison sentence in 1927–1928.

De Gasperi spent the remainder of the dictatorship in the **Vatican** library, mediating between new Catholic movements and the remnants of the old PPI. He was elected secretary of the **Democrazia Cristiana/** Christian Democracy (DC) in 1944 and authored the left-of-center party program published in occupied Rome by the DC's clandestine paper, *Il Popolo*. He served as foreign minister in the second government of **Ivanoe Bonomi** and in the government formed by **Ferruccio Parri** in June 1945. In December 1945, with the concurrence of the **Partito Comunista Italiano**/Italian Communist Party (PCI), De Gasperi became **president of the Council of Ministers**. His ability to work with the PCI in the tense immediate postwar period testifies to his pragmatism. His leadership of the DC enabled the party to outdistance all others in the election of June 1946, whereupon De Gasperi formed a government in conjunction with the **Partito Socialista Italiano/** Italian Socialist Party (PSI) and the PCI.

On his first visit to Washington, D.C., in February 1947, he was able to negotiate considerable economic aid for Italy on the apparent condition that he would expel the two Marxist parties from his government. Inasmuch as he needed their support for the treaty of peace and in the continuing preparation of the 1948 **Constitution**, he could not free himself of them until May 1947, when he formed a new coalition in which the DC was supported by smaller parties of the center-left. The presence of these "lay" parties in the government enabled De Gasperi to prevent ecclesiastical dominance. Even following the DC's huge victory in the April 1948 elections, he persisted with this strategy, which was known as *centrismo*.

In the eight governments that he headed between 1945 and 1953, De Gasperi led Italy to join the **North Atlantic Treaty Organization (NATO)**, consolidated its new democracy, undertook a measure of land reform, and took an active role in the moves toward integrating Europe both economically and politically. In many ways, he was the architect of both his party and its subsequent fundamental choices: Atlanticist, European, and—as **Aldo Moro** was to quote him as saying—"of the center moving toward the left." Outside Italy, he was regarded as one of the primary inspirers of the new Europe that emerged in the 1950s. De Gasperi's reputation has grown over the years; there is today a substantial body of Italian public opinion that believes he should be beatified. *See also* EUROPEAN INTEGRATION; TOGLIATTI, PALMIRO.

DELEDDA, GRAZIA (1871–1937). The only Italian woman writer to win the Nobel Prize in **Literature** (and one of the limited group of women ever to win the world's most prestigious literary award), Grazia Deledda was born in Nuoro (**Sardinia**) in 1871, though from 1898 onward she lived in **Rome**. A self-taught writer, Deledda's many novels depict Sardinian characters in psychological and moral dramas of great intensity. During her lifetime, she was widely compared to Feodor Dostoyevsky, and although this comparison now seems overblown, there is no doubt that her best works—*Elias Portolu* (1903), *Cenere* (*Ashes*, 1904), and *Canne al vento* (*Reeds in the Wind*, 1913)—are powerful works of art that deserve renewed critical attention. Deledda's last work was an autobiography, *Cosima*, which was published after her death in 1937.

DELLA VOLPE, GALVANO (1895–1968). A powerful Marxist thinker, Galvano Della Volpe was born in Imola, near **Bologna**, to an aristocratic family and studied philosophy at Bologna University. After an early career in which he was not immune to the aesthetic appeal of **Fascism**, Della Volpe passed to communism. He was a member of the **Partito Comunista Italiano**/Italian Communist Party (PCI) from 1944 until his death, although he was often in bad odor with the party hierarchy for the unorthodoxy of his Marxism, his outspoken atheism, and his willingness to criticize officially sanctioned thinkers. Della Volpe, who was professor of philosophy at Messina in **Sicily** for almost all of his career, published a large number of dense, difficult books on aesthetics, G. W. F. Hegel, and the philosophy of science. It is as a political philosopher that he is chiefly remembered: The key texts are his *Libertà Comunista* (*Communist Freedom*, 1946) and *Rousseau e Marx* (1957). *Libertà Comunista* was a deliberate attempt—unfortunately written in impenetrable prose—to combat the idea, dear to liberal thinkers like **Carlo Rosselli** and **Guido Calogero**, that socialism and liberalism could be integrated into a single synthesis.

Della Volpe exercised a significant influence on the thinkers of the British and American "New Left" in the 1960s and also nurtured a large number of influential pupils. He died in Rome in 1968.

DE LORENZO, GIOVANNI. *See* SOLO PLAN.

DE MITA, CIRIACO (1928–). Although he was born near **Naples** in Avellino (Campania), De Mita began his political activities while studying law at the Catholic University of **Milan**. In 1956, he was elected to the National Council of the **Democrazia Cristiana**/Christian Democracy Party (DC), and to the Chamber of Deputies in 1963. He first served in a government under **Mariano Rumor** as undersecretary of the interior. Between 1969 and 1973, he was vice secretary of the DC; he also subsequently served as both minister for industry and commerce and minister for foreign trade.

De Mita's political influence was enhanced by his appointment to the Ministry for the South under **Giulio Andreotti** in the late 1970s. In 1982, he was elected secretary of the DC. Despite the extent of his local power base, De Mita led the DC in the direction of factional reform. Factions had always characterized the party inasmuch as they served the electoral needs of the local notables who were at their center. His detractors argue that he was mainly concerned with reforming others' factions, leaving his own still able to function effectively. Whatever the truth of this allegation, the DC performed badly in the 1983 general elections (obtaining a postwar low of just 33 percent), and De Mita's hold over the party became increasingly controversial. For many within the DC, he was too closely identified with the government of national solidarity and the policy of cooperating with the Partito Comunista/Italian Communist Party (PCI) to be trusted.

The 1983–1987 government of **Bettino Craxi** was characterized by intense rivalry between the premier and De Mita, in his role as party secretary of the largest party within the government. In 1988, De Mita was forced to form a government himself. In its short life, it persuaded **Parliament** to approve modest reforms in the premier's office, in local governments, and in parliamentary voting procedures. But *franchi tiratori*—party members who, under cover of the secret ballot, vote against their party leaders' position—from within the DC offered tenacious resistance to more deep-reaching reforms. After the DC elected his rival **Arnaldo Forlani** as its new secretary in February 1989, De Mita was put in an impossible position and was forced to resign as **president of the Council of Ministers** to make room for Andreotti, a figure who was more acceptable to Craxi and the **Partito Socialista Italiano**/Italian Socialist Party (PSI). In 1989, De Mita was made president of the DC, a post from which he resigned in October 1992.

Although widely suspected of complicity in the 1980 Irpinia **earthquake**-relief scandal, De Mita has never been indicted—which makes him a rarity among DC politicians of his generation. He continues to exercise much behind-the-scenes power in the **Olive Tree Coalition**.

DEMOCRATIC PARTY OF THE LEFT (PDS). *See* PARTITO DEMOCRATICO DELLA SINISTRA.

DEMOCRATICI DI SINISTRA/Democrats of the Left (DS). This party was formed in February 1998 from the fusion of the **Partito Democratico della Sinistra**/Democratic Party of the Left (PDS) with several small parties of the center-left. The largest of these were the Federazione Laburista (Labour Federation), the Comunisti Unitari (Unitarian Communists), and the Cristiani Sociali (Social Christians). The party's electoral symbol was changed to reflect its new composition. The PDS's oak tree symbol was retained, but the hammer and sickle symbol at its roots was replaced with the red rose of the socialist movement. The party is a member of the Socialist International and of the Socialist group in the European Parliament.

The DS's first secretary was **Massimo D'Alema**, who became prime minister in October 1998. He was replaced as party secretary by **Walter Veltroni**. Since November 2001, the party secretary has been Piero Fassino, a Piedmontese born in 1949 who served as minister for commerce and minister of justice between 1998 and 2001. Since its foundation, the party's electoral tally has remained fairly stable at around 17 percent of the vote in national political contests (around six million electors). This makes the party second only to **Forza Italia** in terms of domestic political support, but it has proved too little for the DS to hope to dominate the center-left as a whole.

The DS is part of the Unione/Union coalition headed by **Romano Prodi** that won the April 2006 elections and contributes no fewer than nine senior ministers to the government. The party is characterized by very lively internal democracy; there are a great many *correnti* (factions) within the party whose opinions run the full range from liberals (in the European, promarket sense of the word) through to old-fashioned socialists and communists. As a result, the party is not always united. Fassino won the leadership in 2001 only after a hard battle and the contrary votes of nearly 40 percent of the party members. Several of the principal factions are opposed to any attempt to merge the party with other center-left parties to form a broader "Democrat" party incorporating the liberals and Christian Democrats of **Democrazia e Libertà**/Democracy and Liberty (DL). The DS's leadership insists, however, that unity of the center-left is its goal.

DEMOCRATS OF THE LEFT (DS). *See* DEMOCRATICI DI SINISTRA (DS).

DEMOCRAZIA CRISTIANA/Christian Democracy Party (DC). The DC was founded in September 1942. After the armistice on 8 September 1943, the DC took part in the governments that were formed in Allied-occupied Italy. Only in the summer of 1944, however, when the Church threw its unambiguous backing behind the new movement, did the party emerge as a force of genuine weight. After the war, the leader of the DC, **Alcide De Gasperi**, became first foreign minister and then, from November 1945, prime minister. No party other than the DC would hold the premiership again until 1981, a cycle of institutional dominance unmatched by any other party anywhere else in democratic Europe.

The DC's emergence at the core of the Italian political system was founded on the broad appeal of its policies. In the immediate postwar period the party defended the rules governing relations between church and state established by the **Lateran pacts**, evinced a strong commitment to **European integration**, was forcefully anticommunist, and proposed the wider diffusion of private property through land reform and measures to strengthen small owners of all kinds. These policies made the DC the natural party of the peasants, shopkeepers, small businessmen, clerical workers, and self-employed artisans, who constituted a huge proportion of the electorate, but who were less well organized than the manual workers or the big industrialists. The votes cast by these middle-class electors established the DC as the largest party in the country in Italy's first free elections in 1946.

De Gasperi's resolute handling of the **Partito Comunista Italiano**/Italian Communist Party (PCI) gave the DC a positive aura in American eyes. American support for the DC (in the form of campaigns asking Italo-Americans to write to family and friends in Italy encouraging votes for the DC) was instrumental in the party's massive victory in the 1948 elections (48 percent of the vote and an absolute majority of seats), which laid the foundations for the party's subsequent political hegemony. De Gasperi dominated the party until shortly before his death in 1954. Once the De Gasperi era was over, the party's internal ideological divisions (the party encompassed all creeds from Christian socialists to extreme conservatives) burst out as De Gasperi's most dynamic successor, **Amintore Fanfani**, tried to shift the party to the left.

By the end of the 1950s, the party was broadly divided into three main factional blocs, representing the party's left, center, and right, each of which was further subdivided into a vast array of subfactions and individual cabals. Over the next 30 years, although these blocs regularly changed their names and individuals habitually decamped from one faction to another, the basic structure remained approximately the same, and so did the form of politics that these internal divisions entailed. No one faction rode roughshod over the others; every faction (and subfaction, and cabal) was consulted on policy questions, questions of ministerial nominees, and state appointments, and got its share of all available patronage. The center group became the majority in 1958 and remained the party's center of gravity thereafter. In these circumstances, the party leader had to be above all a weaver of compromises. The DC was fortunate that for much of this period its dominant figure was **Aldo Moro**, an artful master of coalition politics.

By the early 1970s, the DC had almost two million members and could count upon a solid 40 percent plurality of the electorate. But this state of affairs was less healthy than it looked. Increasingly out of touch with public opinion, the DC attempted to overturn the 1970 **divorce** law by **referendum** in 1974 and was humiliatingly defeated. The DC seemingly had no answer to the industrial and social strife that paralyzed Italy from 1968 onward. Worst of all, its long hold on power had had predictable effects on public ethics: Major corruption scandals marred the two governments of **Mariano Rumor** in 1973–1974 and would continue to dog the DC until the collapse of the political system in 1993.

In the 1976 elections, the DC just managed to keep ahead of the PCI (39 percent to 34.5 percent) but could not muster a parliamentary majority. The solution was a government of national solidarity between the DC and the PCI in which the latter took no part but agreed not to vote against policies on which the PCI was consulted. This relationship lasted until the PCI leadership felt themselves excluded while, at the same time, facing the disenchantment of many in the rank and file.

In the 1980s, electoral arithmetic forced the DC to relinquish some of its hold on power. In 1981, **Giovanni Spadolini** became the first non-DC premier. In a bid to recapture its central role, the DC elected **Ciriaco De Mita** party secretary in May 1982. De Mita promised to end patronage politics and attempted to put fresh life into the DC's by-now moribund stock of ideas, but the results were disastrous. The party received its lowest ever vote in the June 1983 elections (just under 33 percent) and was forced to allow the PSI's **Bettino Craxi** to assume the premiership. Craxi's ruthless exploitation of his party's position as the fulcrum of Italian politics eventually produced a tacit power-sharing agreement between the DC's leading powerbrokers and Craxi.

The last two governments headed by a member of the DC, **Giulio Andreotti**'s sixth and seventh administrations (July 1989 to June 1992), illustrated in full the malaise of the DC. The party, once a movement of idealistic Catholic democrats, had become a conspiracy to defraud the state. Corruption was rampant at all levels of government, and in southern Italy links between important DC politicians and organized crime were commonplace. Such a party was incapable of resisting the challenges presented by the PCI's renunciation of communist doctrine, new political movements such as the **Lega Nord**, and public demands for political and electoral reform. In the April 1992 general elections, the DC's share of the vote fell below 30 percent, and the party entered into a crisis that proved to be terminal.

The subsequent **Mani pulite** and **mafia** investigations, which revealed the full, astounding extent of political wrongdoing, were the party's death knell. In January 1994, the party was officially wound up and replaced by a new formation with an old name, the **Partito Popolare Italiano**. *See also* BERLINGUER, ENRICO; BRIGATE ROSSE (RB); COLOMBO, EMILIO; *COMPROMESSO STORICO*; CONSTITUTION; COSSIGA, FRANCESCO; DOSSETTI, GIUSEPPE; GLADIO; MARTINAZZOLI, MINO; NORTH ATLANTIC TREATY ORGANIZATION (NATO); *PENTAPARTITO*; SCALFARO, OSCAR LUIGI; SCELBA, MARIO; SEGNI, ANTONIO; SEGNI, MARIO; STRATEGIA DELLA TENSIONE.

DEMOCRAZIA E LIBERTÀ/Democracy and Liberty (DL). Familiarly known as the *Margherita* (Daisy) after its electoral symbol, the DL was constituted in March 2002 from the federation of several centrist parties with, for the most part, Catholic identities. The largest of these was the **Partito Popolare Italiano**/Italian Popular Party (PPI), which was the largest surviving fragment of the old **Democrazia Cristiana**/Christian Democracy Party. The PPI was joined by the Democratici per Prodi/Democrats for Prodi, which, as their name suggests, was the party of **Romano Prodi**'s closest supporters, and Rinnovamento Italiano/Italian Renewal, which was the party associated with the figure of **Lamberto Dini**.

The party leader since March 2002 has been **Francesco Rutelli**, a former Green of strong Catholic beliefs who was the **Olive Tree Coalition**'s candidate for the premiership in the May 2001 general elections. The DL provides eight ministers to the government headed by Romano Prodi elected in April 2006. In electoral terms, the DL is the fourth biggest party in Italy, commanding around 11 percent of the vote (about 3.5 million voters). *See also* CATHOLICISM.

DE NICOLA, ENRICO (1877–1959). President of Italy between 1946 and 1948, Enrico De Nicola was a figure of notable institutional standing in the final years of Italian liberalism. Politically close to **Giovanni Giolitti**, he was elected to Parliament for the first time in 1909. In June 1920, he became speaker of the **Chamber of Deputies**, a post he held until December 1923. Like many liberals, his attitude toward **Fascism** was equivocal. In 1924, he was included in the list of approved Fascist candidates by **Mussolini**, but shortly before the ballot he withdrew his nomination. Despite being nominated to the Senate in 1929, De Nicola played no political role during the Fascist period.

De Nicola returned to active politics after the fall of Mussolini. In the spring of 1944, he resolved the crisis caused by the democratic parties' reluctance to take part in the administration of Allied-occupied Italy so long as **Victor Emmanuel III** retained the throne by suggesting that Prince Humbert should be made Lieutenant-General of the Realm. This scheme paved the way for the creation of the first government of **Ivanoe Bonomi** in June 1944. De Nicola was subsequently elected **president of the Republic** by the **Constitutional Assembly** and oversaw the process of drawing up the **Constitution** of 1948. In that year, he was offered the opportunity to be postwar Italy's first constitutionally elected head of state, but he stepped aside in favor of **Luigi Einaudi**. He was made a life member of the Senate. In 1951–1952, he was briefly president of the Senate and, in 1955, became president of the Constitutional Court, a post he held for two years. He died in his native **Naples** in 1959.

DEPRETIS, AGOSTINO (1812–1887). The quintessential professional politician, Depretis was born in the province of Pavia (Lombardy) in 1812 to a family of wealthy landowners. His political career started in his midthirties when he was elected to the Piedmontese Parliament. Initially a Mazzinian, he remained in opposition until the war of 1859, but then entered into government service, acting as the intermediary in 1860 between the Piedmontese government and the Garibaldini in Sicily. This task was the harbinger of many future conflicts between Depretis and Garibaldi's secretary, the young **Francesco Crispi**.

Depretis's first experience of ministerial office came in the 1860s, as minister for public works, but from 1867 onward Depretis was in opposition. After the death of **Urbano Rattazzi** in 1873, he became the most important figure on the moderate left and led the parliamentary opposition to the economic austerity of **Quintino Sella** and **Marco Minghetti**. In the 1874 elections the left, ably exploiting public discontent with Sella's grist tax, won over 200 seats in the Chamber. In October 1875, Depretis made a famous speech in his hometown of Stradella, in which he outlined the program the left would follow in government. The key points were faithfulness to the **monarchy** and a series of major social reforms, including the abolition of the grist tax, the extension of the right to vote, and compulsory elementary education.

Depretis came to power in the so-called parliamentary revolution of March 1876 when rightist deputies from Tuscany and Lombardy switched their support to the left. Depretis formed a government that included numerous representatives from southern Italy and then called new elections in November 1876. The elections were an immense triumph for the left, which obtained over 400 seats, but were marred by unprecedented government interference with the press and the local electoral authorities.

The left's huge majority soon split into two main blocs: the "purists" headed by Crispi, and the "moderates" led by Depretis. Between 1876 and May 1881, Depretis headed two governments that introduced slowly and incompletely the main points of the 1875 program. Compulsory education between six and nine years of age was introduced in 1877, although it was imperfectly enforced; the grist tax was abolished, but little else was done to improve the lot of the poorest citizens. In 1882, Depretis's third government did finally introduce a reform to the suffrage: The vote was extended to more than 600,000 new electors—7 percent of the population could now cast a ballot. In foreign policy, Depretis was concerned to stay on good terms with Germany and Austria. In 1882, Italy adhered to the **Triple Alliance**, which would remain the focus of the nation's foreign policy until 1915, and began looking for its own "place in the sun" by colonizing territories along the banks of the Red Sea.

Prior to the elections in October 1882, Depretis sensed that he could liberate himself from the "purists" by opening to the right. Accordingly, he appealed to members of the opposition to "transform themselves" into moderate progressives. The maneuver was successful. Led by Marco Minghetti, over 70 former rightists gave their support to the government Depretis set up after the elections. The "purists" protested, but they, too, took part in the government at one time or another. Depretis's political career ended in February 1887 following the disastrous massacre of the Italian expeditionary force at Dogali in **Ethiopia**. *See also TRASFORMISMO.*

DE SANCTIS, FRANCESCO (1817–1883). As a young man, De Sanctis took part in the 1848 uprising against absolutist rule in his native **Naples**. He was imprisoned for two years; after his release he was exiled first to **Turin** and then to Zurich, where he taught Italian literature at the university. He became a member of the Italian **Parliament** and the first minister for **education** of the new kingdom in 1861. He returned to Naples to teach at the university between 1871 and 1877, and became minister for education again in 1878 and 1881, although it cannot be said that he introduced any great curricular or organizational innovations in this post. De Sanctis's importance, however, lies not in the list of public posts that he held but in the quality of his work as a literary historian, which aroused educated Italians to a greater sense of their common literary and cultural heritage—an important step for a new nation. De Sanctis's *Storia della letteratura italiana* (*History of Italian Literature*, 1870–1872) is essentially a history of the culture and civilization of the Italian-speaking peoples from medieval times to the 19th century and is widely regarded as one of the finest pieces of scholarship of its age.

DE SICA, VITTORIO (1902–1974). A matinee idol in the 1930s, Vittorio De Sica transformed himself into one of the greatest film directors in **cinema** history. A native of the Ciociara, the region lying between **Rome** and **Naples**, De Sica began his film career early and by 1930 had appeared in dozens of romantic comedies. He began his directing career in 1940, but it was not until his fifth film, *I bambini ci guardono* (*The Children Are Watching Us*, 1943), that De Sica showed signs of exceptional talent. In 1946, he produced the neorealist classic *Sciuscià* (*Shoeshine*), which portrayed the moving story of two young vagrant shoeshine boys in the streets of war-torn Rome.

De Sica used authentic street children to ensure that his characters behaved naturally, a technique he repeated in his next film, *Ladri di biciclette* (*The Bicycle Thief*, 1948). Ranked in 1952 as one of the 10 greatest films ever made, *Ladri di biciclette* tells the story of Ricci, a desperately poor Roman worker who gets a job as a bill poster. To do the job, however, he needs a bicycle and his is stolen from him on his first day at work. Together with his son Bruno, Ricci scours the streets of Rome and eventually finds the thief but cannot prove his guilt. Frantic to keep his job, Ricci steals a bicycle that has been left outside an apartment building but is caught by an angry crowd. The bicycle's owner does not press charges, and the film ends with Ricci and Bruno walking away into the crowd. They face an uncertain future, but the bond between them has been strengthened by their ordeal. Ricci was played by a factory worker called Lamberto Maggiorani with impressive dignity and restraint, but the movie is stolen by Enzo Staiola's Bruno, the quintessential street urchin.

De Sica approached the heights of *Ladri di biciclette* only once more in his career. In 1951 he made *Umberto D*, a grim story about an aging clerical worker's struggle against destitution and despair. As usual, De Sica used an amateur actor, a professor from the University of **Florence**, as his protagonist. De Sica continued to make films for more than 20 years, but although he worked with some of the world's most talented actors, he never had more than modest critical success until 1970, when his adaptation of **Giorgio Bassani**'s novel *Il giardino dei Finzi-Contini* (*The Garden of the Finzi-Continis*) won the Oscar for best foreign picture. His own performance as an actor in the 1959 film *Il generale della Rovere* was probably the finest of his distinguished career. *See also* LITERATURE; ROSSELLINI, ROBERTO.

DE VECCHI, CESARE MARIA (1884–1959). A lifelong clerico-monarchist, De Vecchi drew close to **Fascism** and to **Benito Mussolini** instrumentally, that is, because he was sure the movement and the Duce could be useful to the conservative causes he supported. Physically distinctive because of his shaved head and extraordinary moustaches, he was often the butt of cruel jokes by other leading Fascists, even after he had been made Count of Val Cismon because of his **World War I** heroism in the battles over that valley.

De Vecchi played an important role during the **March on Rome** in October 1922. While Mussolini awaited news from **Milan**, De Vecchi and **Dino Grandi** went to the capital, where they tried to organize a coalition with nationalist leaders. De Vecchi acted as the crucial go-between in negotiations between the king and the Fascist leader during the final crisis of liberal Italy. His subsequent career as a party leader was distinctly mixed, however. His frequent gaffes as cocommander of the militia (together with **Italo Balbo** after August 1922) included publicly inciting *squadrismo* in his native **Turin**. He was dismissed by Mussolini in May 1923 and sent off to Somalia as governor, whence he returned only after war broke out.

A member of the **Fascist Grand Council**, he endorsed Dino Grandi's motion to deprive Mussolini of office in July 1943 and was subsequently condemned to death. He fled first to a monastery, then to South America, and returned to Italy 10 years later to join the neo-Fascist **Movimento Sociale Italiano**/Italian Social Movement (MSI), in which his monarchist views made him welcome to only some of the party's adherents. He died in **Rome** in 1959. *See also* QUADRUMVIRATE.

DIALECTS. Dialects in Italy are not just regionally distinctive pronunciations of Italian. They are the popular speech of many for whom speaking the literary language as taught in school is a terrible struggle. Yet no inferiority should be imputed. Dialects have their own verb forms and vocabularies. Many have their own theatrical tradition, their own poets, and—most conspicuously—their own songs. Many Piedmontese leaders of newly united Italy, including the king, had to learn Italian as a foreign language.

As the Romans colonized the Italian peninsula, they met Etruscans, Ligurians, Oscans, Illyrians, Phoenicians, and Greeks. (Magna Grecia included Greek colonies in the river valleys of the Italian south, leaving a clear impact on local culture, including speech.) Not surprisingly, the pronunciation of the Latin learned by these people varied significantly. After the collapse of Roman unity and the Germanic, Norman, and Arab invasions between the fifth and ninth centuries, the absence of a political center exacerbated the differences between North and South and further slowed the acceptance of a common speech.

By the Middle Ages a gulf separated the use of Latin as a written language and neo-Latin vernaculars, which, while initially only spoken, came to be written as well between the 11th and 13th centuries. Conceiving all dialects of the Romance languages as derived from Latin helps one see how in Italy (as in France, Portugal, and Spain), one powerful or wealthy region was able to ensure the widened use of its particular Latin dialect. Thus, Castilian became the dialect that the rest of centralized Spain had to accept as the standard, just as Parisian became the standard for unitary France and Tuscan the Italian literary language, for this was the language of Boccaccio, Dante, and Petrarch in the region whose wealth derived from having invented banking and being the major insurer of European trade with the Near and Far East.

In 1945, 50 percent of Italians spoke only a dialect. Before the advent of television, increased school attendance, and the leveling effect on language of commercial films, most Italians found communication between people from differing regions as difficult as between people from separate countries. A Neapolitan and a Milanese can now converse in Italian; 50 years ago, unless they shared a knowledge of French, Latin, or another language, comprehension was difficult.

The vigor of dialects continues at the end of the 20th century, especially in remote areas and among older generations. Spontaneity and intimacy are easiest in the dialect used in the home, among friends, and in the family, and it clearly distinguishes outsiders from those who "belong." Indeed, one's identity seems to depend on ties to territory in the form of ties "to the parish, the club, the neighborhood, the dialect." The global economy may require the loosening of such ties, but the price to be paid has yet to be calculated.

Dialectologists distinguish Gallo-Italic dialects (Piedmontese, Ligurian, Lombard, Emilian-Romagnol) from Venetian (Venetian, Trentino). In central Italy there are several Tuscan and central dialects (Umbrian, Marchigian, Roman) and southern dialects (Campanian, Abruzzese, Molisan, Calabrese, Pulian, Lucanian, and Sicilian). To these must be added the Ladino dialect spoken in Friuli (called *Friulano* in Italian or—in dialect—*Furlans*). Sardinian is closely related to Catalan, the dialect that Francisco Franco tried for decades to stamp out in Spain. See also MINORITIES.

DIAZ, ARMANDO (1861–1928). Born in **Naples**, Diaz can fairly be called modern Italy's most successful soldier since **Giuseppe Garibaldi**, though it must be said that competition for this title is not fierce. After initial training in artillery, in 1910 Diaz was appointed colonel and in May 1912, as commander of the 93rd Regiment, took part in the colonial war against **Libya**, in which he was wounded. He became a major general attached to the general staff under General **Luigi Cadorna**, whom he would later replace as commander-in-chief.

When World War I broke out, Diaz sought a military command and became general in charge of the 49th Division. He distinguished himself both for his tenacity as a commander and for his bravery in battle (he was wounded in July 1917 and won the silver medal for valor). After the disaster of **Caporetto** in November 1917, King **Victor Emmanuel III** made Diaz commander of the Italian army, promoting him over the head of more widely esteemed generals such as **Pietro Badoglio**. Diaz announced his assumption of command with a one-line communiqué to his troops: "I am taking over as Chief of General Staff and I count upon the goodwill and self-sacrifice of everybody."

Diaz obtained the moral effort he asked for. The Italian army held fast through the winter of 1917–1918 on the Piave River, blocking access to the valley of the river Po and to **Venice**, and then in October 1918 broke the Austrian army at the battle of Vittorio Veneto.

Diaz became senator of the realm in February 1918 and after victory was awarded a dukedom and several other military and civil honors. He strongly supported **Fascism** and accepted a post as minister of war in **Benito Mussolini**'s first government. In November 1924, he became a field marshal. He died in **Rome** in February 1928.

DI LAMPEDUSA, PRINCE GIUSEPPE TOMASI (1896–1957). The scion of a noble **Palermo** family, Di Lampedusa is the author of *Il Gattopardo* (*The Leopard*, 1958), arguably the greatest 20th-century Italian novel and one of the greatest historical novels ever written. The book tells the tale of the decline of the ancient Salina family after the **Risorgimento** and the rise of the middle class, represented in the novel by the figure Don Calogero Sedara, the mayor of a small village on one of the Salina family's estates, and his beautiful but unprincipled daughter Angelica. Prince Fabrizio Salina (the "leopard" is his family emblem) allows Angelica to marry Tancredi, his favorite nephew, convinced that the best way to preserve his power and position is to go along with the revolutionary spirit of the times. In a phrase that has become famous as a perfect definition of the perennial Italian vice of *trasformismo*, Tancredi tells his uncle: "If everything is to stay the same, everything has to change." The irony of the novel is that the social structure of liberal Italy does remain the same as before, but the Salinas are replaced by the upstart Sedaras and their ilk. At one point, Salina says that "after us will come the age of the hyenas and the jackals." This brief summary of the novel's plot, however, does not do justice to its thematic and philosophic complexity or its vivid and sensuous descriptions. **Luchino Visconti** brilliantly captured the novel's sad beauty in his 1963 film version.

Despite the book's universal appeal and the author's manifest genius, *Il Gattopardo* was the center of a literary debate when it first appeared. In many ways, conservative in personal philosophy and certainly profoundly pessimistic, the book was dismissed by the **neorealist** establishment in the Italian literary world, and it was only thanks to the efforts of the writer **Giorgio Bassani** that the book saw the light of day in 1959—two years after the author's death. *See also* LITERATURE; SOUTHERN ITALY.

DINI, LAMBERTO (1931–). Economist, banker, and prime minister, Lamberto Dini was born in **Florence** in March 1931. An economist by profession, Dini worked for the International Monetary Fund (IMF) from 1959 to 1975, rising to the position of executive director in 1976. In 1979, he returned to Italy as director-general of the **Banca d'Italia**, a position he held until 1994, when he was persuaded to enter politics as minister of the treasury in **Silvio Berlusconi**'s short-lived first administration (May–December 1994). When Berlusconi's government collapsed, Dini, who had been one of the government's handful of ministerial successes, became President **Oscar Luigi Scalfaro**'s choice to head an interim government of technocrats. Dini shepherded Italy through a difficult year, restoring international confidence in its economic and political stability. His achievements as prime minister seem to have given the former bureaucrat a taste for politics. In February 1996, Dini founded a new centrist party called

Rinnovamento Italiano/Italian Renewal (RI) and campaigned in the April 1996 general elections as an ally of **Romano Prodi**'s **Olive Tree Coalition**/Ulivo. Following Prodi's victory, Dini, who was elected to the Chamber of Deputies as deputy for a Florence constituency, was made foreign minister. The Ulivo's reliance on the Partito di **Rifondazione Comunista**/Communist Refoundation Party (PRC) troubled his conservative political instincts and made the job of reassuring Italy's European partners more difficult.

Between 2001 and 2003, Dini was one of Italy's representatives in the "convention" that drew up a draft constitution for the European Union (EU). *See also* EUROPEAN INTEGRATION.

DI PIETRO, ANTONIO (1950–). An intense, hardworking opponent of political corruption, Antonio Di Pietro was born in the Molise in 1950. He became first a policeman and then, in 1981, a public prosecutor. In 1985, he joined the district attorney's office in **Milan**, where he specialized in corruption investigations. In February 1992, he masterminded the arrest and prosecution of a Milanese businessman with close ties to the **Partito Socialista Italiano**/Italian Socialist Party (PSI) called Mario Chiesa, an event that initiated the **Mani pulite** (Clean Hands) inquiry, which eventually led to the investigation and arrest of thousands of politicians and businessmen all over Italy. Di Pietro became a symbol of Italy's search for social and political regeneration and was the subject of hundreds of flattering profiles in the foreign and domestic press. The high point of the Clean Hands inquiry was Di Pietro's ruthless but brilliant cross-examination of a dozen leading Italian politicians in December 1993 during the trial of a Milanese financier accused of having been the conduit for illegal donations to the political parties.

In 1994, the Mani pulite investigation, and Di Pietro personally, became the targets of violent political opposition as they dug into the financial affairs of the new premier, **Silvio Berlusconi**. Di Pietro resigned in protest at the atmosphere of intimidation surrounding the investigation in December 1994, but, in 1995, he had to survive an investigation into his own conduct as a prosecutor. Cleared of all charges against him, he became minister for public works in the government formed by **Romano Prodi** in May 1996. In the fall of 1996, he once more became embroiled in a web of accusations and inquiries, this time relating to charges that he had given lenient treatment to a Swiss-Italian banker involved in the Clean Hands scandal in exchange for cash. Di Pietro believed that his position as a minister was incompatible with his being under investigation and resigned in November 1996 in order to clear his name. In November 1997, he was elected to the Senate, representing Mugello (Tuscany), where he won 68 percent of the vote.

Di Pietro formed a political movement called L'Italia dei valori/ Italy of Values in time for the 2001 elections, but his list was unsuccessful. In the 2006 elections, Di Pietro joined the Unione/Union coalition led by Prodi. He is currently once again minister for public works.

DI RUDINÌ, ANTONIO STARABBA (1839–1908). A Sicilian conservative, Rudinì came to national attention as mayor of **Palermo**. In 1869, he was briefly minister of the interior under **Luigi Menabrea**. The long sequence of governments of the Constitutional Left then kept him out of office until February 1891, when Rudinì—who had been the undisputed leader of the parliamentary right since 1886— became both prime minister and minister for foreign affairs. His first government was marked by several important events, notably the foundation of the **Partito Socialista Italiano**/Italian Socialist Party (PSI) and the publication of the encyclical *Rerum Novarum*. His government was brought down in April 1892 by parliamentary opposition to his attempts to balance the budget coming from both the military right of **Luigi Girolamo Pelloux** and the parliamentary left of **Giovanni Giolitti**.

Rudinì returned to power in March 1896. His new administration was criticized by the noted economist **Vifredo Pareto** as a "government of gentlemen" who were too well bred to stamp out the corruption revealed during the **Banca Romana** scandal, but, in fairness, Rudinì could also boast some significant achievements. Military spending was capped, the war in **Ethiopia** was brought to an end in October 1896, and civil government replaced military rule in Eritrea. These generally sensible policies were not rewarded at the polls. After the elections of March 1897, Rudinì had to rely on the radicals to stay in office.

Rudinì's second spell as prime minister came to an end as a consequence of the 1898 bread riots, which his government suppressed with severity. At least 80 citizens were killed by troops commanded by General Bava Baccaris in **Milan**. Thousands of people, including several PSI deputies, were arbitrarily arrested and condemned to jail by military tribunals, and emergency laws limiting civil liberties were passed. In June 1898, Rudinì asked that these emergency provisions be made into permanent laws and, when Parliament denied this request, appealed to the king to dissolve the Chamber of Deputies and institute a state of siege by royal decree. This near coup was too extreme even for a conservative court, and Rudinì was obliged to resign. He died in **Rome** in 1908.

DIVORCE. In strongly Catholic Italy, the right to divorce was one of the major social and political issues of the late 1960s and early 1970s. The right to legal separation was first proposed in October 1965 by the socialist deputy Loris Fortuna. Fortuna's bill met fierce resistance from the Church, but, helped by a cross-party pressure group for reform—the "Italian League for the Institution of Divorce"—his ideas gradually won support. In November 1969 a parliamentary coalition of the "lay" parties defeated the opposition of the **Democrazia Cristiana/**Christian Democracy Party (DC) and the **Movimento Sociale Italiano/**Italian Social Movement (MSI) by 325 to 283 votes to pass a law that permitted the state, rather than the Church alone, to authorize the dissolution of a marriage. The so-called *Legge Fortuna* became law in December 1970. Pope Paul VI expressed his "profound regret" for the decision, which the church regarded as a violation of the **Lateran pacts**.

Within six months more than one million Catholics had signed a petition for a **referendum** abrogating the new divorce law, and, in January 1972, the Constitutional Court declared the proposed referendum legitimate. To avoid a divisive social clash over the issue, in February 1972, the political parties resorted to dissolving **Parliament** and calling an early general election (which, by law, may not be held concurrently with a referendum) in order to postpone the referendum vote. In 1973, **Amintore Fanfani**, hoping to make political capital from the issue, turned it into a crusade (he famously warned that homosexual marriage would be legalized if Italians did not turn back the tide of sexual license of which the divorce law was a harbinger). Bowing to the inevitable, president **Giovanni Leone** called a referendum on the issue in March 1974.

The poll, which took place on 12–13 May 1974, illustrated the shift in Italian social mores brought about by the previous two decades of economic growth and social transformation. Some 87 percent of the electorate voted, and a resounding 59.3 percent voted against abrogating the divorce law. Huge numbers of Catholics, taking notice of Pope Paul's studied moderation during the electoral campaign, either abstained or voted in favor of the *Legge Fortuna*. The introduction of divorce has not shaken the foundations of the Italian family. While the number of divorces has greatly increased, the percentage of dissolved marriages remains very low by rich-country standards. Moreover, only 6–7 percent of Italian children are born out of wedlock, compared with figures of 30 percent or more for some industrial democracies. *See also* WOMEN.

DOLCI, DANILO (1924–1997). An advocate of nonviolent resistance and a civil rights activist on behalf of some of Italy's most deprived citizens, Danilo Dolci was born in **Trieste**, the son of a Sicilian father and a Slovenian mother. His entire adult life after 1952, however, was spent fighting on behalf of the peasant and fishing communities of western **Sicily**. His most famous tactic was the so-called strikes in reverse, in which he led hundreds of villagers to repair roads for which funds had been allocated by **Parliament** but not actually allotted. Such nonviolent methods led foreign journalists to call him "the Sicilian Gandhi," a comparison that Dolci always rejected. By embarrassing the Italian state as well as the local notables, he made powerful enemies. In addition, his struggle to gain water rights that were controlled by the local **mafia** added to the precariousness of his position. Yet he continued to organize **cooperatives**, engage in hunger strikes, and agitate for irrigation projects and the dams that they entail. His popularity seemed to protect him from any reprisals by those whom he antagonized.

In 1957, although not a communist, he was awarded the Lenin Peace prize, worth $30,000. The following year he was arrested and tried for unauthorized work done on roads near Partinico and sentenced to eight months in prison. In 1965 and in 1982, he was nominated for the Nobel Prize. In 1967, his allegations that leaders of the **Democrazia Cristiana**/Christian Democracy Party (DC) were guilty of collusion with organized crime led to his conviction for libel and two additional years in prison.

Dolci was a prolific author of political pamphlets and published several volumes of poetry. Long suffering from diabetes, he contracted pneumonia and in his last months was confined to a wheelchair. He died in a Sicilian hospital on 30 December 1997.

DONIZETTI, GAETANO (1797–1848). An astonishingly prolific 19th-century composer, Gaetano Donizetti was born to a poor family in Bergamo in November 1797. With the help of a talented music teacher, Simone Mayr, Donizetti began to study music. In 1815, he went, at Mayr's expense, to study in **Bologna**; on his return in 1817, he was contracted to write operas for the stage (opera was then a popular art form). His first efforts, especially *Il falegname di Livonia* (*The Carpenter of Livonia*) were popular successes. *Chiara e Serafina*, his 1822 debut in **Milan**, was a flop, however. The resilient Donizetti nevertheless bounced back with a string of successful commercial operas performed between 1822 and 1830 in **Naples, Palermo, Rome**, and **Genoa**.

Donizetti moved into a different artistic and commercial league in 1830 when his *Ann Boleyn* was produced at the Carcano theater in Milan and subsequently in Paris and London. The opera established his European reputation, which was confirmed in 1834 (after a string of lesser works) by his *Lucrezia Borgia*, which premiered in Milan to public acclaim and subsequently was staged in Paris. In 1835, he collaborated with the librettist Salvatore Cammarano to write *Lucia di Lammermoor*, the work for which he is today most remembered and which he wrote in a mere 36 days. He was by now one of the most famous composers in Europe, as well-regarded in Naples, Paris, and Vienna as in Milan or Venice.

Donizetti's beloved wife died in 1837. He subsequently contracted syphilis, and this brought on increasing mental instability and eventually a stroke that left the composer paralyzed for the last two years of his life. Donizetti died in Bergamo in April 1848.

DOSSETTI, GIUSEPPE (1913–1996). Born in **Genoa**, this passionately religious man took an active part in the **resistance** to the Nazi occupation even though he always refused to bear arms himself.

Dossetti became chairman of the underground **Comitato di Liberazione Nazionale**/Committee for National Liberation (CLN) in Reggio-Emilia. After the war, he became professor of canonical law and took an important role in the **Democrazia Cristiana**/Christian Democracy Party (DC), serving on its national steering committee and as deputy to **Alcide De Gasperi**. Elected to the **Constituent Assembly**, where he played an important role in drawing up the progressive guarantees of human and social rights that characterize the first part of the Italian **Constitution** of 1948, Dossetti was also editor of the influential periodical *Cronache Sociale*, which, under his direction, opposed Italian accession to the **North Atlantic Treaty Organization (NATO)** and pressed for radical social reforms. He was elected to the Chamber of Deputies in 1948 but left national politics in 1951, despite the fact that he was the leader of the DC's internal opposition to De Gasperi and could count upon substantial support among the party membership: A third of the delegates to the 1949 party congress of the DC voted for his program. In 1956, he ran unsuccessfully for the mayorality of **Bologna**.

Dossetti was a member of the Bologna city council until 1958, but this marked the end of his political life. Taking the vows of priesthood (he was ordained in 1959), he founded a small monastic order and thereafter lived the contemplative life, although in 1959 he did participate in the second Vatican Council as an advisor to Giacomo Lecaro, archbishop of Bologna and a leading exponent of dialogue with communism. Dossetti was silent on political questions until April 1994, when he briefly surfaced to propose that committees for the defense of the Constitution should be formed throughout Italy. He died in Bologna, aged, 83 in December 1996. *See also* INTEGRALISM.

DUCE. *See* MUSSOLINI, BENITO.

DULBECCO, RENATO (1914–). A virologist who won the Nobel Prize in Medicine in 1975, Dulbecco was born in the Calabrian town of Catanzaro and brought up in Imperia in Liguria. He studied biology and medicine at the University of **Turin** and was called up to the army in 1936. He served as a soldier on the Russian front during the war, where he was hospitalized by a wound and sent home. Dulbecco joined the **resistance** as a doctor and served on the Turin **Comitato**

di Liberazione Nazionale/Committee of National Liberation (CLN). In 1947, he left to work in the United States, at the same time as his friend and fellow Nobel prize-winners **Rita Levi-Montalcini** and Salvatore Luria. Dulbecco subsequently worked at the University of Indiana, the California Institute of Technology, the Salk Institute, and, starting in 1962, in London at the cancer institute at Imperial College. He returned to Italy only in 1993 to become president of the Institute of Biomedical Technologies at the National Council for Research in **Rome**.

Dulbeco won the Nobel Prize (shared with Howard Temin and David Baltimore) for his work on "the interaction between tumour viruses and the genetic material of the cell." His work has been a major step forward in the fight to treat and cure cancer. Dulbecco was one of the founders, in 1986, of the human genome project.

– E –

EARTHQUAKES. In seismic terms, Italy is one of the nations most at risk in Europe. There were four major earthquakes in Italy in the 20th century, as well as dozens of minor tremors. The worst quake occurred when Messina (**Sicily**) and its twin city Reggio Calabria were both destroyed on 28 December 1908, with the loss of nearly 100,000 lives—one of the worst natural disasters in European history. This tremor was measured at 7.5 on the Richter scale.

There have been three major quakes more recently. In January 1968, a quake killed 300 people and left hundreds of thousands homeless in western Sicily. In May 1976, more than 1,000 people were killed by an earthquake in Friuli-Venezia-Giulia, near the Yugoslav border. Volunteers came from all over Italy to clear away the wreckage and help the *Friuliani* get back on their feet. In November 1980, a massive tremor (6.8 on the Richter scale) killed 6,000 people in Campania and Basilicata. This terrible natural calamity was compounded by the behavior of Italy's politicians, who turned the disaster into an opportunity to funnel huge sums of relief aid into the area and then to siphon it off to their client networks, friendly businessmen, and organized crime (which carried great electoral weight in the **Naples** region). It has been calculated that over 50 thousand billion lire ($30 billion) were earmarked for earthquake relief, but most of this money was never spent on the reconstruction efforts, and well into the 1990s several thousand refugees continued to live in the prefabricated huts thrown up in the aftermath of the emergency. In September 1997, a series of earthquakes struck Umbria, taking fewer lives but destroying priceless frescoes by Giotto in the church of Saint Francis in Assisi. *See also* MAFIA.

ECO, UMBERTO (1932–). One of the world's leading philosophers and a pioneer in the study of semiotics (the analysis of signs), Umberto Eco is that rarest of birds, a professor who is both internationally respected within the academy and widely read outside. Eco owes his popularity principally to his 1980 novel *Il nome della rosa* (*The Name of the Rose*), a philosophical "whodunit" set in a medieval Italian monastery that quickly sold more than four million copies in numerous languages and became one of the publishing events of recent times. Since 1980, Eco has published several other novels, which have met with less critical and public success, *Il pendolo di Foucault* (*Foucault's Pendulum*, 1988) and *Baudolino* (2002) being perhaps the best-known.

Professor Eco's scholarly works have included monographs on the aesthetics of Saint Thomas Aquinas and medieval aesthetics more generally; the poetics of James Joyce; and, most famously of all, his several books on the theory of semiotics. He was the first Italian to give the Norton lectures on poetry at Harvard University in 1992 and also won the Asturias prize for Communications in 2000. Eco is also a columnist for the weekly news magazine *Espresso*, in which he has a platform for his witty, acute, and occasionally whimsical views on popular culture, politics, and contemporary life in general. Eco, who is a native of Alessandria in Piedmont, lives in **Milan** and teaches at the University of **Bologna**.

ECONOMIC MIRACLE. By 1963, Italy had ceased to be a primarily agricultural country and became a modern industrial state. Between 1950 and 1970, income per capita in Italy grew faster (on average over 6 percent per year) than any other major European country and had arrived at 80 percent of British levels by 1970. Between unification in 1861 and the end of the 1930s, real per capita income in Italy grew by just one-third. Between 1946 and 1963, the years of fastest growth, it doubled. Used to grinding poverty, Italians could only regard this sudden enrichment as miraculous, although, in truth, they had earned it by their own hard work.

Industrially, Italian economic growth was guided by the big private and public corporations. **FIAT** established itself as a mass manufacturer of automobiles, expanding production from a prewar high of 78,000 vehicles in 1938 to more than a million in 1963. The Italian state steel company, Finsider, under the guidance of Oscar Singaglia, became one of the largest and most innovative manufacturers of finished steel products in the world. ENI, the oil and gas business headed by **Enrico Mattei**, gave Italian firms a cheap and plentiful source of fuel. Smaller producers of consumer goods, particularly domestic appliances and textiles, did their share; Italy became one of the world's largest producers of so-called white goods in those years. The chief market was Europe. The creation of the European Economic Community in 1958 opened the markets of northern Europe for the nimble and relatively cheap entrepreneurs of northern Italy, and they took full advantage of the opportunity. Exports grew even faster (approximately 10 percent per year on average) than the economy as a whole, and over 90 percent of sales abroad were in industrial merchandise rather than raw materials or services. Today, more than 70 percent of Italy's exports are to other members of the European Union (EU).

Italy, in short, had become a country that made and sold goods as well as thriving on service sector activities such as tourism. By 1961, nearly 40 percent of the working population was employed in manufacturing and less than 30 percent in agriculture, a historic change from the over 60 percent who had hitherto worked the fields. Between 1958 and 1963, the peak years of the "miracle," nearly one million southerners moved north, mostly to **Turin** and **Milan**, and many hundreds of thousands immigrated to Germany, Belgium, Switzerland, and the United States. But the phenomenon was not limited to the South; the region that lost the largest proportion of its inhabitants to migration was Venetia, whose rural population headed in the thousands to the fatter wage packets provided by the industrial cities of Lombardy. These demographic shifts led to an unprecedented construction boom, during which the outskirts of all of Italy's big cities became disfigured by housing projects hastily thrown up to provide the migrants with apartments. An unforeseen by-product was an upheaval in social mores. Freed from rural traditions, with money in their pockets for the first time, Italians of all classes began to experiment with more liberal sexual conduct, while church attendance declined. The diffusion of television contributed to altering the traditionally communal Italian way of life. Instead of sitting outside in the *piazze*, Italians—like the newly rich citizens of other European countries—became increasingly prone to entertain themselves in front of the flickering screen: More than half of all Italian families had a TV set by 1965.

These economic and social changes left their mark on Italian culture. The disquiet felt by many intellectuals is captured in **Federico Fellini**'s 1957 film *La Dolce Vita*, while the disorientation of the southern migrants is the theme of **Luchino Visconti**'s moving *Rocco e i suoi fratelli* (*Rocco and His Brothers*, 1960). *See also* EUROPEAN INTEGRATION; ISTITUTO PER LA RICOSTRUZIONE INDUSTRIALE (IRI); LAND REFORM; POPULATION.

ECONOMY. Italy has a very anomalous economy. Parts of the country, especially the North, are highly industrialized; the South, by contrast, never fully experienced industrialism and modernization. Italy is a very large economy (the seventh largest in the world), with a high standard of living, yet it is also short of multinational companies. Even Switzerland and the Netherlands, let alone Germany, France, and Great Britain, possess larger numbers of huge firms with worldwide interests.

Italy industrialized late behind steep tariffs imposed by the governments of **Agostino Depretis** and **Francesco Crispi** in the 1870s and 1880s. This mercantilism enabled a domestic steel industry to grow and helped wealthy business interests in the North, but retaliation from other countries, notably France, damaged agricultural exports from **southern Italy**. The massive wave of migration from Italy in the late 19th and early 20th centuries was provoked by agricultural depression in the South that industrial growth in the North could not sufficiently assuage. The figures show clearly that Italy's economic growth was distinctly weaker than Germany's between the 1860s and the outbreak of **World War I**. In 1900, Italy's share of world manufacturing, at 2.5 percent, was exactly the same as it had been in 1860. Germany, meanwhile had improved its share from 4.9 percent to 13.2 percent. Overall GNP increased (measured in 1960 U.S. dollars) from $7.4 billion to just $9.4 billion, although it is true that there was real acceleration in the decade preceding war. In per capita terms, this meant a meager increase, from $301 to $311 (figures from Paul Kennedy, *The Rise and Fall of the Great Powers*. London: Fontana, 1989, 189–190 and 219–220).

The war boosted production in some areas of the economy but added indebtedness and inflation to Italy's economic woes. Despite its rhetoric, **Fascism** never came to grips with Italy's economic problems. **Benito Mussolini**'s obsession with Italy's prestige only compounded Italy's difficulties by making certain decisions, such as the devaluation of the lira, impossible, while the worldwide economic crisis of the 1930s bankrupted Italy's leading investment banks and threw major industries, such as shipbuilding, into crisis. The Fascist state's solution was to nationalize whole swathes of the economy in the **Istituto per la Ricostruzione Industriale (IRI)**.

Italy's share of world manufacturing output was 3.3 percent in 1929; by 1938, on the eve of war, the figure had fallen to just 2.9 percent. Despite the fact that defense spending took almost 15 percent of GNP and living standards were hardly higher than in 1914, Italy's war potential was lower than any other major power. Indeed, Italy was *not* a major power. Under the circumstances, Mussolini's reluctance to enter the war until Nazi Germany's victory seemed certain can be explained by the dictator's awareness of the country's economic weakness. His costly adventures in **Ethiopia** and in the **Spanish Civil War** are less explicable. Italy could not afford Mussolini's **foreign policy**.

After **World War II**, Italy's devastated economy was put back on its feet by the sound money policy followed by the **Banca d'Italia**, which avoided hyperinflation, albeit at heavy social cost, and Marshall Plan aid, which in Italy's case undeniably helped the transition to democracy. In the 1950s, the boom known as the **economic miracle** began. The percentage of the population working on the land finally decreased. Italy became the workshop of Europe, producing light industrial goods for the rapidly expanding European consumer market. The statistics are striking: In 1951, agriculture employed

42.2 percent of the working population; industry 32.1 percent. In 1971, agriculture employed just 17.2 percent; industry, by contrast, had expanded to 44.4 percent. The shift of workers into the service economy began in earnest only in the 1970s.

Postwar Italy made a conscious choice to extend state participation in the economy. Indeed, by the 1970s, Italy was probably the most statist economy outside the communist bloc. In addition to the dozens of firms operating within IRI, which included Ilva (steel), Stet (telephones), and Finmeccanica (an engineering group), the state controlled the energy industry through the Ente Nazionale Idrocarburi (ENI) and dominated the market for credit via its dominating presence in the banking system. Almost the entire banking sector, and all big lending and investment decisions, were in the hands of state-owned banks, which in practice meant the political parties. The economic consequences of such massive state participation were predictable: Italy's biggest companies, especially in southern Italy, became social welfare agencies and political fiefdoms (which is one reason why there are so few multinational Italian firms today). By the 1980s, the state sector was running giant losses.

Contemporaneously, however, the other characteristic feature of the modern Italian economy also appeared. Small businesses, usually family-owned and employing less than 10 employees, began to form industrial districts in which whole communities collaborated in the production of specific products and shared marketing, design, and research costs. The economic growth of Venetia and Lombardy is largely attributable to the success of these companies, which have made Italy a world leader in a vast array of high-quality consumer goods. In 2000, 83.5 percent of Italian manufacturing firms employed less than 10 employees. More significantly, the total of industrial firms employing over 100 workers was less than 1 percent, even though these firms accounted for 55 percent of sales (figures from Martin Bull and James Newell, *Italian Politics.* Cambridge: Polity, 2005, 178).

The inefficiencies of the Italian state, which eroded the competitive edge of the small business sector, was one major cause of the rise of the **Lega Nord**/Northern League (LN). The crisis of Italy's public finances in the 1990s also impelled change. In 1993, Italy began the largest privatization program (larger even than Great Britain's) of any

Western democracy to date. By 2000 numerous banks had been auctioned off, as had the state motorways, Rome airport, parts of ENI, Telecom Italia (as Stet was now known), and Ente Nazionale per l'Energia Elettrica (ENEL), the national electricity agency. Proceeds amounted to 170,000 billion lire, and billions of euros more have since been raised by further sales of stock in ENEL. It is also true that these gains have been offset by huge subsidies to the remaining state enterprises such as Alitalia, the state airline, and the loss-making state railway system.

Italy's main economic need today is transforming its economic model to meet the new challenges emerging from low cost manufacturers in countries such as China, India, and Turkey. Italy's economy is more exposed to competition from emerging nations than Germany's or Britain's, and its political system is less able to implement reforms. The postwar economic boom arguably had a greater transformational effect on Italy than any other European country, but the conditions that made it possible have now vanished. *See also* CASSA PER IL MEZZOGIORNO; CONFINDUSTRIA; CURRENCY; EUROPEAN INTEGRATION; FIAT; PIANURA PADANA; POPULATION; TRADE UNIONS.

EDUCATION. The Italian educational system developed slowly and unevenly. Provision for basic education was sorely neglected in Italy until well after **World War II**, yet the country also possessed outstanding high schools that gave an excellent classical education.

The foundations of public education were two laws passed in 1859 and 1877, which theoretically made public education available to all children aged between six and nine years of age. However, because provision of schools was made the responsibility of municipal governments, which meant small villages had to levy taxes to pay for their own schools, the laws were widely ignored, especially in rural areas and the South. The 1911 census estimated that half the adult population was illiterate. According to Dennis Mack Smith, there were 35 education ministers between 1887 and 1925; obviously, such chopping and changing in the ministry precluded systematic attempts at reform. In 1911, a radical education minister, Luigi Credaro, finally made financing of schools a provincial responsibility and increased state spending on education.

Nevertheless, basic education remained a hit-and-miss affair for many Italians, and illiteracy rates remained strikingly high throughout the Fascist period. The 1923 curriculum reform proposed by the Fascist philosopher **Giovanni Gentile** stressed humanistic education and less rote learning, but its effects were severely limited by Fascist indoctrination in the schools. As late as the 1950s, in defiance of article 34 of the **Constitution** of 1948, many children were educated only to the age of 11, and it was only in 1962 that the center-left government headed by **Amintore Fanfani** introduced both compulsory education until 14 and a common curriculum until that age. The immediate postwar years were also characterized by an acute shortage of teachers. This problem was overcome only in the 1970s, after the baby-boom generation graduated from university.

Today, children start school typically aged six years and stay in primary education for five years. They are usually taught by two *maestre* (most primary school teachers are **women**), one for Italian language and the humanities, the other for science and mathematics. Languages are now widely taught in primary schools, too, with English being the most common second language. Between 11 and 14 years of age, Italians study at *Scuola Media*, where they take a leaving examination to determine their fitness for moving on to the next level. Until 1997, it was possible to leave school once one had passed the *Scuola media* examination, but it is now obligatory to have completed at least one year of secondary studies before dropping out of school. All secondary education is free and is administered by the state, though private (usually religious) schools do exist alongside the state system.

Until recently, Italian secondary schools were divided into academic and professional schools. The most prestigious secondary schools were the preuniversity *licei* (like the French lycée or German Gymnasium). The 14-year-old could choose among the classical liceo, the scientific liceo, fine arts, the conservatory, the pedagogical liceo, and the liceo specializing in foreign languages. Those individuals who did not aim at university studies followed a separate track, concluding their education by studying at technical schools, industrial arts schools, the merchant marine academy, or secretarial and bookkeeping schools (*ragionerie*), although the possession of a diploma from these schools did not exclude pursuing a university career. Recent education reforms, however, have raised technical schools and the *ragionerie* to the status of the *licei*. The goal is to ensure that almost all young Italians are educated academically to 18 years of age.

The school curriculum and teaching methods remain strikingly traditional: The Gentile law, with its emphasis on the humanistic disciplines, still exerts an influence. Students have a very limited choice of electives, and at the traditional *licei* Latin and philosophy are core subjects for all students. Students who fail to achieve satisfactory standards in several subjects may be required to repeat a year, although this practice is much less common than it once was. The school-leaving examination (*maturità*) has oral and written components. Until the late 1990s judgments of candidates' readiness were made by a panel of eight, four from one's own high school and four outside evaluators from other Italian regions. A 1997 reform introduced by the center-left **Olive Tree coalition**/Ulivo all but abolished outside assessment, a move that is widely believed to have lowered academic standards. All students who pass the *maturità* are entitled to automatic entry to a university. *See also* UNIVERSITIES.

EINAUDI, LUIGI (1874–1961). A professor who became the first constitutionally elected president of the Italian Republic in 1948, Luigi Einaudi was the most prominent spokesman in Italy in the 20th century for economic liberalism and for a state whose role was strictly limited to what he called "the government of things." Born in Cuneo (Piedmont) in 1874, the young Einaudi divided his time between his duties as a professor of finance at the University of **Turin** and as editorialist for *La Stampa* and *Corriere della Sera*.

Like **Luigi Albertini**, his editor at the *Corriere della Sera*, Einaudi was an early opponent of **Fascism**. He spoke out against the violence and authoritarianism of **Benito Mussolini**'s movement even before the **March on Rome** and continued his criticisms after Mussolini had come to power. When Albertini was removed from the editorship of the *Corriere* in 1925, Einaudi's long collaboration with the paper also came to an end. There was no place at a Fascist newspaper for a writer who praised free markets and European unification and had signed the manifesto of antifascist intellectuals published by **Benedetto Croce** in 1925. In 1930, an academic review that Einaudi had edited since 1908, *Riforma sociale* (*Social Reform*), was also suppressed by the authorities. Einaudi was able to continue with his scholarly work, however. His key work on economics, *Principi della scienza delle finanze* (*Principles of the Science of Finances*), was published in 1932, and he also was able to write a series of studies on the classical economists.

After the fall of Mussolini in July 1943, Einaudi became rector of the University of Turin, but he was swiftly forced to flee to Switzerland to avoid capture by the Germans. Upon his return to Italy, he was made governor of the **Banca d'Italia**. He was elected to **Parliament** in June 1946 as a member of the **Partito Liberale Italiano/**Italian Liberal Party (PLI) and was soon given important economic responsibilities. In May 1947, Einaudi became budget minister and deputy prime minister in the first postwar government not to include the **Partito Comunista Italiano/**Italian Communist Party (PCI), and he introduced austerity policies that stabilized the plummeting lira. On 10 May 1948, he was elected **president of the Republic**. Einaudi served as president until 1955. He was an active scholar and writer up to his death in October 1961. His *Prediche inutili* (*Useless Sermons*)—reflections on the classical themes of political economy—appeared between 1955 and 1959. These "useless" sermons did not find much of an audience in 1950s Italy, where both the **Democrazia Cristiana/**Christian Democracy Party (DC) and the PCI were in the grip of dirigist economic philosophies, but Einaudi's insistence on limited but efficient government, and his lifelong attachment to the cause of a united Europe, have much more resonance in contemporary Italy. *See also* CARLI, GUIDO; EUROPEAN INTEGRATION; GOBETTI, PIERO.

ELECTORAL LAWS. When Italy was unified in 1861, it inherited the electoral laws of the Kingdom of Piedmont-Sardinia, which elected its **Parliament** through a dual ballot system of single-member constituencies. The Piedmontese system remained in force until 1882, when Italy moved to a plural-member constituency system in which, according to size, constituencies returned two to five deputies and the elector had as many votes as there were candidates to elect. This experiment failed, and a return to the former system took place in 1891, although the threshold for entering the second ballot was now reduced to one-sixth of the votes cast instead of the 30 percent required by the former law.

Universal male suffrage for men over 30 years of age was enacted in Italy in 1912. In 1919, **Francesco Saverio Nitti** introduced proportional representation, a move that allowed **Benito Mussolini**'s nascent Fascist party to gain a foothold in Parliament in 1921. Once in power, Mussolini introduced the "**Acerbo** Law" in 1923. Any party gaining a plurality in the popular vote was guaranteed two-thirds of the seats in Parliament. In 1928 a plebiscitary system was introduced whereby citizens were limited to voting yea or nay to an approved "big list" (*listone*) of approved candidates.

Fully free elections with universal suffrage were introduced in Italy in 1946. In 1953, the **Democrazia Cristiana**/Christian Democracy party (DC) tried to amend the system of proportional representation used in the elections of 1948 by introducing legislation (swiftly dubbed the "swindle law") that gave any coalition that obtained over 50 percent of the vote a substantial "prize" in seats. In the 1953 elections, however, the DC and its allies failed to reach the 50 percent threshold, and the law was never applied. Subsequently, Italy chose its representatives by proportional representation. For the Chamber of Deputies, election was by a convoluted form of the party-list system that guaranteed representation in Parliament to all but the very smallest formations and that awarded seats in strict proportion to the number of votes cast. The result was the fragmentation of the party system and the prevalence of unstable coalition governments. For the Senate, a different system of proportional representation granted greater representation to the larger parties but still meant that the upper chamber contained a plethora of miniparties. An interesting peculiarity of elections for the Italian Senate was—and is—that only adults over 25 years of age may vote.

In the 1980s, dissatisfaction with the electoral system gave birth to a popular movement for electoral reform and to successful **referendums** on electoral reform in June 1991 and April 1993. In the general elections of March 1994, April 1996, and May 2001, both the Chamber of Deputies and the Senate were elected by an electoral law that reserved 75 percent of the seats in both chambers for direct election in single-member constituencies and 25 percent of the seats for election by proportional representation. A German-style "threshold" excluded parties that obtained less than 4 percent of the vote from Parliament. This law worked less well than many expected. Instead of leading to the development of a two-party system on the British or American model, Italy now has a "two-alliance" system of parties (more akin to France's Fifth Republic) in which two broad-based coalitions of mostly small parties confront each other.

Italy returned to proportional representation for the general elections of April 2006, although the winning coalition in the Chamber of Deputies is entitled to a limited "majority prize" to encourage governability. *See also* DE GASPERI, ALCIDE; PANNELLA, MARCO; SEGNI, MARIO.

ENVIRONMENTALISM. As in most other European countries, concern about the quality of the environment began to emerge in Italy in the 1970s and early 1980s. Overbuilding in Italian coastal resorts, increasing pollution in lakes and rivers, the growing problem of smog in the cities, the nascent nuclear program, and a leak in 1976 of dioxin at a chemical plant at Seveso near **Milan** all contributed to an increased interest in environmental issues. Following the success of the German Green Party in the 1983 elections to the Bundestag, local Green associations successfully fielded lists of candidates in the two provinces closest to Germany, Trento and Bolzano, in 1983. In local elections held nationwide in 1985, local Green associations ran candidates in communal and provincial elections all over the country. To capitalize on this upsurge in interest, the "National Federation of Green Lists" was founded in November 1986, and in the 1987 general elections, the federation's symbol was on the ballot paper throughout the country. The federation won 2.5 percent of the vote and elected 13 deputies and two senators. In the fall of 1987, the Greens enjoyed a further triumph when Italians, alarmed by the Chernobyl disaster, voted in a national referendum to end Italy's nuclear power program.

The formation of a rival force, the Verdi arcobaleno ("Rainbow Greens"), which appealed to Greens worried that the environmentalist movement was fossilizing into a traditional political party, did not slow the growth of Green sympathies among the electorate. In the European elections in June 1989, the two lists together obtained over

6 percent of the vote, the apex of Green support in Italy. Although the two rival movements merged in 1990, the Verdi have struggled to maintain electoral support in the changed economic climate of the 1990s. Only 2.8 percent of the electorate voted for Green candidates in the general elections of 1992, a figure that was approximated in the two subsequent electoral tests. In April 1993, the former European commissioner for the environment, Carlo Ripa Di Meana, was appointed national spokesman for the Greens, and until December 1996, when he was deposed as party leader, he represented environmentalists within the **Olive Tree Coalition/**Ulivo. In recent years, the Greens have also made antiwar protest the core of their political platform, opposing, for instance, both the first and second Gulf wars, and in the 2006 elections they formed a common list with the Comunisti d'Italia/Communists of Italy (PdCI).

Unless there is another nuclear or industrial calamity, the Verdi seem destined to remain marginal in Italian political life. Green sentiment, however, has become deeply rooted in Italy. Other single-issue organizations such as the Lega Ambiente (Environmental League), Greenpeace, and the Antivivisection League all have substantial active memberships.

ETHIOPIA. Some 20 years after unification in 1861, Italian governments embarked on a program of imperial expansion. After France had blocked Italian ambitions in Tunisia, Italy made inroads on the Red Sea, occupying several cities in what was to become Eritrea. Between 1887 and 1889, the Italian government aimed at establishing a protectorate over neighboring Ethiopia, to which Britain agreed so long as Italy remained no less than 100 miles from the Nile and did not interfere with the flow of its water. When Menelik, Ethiopian King of Kings, gave France a railway concession in exchange for munitions and other supplies and renounced the 1889 Treaty of Uccialli (which, in the Italian reading, had given Italy a protectorate over Ethiopia), Italy declared war. Menelik's 100,000-strong force roundly defeated the badly led 25,000 advancing Italians at Adowa on 1 March 1896. The immediate consequence in Italy was a wave of popular strikes and protests that forced the government of **Francesco Crispi** to withdraw the army and to resign. In November 1896, Crispi's successor, **Antonio Di Rudinì**, signed a peace that left Italy with Eritrea but recognized the independence of Ethiopia.

Benito Mussolini took Italy's revenge nearly four decades later. After creating border incidents in the unmarked area between Italian Somaliland and Ethiopia, the Duce provoked a brief but bloody war of conquest, opening hostilities on 3 October 1935. Foreign military observers were impressed by the speed of Italy's victory over a territory larger than metropolitan France, its ruthless use of aircraft against civilians, and its use of gas against the poorly equipped Ethiopian army. In May 1936, Addis Ababa fell, and Emperor Haile Selassie fled the country, not to return until British forces recaptured Ethiopia in the course of **World War II**.

Mussolini's victory was also a diplomatic triumph. Playing on the imperial powers' fear of Germany, Mussolini was able to extract from the French a virtual blank check to do as he wished so long as no French colonies were threatened and from the British a policy in the League of Nations of avoiding sanctions that might antagonize the Italian government. The League's threats regarding oil shipments and scrap iron sales did nothing to impede Italian acquisition of those war goods in trade with non-League members, including—conspicuously—the United States. Moreover, League threats enabled Mussolini to portray Italy to the Italian public as the struggling "proletarian" nation facing alone the hostility of the plutocratic European powers.

The conquest of Ethiopia, added to Eritrea (after the war, incorporated in newly independent Ethiopia) and Somaliland, created Italian East Africa, thereby enabling Mussolini to confer on King Victor Emmanuel the title of emperor and to make **Pietro Badoglio** viceroy. For many, the conquest was proof of Mussolini's boast that **Fascism** would show the world that Italy could be a nation of warriors. Subsequent failures in Greece and North Africa in 1940–1941 would prove that such hopes had no military basis. *See also* FOREIGN POLICY; HOARE-LAVAL PACT.

EUROPEAN INTEGRATION. Italians have been numbered among the most vocal supporters of European unification since after 1918, with scholars like **Luigi Einaudi** and the industrialist Giovanni Agnelli being early supporters. Resistance to the nationalist doctrine of **Fascism** was tinged from the start with a belief in the necessity for a federal reorganization of Europe. One of the earliest appeals for a federal European state — the so-called *Manifesto of Ventotene* — was drawn up in 1941 by the antifascist intellectuals Ernesto Rossi and **Altiero Spinelli**. Catholics, in part from idealism, in part from fear of communism, also backed the idea of European unity.

In the 1950s, **Alcide De Gasperi** made European integration one of the core elements of his **foreign policy** and led Italy into the European Coal and Steel Community (ECSC) in 1952. The negotiations that led to the creation of the European Economic Community (EEC), or "Common Market," were begun in Messina in **Sicily** and became law in the Treaty of **Rome** (1958) with the signatures of the governments of France, Italy, West Germany, Belgium, the Netherlands, and Luxembourg. Participation in the EEC brought Italy substantial commercial benefits and was a major factor in the surge of economic growth in 1958–1963 known as the **economic miracle**.

Italy has never quite punched its weight in the European Community (EC) and then the European Union (EU), although it has subscribed to every attempt to expand the powers of "federal" institutions, such as the European Parliament and Commission, at the expense of national sovereignty. In 1987, for instance, dissatisfied with the institutional provisions of the 1986 Single European Act (SEA), Italy symbolically refused to sign the treaty together with the other member states, but waited until a referendum in Denmark had confirmed the treaty.

Some critics argue, however, that Italy's commitment to European unification is in reality somewhat less enthusiastic than its rhetoric suggests. Italy was among the slowest of all member states to implement the single market in goods and services required by the SEA, and even today certain industries and services, notably banking, enjoy a degree of informal protection from European rivals. Italy's state bureaucracy has also failed to exploit the opportunities for growth and industrial development offered by the various European funds for social and economic modernization. Finally, Italy's ability to enforce **immigration** controls required by the Schengen agreements (March 1995) has been called into question, especially by the German government. These agreements eliminate passport and other customs controls at EU borders for EU nationals. Italy's long coastlines, however, offer easy access for clandestine immigrants, who can then move at will to other EU nations. For this reason, Italy only implemented the accords in October 1997.

It is fair to say, however, that the process of European unification has compelled Italy's political parties to adopt deregulating, comptition-inducing policies that they might otherwise not have followed. The privatizations, pension reforms, and austerity policies followed by the governments of **Lamberto Dini** and **Romano Prodi** in the mid-1990s might never have been introduced had there not been the *vincolo esterno* ("external constraint") of the need to participate in European monetary union. A Europe-wide poll taken by the European Commission in May 1997 showed that fully 73 percent of Italians favored the introduction of the European single **currency**, the euro, regardless of the sacrifices entailed.

Nevertheless, it is true that public opinion has cooled toward European integration since 2000. The 2001–2006 government of **Silvio Berlusconi** was, by Italian standards, skeptical of the benefits of the EU. Especially among right-wing voters, enthusiasm for European integration is currently at a postwar low. *See also* ANDREOTTI, GIULIO; BANCA D'ITALIA; ECONOMY; OLIVE TREE COALITION.

EUROPEAN UNION. *See* EUROPEAN INTEGRATION.

— F —

FACTA, LUIGI (1861–1930). Italy's last liberal prime minister, Facta's two administrations in 1922 were the culmination of the lengthy and inexorable decline of liberal institutions in Italy. Facta, who had been minister for justice from January to June 1919 under **Vittorio Emanuele Orlando**, was a supporter of **Giovanni Giolitti**. When, following the resignation of **Ivanoe Bonomi** in February 1922, the **Partito Popolare Italiano**/Italian People's Party (PPI) vetoed Giolitti's nomination by the king, Facta emerged as a compromise candidate for the premiership. After the longest government crisis since 1848, Facta assembled a cabinet that gave three key ministries (finance, education, and agriculture) to the PPI. Six different parties or factions participated in the government, which was approved by **Parliament** on 18 March 1922, with the support of even the **Partito Nazionale Fascista/**National Fascist Party (PNF).

Facta's first administration was characterized by huge Fascist rallies in northern Italy and by unchecked Fascist violence against socialists, **trade unions**, and the PPI. On 10 June 1922, Facta feebly promised the Senate that he would overcome the crisis by applying the law "impartially." The absence of any threat to crack down on Fascist *squadrismo* encouraged the worst violence yet in July–August 1922. Facta's government collapsed in midmonth after Fascist squads devastated the headquarters of the **Partito Socialista Italiano/**Italian Socialist Party (PSI) and PPI in Cremona (Lombardy) and raided the homes of two PPI trade union leaders, Guido Miglioli and Giuseppe Garibotti. In his resignation speech, Facta denied that exceptional measures were needed and blamed local authorities for not enforcing the law. Facta formed a second, almost identical, government on 1 August 1922, promising to restore the "empire of the law." Within days, the Fascists had occupied the city hall in **Milan**, destroyed the offices of *Avanti!*, and started bloody riots in other northern Italian cities. No action was taken to punish these breaches of the law. Further unpunished acts of violence were recorded throughout the country in September and October. Facta again resigned on 27 October 1922, the day of the **March on Rome**, which the central government did not in any serious way oppose. Facta asked the king for emergency powers to repress the Fascist coup. The king refused and appointed **Benito Mussolini** as premier.

How far was Facta culpable for the collapse of parliamentary democracy in Italy? In his defense, it should be said that Italian liberal opinion was demoralized; nothing could have been done to stop the Fascists without giving carte blanche to the PSI, which refused to undertake a permanent commitment to parliamentary democracy. Local **police** authorities under the command of prefects appointed in Rome could have done much more to ensure respect for the law. While all these points are true, an act of will on the part of Facta and his political sponsor, Giolitti, could have saved Italian democracy. As the Fascist writer **Curzio Malaparte** pointed out, the crucial difference between the liberals and the Fascists was that the Fascists were prepared to use violence in pursuit of their ends and the liberals were not. Facta died in his native Pinerolo (Piedmont) in 1930. *See also* FASCISM.

FALCONE, GIOVANNI (1939–1992). The symbol of the Italian state's struggle against the **mafia**, Giovanni Falcone was brutally murdered in a bomb attack on 23 May 1992. He had rapidly risen to national prominence as an assistant district attorney in his native **Palermo**, where he was first the right-hand man of a heroic anti-mafia prosecutor, Rocco Chinnici (murdered by *Cosa Nostra* in 1983), and then, between 1984 and 1987, the lead prosecutor in the huge trial of Michele "the pope" Greco (the boss of the Sicilian mafia) and dozens of other gangsters. Falcone was the first prosecutor to breach the *omertà* (code of silence) that the mafia imposed upon its affiliates, by persuading a senior figure in the underworld, Tommaso Buscetta, to reveal all he knew of the organization's internal workings. In the 1990s, Buscetta was a key witness in the Italian state's investigation into former prime minister **Giulio Andreotti**'s alleged links to organized crime.

In the late 1980s, the efforts of Falcone and his antimafia "pool" of prosecutors in Palermo were hampered by the judicial and political hierarchies in Palermo. Falcone (who survived a bomb attack in June 1989) decided that he could continue the fight against the mafia better from Rome, and, in 1991, with the encouragement of the justice minister, Claudio Martelli, he created the Direzione Nazionale Antimafia/National Antimafia Agency (DNA), a top-level, FBI-style task force that coordinates action against organized crime. Judicial politics prevented Falcone from becoming the first chief of this organization (the post went, instead, to another courageous prosecutor, Agostino Cordova), but the creation of the DNA was the decisive step in the struggle against organized crime. Literally hundreds of gangsters, including the boss of bosses, Toto Riina, have been arrested since 1991. This victory for legality is Falcone's legacy.

Falcone was murdered while traveling between Palermo airport and the city center, by a buried bomb set off by remote control. It blew a huge crater in the highway, killing his wife, Franca, and three bodyguards, as well as Judge Falcone. The grief and rage that were felt throughout Italy at his death had profound political implications, leading directly to the election of **Oscar Luigi Scalfaro** as **president of the Republic** and stimulating growing public frustration with a political system that had for years tolerated and even collaborated

with the bosses of *Cosa Nostra. See also* DEMOCRAZIA CRIS-
TIANA (DC); MANI PULITE; ORLANDO, LEOLUCA; SICILY.

FALLACI, ORIANA (1929–2006). Born in **Florence**, Oriana Fallaci
was one of the few journalists and contemporary political commentators to make the language leap and reach a genuinely international
audience. She was briefly a partisan during **World War II** and, after
training as a journalist in the 1950s, became a war correspondent,
covering events in Latin America, Vietnam, and elsewhere. She was
shot by the Mexican armed forces in 1968 when she was covering the
student disturbances in that country. She was a regular writer for the
Italian magazines *Epoca* and *Europeo* and also for prestigious American publications such as the *New Yorker*. Her books have been translated into many foreign languages and published all over the world.

In the 1970s, especially, Fallaci won a reputation for interviewing
the world's leading politicians. Henry Kissinger, Indira Gandhi, Lech
Walesa, Willy Brandt, and Yassir Arafat are just some of her inter-
viewees. Some of her interviews themselves made history. Kissinger
admitted that the Vietnam War had been a mistake in an interview
with her; Portuguese communist leader Alvaro Cunhal expressed less
than enthusiasm for democracy in an interview with her and greatly
weakened his party's position prior to the crucial 1975 elections.

In recent years, Fallaci became controversial for her outspoken
(and in the opinion of many) racist views on Arabs and Islam. Her
book *La Rabbia e l'orgoglio* (*The Rage and the Pride*, 2001), written
after 9/11, aroused widespread condemnation and several lawsuits for
its offensive material. The book was loved by right-wing parties such
as the **Lega Nord/**Northern League (LN) and was a huge best-seller
in Italy. Fallaci died in Florence in September 2006. *See also* PRESS.

FANFANI, AMINTORE (1908–1999). Born in Arezzo (Tuscany),
Fanfani was a boyhood founder of his hometown's branch of **Azione
Cattolica**. After serving in the army in **World War I**, he attended
Milan's Catholic University of the Sacred Heart in the 1920s, taking
his research degree in economics in 1932. He joined the **Partito
Nazionale Fascista/**National Fascist Party (PNF) in 1933, then
Catholic University's faculty, where he served until 1955, when he
was appointed to the University of **Rome**, a position he held until

1983. As an economist, he wrote the standard textbook for Italian secondary schools on fascist **corporatism**.

Fanfani shifted adroitly to the political center during the war. He became a member of the inner circle of the **Democrazia Cristiana/** Christian Democracy Party (DC) in 1946, when he was chosen to serve on the steering committee of the party and was elected to the **Constituent Assembly** in 1946. He served under **Alcide De Gasperi** and **Giuseppe Pella** between 1948 and 1953 as minister for agriculture and minister for the interior. Finally, after an unsuccessful attempt at forming his own government, he was chosen party secretary in July 1954. In that post, he quickly showed himself able to match the organizational and technical skills of the **Partito Comunista Italiano/**Italian Communist Party (PCI). Younger Parliament members anxious to ride on his coattails were dubbed, in the press, *Fanfaniani*. His faction within the DC, Iniziativa democratica (Democratic Initiative) was a major force until its rise was checked by the emergence of the *Dorotei*, a center-right faction within the DC alarmed by Fanfani's dynamism who preferred the more cautious talents of **Aldo Moro**.

In the 1950s and 1960s, Fanfani was a statesman of genuine international standing. For instance, he was one of the few European statesman singled out for high praise by Charles de Gaulle in his memoirs (having played an active mediating role in the 1961–1962 argument between De Gaulle and the rest of the European Community over the desirability of creating a "Union of States" with powers over foreign and defense policy). He was prime minister three times between July 1958 and May 1963 and was the strongest exponent of the **opening to the left**, which would bring the **Partito Socialista Italiano/**Italian Socialist Party (PSI) into the government. In June 1961, he discussed the question of bringing the PSI into the government with the newly elected John F. Kennedy; without the acquiescence of the U.S. government this move would not have been taken. More generally, he backed a modernizing agenda of economic and social reforms. Fanfani and the DC were heavily defeated in the 1963 elections, however, and he was replaced by his rival, Moro. He was compensated by becoming foreign minister and, in 1965, president of the United Nations General Assembly.

In 1968, he was elected to the Senate and in 1972 was made senator for life. He again served as party secretary between 1973 and 1976; in the latter year, he was elected to preside over the Senate. One might have expected Fanfani's career to terminate here, but, in fact, he continued to take an active part in politics almost until the 1990s. In 1974, he led the attempt by Catholic conservatives to overturn the law on **divorce**, warning the Italians—in lurid terms—that sexual morality would be undermined if the institution of marriage were threatened. Following President **Giovanni Leone**'s resignation in June 1978, Fanfani served as **president of the Republic** pro tempore for three weeks. In both 1982 and 1987, he formed stop-gap governments during moments of political crisis in the parliamentary majority. Fanfani, in short, did not shirk responsibility. His last government office, at the age of 80, was as budget minister in the turbulent administration led by **Ciriaco De Mita** (April 1988 to July 1989). Fanfani died in Rome in November 1999. *See also* EUROPEAN INTEGRATION; NENNI, PIETRO; REFERENDUMS.

FARINACCI, ROBERTO (1892–1945). Before **World War I**, Farinacci was a railway worker and prominent labor boss in the Lombardy town of Cremona. A street-fighter called by a British historian "one of the more illiterate and brutish of the hierarchy," he was rooted in the original revolutionary syndicalist left of the early Fascist movement and was one of the first members of the **Partito Nazionale Fascista**/National Fascist Party (PNF). Farinacci consistently preferred antibourgeois, antiestablishment rhetoric and violence so long as it was performed by the PNF. Farinacci's reliance on violence is illustrated by two episodes. During the punitive expedition against **Milan**'s socialists on 3–4 August 1922, Farinacci not only broke up the presses of *Avanti!* but also evicted the socialist city government, having **Gabriele D'Annunzio** himself address the crowd from the city hall. Similarly, when the acting Italian high commissioners—appointed by the government in **Rome** to woo the newly absorbed German-speaking population of Alto Adige—pursued policies calculated to that end, Farinacci and allied nationalists rejected this "weak" approach. Under Farinacci's direction, squads forcefully seized local government offices in Alto Adige.

Farinacci was also corrupt. With a fraudulent university degree in law (he had attended few lectures and allegedly submitted another's dissertation), he actually began offering his "legal" services as an "insider" influence peddler. He nevertheless acted as defense counsel for the Fascist thugs accused after the murder of **Giacomo Matteotti** and burnished his image with hard-line Fascists by doing so.

Farinacci sided neither with **Benito Mussolini** nor with the 19 rebels who deposed the Duce at the fateful meeting of the **Fascist Grand Council** on 25 June 1943. He was nevertheless consistent in his loyalty to the Duce. Farinacci was captured and executed by partisans at Vinercate, near Milan, on 28 April 1945. *See also* FAS-CISM; *SQUADRISMO*.

FASCISM. Contemporary Italian history is dominated by the Fascist *ventennio* (20-year period), when **Benito Mussolini** led a dictatorship characterized by single-party rule, a pervasive, would-be totalitarian state, a cult of violence and war, and military adventurism.

The Fascist period can usefully be divided into five phases. The first phase was the creation of the movement. Italian Fascism was born on 23 March 1919, at a meeting in Piazza di San Sepolcro, Milan, when Mussolini launched the Fasci Italiani di combattimento/ Italian Combat Leagues, which became the **Partito Nazionale Fascista**/National Fascist Party (PNF) in 1921. In this first phase, Italian Fascism appealed largely to veterans angry with the corruption and indecision of Italy's traditional elites. The movement's first platform, written by Mussolini himself, was a blend of socialism and nationalism. It seemingly had little electoral appeal. In the elections of November 1919, Mussolini personally obtained less than 5,000 votes, while the **Partito Socialista Italiano**/Italian Socialist Party (PSI) and the Catholic **Partito Popolare Italiano**/Italian Popular Party (PPI) attracted mass followings. The poet **Gabriele D'Annunzio**, who had seized the contested Adriatic city of **Fiume** with a private army, seemed a more likely authoritarian leader than Mussolini in 1920.

Fascism gained strength between 1920 and 1922 because it became the means by which the PSI's growing power was smashed, especially in the agricultural areas of the Po River valley, Tuscany, and

Apulia. Fascist squads, headed by local warlords or *Ras*, at Mussolini's instigation waged war against organized labor and the political left. PSI newspapers, offices, and cultural organizations were raided and burned; strikes were broken by strong-arm tactics. Hundreds of people were killed and thousands were savagely beaten or were humiliated by being given a strong dose of castor oil. Rather than repress the Fascists, however, **Giovanni Giolitti** sought to co-opt Mussolini by including the PNF in the **blocco nazionale** during the May 1921 general elections. Neither Giolitti nor his successors, **Ivanoe Bonomi** and **Luigi Facta**, were prepared to use the full weight of the state against the squads. By the spring of 1922, Fascist squads were taking part in "punitive raids" against entire cities (**Bologna**, Cremona, Ferrara) to chase out their elected governments and install temporary reigns of terror.

In October 1922, when King **Victor Emmanuel III** made Mussolini premier rather than risk a conflict with the Fascists who had marched on **Rome**, co-option was taken to a new level. Mussolini consolidated his hold on power by passing the **Acerbo** law, but only moved decisively against the political opposition after the kidnapping and murder of **Giacomo Matteotti** in June 1924. For six months, the democratic opposition boycotted **Parliament**, until Mussolini's leading *Ras* warned him to take action or risk a rebellion in their ranks. On 3 January 1925, Mussolini took responsibility for the killing and began the process of dismantling the liberal state.

Italy under Fascism was a dictatorship, but, despite the fact Mussolini invented the word "totalitarian," Mussolini's rule was not absolute. Theoretically, there was to be no pluralism but rather a single party. The state, the **economy**, and the society were to be bureaucratically, hierarchically, and totally organized, integrating all activities —whether in religion, commerce, arts, leisure hours, or the breeding of children—in subordination to the party-state. The slogan "tutto nello Stato, niente senza lo Stato, tutto per lo Stato" (everything within the State, nothing without the State, everything for the State) illustrated the goal. In fact, there were conspicuous areas of national life in which the intrusion of the state was relatively limited. The **monarchy**, big business, and, above all, the Church all retained considerable autonomy. By contrast, manual workers were robbed of independent **trade unions**; young people were militarized from the earliest age in the *Balilla* and the *Avanguardisti*; and ordinary citizens spent their leisure in social, sporting, and cultural activities organized by the Istituto nazionale del dopolavoro. Professional advancement, especially as a civil servant, was impossible without PNF membership. Intellectual life was rigidly monitored. University professors were asked to pledge their faith to Mussolini (almost all did), and unauthorized political or cultural activity was sternly punished.

Nevertheless, Mussolini's hold on power did not rely on repression and propaganda alone. Both in Italy and abroad, Fascism evoked widespread admiration for its achievements. The launching of great ocean liners (the *Rex* and the *Conte di Savoia*), the more vaunted than real improvement in the punctuality of the rail network, the exploits of **Italo Balbo** and his fellow aviators, the draining of the Italian marshlands, and the athletic triumphs of the boxer **Primo Carnera** and the Italian national soccer team all added to Italy's self-esteem. More important, Fascism was widely perceived as having created, in **corporatism**, an imaginative structure for dealing with the industrial turmoil sweeping the world.

From the early 1930s onward, Mussolini strove to radicalize the regime. Such practices as giving the Fascist salute instead of shaking hands, using the "virile" *voi* (second person plural) instead of the apparently effete *lei*, and marching with the *passo Romano* (goosestep) were introduced. By the mid-1930s, Mussolini was both a competitor and a reluctant admirer of what Adolf Hitler was achieving in Nazi Germany. **Racial laws** against the Jews were introduced in 1938; before then, Fascism had not been especially discriminatory toward Italy's highly integrated Jewish community, and, indeed, many Jews had actually been active Fascists.

Claiming that war, for men, was like childbirth for **women**, Mussolini launched a war of conquest against **Ethiopia** in 1935 and sent a large expeditionary force to assist Francisco Franco's military revolt in Spain. Such actions brought him closer to Hitler. In October 1936, the **Rome-Berlin Axis** was signed; in May 1939, the Axis became the Pact of Steel. Italy did not join the war until June 1940, however, when France was beaten and Great Britain was on the ropes. Italy conducted a strikingly unsuccessful **parallel war** against Britain in North Africa and against Greece. In both cases, Italy had to be rescued by German arms after huge losses.

Fascism's wartime losses were what brought the system down. After the invasion of Italian territory in July 1943, the **Fascist Grand Council** voted on 25 July 1943, to deprive Mussolini of command of the war effort. After Mussolini's fall, Italy was divided between invading Allied and Nazi armies, with Mussolini heading the puppet **Republic of Salò** in northern Italy. The *ventennio* was over, although it left political scars that smart to this day. *See also* ACCADEMIA D'ITALIA; AVENTINE SECESSION; COMITATI DI LIBERAZIONE NAZIONALE (CLN); CROCE, BENEDETTO; FARINACCI, ROBERTO; FEDERZONI, LUIGI; FOREIGN POLICY; GENTILE, GIOVANNI; GRANDI, DINO; ISTITUTO PER LA RICOSTRUZIONE INDUSTRIALE (IRI); LATERAN PACTS; MARCH ON ROME; MOVIMENTO SOCIALE ITALIANO (MSI); QUADRUMVIRATE; PAPACY; RESISTANCE; ROCCO, ALFREDO; SPANISH CIVIL WAR; *SQUADRISMO;* STARACE, ACHILLE; WORLD WAR I; WORLD WAR II; YOUTH MOVEMENTS, FASCIST.

FASCIST GRAND COUNCIL. The law instituting the Gran Consiglio del Fascismo on 28 December 1928, intended it to be "the supreme organ entrusted with the prescription and coordination" of the regime's activities. The head of government (i.e., **Benito Mussolini**) was, by right, the president of the Grand Council, making this law the final step in the creation of his personal dictatorship. The normal prerogatives of a chairman, that is to say, setting the agenda and convening meetings, were spelled out in the law, a fact that makes clear the intention to leave all initiatives in the hands of the Duce. He could designate the secretary of the **Partito Nazionale Fascista/** National Fascist Party (PNF), already the secretary of the Grand Council, as his surrogate, but the initiative lay with the head of government.

Automatic membership fell to the members of the **Quadrumvirate**, to former secretaries of the PNF, and to those cabinet members who had been members of the government for the entire three years since the Fascist "revolution." Additional members pro tempore included the presidents of each house of Parliament and of the Chamber of Corporations (after the corporate system displaced the parliamentary houses); current cabinet officers; the general in command of the militia; the members of the PNF executive committee; and the presidents of the **Accademia d'Italia**, of the Fascist Institute for Culture, of the Special Tribunal for crimes against the state, and of the Confederazione Italiana Sindacati Nazionali Lavoratori/Italian Confederation of National Workers' Unions (CISNAL). The party apparently had absorbed the state.

Structural or constitutional changes were put within the purview of the Grand Council, but no such changes were introduced until the regime's end, brought about when Mussolini agreed to call a meeting of the Council on the afternoon of 24 June 1943. It was the first meeting of the Council to be held since December 1939; not even when Mussolini assumed the command of the country's armed forces in 1940 did a meeting take place. There, **Dino Grandi** advanced a motion to restore power to conduct the war to the throne; it was carried by a 19 to 7 majority with one abstention. Those in favor included **Giacomo Acerbo**, **Galeazzo Ciano**, **Giuseppe Bottai**, and **Luigi Federzoni**, as well as **Emilio De Bono** and **Cesare De Vecchi**, both members of the **Quadrumvirate**. This action enabled King **Victor Emmanuel III** to have Mussolini arrested and put into "protective custody." *See also* FASCISM.

FEDERAZIONE UNIVERSITARIA CATTOLICI ITALIANA/ Catholic University Graduates' Movement of Italy (FUCI). Organized in 1896 as a part of **Azione Cattolica**/Catholic Action (ACI), FUCI provided a useful link between the nascent Christian democracy movement and university students. This necessarily drew them close, in political inspiration, to **Luigi Sturzo** and **Romolo Murri**. The autonomy of the *fucini*, most of whom were liberal Catholics, brought them into conflict with the more staid ACI, which was virtually an instrument of the **Vatican**. The close association with the **Partito Popolare Italiano**/Italian People's Party (PPI) brought FUCI under close scrutiny by the Fascist authorities after 1922 and led to its eventual dissolution in 1931. After reorganization (between 1935 and 1939) under the leadership of Giovanni Battista Montini (later Pope Paul VI) and such prominent laymen as **Aldo Moro** and **Giulio Andreotti**, FUCI became once again an assembly of liberal Catholics and a training ground for many of the political leaders of postwar Italy.

A special section of FUCI was organized in 1934, the university degree-holders' federation—FUCI laureati (the *laurea* is the Italian university degree). They published a weekly magazine called *Azione Fucina* and, beginning in 1935, an intellectual review called *Studium*. To many in the regime, it was clear that *fucini* were engaged in little less than the preparation of a new elite to incorporate Catholic social doctrine into a new political order at the propitious moment, despite their outward conformity to regime requirements. *See also* CATHOLICISM; EDUCATION; FLORENCE; GONELLA, GUIDO.

FEDERZONI, LUIGI (1878–1967). Born in **Bologna**, Federzoni became the leader of the Italian nationalist association in 1910, which campaigned for Italian colonial expansion. Together with **Enrico Corradini**, in 1911 Federzoni founded the influential weekly *L'idea nazionale*, in which he published a famous attack on freemasonry in April 1913.

Federzoni became a parliamentary deputy in 1913 but nevertheless enrolled in the armed forces in 1915. In 1922 he became minister for the colonies in **Benito Mussolini's** first government. Following the disappearance of **Giacomo Matteotti** in June 1924, Federzoni was one of four ministers who resigned from Mussolini's government, publicly requesting that the Fascist leader seek "national conciliation." A few days later, however, Mussolini made Federzoni minister for the interior, a post that he was forced to resign in 1926 after public criticism following two attempts on Mussolini's life, which made his position untenable. He was minister for the colonies once more until 1929.

Federzoni held several prestigious offices in the 1930s. He was president of the Senate from 1929 until 1939, editor of the Fascist literary periodical *Nuova antologia*, and, from 1938, the president of the **Accademia d'Italia**. A member of the **Fascist Grand Council**, he was one of 19 Fascist leaders who signed the motion put by **Dino Grandi** asking King **Victor Emmanuel III** to resume his powers, thus isolating Mussolini who, on the same afternoon (25 July 1943), was put into "protective custody" by order of the king and, after provisional imprisonments, was incarcerated on Gran Sasso in the Abruzzi mountains. After the ex-Duce was liberated (12 September) by German commandos and established in the northern city of **Salò**, a half-dozen of the Grandi motion signers were tried for treason, Federzoni among them. He was condemned to death but managed to flee to Portugal. For his role in **Fascism**'s rise he was sentenced to life imprisonment after liberation in 1945 but was amnestied, and after a period of exile in Portugal and Brazil, he returned to Italy. He spent the last two decades of his life peacefully writing his memoirs. He died in **Rome** in 1967.

FELLINI, FEDERICO (1920–1993). Born in the provincial seaside town of Rimini, Federico Fellini began his career in the cinema as a writer for popular comedians in the 1940s. His first solo film was *Lo sceicco bianco* (*The White Sheik*, 1953), which was followed by *I vitelloni* (*The Spivs*, 1953). This latter film won the Silver Lion at **Venice** and affirmed Fellini's critical reputation. His next film, however, established Fellini as one of the best directors in the world. *La Strada* (*The Road*, 1954), which starred Fellini's wife, Giulietta Masina, is a film of almost unbearable pathos. It is the story of a simple peasant girl called Gelsomina (Masina) who is sold to a circus strongman called Zampanò (Anthony Quinn). Zampanò's brutish behavior drives Gelsomina to her death, at which point Zampanò realizes the extent of his attachment for her. He realizes, in short, what it is to be fully human. Too poetic for Italy's neorealist critics, the film won more than 50 awards, including the Silver Lion and the Oscar for best foreign picture.

La Strada was the beginning of Fellini's creative peak. Over the next eight years he enjoyed an astonishing burst of sustained creativity. *La notti di Cabiria* (*The Nights of Cabiria*, 1956), a touching film about a prostitute, was followed by *La dolce vita* (*The High Life*, 1959), which was both an ironic comment on high life during the Italian **economic miracle** and, more deeply, a meditation on how human beings should live. *Otto e mezzo* (*Eight and a Half*, 1962) is an equally complex film about a film director wrestling with his conscience. The latter two films provided Marcello Mastroianni with two of his greatest roles.

It is widely agreed that Fellini's work fell off after the early 1960s. His films became uneven, repetitive, and overly grotesque, although this does not mean that they are unrelieved failures. The surreal brilliance of the ecclesiastical fashion show, complete with roller-skating priests, saves the otherwise somewhat episodic *Fellini's Roma*

(1972). The autobiographical and profoundly touching *Amarcord* (1973) won the Oscar for best foreign picture. Fellini's death in November 1993 was marked by national mourning: Hundreds of thousands of people lined the streets of **Rome** to pay their last respects to the most poetic Italian artist of any genre in the postwar years. *See also* CINEMA.

FERMI, ENRICO (1901–1954). One of the finest theoretical physicists of the last century, Enrico Fermi was one of the fathers of the atomic bomb and a pioneer in the field of nuclear fission. Fermi was born in **Rome** and was educated at the universities of Pisa and Göttingen. In 1926, when he was still in his midtwenties, he returned to Italy to become professor of theoretical physics at the University of Rome. Initially, Fermi cooperated with the Fascist regime, accepting membership in the **Accademia d'Italia**. In 1938, Fermi was awarded the Nobel Prize in recognition of the lasting importance of his work in atomic structure and the nature of radioactivity. **Benito Mussolini**'s increasingly pro-Nazi policies had long been causing Fermi, whose wife was Jewish, great anguish and—after receiving the prize in Stockholm—he fled to the United States.

In 1942, he was one of the group of scientists at the University of Chicago who produced the first controlled nuclear chain reaction. In the closing years of the war, he worked on Project Manhattan and played a crucial role in ensuring that the Allies, rather than Nazi Germany, won the race to build nuclear weapons. After the war, Fermi returned to the University of Chicago to pursue his research on the behavior of neutrons. He died in Chicago in 1954. The chemical element Fermium (Fm), which is produced artificially in thermonuclear explosions, was named in his honor. *See also* RACIAL LAWS.

FERRARI, ENZO (1898–1988). The founder of the world-famous sports car and motor racing firm, Enzo Ferrara was born in Modena (Emilia-Romagna). After only limited schooling and service in the army during **World War I**, Ferrari began racing in the 1920s and enjoyed a successful career at the national level. In 1929, he opened *La Scuderia Ferrari* (Team Ferrari), with the sponsorship of the local textile industry. Over the next 20 years, some of the greatest drivers of the age, including Tazio Nuvolari, drove for the *cavallino* *rampante* (the prancing horse that is the symbol of all Ferrari cars). In 1947, Ferrari constructed his first Grand Prix car (previously, he had used Alfa Romeos); in 1951, a Ferrari won the British Grand Prix—the first of more than 500 victories that make Ferrari the most successful of all racing teams. In 1952 and 1953, Ferrari driver Alberto Ascari became world champion—the first of eight such championships during Ferrari's lifetime.

In the 1950s, Ferrari began making sports cars for road use. The Ferrari *Gran Turismo*, inspired by the famous Pininfarina car design company, is one of the most cherished cars ever to take the road. Ferrari cars dominated at Le Mans and at other distance races throughout the 1960s. The firm needed extra capital to maintain its competitiveness, however. In 1969, Ferrari sold 50 percent of the firm to **FIAT**, which became majority stakeholder after his death. In the mid-1970s, led by the Austrian driver Niki Lauda, Ferrari won the world championship three times in succession, but then a long drought set in as British teams (McClaren, Williams) using French and Japanese engines (Renault, Honda) came to dominate world motor racing. Ferrari returned to a dominant position only a decade after its founder's death in August 1988.

FIAT. The Fabbrica Italiana Automobili Torino is one of the world's largest producers of motor vehicles. Founded in 1899 by Giovanni Agnelli and an off-beat aristocratic inventor, Count Emmanuele Bricherasio di Cacherano, the nascent Italian auto industry rapidly achieved a reputation for making "horseless carriages" of high quality. Agnelli survived two trials, in which he was accused of fraud and ramping FIAT's share price, to emerge as the undisputed owner of the company by 1911, the year in which his close friend and political patron, **Giovanni Giolitti**, made him *cavaliere al merito di lavoro* (an award for businessmen similar to a British knighthood).

World War I was a bonanza for FIAT, which became the main supplier of vehicles and airplanes to the Italian army and also diversified into the manufacture of machine guns. By 1918, FIAT had become Italy's third-largest industrial concern. By the early 1920s, even visiting Americans recognized that FIAT's **Turin** car plant was among the most technologically advanced in the world.

Agnelli was one of the first people in Italy to recognize **Benito Mussolini**'s rising star, and he helped to finance Mussolini's newspaper *Popolo d'Italia* during the war. In 1923, Mussolini appointed Agnelli to the Senate. But FIAT's relations with the regime were never especially warm. Agnelli only joined the **Partito Nazionale Fascista/**National Fascist Party (PNF) in 1932. Nevertheless, FIAT's sales continued to grow in the 1930s and 1940s largely because of orders of military equipment from the Italian and German governments. When Agnelli died on 16 December 1945, he left a fortune estimated at $1 billion 1945 U.S. dollars.

Agnelli was succeeded as head of FIAT by Vittorio Valletta, a diminutive professor of banking who built the Turin carmaker into a global giant. Under Valletta's stewardship, FIAT mass-produced the cheap minicars (especially the FIAT 600 and FIAT 500) that came to symbolize the **economic miracle**. Owning a car had been a novelty in prewar Italy. By 1966, when Valletta stepped down, Italy had some of the most congested roads in the world, and FIAT was the world's fifth largest manufacturer of motor vehicles, deriving the maximum benefit possible from its protection of its domestic market.

Valletta's place was taken by Giovanni Agnelli's grandson, Gianni. Born in 1921, Gianni had served in the Italian army on the Russian front. After his grandfather's death he became one of the world's most notorious playboys. Agnelli proved unable to cope with the oil crisis and the degeneration of labor relations in Italy, and by the mid-1970s the company was in a potentially terminal crisis. The appointment in 1979 of a tough professional manager, Cesare Romiti, to run FIAT's day-to-day operations, while Agnelli concentrated on lobbying and strategic policy, arguably put the company back on track. In October 1980, Romiti announced thousands of layoffs and then sat out the inevitable strike until the **trade unions** caved in.

Shortly afterward, the company produced the award-winning FIAT Uno, which quickly became Europe's best-selling car, and car manufacturing once more became a cash cow for the group as a whole. In 1986, the company ruthlessly exploited its political connections to ensure that Ford did not buy the luxury Alfa Romeo from the Italian state's **Istituto per la Ricostruzione Industriale/**Institute for Industrial Reconstruction (IRI). Instead, just as FIAT had acquired Lancia, it soon added Alfa Romeo to its product line, then Ferrari. Aircraft, buses, trucks of all sizes (marketed as Iveco), and robotics completed the offerings of this multinational giant.

Despite a severe financial crisis in the first years of this century, which caused FIAT to be the subject of repeated takeover rumors, the company is still one of Europe's largest automakers and one of Italy's largest employers, providing tens of thousands of well-paid manual jobs both in Turin and **southern Italy**. Market share in Italy, which had plummeted from the 60 percent or more that the group enjoyed as late as the 1980s, has stabilized at just over 30 percent. Joint enterprises in Eastern Europe, South America, and Asia add to FIAT's scope. One of Italy's leading newspapers, the Turin-based daily *La Stampa*, has been part of the FIAT empire since 1920, and the Juventus soccer team is also associated with the Agnelli family and the FIAT group. *See also* CALCIO; CONFINDUSTRIA; EUROPEAN INTEGRATION; PRESS.

FINI, GIANFRANCO (1952–). Architect of the recent transformation of the neofascist **Movimento Sociale Italiano/**Italian Social Movement (MSI) into a new, conservative party, Gianfranco Fini is one of the smoothest performers in contemporary Italian politics. In the 1980s, the **Bologna**-born Fini was controversially chosen by **Giorgio Almirante** as his successor. Accordingly, in 1987, Fini became party secretary; after Almirante's death, he assumed the leadership of the MSI's conservative wing. In 1990, at a party congress in **Rome** that was marred by fisticuffs between the factions, the MSI elected **Giuseppe "Pino" Rauti**, the ideologue of so-called fascism of the left, to the secretaryship, although Fini's outstanding final speech consolidated his personal standing within the movement. Rauti's attempt to transform the MSI into a campaigning anticapitalist force quickly proved itself a failure with the MSI's ultraconservative electorate, and Fini returned to the party leadership in time for the collapse of the party system in 1992.

In December 1993, when he was narrowly defeated for the mayorship of Rome, Fini proved that there was a reservoir of former **Democrazia Cristiana/**Christian Democracy Party (DC) voters who were willing to vote for the MSI if the movement presented itself as a party of Catholic conservatives that had turned its back on its Fascist past. In a masterstroke of political presentation, Fini put together an electoral pact called the **Alleanza Nazionale**/National Alliance (AN). Apart from a few former DC rightists and a handful of conservative professors, the pact was the MSI by another name. In alliance with **Silvio Berlusconi** in the "Good Government Pole," the AN obtained twice as many votes as the former MSI in the general elections of March 1994 and entered Berlusconi's short-lived government.

Fini, who tainted his growing reputation by calling **Benito Mussolini** the "greatest statesman of the 20th century" shortly after the 1994 poll, completed the transformation of the MSI into the AN in January 1995 at a conference in Fiuggi, near Rome, that explicitly rejected core aspects of the MSI's ideological heritage. This process of intellectual democratization was carried on at a second conference in Verona in 1998. Fini has also worked hard to distance the party from the anti-Semitic heritage of the 1938 **racial laws**. Making atonement for the past, Fini has visited Israel, and as foreign minister during the latter stages of the 2001–2006 Berlusconi government tilted Italian government policy in a pro-Israeli direction.

The AN remains a medium-sized party that has underachieved in electoral terms. Fini's achievement, however, has been to legitimize the postfascists as an authentic mainstream conservative party. As recently as the late 1990s, Fini's appointment as foreign minister would have aroused ferocious debate throughout the European Union (EU). *See also* CASA DELLE LIBERTÀ (CDL).

FIUME (Rijeka). The city of Fiume, on the Dalmatian coast, became the object of a major diplomatic crisis after the 1919 Paris peace conference failed to hand the city over to Italy. Fiume had a large Italian population, but it had not been promised to Italy in the 1915 **Treaty of London**. When, in June 1919, it became clear that U.S. President Woodrow Wilson favored giving the town to the new state of Yugoslavia, Italian nationalist opinion was outraged. In July 1919, there were clashes between the local Italian population and French soldiers garrisoning the town. Several French soldiers were killed. Italy was criticized by a commission of the wartime allies for its behavior and forced to reduce the number of its own troops in the town. The nationalists began to assemble a legion of volunteers to seize the city, and on 12 September 1919, 2,500 "legionaries" led by the poet **Gabriele D'Annunzio** seized the city. Initially, the Italian government issued only a formal condemnation of this act; it hoped to use the nationalist fervor to put pressure on Britain, France, and the United States. Wilson held firm, however.

D'Annunzio proceeded to rule the city as a personal fief until December 1920. His dictatorship was brought to an end by the Treaty of Rapallo in November 1920, which, among other decisions, declared Fiume to be a free city and awarded the town of Zara (which D'Annunzio had occupied in November 1919) to Italy. The Italian government accepted these terms; D'Annunzio did not. On Christmas Eve 1920, Italian troops attacked Fiume and after four days of fighting succeeded in overcoming the resistance of the legionaries. The loss of Fiume was treated by nationalist opinion as evidence that Italy had been repaid for her suffering during the war with a "mutilated peace." There is no doubt that the credibility of Italy's traditional political class was gravely weakened by the crisis and that the rise of **Fascism** owed much to the liberal state's failure to obtain the port for Italy.

Ironically, the city of Fiume became Italian within a few years. One of the first major successes of **Benito Mussolini**'s conduct of foreign affairs was a treaty of friendship, signed in Rome on 27 January 1924, between Italy and the new kingdom of Yugoslavia. By the terms of this treaty, Italy gained, as well as Fiume, great influence in the Danubian basin. In gratitude, King **Victor Emmanuel III** made Mussolini a member of the *Ordine dell'Annunziata*, the highest honor of the realm. Fiume remained Italian until after **World War II**. *See also* FOREIGN POLICY.

FLORENCE (Firenze). King **Victor Emmanuel II** moved Italy's capital from **Turin** to this Tuscan city in 1865, and for the next five years, until the occupation of **Rome**, Florence remained the capital. Florence is one of the most architecturally beautiful and historically important cities in the world. The artistic heritage accumulated by the leading Florentine families during the Renaissance and displayed ever since in its museums—the Uffizi, the Bargello, the hidden gallery over the Ponte Vecchio—are testimony to the city's central place in European cultural history. Filippo Brunelleschi, Dante Alighieri, Galileo Galilei, Niccolo Machiavelli, Michelangelo, and Giorgio Vasari are all part of the city's history. During its prime, little trade between Europe and the East took place that was not financed by Florentine bankers and insured by Florentine entrepreneurs.

The city was ruled by the Medici family for most of the 300-year period between 1434 and 1737, when the city became the capital of the Grand Duchy of Tuscany under the rule of Francis Stephen of Lorraine, the future emperor of Austria (1745). In 1786, the city abolished the death penalty long before most of Europe. During the Napoleonic period, the French gave the Duchy first to the family of the Duke of Parma (the so-called kingdom of Etruria) and then annexed it directly. The Lorraine family was restored after the Congress of Vienna (1814–1815) but ruled only until 1860, when Florence became part first of Piedmont-Sardinia and then of Italy.

Florence was a center of Fascist activity but also of resistance to the dictator during **World War II**. After the fall of **Benito Mussolini** and the beginning of the civil war of 1943–1945, Tuscan partisans harassed the German garrison so that the **resistance** might be in control of their city when Allied forces entered. The city was divided among four commands to avoid conflicts among the partisans of the main political parties. Repressive measures ordered by German General Albert Kesselring reflected his conviction that irregular, hence illegal, belligerence by those who should be noncombatants could be stopped by preventive hostage-taking, reprisals, public hangings, and home burnings. These measures, however, served to draw Tuscans closer together despite class, political, and social differences.

Florence was the first, but not the last, Italian city to have been brought under partisan control prior to the arrival of Allied armies. When Allied political teams arrived on 13 August 1944, equipped with lists of Italian liberal notables, aristocrats, and Catholics to fill administrative jobs, they found that the local **Comitato di Liberazione Nazionale**/Committee of National Liberation (CLN) had effectively organized city government to perform municipal chores ranging from garbage collection to water supply. The Allies saw the wisdom of treating the CLN delegates as legitimate interlocutors rather than risking the city's entire population turning against the liberators. The partisans had made clear that they would not accept being treated as mere auxiliaries.

Since the war's end, Florentine political life has been no less interesting than its wealth has been impressive. Between 1960 and

1962, Florence was one of those cities that "opened to the left," and its municipal government has since then more frequently been in the hands of left majorities than not. In November 1966, the city's art treasures were badly damaged by the flooding of the Arno River, which runs through the city. In 1993, the treasures of the Uffizi galleries were again put at risk after a random bomb attack, attributed to the **mafia**, caused widespread damage.

FO, DARIO (1926–). Dario Fo was born on 24 March 1926, near Lake Maggiore (Leggiuno Sangiano in Lombardy). Long a showman, playwright, designer, monologuist, director, actor, clown, and satirist, Fo—no less than the Italian intellectual community—was astonished to learn that he was to receive the Nobel Prize in Literature in 1997, bringing to six the number of Italians to be so honored. Most of Fo's work (including 70 plays) consists of poking a carefully aimed thumb in the eye of those in authority, as well as of terrorists, popes, and tycoons, all of whom are—in Fo's view—obtuse, at the very least. His plays have been likened to an absurdist type of British kitchen-sink drama. His most famous play, *La morte accidentale d'un anarchico* (*The Accidental Death of an Anarchist*, 1970) has been translated and staged all over the world. He has been allowed entry into the United States only once, in 1984. On two earlier occasions he and his wife since 1953, the actress Franca Rame, had been denied U.S. visas because of his leftist associations and long membership in the **Partito Comunista Italiano**/Italian Communist Party (PCI).

The **Vatican** has an equally negative view of Fo, having been the target of his humor on more than one occasion. *L'Osservatore Romano* deplored the action of the Swedish Academy, for having selected this author "of questionable works." The Swedish Academy, however, described this perfect jester as blending "laughter and gravity" in ways that reveal injustices and abuses by those in charge anywhere. *See also* LITERATURE; LOTTA CONTINUA; LUZI, MARIO; STRATEGIA DELLA TENSIONE.

FOIBE. The *foibe* are bulblike fissures in the ground that widen out to form a cave below. They are a common geological feature in Istria, Dalmatia, and the province of **Trieste**. During and immediately after **World War II**, these caves were used as dumping places for the thousands of Italians killed by Yugoslav partisans in a policy of deliberate ethnic cleansing in May–June 1945. Josip Brod Tito, the Yugoslav leader, was determined to eliminate resistance from the Italian community of Istria and to terrify Italian speakers into silence or flight. The bodies of the victims were thrown into the *foibe* to hide the extent of the massacre. The true numbers of Italians killed will never be known, but the likeliest figure (much contested by revisionists) is around 10,000. Tens of thousands of Italians fled Istria at the same time. For many years, the need to maintain good relations with the Yugoslav government led to the subject of the *foibe* being taboo, especially on the left, but the collapse of Yugoslavia and the subsequent civil war have reopened the subject. It should also be added that the brutal behavior of Italian troops in Croatia and Slovenia during the early part of the war had aroused the deep animosity of the local Slav population.

FOREIGN POLICY. Italy's foreign policy has generally had clear, but unassertive, objectives. Before unification, the lack of cohesion among ministates and principalities under Austrian, Spanish, or Pontifical jurisdiction made unrealizable any territorial ambitions on the part of those few states that were autonomous. Moreover, a paucity of industrial raw materials and the vulnerability of two long coastlines warranted a certain modesty. After the peninsula's unification, however, the aim became to establish Italy's credentials as a power by pursuing a colonial policy in **Ethiopia** and in **Libya**.

Successive governments also negotiated the so-called **Triple Alliance**, tying Italy to Germany and Austria-Hungary. However, Italy increasingly chafed at the limitations of the Triple Alliance. Calculating that Italy's security required control over the mountain passes to its north and the absence of a rival power on the Adriatic, the Italian government competed for influence with Austria in the Balkans. It was calculated that Austria would see no reason to share either mountain passes or seas with the Italians in the case of a joint victory in a European war. On the other hand, a victorious Anglo-French alliance would surely have no objection to parceling out formerly Austrian holdings to an Italian ally.

These considerations combined with resurgent nationalism in the spring of 1915 and led to Italy entering the war on the side of Great

Britain, France, and Russia, rather than Austria and Germany. Italy's trust in the Allies proved misplaced, however. Italy gained the Brenner frontier with Austria (and thus absorbed a large German-speaking minority), but its other territorial gains were meager. Disillusionment with Italy's treatment contributed greatly to the public mood that made **Fascism** possible.

Under Fascism, similar objectives prevailed. **Benito Mussolini** sought to project Italy as a power convincingly enough to make it not only respected but actively feared. Boldness and initiative led Mussolini's Italy to be the first state to recognize the Soviet government (1924), to establish good relations with Yugoslavia and expand Italian influence in the Danubian basin, to shell the island of **Corfu**, and gradually to absorb **Albania**. On the other hand, Mussolini was a valued member of the European elite and was much courted by Britain and France. Mussolini signed the 1925 **Locarno Pact** guaranteeing Belgian and French frontiers (while remaining silent about Germany's eastern frontiers, to which the guarantees did not extend). In March 1933, Italy signed the **Four Power Pact** with France, Germany, and Great Britain. The Duce hoped thereby to ensure Italy's place among the European Great Powers, which would reduce the influence of small powers in the League of Nations. At **Stresa** in April 1934, Mussolini signed a Treaty with Britain and France in response to Germany's repudiation of the Locarno Treaties and of the disarmament clauses of the Treaty of Versailles. Italy mobilized troops during the attempted Nazi coup in Austria in 1934.

Mussolini's ambitions grew steadily, and the refusal of British and French public opinion to allow him a free hand in Ethiopia gradually caused him to move into Adolf Hitler's camp. Both Italy and Germany backed General Francisco Franco's insurrection in Spain. In September 1936, Hitler invited Mussolini to Germany for a state visit and to watch German army maneuvers, hoping to convince the Duce that Germany would certainly triumph in any European war. The visit took place just three months after the opening of hostilities in Spain and just six months after Germany had reoccupied the Rhineland, contrary to both the Versailles and Locarno Treaties. Hitler succeeded so completely in flattering his guest's vanity that within a month the **Rome-Berlin Axis** had been formed (25 October 1936).

By March 1938, Italy was so deeply committed to a Fascist victory in Spain that Mussolini could not oppose the German absorption of Austria, a fact that at one stroke erased Italy's only concrete gain from its participation in **World War I**. In place of the Austrian rump state and its weak successors beyond the mountains ringing Italy, there was a new Germanic empire far more powerful and more expansionist than the Habsburgs had been. However, Mussolini's admiration of Germany's might led him to accept the Pact of Steel (May 1939), which bound Italy to Germany by military obligations that Italy was in no position to honor. Moreover, even a victorious Germany would be unlikely to satisfy what Mussolini defined as Italy's needs, and any German defeat must necessarily bring Italy down as well. In short, the Pact of Steel was Mussolini's undoing. He delayed Italian entrance into the war until he thought that victory was near but then embroiled Italy in a **parallel war** in Greece and North Africa that bankrupted the nation and exposed fascism's empty boast of military might.

Since 1945, Italy's policies have consistently aimed at identifying Italy as an Atlantic power and hence a loyal member of the **North Atlantic Treaty Organization (NATO)**. Italy still hosts several major NATO bases and during the Cold War was one of the United States' most reliable allies—so much so, indeed, that Italy was nicknamed "NATO's Bulgaria." The extent of Italian subservience to the United States can be exaggerated, however. Italy's "Mediterranean vocation" (and need for oil and gas) has led it to seek good relations with the Arab states to its south; during the 1950s, Italy was one of the first Western European states to establish good relations with the Soviet Union, and Italy's Europeanism has been even more central than Atlanticism in its foreign policy.

Italy's aim is to become one of the motors of the integration of Europe. It has consistently supported increased powers for the institutions of the European Community, even when this meant making economic sacrifices. The 1958 treaty establishing the European Economic Community (EEC) was proposed at Messina (**Sicily**) in June 1955, drafted by the foreign ministers of the six member states at **Venice** in May 1956, and signed in **Rome** in March 1957. The **Democrazia Cristiana**/Christian Democracy party (DC) was a stalwart backer of the European project. From the 1970s onward, the tacit approval of the **Partito Comunista Italiano**/Italian Communist Party (PCI) was also given to Italy's membership in the Community, although the PCI was initially a stern critic of both NATO and European unity.

In recent years, Italy has become one of the United Nations' (UN) most active member states in peacekeeping missions around the globe; more than 9,000 Italian troops were employed in such missions at the end of 2006. Italian troops and service personnel were deployed in Albania in 1997 with the goal of preventing a collapse of that country. Italy also made a substantial contribution to the postwar reconstruction of Iraq in 2003. In September 2006, Italy contributed over 2,000 soldiers and several warships to the international force deployed in southern Lebanon to police the ceasefire between Israel and Hezbollah. As one of the few countries enjoying good relations with both the Arab world and Israel, Italy was uniquely placed to broker a peace deal between Israel and Lebanon. Italy's high profile in peacekeeping is not solely motivated by humanitarian goals; it openly aspires to a permanent place on an enlarged UN Security Council. *See also* COLOMBO, EMILIO; EUROPEAN INTEGRATION; DE GASPERI, ALCIDE; FIUME; LONDON, TREATY OF; PRINETTI-BARRÈRE NOTES; SFORZA, CARLO; TRIESTE; VISCONTI-VENOSTA, EMILIO; WORLD WAR II.

FORLANI, ARNALDO (1925–). A parliamentarian from 1958 to 1994, Arnaldo Forlani was leader of the **Democrazia Cristiana/** Christian Democracy Party (DC) from 1989 to 1992. During that period, his ambition to become **president of the Republic** was dashed, and the DC was crushed by bribery scandals. Forlani is a native of Pesaro, a middle-sized city in the Marches, his constant electoral base. He was elected to **Parliament** in 1958 and took office in the late 1960s, first as minister for state participation in industry and then for relations with the United Nations. In 1969, he became party leader, a post he held until 1973.

In 1973, Forlani briefly became secretary general of the European Christian Democratic Union, but he was soon called back to high office in Italy, becoming minister of defense (1974–1976), foreign minister (1976–1979), and, finally, prime minister from October 1980 to June 1981. During the first premiership of **Bettino Craxi**, Forlani was vice premier. Forlani became party leader once more in February 1989, when the DC's center faction, with the support of the faction of **Giulio Andreotti**, combined to vote out the then leader (and prime minister), **Ciriaco De Mita**. This move, which was strongly backed by Craxi, handed the reins of power in Italy over to the so-called CAF (Craxi-Andreotti-Forlani). The three men governed—or misgoverned—the country until the electoral and judicial disasters of 1992–1993.

Perhaps because Craxi feared him less than Andreotti, Forlani was the triumvirate's choice to become president after the resignation of **Francesco Cossiga** in April 1992. Forlani obtained only 469 votes, 40 less than the required quota, and 80 less than the government parties theoretically controlled. Even after frantic arm-twisting by party whips, Forlani's vote only increased by 10 in a subsequent ballot, and he was forced to drop out of the contest. His defeat symbolized the CAF's loss of control over the newly elected Parliament.

Had Forlani won the presidency, he would have appointed Craxi prime minister, and the world would never have heard of the **Mani pulite** ("Clean Hands") investigation. Forlani himself was drawn into the bribery scandals and, in December 1993, was subjected to a ruthless cross-examination by **Antonio Di Pietro** when he was called as a witness to explain bribes paid to the DC by the chemical company Enimont. Forlani literally frothed at the mouth as he frantically tried to avoid the prosecutor's pointed questions. He left the witness box with his political career in ruins. *See also PENTAPARTITO.*

FORTIS, ALESSANDRO (1842–1909). Born in Forlì in Emilia-Romagna, as a young man Alessandro Fortis took part in **Giuseppe Garibaldi**'s campaigns to liberate the Trentino in 1866 and **Rome** in 1867. A moderate republican and antimonarchist in his youth, Fortis was elected to the Chamber of Deputies in 1880 and became increasingly connected with **Francesco Crispi**. He initially served in the government of General **Luigi Girolamo Pelloux (June 1898–May 1899)** as minister of agriculture but joined his fellow republicans in opposing the restrictions on political activity and free speech proposed by Pelloux. After the turn of the century, Fortis's ally of choice became **Giovanni Giolitti**, whose liberal reformism was closest to Fortis's own political views. When Giolitti's second administration resigned in March 1905, Fortis followed him as prime minister. His

tenure in this office was characterized by a lengthy guerrilla war in
Parliament between Fortis and his conservative rival, **Sidney Sonnino**. Fortis's plans to introduce a partial nationalization of the railways and to conclude a trade agreement between Italy and Spain that
would have slashed Italian tariffs on Spanish wine met with fierce
parliamentary and public opposition. The tariff bill was defeated in
Parliament, causing Fortis to reshuffle his government in December
1905. His government eventually fell in February 1906, despite Giolitti's support.

Fortis visited Calabria and **Sicily** in September 1905 to examine
firsthand the extent of **earthquake** damage. Shortly afterward he put
forward a special law to aid these regions. This was the first real
recognition by the Italian state of the fundamental problems underly-
ing southern underdevelopment. Fortis died in Rome in 1909.

FORZA ITALIA. This wholly new party was born in the fall of 1993,
when **Silvio Berlusconi** ordered his marketing strategists to prepare
his entry into politics. In December 1993, thousands of Forza Italia
"clubs" were begun in cities and towns all over the country. Some
15,000 groups had been formed by the end of January 1994, when
Berlusconi officially announced his intention to run for **Parliament**.

Berlusconi was well aware that the "clubs" did not constitute a
genuine party organization. He accordingly allied his new movement,
and his three national television networks, with the **Lega Nord/**
Northern League (LN) in the so-called Liberty Pole alliance (*Polo
delle libertà*) and with the **Alleanza Nazionale/**National Alliance
(AN) in the "Good Government Pole" (*Polo del buon governo*) in
electoral districts in southern Italy. Two smaller parties, the Unione
di Centro/Center Union (UDC) and the Centro Cristiano Democra-
tico/Christian Democratic Center (CCD), also struck electoral pacts
with Forza Italia. Berlusconi's television networks propagated the
idea that these electoral pacts stood for radical deregulation of the
private sector and promised that Berlusconi would use his business
skills to create one million jobs within a year. The rival left-wing alliance parties, meanwhile, were portrayed as communists who would
snuff out private enterprise and tax the savings of the middle class.

These tactics paid off. Less than four months after its foundation,
Forza Italia became the most widely supported party in Italy, with 21

percent of the vote. In terms of parliamentarians, however, Forza Italia was underrepresented, with 99 seats in the Chamber of Deputies and 32 senators. Forza Italia's deputies, moreover, were lacking in political experience (only 15 percent had had any political background prior to joining Berlusconi's movement) and did not provide Berlusconi with a pool of ready ministerial talent. It is a measure of Forza Italia's artificial nature that Berlusconi, to fill his party's quota of ministerial appointees in the government that he formed in May 1994, was forced to give top ministerial jobs to individuals from his own corporation and to outside experts, such as **Lamberto Dini**, who had nothing to do with Forza Italia or with Berlusconi himself. Italians began to call Forza Italia *un partito azienda* (a company party).

Forza Italia has nevertheless remained Italy's most strongly supported political party. During the 1996 general elections, it slipped to 20.6 percent of the popular vote and briefly lost its primacy, but in every other major national electoral test since 1994 it has emerged as the largest party, obtaining over 30 percent of the national vote in the 1994 European elections and 29 percent in the 2001 general elections. In 2006, Forza Italia scored 23 percent, defying the predictions of commentators who had expected it to fall to under 20 percent again.

Forza Italia's local organization remains lackluster in many parts of Italy. Berlusconi's trusted associates continue to direct its national operations, and party democracy is limited (it is not imaginable, for instance, that Berlusconi's leadership could be challenged). Forza Italia, in short, is arguably more like the electoral organization of a U.S. senator than a traditional European mass party. *See also* CASA DELLE LIBERTÀ (CDL).

FOSCOLO, UGO (1778–1827). A kind of Italian Shelley, Ugo Foscolo was a poet, classical translator, and patriot who was born to an Italian father and a Greek mother on the isle of Xante. He grew up in the then Venetian town of Spalato (modern-day Split, in Croatia), then moved to Venice. His first significant work, a pamphlet entitled *Bonaparte Liberatore* (*Bonaparte the Liberator*), was written in **Venice** in 1797 and celebrated the victory of the French revolutionary armies that occupied northern Italy and established the Cisalpine Republic in 1796. Foscolo moved to **Bologna** and **Milan** to take part in political activity in 1797 and fought bravely in defense of the Cisalpine Republic in 1799 when the Austro-Russian forces strove to restore absolutist rule in northern Italy. Foscolo subsequently served for some years in the French army in both Italy and France itself.

Foscolo's literary masterpiece, his 1807 collection *Dei Sepolcri* (literally, *On Tombs*), was written after Napoleon had crowned himself king of Italy—a move that Foscolo, a former Jacobin, made no protest against. When Napoleon was defeated, Foscolo was treated kindly by the Austrians, despite the fact that he was by now one of the most well-known and most outspoken nationalists in Italy. In March 1815, however, he fled to Switzerland, and from there to England, rather than accept the restoration of Austrian rule in Venetia and Lombardy. In England, he tried to live like a gentleman, but before long he had become a chronic debtor, with a string of mistresses and illegitimate children to maintain or, more usually, to neglect. This last period of his life saw him produce some of his best work, however. His essay *Discorsi sulla servitù d'Italia* (*On the Servitude of Italy*, 1819) immensely influenced the young **Giuseppe Mazzini**, while his many essays on Italian literature, especially on Dante, are still regarded as important works of criticism today. Foscolo died in disgrace and poverty in Burnham Green, near London, in September 1827. In 1871, after the liberation of **Rome**, the poet's remains were transferred to Italy, and Foscolo was interred in the vaults of Santa Croce Church in **Florence**, a building he had described as the last resting place of many "Italian glories" in *Dei Sepolcri*.

FOUR POWER PACT. A four power pact was first proposed by **Benito Mussolini** in the aftermath of the failure of the London Economic Conference, prepared under the auspices of the League of Nations, in 1933. Mussolini argued that it would be better if Britain, France, Germany, and Italy established a directory of great powers to decide European questions among themselves instead of relying on the League. In particular, they should revise the territorial boundaries established at Paris in the aftermath of **World War I**. Mussolini's initiative was received more warmly by the British than the French. It was received most warmly of all by the Germans and the Hungarians, both of whom felt they had been gravely wronged in 1919–1920. The beneficiaries of the peace treaties, above all Yugoslavia, Czechoslovakia, and Poland, were vehement in their opposition. Eduoard Benes, the premier of Czechoslovakia, was especially outspoken in resisting the pact. France, the chief ally of these powers, responded with a counterproposal that insisted that territorial changes could only be carried out after a unanimous vote of the Council of the League, but that the four nations would collaborate together to settle outstanding disputes. A pact enshrining these sentiments was signed in June 1933, but only Germany and Italy ratified it. An angry Mussolini threatened in December 1933 that "His majesty, the cannon" would have to resolve disputes in the absence of the pact.

There is a macabre sense in which Mussolini's proposal was farsighted, however. The policy of appeasement followed by the British and French governments, which culminated in the revision of Czechoslovakia's borders by the four powers at Munich on 30 September 1938, was an example of the kind of diplomacy through which Mussolini was hoping to stabilize Europe. *See also* AXIS, ROME-BERLIN; FOREIGN POLICY; STRESA FRONT.

FUTURISM. A literary, artistic, and cultural movement founded in the first decade of the 20th century, futurism combined genuine artistic radicalism with a love of violence, power, and speed that led futurist thinkers and writers to extol the virtues of war and to embrace Fascism as their political creed.

The essence of futurism was its celebration of the beauty of modernity. A racing car could be as beautiful as a race horse, electric pylons as beautiful as trees or mountains. Literature and art should not, in short, be restful or contemplative, but should capture the noise, bustle, drama, and violence of industrial cities. In the words of the futurist manifesto published by **Filippo Tommaso Marinetti** in the French newspaper *Le Figaro* in 1909, the futurists wanted to "sing" of "the vast crowds energized by work, pleasure, or protest," to depict the "vibrant nightly fervor of the arsenals and workplaces lit by violent electric moons," the "bridges arched across rivers like gigantic gymnasts," and the "locomotives . . . like enormous steel horses in a harness of tubes." Despite the vigor and exuberance of Marinetti's prose in the manifesto, these tasks were fulfilled more memorably by artists such as **Umberto Boccioni**, Carlo Carrà, and Giacomo Balla than by the writers associated with the futurist cause.

Ideologically, the futurists subscribed to the antidemocratic philosophy of violence and power worship traceable to Friedrich Nietzsche and popularized by Georges Sorel. Like the dadaists, they were hostile to traditional and classical forms in art, architecture, and esthetics. "The sound of a racing car engine is more beautiful than the greatest symphony" was a part of the futurist manifesto. **Giovanni Papini**, the editor of *Leonardo*, was the most prominent Italian thinker to fall under the sway of such ideas. Marinetti's manifesto, however, expressed the political thinking animating the futurists succinctly: "We want to glorify war—the world's only form of hygiene—militarism, patriotism, the destructive gestures of the anarchists, the fine ideas for which men die, and contempt for **women**." With a philosophy such as this, futurist intellectuals mostly became enthusiastic Fascists, although their ardor cooled as **Benito Mussolini**'s regime became increasingly institutionalized and conservative in the 1930s. *See also* FASCISM; LITERATURE.

– G –

GARIBALDI, ANITA (1821–1849). The Brazilian-born first wife of **Giuseppe Garibaldi**, Anita Garibaldi (Anna Maria Ribeirao da Silva) was a heroine of the struggle for Italian unification. Already married when she met the Italian adventurer in 1839, she and Garibaldi had two sons and a daughter together. Both sons became prominent soldiers and statesmen on the model of their father. Menotti (1840–1903) was born out of wedlock (Garibaldi and Anita were only able to marry after the death of her first husband in 1842). He fought with his father in the "Expedition of the Thousand" to Sicily and won a gold medal for gallantry in the war against Austria of 1866. From 1876 to 1900, he was a parliamentary deputy. The second son, Raced (1847–1924), was also a war hero and adventurer who served in Parliament and took a leading role in the Italian–Turkish war when he was over 60 years old.

Anita Garibaldi is remembered today, however, less for the exploits of her children than for her own extraordinary bravery and devotion. In 1849, against Garibaldi's will, she followed him to **Rome** and took part in the defense of the city against the French army. She accompanied him on the tragic retreat through the Papal States to Ravenna, where, overcome by exhaustion and hunger, she died when she was not yet 30 years old. Lodged between petrochemical plants and the Adriatic, the small hut in which she was ravaged by fever is still standing and is the object of sporadic pilgrimages.

GARIBALDI, GIUSEPPE (1807–1882). Born in Nice to a sea captain father, the young Garibaldi was a professional revolutionary. He took part in the Mazzinian uprising against the Piedmontese monarchy in 1834 and, following its suppression, was condemned to death for his role in the fighting. Garibaldi, however, had fled to Brazil. There, he met his first wife, Anita, and fought gallantly for six years (1836–1842) on behalf of the South Rio Grande republic, trying to achieve independence. Garibaldi ended the war as admiral of the would-be republic's small fleet. In 1846, he organized and commanded the Italian legion that fought for Uruguay in its war against Argentina. Garibaldi's reputation as the "hero of two worlds," and his familiar penchant for South American peasant garb, dates from this period.

News of the 1848 revolutions, however, prompted his return to **Turin**. Garibaldi fought bravely against the Austrians in Lombardy and in defense of the Roman republic in the spring of 1849. Together with a faithful band of volunteers and Anita, Garibaldi broke out of **Rome** and retreated toward **Venice**, which was still resisting Austrian rule. After suffering heavy casualties, they were forced to take refuge in the swamps surrounding Ravenna, where Anita died of exhaustion.

Garibaldi, at the lowest ebb of his fortunes, was expelled from Piedmont-Sardinia and was forced to lead the life of an exile once more. He worked briefly as a candle-maker in Camden, New Jersey, before returning to Europe in 1854. He established himself in a house on the Sardinian Island of Caprera and gradually became more politically realistic. Under **Camillo Benso di Cavour**'s influence, Garibaldi accepted that the Piedmontese **monarchy** offered the best hope of unifying Italy. This renunciation of his Mazzinian and revolutionary principles restored him to favor in Turin, and in 1859 Garibaldi was made a general in the Piedmontese army.

Garibaldi was violently critical of the Treaty of Villafranca. In January 1860, he endorsed the latest venture launched by **Giuseppe**

Mazzini, the "Action party," which openly espoused a policy of liberating southern Italy, Rome, and Venice by military means. To this end, in the spring of 1860, Garibaldi led a corps of red-shirted patriots from **Genoa** to the assistance of a Mazzinian uprising in **Palermo**. The "Expedition of the Thousand" is the most famous of all Garibaldi's military exploits. After landing near Palermo with the support of ships from the British fleet, Garibaldi swiftly took command of the island. On 14 May 1860, he became dictator of **Sicily** and head of a provisional government that was largely dominated by a native Sicilian who would play an important role in the political future of Italy, **Francesco Crispi**.

With the support of thousands of Sicilian peasants and workers, Garibaldi then invaded the Italian mainland, intent on marching on Rome. He entered **Naples** in September 1860. He was joined there by the principal republican theorists, Mazzini and **Carlo Cattaneo**, and for a brief moment it looked as if the process of Italian unification would take a radical turn. Cavour's shrewdness enabled him to outmaneuver Garibaldi. Piedmontese troops invaded the Papal States, blocking the road to Rome. Garibaldi decided not to compromise Italian unity by risking a conflict with the Piedmontese. On 26 October 1860, he consigned southern Italy to the monarchy.

Garibaldi, however, was unable to consider Italian unification complete while Rome remained under clerical domination, protected by French troops. He became a thorn in the side of the first Italian governments by carrying on his own independent foreign policy. In 1862, Garibaldi returned to Sicily to raise another army of volunteers willing to march under the melodramatic slogan "Rome or Death." The outraged reaction of Napoleon III compelled the Italian government to intervene, and Garibaldi's advance was halted by Italian troops at Aspromonte in Calabria. There was a skirmish, and Garibaldi was shot in the foot. Garibaldi was briefly imprisoned, but his international fame (especially in England, to which he made a triumphal visit in 1864) soon led to his release.

In 1866, Garibaldi led Italian troops in the Trentino, liberating a great part of the Italian-speaking territory under Austrian rule before being ordered to relinquish his gains upon the end of the hostilities between Prussia and Austria. His short reply amply conveyed his disgust at the command: Garibaldi sent a one-word telegram saying *obbedisco* (I obey). His exploits in the Trentino were a prelude to further impolitic attempts to take Rome in the fall of 1867. Escaping from house arrest on Caprera, he joined 3,000 waiting volunteers in Tuscany. The courage of his amateur troops, however, was no match for the French army defending Rome, and at the small but bloody battle of Mentana on 3 November 1867, Garibaldi was decisively beaten. Once more, he was forced into exile on Caprera.

Garibaldi played no role in the liberation of Rome in 1870. His last campaign was on behalf of the French Republic. Garibaldi led a corps of Italian volunteers at the battle of Dijon in the fall of 1870, and his efforts were a useful contribution to what was the only French victory of the Franco–Prussian War. In his last years, Garibaldi dedicated himself to writing his memoirs (and heroic poetry) and became a declared socialist. He died on Caprera in 1882, but his myth has been a powerful influence on Italian political life ever since. *See also* RESISTANCE; RISORGIMENTO.

GENOA (Genova). One of Italy's largest cities, with a current population of over 600,000 inhabitants, Genoa has long been one of the most important ports in the Mediterranean. In the Middle Ages, Genoa, while nominally part of the Holy Roman Empire, was actually a free republic governed by a rudimentary form of representative government. It possessed a powerful navy and controlled the whole of the Tyrrhenian sea, as well as colonial outposts in the Middle East and Turkey. Victories against Pisa (1284) and **Venice** (1298) left it without rivals. Genoa squandered its good fortune and less than a hundred years later was under first French dominion and then rule from Milan. Genoa retained its proud maritime tradition, however. The most famous sailor in history, Christopher Columbus, was a native of Genoa. In the 15th and 16th centuries, as part of Spanish empire, Genoa flourished, and the city's many splendid *palazzi* date from this period. The historical center of Genoa is recognized as a world heritage site by the United Nations.

Genoa's modern history began in 1797, when the so-called Ligurian republic was formed. Genoa was incorporated into France during the Napoleonic epoch and later, after the **Congress of Vienna**, became part of the kingdom of **Sardinia**. The Genoese became ardent Italian patriots under the rule of the House of Savoy: **Giuseppe**

Garibaldi sailed to **Sicily** from the Genoa shore in 1860, and many of his red-shirted volunteers were Ligurians. Genoa became a rich industrial port at the end of the 19th century, importing and exporting the products needed and produced by **Milan** and **Turin**.

A working-class town, it was a center of partisan activity during **World War II**, being awarded a gold medal for valor, and in 1960 erupted in protest when the neofascist **Movimento Sociale Italiano**/Italian Social Movement (MSI) provocatively chose to hold its annual conference there. In more recent times, the decline of local industries such as ship-building has caused severe poverty in some parts of the city, although even today the port, which is the second-biggest in the Mediterranean after Marseilles, remains a big employer. The port area has been renovated in recent years; its centerpiece is the giant aquarium, which attracts hundreds of thousands of tourists every year. In July 2001, the G8 summit of world leaders was held in Genoa. The visit provoked widespread riots by antiglobalization activists from all over Europe and a violent reaction by the **police**. *See also* TAMBRONI, FERNANDO.

GENTILE, GIOVANNI (1875–1944). Born in Trapani (**Sicily**), Giovanni Gentile was both a philosopher of great distinction and a cultural propagandist on behalf of the Fascist regime. His early studies were done at Italy's most renowned institute of higher education, the *Scuola Normale* in Pisa, where he developed parallel interests in German idealism and the philosophy of Karl Marx. He disparaged all forms of positivism, materialism, or utilitarianism and was opposed to the political manifestations of such broad philosophical currents as socialism and laissez-faire liberalism, but he remained unusually aloof from political activity until **World War I**. During the war, which he enthusiastically supported, Gentile published what is arguably his most important philosophical treatise, *I fondamenti della filosofia di diritto* (*The Fundamentals of the Philosophy of Law*, 1916). It was in this book that he introduced the concept of the "moral state," which rested on the belief that the individual only fully realizes himself when he obeys a state whose purposes are good. Service and sacrifice to the community, in this ethic, are higher virtues than independence and the pursuit of individual happiness. The implications of this position are obvious.

By the end of the war, Gentile was associated politically with the nationalists. In October 1922, **Benito Mussolini** invited the philosopher to join his first cabinet. Gentile accepted and, in 1923, became both a member of the **Partito Nazionale Fascista/**National Fascist Party (PNF) and a senator. As minister, he was responsible in May 1923 for an important educational reform that laid the basis for the modern Italian school and university system. He was also responsible for the infamous "loyalty oath" that all Italian teachers, at whatever level, were asked to sign. Doing so pledged signatories to teach all their courses in such a way as to promote **Fascism** and its values. Only a handful refused.

Gentile resigned from the government in June 1924 after the murder of **Giacomo Matteotti** but remained the regime's most respected cultural and philosophical voice. In 1925, in opposition to his former mentor, **Benedetto Croce**, Gentile published a manifesto, signed by **Filippo Marinetti** and **Luigi Pirandello**, among others, urging on intellectuals a moral commitment to Fascism's historical mission. In the same year, he wrote *Che cosa è il fascismo* (*The Nature of Fascism*), a highly readable short account of what he understood to be Fascism's objectives and ideals. It is probable that Mussolini used parts of this essay in preparing his article on Fascism for the *Italian Encyclopedia*, of which Gentile was the editor. Gentile was president of the Institute of Fascist Culture and was a member of the **Fascist Grand Council** until 1929. In 1944, he became the last president of the **Accademia d'Italia** (Italian Academy). The encyclopedia was a huge undertaking and occupied most of Gentile's scholarly energies between 1929 and 1936. Most of Italy's leading intellectuals contributed, with the conspicuous exception of Benedetto Croce.

Gentile lost much direct political influence after the **Lateran pacts** in 1929, which he opposed on doctrinal grounds. He never renounced Fascism, however, even after Mussolini's downfall. After some hesitation, Gentile backed the **Republic of Salò**, and this cost him his life. In 1944, he was assassinated in **Florence** by a squad of partisans. *See also* EDUCATION; RESISTANCE; UNIVERSITIES.

GENTILONI PACT. Alarmed by the prospect of a victory of the **Partito Socialista Italiano/**Italian Socialist Party (PSI) in the elections of October 1913 (which were both the first elections held with universal male suffrage and the first in which the Church allowed openly Catholic candidates to run), the president of the Unione Elettorale Cattolica (The Catholic Electoral Union), Count Vincenzo Ottorino Gentiloni, devised an electoral arrangement to maximize Catholic influence. Liberal candidates who promised to support Catholic schools and religious instruction in the public schools, would oppose the introduction of divorce, and agreed to several other key issues for "confessional" voters were offered the backing of the network of Catholic social organizations and parish clergy. The strategy was a striking success. Nearly 30 Catholic candidates were elected, and Gentiloni claimed that over 200 liberal candidates owed their victories to Catholic votes. Only 79 socialists of different denominations were elected, and the *Osservatore Romano* argued that "the party of subversion" would have won at least a hundred more deputies had the Church not intervened. Many embarrassed liberal deputies later denied having reached an explicit accord with Gentiloni. Whatever the truth of their denials, the Gentiloni pact signaled that the Church was the only institution with sufficient nationwide organization to contest the growing strength of the workers' movement. For better or worse, the Church had reentered Italian politics. *See also* CATHOLICISM; GIOLITTI, GIOVANNI; GUARANTEE LAWS; PAPACY.

GIANNINI, GUGLIELMO. *See QUALUNQUISMO.*

GIOBERTI, VINCENZO (1801–1852). The radical political ideas of the Catholic philosopher Vincenzo Gioberti constrained him to live the life of an exile for much of his adult life. In the early 1830s, the young priest joined the clandestine organization *Giovine Italia* (Young Italy) and after a period of imprisonment was forced to move to Brussels in 1833, where he wrote and published several works of theology and philosophy. In 1843, he published his most famous work, *Del primato morale e civile degli italiani* (*The Moral and Civil Primacy of the Italians*), a book that gave birth to so-called neoguelphism. In retrospect, it might seem incredible that this somewhat obscure book, which argued that **Catholicism**, symbolized by the **papacy**, was the heart of the primacy of Italian culture, should have aroused such passionate interest and debate. But Gioberti added a political dimension to his work by suggesting that it followed from his thesis that the most natural political form for Italy was a federation of sovereign principalities presided over by the pope. This proposal was intellectually problematic since it in effect nationalized and politicized the supposedly universal and spiritual Church; at the same time, it presented political problems because its nationalist tone challenged Austrian rule. The huge success of his book launched Gioberti on a political career. Gioberti returned to **Turin** (his place of birth) after Charles Albert conceded a constitution to liberal opinion in March 1848. Gioberti rapidly became one of the principal political figures in the Piedmontese capital. He was elected to Parliament and after the Piedmontese defeat at Custoza in July 1848 became first a cabinet member and then prime minister. Consistent with his ideas, Gioberti strove to improve relations with the papacy, but the plan was overtaken by the revolution in **Rome** in November 1848 and the defection of the pope to **Naples**. After the defeat of the Piedmontese army at Novara, Gioberti took refuge once more in exile, fleeing to Paris, where he remained until his death in 1852. *See also* REVOLUTIONS OF 1848; RISORGIMENTO.

GIOLITTI, ANTONIO (1915–). Grandson of **Giovanni Giolitti**, Antonio Giolitti was a hero of the wartime **resistance** (he was wounded and almost killed in combat in 1944), who began his political career in the **Partito Comunista Italiano**/Italian Communist party (PCI). He was elected to the **Constituent Assembly** in 1946 and served as a deputy for the PCI until 1953. In 1956, he was the most prominent leader of the party to resign his membership following the Soviet repression of the democratic revolution in Hungary. The PCI backed the Soviet line and denounced the Hungarian revolutionaries as fascists and reactionaries intent on the abolition of socialism. Giolitti, along with many of the party's intellectuals, could not stomach the party line on this issue. Membership in the PCI was for him no longer compatible with the ideas and objectives that he regarded as necessary for the victory of socialism. He joined the **Partito Socialista Italiano**/Italian Socialist party (PSI) in 1957 and became a PSI deputy in the elections of 1958. Giolitti served as budget minister at various times between 1963 and 1974 and then in 1977 became European commissioner for regional policy during the presidency of

Roy Jenkins, a post that he retained until 1985 under Jenkins's successor, Gaston Thorn. Giolitti, disturbed by the policies of **Bettino Craxi**, made his peace with the PCI in 1987 and served until 1992 as a senator for the independent left. Unusually for an Italian politician, he has published his memoirs, which are an important source for contemporary historians. *See also* CARRISTI; EUROPEAN INTEGRATION.

GIOLITTI, GIOVANNI (1842–1928). Giolitti's legacy is much contested, but no one doubts that this statesman from Mondovì in Piedmont made a critical contribution to Italian history. Giolitti entered politics in 1882 after a brilliant career in the finance ministry. In 1889 he was entrusted with the post of treasury minister by **Francesco Crispi**, and in 1892 he briefly held the office of prime minister. His appointment was controversial since he was the first politician to reach the highest office who had played no role in the **Risorgimento**. His first premiership, however, was ended by the **Banca Romana** scandal, which was manipulated by his political rivals to make his position untenable. Giolitti returned to politics in 1897, but only in 1901 did he return to ministerial office. During his tenure as minister of the interior, Giolitti was severely criticized by industrialists and landowners for his lax attitude toward **trade unions**. Giolitti believed that the state should take no side in the class conflict and strongly defended the right to strike. He once told a landowner who complained in the Senate of having to plough his own fields that he should continue—for by so doing, he would realize how hard the peasants worked and would pay them more. Only a more equal distribution of income, Giolitti believed, would bring an end to the civil strife that had been plaguing Italy since the mid-1890s.

Giolitti succeeded **Giuseppe Zanardelli** as prime minister in 1903; for most of the next 20 years, he dominated Italian political life. Giolitti added to the liberal reforms initiated by Zanardelli. His several prewar administrations opened a dialogue with the labor movement, nationalized the railways in 1909, and introduced universal male suffrage with the electoral reform of 1912. Italy meanwhile joined the race of the European nations for "a place in the sun" by waging war with Turkey in 1911–1912 and seizing **Libya** as a colony. Yet these achievements are overshadowed by what was not done. Giolitti did not campaign for the reform of the social injustices that were pushing the peasants and workers toward revolutionary doctrines and shrank from using the state to enforce the privileges of the wealthy. This position was an understandable one, but one that ultimately appeared as weakness.

Giolitti was a master of the dark art of *trasformismo*. The Giolittian system of politics was a skillful balancing act that required him to incorporate radicals, republicans, moderate socialists, and finally Catholics into his governing coalition. His acceptance of the **Gentiloni pact** was a step too far for the radicals, however, and Giolitti was forced to resign on the eve of war. Giolitti opposed Italian entry into **World War I** and was widely suspected of working with the Austrians and Germans to prevent Italy's renunciation of the neutrality it adopted in August 1914. His opposition to the war derived from his sensitivity to Italy's military and economic weaknesses; he truly believed that the war might end with the Germans marching into **Milan**. So far as Giolitti was concerned, the Austrians and Germans had offered *parecchio* (a great amount) to ensure Italy's neutrality, and he could not see the point of spilling blood to obtain more. This calculating mentality was typical of Giolitti and flew in the face of the widely prevalent irrationalism and its consequent exaltation of action over reflection, an attitude soon elevated to dogma in the Fascist regime.

Giolitti returned to power only in 1920–1921, just as disillusionment with the peace settlement and mounting industrial unrest were bringing the fundamental problems of liberal Italy to the crisis point. Bravely, Giolitti put an end to the occupation of **Fiume** by the band of adventurers led by **Gabriele D'Annunzio**, but it can be argued that he was far too tolerant of **Fascism**. Giolitti seemingly believed that **Benito Mussolini** could be tamed and would both restore order and initiate social reforms. Events gradually robbed him of this illusion and convinced him to pass to the opposition. Until his death in **Turin** in 1928, Giolitti was an outspoken critic of the new regime. *See also* BISSOLATI, LEONIDA; BLOCCO NAZIONALE; MARCH ON ROME; PARTITO SOCIALISTA ITALIANO (PSI); TURATI, FILIPPO.

GIRO D'ITALIA. Second only to the Tour de France in cycling prestige, the Giro d'Italia takes place every year in May. The first event took place in 1909, with eight stages for a total of 2,448 kilometers. The first winner was Luigi Ganna, who also won the following year. His prize was the then magnificent sum of 5,325 lire. Italians dominated the race until the 1950s. The first foreign winner was Hugo Koblet of Switzerland in 1950. Koblet was followed by another Swiss, Carlo Clerici, in 1954, and then by the Luxembourger Charly Gaul, who won in 1956 thanks to a historic stage victory on Monte Bondone near Trento during a blizzard. Gaul also won in 1959. The 1960s and early 1970s were dominated by "the cannibal," Eddie Merckx of Belgium, who won five times between 1968 and 1974, including three consecutive victories between 1972 and 1974. Merckx shares the overall record for victories with two Italians, **Fausto Coppi** and Alfredo Bindi, who is the only other cyclist to win three Giri in a row (1927–1929). In recent years, Italians have begun to dominate the event again: All 10 races from 1997 to 2006 were won by Italian cyclists, although this is in part due to the fact that the crowded calendar of modern cyclists has led to some of the leading non-Italian stars deserting the race to prepare for the Tour de France.

The Giro is organized each year by Italy's best-selling sporting newspaper, *La Gazzetta dello Sport*, which is printed on pink newspaper. The leading rider therefore wears a pink jersey. The race, especially the dramatic mountain stages in the **Alps** and the Dolomites, is watched by hundreds of thousands of people each year and by millions on television. Cycling, after soccer (**calcio**), is Italy's most passionately followed sport.

GIUSTIZIA E LIBERTÀ/Justice and Liberty (GL). An antifascist organization founded in Paris in 1929 by **Carlo Rosselli**, **Gaetano Salvemini**, and several other intellectuals, Giustizia e Libertà has a proud place in Italian history. Under the headline "we shan't win in a day, but win we shall," the movement's journal (also called *Giustizia e Libertà*) declared itself to be a revolutionary organization of republicans, liberals, and socialists committed to liberty, a republican form of government, and social justice. In July 1930, the movement publicized these ideals by launching a leaflet drop over the cathedral square in **Milan** from an airplane purchased by Rosselli. This dramatic gesture caused the authorities to crack down; in October 1930, the leading organizers inside Italy, **Ferruccio Parri**, Ernesto Rossi, and Riccardo Bauer, were arrested. Rossi and Bauer were sentenced to long prison terms in May 1931. In November, GL joined the so-called antifascist concentration uniting all the political forces in exile. The *giellisti*, as the movement's members became known, were made responsible for organizing **resistance** to the regime inside the country. This pact lasted until May 1934, when Rosselli broke with the major party in the antifascist concentration, the **Partito Socialista Italiano** /Italian Socialist Party (PSI) because of its increasing closeness to the **Partito Comunista Italiano**/Italian Communist Party (PCI).

The movement was seriously harmed by the brutal murder of Carlo Rosselli and his brother, Nello, in 1937. Nevertheless, clandestine cells of Giustizia and Libertà were established in northern Italy, in particular, and former *giellisti* later became influential figures in both the PSI and the **Partito d'Azione**/Action Party (PdA) after the fall of the regime. *See also* SPANISH CIVIL WAR.

GLADIO. Ostensibly a secret network of nearly 50 underground armed squads that would have organized resistance to an eventual Soviet invasion of Italy, Gladio (a *gladio* was the short, double-edged and pointed sword used in ancient Rome by the infantry and in the arena) is one of the many murky chapters in Italian Cold War history. The networks were discovered accidentally in 1990 during a judicial investigation in **Venice** into the murder of a policeman. Pressed by the leadership of the **Partito Comunista Italiana**/Italian Communist Party (PCI), who suspected that the squads had existed to organize subversive activity in the event of a Communist electoral victory, the then premier, **Giulio Andreotti**, first claimed that the networks had been disbanded in 1972. Subsequently, in October 1990, he was forced to admit that the squads were still in being. Furthermore, no fewer than 12 of the squads' 150 arms caches had been rifled by unknown hands. In January 1991, the gladiators' names were revealed, and it swiftly became clear that a substantial proportion had links to neofascist groups.

It is widely believed in Italy that Gladio was not a **North Atlantic Treaty Organization (NATO)** initiative, as the Andreotti government claimed, but was instead a Central Intelligence Agency (CIA) undercover operation in collaboration with the Italian secret service to subvert a PCI government, even if legitimately elected. There are certainly some grounds for believing this hypothesis. NATO headquarters initially denied its involvement and only retracted its denial after arm-twisting by the Italian government. The only first-rank Italian politicians to have been fully informed of the networks were Andreotti and President **Francesco Cossiga**, both of whom were notoriously close to the secret services, while other equally important, but less conspiratorial, politicians, such as **Amintore Fanfani**, were seemingly not informed at all.

Whatever the truth of Gladio's origins and purpose, the discovery of the network immediately led to a major institutional crisis as Cossiga used every power at his command to suppress an independent inquiry into his role in the affair. Most disturbing of all, the revelation that the Italian state had been arming squads of right-wing extremists hinted at an ominous explanation for the wave of neofascist terrorism, the so-called **strategia della tensione** (strategy of tension) in the 1970s that culminated in the bomb attack at the **Bologna** railway station on 2 August 1980.

GOBETTI, PIERO (1901–1926). In his tragically brief life, Piero Gobetti was the author of some of the most thought-provoking political philosophy written in Italy in the 20th century. Born in **Turin** in 1901, he was a child prodigy—**Antonio Gramsci** made him the theater critic of the journal *Ordine nuovo* when he was just 18 years old. While still a student, he founded and edited the antifascist periodical *Rivoluzione liberale* (*Liberal Revolution*), which was banned by **Benito Mussolini** in 1925. In 1923, he became a publisher: "Piero Gobetti editore" specialized in printing works by antifascist writers, including the poet and future Nobel laureate **Eugenio Montale**. Gobetti's most famous essay, also called *La rivoluzione liberale*, was published in 1924; his other works include *Dal bolscevismo al fascismo* (*From Bolshevism to Fascism*, 1923) and *Risorgimento senza eroi* (*The Risorgimento without Heroes*, 1926). Gobetti's thought was characterized by an abiding faith in individualism and a profound suspicion of all bureaucratic and hierarchical forms of society. For this reason, he famously identified the Bolshevik revolution in Russia as "an experience in liberalism," since he regarded the Soviets established in St. Petersburg and Moscow as the embryo of a higher, more dynamic form of democracy than the parliamentarianism that had delivered Italy into the hands of Mussolini.

The violence of the Fascist squads forced Gobetti to immigrate to Paris in January 1926, where he died from the effects of a beating only a few weeks after his arrival. He was survived by his wife, Ada Prospero, who became a leading figure in the **resistance** to **Fascism**.

GOLGI, CAMILLO (1843–1926). Born in the small mountain village of Corteno, near Brescia (Lombardy), Camillo Golgi won the Nobel Prize in Medicine in 1906 (the same year **Giosue Carducci** won the literature prize). Golgi studied at the University of Pavia in the 1860s and after graduating in 1865 worked as a doctor, winning in 1872 a public examination to become *primario* (head doctor of a ward) at the Abbiategrasso hospice for the terminally ill in **Milan**. It was while he was working there that Golgi made his first crucial discovery, which he published in a paper called "On the Structure of Brain Grey Matter." This discovery was the so-called black reaction, the fact that by staining nervous tissue with silver nitrate, it was possible to see nerve cell structure in its entirety. "Golgi staining" is still used by doctors and researchers today. In 1876, Golgi was appointed professor of histology at Pavia University; in 1881, he became professor of general pathology. Over the next three decades, he made Pavia a center of world-class research in medicine, nurturing the careers of numerous outstanding young researchers.

Golgi's discovery of black reaction set off a major scientific debate and was regarded as a crucial breakthrough in the field. He was subsequently to make many more discoveries. The distinction he made between the two types of nerve cells is standard today; they are known, in fact as "Golgi type 1" and "Golgi type 2" neurons. Golgi also made a fundamental contribution to the cure of malaria by understanding the cycle of the disease and by experimenting with quinine as its cure. In 1897–1898, Golgi discovered the so-called Golgi apparatus, a major breakthrough in cell biology that was, however, only confirmed in the 1950s and 1960s by the use of electron microscopes. In 1906, Golgi shared the Nobel Prize with the Spanish physiologist Santiago Ramon y Cajal.

Golgi was rector of Pavia University and became a senator in 1900. He died in Pavia in January 1926.

GONELLA, GUIDO (1905–1982). A journalist from Verona, Guido Gonella first made his name in the Catholic students' movement, the **Federazione Universitaria Cattolici Italiana**/Catholic University Graduates' Movement of Italy (FUCI). Members included many postwar leaders of the **Democrazia Cristiana**/Christian Democracy Party (DC), such as **Aldo Moro** and **Giulio Andreotti**. Like Andreotti, Gonella became one of the young Catholic intellectuals close to, and inspired by, **Alcide De Gasperi**.

As early as 1932, Gonella was the managing editor of the bi-monthly *Illustrazione Vaticana*, a journal used to disseminate De Gasperi's views. He was also editor of *Rassegna Internazionale di documentazione*. Because of these journals' purported antifascist slant, Gonella was arrested in 1939 on the eve of war in Poland. Catholic opinion favored Poland, but the Fascist regime was allied to Germany. Gonella was sentenced to a spell of "political surveillance," but he was still able to became assistant editor of *L'Osservatore Romano*, the influential **Vatican** daily newspaper. In 1943, he founded *Il Popolo*, which was to become the daily broadsheet of the DC. He remained at its helm until 1946. In the DC, his role included writing much of the program at the party's initial convention. From a Catholic background shared by his fellow DC militants, Gonella wanted to establish for his party a mass base among those who had been the backbone of the Fascist movement: small property owners and the lower middle class, who feared the Bolshevik menace. Artisans, shopkeepers, small businessmen, and white-collar workers sought assurances that Catholic morality and property rights would not suffer and that individual initiative would be protected from monopoly capitalism as well as from the ideological zeal of the left.

Gonella was elected to the **Constituent Assembly** and subsequently to the Chamber of Deputies in the first **Parliament** of the new republic. Consistently reelected to Parliament, he served as minister of **education** in De Gasperi's first five governments (1946–1951) and was also political secretary of the DC between 1950 and 1953. He subsequently served in almost every government until the 1972–1973 cabinet formed by **Giulio Andreotti**. He did not, however, serve in the mid-1960s administrations of Aldo Moro that carried out the **opening to the left**. Gonella was elected to the Senate in 1972 and served as a senator, and, after 1979, as a member of the first elected European Parliament, until his death in 1982. *See also* PRESS.

GORIA, GIOVANNI (1943–1994). Republican Italy's youngest-ever **president of the Council of Ministers** (prime minister), Goria was a native of the Piedmont town of Asti. His national political career began in 1976, when he was elected to the Chamber of Deputies; his ministerial career began just a few years later. In December 1982, Goria became minister for the treasury and held this post until his accession to the premiership in July 1987. During his spell as treasury minister, a huge increase in public spending took place, and the Italian state regularly ran annual budget deficits of 12–14 percent of GDP.

As prime minister, Goria soon discovered that he had little or no power to implement cuts in spending or to follow any constructive policies at all. Closely allied to **Ciriaco De Mita**, the then secretary of the **Democrazia Cristiana**/Christian Democracy Party (DC), Goria found that his government was hostage to the campaign being waged against De Mita by the **Partito Socialista Italiano**/Italian Socialist Party (PSI), and by the DC leader's own rivals within the party. His nine months as prime minister were a period of permanent political crisis in which Goria himself aged visibly. His treatment by the **press** was quite ruthless: To symbolize Goria's political nullity, one cartoonist began to represent the prime minister by drawing only his trademark wavy hair and full beard. Goria's government collapsed in March 1988. He returned to ministerial office only in 1991, as agriculture minister, and took the more prestigious post of finance minister in the administration formed by **Giuliano Amato** in June 1992. He resigned in January 1993 after he was briefly placed under investigation by the judiciary of his native Asti. He died there in May 1994.

GRAMSCI, ANTONIO (1891–1937). Born in Cagliari, **Sardinia**, Gramsci overcame a serious childhood accident and his family's limited economic means to attend the university in **Turin**. It was here that he began his involvement in politics, joining the **Partito Socialista Italiano**/Italian Socialist Party (PSI) in 1913, and becoming a member of the editorial staff of the party paper *Avanti!* After the

Bolshevik revolution in Russia, Gramsci founded *Ordine nuovo*, a periodical distributed mostly in Turin that published pro-Soviet views and took issue with what Gramsci saw as the timidity and futility of the PSI and organized labor in the face of the growing Fascist menace. *Ordine nuovo* subsequently became the official paper of the **Partito Comunista Italiano**/Italian Communist Party (PCI) after its formation in January 1921, and Gramsci, as editor, became a member of the new party's central committee, as well as a parliamentary deputy in 1924.

Gramsci disapproved of the PCI's intransigent insistence upon an impractical policy of armed resistance to the Fascists. Gramsci wanted to build a mass party that united the northern workers, the southern peasantry, and middle-class progressives against **Fascism**. His more moderate line prevailed. In 1926, the party's third congress, held in secret in Lyon, France, chose him as its new leader. Unlike his close friend from the university and successor as leader of the PCI, **Palmiro Togliatti**, Gramsci was unable to refrain from criticizing the degeneration of the Soviet regime. In October 1926, he condemned the dictatorial tendencies of the Soviet party in a famous letter to its central committee, which Togliatti, the Italian representative in Moscow, deliberately suppressed.

Shortly afterward, Gramsci bravely reentered Italy to oppose **Benito Mussolini**'s repressive laws against the **press** and political freedom, but he was arrested on 8 November 1926, before the parliamentary debate could begin. In 1928, he was sentenced to over 20 years of imprisonment. Between 1928 and 1933, he was held in a jail in the southern city of **Bari**. While in prison, his health began to fail. International interest in his case caused the authorities to allow Gramsci to leave prison briefly in 1934, returning to jail in 1935. Finally released in April 1937, he died of a brain hemorrhage in the same month. He was survived by his wife and two children, who were living in the Soviet Union.

During his confinement, Gramsci wrote copiously on philosophical, political, historical, and social questions. When, after the war, his prison letters and notebooks were published by the progressive publisher Einaudi of Turin, it became clear that, despite the difficulties of his style, Gramsci was a thinker of the first order. In his view, it was a mistake to believe that there could be only one way to achieve the ultimate goal of socialism; each country would have to find its own individual road to achieving a socialist society. This idea assumed immense political importance after 1945, when Togliatti used it to justify the PCI's relative independence from Moscow. Eventually, the notion of "many roads to socialism" undergirded the *compromesso storico*. In Italy, Gramsci considered that socialism would only supersede capitalism after the PCI had attained cultural "hegemony" by controlling and shaping the means of intellectual production and hence the formation of ideas.

GRANDI, DINO (1895–1988). A lawyer from Imola, Dino Grandi was simultaneously intelligent, violent, and an eager social climber. He was a powerful provincial action-squad leader in Emilia-Romagna who was elected to **Parliament** in May 1921. After **Benito Mussolini** took power, Grandi became undersecretary at the Ministry of Foreign Affairs and, from September 1929, foreign minister. He remained at that post for three years at which time Mussolini resumed direction of foreign affairs, sweetening Grandi's dismissal by making him ambassador to the United Kingdom where he became known for his gentlemanly love of golf, his belligerent posturing at the London Naval Conference (1930), and his reassurances to the British government in 1935 concerning Italian intentions in **Ethiopia**. In his eagerness to feed the Duce's vanity, Grandi exaggerated his reports of British admiration for Mussolini and consistently told the Italian dictator what he most wanted to hear. Mussolini repaid him by failing to keep him apprised either about initiatives in Ethiopia or, eventually, in Spain. As a result, Grandi was often ill-informed, forcing him to fabricate quite transparently. His standing in British circles declined steadily. He returned to Italy in 1939.

Grandi supported Mussolini's decision to enter the war in June 1940. Subsequently, after the disasters in Greece, North Africa, and Russia were capped by the Anglo-American invasion of Sicily, the demoralization of the Italian army was complete. It was clear that changes were urgently needed. On 24–25 July 1943, Mussolini opened the first wartime meeting of the **Fascist Grand Council** with a rambling speech in which it became clear that he had no policy objectives. Grandi led the revolt of those who believed that Mussolini's powers had to be curbed, even though to this day it is not clear that they realized that they were about to provoke the Duce's downfall, by proposing that the king should resume his role as supreme military commander. Mussolini allowed Grandi's motion to come to a vote; the Grandi motion carried handily, 19 in favor, seven opposed, and one abstention. The meeting ended at 3:00 A.M. after nearly 10 hours of argument. Mussolini was arrested later the same day.

Grandi escaped to Portugal in August 1943 and was sentenced to death in absentia by the **Republic of Salò** at Verona in January 1944. He lived in Portugal and Brazil until the 1960s, then returned to Italy under a presidential amnesty. He died in **Bologna**. *See also* QUADRUMVIRATE.

GRAZIANI, RODOLFO (1882–1955). Born in Frosinone just south of **Rome**, Graziani finished **World War I** as a colonel but left army service for private life after that war. He returned to active duty in 1922 and was sent to **Libya**, where he coordinated efforts at putting down Senussi irregulars, who had effectively slowed Italian colonization. By 1930, he had hanged their leaders in front of what remained of their clans after 60,000 of their number had been killed. When he returned to Italy in 1934, it was as a general commanding an army corps.

In the following year, he was sent to **Ethiopia** to prepare the attack on that country. His brutal success in subduing the Ethiopian forces—including the use of poison gas—led to his promotion to marshal. In 1936, he replaced his archrival, **Pietro Badoglio**, as viceroy of Ethiopia. When Graziani was repatriated in 1937, he was styled Marquis of Neghelli.

In 1939, Graziani became chief of the General Staff, and in 1940 he was put in command of Italian forces in North Africa. They numbered over 300,000 but were still equipped with rifles of an 1891 design and had but 160 aircraft at their disposal. Accustomed to putting down nomadic tribesmen and inordinately proud of having been the first commander ever to use armored vehicles in the desert, Graziani realized too late that the party placemen around him in command positions were lacking in military experience. Far less numerous British and Commonwealth forces (two divisions faced Graziani's 10) were better led and far better organized, so much so that early in January 1941 they forced Graziani to retreat so rapidly that he was relieved of his duties and summoned to Rome by a Commission of Inquiry.

Deprived of his command, Graziani resumed private life until September 1943, when he rejoined **Benito Mussolini** in the **Republic of Salò**, in which he served as defense minister. On being captured by the advancing Allies, he avoided execution but was tried by Italian courts in 1948 and sentenced to 19 years' imprisonment for "collaboration with the German invader." Amnestied after just five years, he became honorary president of the **Movimento Sociale Italiano/** Italian Social Movement (MSI). He died in 1955 in Rome. *See also* LIBYA.

GRONCHI, GIOVANNI (1887–1978). Born in Pontedera (Pisa), by his early twenties this Tuscan schoolteacher was among those liberal Catholics who eventually formed the **Partito Popolare Italiano/**Italian People's Party (PPI) in 1919. After **World War I**, he was active in **Azione Cattolica/**Catholic Action (ACI); by 1922, Gronchi was at the head of Catholic labor unions. He publicly opposed Pius XI's involving *Azione Cattolica* in labor questions, fearful that it would inevitably lead to **trade unions'** subordination to the regime. When Gronchi realized the futility of his struggle for autonomy, he repeatedly warned that tying the Church closely to the regime could only damage the Church, the worker, and the nation, should Fascist militarism and incompetence lead to disaster. Moreover, he argued that the new state, far from being consonant with Catholic doctrine as expressed in *Rerum Novarum*, was an instrument for the imposition of the state's will. Dissenting from the pope's policies, Gronchi withdrew from political activity until 1943.

In September 1943, the new government of **Pietro Badoglio** made it possible for party life to resume. Gronchi soon emerged as a major figure in the nascent **Democrazia Cristiana/**Christian Democracy Party (DC). Gronchi was a conspicuous figure on the left of the DC and eventually broke with the more centrist position of **Alcide De Gasperi**. He advocated an independent Italian foreign policy within Western Europe and an "opening" to the socialists. By combining their strength, the Catholic and socialist masses could, in his view, create a left Catholic regime in Italy. In 1955 these progressive political views attracted the combined votes of the **Partito Comunista Italiano/**Italian Communist Party (PCI) and the **Partito Socialista Italiano/**Italian Socialist Party (PSI) and allowed the DC to propel him into the presidency of the republic, where he remained until 1962, when he became a life senator. While president, his official trip to the Soviet Union in February 1960 exposed him to criticism from the nationalist and conservative right. Active in the Senate as he had been in the party, he served on the foreign affairs committee and—in the last **Parliament** of his life (he died in **Rome** in 1978)—on the defense committee. *See also* TAMBRONI, FERNANDO.

GUARANTEE LAWS. Following the occupation of **Rome** in 1870, relations with the **papacy** became the major concern of the Italian government. Pope Pius IX was determined to maintain control of at least a symbolic portion of the city. This no Italian government would allow, for fear of foreign involvement (Pius asked Prussia to intervene on his behalf in the summer of 1870). A generous settlement was necessary. In May 1871, the Italian state unilaterally recognized the pope as a head of state, conceded his right to free communication with foreign Catholics, gave diplomatic recognition to foreign ambassadors at the **Vatican**, and offered a substantial annual subsidy (later refused) for the papal court's expenses. The government also renounced some of its powers over the nomination of bishops within Italian territorial boundaries, although it was prevented from abolishing all jurisdiction over Church affairs by the strongly anticlerical majority in Parliament.

These *guarentigie* (guarantees) were greeted with hostility by Pius IX. For the next 50 years, Pius IX and his successors treated themselves as prisoners of conscience and refused to go outside the walls of St. Peter's. Pius also unsuccessfully attempted to persuade the Catholic nations of Europe to maintain their embassies at **Florence**, the former capital, not Rome. A papal ban forbidding Catholic heads of state to visit Rome was enacted and remained in force until 1920. Pius's reaction was not mere pique. The pope could not afford to bow to the law for fear that foreign countries would use his subordination to the Italian state as an excuse to interfere with his spiritual powers over their Catholic citizens. Even without the pope's participation, however, the guarantees provided a modus vivendi between church and state until they were superseded by the **Lateran pacts** in 1929. See also CATHOLICISM; GENTILONI PACT.

– H –

HISTORIC COMPROMISE. *See COMPROMESSO STORICO.*

HOARE-LAVAL PACT. Sir Samuel Hoare served as British foreign minister in 1935 in the government of Samuel Baldwin. His opposite number in France was Pierre Laval. At the beginning of December 1935, Hoare and Laval agreed to resolve the international crisis provoked by **Benito Mussolini**'s invasion of **Ethiopia** in October by offering to cede to Ethiopia a port in British Somaliland if Emperor Haile Selassie would cede to Italy the Ogaden and Tigray. Furthermore, Britain and France would recognize Italian economic paramountcy in the rest of Ethiopia. In substance, the Ethiopian government was asked to surrender two-thirds of its territory and give Italy a de facto protectorate over what remained.

This offer was not rejected out-of-hand by Mussolini, though he really wanted a formal Italian protectorate. Before negotiations could resume, the Hoare-Laval proposals were leaked to the French press. The result was a furor, especially in Britain. Baldwin dismissed Hoare (who was to resume a political role a few years later as British ambassador to Spain), blaming the initiative on Laval; British distrust of the French increased. Thus, not only was Mussolini in a position to conquer the territory, but the onus for the breakdown of negotiations could be put on the democracies. By May 1936, the Italian army had entered Addis Ababa, the capital of Ethiopia. In July, the League of Nations lifted sanctions against the aggressor. Mussolini was able to claim that Italy had stood up to 60 nations arrayed against it. *See also* FOREIGN POLICY; FOUR POWER PACT.

HOUSE OF FREEDOMS. *See* CASA DELLE LIBERTÀ (CDL).

– I –

IMMIGRATION. Italy is one of the chief destinations of migrants from Albania, Africa, China, Eastern Europe (especially Romania), and the Philippines. Its lengthy coastline invites a commercial traffic of clandestine immigration, and there have been many tragic drownings when boats carrying would-be migrants capsized. More than 2.3 million immigrants, almost all of them comparatively recent arrivals, possessed a *permesso di soggiorno* (residency permit) in January 2005.

This influx of migrants, who have been drawn to Italy by the economic difficulties of Africa and Eastern Europe, the ease with which immigrants can obtain undocumented work on the black market, and the shortage of Italians willing to do jobs involving hard manual labor, has turned Italy into a multicultural society in the space of little more than a decade. As recently as the early 1990s, Italy was a highly homogeneous society. Immigration has been regulated by a series of laws (the "Martelli law" of 1990, the "Turco-Napolitano" law of 1997, and the "**Bossi-Fini**" law of 2002) that have tried to regulate the phenomenon and, more recently, appease growing anti-immigrant sentiment. Political parties such as the **Lega Nord**/Northern League (LN) have capitalized on some of the social problems worsened by the recent migratory wave (petty criminality, prostitution, etc.) to campaign against the multicultural society more generally. On the other hand, in many cities, language and job-training programs are available, as are municipal centers to offer assistance in finding housing and in adjusting to Italian life.

Although the political parties of the right dislike immigration, there is little doubt that Italy needs to accommodate itself to the reality of becoming a less homogeneous society. Italy has one of the lowest demographic growth rates in the world and needs migration to maintain its standard of living. *See also* POPULATION.

INGRAO, PIETRO (1915–). Born in Latina province near **Rome**, Ingrao began a lifetime of antifascist activity in adolescence. After joining the **Partito Comunista Italiano**/Italian Communist Party (PCI) in 1940, he earned the distinction of being sought by the Fascist police because he had become one of the leaders of the clandestine communist group operating in Rome. From a temporary safe house in Calabria, he managed to reach **Milan**, where he became one of the editors of the clandestine newspaper *Unità*, a post in which he was confirmed for 10 years beginning in 1947.

From his first election in 1948 to 1992, Ingrao served steadily as a member of the Chamber of Deputies. In 1963, he was chosen vice president of the Communist Parliamentary Group. Five years later, he was elected president of the Parliamentary Group and retained that post until 1972, when he was put in charge of interregional coordination. In 1975, he became director of the party's Study Center for State Reform. He was elected to serve as president of the Chamber of Deputies between 1976 and 1979, and when he was redesignated for that post he refused in order to serve on the Committee for Constitutional Affairs.

Ingrao, long identified as one of the most influential members of the Central Committee, left the party in 1993. At the **Bologna** convention of the PCI in 1991, Ingrao struggled to retain much of the traditional symbolism of the West's leading communist party. While he did not carry the day, it was clear that he spoke for much of the working-class base of the party. Ingrao supported the **Partito di Rifondazione Comunista**/Communist Refoundation (PRC) in the 2004 European elections. He remains proud of the communist heritage of the Italian left.

INTEGRALISM. The devout of any faith who advocate the application of its sociology and teachings to political and social life are "integralists," since they seek to integrate faith and policy. Islam is not alone in this view: It exists as well in Roman Catholic states, Italy being a case in point. Beginning in 1948, Luigi Gedda organized civic committees that were meant to check the perceived threat of Bolshevism by ensuring the coherence of the Catholic vote as part of **Azione Cattolica**/Catholic Action (ACI), which also organized newly enfranchised **women**. By 1949, Italian Catholics voting for Marxist parties risked excommunication. These initiatives linked the Roman Catholic Church with the right-most wing of the **Democrazia Cristiana**/Christian Democracy Party (DC).

The most aggressive Catholics were often active in the cities deep in the "Red Belt" of Emilia-Romagna and northward. Cardinal Lercaro of **Bologna**, for example, with the support of local industrialists, had small trucks and school buses converted into mobile chapels (the famous *cappelle volanti* or flying chapels) that, together with a priest, would drive on Sunday mornings into working-class neighborhoods, there to play over loudspeakers recordings of church bells and hymns while serving mass to passersby. Others sought expression through a faction of the early DC ably led by Professor Giorgio La Pira and

Giuseppe Dossetti, an ex-partisan member of the **Constituent Assembly**. *See also* CATHOLICISM; GONELLA, GUIDO.

IOTTI, LEONILDE (1920–1999). The first woman ever to become president of the Italian Chamber of Deputies, "Nilde" Iotti was born in Reggio Emilia (Emilia-Romagna). She became a communist activist while in her teens, and in 1946 she was one of the very few women elected to the **Constituent Assembly**. After the war, she was elected to the Central Committee of the **Partito Comunista Italiano/** Italian Communist Party (PCI) and to its *direzione*, or inner cabinet, and played an important role in making party policy, especially on **women**'s issues. Iotti was in fact even closer to the heart of the PCI's leadership than these institutional posts suggest: She was the companion of **Palmiro Togliatti**, the party leader, until his death in 1964. In **Parliament**, she was especially active in the struggle to obtain a **divorce** law during the late 1960s and then to defend the law from a **referendum** challenge in 1974.

Iotti became deputy president of the Chamber in 1972, and in 1979 replaced another communist, **Pietro Ingrao**, as the Chamber's president. She held the post until 1992. In 1987, during a lengthy and confused government crisis, Iotti was briefly given an exploratory mandate by President **Francesco Cossiga** to form a new government. Although her attempts failed, it was the first time that a member of the PCI had been entrusted with this task. Iotti died in **Rome** in December 1999.

IRREDENTISMO. The occupation of **Rome** in 1870 still left a number of "unredeemed" Italian territories such as the Trentino and **Trieste**. In 1877, the radical politician Matteo Renato Imbriani formed, with the patronage of **Giuseppe Garibaldi**, an association called L'Italia irredenta, whose goal was the liberation of these "unredeemed" territories from Austrian rule. The Italian government's refusal to push Italy's claims at the Congress of Berlin (1878) and the pro-German foreign policy followed by the administrations of **Agostino Depretis** and **Francesco Crispi** after the signature of the Triple Alliance in 1882 led the association to become one of the main opposition forces in liberal Italy. An offshoot of the association, the "Committee for Trento and Trieste," was banned by Crispi in 1889. Subsequently, clubs of citizens named in honor of an Italian nationalist from Trieste, Guglielmo Oberdan, who had been hanged by the Austrians, were also banned.

After 1900, the movement became more prone to violence and illegality, and many irredentists transmuted their beliefs into nationalism and even imperialism. *Irredentismo* was at the bottom of the decision of many socialists, radicals, and republicans to support the war in 1914, although unlike the nationalists, the irredentists were usually in favor of entering the war on the side of the Entente. By 1919, when **Gabriele D'Annunzio** seized **Fiume** to general popular approval, the movement had lost its authenticity. **Benito Mussolini** also used the rhetoric of *irredentismo* to justify Italian adventures in Dalmatia, **Albania**, and the eastern Mediterranean—a perversion of the original ideal.

ISTITUTO PER LA RICOSTRUZIONE INDUSTRIALE/Institute for Industrial Reconstruction (IRI). For most of the latter half of the 20th century, the state holding company, IRI, held a central position in the Italian economy. The company was set up in 1933, as the Fascist administration struggled to rescue the country's financial system from the huge losses the principal investment banks had incurred lending to Depression-hit manufacturing firms. In essence, the state bailed the banks out and was left with a ragbag of industrial companies whose activities included steel, shipbuilding, electricity generation, and telephones. The initial goal was to restore IRI's component parts back into private ownership as soon as their profitability warranted it, but in 1937 the regime's increasingly belligerent foreign policy goals led it to desire greater control over economic production, and IRI, with the cooperation of the industrial elite, was thus used to coordinate the Italian state's (somewhat inefficient) transition to a war economy.

After the war, IRI's member firms employed almost 100,000 people and faced immense problems readjusting to a peacetime economy. After a decade of drift, the Italian government acted, establishing, in December 1956, the Ministry for State Participation in Industry, which created a three-tier system of control for state-owned businesses. The bottom, operating tier was occupied by individual joint-stock companies, which were grouped into *enti di gestione* (management structures) answerable to the ministry and wholly owned by it. The *enti di gestione*, of which IRI was the biggest, were supposed to be run as ongoing economic concerns, with the government providing strategic direction. In particular, from 1957 onward, IRI was directed to spend at least 40 percent of its capital investment budget in **southern Italy**.

IRI itself was divided into six main *società finanziarie* (financial holding companies). These controlled the company's telephone, shipping, engineering, shipbuilding, steel, and electricity generation activities. In addition, the company controlled a number of banks, the state television service, and the national airline, Alitalia. By the early 1960s, IRI controlled nearly 7 percent of total manufacturing output, and its largest subsidiary, Finsider, the steel company, had become one of the highest producing steel corporations in the world.

The early 1960s were the high point of IRI's success. Gradually, the shortcomings of state-controlled enterprises everywhere began to take a toll on the institution's efficiency. Investment decisions were too often taken for political reasons; layoffs were avoided; **over-generous** pension, job security, and fringe benefit rights were awarded to the workforce; bureaucratic empire building took place; and strategic decision making, which required broad ministerial, union, and managerial consensus, was slow and unresponsive to changes in market demand. By 1982, when **Romano Prodi** took over as chairman of the company, IRI was losing 3 trillion lire every year and had 35 trillion lire of accumulated debt. Prodi imposed a measure of financial discipline and attempted to solve the debt problem by asset sales, but his plans swiftly ran into political opposition. In 1986, Prodi wanted to sell off the Alfa Romeo car firm to the American carmaker Ford, but the government intervened and forced him to sell the company to **FIAT** instead. When Prodi's political backer, **Ciriaco De Mita**, was forced from power in 1989, the privatization program was halted completely, and Prodi lost his job. The European Union (EU) has succeeded, however, where Prodi failed. The need to meet EU guidelines has led to significant privatizations since 1992, notably in the telecom sector, although skeptical Italian economists claim that not enough has been done to liberate the newly privatized firms from political control. *See also* ECONOMIC MIRACLE; ECONOMY; EUROPEAN INTEGRATION; OLIVE TREE COALITION.

– L –

LABRIOLA, ANTONIO (1843–1904). One of the most prominent Marxist philosophers of the late 19th century, Antonio Labriola was the son of a schoolteacher from Cassino (Campania). A brilliant student who won prizes for essays on Spinoza and Greek interpretations of Socrates's thought before he was 30 years old, Labriola became *ordinario* (full professor) of history in 1877. Labriola's conversion to socialism was a slow process. The seemingly scientific approach of Marxism to social questions, his disgust at the increasingly corrupt form of parliamentary democracy practiced in liberal Italy, contacts with workers' study groups, and the intolerance of right-wing students toward his ideas (Labriola was forced to abandon a course on the French Revolution in February 1889 by riotous students) were the chief factors that led him to embrace the socialist cause, which can be dated to a speech he gave to a study group of Roman workers in June 1889.

In the 1890s, Labriola established an international reputation as a Marxist theorist. Between April 1895 and 1897, he published three long essays on historical materialism in the journal *Devenir Social*, edited by the French theorist Georges Sorel. In these essays, Labriola introduced the notion of Marxism as a practical doctrine—a guide to understanding historical development rather than a dogma—that would later be taken up by **Antonio Gramsci**. In Italy, the same essays were edited for publication by **Benedetto Croce**, and they had an enormous influence on Croce's early thought.

Despite his doctrinal flexibility, Labriola was hostile to the reformism of **Filippo Turati**. He opposed the **Partito Socialista Italiano/**Italian Socialist Party's (PSI) collaboration with the forces of Italian liberalism and evinced at times an intemperate hostility toward the Italian bourgeoisie. Paradoxically, however, he supported the imperialist adventures of the Italian state in **Libya** and East Africa, arguing somewhat coldly that imperialism was a necessary stage in the development of European capitalism, from which Italy could not refrain without condemning itself to social backwardness. Labriola died of throat cancer in 1904.

LABRIOLA, ARTURO (1873–1959). The most noted Italian follower of the French syndicalist Georges Sorel, Labriola was viewed as a

226 • LA MALFA, UGO

heretic by the socialist movement in Italy, which he had joined in 1895, the year he received his *laurea* in jurisprudence from the University of **Naples**. Syndicalist thinking was one of the mainsprings of the general strike of September 1904, in which Labriola played an important organizational role. His contempt for parliamentary democracy and the pacific resolution of political disputes that pervaded the thinking of the Italian right in the early 20th century runs through his prewar writings. Unsurprisingly, in his periodical, *Avanguardia socialista (The Socialist Vanguard)*, published between December 1902 and October 1906, and in his many books and pamphlets, he espoused an interpretation of Marxism that differed from both the moderate social democracy of **Leonida Bissolati** and the mainstream of the **Partito Socialista Italiano**/Italian Socialist Party (PSI), which believed that socialism would occur through revolutionary action only when historical conditions were ripe.

Labriola, like Sorel and the young **Benito Mussolini**, believed that the working class should accelerate the historical process and smash the institutions of the state through violent action by the trade unions. He was "intransigently revolutionary," having bolted from the PSI in 1907. Elected to **Parliament** in 1913 as an independent socialist, he found convoluted reasons for defending Italy's war against Turkey and Germany and Austria. He accepted the post of minister for labor in the last government of **Giovanni Giolitti** in 1921 and yet opposed **Fascism** both in Parliament and in a much-discussed book, *La dittatura dei borghesi (The Dictatorship of the Middle Class*, 1924). Labriola was dismissed from his appointment as a professor at the University of Messina for having criticized the regime. Thereupon, he immigrated to France and Belgium and lived in exile until the 1935 invasion of **Ethiopia**, which he openly supported, induced him to return.

After the fall of Fascism, Labriola resumed an active political role. He was elected to the **Constituent Assembly** in 1946 and became a life senator in 1948. In 1956, he was elected to the Naples city council as an independent on the list of the **Partito Comunista Italiano/** Italian Communist Party (PCI). He died in his native Naples in 1959.

LA MALFA, UGO (1903–1979). One of Italy's most honest and talented postwar leaders, the **Palermo**-born Ugo La Malfa was an exponent of a socially humane brand of liberal capitalism that found few adherents in postwar Italy. As a student, he distinguished himself by both scholarly brilliance and antifascist activism (he was arrested briefly in 1934 and took part in the clandestine movement **Giustizia e Libertà**). A founder of the **Partito d'Azione/**Action Party (PdA) in 1942, he was its representative in the **Comitati di Liberazione Nazionale/**National Liberation Committees (CLN) after the Italian surrender in September 1943.

La Malfa's ministerial career began immediately after the war. He was minister for transport under **Ferruccio Parri** and for foreign trade in the first of **Alcide De Gasperi**'s eight governments (November 1945–June 1946).

Discontented with the policies being followed by Emilio Lussu, leader of the PdA, La Malfa—together with Parri—left the party in February 1946 to form the "Movement for Republican Democracy," which later merged with the **Partito Repubblicano Italiano/**Italian Republican Party (PRI). Over the next 30 years, La Malfa came to symbolize the tiny PRI, whose reputation for being the "conscience" of the Italian center-left owed much to La Malfa's intellectual rigor and personal integrity. He became party leader in 1965 after a period as budget minister under **Amintore Fanfani** (1960–1963). La Malfa was the minister responsible for the policy of austerity that followed the 1973 oil shock. He served as vice premier under **Aldo Moro** between 1974 and 1976, and continued to preach a message of fiscal prudence. The need for financial stability led La Malfa to become Italy's most vocal exponent of entry into the European Monetary System in 1979.

President **Sandro Pertini** offered La Malfa the chance to form a government in March 1979. Blocked by the **Democrazia Cristiana/**Christian Democracy Party (DC), whose members distrusted his reforming zeal, La Malfa was forced to accept second best and become vice premier and budget minister under **Giulio Andreotti**. La Malfa immediately proposed large spending cuts but did not live long enough to put them into effect. Tired out by overwork, he died suddenly in **Rome** in the spring of 1979. His son, Giorgio, has followed in his father's footsteps, becoming budget minister under **Francesco Cossiga** in 1981 and leader of the PRI since 1987.

LA MARMORA FERRERO, ALFONSO (1804–1878). One of four brothers, all of whom rose to the rank of general in the Piedmontese army, Alfonso La Marmora was the first military officer to become prime minister of Italy, in September 1864. He had earlier served as prime minister of the Kingdom of Sardinia for six months in 1859, after the peace of Villafranca and the subsequent resignation of **Camillo Benso di Cavour**. During his first spell in office, a law unifying local administration throughout the country was promulgated. Building on earlier laws presented by **Urbano Rattazzi** in 1863, the new local government arrangements established tight central control over the peninsula. In addition, Italian law was harmonized with Sardinian law in matters of public health, the classification of roads, railways, canals, and other public works. During La Marmora's period as premier (he continued to govern until June 1866, interrupted only by a brief government crisis in December 1865), the new civil code was introduced. The code, which has been in force since January 1866, permitted civil marriage for the first time but backed away from introducing **divorce**. The judicial inferiority of **women** and children born outside marriage was established.

La Marmora gave up politics in June 1866 to lead the Italian forces in the war against Austria. Despite his creation of the **Bersaglieri**, his military leadership was less than inspiring: Italian troops under his command were defeated at Custoza in June 1866, largely as a result of his errors as a commander. After the war, La Marmora was the target of bitter public criticism both for his conduct in the field and for the wider failure of his governments to prepare the new kingdom's armed forces. He retired into seclusion, emerging only in 1870 when King **Victor Emmanuel II** made him Lieutenant of **Rome**. He died in **Florence** in 1878.

LAND REFORM. One of the most contentious measures introduced in the immediate postwar period, the 1950 land reform was a major step in the modernization of Italian agriculture and reduced the political power of the landowning class in southern and central Italy. Pressure for land reform arose after the death of **Benito Mussolini** when peasants in **Sicily** and other parts of Italy occupied and began to cultivate land left fallow by absentee landlords. Fausto Gullo of the **Partito Comunista Italiano**/Italian Communist Party (PCI), as minister for agriculture in Allied-occupied Italy, introduced a series of decrees in 1944 that allowed peasant cooperatives to take over arable land left uncultivated by its owners. Over the next two years, tens of thousands of peasants formed **cooperatives**, and a considerable quantity of land was put to productive use. Gullo's decrees met with uncompromising opposition from the **Democrazia Cristiana**/Christian Democracy Party (DC), worried that the PCI would reap a harvest of votes among the rural poor, and from the **Partito Liberale Italiano/** Italian Liberal Party (PLI).

Under **Antonio Segni**, minister for agriculture in the cabinet formed by **Alcide De Gasperi** in July 1946, the legal balance was restored to favor the landowners. In 1949, grievances boiled over and all of **southern Italy**, save Calabria and Basilicata, saw mass occupations of private land. The police intervened to defend private property, and a number of people were killed. Such repressive tactics only exacerbated tensions in the **Mezzogiorno** and won the DC no friends in Washington. Starting in May 1950, therefore, De Gasperi and Segni promoted three laws (one for Sicily, one for Calabria, and one for the marshland areas near **Rome** and the Po River valley) that aimed to break up the great estates and redistribute the land among the peasants who worked it. State land development agencies were created to improve uncultivated terrain and to sell it, at discounted prices, to landless peasants. Generous land improvement grants were provided, and the Italian government made an expensive effort to provide infrastructure for normally neglected rural regions.

Over the next two decades, agricultural productivity rose dramatically in Italy, and the net harvest of the main crops (grain, grapes, vegetables) increased despite a sharp fall in farm workers as peasants migrated to the booming factories of the industrial cities and to northern Europe. Such gains in production, however, were due less to the land reform, which affected only a few hundred thousand people directly, than to the huge investments poured into agriculture by the DC in the 1950s and 1960s. By the 1970s, more than one-third of the average farmer's income came from state subsidies, and unsurprisingly, the agricultural producers' associations (*consorzie*) became a bastion of support for the DC. *See also* CASSA PER IL MEZZOGIORNO; *LATIFONDI*; SOUTHERN ITALY.

LANZA, GIOVANNI (1810–1882). By training, a doctor of medicine, Giovanni Lanza's historical legacy was the stiff and painful cure that he gave to the Italian economy during his premiership from 1869 to 1873. Elected to the Piedmontese Parliament for the first time in 1849, he served as minister of education and minister of finance under **Camillo Benso di Cavour** in the 1850s. After reunification he became one of the leading figures of the parliamentary right. He was minister of the interior in 1864 in the **La Marmora** government but resigned in opposition to the grist tax (*dazio sul macinato*) imposed by **Quintino Sella**.

Lanza became premier in 1869. In economic policy, he and his treasury minister, **Marco Minghetti**, struggled to put the nation's accounts in order; in **foreign policy** Lanza successfully persuaded King **Victor Emmanuel II** not to side with the French in the Franco–Prussian War. Instead, Lanza took the opportunity to complete the unification of Italy by occupying **Rome** and proclaiming it the capital on 27 March 1871. Lanza unsuccessfully tried to put relations with the Church on a firm footing after the occupation of Rome. The **guarantee laws**, though not recognized by the Church, served as a modus vivendi between the spiritual and temporal powers within the Italian state until the **Lateran pacts** in 1929. Lanza was forced to resign in 1873. He continued to serve as deputy for his native Casale Monferatto (Piedmont) until his death in 1882. *See also* CATHOLICISM.

LATERAN PACTS. The Lateran pacts were an agreement reached between **Mussolini** and Pope Pius XI that replaced the **guarantee laws** of 1871 as the basis for church-state relations in Italy. They were the fruit of a lengthy period of secret negotiations among Pius, the Vatican's foreign minister, Cardinal Pietro Gasparri, **Benito Mussolini**, and the Fascist justice minister, **Alfredo Rocco**. Negotiations began in August 1926, but ran into serious difficulties over **education**, which the Church was not prepared to wholly cede to the Fascist state. Eventually, in February 1929, in the Lateran Palace in Rome, Mussolini and the pope came to a deal that granted unique privileges within the state to the Catholic Church.

The agreement consisted of three separate pacts. The first was a treaty of mutual recognition between the Vatican and the Italian state, whereby Italy acknowledged the territorial rights of the pope over the Vatican palaces and a number of other churches in **Rome**, and accepted that the Vatican was an independent state that could maintain diplomatic relations with other states even during times of war. The pope, in return, recognized the kingdom of Italy. A financial convention appended to the treaty constrained Italy to pay substantial reparations for Church property expropriated after the **Risorgimento**.

An additional concordat established the role that the Church would play in the civil life of the nation. Here, too, the Church won substantial concessions. Mussolini recognized that **Catholicism** should be the official state religion; the state's existing veto power over episcopal appointments should be reduced to a consultative power only; religious instruction would be provided at all levels of primary and secondary education (though not in the **universities**); the Church would be permitted to organize youth associations, including **Azione Cattolica**/Catholic Action (ACI) and the Boy Scouts; and church weddings would have civil recognition. The concordat effectively gave the Church legal autonomy from the totalitarian state. It was greeted with consternation by many Fascists, notably **Giovanni Gentile** and **Roberto Farinacci**. Catholic democrats like **Luigi Sturzo**, **Giovanni Gronchi**, and **Alcide De Gasperi**, by contrast, worried that the Church would become too closely identified with **Fascism**. Pius XI, however, was satisfied. The pacts were a legal bulwark of genuine strength against Fascist encroachment on the Church's traditional activities.

The Lateran pacts were subsequently affirmed—with **Partito Comunista Italiano**/Italian Communist Party (PCI) support—in Article 7 of the 1948 **Constitution**, which reiterates the independence and sovereignty of the Catholic Church and, in paragraph 2, states: "Relations between [state and the church] are governed by the Lateran pacts. Alterations of these pacts, if accepted by both parties, shall require no constitutional amendments."

In 1984, the pacts were renegotiated to give full status to church weddings so long as they conformed with civil law. Vatican annulments of marriages were made reviewable by Italian courts; religious teaching in Italian public schools was left to the discretion of parents; limited tax exemptions were granted to Church properties with a strictly religious function; state stipends to the clergy were ended;

and it was agreed that all disputes between the Vatican and Italy were to be settled in Italian courts, a concession that established the primacy of Italian law. This tilting of the balance toward the state reflects Italy's increasing secularization. *See also* PAPACY.

LATIFONDI. As late as the 1940s, land tenure in **southern Italy** was based on the tradition of the *latifondo*, or large estate. Such estates practiced an essentially feudal system in which the landowner was entitled to most (as much as 75 percent even after 1945) of the crops raised on his land. Tenants had no permanent right to the terrain they cultivated, but usually rented, for a fixed period of time, several thin strips of land, often far apart from each other, to which they had to walk every working day. Richer peasants sublet such strips to poorer ones, whose entire income thus depended on tilling a patch of (often poor) land on behalf of two classes, both of which were profiting from their labor. The peasants were in constant competition with each other for the best strips of land and for the favor of the landowner's *campieri* (overseers) and *gabellotti*, responsible for tax collection on behalf of the landlord. The *campieri* enforced compliance and kept wages low among agricultural laborers, the most oppressed of all Italian social categories. Incomes among the landlords, meanwhile, were huge, but only rarely were they ploughed back into farm modernization.

The social costs of this system were enormous. Southern Italy had a grim rural standard of living by the end of the Fascist period: Hundreds of thousands of peasants lived in one-room homes, without running water or electricity; few southerners had been able to accumulate capital, and hence there was a minuscule entrepreneurial middle class able to lead an economic resurgence; and a cultural pattern of dependency on the powers that be had been established. Perhaps most seriously of all, the **mafia** was a product of the *latifondi*. The landowners and the *gabellotti*, anxious to preserve their positions, paid "men of honor" to intimidate upstart laborers. Convinced that "there is neither law nor justice except by one's own initiative," to quote an old Calabrian saying, many Sicilians and Calabrians became *mafiosi*, a grim and risky form of social mobility.

The social injustice engendered by the *latifondo* system periodically caused political turmoil in southern Italy. In the mid-1890s, when the government's trade policies deprived Sicily of its traditional French market for sulfur exports, with a resultant shift of labor from mining to already overcrowded agriculture, the result was a series of peasant uprisings that were savagely repressed by an invading army of more than 80,000 troops. Under **Fascism**, the landowners' privileges were preserved by the full weight of the state.

After the fall of **Benito Mussolini**, however, the peasantry of the Mezzogiorno were politicized by the **Partito Comunista Italiano/** Italian Communist Party (PCI). In a series of decree laws, the PCI agriculture minister in the government of **Ivanoe Bonomi**, Fausto Gullo, authorized peasant **cooperatives** to take over vast swaths of uncultivated land used by the landowners for hunting, limited the landowners' tithe to 50 percent, banned the *gabellotti*, and established state-owned grain stores to which the peasants could take their produce. These policies were wildly popular with the peasants (and account for a good deal of residual leftism in the rural South even today) but were met by unrelenting opposition and widespread violence from the landlords and political obstruction from the **Democrazia Cristiana/**Christian Democracy Party (DC). The decrees were soon ruled illegal by the high courts, and the peasants had to wait until the agricultural reform of July 1950 for serious improvement in their conditions of life. *See also* CASSA PER IL MEZZOGIORNO; DE GASPERI, ALCIDE; LAND REFORM.

LEGA NORD/Northern League (LN). Lega Nord is the name taken in February 1991 by a confederation of regional leagues campaigning for a federalist reform of the Italian **Constitution**, fiscal reform, privatization, and strong anti-immigrant measures. By far the most important of the leagues was the Lega Lombarda/Lombard League, which redefined localist feeling in much of northern Italy in the 1980s. Formed in 1982, the Lega Lombarda was initially regarded as a political oddity. However, the skillful leadership of **Umberto Bossi**, the worsening corruption of the Italian political system, the growing influx of non-European migrants, and unscrupulous "antisoutherner" rhetoric added to the League's appeal. In the 1987 general elections, Bossi was elected to the Senate.

The real electoral breakthrough, however, came in local elections in May 1990. Exploiting dissatisfaction with the party system, the

Lega Lombarda won 19 percent of the vote in Lombardy; autonomy candidates did unprecedentedly well in other parts of the North. In August 1991, Bossi proposed the division of Italy into three self-governing and fiscally independent "macroregions": the North, the South, and the Center. In the 1992 general elections, the LN took 8 percent of the national vote (17 percent in the North) and became Italy's fourth largest party, with more than 50 representatives in the Chamber of Deputies. Bossi himself was the most popular candidate in the country, receiving more than 250,000 preference votes. In local elections in June 1993, the Lega Nord won the mayoral race in **Milan**, with over 40 percent of the poll.

However, three factors prevented the LN from replacing the **Democrazia Cristiana**/Christian Democracy Party (DC) as the natural home for Italy's middle-class electorate. First, its appeal stopped at the river Po: only northern voters showed any interest in the League's ideas. Second, in December 1993, Bossi was charged with (and eventually found guilty of) accepting an illegal donation to the party funds. The charge was trivial by comparison with the financial abuses committed by Italy's political old guard, but the episode tarnished his claim of opposing the "money politics" of the traditional parties. Third, and most important, the rise of **Silvio Berlusconi**'s party, **Forza Italia**, denied the Lega Nord a firm hold on conservative, middle-class voters.

The LN fought the March 1994 general elections as part of the "Liberty Pole"— the right-wing electoral alliance formed by Berlusconi in the North of Italy. In numerical terms, the LN secured slightly fewer votes than in 1992. Its parliamentary representation, however, thanks to the introduction of first-past-the-post voting, increased enormously, to more than 100 deputies and 50 senators. The League was awarded a deputy prime ministership, several key ministerial positions, and the presidency of the Chamber of Deputies, but it was soon at odds with Berlusconi and with the former fascists of the **Alleanza Nazionale**/National Alliance (AN). The LN, despite its strident right-wing rhetoric on social questions, is strongly opposed to the centralized, corporatist state traditionally supported by Italian **Fascism**. Accordingly, in December 1994, Bossi brought down the government in a vote of confidence. This move split his own party and led to a challenge to his leadership in February 1995.

To everybody's surprise, however, the LN was able to fight the April 1996 elections without allies and remain the largest party in Italy's alpine regions. Overall, the party took 10 percent of the national vote and even won many electoral districts directly. Bossi celebrated this by threatening to create a new state, to be called "Padania," from the regions of northern Italy, and in September, after a symbolic journey down the river Po, he "founded" the new republic.

The initial euphoria over "Padania," however, was the high spot of the LN's success. Its support began to fall away in the late 1990s, and the League was forced back into an electoral alliance, the **Casa delle Libertà**/House of Freedoms (CDL), with Berlusconi. The League obtained less than 4 percent of the vote in the May 2001 elections and became a loyal but subordinate member of the government formed by Berlusconi after that vote. The League used its place in government to press for "devolution" of powers to the regions in the context of a wider reform of the **Constitution**. It was hampered, however, by Bossi's serious illness from 2004 onward. The Italian electorate rejected the constitutional reform in a **referendum** held in June 2006.

The LN has been increasingly tarred with the brush of political extremism in recent years. Its senior figures, including several ministers, have engaged in incendiary rhetoric against Islam and Italy's growing immigrant population. The LN, as a result, is now widely regarded as a far-right party akin to the French Front National. *See also* IMMIGRATION, ELECTORAL LAWS; REGIONALISM.

LEGAL SYSTEM. Most Italians, legally trained or not, take pride in the fact that the basis of the most widely adopted legal system in the non–Anglo Saxon world is, in fact, Roman law and the medieval glosses prepared by those who systematized it, the glossators. Its crowning modern achievement is the French Civil Code, of which the Italian Codice Civile is a virtual translation.

Some differences between the civil (or Roman) law and the English common law used in former English colonies are worth explicating. Prosecutors are part of the career magistracy, as are prefects, magistrates, notaries, and praetors. Competitive examinations provide the entrance route. Plea bargaining is out of the question because courts seek the truth rather than an accommodation between contending interests. In response to the **Brigate Rosse** and to the difficulty of finding evidence against members of the mafia, Italy has recently begun offering lower penalties for *pentiti*, repentant wrong-doers who turn state's evidence. Procedure follows the premise of an accusatorial trial (or inquisitorial), perceived as an improvement over vengeance taken with one's own hands for a wrong.

Courts use only written evidence, allowing no surprise witnesses. The right to appeal a judgment is guaranteed, the first on both law and facts but the last on law only. The result is slow trials and long waits to appear on a court's calendar. Thus, by the 1980s, great demand for the modernization of penal procedure led to adopting some elements of Anglo-American procedure, drawn from an entirely different tradition, culture, and set of assumptions.

Canon law of the Roman Catholic Church is still studied in all faculties of jurisprudence. A third element of contemporary Italian law (in addition to Roman law and canon law) is the commercial law of the Italian city-states that dominated medieval trade between Europe and the eastern Mediterranean. This is the element in Roman law that is not scholars' law but is pragmatic, drawn by businessmen who had formed guilds and had devised appropriate rules. Commercial law, applied by merchants rather than ecclesiastics or royally appointed temporal judges, spread to all of Europe.

Civil law studies address a civil code, commercial code, code of civil procedure, penal code, and code of penal procedure. All were meant to be complete and coherent, accessible to all literate persons without regard to specialized legal training. The modern nation-state gave rise to the view that the highest source of law was statutory, followed by administrative regulations, then customary usage and such general principles of natural law as good faith, public order, and morality.

Aside from conciliators (for small claims) and praetors (who also hear labor cases), the tribunal of the first instance is followed by an appeals court, then by the Court of Cassation, which can quash a decision and remand to a lower court for a new hearing on points of law. Since **World War II**, an added Constitutional Court reflects the need to ensure the constitutionality of new legislation. Most trials are heard by a panel of judges rather than by a jury. The entire system is supervised by the Consiglio Superiore della Magistratura/High Council of the Magistracy (CSM).

In penal procedure, an accused who has been arrested by the police faces an investigating magistrate, who may call witnesses, effect confrontations and reenactments, and warrant phone taps and mail-opening to compile a dossier, which is then examined by both sides.

Administrative courts are seated in each regional capital as the Tribunale Administrativo Regionale/Regional Administrative Court (TAR). Appeal may be made to the Consiglio di Stato (Council of State), the highest administrative tribunal.

Court	Number of Courts	Number of Judges
Cassation	1	7
Appeal	23	5
Assize	91	2 (+ 6 laypeople)
Tribunals of First Instance	156	3
Praetors	893	1
Conciliatori	8,000	1

LEONE, GIOVANNI (1908–2001). Born in **Naples**, Giovanni Leone was a convinced Fascist who fought bravely in **World War II** and campaigned on behalf of the **monarchy** during the 1946 **referendum**. An academic lawyer by training, Leone was a student of **Enrico De Nicola**, who was to be the first president of Italy. The young Leone took degrees in law as well as in political and social sciences and began his own academic career at the University of Naples in 1933 as a *libero docente* in criminal law and procedure. Attaining the rank of professor in only two years, he was given tenure in 1936 with an appointment at the University of Messina. His academic career subsequently took him to Bari, Naples, and **Rome**.

In 1944, Leone enrolled in the **Democrazia Cristiana**/Christian Democracy Party (DC) and served for a year as political secretary of the Naples section. In 1946, he was elected to the **Constituent Assembly** and, in 1948, to the first republican **Parliament**. In 1950, he was made vice president of the Chamber of Deputies. He replaced **Giovanni Gronchi** as president of the lower house when the latter was elected head of state.

In 1963, Leone formed a government to steer the budget through Parliament. His first candidacy (in 1964) for the presidency of the republic was unsuccessful, although he was his party's official nominee.

The victor, **Giuseppe Saragat** of the **Partito Socialista Democratico Italiano/**Italian Social Democratic Party (PSDI), made Leone a life senator. In June 1968, Leone followed **Aldo Moro**'s third government, forming a *monocolore* cabinet (i.e., one made up entirely of deputies from a single party). It survived until November of that year. In December 1971, he was elected **president of the Republic**. In September 1974, he was the first head of state to be invited to the White House by President Gerald Ford.

Inquiries in the U.S. Senate led to newspaper assertions that, like industrial leaders elsewhere in the world, several Italian ministers and President Leone had accepted bribes from the Lockheed Corporation to facilitate aircraft sales to the Italian Air Force. Leone resigned his office in June 1978 under this cloud of scandal, making way for **Alessandro Pertini** to become president. As a life senator, however, he retained his seat in Parliament. Leone died in Rome in November 2001.

LEONE, SERGIO (1929–1989). The inventor of the "spaghetti Western," Sergio Leone was uniquely able to make films that were both a critical and a box office success. Born in **Rome**, Leone was what Italians call a *figlio d'arte* insofar as both his father and mother were prominent figures in the Italian silent cinema. After a lengthy apprenticeship in Hollywood (he made more than 50 films as an assistant director), in 1964, Leone directed the seminal Western *A Fistful of Dollars* under the pseudonym "Bob Robertson." This film, which starred Clint Eastwood as "the man with no name," cost less than $200,000 to make but revived the Western genre in a new, more brutally realistic, form. The film's sequel, *For a Few Dollars More* (1965), was equally successful.

Leone, by now internationally famous, was able to make the two big-budget Westerns that permanently established his reputation as one of the great contemporary film directors: *The Good, the Bad, and the Ugly* (1966) and *Once Upon a Time in the West* (1968). Complex, violent, and philosophical, these movies combined art and entertainment with outstanding skill. The same is true of Leone's last film, the epic gangster movie *Once Upon a Time in America* (1984). This saga of a band of Jewish gangsters was a lengthy and complicated study in themes of friendship and betrayal. Drastically cut by its American distributors, the film, when seen in its entirety, can only be described as an intellectual and visual triumph. Leone died in Rome in 1989. *See also* CINEMA.

LEOPARDI, GIACOMO (1798–1837). The precocious son of a noble southern Italian family, Giacomo Leopardi was the greatest Italian poet of the 19th century and one of the finest romantic poets in any language. Born near Macerata (Marches), Leopardi was an introspective, studious, sickly boy who practically lived in his erudite father's capacious library from the age of 11 until his late teens, teaching himself Greek, astronomy, classical history, and poetry. By 1815—still only 17 years of age—he translated Homer and Virgil and wrote an essay on the "popular errors of the ancients" worthy of a first-rate classical scholar. The first poems that Leopardi would later include in his *Canti* (*Lyrics*, 1831) were written around 1819: "*L'infinito*" ("Infinity") is best known, with its haunting final stanza: "*Cosi tra questa immensità s'annega il pensier mio/e il naufragar m'è dolce in questo mare*" ("Thus, in this immensity, my thought drowns and to drown seems sweet to me, in this sea").

By the time he wrote this poem, Leopardi was desperate to lead a less cloistered life away from home. His father eventually allowed his son to move to an uncle's house in **Rome**, where the young poet hoped to find a job. The experience was a disappointment, however, and Leopardi soon returned home. In 1825, he moved to **Milan**, where the publisher Stella had invited him to edit a volume of Cicero's collected works. Stella published Leopardi's main collection of philosophical reflections, *Operette morali* (*Moral Essays*) in 1827 and two anthologies of Italian renaissance prose and poetry. The next three years were the peak of Leopardi's mature poetic gift: In 1828, he wrote "*Il Risorgimento*," and the following year the collection of poems known as *Grandi Idilli* (*Great Idylls*). The most famous of these is perhaps "*La quiete dopo la tempesta*" ("The Quiet After the Storm"). Between 1830 and his death in 1837, Leopardi's failing health and a succession of unhappy love affairs inspired a final creative burst; his last poems were written on the slopes of Vesuvius, overlooking cholera-ridden **Naples**.

LEVI, CARLO (1902–1975). A gifted painter as well as an outstanding writer, Carlo Levi's principal legacy is the famous novel *Cristo si è fermato a Eboli* (*Christ Stopped at Eboli*, 1945). This autobiographical novel tells the story of a northern Italian intellectual who is confined to a small, remote village in rural Calabria by the Fascist government. The book's moving portrayal of the peasants' economic and cultural backwardness yet great personal dignity swiftly won it a worldwide audience. It remains one of the most translated postwar Italian novels even today.

Levi had already established his reputation as an artist by the time he wrote his classic novel. Before his arrest and exile for antifascist activity in 1935–1936, he had been one of the founders of the "group of six," a school of painting in **Turin** that, in open contrast to the preferences of the regime, attempted to bring French influences such as impressionism and fauvism to bear on their work.

Levi was elected to the Senate as a member of the **Partito Comunista Italiano/**Italian Communist Party (PCI) in 1963. He died in **Rome** in 1975. *See also CONFINO*; NEOREALISM.

LEVI, PRIMO (1919–1987). A Jewish Italian from **Turin** who initially specialized in chemistry, Levi's documentary novel, *Se questo è un uomo* (translated as *If This Is a Man*, 1947), is regarded as one of the classics of holocaust **literature** and has been one of the most widely debated books of the century. The book is based on Levi's own experiences after he was deported to Auschwitz in 1944. In 1963, he wrote a sequel to the book, *La Tregua* (*The Truce*), which described his homecoming through war-torn Eastern Europe after the end of hostilities. The highlights of Levi's later work were *Il sistema periodico* (*The Periodic System*, 1975) and *La chiave a stella* (*The Wrench*, 1978). The former of these consists of 21 short stories that narrate the difficulties of Levi's generation during **Fascism**; the second novel, which is thematically experimental, is a series of involved accounts by a skilled manual worker of how he overcame various complex technical problems. *La chiave a stelle* won the Strega prize, Italy's most prestigious literary award. His last novel, *Se non ora, quando?* (*If Not Now, When?* 1982) won the scarcely less prestigious Viareggio and Campiello prizes. Levi committed suicide in 1987 by throwing himself down the stairwell of his Turin home. *See also* RACIAL LAWS.

LEVI-MONTALCINI, RITA (1909–). An eminent neurobiologist, Rita Levi-Montalcini won the Nobel Prize in Medicine in 1986 for her groundbreaking work on nerve growth factor (NGF), a protein that governs the development and differentiation of nerve cells. The Nobel foundation said that the discovery of NGF was a classic example of how an "acute observer" can "extrapolate a clear theory from apparent chaos."

The Nobel prize was the climax of a glittering career that had begun in harsh circumstances. Deprived of her university position by the 1938 **racial laws**, Levi-Montalcini was forced to flee first to Belgium, then (after the Nazi invasion of that country in 1940) to a clandestine refuge in **Florence** for the duration of the war. After the city was liberated she worked as a doctor until 1947 when, at the age of almost 40, she got the chance to go to Washington University, Missouri, as a researcher. She stayed at Washington until retirement in 1977, although from 1961 onward she combined her professorship with the directorship of the Italian Institute of Cell Biology. Levi-Montalcini continued to do original work in neurobiology until well into the 1990s.

Levi-Montalcini was the first woman to be president of the *Enciclopedia Italiana* and, in recent years, has been active in promoting environmentalism and the cause of **women**'s rights. In August 2001, **Carlo Azeglio Ciampi** made her senator for life of the Italian Republic. This has proved to be no sinecure. In May 2006, the newly formed government of **Romano Prodi** survived its initial vote of confidence in Parliament thanks to her vote. *See also* DULBECCO, RENATO.

LIBYA. In the 16th century, the Ottoman Turks combined Tripolitania, Cyrenaica, and Fezzan to form Libya. Two hundred years later, a Libyan dynasty established independence from Turkey. Turkish control was reestablished in 1835.

By 1887, Italy had secured the acquiescence of Europe's Great Powers for eventual Italian initiatives in Libya. Following France's annexation of Morocco in 1911, the Italian government insisted on a counter for French gains. In October 1911, Italy landed troops and quickly proclaimed the annexation of Libya; **Giovanni Giolitti** proclaimed on the eve of the landing that the invasion was a "historical inevitability." Within months, 150,000 Italian settlers had arrived in Libya. Libya was proclaimed to be under "the full and entire sovereignty of the kingdom of Italy" on 5 November 1911. Determined resistance, initially by Turkey's Enver Bey, continued until 1931, however, when Italian forces under **Rodolfo Graziani** captured and executed the Senussi leader, 'Umar al-Mukhtar.

Italy carried the war against Turkey into the eastern Mediterranean. In April and May 1912 Italian warships entered the Dardanelles and shelled, then occupied, the island of Rhodes and some of the Dodecanese Islands. By the fall, several Balkan states had declared war on Turkey, leading it to sign the Treaty of Lausanne with Italy on 18 October 1912. Under its terms, Italy was to end its occupation of the islands (which it failed to do) in exchange for the Turks leaving Tripoli (although they were to retain religious primacy by appointing a caliph).

Libya's role in **World War II** was as a springboard for Italian moves against Egypt—and subsequently, as a theater of Italian military debacles. Italy's armed forces suffered a series of disastrous defeats in Libya, and the territories were liberated by the British. Libya was recognized as an independent state after Italy signed the peace treaty with the Allies in February 1947. Subsequently, the United Nations established Libyan independence from Italy (1951) under a Senussi monarch, Idris I. By 1969, oil revenues had inspired a group of ambitious army officers, led by Mu'ammar Gadafi, to overthrow the monarchy in favor of "modernization." One of Gadafi's first acts, between January and July 1970, was to seize all property belonging to Jews and to 35,000 Italians. While the Jewish community was compensated with 15-year bonds, the Italian community was denied any compensation as reparations for the depredations Libya had suffered during Italian rule. Relations between the two countries became extremely strained, although in February 1974 Italy and Libya signed an accord in **Rome** that committed Libya to send to Italy 30 million tons of oil (up from 23 million) in exchange for technical assistance in building petrochemical facilities and shipyards, and improving agriculture. *See also* BADOGLIO, PIETRO; BALBO, ITALO; FOREIGN POLICY.

LIRA. *See* CURRENCY.

LITERATURE. Modern Italian literature can best be summarized by an account of its principal literary movements. In the period covered by this dictionary, the first important movement is Romanticism, which in Italy at least was associated with the **Risorgimento** and passionate national feeling. The most famous Romantic poets are **Ugo Foscolo** and, of course, **Giacomo Leopardi**, who nevertheless returned to classicism in his later works. **Alessandro Manzoni**, the author of *I Promessi Sposi* (*The Betrothed*, 1827), was both a great novelist and an ardent evoker of *Italianità*. In poetry, a neoclassical reaction to Romanticism emerged in the work of **Giosue Carducci**, who was the first Italian to win the Nobel Prize in Literature.

At the end of the 19th century *Verismo* (naturalism), with its photographic realism and commitment to picturing life objectively, produced two significant writers, the Sicilian **Giovanni Verga** and the Sardinian **Grazia Deledda**, who also won the Nobel Prize. Both are fine writers, but their work is less powerful than that of their French contemporary, Émile Zola. A contemporary writer working in the tradition of *Verismo* is **Elsa Morante**. Her novels, with their child protagonists acting as the voice of innocence and imagination in the face of the horrors of history and the adult world, have yet to be fully discovered outside Italy and France. In general, the post-1945 tradition of **neorealism**, though more overtly political, shares some core features of *Verismo*. **Cesare Pavese**, Beppe Fenoglio, and **Vasco Pratolini** are well-known neorealist writers. But for stark depictions of the realities of everyday life, no Italian novelist has matched the brilliance of the film directors working in this genre. The classic neorealist novel is really **Vittorio De Sica**'s film *Ladri di biciclette* (*The Bicycle Thief*, 1948).

Decadentism, whose exponents included the poet and novelist **Gabriele D'Annunzio**, the poet Giovanni Pascoli, and the novelist **Italo Svevo**, was an early 20th-century literary movement whose writers were fascinated by the decay of European society; their work was much more subjective and concerned with their protagonists' inner states and emotions than naturalist writers. Once again, Italy's writers, while important, do not match the finest French writers (Baudelaire, Rambaud, Proust) of this genre. The exception is **Luigi Pirandello**, who can be associated with decadentism but whose work transcends any individual school. There is no doubt of Pirandello's status, despite his political leanings toward **Fascism**, as one of the most profound writers in any language in the 20th century.

Futurism was another literary and artistic current that had Fascist leanings. The movement glorified war and violence and delighted in the power and dynamism of modern life. In addition to the movement's founder, **Filippo Marinetti**, the most gifted writer associated with the movement is probably the poet Aldo Palazzeschi.

Italian literature in the 20th century fared well in two of literature's main fields, poetry and the novel. There were three main poetic movements: the crepuscular movement, which was allied in spirit to decadentism; futurism; and hermeticism, which was characterized by a rejection of D'Annunzian bombast and by the use of simple words in dense, allusive, complex phrases. **Mario Luzi** and **Giuseppe Ungaretti** are the most famous writers in this last school, but both have to bow to **Eugenio Montale**, who is unquestionably one of the great poets of the last century. The work of **Salvatore Quasimodo**, who, like Montale, also won the Nobel Prize, is perhaps less venerated today.

This short account can only hint at the richness of the Italian literary tradition and the wealth of styles it has produced. **Ignazio Silone** was a politically sophisticated writer with deep roots in the Abruzzi countryside whence he came; **Italo Calvino** was a master of *favole* (fables); **Leonardo Sciascia** wrote about both **Sicily** and the sophistication of human depravity in beautiful, subtle prose; **Giuseppe Tomasi Di Lampedusa**'s *Gattopardo* (*The Leopard*, 1958) must be one of the richest pictures of decadence written in recent times. **Umberto Eco**'s *Il Nome della Rosa* (*The Name of the Rose*, 1980) is a philosophical mystery story of great intellectual power. The plight of Jewish Italians after the 1938 **racial laws** is the political background to the works of **Giorgio Bassani** and **Primo Levi**.

The theatrical tradition is much less strong. Pirandello aside, only **Dario Fo**, who is a remarkable clown and satirist but probably not a great writer, and the Neopolitan playwright Eduardo De Filippo have achieved an international reputation.

Italian literary life remains varied and challenging in style and content today. One reason may be that Italy is exceptionally open to works in translation. The best English, French, and German novels are instantly translated into Italian. American models exercised a large influence on Italian writing in the post-1945 period. Latin American "magical realists" have also left their mark. Translated works are often more "popular" than Italian writers. Popular writing does exist in Italy—its outstanding exponent was Giovanni Guareschi—but there is no Italian equivalent of John Grisham, Agatha Christie, or Tom Clancy. The lack of children's writers is striking. Italian children fed up with reading either dated fables or *filastrocche* (nursery tales) have taken enthusiastically to the stories of Harry Potter. *See also* CINEMA; COLLODI, CARLO; DE SANCTIS, FRANCESCO; LEVI, CARLO; MALAPARTE, CURZIO; MORAVIA, ALBERTO.

LOCARNO PACT. The central accord of the Locarno Pact, signed on 1 December 1925, was the Pact of Western Security, which Italy signed together with Belgium, Great Britain, France, and Germany. The powers signing the pact guaranteed "jointly and severally" the western borders created by the Treaty of Versailles and pledged themselves on principle to the arbitration of disputes and rapid reference to the Council of the League of Nations rather than aggressive war. Italy signed the Locarno Pact for two main reasons. First, **Benito Mussolini** liked being placed on a par with France and Britain as a signatory. Second, he did not want Italy to be isolated in Europe. Mussolini did not demand that the Brenner frontier with Austria be included in the pact, although he was insistent that Italy would act to prevent Austro-German unification. Locarno represented a moderate shift in foreign policy by Mussolini after the intemperance of the **Corfu** incident in 1923. *See also* FOREIGN POLICY.

LOMBARDI, RICCARDO (1901–1984). One of the founding members of the **Partito d'Azione**/Action Party (PdA) in 1942, Riccardo Lombardi was born in Enna (**Sicily**). He was the PdA's representative in the Comitato di Liberazione Nazionale-Alta Italia/National Liberation Committee-Northern Italy (CLNAI) and was one of the resistance leaders who negotiated the unconditional surrender of the **Republic of Salò** with **Benito Mussolini** in April 1945. Following these negotiations, Lombardi was appointed prefect of **Milan** by the CLNAI. One of his first tasks was to save the bodies of Mussolini and his mistress, Clara Petacci, from further vilification by the crowd that had strung them up in Piazza Loreto.

Lombardi served as transport minister in **Alcide De Gasperi**'s first postwar government (December 1945–July 1946) and was elected to the **Constituent Assembly** as a member of the PdA. He was the secretary of the PdA until its dissolution in 1947. Lombardi was reelected to the Chamber of Deputies in 1948 as a member of the **Partito Socialista Italiano**/Italian Socialist Party (PSI). He edited the party daily, *Avanti!*, in 1949–1950, and rapidly became the theoretical voice of the PSI's left wing and a major rival within the party to **Pietro Nenni**. Lombardi reluctantly agreed to the PSI's decision to form a coalition government with the **Democrazia Cristiana**/Christian Democracy Party (DC) in 1963; he theorized that the PSI would be able to undermine the capitalist system in Italy from within the state by promoting radical social reforms. He did not take ministerial office, however, and thus was unable to press his case. His position was further weakened by the loss of **Lelio Basso** and others of the party's far left, who left the PSI to form the Partito Socialista Italiano d'Unità Proletaria/Italian Socialist Party of Proletarian Unity (PSIUP) in 1964. Lombardi remained the focal point of the PSI's left throughout the 1960s and 1970s, but his supporters were only a minority faction within the party. Lombardi was briefly president of the PSI in 1980. He died in **Rome** in 1984.

LOMBROSO, CESARE (1835–1909). Born in Verona, Lombroso was a pioneer in the field of criminology. His early career was as an army surgeon, but he subsequently became professor of mental illness at the University of Pavia and, influenced by Darwinian ideas of natural selection, began to develop his ideas on inherited criminal traits. Unlike the theologically inspired experts of the time, Lombroso did not believe that crime was due to the innate wickedness of humanity. Rather, he argued in his book *L'Uomo Delinquente* (*Criminal Man*, 1876) that criminals were genetically (as we would say today) disposed to crime. Lombardo argued that the born criminal could be identified by certain physical characteristics (large jaws, shifty eyes, long arms, flattened noses). Criminals were human beings who had degenerated rather than evolved.

The positive aspect of this theory was that Lombroso argued that criminals should be treated humanely and that the death penalty should be abolished. He advocated a prison regime that tried to rehabilitate its inmates. The negative aspect of Lombroso's work was that it spilled over into racial theorizing. Like many other theorists of his time, Lombroso believed that science had demonstrated that Europeans were a superior race that had evolved further than the rest of the species. The eugenics movement, the attempt to breed a higher form of humanity, regarded Lombroso's work as fundamental.

Lombroso also advanced the interesting theory that artistic genius is closely connected to insanity. His work with psychiatric art was regarded as a groundbreaking attempt to understand the workings of the mind. Lombroso died in **Turin** in October 1909.

LONDON, TREATY OF. The agreements signed in London on 26 April 1915, induced Italy to join the war as an Anglo-French ally with the objective of neutralizing Austria. At war's end Italy was to gain control over South Tyrol, Trentino, Gorizia, Gradisca, **Trieste**, Istria, and portions of the Dalmatian Coast. It was also to get a protectorate over Durazzo (Albania), sovereignty over the Dodecanese Islands, and—in Asia Minor—Adalia, if Turkey should be partitioned in Asia. Moreover, if Great Britain and France divided Germany's colonies, Italy would receive compensation enlarging **Libya**, Eritrea, and Somalia.

In return, Italy pledged to go to war within a month of signing, that is, before 26 May 1915. Not only was the text of this treaty not discussed in **Parliament**, it was not made public until Russian archives had been opened by the communists in the last year of the war and many documents were published in the neutral Swedish press.

Once the United States entered the war and Russia had withdrawn (after the 1917 Revolution and the Treaty of Brest-Litovsk), the Treaty of London was a dead letter. The United States had not been a signatory so was not bound to overlook the contradictions between the treaty and President Woodrow Wilson's 14 Points, which promised Serbia access to the sea and national self-determination. Italy's fury when it became clear that the Paris peace conference would renege on the Treaty of London knew no bounds. Italian nationalists deplored the "mutilated peace" and Premier **Vittorio Emmanuele**

Orlando left Paris in disgust in April 1919 (although he later returned to the conference table).

In 1916, the Sykes-Picot agreement between Britain and France regarding oil-rich territories in the Middle East excluded Italy, thus necessitating a special treaty to placate Italian interests. This was the Treaty of St. Jean de Maurienne (17 April 1917), which promised Italy Smyrna as well as Adalia—thus, for the first time, showing a readiness to put Ottoman Turks under foreign rule. The treaty was never ratified, and the failure to give Italy a foothold in the Middle East also served as a grievance for postwar Italian governments. *See also* FIUME; WORLD WAR I.

LONGO, LUIGI (1900–1980). After serving as a soldier in World War I and studying engineering, Luigi Longo joined the **Partito Socialista Italiano**/Italian Socialist Party (PSI), where he worked on the party newspaper and took part in the **Turin** factory occupations of 1920. At the Livorno (Leghorn) Congress of the PSI in 1921, he supported the minority who wished the PSI to enter the Communist International on Lenin's terms and who split away to form the **Partito Comunista Italiano**/Italian Communist Party (PCI). In 1922, Longo was one of the PCI's delegates to the International's Fourth Congress. Between 1923 and 1924, he was arrested twice but served less than a year in prison. In 1927, he escaped persecution by fleeing to France, where he lived until 1932, with the task of providing falsified documents to those who were to enter Italy to conduct antifascist activity. Between 1933 and 1935, he was sent to the USSR as a representative of the PCI. There, he became a member of the political committee of the Comintern.

During the Spanish Civil War, Longo served in the Garibaldi Battalion and was the political commissar of the Second International Brigade, which had the distinction of inflicting a serious defeat on the Italian expeditionary force at Guadalajara. At the end of 1936, he became inspector general of the 50,000-man International Brigades and took part in the final defense of Madrid.

In 1938, Longo was arrested in France and turned over to the Italian authorities, who imprisoned him for five years. Freed in September 1943, he directed the PCI's partisan activity in **Rome** and was one of the leaders of the **resistance** against the Germans. For his efforts, he was awarded a Bronze Star by the U.S. government. Elected to the **Constituent Assembly** in 1946, he served in the first **Parliament** and was repeatedly reelected thereafter. For 10 years, beginning in 1956, he was joint editor (with **Alessandro Natta**) of the PCI's main theoretical journal, *Critica Marxista*. A lifetime of party service led to his succeeding **Palmiro Togliatti** as party secretary in August 1964. During Longo's tenure as leader, the PCI took its first tentative steps away from pro-Soviet orthodoxy by strongly criticizing the Russian suppression of the Prague Spring in 1968. Longo died in Rome in 1980.

LOTTA CONTINUA. The extraparliamentary left parties or "ultras" of the 1960s and 1970s included the Movimento Studentesco (Student Movement), Servire il popolo (Serve the People), Avanguardia Operaia (Workers' Vanguard), Potere Operaio (Worker Power), **Il Manifesto** (The Manifesto), Autonomia Operaia (Worker Autonomy), Lotta Operaia (Workers' Struggle), and Lotta Continua (Constant Struggle), which was the largest. All of these groups were quick to criticize both the **Partito Comunista Italiano**/Italian Communist Party (PCI) and national **trade unions** as being too ready to compromise for the sake of stability and industrial peace.

Lotta Continua was founded in the autumn of 1969. The movement's weekly newspaper was published for the first time in November of the same year. In 1972, its third national conference decided that the movement should press for a "general conflict" with the bourgeois state. What this meant in practice was that some members of the movement robbed banks, incited manual workers to violence against factory foremen and managers, and condoned some of the early outrages of the **Brigate Rosse**/Red Brigades (BR). Only in October 1972 did the majority faction of Lotta Continua admit that terrorism was a mistaken strategy and that it should be condemned.

Lotta Continua was a masculine, even sexist organization, despite its leftist politics. By 1976, **women** who were dissatisfied with their roles occupied meeting halls and held countermeetings and assemblies; at the Rimini Congress in October 1976 women members openly rejected the movement, obliging the leadership to agree that the basic assumptions of the organization had to be reexamined. Although its newspaper continued to appear, Lotta Continua dissolved.

A residual group, joined by the remnants of others in similar straits, drifted into Democrazia Proletaria, a party that held seats in **Parliament** from the elections of June 1976 until the mid-1990s. However, not all of Lotta Continua's members chose the left. Several ended up close to **Bettino Craxi** and have since become court intellectuals for **Silvio Berlusconi**.

The memory of Lotta Continua remains a highly contested one because of the movement's alleged role in the death of a policeman, Luigi Calabresi, whom the movement accused of having killed an anarchist called Giuseppe Pinelli, accused (wrongly, it is now clear) of the 1969 bomb blast at Piazza Fontana in **Milan**. (Pinelli "fell" out of a fourth floor window; his case is the subject of **Dario Fo**'s *Accidental Death of an Anarchist*). Calabresi eventually sued Lotta Continua, but the case was never fully heard because the judge was overheard saying he believed Calabresi to be guilty of murdering Pinelli. In May 1972, Calabresi was gunned down in the street. Lotta Continua celebrated his death as an act of justice. In 1988, two of the movement's former leaders, Adriano Sofri and Giorgio Pietrostefani, were accused of ordering Calabresi's murder along with Ovidio Bompressi, a militant in the movement, who was accused of actually pulling the trigger. The chief witness was the driver of the getaway car, one Leonardo Marino.

Sofri, Pietrostefani, and Bompressi were sentenced to 22 years in prison. The three men were condemned definitively in 1997 and began prison sentences. Marino was given 11 years and did not serve a day in jail. Grave doubts have been expressed by many observers about the validity of Marino's confession, and Sofri's confinement has become a major political issue. *See also* SESSANTOTTO, IL; STRATEGIA DELLA TENSIONE.

LUZI, MARIO (1912–2005). One of the greatest Italian poets of the 20th century, Luzi was widely expected to win the Nobel Prize. In 1997, when the prize went to the controversial playwright **Dario Fo**, Luzi was unable to hide his disappointment and sniffed that the prize itself had been devalued. Luzi was compensated in October 2004 with the conferral of a life senatorship by **Carlo Azeglio Ciampi** for his "extraordinary literary and artistic merit."

His achievement is not in doubt. Luzi was the last significant exponent of *ermetismo* (hermeticism), a Florentine school of poets that strove to avoid the rhetorical excess of the Italian poetic tradition but to make complex, obscure use of simple words and that prized poetry for its expressiveness rather than its power to communicate ideas. As a poet, translator, and critic, Luzi was one of contemporary Italy's most influential and prolific writers. Highlights of his poetic career include *Avvento Noturno* (*Night-time Occurrence*, 1940); *Nel Magma* (1963), whose subject matter is the daily life of contemporary Italian society and which has a highly conversational style; and *Ceneri e ardori* (*Ashes and Passions*, 1997). Luzi was professor of French **literature** at the universities of Urbino and his native **Florence**; he died in Florence in February 2005. *See also* MONTALE, EUGENIO.

LUZZATTI, LUIGI (1841–1927). Born in **Venice**, Luigi Luzzatti was a long-serving politician in prefascist Italy. After an early career in academic law he entered **Parliament** in 1871, where he remained until 1921. A moderate conservative, he was minister for the treasury under **Antonio Starabba Di Rudinì**, **Giovanni Giolitti**, and, briefly, **Sidney Sonnino**.

Luzzatti was caretaker prime minister between 1910 and 1911. His spell as prime minister was dominated by the question of extending the suffrage. Luzzatti proposed to reduce the severity of the norms for ascertaining electors' educational standards, to introduce nationwide state elementary education, and to introduce election for a part of the Senate. In addition, he proposed making the vote a compulsory duty. These proposals initially won him widespread parliamentary support (his government was backed by 386 deputies, including the **Partito Socialista Italiano**/Italian Socialist Party [PSI]), but, by December 1910, the PSI and radicals in the Parliament had decided that these proposals did not go far enough. His government fell over the electoral reform issue in March 1912, and he was replaced by Giolitti, who introduced universal male suffrage. Nominated to the Senate in 1921, Luzzatti died in **Rome** in 1927. His memoirs are a source of great importance for historians.

– M –

MAFIA. The Sicilian mafia originated during the rule of the Bourbons. In a society where the state existed merely to collect taxes and preserve the privileges of the nobility and the large landowners, justice was a matter for individuals, and the *mafioso* ("man of honor") who would defend his family's property and avenge insults to the family name or its **women** became the most respected man in his community. According to the Italian scholar Pino Arlacchi, *mafiosi* passed through two stages in their social development. In the first, "anomic" stage, they established themselves as men to be feared by virtue of their ferocity in conducting *vendette*. Thereafter they performed the role of government in the small village or the neighborhood in which they lived. The *mafioso* and his "family" or "clan" of friends provided protection from thieves and bandits, punished social deviants, and acted as mediators, patching up quarrels over seduced daughters and marriage dowries before they led to bloodshed. They brooked no interference and dealt brutally with informers, giving rise to the phenomenon known as *omertà*, which prohibits collaborating with "outsiders," that is, the Italian state or its judiciary or **police**. Men of honor were courted by the political class, especially after the introduction of universal male suffrage in 1912. Becoming a "man of honor" could arguably be seen as a dangerous form of social mobility, a way for the most ruthless peasants to emerge as social leaders.

Benito Mussolini waged war on the mafia clans after his accession to power in 1922. Thousands of Sicilians, whether or not proven to be *mafiosi*, were arrested and sent into internal exile. The arrival of the Allies in 1943, however, gave the leading mafia bosses a new lease on life. Assuming that imprisoned *mafiosi* were antifascists, the British and American armies released and even gave political responsibilities to well-known men of honor.

Italy's postwar **economic miracle** reduced the power of the traditional mafia. Fewer young Sicilians were tempted into becoming men of honor, and the (relative) modernization of social and sexual mores and customs meant that the clans lost their mediating function. The word "mafia" increasingly became associated with criminal gangs trafficking in contraband cigarettes and, from the 1970s onward, drugs. The Italian state fought these gangs with zeal. By the end of the 1960s, **Sicily** was a more law-abiding place than at any previous time in its modern history.

Three factors saved the mafia from extinction. First, the economic miracle came to an end in the 1970s. Second, the gangs became entrepreneurs and used the proceeds from their illicit activities to buy up large sections of the economy of **southern Italy**, especially in low-technology construction, agriculture, tourism, and transport. Aside from providing services that are illegal, such as prostitution, intimidation of competitors, and contract-rigging, the mafia's activities include legitimate businesses and investments, particularly in construction industries. Third, the degeneration of the Italian political class allowed the mafia to regain its influence over the political process: In exchange for votes, the politicians funneled public works contracts to companies beholden to—if not owned by—the mafia. In exchange for campaign funds and the delivery of votes, political figures offered protection against investigation and a share of public contracts.

It is no exaggeration to say that by the 1980s political life in three southern Italian regions—Campania, Calabria, and **Sicily**—was heavily influenced by local crime bosses. Politicians who crossed the leading clans, such as Piersanti Mattarella, the president of the Sicilian regional government, were brutally murdered, as was a grisly list of judges and policemen. The early 1980s also saw the emergence of the Corleonesi. Led by Toto Riina and Bernardo Provenzano, they exterminated the older clans. In **Naples** and Calabria (where the criminal gangs are known as the *Camorra* and the *'ndrangheta*, respectively), the domination of the political-criminal elite was arguably even more complete. **Earthquake** relief funds, together with the profits to be made in narcotics dealing, added further to the sums at stake and contributed to the viciousness of the struggle among rival clans for dominance.

The Italian state's fight against the mafia was led by a determined prosecutor, **Giovanni Falcone**, who persuaded several mafia associates to break the ancient code of *omertà* and turn state's evidence (the so-called *pentiti*). A huge trial of literally hundreds of gangsters between 1984 and 1987 (the so-called *maxiprocesso*) concluded in a personal triumph for Falcone and the imposition of 19 life sentences. Despite this triumph, the antimafia judges and policemen of southern

Italy were denied the political backing that they needed to prosecute the battle efficiently. By the early 1990s, lawlessness had reached unprecedented levels. In February 1992, Salvo Lima, a **Palermo** boss politician close to **Giulio Andreotti**, was gunned down. His death was widely seen as an admonition to the political class. Later in the same year, Falcone and his colleague Paolo Borsellino were murdered by car bombs.

The Italian state at last acted with vigor. The heads of the Corleonesi, including Toto Riina, were hunted down in 1993, as the collapse of the **Democrazia Cristiana/**Christian Democracy Party (DC) robbed the gangs of their political protection. Riina was eventually sentenced to 11 life sentences. Although there have been intermittent cases of alleged political collusion between politicians and the mafia in Sicily and Naples since the mid-1990s, and although the use of *pentiti* in trials has provided increasingly dubious results, notably in the case of Andreotti, it is fair to say that the Italian state has restored much of its authority.

MAGRIS, CLAUDIO (1939–). One of Italy's greatest living writers, Claudio Magris was born in **Trieste** in 1939. An academic authority on the history and **literature** of Germany and central Europe, he is also an essayist, novelist, translator, and critic. In the great tradition of central European intellectuals, he prefers to write in the remarkable Habsburg-era cafés of Trieste rather than in his study. He is fascinated by the rich cultural milieu of central Europe (for which Trieste was both the port and meeting place). Magris's classic work, *Danubio* (*Danube*, 1986), about a voyage down the river in which every stopping place gives birth to a profound diary of philosophical reflections, was translated into nearly 20 languages and is widely regarded as a modern literary classic. In June 2004, Magris won the prestigious Prince of Asturias Award for Literature; the Spanish jury cited for special praise his understanding of a Europe that was "diverse and without frontiers, cohesive and open to dialogue between cultures." Magris's *Microcosmi* won the important Strega literary prize in 1997. Magris was briefly a senator (1994–1996), but he has been less deflected from his work by party politics than have most of Italy's leading intellectuals.

MALAGODI, GIOVANNI (1904–1991). The scion of a well-established liberal family (Malagodi's father, Olindo, was a prominent journalist and Anglophile who was appointed to the Senate), Malagodi's initial career was in international banking. After the war, he was one of the technical experts who contributed to the drawing up of the Marshall Plan and, in the late 1940s, represented the Italian government as minister plenipotentiary in international trade negotiations. In 1950, Malagodi became a top functionary, chairing the committee on the labor market of the Organization for European Economic Cooperation (OEEC).

Malagodi's political career began in 1953 when he was elected to **Parliament** for the **Partito Liberale Italiano**/Italian Liberal Party (PLI). He became leader of the PLI in 1954 and held the post until he became treasury minister under **Giulio Andreotti** in 1972. This was his only ministerial experience; his staunch opposition to statist and interventionist economic policies prevented the PLI from cooperating with the governments of the center-left preferred by such **Democrazia Cristiana**/Christian Democracy Party (DC) leaders as Amintore Fanfani and Aldo Moro in the 1950s and 1960s. Despite his economic conservatism, Malagodi was strongly in favor of liberal social reforms such as **divorce**.

Malagodi became honorary president of the PLI in 1976. He was elected to the Senate in 1979 and was briefly president of the upper chamber in 1987. He died in **Rome** in April 1991.

MALAPARTE, CURZIO (pseud. Kurt Erich Suckert, 1898–1957). An intriguing figure, Malaparte (who Italianized his name during his service as a volunteer in the Italian army in 1915) was an active Fascist in his native Tuscany. In 1924, he founded a review, *La Conquista dello stato* (*The Conquest of the State*), which became the theoretical journal of the revolutionary wing of the **Partito Nazionale Fascista**/National Fascist Party (PNF) headed by **Roberto Farinacci**. High in the esteem of the Duce, he was sent to the Soviet Union as a correspondent, which led him to write *L'Intelligenza di Lenin* (*The Intelligence of Lenin*, 1930), a book full of scarcely disguised admiration for Soviet totalitarianism. He became editor of the **Turin** newspaper *La Stampa* in 1929 but was hounded from his job by **Benito Mussolini** for publishing too many articles critical of Fascist industrial policy. This, at any rate, was Malaparte's explanation.

Exiled in Paris, Malaparte wrote the Europe-wide best-seller *Technique du Coup d'état* (*Technique of the Coup d'Etat*, 1931), which described recent seizures of power in various European countries and argued that the essential element of political power was the willingness to use violence in pursuit of one's ends. Malaparte argued, for instance, that Mussolini had been successful less for his own merits than because of the spinelessness of Italy's liberals, who had been unwilling to defend their own values and state. Such a position did nothing to enhance his standing with the Fascist dictator. Malaparte also disparaged Adolf Hitler and the Nazi movement, and extracts from his book were used as propaganda material by the antifascist parties in the German elections of 1932. *Technique du Coup d'Etat* was banned in Italy and burned in Germany. Malaparte was arrested upon his return to Italy in October 1933 and served several years of confinement in the mid-1930s. He was a correspondent in Russia and Finland during the war. After the war, he embraced the Chinese brand of communism and had just returned from a visit to Red China—one of the first foreigners permitted to see the Maoist state—when he died from cancer in 1957.

Malaparte's literary output was vast, but three books in particular have withstood the test of time: *Kaputt* (1944), *La Pelle* (*The Skin*, 1949), and *Maledetti toscani* (*Damned Tuscans*, 1956). In addition to his prodigious literary output, Malaparte also designed his own house on the Isle of Capri. It is still regarded as a classic example of modernist architecture. *See also* LITERATURE.

MALFATTI, FRANCO MARIA (1927–1991). A **Rome**-born journalist whose early political activity was in the faction of the **Democrazia Cristiana**/Christian Democracy Party (DC) headed by **Giuseppe Dossetti**, Malfatti was an important figure in Italian political life in the 1970s and 1980s. He became a parliamentary deputy in 1963 and served as a junior minister between 1963 and 1969 under both **Aldo Moro** and **Giovanni Leone**. In 1969 he became minister for the state industries and then minister for the postal service and telecommunications.

For a man still only in his early forties, his career was progressing well, but in July 1970 he was overpromoted when he became the third president of the European Commission, following in the footsteps of Walter Hallstein of Germany and Jean Rey of Belgium. Malfatti lasted less than two years, during which time the European Community (EC) made a number of important policy innovations, including the decision to admit Great Britain, Denmark, Ireland, and Norway and to take a more assertive common approach in foreign affairs. In March 1972, however, Malfatti resigned to be a candidate in Italian parliamentary elections. He was widely perceived to have placed his personal political ambitions before the European cause, and his behavior created a definite prejudice against future Italian candidates for top European jobs.

Malfatti served as minister for **education** between July 1973 and March 1978, an unenviable task because these were years of sometimes violent upheaval in both the schools and the universities. He became finance minister subsequently and served as foreign minister in the government of **Francesco Cossiga** between August 1979 and January 1980, resigning for health reasons. Malfatti died in Rome in December 1991. *See also* EUROPEAN INTEGRATION.

MANIFESTO, IL/The Manifesto. Initially a weekly from its beginnings in June 1969, *Il Manifesto* became a daily newspaper in 1971 and continues to maintain a substantial readership among students and politically active workers even today. The main goal of its renegade founders, Luigi Pintor, Aldo Natoli, and Rossella Rossanda—all deputies of the **Partito Comunista Italiano**/Italian Communist Party (PCI)—was to press for a definitive break between Italian communism and the Soviet Union. After the fifth issue of the paper argued that the PCI's response to the Soviet invasion of Czechoslovakia had been insufficiently critical, the group was accused of factionalism by the central committee of the PCI and expelled. In the 1970s *Il Manifesto* was the newspaper of choice for the many individuals and groups who felt that the PCI had lost its revolutionary ideals and had become integrated into the political system. *See also* LOTTA CONTINUA; PRESS.

MANI PULITE. The "Clean Hands" investigation into corruption began in **Milan** in February 1992 with the arrest by prosecutor **Antonio Di Pietro** of Mario Chiesa, a **Partito Socialista Italiano**/Italian Socialist Party (PSI) politician with close links to the party leader, **Bettino Craxi**. Chiesa's arrest triggered corruption inquiries all over the country, but the Milan "pool" of prosecutors would remain the spearhead of the investigations into illicit activities by politicians over the next three years.

In retrospect, the "Clean Hands" investigation developed in five main phases. The first phase was the easiest: the discovery of the corruption surrounding public works contracts in Milan and dozens of other cities all over Italy. By the fall of 1992, literally thousands of businessmen had confessed to paying politicians. Soon, dozens of politicians at the local and regional levels, as well as parliamentary deputies from all the main parties, had been indicted on charges of corruption, extortion, and illegal financing of the political parties.

The second phase of the investigation, by the Milanese prosecutors in particular, of the leadership of the PSI, was the one that brought down the political system. By the end of April 1993, the Milan "pool" had asked **Parliament** for authorization to indict Bettino Craxi on diverse counts of corruption and extortion. When Parliament refused to lift immunity, there were street demonstrations all over Italy and the one-day-old government of **Carlo Azeglio Ciampi** collapsed ignominiously. During the summer of 1993, the investigation spread into health care contracts. When a government official responsible for authorizing new pharmaceuticals for the Italian market was arrested in his home, the police discovered thousands of Kruggerrands and other gold coins, gold ingots, and Swiss bank accounts worth tens of millions of francs. The health minister, Francesco De Lorenzo of the **Partito Liberale Italiano**/Italian Liberal Party (PLI), was also arrested and charged with organizing rake-offs from the public money being spent to combat AIDS.

It was clear that none of the former parties of government was clean (and the opposition **Partito Democratico della Sinistra**/Democratic Party of the Left had not escaped unscathed either). In December 1993, Antonio Di Pietro used the trial of Sergio Cusani to put the entire Italian political class on trial. Cusani was a Milanese financier who had disbursed "the mother of all bribes" (150 billion lire) from the chemical company Enimont. One by one, the heads of the main political parties were called as witnesses and subjected to merciless cross-examination. In front of some of the largest television audiences in Italian history, they collectively admitted to taking immense sums. The treasurer of the DC, Senator Severino Citaristi, admitted in court that the DC had raised 85 billion lire a year in illicit contributions like the one from Enimont. Even **Umberto Bossi** admitted that he had received an undeclared "donation" from Enimont to help the activities of the **Lega Nord**.

The Cusani trial was the apex of the third phase of the Mani pulite investigation. In 1994, the fourth phase began when attention shifted to the media empire of **Silvio Berlusconi**. In November, it was officially announced that Berlusconi, who was by now prime minister, was under investigation. The Milanese judges also began investigating Berlusconi's personal lawyer, Cesare Previti, who was accused of corrupting judges in **Rome** on Berlusconi's behalf.

The Milan prosecutors found themselves increasingly on the defensive after Berlusconi came to power. Di Pietro was forced to resign to defend himself against allegations of personal wrongdoing; the other judges were abused by the political parties and the **press**. Politicians across the political spectrum accused prosecutors throughout the country of usurping political power in order to establish "a republic of judges." Berlusconi's newspapers talked of judges with "red robes" who were doing the bidding of the Left. Corruption was all but openly defended as having been necessary to combat the well-funded **Partito Comunista Italiano**/Italian Communist Party (PCI), which received under-the-counter funding from the **cooperative** movement and the USSR.

The combination of political opposition and Italy's notoriously slow legal process has resulted in many politicians escaping all but scot-free. Most politicians who admitted to taking bribes for their parties managed to escape with suspended sentences or plea bargains; some have even returned to political life at the local or even national level. Berlusconi, the biggest fish caught by the investigations, used his political power retrospectively to decriminalize some of the charges upon which he had been found guilty. Corruption, while not as ubiquitous as in the 1980s, remains a serious problem in Italy today. *See also* LEGAL SYSTEM; MAFIA; *PENTAPARTITO*.

MANIN, DANIELE (1804–1857). A lawyer born into one of **Venice**'s noblest families, Daniele Manin became one of the symbolic figures of Italian nationalism. Briefly arrested by the Austrians in January 1848, he became the focus of the nationalist uprising in the city. At the end of March, after a tumultuous fortnight of street conflict, a republic was declared, with Manin being chosen as the first president of the new state. However, in July 1848, when the Venetian national assembly voted for unification with the Kingdom of **Sardinia**, the antimonarchist Manin resigned from the presidency. In 1849, when Austrian victories over the Kingdom of Sardinia left Venice without allies, Manin heroically guided the city's resistance. The city was blockaded by the Austrians at the end of May 1849 and resisted— until the end of August—land, sea, and aerial bombardment (by lighter-than-air balloons) and a serious outbreak of cholera. Under the terms of the armistice, Manin and some 40 other citizens were compelled to leave the city. He immigrated to France, where he lived in poverty. In 1856, he was persuaded by **Camillo Benso di Cavour** to set aside his distrust of the Sardinian royal family and accept the presidency of the Italian National Society, a body uniting all strands of the nationalist movement except the Mazzinians, which pledged itself to unite Italy under the direction of the Kingdom of Sardinia. Manin died the following year. His son, Giorgio, took part in **Giuseppe Garibaldi**'s expedition to **Sicily** in 1861 and became aide de camp to King **Victor Emmanuel II**.

MANZONI, ALESSANDRO (1785–1873). Born in **Milan**, Manzoni was the grandson of **Cesare Beccaria**, the enlightenment philosopher and jurist. As a writer, his most creative period was between 1812 and 1827. In these years, he wrote his most influential poetry and plays and, after 1821, began working on the huge manuscript of *I promessi sposi* (*The Betrothed*), which was originally called *Fermo e Lucia*. The novel was published in 1827.

I promessi sposi tells the story of two weavers, Renzo and Lucia, who wish to marry but whose love is endangered by Don Rodrigo, a libertine who has other plans for Lucia. The couple flee, are separated, and undergo seemingly endless vicissitudes, but are eventually reunited in happy married life. Summarized so briefly, the novel might seem to be a mere melodrama. In fact, it was a momentous step for Italian **literature**. For the first time since Boccaccio, ordinary people took the stage in Italian literature, speaking in their native language and being described faithfully as dignified individuals rather than as caricatures. There was nothing artificial or rhetorical about Manzoni's style, while the powerful Christian humanism suffusing the novel was an equally radical innovation for the time. *I promessi sposi* remains a subject of compulsory study in Italian schools.

After the publication—and immediate public and critical success—of *I promessi sposi*, Manzoni fell silent. He was made a life senator in 1861. He dedicated his later years to writing a historical essay comparing the French Revolution with the **Risorgimento**. This work was published after his death in Milan in 1873. *See also* VERDI, GIUSEPPE.

MARCH ON ROME. In Fascist myth-building, few events were as exalted as the March on **Rome**. In fact, the March on Rome was less a coup d'état than a capitulation by the Italian political elite, a capitulation, moreover, in which **Benito Mussolini** played only a minor part.

The failure of successive governments after **World War I** to combat the reign of terror imposed by Fascist *squadrismo* led the **Partito Socialista Italiano**/Italian Socialist Party (PSI) to proclaim a general strike in August 1922. This move played directly into Mussolini's hands. He was now able to announce that the Fascist squads stood ready to break the strike if the government did nothing; the squads could thus be presented as forces of law and order. On 3 August 1922, the Fascist blackshirts took over many cities in the North, most conspicuously **Milan**, where they burned the buildings of the socialist newspaper *Avanti!* and smashed its presses. Mussolini subsequently asserted that "in 48 hours of systematic, warlike violence, we won what we would never have won in 48 years of preaching and propaganda." The credibility of the PSI was shattered, as was the authority of the state. The PSI split in early October 1922, with the expulsion of **Filippo Turati** and the reformists willing to back a government that would fight the Fascist menace. In early October, the Fascist squads invaded Trentino and Alto Adige, pledged to "de-Austrianize" the local inhabitants. The nationalist Right now began openly to position itself for cooperation with the Fascists, should Mussolini take power.

Christopher Seton-Watson has written that three obstacles now stood in Mussolini's way: the king, the army, and **Gabriele D'Annunzio**, the hero of the occupation of **Fiume**. King **Victor Emmanuel III** was personally skeptical of Mussolini's movement but feared for his throne if he came out openly against **Fascism**. The army was full of Fascist sympathizers but would not break its oath to serve the king. D'Annunzio, who was friendly with Facta, might emerge as the dictator who forestalled the Fascists' triumphal march. Premier **Luigi Facta** and **Giovanni Giolitti** planned a patriotic rally for 4 November 1922, that would have launched a new party, incorporating the **Partito Popolare Italiano**/Italian Popular Party (PPI) and the reformist socialists and that would have had D'Annunzio's support. Mussolini feared that such a government would use authoritarian means to repress the squads. On 22 October 1922, at a Fascist congress in **Naples**, he said that he merely wanted to regenerate the Italian state and would take part in a new government if he received five ministerial portfolios, including foreign affairs. On 25 October 1922, however, D'Annunzio announced that he would not attend the patriotic rally.

Mussolini decided to act. On the night of 28 October 1922, while Mussolini himself remained barricaded in the offices of his newspaper, *Il Popolo d'Italia*, Fascist squads took over most of north and central Italy. Civil authority crumbled. Operating from the town of Perugia, Mussolini's chief henchmen, the **quadrumvirate**, mobilized squads from provincial cities to proceed in "columns" upon Rome. Loyal troops were waiting for them at the gates of Rome. Premier Facta asked the king to declare a state of siege on 28 October 1922. The king at first acquiesced, then changed his mind. The king's refusal to make good on that undertaking reflected the repugnance he felt for civil war. He was also concerned lest his dashing cousin, the Duke of Aosta, who was on good terms with the Fascists, might plot to depose him. On the evening of 29 October 1922, the king sent for Mussolini, who arrived by train on the morning of 30 October. He formed a government of Fascists and nationalists later the same day. The Fascists were allowed to march through Rome. There was some fighting between workers and the Fascists, but this was the only bloodshed of Mussolini's extraordinary coup. The London *Times* spoke of a "salutary" response to Bolshevism and the *New York Tribune* hailed the victory of the "Garibaldi in a Black Shirt."

MARCONI, GUGLIELMO (1874–1937). The inventor of the wireless, Guglielmo Marconi was not only one of the most important scientists of the 20th century but an adept businessman and diplomat. Born into a well-off family from **Bologna** (Emilia-Romagna), Marconi was attracted to the physical sciences from his earliest youth. Unable to find financial support for his ideas in Italy, in 1896, he patented the first prototype of the wireless in England. In 1901, he successfully sent a transatlantic message between Britain and the United States. This feat, which at the time seemed little short of miraculous, won Marconi the Nobel Prize in Physics in 1909.

Marconi was far from being an ivory tower academic. He had founded a company to exploit his discoveries commercially as early as 1897, and as the military and commercial implications of wireless technology were realized, he became an important political figure. Between 1912 (the year in which he was nominated as senator) and 1915, he played a key role in Anglo-Italian relations and in the negotiations that eventually led to Italy joining the war on the side of the Entente. In 1919, he was one of the Italian delegation to the Paris peace conference.

Marconi joined the **Partito Nazionale Fascista**/National Fascist Party (PNF) in 1923. The regime showered honors upon him, including the presidency of the **Accademia d'Italia**. He died in **Rome** in July 1937.

MARINETTI, FILIPPO TOMMASO (1876–1944). Born in Alexandria, Egypt, and educated in French language schools, Marinetti was caught up in the "free style" poetry that was coming into vogue at the turn of the century. Between 1902 and 1908, he wrote three collections of poetry in free verse. Faced with the social tension between dreams and reality, Marinetti chose the urban, technological, industrial reality, and the mystique of the superman. His *Mafarka le futuriste* (*Mafarka the Futurist*, 1910) pointed the way toward what was to become the futurist movement. He defined it in his *Manifesto* of 1909. "We sing the love of danger, courage, rashness, and rebellion

... [not] thoughtful immobility and ecstasy [but] the new beauty of speed ... we glorify war, militarism and patriotism." The breaking of constraining rules, being agitated and nervously aware—these were the elements of **futurism**, identifying order and tradition with the dead past. Museums, libraries, and elite schools should be closed (or, indeed, burned) and the pope expelled from **Rome**. Futurist libertarians were able to satisfy the apparent longing among many of the young generation for a party of the right that would free Italy from the status of being an "also-ran" and from alternating between being imitation-French and imitation-German.

Marinetti was a "Fascist of the first hour" and was present at the initial meeting in **Milan**'s Piazza di San Sepolcro. He was elected to the central committee of the Fascist movement (still not yet a party) in the founding session of 23 March 1919. **Benito Mussolini** welcomed Marinetti's support in the early years, but when faced with choosing between Catholic support and the support of the futurists, he found no difficulty in turning his back on Marinetti, who resigned from the central committee of the Fascist party in June 1920 because of what he saw as the transformation of **Fascism** by its appeasement of the Church.

Marinetti nevertheless never broke with the regime. He accepted being named among the first appointees (all chosen by Mussolini himself) to the newly created **Accademia d'Italia** (and became its president during the war) and associated himself with the regime's propaganda activities. It was Marinetti's voice, for instance, that announced the dramatic return to Italy of **Italo Balbo** and the Air Armada from its New World visits in August 1933.

Marinetti volunteered to fight in the war against **Ethiopia**. When Italy went to war with the Soviet Union, Marinetti, who was in his midsixties, rejoined his regiment on the Don River. Subsequently, he joined Mussolini at **Salò**. His death in Bellagio (Como) in 1944 was honored by a state funeral. *See also* BALBO, ITALO; LITERATURE.

MARTINAZZOLI, MINO (1931–). The last secretary of the **Democrazia Cristiana**/Christian Democracy Party (DC) before its demise in January 1994, Mino Martinazzoli had long been the party's conscience. Born in the province of Brescia (Lombardy), Martinazzoli made his way into national politics via local politics. He was elected to the Senate in 1972 and was reconfirmed in the subsequent elections of 1976 and 1979. In 1983, he switched houses and was elected to the Chamber of Deputies. Martinazzoli served as minister of justice in the first government of **Bettino Craxi**, and as minister for defense under **Giulio Andreotti** between 1989 and 1991. In October 1992, the DC turned to him in desperation as the corruption investigations grew in intensity and the full extent of the DC's misgovernment became clear. As party secretary, Martinazzoli did his best to revive the DC, but its electoral fate was sealed by the allegations of links between leading DC politicians and the mafia in the spring of 1993. After an electoral calamity in local elections in June 1993, and further, even graver, defeats in November–December 1993, Martinazzoli decided that the DC was beyond saving. Although the party's right split away to form the Centro Cristiano Democratico/Christian Democratic Center (CCD), he and the majority of the former DC transformed its remnants into the **Partito Popolare Italiano**/Italian People's Party (PPI), apparently hoping that the revival of that name would provide the party with new vigor and renewed credibility.

That was not to be. The 1994 elections were something of a disaster for the PPI, which overestimated its electoral support and was not able to hold the balance of power in the new **Parliament**, as Martinazzoli had hoped. Martinazzoli was replaced as party leader by **Rocco Buttiglione** after the elections. He returned to local politics and in April 1995 was elected first mayor of Brescia and subsequently member of the Lombardy regional assembly.

MATTEI, ENRICO (1906–1962). Enrico Mattei was founder and head of the great oil and natural gas multinational, Ente Nazionale Idrocarburi (ENI). He was born in the Marches, the son of a police officer. He left school at 15 and, after working in a tannery, went to **Milan** as a salesman of German industrial equipment. Before 1940, he established his own chemical company. After 1945, he became prominent in the **Democrazia Cristiana**/Christian Democracy Party (DC).

After the war, he was put in charge of the moribund agency that had been established under the Fascists, Azienda Generale Italiana Petroli (AGIP). Mattei transformed AGIP by the intensive exploitation of the methane gas discovered in the Po Valley a few years after the war. The appetite of private firms was whetted by the prospect of abundant cheap energy, but Mattei, aided considerably by Prime Minister **Alcide De Gasperi**, succeeded in ensuring that all Po Valley natural gas exploitation would be under the control of ENI, created for this purpose in February 1953.

A financial buccaneer, Mattei managed to build an empire in the next decade that created such spin-offs as petrochemicals, motels, restaurants, steel oil-ducts, construction contracting, textiles, nuclear power, and research. His accomplishments required cutting through the bureaucratic "red tape" of Italy's patrimonial tradition, and Mattei was not always scrupulous in his methods.

Mattei's willingness to offer Arab oil producers terms far more favorable than those of the Anglo-American "Seven Sisters" made him many foreign enemies. At his bidding, Italy also became a big buyer of Soviet gas from the mid-1950s onward. His support for the Algerian independence movement led to his execution being ordered by the Organisation Armée Secrete/Secret Army Organization (OAS), the private army of French settlers who took up arms against France to induce the government to keep Algeria French. It is no exaggeration to say that Mattei was conducting his own de facto **foreign policy** by the end of the 1950s.

In October 1962, his private airplane crashed on a flight from **Sicily** to Milan. The **mafia**, the Central Intelligence Agency (CIA), the international oil cartel, and the OAS were all accused of having caused his death in the press, in novels, and in films (such as *Il Caso Mattei* by **Francesco Rosi**, 1972).

MATTEOTTI, GIACOMO (1885–1924). A socialist martyr, Giacomo Matteotti's murder by the Fascists led to the definitive end of liberal Italy and the advent of **Benito Mussolini**'s dictatorship. Matteotti was born in Rovigo, near **Venice**, the son of a lower middle-class family. He studied law and seemed embarked on a career as a jurist, but his socialist sympathies led him toward political activism and journalism. He opposed **World War I** but was nevertheless called up and served in the army for three years. In 1919, he was elected to Parliament as a deputy for the **Partito Socialista Italiano**/Italian Socialist Party (PSI). Matteotti belonged to the reformist wing of the PSI, however, and in 1922 he joined **Filippo Turati** in forming the Partito Socialista Unitaria/United Socialist Party (PSU), becoming its secretary and chief organizer.

In 1923, Matteotti published a searing condemnation of **Fascism**'s intellectual and economic pretensions, *Un anno di dominazione fascista* (*A Year of Fascist Domination*), and, in May 1924, he made a historic speech in the Chamber of Deputies denouncing the electoral frauds and acts of intimidation that had falsified the 1924 elections throughout Italy. On 10 June, five Fascist *squadristi* kidnapped him as he walked along the banks of the Tiber in **Rome**. His body was found two months later.

Matteotti's murder provoked the liberal and democratic opposition to walk out of **Parliament** on 13 June, and the widespread disgust with the violence and illegality of the Fascist militias might have brought Mussolini down. In the end, however, the *delitto Matteotti* (the Matteotti crime) served to consolidate Mussolini's power. After Mussolini was directly accused (December 1924) of having ordered Matteotti's murder, he accepted political responsibility for the killing in a bold speech in January 1925. This was a prelude to the widespread closings of "subversive" publications and organizations, indiscriminate arrests of critics, and the abolition of competitive elections. Together, these measures—given the proven illegalities of the action squads—ended all remnants of liberal democracy in Italy. *See also* AVENTINE SECESSION.

MAZZINI, GIUSEPPE (1805–1872). One of the most influential political theorists of the 19th century, Giuseppe Mazzini was born in **Genoa**, where he studied law and philosophy and developed the advanced republican and democratic ideas that he propounded for the rest of his life. He became a member of the *carboneria* in 1827. In November 1830, he was betrayed by an informer and served four months in jail. Prison was followed by exile to Marseilles where, in 1831, he founded a new clandestine movement, Giovine Italia. In a sense, Giovine Italia can be seen as a prototype for the revolutionary parties of the 20th century. Mazzini demanded great commitment and personal virtue from the movement's members, insisted that the point of political theorizing was to provide not sterile discussions but a guide for action, and underlined the need for a dictatorship of the revolutionary elite in the immediate aftermath of a revolution. In concrete terms, Giovine Italia (which gave birth to similar movements in Poland, Germany, and Switzerland) achieved little. An abortive uprising in Piedmont-**Sardinia** in 1834 was its only serious attempt to upset the absolutist order, and the movement had disintegrated by 1837.

Mazzini was the first Italian revolutionary to pay attention to the needs of the urban working class. Strongly influenced by English Chartism (he lived at length in England), Mazzini argued in strikingly similar terms to Marx that the Industrial Revolution was producing a two-class system in which the worker, "denied land, capital and credit," was a slave at the mercy of the property-owning class. Unlike Marx, however, Mazzini thought that this divide could be filled by a democratic government instituting concrete social reforms to improve wages and conditions and reduce the working day. He was, in short, an early social democratic reformist.

No democratic revolution was possible in Italy while the Austrians continued to hold much of the country. Accordingly, in 1848, Mazzini argued in favor of national unity against the common enemy and temporarily made his peace with the monarchy of Piedmont-Sardinia. In March 1849, Mazzini rushed to **Rome**, anticipating a revolutionary upheaval directed against the **papacy**. He was immediately made a parliamentary deputy and became one of the triumvirate of leaders in charge of the city's defenses against the advancing French forces. Mazzini drew up the republican Constitution that was symbolically promulgated on the day that Rome was forced to surrender. Expelled from Rome, he was forced, once more, into exile, in Switzerland and England.

In the 1850s, Mazzini lost influence over the nationalist movement. In 1853, he started a new revolutionary movement called the Partito d'Azione/Action Party, but its one attempt to promote simultaneous insurrections in Genoa and **Naples** in 1857 ended in disaster. An expeditionary force led by the anarcho-socialist Carlo Pisacane was slaughtered by angry peasants near Salerno; Mazzini had to flee from Genoa with the police on his trail. As a consequence, frustrated former Mazzinians such as **Giuseppe Garibaldi** joined the Italian Nationalist Society with its motto "For Italy and Victor Emmanuel." Mazzinians were responsible for the uprising in **Palermo** in 1860 that led to the expedition of Garibaldi's "Thousand." The policies enacted by Garibaldi's dictatorship in **Sicily** were also Mazzinian in inspiration and were enforced by one of his most loyal followers, **Francesco Crispi**. Mazzini himself, however, played only a relatively minor role in the unification of 1860. In September 1860, he went to Naples, intent on launching the idea of a national Constituent Assembly that would freely decide whether or not to accept annexation by Piedmont-Sardinia, but nothing came of this plan.

In the last decade of his life, Mazzini was deserted by Francesco Crispi and others among his few remaining supporters, who became royalists and leaders of the constitutional left. He was sharply criticized by Italy's nascent workers' movements. In 1870, he was arrested while attempting to promote an uprising in Rome. Released after the liberation of the capital, he lived the last few months of his life in Pisa under the pseudonym Dr. Brown. *See also* REVOLUTIONS OF 1848, RISORGIMENTO.

MEDIA. Italian television first went on the air in January 1954. The new state-owned service, the Radio Autodiffusione Italiana (RAI), transmitted fewer than 1,500 hours of programs in the first year of service, and viewers were numbered only in the tens of thousands. This number increased rapidly as the **economic miracle** brought the cost of a television set within the reach of ordinary middle-class Italians (four million Italian families possessed television sets by 1964). In the early years of Italian broadcasting, the most popular programs were reproductions of American game shows such as *Double or Quits* and the *Sixty-Four Thousand Dollar Question*. The star of these shows, a young Italian American named Mike Buongiorno, remains one of Italy's most popular television personalities today. Nevertheless, there was also a public service element to early Italian broadcasting. Starting in 1959, RAI produced a program called *Non è mai troppo tardi* (*It Is Never Too Late*) that taught hundreds of thousands of Italians to read more fluently and to obtain the elementary school leaving certificate.

For the first seven years only the first channel, RAI-1, was broadcasting; but, in 1961, a sister channel, RAI-2, appeared. RAI-3 came on the air in 1979 (there are also three parallel radio channels). In the 1980s, RAI's monopoly over nationwide broadcasting was broken by an upstart entrepreneur, **Silvio Berlusconi**, who—beginning with a local TV station in **Milan**—rapidly expanded to build three national networks called Rete 4, Canale 5, and Italia 6. A politically sanctioned duopoly emerged, which has made Italy one of the least advanced countries in the industrialized world in the increasingly crucial field of entertainment technology and services. On a typical evening during primetime, 80 percent of the viewing public are watching either RAI (which retains a slight lead) or Berlusconi's three channels. This situation continues despite several sentences by the Constitutional Court, which has found that the existing duopoly infringes article 21 of the **Constitution**, and a June 1995 referendum in which Italians voted by 55 to 45 percent to privatize the RAI.

RAI is one of the most politicized television companies in the democratic world. During the 1980s, the three RAI channels, and especially their news programs, were fiefs of the main political parties, with RAI-1 being dominated by the **Democrazia Cristiana**/Christian Democracy (DC), RAI-2 by the **Partito Socialista Italiano**/Italian Socialist Party (PSI), and RAI-3 by the communists. The five-person board of directors in charge of the RAI is composed of nominees from the main political parties, and the governing coalition ensures it has a majority. During the Berlusconi government of 2001–2006, there were several cases of leading journalists being squeezed out of their posts because they were regarded as hostile to the premier.

Italian television is also highly politicized in content: A huge number of talk shows and discussion programs deal with political topics. One of these, *Porta a Porta* (*Door to Door*), hosted by the journalist Bruno Vespa, has been called the "third chamber" in Italy's democracy, since so many politicians appear on it. In 2001, Silvio Berlusconi signed a five-point "contract with the Italians," listing five pledges that his government intended to keep, live on the show.

High union costs and Berlusconi's reliance on cheap American imports (which are dubbed into Italian; no subtitles are used) have also ensured that none of the television companies has achieved a particularly good record in producing quality programs of its own. Italy is one of Hollywood's biggest export markets.

Television has generated a large media industry, which is also largely controlled by Berlusconi. Publitalia, which Berlusconi owns, has a stranglehold on the advertising market; Mediaset, Berlusconi's media group, also owns *Sorrisi e canzoni* (*Smiles and Songs*), the leading national magazine specializing in listings and gossip about the stars. *See also* EDUCATION; PRESS.

MENABREA, LUIGI FEDERICO (1809–1896). Born in Chambéry, in the Savoy region of modern-day France, Luigi Federico Menabrea was a distinguished engineer who served in the engineering corps of the Sardinian army. Elected to the Parliament of Piedmont-**Sardinia** in 1848, he swiftly became one of the leaders of the *destra storica* (the historic right). He served as minister for the navy and for public works in the early 1860s and as ambassador to Vienna in 1866. At the end of October 1867, Menabrea formed his first government, which lasted little more than a month. During this month, **Giuseppe Garibaldi** was defeated at the battle of Mentana, outside **Rome**, by French forces. Menabrea's administration subsequently came under fire from Italian patriots for doing too little to make Rome the capital of Italy. The huge debts incurred by Italy during the war with Austria in 1866, and fear of a further war with France if the Roman question were pushed too hard, led Menabrea to choose a course of prudence.

His second and third cabinets (January 1868 to May 1869, May 1869 to December 1869) concentrated on restoring the public finances. During Menabrea's tenure, the notorious grist tax on milled grain was introduced in January 1869. Menabrea's government also privatized the state tobacco industry, selling it to a consortium of Italian and foreign bankers. Both decisions were unpopular. The former led to widespread rioting in rural areas, which the government suppressed at the cost of over 200 lives; the latter, to predictable accusations of corruption. Nevertheless, they were the beginning of a period of austerity that enabled the Italian state to put its finances on a sound footing by the mid-1870s. Menabrea served as ambassador to France and Great Britain for the remainder of his career. He died in his native Savoy in 1896.

MESSNER, REINHOLD (1944–). Born in the Alto Adige town of Bressanone (Brixen), Messner is probably the most famous living mountaineer. An ardent **environmentalist**, he insists that climbers should scale peaks, not dominate or damage them. As a result, he has always used the minimum possible artificial assistance on his many climbs. In 1986, Messner was the first climber to scale all 14 peaks over 8,000 meters high in the world; in 1978 he was the first climber, together with his friend Peter Hebeler, to climb Everest without oxygen; and, in 1980, he climbed Everest alone without oxygen. In all, he has climbed several thousand peaks, with more than a hundred of his ascents opening fresh paths for climbers to follow. His life has not been free of controversy, however. During the descent from Nanga Parbat (8,125 meters) in 1970, his brother Günter was killed, and Messner was unjustly accused of having left his brother in the lurch (Messner himself lost his toes to frostbite during this descent).

Messner has achieved several other remarkable feats of exploration. In 1990, he became the first man to cross the Antarctic without using either dogs or mechanized transport; in 2004, he crossed the Gobi Desert on foot. Between 1999 and 2004, he served as a deputy for the Greens in the European Parliament.

MEZZOGIORNO. *See* SOUTHERN ITALY.

MILAN (Milano). Milan is an ancient city. It has been an important municipal center since Roman times and, in AD 285, *Mediolanum*, as the Romans called it, became the capital city of the western half of the Roman Empire. The city's modern history began in 1737, after the War of the Spanish Succession, when the peace of Utrecht assigned Milan to Austria. In the next century, under Napoleon, Milan was to enjoy relative freedom, becoming the capital of the Republic of Italy in 1802, then of the Kingdom of Italy in 1805. The Milanese, therefore, were disgruntled by the decision of the Congress of Vienna in 1815 to restore Austrian rule. Milan was the center of the **revolutions of 1848** in northern Italy. It was liberated by the Piedmontese army in 1859. In the late 19th century Milan was the stronghold of Italian socialism and trade unionism. Prior to the rise to power of **Fascism** in 1922, the city was the setting for fierce street battles between the **Partito Socialista Italiano**/Italian Socialist Party (PSI) and **Benito Mussolini**'s squads. In 1945, the city's working class liberated the city without waiting for Allied forces.

Since 1945, Milan has become Italy's premier commercial, financial, and manufacturing center. More than four million people live in the city of Milan and its hinterland, and measured by the proportion of its citizens who work in manufacturing, Milan has become one of the most highly industrialized areas in the world. The high levels of industry have brought both an enviably high standard of living—the per capita value of the city's product is approximately € 30,000—and a less enviable reputation for pollution, chaotic traffic, and urban sprawl. Political corruption has also marred the city's image. In 1992–1993, the city was the center of the **Mani pulite** investigations into political wrongdoing that eventually led to the disgrace of the PSI leader (and Milanese political boss) **Bettino Craxi**. *See also* LEGA NORD (LN); RISORGIMENTO.

MINGHETTI, MARCO (1818–1886). Born in **Bologna**, Marco Minghetti was a close collaborator and friend of **Camillo Benso di Cavour**. He served as minister of the interior under Cavour in 1860–1861 and rose to be prime minister in March 1863. In this role, he signed, in 1864, the treaty with Napoleon III that led to the withdrawal of all French forces from Italy in exchange for a guarantee of the pope's authority over **Rome**. The treaty also established **Florence** as the capital of Italy. This treaty was wildly unpopular with Italian nationalists and radicals, notably **Giuseppe Garibaldi**, and with the deputies of the parliamentary left. Popular feeling against the treaty brought Minghetti's administration to an end in September 1864.

Minghetti occupied no further cabinet posts until July 1873, when he succeeded **Giovanni Lanza** as premier and also held the key post of finance minister. In office, Minghetti followed a policy of unremitting rigor that balanced the nation's books within three years. This financial rectitude naturally had political costs: Minghetti's unpopular policies were one of the principal causes of the so-called parliamentary revolution that brought **Agostino Depretis** and the left to power in 1876.

Minghetti led the parliamentary opposition from 1876 to 1882. In that year, however, he and his faction in Parliament shifted their support to Depretis, allowing the premier to "transform" the political situation by forming a centrist majority. Minghetti died in **Rome** in 1886.

MINORITIES. Linguistic minorities in Italy abound. Many Italians speak so-called standard, school-taught Italian (*la lingua letteraria*) as a second language; second, that is, to their spoken language, which is their local **dialect**. As late as 1945, 50 percent of Italians spoke only a dialect. Widespread exposure to films and television and longer school attendance have greatly reduced the influence of dialects on young Italians. Nevertheless, there remain several non-Italian linguistic groups scattered throughout the peninsula. Albanian and Greek are spoken by small communities in several regions of **southern Italy**, and there is a small Slovenian community in Friuli. The largest linguistic communities, however, are the Germans of Trentino-Alto Adige, the Sardinians, and the *Ladini*, who inhabit the eastern Alps and Friuli.

In the last 20 years, these linguistic minorities have been surpassed in numbers by ethnic minorities created by **immigration**. Albanians, Arabs from North African nations such as Tunisia and Morocco, black Africans, Chinese, Poles, Romanians, Russians and Kurds all form sizeable ethnic groups within the general **population**.

Historically, the German-speaking minority in Alto Adige (Süd Tirol) has been the source of the most political problems. Italy acquired the minority only as a result of its insistence, after **World War I**, on a frontier at the Brenner pass, instead of settling for the incorporation of the largely Italian Trentino alone. Only 3 percent of the population of Alto Adige was Italian speakers. Under **Fascism**, a policy of forcible Italianization was carried out. Place names were Italianized, tens of thousands of Italians were encouraged to migrate to the province, and German speakers were actively discriminated against in the public services. In 1939, Benito Mussolini and Adolf Hitler agreed to allow the German speakers a choice between staying under Italian domination or immigrating to the Third Reich. Those who chose to stay, the so-called *Dableiber*, were often condemned as traitors. Those who left, the *Optanten*, were regarded by many as Nazis. After **World War II**, the Italian Republic tried to solve the problems of Alto Adige by throwing money at them, but deep divisions still remain. The two linguistic communities are not integrated (there are even separate kindergartens for Germans and Italians), and all jobs in the public services are allocated proportionally in accordance with linguistic origin among Germans, Italians, and members of the *Ladino* community. Italians wishing to work for the state must also possess the *patentino*—a license proving linguistic competence in German. *See also* REGIONALISM; SÜD TIROL VOLKSPARTEI.

MODIGLIANI, AMEDEO (1884–1920). One of the most distinctive 20th-century artists, Amedeo Modigliani was born into a wealthy Jewish family from Livorno (Leghorn) on the Tuscan coast but spent most of his adult life in Paris, where he began working as a sculptor and was greatly influenced, like many artists of the time, by African art. His life in Paris was the classic tale of the neglected genius: He had only one one-man show in his lifetime, and that was swiftly shut down by the police on the grounds of obscenity. He was interested in the work of Paul Cezanne but otherwise was little influenced by either the principal movements in the art world (fauvism, **futurism**, and cubism) or the left-wing politics of the Parisian art scene.

The last five years of his brief life were the most memorable for his artistic production. In these years, Modigliani painted the portraits and the strikingly erotic (some would say pornographic) nudes that established his artistic reputation. His *Portrait of Leopold Zborowski* (1916), epitomizes his uniquely stylized form of portraiture. Zborowski, Modigliani's closest male friend, sits in the center of the canvas, a bulky figure in a brown suit, whose shoulders taper like a wine bottle to a perfectly oval-shaped head. Detail is reduced to a minimum: The eyes are no more than a dab of unexpressive green, the sitter's hair and beard are merely precisely defined areas of brown paint, the face is absolutely flat, the skin of the face is unwrinkled and almost monochromatic, the brown suit has a virtually indistinguishable lapel but no other adornment, and the background is an unfeatured grey-green cloth or curtain. Yet the picture conveys both an undeniable sense of character—one perceives Zborowski's poise and intellect—and a powerful sense that the sitter has been accurately represented.

From about 1912 onward, Modigliani was chronically addicted to alcohol and hashish. Several glasses of whisky were required to set his creative gifts in motion; he made a conscious philosophy out of living a life of excess. He died of tubercular meningitis in 1920. His last companion, Jeanne Heburtane, killed herself the following day.

MODIGLIANI, FRANCO (1918–2003). Born in **Rome**, Modigliani was forced to leave Italy after the introduction of the 1938 **racial**

laws. He went to the United States and became a successful teacher of economics at the University of Illinois and then professor of economics and finance at the Massachusetts Institute of Technology. Modigliani was awarded the 1985 Nobel Prize for economics for two works he had produced in the 1950s. The first of these was concerned with the human propensity to save. Before Modigliani's work, it had been taken for granted that human beings saved during their working life to be able to consume during their retirement. Modigliani showed that this was not so, and that a broad range of factors influenced savings decisions. His second great innovation, the "Mo-Mi theory" (so-called because the theory was developed together with the American economist Merton Miller), overturned the commonplace notion that it was better for a firm to finance its growth by taking out loans rather than issuing shares. Modigliani and Miller showed that company value is not dependent on financial structure so much as on current perceptions of the company's future profits.

Although he took out American citizenship in 1946, Modigliano remained interested in his native country and was a frequent commentator on Italy's recurring economic crises until his death. He was a particularly outspoken critic of the large government deficits being accumulated by the Italian state. In 2003, he opposed the decision of the Anti-Defamation League to honor **Silvio Berlusconi**, who, Modigliani contended, had sought to exculpate **Benito Mussolini** for his treatment of Italy's Jews. Modigliani died in Cambridge, Massachusetts, in September 2003.

MOMIGLIANO, ARNALDO (1908–1987). Widely regarded as one of the greatest 20th-century scholars of classics and of the ancient world, Arnaldo Momigliano was born in the province of Cuneo (Piedmont) in 1908. Momigliano, already a professor, was forced to flee Italy in 1938 because the introduction of the **racial laws** meant he, as a Jew, was unable to continue his career. He left for England where he taught at Bristol University and then at University College, London, where he was professor from 1951 to 1975. Momigliano was also visiting professor for more than 20 years (1964–1987) at Chicago University. He was knighted by Queen Elizabeth II in 1974 for his contributions to scholarship.

Isaiah Berlin, surely a convincing witness, called Momigliano a "great scholar," and in fact Momigliano's work ranged over the entire historical traditions of Greece, Rome, Persia, and old testament Judea. He wrote of the birth of the early church and biographies of Philip of Macedon and the emperor Claudius, and in Italian left 11 volumes of collected essays of "Contributions to the History of Classical Studies and of the Ancient World." In particular, Momigliano was an unrivalled expert on the historiography of the ancients and of the Greek historians Herodotus and Thucydides. Momigliano taught in Pisa, at the *Scuola Normale*, in his final years. He died in **Rome** in 1987.

MONARCHY (House of Savoy). One of Europe's oldest ruling families, the lineage of the dukes of Savoy stretches back to the Middle Ages. Though theoretically subjects of the Holy Roman Empire, the Savoy family enjoyed great autonomy and, from **Turin**, governed Chambéry and Annecy in modern-day France and a substantial tract of territory straddling the **Alps**, and territories within the modern Italian regions of Piedmont, Aosta, and Liguria constituted the dukedom's boundaries. The dukes achieved regal status as a result of the enterprising Duke Amadeus II (Amadeo II, 1675–1730), who deserted King Louis XIV of France at a crucial moment in the War of Spanish Succession and was rewarded for his behavior by elevation to kingship and the addition of the island of **Sicily** to Savoyan territory in 1718. In 1720, under Austrian pressure, he was obliged to exchange Sicily for **Sardinia**. His heirs were henceforth known as the Kings of Sardinia, although many historians refer to the state as Piedmont-Sardinia to reflect the fact that Turin continued to be the administrative and social capital of the new state. The new state added to its domain during the War of the Polish Succession, when Charles Emmanuel III, the son of Amadeus II, defeated the Austrians and conquered Lombardy, although at the peace of Vienna in 1738 he was obliged to give Lombardy back in exchange for the province of Novara and other minor territorial gains.

As the primary power in Lombardy and Venetia, Austria was a long-standing enemy of the Savoy family. Nevertheless, the family was an absolutist dynasty, and the Savoys therefore rallied to the side of imperial Austria against the challenge of revolutionary France after 1789. Napoleon defeated the Austro-Piedmontese forces at the battle of Mondovi in 1796; two years later, Charles Emmanuel IV of Savoy was forced to flee to Sardinia when French forces occupied Turin. The Savoys, in the person of King Victor Emmanuel I, were only restored to their throne in 1815 at the **Congress of Vienna**.

The importance of the Savoy family, of course, is that they became the ruling family of all Italy. Victor Emmanuel I was succeeded on the throne of Sardinia by his pro-Austrian brother, Charles Felice (reigned 1821–1831), and only after that by his son, **Charles Albert** (1831–1849). Italian unification was achieved during the reign of **Victor Emmanuel II** (1849–1878). His son, Humbert I (1878–1900), was a reactionary who backed the conservative governments of the 1890s and was killed by an emigré anarchist who returned from the United States with the express intention of avenging the innocent peasants and workers slaughtered by Italian troops during the Sicilian uprisings of 1894 and the Milanese bread riots in 1898.

Humbert's son, **Victor Emmanuel III** (1900–1946), initially backed relative progressives in the Italian political establishment but ultimately acquiesced in the accession to power of **Benito Mussolini**. His son, Humbert II, was king for two months in 1946 prior to the **referendum** on the future of the monarchy. By a very close margin (12.7 million votes to 10.7 million, with 1.5 million invalid votes), Italy elected to become a republic.

The Savoy family was subsequently debarred from ever setting foot in Italy again, though this ban was lifted in 1997. Even today, many Italians, particularly in the North, regard the Savoy family as traitors and unpunished war criminals. There is no monarchist political party in Italy today, although there is a surprising amount of public interest in the Savoy family's jet-set lifestyle. *See also* BADOGLIO, PIETRO; MARCH ON ROME; NAPOLEONIC ITALY; REVOLUTIONS OF 1848.

MONETA, ERNESTO TEODORO (1833–1918). Moneta, a Milanese, won the Nobel Peace Prize in 1907, the only Italian to have done so. He was an ardent nationalist who fought with **Giuseppe Garibaldi** during the wars of liberation 1859–1860 and in the war against Austria in 1866. He became a journalist and as editor of one of Italy's most important daily newspapers, *Il Secolo*, between 1867 and 1895, was a powerful influence on public opinion. He was strongly anticlerical (though a religious believer) and sought to mitigate the anti-Austrian and anti-French fervor of the Italian masses.

Moneta published a four-volume work entitled *Le guerre, le insurrezioni e la pace nel secolo XIX* (*Wars, Insurrections and Peace in the Nineteenth Century*) between 1903 and 1910. He also edited a prestigious fortnightly journal called *La Vita Internazionale*, which attracted contributions from the leading radical and socialist intellectuals of the day. The theme of his later work was the futility of war: its inevitable failure to provide worthwhile solutions for human problems. Moneta served as Italy's representative on the International Peace Bureau from 1895 onward and founded the Società per la pace e la giustizia internazionale (Society for International Peace and Justice) in 1887. The society's objectives were to educate popular sentiment in favor of ending war; favor the brotherhood of all peoples; propose arbitration as a solution for human conflicts; and abolish standing armies and replace them with "armed nations." Moneta strongly opposed Italy's colonial adventurism in **Libya** but supported Italy's entrance into **World War I**. His pacifism remained conjugated with patriotism: He insisted that world peace did not mean the dissolution of nations in a cosmopolitan melting pot, but rather the integration of nations into a just international order. Moneta died of pneumonia in **Milan** in 1918.

MONTALE, EUGENIO (1896–1981). One of the greatest 20th-century poets, Eugenio Montale became the fifth Italian in that century to win the Nobel Prize in **Literature**. Montale established his reputation in 1925 when the antifascist publisher and political theorist **Piero Gobetti** printed his remarkable collection *Ossi di seppia* (*Cuttlefish Bones*). Along with Eliot's *Wasteland* (which Montale translated into Italian), the poems in *Ossi di seppia* are perhaps the most poignant expression of the malaise experienced by the generation who had survived **World War I**. Spare in style, self-consciously rejecting the pompous, rhetorical forms popularized by **Gabriele d'Annunzio**, they also refused to make any concessions to the ardent, committed poetry prized by **Fascism**.

Montale "discovered" **Italo Svevo** in a famous essay in 1925, and as one of the principal figures connected with the literary magazine

Solaria, he played an important role in preserving independent Italian literature during the dictatorship. His relations with the regime were never easy, and in 1939 his refusal to swear allegiance to **Benito Mussolini** led to his losing his job at a Florentine literary foundation. In the same year, he published his second great collection of poems, *Le occasioni* (*Occasions*).

After **World War II**, Montale worked as a cultural and music critic (his collected short essays and criticism were published in Italy in 1996) for *Corriere della sera* and produced a masterful collection of poems, *Il Bufera e altri* (*The Storm and Others*) in 1956. The death of his wife in 1963 inspired him to write a series of lyric poems that were later collected in *Saturna* (1971).

Honors were showered on Montale in his last years. He became a life member of the Italian Senate in 1967 and, in 1975, became a Nobel laureate for literature. He died in **Milan** in September 1981.

MONTANELLI, INDRO (1909–2001). Perhaps the most famous Italian journalist of the 20th century, Indro Montanelli fought a long intellectual battle against Italian communism but in the mid-1990s became one of the sternest critics of the right-wing politicians who had emerged in Italy since the collapse of the **Democrazia Cristiana/** Christian Democracy Party (DC) in 1992–1993.

Born near **Florence**, Montanelli, who was an ardent Fascist in his youth, made his name as a war correspondent for the *Corriere della sera* in Finland during the winter of 1939–1940. For most of the immediate postwar years Montanelli was the chief columnist for the *Corriere*, but, in 1974, dismayed by the paper's increasing willingness to compromise with the **Partito Comunista Italiano/**Italian Communist Party (PCI), he left the Milanese daily to found a new newspaper, *Il Giornale nuovo*, which he edited until January 1994. At *Il Giornale*, Montanelli was vehemently critical of both the PCI and the DC, whose corruption and political malpractice he denounced in brilliant, incisive prose. He nevertheless continued to urge his readers to "hold their noses" and vote for the DC so long as there was any risk of the PCI's taking power. Montanelli's defense of the DC made him unpopular with the radical left in the turbulent 1970s; in June 1977, he was shot in the legs by zealots of the **Brigate Rosse/**Red Brigades (BR).

Montanelli's career as editor of *Il Giornale* was brought to an end by his refusal to condone and support the political career of **Silvio Berlusconi**, the paper's owner. Berlusconi brusquely sacked Montanelli, and the veteran journalist was forced to start a new broadsheet, *La Voce*, which soon failed. Montanelli continued to play an active role in Italian public life and to publish regular articles on the political scene until his death in July 2001. In addition to his journalism, he was the author of numerous works of popular history including a multivolume best-selling history of Italy, as well as several plays and stories. *See also* PRESS.

MONTESSORI, MARIA (1870–1952). One of the 20th century's most famous and innovative educational theorists, Maria Montessori was born in Ancona (The Marches). The so-called Montessori method, which has been used in experimental schools all over the world and has had a huge impact on curricular and school reform in all advanced industrial countries, prizes the use of didactic materials that spontaneously awaken the curiosity of young children and also incite them to learn. It was thus in opposition to the highly disciplined and teacher-centered methods common in the early part of the 20th century. Children taught by the Montessori method are encouraged to read, write, and develop spatial skills at a very early age. This aspect of the method has led to criticism from educational progressives, who believe that early **education** should allow children to adjust to their environment and experience rather than fostering precocious academic achievement.

As one would expect from someone who put so much emphasis on free inquiry and curiosity, Montessori was no friend of the Fascist regime. Rather than endure the dictatorship, she left Italy and eventually established herself permanently in the Netherlands. She died near The Hague in 1952. *See also* WOMEN.

MONTI, MARIO (1943–). Born in Varese near the border of Lombardy with Switzerland, Mario Monti has enjoyed a distinguished career as an economist, a university administrator, and a European commissioner. Monti's academic career mostly took place at the University of **Turin** and at the Bocconi University in **Milan**, a private school that specializes in the social sciences and in preparing business leaders. In 1985, he became professor at the Bocconi and between 1989 and 1994 was the university's rector. He became president of the Bocconi in 1994.

In the 1980s, Monti was called upon to serve on numerous parliamentary and government committees of inquiry, most notably the Spaventa Commission on the national debt and public finances (1988–1989). The combination of his academic reputation and public service led to his being nominated to the European Commission by the first government of **Silvio Berlusconi** in 1994. He took over as commissioner responsible for the internal market, financial services, customs, and tax questions in January 1995. In 1999, he was named to the crucial post of Competition, responsible for approving or blocking mergers throughout the European Union (EU) and monitoring monopolistic behavior within the internal market. This role gave Monti a high public profile since he was called upon to adjudicate in a large number of prominent cases, most notably the decision to fine Microsoft for uncompetitive behavior. His successful handling of the job won him the nickname, "Super Mario."

The second Berlusconi government, for internal political reasons, did not renew Monti's seat on the Commission in 2004, preferring **Rocco Buttiglione**. Monti is one of the founding members of Bruegel, a think tank on policy making in the EU, and a regular commentator in Italian and other European newspapers. It is widely thought that Monti could emerge as prime minister in the future. Like **Lamberto Dini** in the 1990s, he is respected by both the left and the right in Italian politics. See also EUROPEAN INTEGRATION.

MORANTE, ELSA (1918–1985). An important figure in postwar Italian fiction, Elsa Morante was the author of four major novels, *Menzogna e Sortilegio* (*The House of Liars*, 1948), *L'Isola di Arturo* (*Arturo's Island*, 1957), *La Storia* (*History: A Novel*, 1974), and *Aracoeli* (*Aracoeli*, 1982). Childhood recurs as an obsessive theme in all her works, and child characters are often employed as a foil to expose the corruption and alienation of the adult world. Morante became famous almost overnight with the publication of *La Storia*, which became a best-seller and stirred a huge debate between those critics who condemned its profound pessimism and those who praised Morante's warmth toward the ordinary people who are history's principal victims. Initially more successful in France than in Italy, few would now doubt that Morante is one of the most important contemporary Italian novelists and one of the most talented **women** writers to emerge in any language since 1945. She died in her native **Rome** in 1985. *See also* LITERATURE; MORAVIA, ALBERTO.

MORAVIA, ALBERTO (pseud. Alberto Pincherle, 1907–1990). One of Italy's most prolific and controversial contemporary writers, Alberto Moravia was an exceptionally precocious novelist. *Gli indifferenti* (*The Indifferent*, 1929), his first novel, was published when he was hardly more than 20 years old. Many still regard this study of bored, corrupt, worthless, and indecisive upper-class Romans as his best work. Its sexual frankness won it a large audience, but its merciless depiction of the feebleness and rottenness of the Italian ruling class aroused the censure of the regime, and Moravia was obliged to leave Italy for exile in Mexico and the United States.

Several of Moravia's later novels were turned into films, the most successful being *Il Conformista* (*The Conformist*, 1952); **Bernardo Bertolucci** won his first Oscar for an adaptation of it. The influence of Moravia's novel *La Noia* (literally "Boredom" but translated as *The Empty Canvas*) is very evident in the films of **Michelangelo Antonioni**. Both of these novels were of the same existentialist genre as *Gli indifferenti*, but Moravia also wrote several realist novels, the best of which is probably *La Romana* (1947). Moravia was close politically and personally to the leaders of the **Partito Comunista Italiano**/Italian Communist Party (PCI). In the 1960s, he made a much-publicized visit to revolutionary China and wrote a somewhat naive account of what he saw there. In 1986, he married the young Spanish novelist Carmen Llera; he had previously been married to the Italian novelists **Elsa Morante** and Dacia Moraini. Moravia died in **Rome** in 1990. *See also* CINEMA; LITERATURE.

MORETTI, NANNI (1953–). A talented, though highly political and somewhat narcissistic, film director, Nanni Moretti was born in Brunico (Alto Adige) but has lived all his life in **Rome**, which is also the location of many of his films. Moretti is also an accomplished actor and documentary film maker and was a semiprofessional water polo player, which helped him with the setting of his film *Palombella Rosso* (1989).

Moretti's career began with two critically acclaimed art-house movies, *Ecce Bombo* (1978) and *Bianca* (1984), but commercial as well as critical success arrived in the 1990s with a series of well-regarded films. In *Il Portaborsa* (directed by Daniele Lucchetti, 1991), Moretti played the part of an unscrupulous politician who employs an idealistic Neapolitan intellectual (Silvio Orlando) as a speechwriter. Orlando and Moretti brilliantly complement each other in what is one of the most illuminating political movies made in Italy in recent years. As a director, Moretti made and starred in *Caro Diario* (*Dear Diary*, 1993) and *Aprile* (*April*, 1998). These films are superbly scripted and developed, but as with Woody Allen, one cannot help but conclude that the film's main subject is the director's own personality. By contrast, *La Stanza del Figlio* (*The Son's Room*, 2001), which won the Palme d'Or at the Cannes film festival, is a subtle depiction of how a highly rational, progressive, upper-class family deals with the trauma caused by the accidental death of their son.

In the most famous scene in *Aprile*, Moretti's character is watching **Massimo D'Alema** debating with **Silvio Berlusconi** on television and urges him to "say something left-wing; say something not even left-wing, just civilized." Since Berlusconi's victory in the 2001 elections Moretti has become a political activist of some importance and has been an outspoken critic of the official parties of the center-left. In 2002, together with a number of other public intellectuals, he launched the *girotondo* movement (so-called because its first public protest was to form a ring of people holding hands around the **Parliament**) to press for a more ethical public life and for a less accommodating line toward Berlusconi on the part of the political Left. Moretti's most recent film, *Il Caimano* (*The Caiman*, 2006) is a film about a filmmaker making a film about Berlusconi. *See also* CINEMA.

MORO, ALDO (1916–1978). Born in Apulia, the heel of the Italian boot, Moro became a professor of law and criminal procedure at the University of **Bari**. During the war years, he was simultaneously president of the **Federazione Universitaria Cattolici Italiana/** Catholic University Graduates' Movement of Italy (FUCI); a member of the Catholic Movimento Laureati (Graduates' Movement) and editor of *Studium*, its major publication; and a member of the Gioventù Universitaria Fascista/Fascist University Youth (GUF).

Elected to the **Constituent Assembly** and subsequently to the first republican Parliament, Moro was identified with **Alcide De Gasperi**, in whose fifth government Moro was made undersecretary for foreign affairs. Consistently reelected to the Chamber of Deputies, by 1953, he was floor leader of the **Democrazia Cristiana**/Christian Democracy Party (DC). He was minister of education in the 1958 government headed by **Amintore Fanfani**. In 1959, he became secretary of the DC. In this role he was instrumental in achieving the **opening to the left** and creating a coalition with the **Partito Socialista Italiano**/Italian Socialist party (PSI). Moro headed a government that included the PSI between 1963 and 1968. By 1976, he had been prime minister five times.

Moro also served as minister for foreign affairs in governments headed by **Mariano Rumor** (1969–1970; 1973–1974), **Emilio Colombo** (1970–1972), and **Giulio Andreotti** (1972). It was in this capacity that he met Henry Kissinger, who described Moro as wily, imperceptibly maneuvering, and the most formidable among the DC leaders. Moro was indeed the supreme party strategist and a man of extraordinary intellectual subtlety. His detractors described him as obfuscating. Some of his more elliptical formulations are still quoted, for example, "parallel convergences."

In the politically troubled 1970s, Moro was chief architect of the *compromesso storico*. Without his flexibility, the **Partito Comunista Italiano**/Italian Communist Party (PCI), and its leader, **Enrico Berlinguer**, might have been cold-shouldered. Moro was accordingly regarded by the far left as the symbol of the party regime (a regime that was held to include the PCI). In their boldest move, the **Brigate Rosse**/Red Brigades (BR) kidnapped Moro in broad daylight on 16 March 1978. After bitter quarrels over his fate, BR leaders offered to negotiate with the government for his release. The offer was rejected, despite the fact that Moro himself wrote several letters to DC leaders pleading with them to save his life. Moro was put on "trial" by the terrorists, found "guilty" on 15 April 1978, and "executed." His body was left in the trunk of a small automobile in central **Rome**, midway between PCI national offices and the national headquarters of the DC in Piazza del Gesù, on 9 May 1978.

Moro's murder produced vitriolic exchanges among political lead-ers of all parties, but most especially within the DC. The **police** and the political elite were immediately accused of not having done enough to discover Moro's prison. The subsequent publication of fur-ther letters he had written during his imprisonment, in which he was bitterly critical of the efforts being made to get him released, only ex-acerbated the polemic surrounding his death. The Sicilian writer **Leonardo Sciascia**'s book *L'Affaire Moro* is perhaps the most fa-mous contribution to this debate. For Sciascia, who was a member of the parliamentary commission of inquiry into Moro's death, the most "monstrous thought" of all was that "someone had died at the right moment." *See also* COSSIGA, FRANCESCO.

MOSCA, GAETANO (1858–1941). One of the democratic age's most uncomfortable thinkers, Gaetano Mosca is chiefly remembered today for his conviction that democratic regimes—like all other types of regime—are controlled by elites, who manipulate public opinion and the levers of power for their own ends.

Born in **Palermo** in 1858, Mosca's critique of democracy first sur-faced in his 1884 work *Teorica dei governi* (*Theory of Governments*). But it was his 1896 work, *Elementi di scienza politica* (*Elements of Political Science*), that established his reputation. For Mosca, who by now was a close advisor of the conservative statesman **Antonio Starabba Di Rudinì**, the rhetoric of popular sovereignty was simply a device used by Machiavellian politicians to facilitate their own pur-suit of power. Moreover, paucity of political sophistication, shaky in-stitutions, and a high tolerance for political corruption meant that democratic reforms were a gift horse that should be carefully exam-ined for unscrupulous agitators willing and able to exploit popular prejudices and ignorance. For this reason, Mosca, who was elected to **Parliament** in 1909, opposed the introduction of universal male suf-frage in 1912.

Mosca, however, must be regarded as a liberal-conservative, not as a protofascist or a reactionary (his most famous pupil, **Piero Gobetti**, described him as a "conservative gentleman"). His objection to de-mocracy was precisely that it increased the likelihood that an antilib-eral elite would come to power—and post-1918 politics in Italy hardly persuaded him to question this analysis. Like **Benedetto**

Croce, Mosca was initially inclined to give **Benito Mussolini** the benefit of the liberal doubt, but, by 1925, he had passed to the opposition. Mosca signed the manifesto of antifascist intellectuals published by Croce in the newspaper *Il Mondo* on 1 May 1925. Mosca's final years were spent finishing off an enormous history of political thought, which was published in 1933. He died in **Rome** in 1941.

MOVIMENTO SOCIALE ITALIANO/Italian Social Movement (MSI). Survivors of the **Republic of Salò** joined returning veterans, former war prisoners, and nostalgics for **Fascism**'s certainties to found the MSI in December 1946. **Giorgio Almirante**, the party's first secretary, had been a member of the *Decima mas* (former naval personnel of the Motoscaf Antisommergibile/Antisubmarine Patrol Boats, who were used in the republic to find, arrest, and massacre Italian partisans), and preferred violent confrontations to political compromise. At Salò, the original hundred party members (including Almirante) grew to 4,000, led by Roman Prince Junio Valerio Borghese, who refused to be subordinate either to the Germans or to Fascist party functionaries. The presence of additional right-wing groups, such as the monarchists and factions within the newly formed MSI, made cohesion difficult.

Despite his undeniable abilities and skill as an orator, Almirante was replaced in 1950 by Augusto De Marsanich, who was determined to make the party an accepted player in the Italian Republic. The MSI continued on this path under the leadership of Arturo Michelini, chosen in 1954, whose network of contacts in his native **Rome** provided entry to both **Vatican** and bourgeois Roman circles. Events surrounding the government of **Fernando Tambroni**, however, made it difficult to put the MSI at the core of a parliamentary right.

When Michelini died unexpectedly in 1969, the party chose Almirante to replace him. He began to combine the strategies of anti-regime agitation with the pursuit of legitimation as the party of "law and order." Almirante managed to tie to himself **Giuseppe Rauti**, the hotheaded street fighter and founder of the neo-Nazi movement Ordine Nuovo. A few senior military officers (Admiral Birindelli, General Giovanni De Lorenzo, and General Vito Miceli) were drawn to the party after the 1972 merger with the monarchists of the Destra Nazionale/National Right (DN), thus creating the MSI-DN.

By 1980, the MSI had put aside the cudgel in favor of the double-breasted suit, becoming the party of opposition to (leftist) terrorism, the drug culture, abortion, and **divorce**, and—with similar energy—becoming the advocate of a French-style presidency for Italy. Almirante visited the United States and even paid homage at the funeral of **Enrico Berlinguer** in the Rome headquarters of the **Partito Comunista Italiano**/Italian Communist Party (PCI). The reborn MSI-DN offered corporatism as an alternative to unbridled capitalism. A strong state, hierarchy, discipline, authority and obedience, acceptance of the Fascist years as an integral part of Italy's recent past and not an anomaly: These core beliefs purported to defend the "dignity and interests of the Italian people" in the Mediterranean, Europe, and the world.

Before Almirante died in the spring of 1988, he led the MSI to elect as secretary **Gianfranco Fini**, born seven years after **World War II**. Fini has held that position since 1988, except for the period January 1990 to July 1991, when Rauti was secretary. Fini's program included the death penalty, lower taxes, harsh anti-immigrant legislation, and revision of the 1975 Treaty of Osimo settling the borders with Yugoslavia. Fini was the last leader of the MSI. Under his guidance, the party transformed itself into the **Alleanza Nazionale**/National Alliance (AN) in 1994–1995 in an attempt to make the neofascist movement a pole of attraction for the many conservative voters disillusioned by the moral decline of the DC and alarmed by the growing strength of the Italian left. *See also* IMMIGRATION; SOLO PLAN; STRATEGIA DELLA TENSIONE.

MURRI, ROMOLO (1870–1944). Born in the Marches, this leader of radical **Catholicism** in pre-1914 Italy had become a priest in 1893. Like many young priests born after the **Risorgimento**, he chafed under the Church's ban on political activity and found the **Vatican**-approved social movements (the most important of which was the so-called Opera dei congressi) intolerably conservative. Beginning in 1898, Murri edited a magazine, *Cultura sociale*, a Catholic rival to the Socialist Party's intellectual journal *Critica sociale*. Spurred by the state's repression of workers' movements throughout Italy in 1898–1899, Murri's critique of Italian society assumed nearly Marxist tones—so far as he was concerned, the state was merely the expression of the desires and ideas of the property-owning classes, an essentially repressive organization that had to be transformed into *una democrazia cristiana* (a Christian democracy).

Disenchanted with the conservatism of the Vatican, Murri founded the Lega Democratica Nazionale/National Democratic League in 1905. The new movement openly proclaimed its intention to recruit young working-class activists who would spread democratic and socialist ideas within Catholic organizations in Italy. Displeased, the Church banned priests from participating in the new movement and eventually suspended Murri from the priesthood in 1907, after he openly called for state supervision of religious schools and the ending of religious instruction in elementary schools. Undaunted, Murri was elected to **Parliament** as a radical for his native Ascoli Piceno (Marches) in 1909. The Church responded by excommunicating him.

Murri's hostility to Giolittian liberalism and the influence of the philosophy of **Giovanni Gentile** later caused his political views to turn to the right. He won the plaudits of the Fascist hierarchy by publishing a paean to the strong state entitled *La conquista ideale dello stato* (*The Ideal Conquest of the State*, 1923). After the publication of this book, **Piero Gobetti** dismissed him as "the perfect example of a failed prophet." He was reconciled to the Church in 1943 and died the following year. See also GIOLITTI, GIOVANNI.

MUSSOLINI, BENITO (1883–1945). Mussolini was born in the foothills of the Apennines in Predappio (Romagna). His father and grandfather were both peasants who were jailed for their commitment to the nascent socialist movement, while his mother was a schoolmistress and a devout Catholic. Mussolini, though a voracious reader, seems to have been an ill-tempered child who was twice suspended from school for knifing fellow students. After leaving school he had a number of teaching appointments, but everywhere he went he managed to antagonize the authorities. After fleeing to Switzerland and France to avoid military service in 1903–1904, his political activities and riotous conduct led to his being arrested and expelled. Fascist historians subsequently misrepresented this ignominious period in Mussolini's life by asserting that he had studied at the University of Geneva. A general amnesty for deserters, however, allowed him to repatriate and clear his record by 18 months of military service. While Mussolini was serving in the military, his mother died. Mussolini returned to Predappio as soon as his period of conscription was over and became both a (rather incompetent) schoolteacher and a socialist activist of growing notoriety.

In 1909, Mussolini immigrated once more, this time to the Trentino (then under Austrian rule) where he honed his growing skills as a propagandist as editor of *Il Popolo* (*The People*), an irredentist newspaper published by the leader of the Italian community, **Cesare Battisti**. Repeatedly arrested by the Austrian authorities, Mussolini's inevitable expulsion only enhanced his standing among Italian nationalists.

Mussolini opposed the war in **Libya**, which the reformist majority of the **Partito Socialista Italiano**/Italian Socialist Party (PSI) had backed, and served a five-month prison sentence in 1911 for antiwar activities. One of his cellmates was **Pietro Nenni**. On his release, Mussolini was determined to wrest control of the PSI from the reformists. Taking advantage of the membership's hostile reaction to a visit to the royal palace made by **Leonida Bissolati** to congratulate the king on escaping from an assassination attempt, Mussolini made a violent speech against Bissolati's policy of obtaining social reforms through cooperation with the Italian state. Mussolini's motion to expel Bissolati and the other leaders of the PSI's moderates achieved an unexpectedly large majority, and Mussolini briefly became the party's dominant personality.

Mussolini became editor of the party newspaper, *Avanti!* In 1914, he was torn between the party line of neutralism and the will to intervene. His hope appears to have been that a military bloodbath would stimulate revolutionary conditions. Unilaterally, he changed the editorial policy of the paper to one backing interventionism, but he was unable to carry the party leadership with him and was expelled. Undaunted, Mussolini launched a paper of his own, *Il Popolo d'Italia* (*The People of Italy*), in November 1914, with substantial financial aid from businesses in the war industries. By 1915, he had become an expansionist, advocating the creation of an Italian empire in the eastern Mediterranean and Middle East. Mussolini was called up in September 1915 and seems to have performed his duties as a soldier competently, being promoted to corporal, but without particular distinction. In February 1917, he was wounded by an accidental explosion during grenade training; Fascist hagiographers would later make much of this injury and claim that the war began to go badly for Italy when Mussolini was constrained to leave the front! Mussolini returned to *Il Popolo d 'Italia*, where he took an increasingly nationalist and populist line and abandoned socialism, as he himself put it, with a "sigh of relief."

In March 1919, Mussolini founded the Fasci Italiani di Combattimento. The new movement had no clear ideology; Mussolini's speeches and articles drew upon a mishmash of anarchist, socialist, nationalist, and syndicalist themes. But the movement's appeal for action, which it backed up by a campaign of terror against the PSI in the streets and fields of Italy, appealed to Italy's numerous disaffected former soldiers, and Mussolini showed great skill in trimming his tactical sails to suit the needs of the moment. He became prime minister in October 1922 after the **March on Rome**, but governing with respect for democracy was not the hallmark of his premiership. In his first speech to **Parliament**, he made clear his contempt for the institution, saying that he could have bivouacked his blackshirts in "*quest'aula sorda e grigia*" ("this deaf, gray hall"). Fascist bullyboys terrorized the rival parties; the opposition leader **Giacomo Matteotti** was murdered; and all opposition parties, newspapers, and independent political activity was banned in 1925–1926. He had become Duce, the leader, and his word was law.

Like the rulers of Soviet Russia, Mussolini set out to create a new man for a new century, but his methods seem somewhat infantile in retrospect. Great emphasis was put on flag-waving rallies, grandiose architecture, and educational propaganda. Mussolini himself struck heroic poses; spoke to what the Fascist press called "oceanic crowds" of carefully choreographed enthusiasts; and launched symbolic battles for grain, land reclamation, and fertility. Quite a number of foreign visitors were taken in by the facade: Winston Churchill and a stream of other eminent upper-class British visitors regarded Mussolini as one of the great men of the age. In retrospect, however, we can see that he was merely a semi-intellectual with a gift for propaganda and political intrigue. Mussolini was extremely skilled at making sure that rivals for influence within the Fascist movement, such as **Italo Balbo**, were promoted to jobs distant from the power centers in Rome. Above all, although he invented the word, he was not a totalitarian dictator on the model of Josef Stalin and Adolf Hitler, though he may have liked to have been. He was much less ruthless, less obsessed, and more human, and Fascist Italy was consequently a much more livable place than the terrible dictatorships of Nazi Germany and Communist Russia.

Mussolini was also prone to vainglory. His downfall can ultimately be traced to the fact that he began to believe his own propaganda. Contemptuous of democratic Britain and France, puffed up by Italy's bloody military victory in **Ethiopia**, his ego flattered by Hitler's skillful diplomacy (notably during a five-day official visit to Germany in September 1937 and Hitler's return visit in April 1938), Mussolini threw in Italy's lot with Nazi Germany. Mussolini soon became the junior partner in Hitler's plans, though the German dictator continued to the end to regard the Duce with esteem and friendship. As the war progressed, Mussolini, who was also suffering from a serious stomach illness, proved to be an inadequate war leader: out of touch with reality and unable to direct the war effort with the energy and rationality that the Fascist system, in which power was entirely concentrated in the Duce's own hands, demanded. When, after the Allied invasion of **Sicily** in July 1943, the **Fascist Grand Council** deposed Mussolini, there was no popular protest—even among active Fascists. *Il Popolo d'Italia*, announcing the news, simply replaced Mussolini's photograph on the front page with one of Marshal **Pietro Badoglio**.

Mussolini was rescued by the Germans from his hotel-prison on top of the Gran Sasso mountain in September 1943. For the last two years of his life he ruled the puppet **Republic of Salò** and must bear great responsibility for the savagery of the civil war fought in northern Italy in those years. On 28 April 1945, as Mussolini, his mistress Clara Petacci, and a handful of diehards were trying to escape into Switzerland, they were captured by partisans and summarily executed; Mussolini was hung by his heels in Milan's Piazza Loreto, where his corpse was vilely treated by the crowds. *See also* AXIS, ROME-BERLIN; CORPORATISM; DE FELICE, RENZO; FACTA, LUIGI; FASCISM; FOREIGN POLICY; MONARCHY; PARTITO NAZIONALE FASCISTA; QUADRUMVIRATE; RACIAL LAWS; RESISTANCE; SPANISH CIVIL WAR; VICTOR EMMANUEL III; WORLD WAR II.

MUTI, ETTORE (1902–1943). A flamboyant figure from Ravenna on the Adriatic, Ettore Muti was secretary of the **Partito Nazionale Fascista**/National Fascist Party (PNF) between 1939 and 1941. A close friend of Galeazzo Ciano, son-in-law of **Benito Mussolini**, Muti was somewhat childish in the Duce's company. His courageous service in the **Arditi** in **World War I** had led to frequent decoration. After becoming party secretary, his penchant for wearing all his medals on any and every occasion resulted in his being ironically described as having "the most magnificent chest in Italy." Undeniably brave, he had also participated in **Gabriele D'Annunzio**'s occupation of **Fiume**. Both in the war in **Ethiopia** and in the **Spanish Civil War**, he was Ciano's copilot in bombing raids. He lost a hand and an eye in the Spanish Civil War, for which he was awarded a gold medal.

Memorialist Fidia Gambetta described Muti's penchant for driving his Bugatti two-seater at breakneck speeds into the main square of small Italian towns. The scene was reproduced by **Federico Fellini** in his film-memoir, *Amacord* ("I remember" in Romagnole dialect). Muti's limited administrative abilities led to his dismissal in May 1941 and his replacement by Adelchi Serena, who was, in turn, replaced by a young, unknown, and administratively inexperienced law student, Aldo Vidussoni.

When **Pietro Badoglio** came to power in July 1943, he had Muti arrested at his seaside villa in Fregene, near **Rome**. Muti was allegedly killed while attempting to escape, but it was widely believed that the new government had murdered a potentially dangerous enemy. As a result, Muti became a cult figure for diehard opponents of the Badoglio regime. *See also* FASCISM.

– N –

NAPLES (Napoli). Italy's third-largest city, with nearly 1.5 million inhabitants, Naples is the center of a conurbation that stretches along the coast and includes such important towns as Erculano (site of the ancient town of Pompeii), Torre Del Greco, and the famous village of Sorrento. Its population density, at nearly 3,000 inhabitants per square kilometer, is one of the highest in the world; only Hong Kong and a handful of other cities in Asia are more crowded. The islands of Capri and Ischia, famous for their natural beauty, are also part of the province of Naples. Mount Vesuvius, a huge active volcano, looms over the city.

The city's history has been turbulent. It was founded in the fifth century BC. In 327 BC, it became a self-governing province of the Roman Empire. After the empire's fall, Naples was successively occupied by the Goths (AD 493) and the Byzantine Empire (AD 536). Gradually the city achieved greater independence and became an important trading center. Both Lombards and Saracens tried to conquer Naples for this reason, but it was not until AD 1138, when the Normans captured the city, that Naples succumbed. In the later Middle Ages the Kingdoms of Aragon, France, and Spain successively ruled Naples.

The city's modern history began with the Spanish, whose corrupt rule, many argue, left a trace on the political culture of the city that endures today. In 1647, the city rose in revolt against Spanish misgovernment. In 1734, after a brief period of Austrian rule, Charles of Bourbon became monarch of an independent Kingdom of Naples that lasted until French troops occupied the city in 1798. In 1799, the people of Naples established a republic, but Bourbon troops supported by the British fleet crushed the nascent democracy. Napoleon reoccupied Naples in 1806. For two years, Joseph Bonaparte, Napoleon's brother, ruled the city; after Joseph became king of Spain, his place was taken by one of Napoleon's most successful generals, Joachim Murat. After the fall of Napoleon in 1814–1815, the Austrians restored the Bourbons to power in what became known as the Kingdom of the Two Sicilies. In both 1820 and 1848, the city was the center of uprisings against absolute rule that were suppressed by the Austrian army. The city was finally liberated by **Giuseppe Garibaldi** in 1860. During World War II, the city's insurrectionary traditions came to the fore once more: In four days of bloody street fighting (28 September to 1 October 1943), the people of Naples managed to liberate the city from its Nazi occupiers in advance of the Allies' arrival.

Despite its glorious history, Naples has a reputation for being one of Europe's problem cities. The ubiquitous *Camorra* (the Neapolitan **mafia**) and exceptionally high rates of poverty are the most troublesome issues. Illegal construction, insane traffic, widespread political corruption, and decaying infrastructure are additional concerns. *See also* EARTHQUAKES; NAPOLEONIC ITALY; SOUTHERN ITALY.

NAPOLEONIC ITALY. The idea of a united Italy first took concrete political form under the rule of Napoleon Bonaparte. In 1793, the Papal States, the Kingdom of **Naples**, and the absolutist rulers of northern Italy declared war on revolutionary France. Commanded by Napoleon, the French invaded what is today Piedmont and defeated the Austro-Piedmontese army at the battles of Millesimo and Mondovì. The peace of Paris between France and Piedmont-**Sardinia** (May 1796) assigned Nice and Savoy to France, and after further defeating the Austrians at Lodi, northern Italy was reorganized on republican lines. In July 1797, the Cisalpine Republic was founded, with the tricolor as its flag, uniting all of northern Italy from the French border to Emilia-Romagna. In October 1797, the Treaty of Campo Formio ceded Venetia to Austria in exchange for Austrian recognition of the revolutionaries' gains.

In 1798, Napoleon continued his conquests in **southern Italy**. The Papal States and Naples were occupied and briefly transformed into a republic, Piedmont itself was occupied by French troops, and Pope Pius VI was forced to move to France. Internal developments in France, however, allowed the Austrians, aided by the English navy and the Russian army, to launch a counterattack in 1799 and reconquer most of the peninsula after bloody fighting, especially in Naples. In 1800 Napoleon launched his second Italian campaign and destroyed the Austrian army at Marengo. The subsequent peace of Luneville in 1801 assigned the duchies of Parma and Piacenza to Piedmont and the isle of Elba to France. The Pope was restored to his throne in Rome, but **Bologna**, Ferrara, and Ravenna were retained by the Cisalpine Republic. The following year, the Cisalpine Republic became the republic of Italy, with **Milan** as its capital. The Napoleonic legal codes were introduced throughout the republic in 1805, just two years after their introduction in France. Also in 1805, Napoleon turned the republic of Italy into a kingdom and took the crown. The new kingdom's territories were extended at the peace of Pressburg between France and Austria to include Venetia and Istria (Istria is now part of Croatia). The following year, Napoleon invaded

Naples and appointed his brother Joseph to the throne. In 1808, French troops occupied the Papal States and took the pope prisoner once more. In 1809, the Trentino was occupied. All of modern-day Italy except **Sicily** had been united into one kingdom, and although Bonaparte by now had become as much a crowned prince as any of the continent's hereditary monarchs, a culture of assertive nationalism as well as of liberal and constitutionalist thinking had been injected into Italy's politically influential classes. The subsequent attempt to restore absolute monarchy at the **Congress of Vienna** in 1814–1815 flew in the face of these decisive developments. *See also* PAPACY.

NAPOLITANO, GIORGIO (1925–). A native of **Naples**, Giorgio Napolitano joined the **Partito Comunista Italiano**/Italian Communist Party (PCI) in 1945 after a period of youthful antifascist activity. He was elected to the Chamber of Deputies for the first time in 1953 and represented first the PCI, then the **Partito Democratico della Sinistra**/Democratic Party of the Left (PDS) in **Parliament** for most of the next 40 years. Napolitano remained in the PCI after the Soviet Union's crushing of the 1956 revolution in Hungary, though he has written that the decision to stay within the communist movement was very difficult. He was, nevertheless, closely identified with the PCI's social-democratic wing, the so-called *miglioristi* (reformers), and their leader, **Giorgio Amendola**. In the 1970s and early 1980s, he was the chief theoretician of the PCI's move away from the Soviet bloc and its adoption of a **foreign policy** that defended international institutions and criticized Soviet expansionism. Napolitano believed, as he argued in a famous 1979 book, that the PCI was wallowing "in the middle of the ford" between communism and social democracy. In domestic policy he was a strong proponent of an electoral alliance with the **Partito Socialista Italiano**/Italian Socialist Party (PSI). The PSI's integration into the structure of political power in the 1980s, however, rendered this project impossible. Neither **Bettino Craxi** nor the majority of the PCI's membership would have been willing to turn it into a political reality.

Napolitano has held several of the highest positions in the Italian state. Between 1981 and 1986, he was the PCI's floor leader in the Chamber of Deputies, and, between 1992 and 1994, he was president of the Chamber of Deputies. In May 1996, he became minister for the interior in the center-left government formed by **Romano Prodi** and in this role was instrumental in passing an important (and relatively liberal) **immigration** law. In 2005, president **Carlo Azeglio Ciampi** made him life senator. After the elections of April 2006, Napolitano succeeded Ciampi as **president of the Republic**, although he was elected with the votes of the center-left forces in Parliament only.

NATIONAL ALLIANCE. *See* ALLEANZA NAZIONALE (AN).

NATTA, ALESSANDRO (1918–2001). Born in Imperia (Liguria) in the last year of **World War I**, Natta studied literature at the University of **Genoa** before he began teaching in an Imperia secondary school, then became an artillery lieutenant in **World War II**. He was wounded in action against the Germans after Italy's surrender to the Allies on 8 September 1943, was taken prisoner on Rhodes, and was sent to a series of prison camps. After the war he joined the **Partito Comunista Italiano**/Italian Communist Party (PCI), returned to his teaching duties, served on his local city council, and in 1948 was elected to the Chamber of Deputies. Natta's party work was primarily as an intellectual and theorist: He edited *Rinascita*, was co-editor with Luigi Longo of *Critica Marxista* between 1956 and 1966, and served on the Central Committee as well as on the Steering Committee of the PCI.

A reliable party functionary, Natta was made general secretary (party leader) upon **Enrico Berlinguer**'s untimely death in 1984. He was confirmed in that post at the **Florence** Congress of the PCI in April 1986. Like others who try to lead by consensus, he seemed torn between the forces that were wrenching the party apart, one pulling in the direction of renewed Stalinist-Leninist orthodoxy and the other toward northern European social democracy, anathema to the party's left. However, PCI losses in the 1987 elections weakened his position, and a subsequent heart attack in 1988 brought about his resignation. His place was taken by **Achille Occhetto**. At the all-important **Bologna** Congress, in February 1991, where the PCI was transformed into the **Partito Democratico della Sinistra**/Democratic Party of the Left (PDS), Natta—like **Pietro Ingrao**—was among the nostalgics reluctant to give up the symbolism of the largest Western Communist party.

Unsympathetic observers have remarked on the "grayness" of one who was essentially a party worker and who lacked the charisma that had characterized Berlinguer. Tempted by the possibilities opened, on the one hand, by unity on the left with the **Partito Socialista Italiano/**Italian Socialist Party (PSI) and, on the other, by collaboration with the **Democrazia Cristiana/**Christian Democracy (DC), Natta proved unable to make a clear choice or to articulate a clear party position.

NATTA, GIULIO (1903–1979). Born in Imperia near **Genoa**, Giulio Natta was awarded the Nobel Prize in Chemistry in 1963 and was the long-time director of the department of industrial chemistry at Milan's Politecnico University. Natta's work in the field of macromolecular structure, especially polymers, led in 1953 to the invention of isotactic polypropylene. This was not just ivory tower theorizing, but work with enormous practical advantages. Without Natta's work we would today not have (or would have waited for) industrial packaging, disposable diapers, cling-film, and dozens of other uses of plastic. In effect, Natta's work transformed the study of polymers from an academic inquiry into a huge opportunity for the chemical industry. Natta produced some 700 scientific papers during his life; the Nobel was just the greatest of dozens of prizes awarded to him during his career. He died in Bergamo (Lombardy) in May 1979.

NEGRI, ANTONIO (1933–). Regarded by some as a *cattivo maestro* (corrupting teacher), by others as a hero of the struggle against globalization and the imperial ambitions of the United States, Antonio "Toni" Negri is one of the most influential intellectuals of the postwar Marxist left anywhere in the world. Born in Padua (Padova), where he also took his degree in philosophy, Negri hails from a tradition of progressive **Catholicism**, and as a student was actually a prominent member of the youth organization of **Azione Cattolica/**Catholic Action (ACI). In the 1960s and early 1970s, Negri was involved in a series of intellectual groups, the most important of which was Potere Operaio (Worker's Power). In 1977, which in

Italy was a replay of 1968, Negri's articles and books were textbooks for would-be faculty revolutionaries.

In April 1979, Negri, who by now was professor of political theory at Padua, was arrested and charged with being the mind behind the actions of **Brigate Rosse**/Red Brigades (BR). No proof was provided of his direct collusion in the BR's murders, although his intellectual influence on the BR's public statements was obvious. Negri nevertheless remained in jail under the "special laws" adopted to fight the terrorists.

Negri's case was taken up by the **Partito Radicale**/Radical Party (PR) in the early 1980s, and in 1983 Negri was elected to **Parliament** on the PR's ticket. Rather than campaign for other prisoners, Negri, now out of prison and possessing parliamentary immunity, fled to Paris, to the rage of the PR's leader, **Marco Pannella**, who was a personal friend. In 1984, Negri was condemned to a long sentence of imprisonment for subversion. The French government refused to extradite him, regarding him, in effect, as a political exile. Negri remained in Paris until 1997, when he returned to Italy and served six years in **Rome**'s Rebibbia jail until his release in the spring of 2003.

While he was in prison Negri wrote, together with the American intellectual Michael Hardt, his most famous book to date, *Empire*, which was published in English in 2000 and then in Italian and more than 20 other languages. The argument of this very long, dense, and complex book is that the phenomenon of globalization is rapidly eroding the power of the nation-state, and that imperialism has not disappeared but has been transferred to the network of international institutions that have been created in recent decades. *Empire* has led to comparisons with Karl Marx and to Negri's inclusion in a list of the 25 most influential living thinkers published by the *Nouvel Observateur* in January 2005.

NENNI, PIETRO (1891–1979). The dominant figure in the **Partito Socialista Italiano**/Italian Socialist Party (PSI) for much of this century, Pietro Nenni began his political career in his native province of Forlì (Emilia-Romagna) as a militant of the **Partito Repubblicana Italiano**/Italian Republican Party (PRI). One of the organizers (**Benito Mussolini** was another) of a series of strikes and public protests against Italy's 1911 colonial war in **Libya**, Nenni was arrested and

sentenced to several months' imprisonment. His opposition to war
was not repeated in 1915, however. In line with his party, Nenni supported intervention and served at the front as an infantryman. This
experience made him strongly critical of the PSI's hostility to the
war. In 1919, Nenni was even one of the founding members of
Bologna's *fascio di combattimento* (Combat Veterans' League).

Instead of Nenni evolving into a Fascist, however, his experience
during the turbulent "red biennial" (1919–1921) caused him to reex-
amine his most fundamental ideological views and to edge toward
reconciliation with the PSI. Nenni became a journalist for the PSI
daily *Avanti!* in 1921 and, in December 1922, as editor of the paper,
opposed the party leadership's attempts to woo Moscow by merging
with the breakaway **Partito Comunista Italiano**/Italian Communist
Party (PCI). Believing, pragmatically, that the PSI should rather concentrate on rallying all of Italy's democratic forces against the common Fascist enemy, Nenni became an isolated figure and, in 1925,
was forced to resign from the paper's editorial board. The following
year, he took refuge in France.

While in exile in Paris, Nenni was the architect of the reunification
of the reformist and "maximalist" wings of the Italian socialist move-
ment in 1930. He became party leader in 1933 and also editor of
Avanti! Despite his past hostility to the PCI, Nenni supported the
"Popular Front," fighting personally in the International Brigade in
Spain. His antifascist activities were interrupted in 1941 when he was
taken prisoner by the Germans and handed over to the Italian gov-
ernment, which imprisoned him on the island of Ponza (Campania).
His daughter, Vittoria, was less fortunate; she died in Auschwitz in
July 1943.

Released from prison, Nenni took a leadership role in the **Comitato di Liberazione Nazionale** Alta Italia/National Liberation Committee-Northern Italy (CLNAI). Under his direction, the PSI—unlike
the PCI—refused to join the cabinet of **Ivanoe Bonomi**. In
April–May 1945, Nenni was the primary contender to head the new
all-Italian government. The British viewed this prospect with frank
horror, and **Ferruccio Parri** was eventually chosen as prime minister. Nenni did become vice premier and minister in charge of organizing the elections to the **Constituent Assembly** in the first administration formed by **Alcide De Gasperi** in December 1945.

The PSI fought the elections of June 1946 in the company of the PCI, emerging as the second-largest party in Italy after the **Democrazia Cristiana**/Christian Democracy Party (DC), with 20 percent of the vote. Nenni had the sensitive post of foreign minister in De Gasperi's second administration but was unable to follow a pro-Soviet foreign policy. Within a few months, the wily De Gasperi had reshuffled his government to exclude both the PCI and the PSI.

Nenni became increasingly convinced in the 1950s that the PSI had to assert its independence from the PCI. After regaining the party leadership in 1953, he seized the opportunity provided by the Soviet crushing of the Hungarian revolution in 1956 to inch away from the PCI and eventually, between 1960 and 1963, to join the DC in government. Nenni believed that the PSI's participation would lead to major changes in the structure of Italian society, but he overestimated the extent to which the PSI could make its voice count. Nenni was the principal architect of the failed attempt to merge the **Partito Socialista Democratico Italiano**/Italian Social Democratic Party (PSDI) with the PSI between 1966 and 1968. He died in **Rome** in 1979. *See also* OPENING TO THE LEFT; TAMBRONI, FERNANDO.

NEOREALISM. The goal of neorealist writers and artists was to represent ordinary working-class life faithfully and find poetry in the lives of the poor and oppressed. This emphasis on working-class experience was influenced by the theories of the communist philosopher **Antonio Gramsci**, who believed that culture in Italy had always been hegemonized by the elite and that the communist movement needed to produce a "national-popular" literature of its own. The neorealists were also influenced by the sometimes grim realism of American writers such as John Steinbeck, Ernest Hemingway, and John Dos Passos.

Among the film directors who worked in the neorealist idiom were **Vittorio De Sica**, **Roberto Rossellini**, and **Luchino Visconti**. These directors used ordinary citizens in preference to established actors, allowed the use of **dialect** instead of literary Italian, and set their films in working-class settings. The main subject matter of neorealist novels and reportage was working-class and peasant life during the war and the **resistance** to the Nazis. **Carlo Levi, Primo Levi, Italo**

Calvino, and **Cesare Pavese** are four remarkable writers on these themes.

Many of the leading intellectuals associated with neorealism were socialists or communists, but almost without exception they found the **Partito Comunista Italiano**/Italian Communist Party (PCI) too insistent in its demands that their realism be transformed into socialist realism, that is, propaganda. The short-lived neorealist literary periodical *Il Politecnico* was soon the target for ideologically motivated attacks by the leader of the PCI, **Palmiro Togliatti**, and by the PCI's stable of politically orthodox critics and scholars. *Il Politecnico* was all but boycotted by the PCI and its sympathizers and had to close in 1947.

By the early 1950s, the best neorealist artists were chafing at the genre's limits. Rossellini and Visconti increasingly made visually beautiful films with psychological themes set (often) in upper-class settings. Pavese's last novel before his suicide, *La Luna e i falò* (*The Moon and the Bonfires*, 1950), was introspective and nostalgic in tone. Calvino increasingly became a *favolista*, or writer of fables. Few of the Italian writers and directors of the first rank who emerged in the 1950s were neorealist in approach. For all neorealism's limits, however, in the hands of its finest artists, the suffering, poverty, and endurance of the Italian working class was transmuted into artistic form. See also CINEMA; LITERATURE.

NICOTERA, GIOVANNI (1828–1894). Born in Catanzaro (Calabria), Giovanni Nicotera was a hero of the struggle against absolutism in the Kingdom of the Two Sicilies. In 1857 he was sentenced to death for his part in the abortive attempt of a group of revolutionaries, led by Carlo Pisacane, to raise an insurrection in southern Italy; this sentence was commuted to life imprisonment on the isle of Favignana, off **Sicily**. Nicotera was rescued by **Giuseppe Garibaldi**'s forces in June 1860.

Nicotera was elected to **Parliament** in 1861, but he continued to support Garibaldi's efforts to complete the reunification of Italy. Nicotera was at Garibaldi's side during the clash with the Italian army in Aspromonte in 1862, in Garibaldi's successful campaign against the Austrians in the Trentino in 1866, and at the disastrous battle of Mentana in 1867.

Nicotera gradually abandoned the radicalism of Garibaldi and compromised with the Italian state. When the parliamentary left took power in 1876, Nicotera became minister of the interior under **Agostino Depretis**. His support for Depretis did not extend to accepting the policy of *trasformismo*, and, during the 1880s, Nicotera was one of the leaders of the parliamentary opposition to Depretis's center-right government. Nicotera served as interior minister under **Antonio Starabba di Rudinì** in 1891–1892, and, in his final years, the authoritarian and nationalistic policies propounded by **Francesco Crispi** increasingly attracted him. Nicotera died in Vico Equense (**Naples**) in 1894.

NITTI, FRANCESCO SAVERIO (1868–1953). One of the few politicians of national standing to emerge from the rural southern region of Basilicata (another is **Emilio Colombo**), Francesco Saverio Nitti entered politics in 1904 after a career as a university teacher of jurisprudence. He served as a minister in **Giovanni Giolitti**'s governments from 1911 to 1914, and in 1917 became minister of the treasury in the government of **Vittorio Emanuele Orlando**.

Nitti succeeded Orlando as prime minister in June 1919 and was forced to deal with a country that was on the point of institutional and social collapse. He vainly tried to hold together a territory ravaged by the economic costs of the war; the violence and nationalism of the disillusioned former soldiers enrolled in the Fasci italiani di combattimento, precursor of the **Partito Nazionale Fascista**/National Fascist Party (PNF); and the rising tide of working-class revolutionary syndicalism, but the effort was too much for him. His failure to deal with the challenge posed to his authority by **Gabriele D'Annunzio**'s seizure of **Fiume** in the summer of 1919 was symptomatic of his entire experience as prime minister. Nitti's professorial, abstract, rational approach to government was simply inadequate for the demands of the time. In June 1920, he was forced to hand over the reins of government to Giolitti.

Nitti was willing to give **Fascism** a chance to prove itself, but his tolerance was not reciprocated. Forced to flee abroad on the eve of the 1924 elections, he spent the years of **Benito Mussolini**'s dictatorship in exile—and was even briefly held prisoner by the Nazis in 1943. He returned to Italy in 1945, and together with **Benedetto**

Croce, Vittorio Emanuele Orlando, and **Ivanoe Bonomi**, fought the elections of June 1946 under the colors of the so-called Unione Nazionale/National Union Party. Nitti was elected to the **Constituent Assembly**, but he was only able to play a marginal role in a Parliament dominated by the **Democrazia Cristiana/**Christian Democracy Party (DC).

Nitti was made a life senator in 1948 and in his elder statesman's role was an opponent of the Italian decision to sign the North Atlantic Treaty in April 1949. He died in **Rome** in 1953. In addition to his long political career, Nitti was the author of several interesting, if not particularly profound or original, works of political philosophy during his years in exile.

NORTH ATLANTIC TREATY ORGANIZATION (NATO). Italy signed the North Atlantic Treaty on 4 April 1949. The decision to enter the Western alliance was a hugely controversial one in an ideologically divided nation. In a parliamentary debate shortly before the signature of the pact, **Palmiro Togliatti** had declared that Italian communists would be "traitors" if they did not do everything possible to protest against a treaty that he condemned as an "imperialist intrigue" against the Soviet Union. Socialist and communist deputies attempted to filibuster the acceptance of the treaty, and huge demonstrations were mounted across the country. Even some members of the **Democrazia Cristiana/**Christian Democracy (DC), notably **Giuseppe Dossetti**, were lukewarm about the treaty. Nevertheless, the Chamber of Deputies approved membership on 17 March 1949, by a vote of 342 to 170, with 19 abstentions. The Senate voted 183 to 112 (among the "no" votes were two relicts of prefascist Italy, **Vittorio Emmanuele Orlando** and **Francesco Saverio Nitti**). From March 1949 onward, adherence to NATO has been a key test for fitness to be a member of government. The **opening to the Left** could not have taken place in the mid-1960s had the **Partito Socialista Italiano/**Italian Socialist Party (PSI) not recognized, at its Party Congress in 1961, that equidistance between East and West was no longer a tenable position.

Italy has always been a reliably subordinate NATO partner; indeed, during the Cold War, it was regarded as "NATO's Bulgaria." The Mediterranean Command of the organization is in **Naples** and large NATO bases were constructed in **Sicily**, Friuli, Apulia, Tuscany, and elsewhere. Italy was one of the first NATO members to accept cruise missiles on its soil in the early 1980s, although there were huge demonstrations in September 1983 when the missiles began to be deployed. The **Olive Tree Coalition**/Ulivo government headed by **Massimo D'Alema** backed NATO's bombing of Serbia during the 1999 Kosovo crisis in the face of determined opposition from the pacifist movement within Italy. NATO membership compensates for Italy's miserly spending on defense. Italy spends approximately 2 percent of GDP on its armed forces. This is significantly less than Great Britain and France, though slightly more than Germany. *See also* GLADIO.

– O –

OCCHETTO, ACHILLE (1936–). Although born in **Turin**, Achille Occhetto has long represented **Palermo** (**Sicily**) in the Chamber of Deputies. Elected to the Central Committee of the **Partito Comunista Italiano**/Italian Communist Party (PCI) in 1979, it was to Occhetto that the PCI turned when it faced crisis in the late 1980s. In July 1988, he was chosen to replace **Alessandro Natta** as party secretary by the central committee, a post in which he was confirmed by the Eighteenth Congress of the PCI in March 1989. At this congress, the party, at Occhetto's behest, did away with all references in the party statute to Marx, Lenin, and former leader **Palmiro Togliatti** and greatly expanded its leadership cohort to allow the influx of new, more reform-minded individuals. In November 1989, after the collapse of the Berlin wall, Occhetto realized that these changes were insufficient and led the process of renewal by which the PCI was transformed between 1989 and 1991 into the **Partito Democratico della Sinistra**/Democratic Party of the Left (PDS).

In the general elections of March 1994, Occhetto was the architect of the so-called Progressive Alliance, a motley collection of left-wing parties that did not possess enough general appeal to win centrist votes. Although the PDS improved its individual share of the vote, the alliance as a whole fared poorly. In elections to the European Parliament three months later, the PDS was defeated even more clearly.

After this second rebuff, Occhetto resigned as secretary of the PDS and was replaced by **Massimo D'Alema**.

Occhetto's fundamental vision was to turn the PDS into a radical, campaigning movement that would expand and improve the conditions of **women**, immigrants, and the lowest paid. He has never renounced this vision and, indeed, has watched the subsequent evolution of the ex-PCI with some disdain. In the highly regulated, high taxation Italy of the 1990s, Occhetto's approach was destined to failure. The magnitude of his achievement, however, has been understated by many commentators. Had Occhetto not had the drive to make the necessary break with communism in 1989, the PCI would have seemed an unbearable anachronism in the Italian political crisis of 1992–1993.

Occhetto is currently a member of the European Parliament, where he sits as a member of the Socialist Group.

OLIVE TREE COALITION/Ulivo. This name was chosen by the broad coalition of a dozen center-left parties assembled, under the leadership of **Romano Prodi**, in the spring of 1995. The Olive Tree Coalition governed Italy between the general elections of April 1996, when it obtained 284 seats in the Chamber of Deputies, and the government crisis of autumn 1998, when Prodi's cabinet was brought down by the contrary vote of the **Partito di Rifondazione Comunista**/Communist Refoundation (PRC), which had previously provided the Coalition with a slender parliamentary majority.

Despite the difficulties caused by the Olive Tree Coalition's heterogeneous character—conservatives, ex-communists, socialists, environmentalists, neoliberals, and Catholic centrists were all represented within the government—it should be said that Prodi's cabinet scored some useful policy triumphs. Laws proposing the devolution of power to local tiers of government were enacted in 1997, an overdue reform of the **education** system was begun, and public aid was directed toward economic blackspots in **southern Italy**. Most important, public finances were brought under control by a prolonged period of austerity, and Italy, as a consequence, was allowed to participate in using the single European **currency**, the euro, from 1999 onward. Prodi's difficulties began once entry to the euro had been attaained.

The Ulivo has been somewhat revived since 2004 by the Italian center-left's decision to choose Prodi as their prime ministerial candidate in the elections of 2006. Today it refers to the formal political alliance between the **Democratici di Sinistra**/Democrats of the Left (DS) and **Democratici e Libertà** (a coalition based on the former **Partito Popolare Italiano**/Italian Popular Party (PPI) and the much smaller "Democrats for Prodi"). Led by Prodi, the Olive Tree Coalition allied itself with the PRC and with several other parties of the center and far left to win the April 2006 elections, albeit by the narrowest of margins. The idea that the Ulivo should be transformed into a single "Democrat" party has been much discussed but as yet has not been acted upon. *See also* BERTINOTTI, FAUSTO; D'ALEMA, MASSIMO; EUROPEAN INTEGRATION; RUTELLI, FRANCESCO.

OPENING TO THE LEFT (l'apertura a sinistra). This term describes attempts made in the early 1960s by several leaders of the **Democrazia Cristiana**/Christian Democracy Party (DC) to broaden the consensus in the Italian polity by including the **Partito Socialista Italiano**/Italian Socialist Party (PSI) in the government. Between 1961 and 1963, with due attention to the international implications (particularly U.S. opinion), the PSI was gradually brought into the governments headed by **Aldo Moro** (1963–1968). They stayed in power with the DC until 1972. The historic compromise that Moro wove in the 1970s with the **Partito Comunista Italiano**/Italian Communist Party (PCI) and its leader, **Enrico Berlinguer**, can be seen as an attempt to repeat the strategy. In neither case did the strategy fully succeed; many commentators, indeed, have seen the opening to the left as an example of the perennial device of *trasformismo* and have depicted it as a means by which the DC drew the fangs of radical forces for change in Italian society.

ORLANDO, LEOLUCA (1948–). One of the most flamboyant and courageous personalities of recent Italian politics, Leoluca Orlando made his reputation as a reformist **Democrazia Cristiana**/Christian Democracy Party (DC) mayor of **Palermo**. An academic lawyer, Orlando entered Sicilian politics in the 1970s and swiftly became one of the most outspoken critics of the DC's established leadership on the island. In 1985, he became mayor of Palermo for the first time, at the head of a conventional five-party alliance that included all the DC's national allies. In 1987, he broke with the **Partito Socialista Italiano**/Italian Socialist Party (PSI) and formed a new administration that included the Greens and representatives from the numerous civic renewal groups and anti**mafia** initiatives that had sprung up in the city during the 1980s. In 1989, he added the **Partito Comunista Italiano**/Italian Communist Party (PCI) to his majority. This "Palermo spring" won Orlando national attention; his increasingly unambiguous accusations that leading DC politicians such as **Giulio Andreotti** were collaborating with the mafia made him notorious. Orlando became a hero for Italy's liberal press, but some skeptics, notably the Sicilian writer **Leonardo Sciascia**, regarded him as an opportunist who was making his career as a "professional opponent of the mafia."

Orlando broke with the DC in 1990 and launched a new political party, **La Rete**, in October of that year. He was elected to the Chamber of Deputies in April 1992 with an enormous number of personal preference votes, and, in November 1993, won the mayoralty of Palermo for La Rete by a plebiscite-like 75 percent majority, but his party has failed to take root outside of Palermo. Orlando resigned from the mayorality in December 2000 to campaign for the regional elections, in which he was the center-left's candidate for the regional presidency. The candidate of the **Casa delle Libertà**/House of Freedoms defeated him easily, however. Orlando was elected to the Chamber of Deputies in April 2006. *See also* FALCONE, GIOVANNI; SICILY.

ORLANDO, VITTORIO EMANUELE (1860–1952). A Sicilian professor of law, Orlando was a member of several prefascist cabinets, rising to the post of minister of the interior during **World War I**. In 1917, he became prime minister himself when the **Caporetto** disaster brought about **Paolo Boselli**'s resignation. A better risk calculator than his predecessor, he ordered Italian forces to counterattack in late October. By the end of the month, Italian forces with British reinforcements inflicted a major defeat on the Austrian army at Vittorio

Veneto and, on 5 November (nearly a week before the armistice in France), the guns were silenced on the Austrian front. Orlando was called the "President of Victory" and became one of the "Big Four," together with Woodrow Wilson, Georges Clemenceau, and David Lloyd George, charged with making the postwar settlement.

Italy and Orlando cut something of a bad figure in the Paris negotiations. Italy's failure to obtain the full territorial gains promised to it by the 1915 **Treaty of London** led to the Italian delegation's storming out of the French capital in April 1919 and retiring to **Rome**. Orlando seemingly assumed that the Allies would offer terms to persuade him to return. Instead, Orlando and Foreign Minister **Sidney Sonnino** eventually returned to Paris, barely in time for the German signature on the Treaty of Versailles.

Italy did in fact obtain the Brenner frontier with Austria and Trieste. It was hardly the "mutilated peace" that Italian nationalists condemned. Orlando's resentments were nourished by the question of **Fiume** (Rijeka), which Italy coveted, and the Dalmatian coast. The subsequent Treaty of Lausanne with Turkey (July 1923) confirmed Italian sovereignty over the Dodecanese Islands, which had been exercised de facto since 1912. Nevertheless, the perception that the settlement had been mishandled and Italy denied its just deserts led to Orlando being turned out by Parliament in a humiliatingly lopsided vote, 262–78. His successor, **Francesco Saverio Nitti**, had the good sense to abort a naval expedition to annex Soviet Georgia that Orlando had devised.

Orlando's relationship with **Fascism** was initially ambiguous. Like many Italian liberals, Orlando feared the Fascists less than he feared the socialist menace and the influence of the **Vatican**. Nevertheless, by 1925 he had realized the futility of his hopes. He broke with **Benito Mussolini** and resigned from **Parliament** and from all political activity. When the regime required university professors to pledge allegiance to Mussolini in 1931, only 11 in the entire system refused and resigned their posts. One of them was a by now elderly Orlando. In 1944, the government of **Ivanoe Bonomi** named Orlando president of the Chamber of Deputies. In 1948, he became a life senator, a position he held until his death.

– P –

PACINI, FILIPPO (1812–1883). Born in Pistoia (Tuscany), Filippo Pacini became famous after his death as the discoverer of cholera. He showed great aptitude for the natural sciences from an early age and in 1830 began his studies at medical school. While still a medical student, he discovered "Pacinian corpuscles," which established his reputation within the scientific community. In 1849, only 37 years old, he became professor of general and topographic anatomy at the University of **Florence**.

Cholera raged in Florence in the early 1850s, and Pacini began to study the disease. In a paper published in 1854 entitled "Microscopical observations and pathological deductions on cholera," Pacini affirmed that cholera was a contagious disease provoked by living organisms (that he called "vibrions") that destroyed the intestines and caused massive loss of fluid. Pacini's work was almost unknown at the time; the great German scientist Robert Koch would win the Nobel Prize in 1905 for arriving at identical conclusions in the 1880s in work that was much more widely publicized. Pacini's prior claim was recognized only in 1965, and the organism that causes cholera is now officially known as *Vibrio cholerae Pacini 1854*.

Pacini was a pioneer in the field of microscopical research and personally built, together with his fellow scientist Giovanni Battista Amici, some of the most advanced instruments of the time. These are today housed in the Museum of the History of Science in Florence. Pacini died in Florence in July 1883.

PAGANINI, NICCOLO (1782–1840). Born in **Genoa** (Genova), Paganini was a violin virtuoso who became famous across Europe for the passion and the skill of his playing, which was so striking that it was rumored to be the result of a pact with the devil. His technical genius transformed the development of the instrument, and his artistic impact on such important composers as Brahms, Liszt, Chopin, and Berlioz is well-documented. His own compositions were far from negligible: The most admired are the 24 Caprices for violin and guitar and, especially, his second violin concerto. Paganini was also a guitar virtuoso and was one of the first musicians to compose for this instrument. The culmination of Paganini's career was his series of concerts at the imperial court in Vienna (1828) and his tours of London and Paris (1831–1834).

The quintessential romantic artist, Paganini had a turbulent private life, enjoying numerous affairs with aristocratic patronesses and spending a fortune on prostitutes and gambling. His frenetic life worsened the throat cancer that brought about his death in Nice in 1840. Paganini's name is venerated in Genoa, where each year since 1954 an international violin prize, the "Premio Paganini," has been awarded. The winner is permitted to play the "cannon," Paganini's personal violin, which was made in 1743.

PALERMO. The largest city in **Sicily** with over 700,000 inhabitants, Palermo is the island's political center and principal port. Founded around 700 BC by the Phoenicians, Palermo is one of the oldest cities in the world. Part of Carthage from 480 BC to when it became part of the Roman Empire in 254 BC, Palermo has endured wave after wave of foreign conquest. The Vandals, Goths, Byzantines, Arabs, and Normans all conquered the city after the fall of the Roman Empire. The last two invasions, in particular, left an indelible architectural impression on the city. The "Palace of the Normans," one of the finest buildings in Italy, is a ninth-century Arab building that was restructured by the Normans in the twelfth century.

The city's modern history can be said to have started in 1738, when the city became a possession of the Bourbons. In 1820, Palermo revolted against rule from **Naples** (the capital of the Bourbon Kingdom of the Two Sicilies), but the populist uprising was put down by troops sent by the constitutional liberal government of Naples, which itself was crushed by the Austrians shortly afterward. In 1831, there were further riots in Palermo against Bourbon rule, and then, in 1848, an insurrection in Palermo was the trigger that set off the famous "year of revolutions" throughout Europe. In 1860, the city's people rebelled again, ensuring victory for the redshirts of **Giuseppe Garibaldi**.

The contemporary city has been scarred by persistent misgovernment and by the pervasive presence of the **mafia**. Probably nowhere in Italy has the link between the political class and organized crime been so strong. Since the early 1970s, in particular, Palermo has been the scene of a dozen so-called "excellent crimes," the murders of judges, politicians, or police commanders opposed to the mafia. In

1992 alone, the mafia killed judges Paolo Borsellino and **Giovanni Falcone** and gunned down Salvo Lima, a politician close to **Giulio Andreotti** who was widely reputed to have been the mafia's political facilitator in **Rome**. Nevertheless, resistance to the mafia has taken political form. The "Palermo spring" of the late 1980s and early 1990s turned **Leoluca Orlando** into a politician of national status. Orlando has been *sindaco* (mayor) of Palermo for most of the last two decades, and, under his leadership, civil society has asserted itself and the mafia's hold has been greatly reduced.

PANNELLA, MARCO (1930–). The historic leader of the **Partito Radicale/**Radical Party (PR), Marco Pannella is a political showman who has nevertheless changed Italian history. He cut his political teeth as a student activist in the 1950s and was one of the PR's founding members in 1956. He became leader in 1962 and for the last 45 years has been a constant presence in Italian political life, campaigning for changes to the **divorce** laws, a more liberal abortion law, electoral reform, and action against a vast range of domestic and international abuses and injustices. The important constitutional role occupied by **referendums** in Italy is largely due to Pannella's single-minded use of the referendum as an instrument for achieving social reforms.

Pannella was first elected to Parliament in 1976 and led the PR's minuscule delegation in the Chamber of Deputies until the 1992 elections, which the PR fought under the name of the *Lista Pannella*. Under his leadership—though reign may well be a more fitting description—the PR was regarded as a libertarian fringe group, and as such it became popular with the urban, university-educated young. In 1994, however, after the collapse of the **Democrazia Cristiana/** Christian Democracy Party (DC) and its system of dominance, Pannella allied his movement with **Silvio Berlusconi**'s right-wing coalition and engaged in a spirited defense of the indicted leaders of the old regime. This perverse move robbed the veteran radical of credibility with his electoral constituency, and Pannella's fortunes ebbed visibly.

Pannella nevertheless adds his own particular spice to the already highly flavored dish of Italian politics. His volcanic television monologues; his penchant for chaining himself to railings; his frequent hunger strikes; the Radical Party's candidacy of Cicciolina, a porno star; and his cannabis "smoke-ins" have all made him one of Italy's most recognized public figures. *See also* BONINO, EMMA; NEGRI, ANTONIO.

PAPACY. Since Italy became a unified nation in 1861, there have been 11 popes. All but two (the current incumbent, Benedict XVI, and his predecessor, John Paul II) have been Italian. The moral teachings and political opinions of these men have exercised an enormous influence on Italian politics and society.

Pius IX (pope, 1846–1878). Giovanni Maria Mastai Ferretti was born in Senigallia (the Marches) in 1792. Initially regarded as a liberal, he was forced to flee from **Rome** during the 1848 revolution. Restored to his throne by French troops in 1849, he became a rigid conservative. Chiefly remembered for pronouncing the doctrine of papal infallibility in 1869, he rejected all attempts by the Italian state to reach a compromise on the role of the Church within Italy after the occupation of **Rome**.

Leo VIII (pope, 1878–1903). Vincenzo Gioacchino dei conti Pecci was born near Rome in 1810. More genuinely liberal than his predecessor, he nevertheless refused to acknowledge the authority of the Italian state over Rome and defined himself as the "prisoner in the **Vatican**." He barred Catholics from participating in Italian political life. His main doctrinal innovation was the encyclical *Rerum Novarum,* which criticized free market economics as well as socialism.

Pius X (pope, 1903–1914). Giuseppe Melchiorre Sarto was born in the province of Treviso (Venetia) in 1835. In terms of his influence on Italian life, he is chiefly important for giving his tacit consent to the so-called **Gentiloni pact**, by which the Church indicated a list of conditions that liberal candidates should respect in order to be assured of Catholics' votes. He was sanctified in 1954.

Benedict XV (pope, 1914–1922). Giacomo Della Chiesa was born in **Genoa** (Liguria) in 1854. He is most famous for his condemnation of **World War I** as a "useless slaughter" in 1917. Within Italy he promoted the formation of the **Partito Popolare Italiano/**Italian Popular Party (PPI) in 1919.

Pius XI (pope, 1922–1939). Ambrogio Damiano Achilli Ratti was born near **Milan** in 1857. As pope, his primary duty was maintaining the Church's independence from the Fascist regime. The **Lateran pacts**, signed in February 1929, succeeded in this objective, though liberal Catholics believed that they made the Church an accomplice of **Benito Mussolini**'s repressive rule. Violently anticommunist, Pius XI backed the Fascist side during the **Spanish Civil War** (1936–1939).

Pius XII (pope, 1939–1958). Eugenio Pacelli was born in Rome in 1876. He strove to keep Italy out of **World War II** and preached a negotiated end to the conflict at every opportunity. Widely criticized for not having condemned Hitler's persecution of the Jews with sufficient vigor, Pius undertook an anticommunist crusade after 1945, interfering directly in Italian domestic politics by threatening to excommunicate communist voters and by mobilizing the clergy in support of the **Democrazia Cristiana**/Christian Democracy Party (DC).

John XXIII (pope, 1958–1963). Angelo Giuseppe Roncalli was born in Bergamo (Lombardy) in 1881. As pope, he initiated a period of liberalization for the Church. He prompted the liturgical and doctrinal renewal of the Second Vatican Council between 1961 and 1965, giving it the specific task of "enabling the Church to contribute more usefully to solving the problems of modern life." Domestically, he sought to disengage the Vatican from Italian politics. His popularity soared after he visited Italian prisons and showed a humility at one with his humble origins. Politically, he followed a policy of detente toward the communist bloc.

Paul VI (pope, 1963–1978). Giovanni Battista Montini was born in Brescia (Lombardy) in 1897. Paul was the first pope to make pastoral visits overseas, visiting Israel in 1964 and several other countries in the following years. Within Italy, he refrained from turning issues such as **divorce** and abortion into a crusade, while affirming the Church's objections to liberalization in these matters.

John Paul I (pope, 1978). Albino Luciani was born in the province of Belluno in 1912. A much-loved figure who spurned traditional pomp and ceremony during his investiture, John Paul was expected to renew the policies of Pope John XXIII. His sudden death in September 1978, after just 34 days as pope, put an end to these hopes.

John Paul II (pope, 1978–2005). Karol Wojtyla was born in Wadowice (Poland) in 1920. He was the first non-Italian pope since the Dutchman Hadrian VI (1521–1523). He played a significant role in supporting Poland's *Solidarnosc*, which accelerated the disintegration of the Warsaw Pact system and even of Soviet communism. Despite his theological conservatism, John Paul won rueful respect from progressives in Italy for his opposition to the Gulf War and for his strictures against the materialism of modern life. He was the target of an unsuccessful assassination attempt in May 1981. His death in April 2005 was greeted by popular mourning in Italy.

Benedict XVI (pope, 2005–). Joseph Alois Ratzinger was born in Marktl-am-Inn (Germany) in 1927. A theological conservative, Ratzinger beat several strong Italian candidates during the conclave of cardinals. In September 2006, he made controversial remarks about Islam that led to an uproar in the Arab world.

PAPINI, GIOVANNI (1881–1956). A self-taught intellectual of formidable energy and power but little precision, Giovanni Papini was a tireless editor and literary entrepreneur. Nevertheless, he is chiefly remembered today for his paean of praise for **Fascism**, *Italia mia* (*My Italy*, 1941).

Born in **Florence**, Papini came to public attention as a literary figure between 1903 and 1907 as the editor of the little magazine *Leonardo* and as a contributor to *Il Regno*, a review edited by **Enrico Corradini**. A violent nationalist, Papini was also attracted by pragmatism, which, unlike American philosophers, such as John Dewey and William James, he interpreted as an ideology of power that would lead to the "twilight of the philosophers" rather than as a practical tool for the achievement of social reform.

After experimenting with nationalism and **futurism**, Papini turned to the Church, becoming a devout Catholic in the 1920s. He also started his final literary venture, *Frontespizio*, and warmed somewhat to **Benito Mussolini**. After he was invited to join the **Accademia d'Italia** (1937), he became an ardent admirer. *Italia mia* was one of the low points of intellectual fellow-traveling with Mussolini's regime. A tirade of invective against plutocratic Britain and the sinister forces of freemasonry and Jewry, and a plea for Italy to achieve its historical role and reemerge as the guiding hand in European civilization, the book was a study in the power of nationalist ideology to detach its followers from the moorings of common sense. By the end of the war, however, the Florentine intellectual had come to realize that the irrationalist philosophy he had propagated throughout his life had been one of the causes of the immense destruction that was all around him. He did not support the **Republic of Salò**. Papini died in Florence in 1956.

PARALLEL WAR. At the time of the formation of the "Pact of Steel" (6–7 May 1939), Italian General Ugo Cavallero gave German Foreign Minister Joachim von Ribbentrop a memorandum for the Führer, Adolf Hitler, from **Benito Mussolini**, informing him that Germany's chief ally would not be able to enter a European war at any time before 1942 unless Germany agreed to replace the military supplies that Italy had used in **Ethiopia** and in the **Spanish Civil War**. Mussolini wanted to conduct, at a moment of his own choosing, a war parallel to Hitler's but independent of Hitler's attempt to consolidate Germany's position in northern Europe. Italy's ambitions focused on the Mediterranean and the Balkans.

German moves into Slovakia (in March 1939) induced Mussolini to anticipate his planned invasion of **Albania**, the better to demonstrate to Hitler his capacity for autonomous action. When Hitler made war on Poland and within weeks had forced it to submit, and then crushed Norway, the Low Countries, and France, Mussolini saw the prospect loom of a reordering of Europe's power relations without Italy's participation. Hence, he declared war on Britain and France on 10 June 1940, so that "a few thousand [Italian] dead" would entitle him to a seat at the peace settlement that he believed to be imminent. The result of this military intervention was that Italy was embroiled in disastrous wars with Britain in North Africa and with Greece that went so badly Germany had to intervene to prevent a total debacle. *See also* WORLD WAR II.

PARETO, VILFREDO (1848–1923). One of the most important economists of the 19th century, Vilfredo Pareto was also a challenging sociologist and political economist. For economic theorists, Pareto is chiefly remembered as the inventor of the so-called Pareto optimalization in 1906, which describes efficient and inefficient states in a market economy. Pareto was also one of the leading proponents of laissez-faire theories after the Italian state's adoption of protectionism in 1887. He did not shirk political polemic: In June 1896, in a devastating article, he ironically attacked numerous leading politicians, and in particular **Antonio Starabba di Rudinì**, as heading a "ministry of gentlemen," for not having investigated the role played by political corruption in the **Banca Romana** scandal.

As a sociologist, Pareto's reputation rests upon his colossal (2,000 page) *Trattato di sociologia generale* (*Treatise of General Sociology*, 1916). The central theme of his work in social theory was that human history is nothing other than a perpetual struggle between elites to obtain power or to conserve it. Political ideologies (such as liberalism or conservatism or socialism) are merely elaborate justifications with which the elites mask their intentions from others and even from themselves. Pareto believed, moreover, that contemporary Europe was guided by a uniquely inept ruling class that did not even defend its own values with energy and was destined to yield to the rising power of the working class.

Pareto's academic career was largely spent in Switzerland. He took the chair in political economy at the University of Lausanne in 1893. In his final years, he lived at Celigny on the shores of Lake Geneva. He died there in 1923. See also MOSCA, GAETANO.

PARLIAMENT. Since unification in 1861, with a brief hiatus between 1939 and 1943, the Italian Parliament has been composed of a **Chamber of Deputies**, elected initially by a very restricted form of suffrage and since 1946 by all adults over 18 years of age, and a Senate.

The Chamber was housed between 1861 and 1865 in Palazzo Carignano in **Turin** and then, after the capital moved to **Florence**, in Palazzo Vecchio. When the capital was moved to **Rome** in 1871, the Chamber was housed in Palazzo Montecitorio and remains there today. Between 1939 and 1943, the Chamber was abolished and replaced by the Camera dei fasci e delle corporazioni (Chamber of Fascists and Corporations). Membership was limited to members of the national council of the **Partito Nazionale Fascista**/National Fascist Party (PNF), members of the **Fascist Grand Council**, and 500 representatives of the corporations.

The Senate was nominated by the king until 1948. The **Statuto Albertino** allowed the king to choose senators for life from 21 different categories of profession, including bishops, experienced parliamentary deputies, judges, ambassadors, and artists and thinkers who had shown exceptional merit. Senators had to be over 40 years of age. After unification, the power to nominate senators passed more and more into the hands of the government and the prime minister of the day, although formal power remained with the king. **Camillo Benso di Cavour** managed to get nearly 160 senators nominated, and the Senate was gradually filled with eminent figures from outside Piedmont (each influx of new nominees was called an *infornata*, or "bake"). When the capital moved to Rome, the Senate was housed in Palazzo Madama, by an odd coincidence the same name as the building that had housed it in Turin, and it is still there. The Senate was much more conservative than the Chamber during the period 1861–1922, and many inconclusive plans were hatched to reform it and make it more representative of the country's new middle class, but during the Fascist period it paradoxically gained more independence, and some of the Fascist regime's most public critics, notably **Luigi Albertini** and **Benedetto Croce**, were protected by their membership.

The Italian Parliament today consists of a Chamber of Deputies of 630 members elected by universal suffrage and a Senate of 315 elected members plus life senators (ex-presidents of the republic and up to five presidential nominees named for "social, scientific, artistic, or literary" merit). Only citizens over 25 can vote in Senate elections; those who have reached their majority (age 18) may vote for the Chamber.

The Italian Parliament sits for a maximum of five years, although the president can dissolve the legislature if the government of the day is no longer able to command a parliamentary majority. Both chambers of Parliament must give an initial vote of confidence to a government before it can take office. Meeting in joint session, the Parliament also chooses the **president of the Republic** for a seven-year term, as well as 5 of the 15 members of the Constitutional Court. To calm the fears inspired by a strong executive, and the better to ensure a level of representation that **Fascism** had denied, the writers of the **Constitution** of 1948 revived the prefascist parliamentary system with only a few changes. Parliament was given strong powers to curb the executive (including secret voting, which meant that the power of party whips to coerce their deputies into obedience with the party line was greatly reduced), and an extremely representative system of proportional representation was adopted. In a society as divided as Italy is by region, economic function, and class, this decision ensured that politics would be conducted by multiparty coalitions. All laws must be approved by both chambers of Parliament, and there is also a powerful committee system.

The parties of Italy's Parliament can be said to have been grouped into five main categories between 1946 and 1994: the Catholics, the "lay" parties, the Marxist left, the neofascists, and the regionalists. Before the corruption scandals in the 1990s, the **Democrazia Cristiana**/Christian Democracy Party (DC) regularly received around 40 percent of the vote. The Marxist left also usually polled almost 40 percent of the electorate. Since both the neofascists and the communists were regarded as "antisystem" parties, coalitions had to be built around the DC, with the cooperation of the "lay" parties and of the **Partito Socialista Italiano**/Italian Socialist party (PSI) whenever that party was willing to move into the mainstream.

The current Parliament is as thronged with miniparties as ever. There are more than a dozen parties represented, the largest of which, **Forza Italia**, commands only about one-fifth of the available seats. Italy's parties unsurprisingly seem unwilling to vote for an **electoral law** that might reduce their number. *See also* CORPORATISM.

PARRI, FERRUCCIO (1890–1981). Born near **Turin**, Parri fought bravely in **World War I** and was wounded on three occasions. He proved equally brave as an uncompromising antifascist. In December 1926, together with **Carlo Rosselli** and **Alessandro Pertini**, he helped **Filippo Turati** escape from Italy, and he was one of the organizers of the clandestine movement **Giustizia e Libertà**. In October 1930, he was arrested in **Milan** and was sentenced to a period of *confino*. At the end of 1941, Parri acted as the coordinator of the negotiations that led to the formation of the **Partito d'Azione**/Action Party (PdA) in May 1942.

Parri was active both as a diplomat and as a **resistance** commander during the German occupation. In December 1944, on behalf of the **Comitato di Liberazione Nazionale**-Alta Italia/National Liberation Committee-Northern Italy (CLNAI), he signed the agreement by which the British agreed to furnish the partisans operating in northern Italy with arms and money in exchange for a commitment to postwar disarmament and recognition of the government approved by the

Allies. As "Partisan Maurizio," he was one of the heroes of the popular military struggle against the Germans. In January 1945, he was arrested by the Nazis in Milan but was saved from certain death when the Allies required his restitution as a sign of German good faith in secret surrender talks that began in March 1945.

After liberation, the British and Americans realized that they had to respect the "wind from the North" and incorporate the main partisan parties into the provisional government. In June 1945, Parri, whose politics alarmed the British but who was personally greatly esteemed by the Allies, became postwar Italy's first prime minister. His government, however, lasted only until November, when the **Partito Liberale Italiano/**Italian Liberal Party (PLI) and the **Democrazia Cristiana/**Christian Democracy Party (DC)—alarmed by the influence of the left in Parri's administration—withdrew their ministers.

In February 1946, Parri's dislike of the increasingly procommunist position of the PdA led him to join with **Ugo La Malfa** to form the so-called Concentramento Democratico Repubblicano/Democratic Republican Concentration. After receiving just 97,000 votes in the 1946 elections to the **Constituent Assembly**, Parri and La Malfa became members of the **Partito Repubblicano Italiano/**Italian Republican Party (PRI). In 1953, however, Parri broke with the PRI over its support for an electoral reform known as the "swindle law." In the subsequent election, Parri's Unità Popolare/Popular Unity Party obtained 170,000 votes, which tipped the balance and ensured that the swindle law's provisions never came into effect. In 1955, Parri received over 300 votes in the first ballot for the presidency, though eventually **Giovanni Gronchi** was elected. In March 1963, he was made senator for life. He died on 8 December 1981, in **Rome**. *See also* ELECTORAL LAWS; RESISTANCE.

PARTITO COMUNISTA ITALIANO/Italian Communist Party (PCI). Founded in 1921 by a breakaway faction of the **Partito Socialista Italiano/**Italian Socialist Party (PSI), the new party's first leader was **Amadeo Bordiga**, but his doctrinaire approach led to his replacement in 1926 by **Antonio Gramsci**. Gramsci's successor as party leader was **Palmiro Togliatti**. The PCI maintained an underground presence in Italy during the Fascist period and took the lead in organizing **resistance** to **Fascism** during the **Spanish Civil War** and after 25 July 1943.

Togliatti returned to Italy from exile in the Soviet Union in 1944. Under his guidance, the PCI cooperated fully with the conservative governments of **Pietro Badoglio** and **Ivanoe Bonomi** established in Allied-occupied Italy; after the war, the PCI participated in the first two governments of **Alcide De Gasperi**. The international situation dictated this moderate line. Stalin and Churchill had agreed that Italy would fall within the British sphere of interest, and British troops would have crushed any overtly revolutionary activity, but Togliatti seems to have taken conciliation beyond what was necessary. The Italian state was not cleansed of former Fascist functionaries, progressive taxation reforms were not introduced, and the peasants of southern Italy were denied immediate relief. In March 1947 De Gasperi reshuffled his government to exclude the PCI and the PSI without having made any concession of substance to the working class. On the other hand, under Togliatti the PCI became Italy's largest mass party, with nearly two million members, establishing its claim to being the authentic voice of Italian workers.

In international policy, the PCI was closely linked to the USSR. The party defended the Soviet takeover of Eastern Europe, organized immense demonstrations against Italian membership in the **North Atlantic Treaty Organization (NATO)** and the American intervention in Korea, and greeted the news of the death of Josef Stalin with an outpouring of public grief. Only after Nikita Khrushchev's secret speech to the 20th Congress of the Soviet Communist Party in 1956, admitting the scale of Stalin's repressions for the first time, did a serious debate begin about the totalitarian character of the USSR. This debate heated up after the Soviet repression of the Hungarian uprising in the same year. Togliatti backed the Soviet Union, but tens of thousands of party members, especially intellectuals, resigned their membership in the wake of these events.

The PCI shifted perceptibly toward a more moderate position in international affairs after Togliatti's death in 1964. The new leader, **Luigi Longo**, was outspoken in his condemnation of the Soviet Union's 1968 repression in Czechoslovakia. In domestic policy, the decade was dominated by a major theoretical debate between the party's left and right wings. **Pietro Ingrao** on the left argued that the PCI should democratize its internal politics, while the right wing's leader, **Giorgio Amendola**, wanted the PCI to merge with the PSI around a platform of social democratic reforms. The PCI had become the dominant party in several of Italy's regions, and its government was widely regarded as being more efficient and honest than that of the **Democrazia Cristiana/**Christian Democracy (DC). **Bologna**, the PCI's showcase city, was regarded as a model of democratic socialist government by everybody except the Italian extreme left, which believed the PCI had compromised its ideals.

Under the leadership of **Enrico Berlinguer** there was even hope that the PCI would achieve a historic *sorpasso* (overtaking) and obtain more votes than the DC in the 1976 elections. In the event, neither party could form a government; thus the compromise reached allowed the DC to head the government with the PCI's parliamentary support. In the next elections in 1979, the party was relegated to its familiar opposition role. By now, the PCI had become a "Eurocommunist" party, which no longer accepted Moscow's primacy and was critical (though not yet condemnatory) of human rights abuses in the Soviet bloc.

After Berlinguer's death in 1984, he was succeeded by the intelligent but bureaucratic **Alessandro Natta**, who let the party drift until a disaster in the 1987 general election compelled change. The party chose a dynamic young leader, **Achille Occhetto**, and at the Eighteenth Party Congress in March 1989 abandoned all references to Marx, Lenin, and Togliatti in its party statutes.

The collapse of the Soviet client states in Eastern Europe prompted Occhetto to announce (14 November 1989) that he intended to turn the PCI into a leftist party "new even in name." By 3 February 1991, Occhetto had a large majority for replacing the PCI with the **Partito Democratico della Sinistra/**Democratic Party of the Left (PDS). A minority group, unable to renounce the link with communism, formed the **Partito di Rifondazione Comunista/**Communist Refoundation Party (PRC) on the same day. *See also* BERTINOTTI, FAUSTO; BOBBIO, NORBERTO; CARRISTI; COSSUTTA, ARMANDO; *COMPROMESSO STORICO*; IOTTI, LEONILDE; LAND REFORM; *MANIFESTO, IL*; NAPOLITANO, GIORGIO; NENNI, PIETRO; NEOREALISM; SECCHIA, PIETRO; SESSAN-

TOTTO, IL; SILONE, IGNAZIO; TRADE UNIONS; VITTORINI, ELIO.

PARTITO D'AZIONE/ACTION PARTY (PdA). The PdA was founded in May 1942 by a diverse group of radicals, liberals, libertarians, and socialists. Many former members of **Giustizia e Libertà** joined the ranks of the new formation, as did some liberal communists. From the beginning, the party was gravely divided internally over points of political principle. It did have three main areas of common ground, however: It was antifascist, opposed to the bureaucratic and totalitarian form of communism practiced in the Soviet Union, and violently antimonarchical. Unlike the **Partito Comunista Italiano**/Italian Communist Party (PCI), the PdA refused to join the wartime governments set up in Allied-occupied territory by **Pietro Badoglio** and **Ivanoe Bonomi** in the latter stages of the war. Instead the PdA, via its military arm, the "Justice and Liberty Brigade," threw itself into the partisan struggle and bore a disproportionate share of the fighting against the Germans and their Fascist allies. In all, the PdA contributed over 30,000 partisans, perhaps a fifth or a quarter of those active in the partisan struggle, and they suffered heavy casualties: More than 4,000 were killed in action. Only the PCI made a greater contribution to the domestic Italian war against Nazism.

When the war was over, the PdA's commander in northern Italy, **Ferruccio Parri**, was made prime minister. It was said that this would bring a "wind from the North" for radical social change, but the PdA was the smallest and least well-organized party in the postwar coalition, was disliked by both the PCI and the **Democrazia Cristiana**/Christian Democracy (DC), and was soon shunted out of office. The PdA did not even manage to arrive at the elections for the 1946 **Constituent Assembly** as a united force: In February 1946, at the movement's first real congress, Parri and **Ugo La Malfa**, the party's right wing, left the party. In the elections of 1946, the party made a miserable showing and gradually fizzled out.

Why, therefore, regard the PdA as an important political movement? The answer is that it acted as a bridge that enabled the liberal-socialist ideas of the early antifascist resistance to be transmitted into the main postwar political parties. Every major party except the DC, including the PCI, was in some way influenced by the PdA, and it is widely agreed that former *azionisti* have an importance in Italy's intellectual and political development out of all proportion to their numbers. *See also* RESISTANCE.

PARTITO DEMOCRATICO DELLA SINISTRA/Democratic Party of the Left (PDS). Founded in February 1991, this heir to the **Partito Comunista Italiano/**Italian Communist Party (PCI) was the principal leftist force in Italian politics for seven years in the 1990s. The PDS's short history can be divided into two periods. In the first period, the party was led by **Achille Occhetto**. Under Occhetto, the party survived the 1992 general elections, the first after the collapse of communism in the Soviet bloc, obtaining a creditable 16 percent of the vote, and emerged from the **Mani pulite** corruption scandals in better shape than any other traditional party. Proposing itself at the head of a "Progressive Alliance" of radical parties, the PDS did well in local and regional elections held in late fall 1993. The March 1994 general elections were a different story, however. Occhetto was outperformed on the campaign trail by the new leader of the Italian right, the media entrepreneur **Silvio Berlusconi**, and the Italian left was soundly defeated at the polls by the conservative and populist right. The PDS's own share of the vote nevertheless increased to 20 percent. *See also* CALOGERO, GUIDO.

After further losses in the June 1994 elections to the European Parliament, Occhetto was replaced as leader by his deputy, **Massimo D'Alema**, and the second phase of the party's history began. Under D'Alema, the PDS worked in conjunction with **Romano Prodi** and the more progressive elements of the former **Democrazia cristiana/**Christian Democracy Party (DC) in the **Olive Tree Coalition**. The PDS provided nine senior ministers, including deputy prime minister, minister of the interior, and finance minister, in the cabinet formed by Prodi after the general elections of April 1996. The PDS was, by a narrow margin, the party that attracted most votes nationally in this poll. Under D'Alema, the party's political platform was radically changed. The PDS committed itself to the market economy, privatization, and welfare reform, policies far from its communist heritage. D'Alema also tried to broaden the party to encompass small parties from the noncommunist left. In February 1998, the PDS absorbed several of these parties, but in the process changed its own name to the **Democratici di Sinistra/**Democrats of the Left (DS). The new formation retains the PDS's oak tree symbol, but at the roots of the tree, the red rose of European social democracy has replaced the old hammer and sickle emblem of the PCI.

PARTITO DI RIFONDAZIONE COMUNISTA/Communist Refoundation Party (PRC). This group split from the 20th Party Congress of the **Partito Comunista Italiano/**Italian Communist Party (PCI) in February 1991, manifesting its rejection of the party's transformation into the **Partito Democratico della Sinistra/**Democratic Party of the Left (PDS). Led initially by **Armando Cossutta**, and from 1994 by **Fausto Bertinotti**, it has displayed unexpected electoral and organizational resilience. In the 1994 general elections it obtained 6 percent of the poll, a figure that rose in 1996 to 8 percent. The party today boasts 100,000 dues-paying members and more than 30 deputies.

Since April 1996, the PRC has been a necessary but sometimes difficult ally for the **Olive Tree Coalition**. In October 1998, the PRC brought down the first government of **Romano Prodi** when further changes to the welfare system were proposed. The party split, with Bertinotti leading the majority faction of the party into opposition. In the 2001 elections, the PRC fought alone and by taking votes away from the center-left was decisive in handing a large victory to Silvio Berlusconi's **Casa delle Libertà/**House of Freedoms (CDL). The lesson was learned. The PRC agreed to join the Unione/Union, as the new center-left coalition formed by Prodi in 2004 was called, and also agreed to subscribe to a common coalition program. After the Unione won the April 2006 elections, the PRC was rewarded by a place in government and by the election of Bertinotti as president of the Chamber of Deputies. Whether the PRC, whose political ideology is antiglobalization, anti-American, and pacifist can thrive as a party of government is open to question. Since Bertinotti's elevation to an institutional role, the party has been led by Franco Giordano.

PARTITO LIBERALE ITALIANO/Italian Liberal Party (PLI). Formed in 1943, the PLI occupied a minority position on the right of the Italian political spectrum until the political scandals of the 1990s brought about the party's dissolution. Its early leaders included **Luigi**

Einaudi and **Benedetto Croce**, who was elected president of the party in 1946 and was made its president for life in 1947. In November 1945, the PLI colluded with **Alcide De Gasperi** to bring down the government of **Ferruccio Parri**, which the Liberals regarded as ineffectual. The PLI in this period was split between a relatively progressive wing, which was willing to countenance some measure of social and agricultural reform, state regulation of industry, and a republican form of government, and a conservative faction that was prepared to back none of these things. The conservatives were numerically stronger, and the party consequently saw many of its most gifted leaders, notably **Manlio Brosio**, leave to join the **Partito Repubblicana Italiano**/Italian Republican Party (PRI).

In June 1946, the PLI fought the elections in the company of a cluster of survivors from prefascist Italy; together they took just under 7 percent of the vote. In 1948, the party was allied with Uomo Qualunque but obtained less than 4 percent of the ballots cast. The PLI's showing in 1948, in fact, set a precedent that would be repeated until the 1980s: Whenever the threat from the **Partito Comunista Italiano**/Italian Communist Party (PCI) seemed strong, the PLI would lose votes to the **Democrazia Cristiana**/Christian Democracy Party (DC); when the DC was riding high, the prosperous upper-middle-class professionals who constituted the PLI's main base of support resumed their backing for the PLI.

Apart from a brief spell in government in 1954–1955, and again in 1972–1973, the PLI's hostility to state ownership and to the creation of the welfare state kept it out of government until 1981. For most of this period, the PLI was led by a highly respected economist, **Giovanni Malagodi**. The PLI's peak electoral performance came in 1963, when it obtained 7 percent of the votes and 39 deputies in the Chamber.

Despite its conservative economic credentials, the PLI was progressive on social issues. It strongly backed **divorce** and campaigned vigorously to protect the 1970 law instituting divorce rights from a DC-led referendum in 1974. At the end of the 1970s, the PLI began to tilt toward cooperation with the DC, but the PLI's access was blocked by the **Partito Socialista Italiano**/Italian Socialist Party (PSI). The necessity of forming a solid majority eventually led to the formation of the five-party coalition called the *pentapartito*. The

PLI—which by the 1980s could count upon little more than 2 percent of the vote—played a subordinate role in the governments it entered. Nevertheless, several of its chief figures became enmeshed in the bribery scandals of 1992–1993. In the 1994 elections, the party split, with some leading members siding with the center-left and others forming a new party called the Unione di Centro/Center Union, which allied itself with media entrepreneur **Silvio Berlusconi**. *See also QUALUNQUISMO.*

PARTITO NAZIONALE FASCISTA/National Fascist Party (PNF). The PNF was formed in November 1921 as a way of unifying and strengthening the Fasci Italiani di Combattimento/Italian Combat Veterans' Associations, the original Fascists who had joined **Benito Mussolini** at the March 1919 rally in **Milan**'s Piazza San Sepolcro. From 1926 onward, the PNF was the only legal political party in Italy.

Organizationally, the PNF became progressively more hierarchical. The party's first statute (December 1921) provided for a degree of party democracy, but later revisions eliminated the democratic principle and strengthened the role of the Duce himself. In the 1929 statute, the power to choose the party secretary, who himself had sweeping patronage powers over the whole gamut of associations, institutions, cultural bodies, and youth organizations, was taken from the **Fascist Grand Council** and given to Mussolini. The secretary's decisions on appointments had to be ratified by Mussolini himself, who thus found himself at the head of a sprawling organization. Indeed, managing the PNF was one of Mussolini's main tasks.

Party membership, which was reduced by a purge in 1924–1925 under the leadership of **Roberto Farinacci**, expanded in the late 1920s under Augusto Turati to almost a million and then vastly increased as the regime consolidated its hold on power. By the beginning of **World War II**, there were 2.5 million party members, and membership was a necessity for anybody who wished to make a career in public administration.

The PNF and the state overlapped confusingly. From 1926 onward, elected mayors were abolished and local government was carried on by local *Podestà*, who were, of course, senior party members. The party's youth organizations duplicated and shadowed the work of the

education ministry. The Opera Volontaria per la Repression Antifascista (OVRA), or secret police, was effectively the Fascist police, secret and unaccountable to anyone other than Mussolini himself, who allegedly took pleasure in having devised these initials with no publicized meaning, hoping thereby to inspire fear. The Fascist militia, like Hitler's SS, was the party's private army (and, as such, was much resented by the regular army). These parallel structures put the party on the same level as the state, which was apparently Mussolini's design. So successful was he in realizing his design that the chief concern of the Allies after the surrender of Italy on 8 September 1943, was the disbanding of all the institutions and instruments of the PNF. *See also* CORPORATISM; FASCISM; MARCH ON ROME; YOUTH MOVEMENTS, FASCIST.

PARTITO POPOLARE ITALIANO/Italian People's Party (PPI). The PPI was founded by Don **Luigi Sturzo** in January 1919 with the blessing of Pope Benedict XV. The decision to found a mass party open to non-Catholics and, theoretically, independent of the Church hierarchy was the product of the **Vatican**'s growing alarm at the strength of the **Partito Socialista Italiano**/Italian Socialist Party (PSI) after 1918. At the PPI's First Congress in June 1919, Don Sturzo outlined a progressive program that emphasized the need to defend the family; to extend **education**, welfare, and pensions to create a social safety net; to increase the nation's productive powers and divide the nation's wealth more equitably; and to work for peace in the world. The PPI also asked for proportional representation, an elected Senate, and **women**'s suffrage. Proportional representation was in fact introduced in August 1919. The PPI obtained 1.2 million votes in the November 1919 elections, securing 20.5 percent of the total, making it the second-largest group in **Parliament** after the PSI.

By the next spring, the party had 250,000 members and took part in **Giovanni Giolitti**'s last government (June 1920–July 1921). It did not join the antisocialist **blocco nazionale** that was liberal Italy's last-ditch effort to retain its hold on power. In the general elections of May 1921, the PPI repeated its 1919 result and subsequently had three ministers in the cabinet formed by **Ivanoe Bonomi**.

At the party's Third Congress in October 1921 an attempt by the leader of the party's left to commit the PPI to noncooperation with the

Fascists was rejected. The leadership underestimated the threat posed by **Benito Mussolini**. The PPI in fact entered the government formed after Mussolini's coup in October 1922. At the PPI's Fourth Congress in April 1923, the leadership's position toward **Fascism**, as sustained by the head of its parliamentary group, **Alcide De Gasperi**, was clarified as one of "conditional collaboration"—support for the government so long as it kept within constitutional boundaries. This was not enthusiastic enough for one delegate, who declared that Italy should "thank divine providence for sending her a man like Mussolini."

The PPI split over the 1923 **Acerbo** Law, with most of the party abstaining but a small minority voting in favor. Before the vote, Don Sturzo had been pressured into resigning as leader by the Vatican, which was worried that his continuance in office would wreck relations with Mussolini. In the elections of March 1924, the PPI, fighting on an openly antifascist platform, obtained 650,000 votes (9 percent) and 39 deputies. These results made it the largest opposition party. After the poll, the PPI chose De Gasperi as its new leader. Under his direction, the PPI took a prominent role in the boycott of Parliament that followed the murder of **Giacomo Matteotti**. The PPI's deputies attempted to retake their seats in the Chamber in January 1926 but were physically ejected by the Fascist members. The party was suppressed in November 1926. Its leaders were mostly allowed to live an unmolested life and made no attempt to set up a clandestine organization.

In January 1994, the rump of the scandal-hit **Democrazia Cristiana**/Christian Democracy (DC) renamed the party the PPI in a bid to recall the original Christian democratic movement. The party nevertheless did very poorly in the March 1994 elections. After the elections it chose **Rocco Buttiglione** to be its leader, but his divisive strategy caused the party to split in March 1995. The revived PPI merged with supporters of **Romano Prodi** to form **Democrazia e Libertà** (also known, after its electoral symbol, as the *Margherita*, or daisy). Democrazia e Libertà is the second-largest component of the Unione/Union, the governing coalition narrowly elected in April 2006. *See also* PAPACY; *RERUM NOVARUM.*

PARTITO RADICALE/Radical Party (PR). The PR was founded in 1955 by a group of intellectuals drawn from among the disaffected within the **Partito Liberale Italiano**/Italian Liberal Party (PLI) who had grown impatient with the economic conservatism of **Giovanni Malagodi**. Originally hardly more than a club of intellectuals associated with the weekly newspaper *Il Mondo*, the PR nevertheless articulated a penetrating critique of the economic and political tendencies of Italian society. The PR's principal figures, Mario Pannunzio and **Ernesto Rossi**, waged war against the dogmatism of both the Catholic Church and the **Partito Comunista Italiano**/Italian Communist Party (PCI) and against the growing corruption and clientelism of the chief political parties, and argued that the Italian state was interfering too much in the workings of the free market.

In 1962, a generational change in the leadership brought the PR under the control of **Marco Pannella**, who has been the dominant figure in the party ever since. Until the late 1970s, Pannella's small band of activists was merely a **Rome**-based pressure group that agitated for social reforms, but the PR's sponsorship of a **referendum** to liberalize the 1978 abortion law brought genuine electoral popularity, especially among the urban young. In the 1979 general elections, the PR could boast the votes of 3.5 percent of the electorate, up from just 1 percent in 1976, and as much as 7 percent in big cities such as Rome, **Milan**, and **Turin**. The PR also persuaded nearly four million Italians to vote for its amendment to the abortion law in May 1981 — nearly 12 percent of the electorate. Since 1981, the PR has made the referendum its chief political weapon, sponsoring or cosponsoring plebiscites on nuclear power, the judiciary, hunting, and electoral reform, among other issues.

In the 1980s, the PR developed into a campaigning movement that resembled Greenpeace or Amnesty International more than a traditional political party. The PR's primary concerns became world hunger, **environmental** questions, the fight against the death penalty, and the decriminalization of drugs. PR members were allowed to join other parties, and the party essentially became a forum for Pannella. In 1992, the PR actually fought the election as the *Lista Pannella*, which symbolized the unhealthy extent of the PR's enthrallment to its charismatic leader. Also in 1992, the PR staved off extinction by a recruitment drive that attracted 37,000 new subscriptions. This testified to the affection that the increasingly eccentric PR inspired, but this affection was put to the test by Pannella's perverse decision to defend the politicians involved in the corruption investigations, and, in 1994, to side with **Silvio Berlusconi's** right-wing coalition.

Since the late 1990s, an aging Pannella has been superseded by **Emma Bonino**, who is currently minister for European Union affairs in the government of Romano Prodi and who was previously the European Union's commissioner for fishing, human rights, and third world issues. The PR joined with the **Partito Socialista Italiano/** Italian Socialist Party (PSI) to form a joint list called the "Rose in the Fist" during the 2006 general election campaign. The party's main platform today is once again the need for economic deregulation, free trade, and privatization. In this regard, despite the extreme liberalism of the Radicals' stance on social policy, the PR in some ways is the nearest thing to a conservative party that Italy possesses.

PARTITO REPUBBLICANO ITALIANO/Italian Republican Party (PRI). Officially founded in April 1895 (though the party's roots can be traced back to **Giuseppe Mazzini** and the various political movements that he inspired), the PRI was little more than a parliamentary fringe group when **Benito Mussolini** took power. Banned during the dictatorship, the PRI was active in the **resistance** to **Fascism**, although its antimonarchist principles prevented it from taking part in the **Comitati di Liberazione Nazionale/**National Liberation Committees (CLN) after Italy's surrender to the Allies on 8 September 1943.

The PRI was reborn as an organized party in 1946. It obtained 4 percent of the vote in the elections to the **Constituent Assembly** and was subsequently strengthened when **Ferruccio Parri** and **Ugo La Malfa**, and former **Partito Liberale Italiano/**Italian Liberal Party (PLI) leader **Manlio Brosio**, joined the party.

The PRI's policy stance in this period was founded on a progressive attitude toward social and economic reform and hostility to the **Partito Comunista Italiano/**Italian Communist Party (PCI). This stance made the PRI a natural ally for **Alcide De Gasperi**, who— despite the **Democrazia Cristiana/**Christian Democracy Party's (DC) narrow overall majority in the Chamber of Deputies in the May 1948 elections—included the PRI in all his governments. PRI ministers held such portfolios as foreign affairs, defense, and foreign trade at various times and thus enjoyed an influence on national policy out of all proportion to their electoral support. In 1953, the PRI split after the party majority backed the DC's attempt to introduce the so-called *Legge truffa* (swindle law). Ferruccio Parri and the party's left wing deserted the PRI in protest and formed a new group, Unità popolare (Popular Unity), which campaigned against the new law and was decisive in denying the DC the majority it needed to put the law's provisions into effect. The PRI's share of the vote sank to just 1.6 percent in 1953.

Chastened by this experience and by the DC's rightward move after the death of De Gasperi, the PRI played no further governmental role until 1962. Under the leadership (from 1965) of Ugo La Malfa, the PRI acted as the critical conscience of the center-left during the 1960s and 1970s, speaking out against the political parties' increasing power over the institutions of the Italian state and arguing vehemently for social reforms such as **divorce** and abortion. La Malfa, after a contentious spell as treasury minister during the 1973 oil shock became vice premier during the 1974–1976 administration of **Aldo Moro**. La Malfa died in 1979. His place was taken by **Giovanni Spadolini**, who argued that the PRI was capable of providing political leadership, not just moral tone, to Italian government. In the 1983 elections, the PRI's electoral support was its best ever—5.1 percent.

Yet despite the generally high quality of the PRI's ministerial appointees in the 1980s, the party became a powerless spectator as the DC and the PSI struggled for power and patronage. Eventually, in April 1991, the party secretary, Ugo La Malfa's son Giorgio, pulled the PRI out of the governing coalition. The PRI was the cleanest party of government in the first Italian Republic, although it did not emerge unscathed from the bribery scandals in 1992–1993. Still led by Giorgio La Malfa, the PRI has supported both the **Olive Tree Coalition** and **Silvio Berlusconi** since the mid-1990s, but by now it is a mere shadow of its former self.

PARTITO SOCIALISTA DEMOCRATICO ITALIANO/Italian Social Democratic Party (PSDI). The first step toward the creation of a social democratic party in Italy was taken in January 1947 when **Giuseppe Saragat**, motivated above all by his opposition to the power of the **Partito Comunista Italiano**/Italian Communist Party (PCI), led 52 of the 115 Partito Socialista Italiano d'Unità Proletaria/

Italian Socialist Party of Proletarian Unity (PSIUP) deputies in the **Constituent Assembly** to form the Partito Socialista dei Lavoratori Italiani/Italian Socialist Workers' Party (PSLI). In December 1947, this new formation entered the government, with Saragat becoming vice premier. In May 1948, the PSLI fought the elections in the company of the Unione Democratica Socialista/Democratic Socialist Union (UDS), a movement headed by the writer **Ignazio Silone**. The results were promising: In all, the new ticket received over two million votes (7 percent of the electorate).

The PSLI's internal politics were turbulent after the 1948 elections. A further schism in the **Partito Socialista Italiano**/Italian Socialist Party (PSI) led to the formation of a miniparty headed by the former interior minister, Giuseppe Romita, which quickly merged with the UDS and numerous defectors from the PSLI to form the Partito Socialista Unificato/Unified Socialist Party (PSU). The political line of the new party was more neutralist in foreign affairs and more critical of Saragat's policy of cooperating with the **Democrazia Cristiana**/Christian Democracy Party (DC). This fragmentation of Italian social democracy was unsustainable, however, and, in January 1952, a unifying congress took place in **Bologna**, where the PSDI was born. Romita was the first party secretary; the following year, he was replaced by Saragat. The PSDI's electoral baptism came in 1953, when its vote fell to just 4.5 percent.

The PSI's shift away from the **Partito Comunista Italiano**/Italian Communist Party (PCI) and toward the political center after 1962 raised the question of the reunification of Italian socialism. The PSI's votes contributed to Giuseppe Saragat's election as president of Italy in 1964, and, in 1966, the PSI and the PSDI merged into a new party known as the Partito Socialista Unificato/Unified Socialist Party (PSU). The experiment was not a success. The PSU obtained just 14.5 percent of the vote in the elections of 1968, 5 percent less than its two component parties had obtained in the previous electoral test in 1963. The PSU fell apart in July 1969, and, in 1970, the PSDI reformed under the leadership of Mario Tanassi.

Lacking a mass electoral base (over the next 20 years the PSDI's support would never be higher than 5 percent of the electorate), the PSDI became a satellite of the DC and adopted the corrupt and clientelistic policies that were the DC's trademark. In 1976, party leader

Tanassi was accused of having accepted bribes from the American aerospace company Lockheed while minister of defense under Mariano Rumor from 1971 to 1974. He was eventually found guilty and sentenced to two years' imprisonment. Most of Tanassi's successors were little better. One of them, Pietro Longo, was found to be a member of the subversive masonic lodge **Propaganda Due** (P2) and was later arrested on corruption charges. The last two secretaries of the PSDI, Antonio Cariglia and Carlo Vizzini, were swept away by the corruption investigations of 1992–1993. The PSDI took part in every administration between August 1979 and July 1992, but it made no apparent contribution to improving Italy's political and economic life. *See also* OPENING TO THE LEFT.

PARTITO SOCIALISTA ITALIANO/Italian Socialist Party (PSI). The PSI was founded, under the name "Italian Workers' Party," in **Genoa** in 1892. In its early years, the party was dominated by **Filippo Turati** and his companion, Anna Kuliscioff. Turati's reformist socialism came into increasing disrepute with the party's "maximalist" wing. At the party's Eighth Congress in 1912, the revolutionaries, led by **Benito Mussolini**, expelled the party's moderates, and Turati was left to fight an increasingly lonely battle until his own expulsion in 1922. For the most part, the PSI remained faithful to the Marxist view that **World War I** was a product of imperialism that the working class of all nations had the duty to oppose. Earlier—in November 1914—Mussolini had himself been expelled for violating the party's neutralist line on intervention in the war.

The PSI's Marxism did no harm with a working-class electorate inspired by the Bolshevik Revolution in Russia. In the 1919 general elections, the second held under universal male suffrage, the PSI became the largest party, with almost 33 percent of the vote and 156 deputies. This electoral triumph was a prelude to the so-called *biennio rosso* (1920–1922), two years of heated industrial action and street battles between Fascists and socialists.

Resistance to **Fascism** was hampered by the doctrinaire manner of the "maximalists." Even after the Fascists broke a "pact of pacification" signed with the PSI in August 1921, the PSI's leadership refused to join a government that would use force to restore law and order; at the same time, the PSI argued futilely with the **Partito Co-**

munista Italiano/Italian Communist Party (PCI) over whether conditions were ripe for outright revolution. The consequence was that Mussolini seized power, and the PSI, though still theoretically a legal party, was soon subjected to police harassment and the arbitrary arrest of many of its local and national leaders. The party was outlawed, along with the rest of the opposition, in November 1926.

The party's reformist and maximalist wings resolved their differences at a congress of exiles in Paris in July 1930. The architect of this deal was **Pietro Nenni**, who became from this moment onward the chief figure in Italian socialism. Within Italy, however, the PSI became almost moribund during the dictatorship. In August 1943, it was forced to merge with **Lelio Basso's** Movimento di Unita Proletaria/Movement of Proletarian Unity (MUP), to form the Partito Socialista Italiano d'Unità Proletaria/Italian Socialist Party of Proletarian Unity (PSIUP). Lacking organization, the new party soon became subordinate to the PCI within the **resistance**. It did not, however, endorse the PCI's decision to join the government formed by **Ivanoe Bonomi** in August 1944.

The PSIUP participated in the administrations formed by **Ferruccio Parri** and **Alcide De Gasperi** that governed the country prior to the election of the **Constituent Assembly** in June 1946. In the elections, which it fought in alliance with the PCI, the PSIUP obtained 20 percent of the vote and emerged as the second party after the **Democrazia Cristiana**/Christian Democracy Party (DC). The PSI (as it was again called after 1947) continued its "Unity of Action" pact with the PCI until 1953, even presenting joint lists of candidates in 1948, but this close identification with communism did not serve the party's interests. In January 1947, the party's moderates, led by **Giuseppe Saragat**, left the party, weakening its electoral support, and the PCI soon overtook the PSI as the point of reference for the working class.

The PSI definitively broke with the PCI in 1956 after Nikita Khrushchev's secret speech on Stalin's crimes and Soviet suppression of the Hungarian revolution. Nenni, who had been a convinced "frontist," had received a Stalin prize, which he now returned. He then began a flirtation with the DC. In 1963, Nenni took the plunge and entered the cabinet formed by **Aldo Moro** in December of that year. The party remained in office more or less constantly until 1974, but the move was not an electoral success. In the 1968 elections, the PSI and the **Partito Socialista Democratico Italiano**/Italian Social Democratic Party (PSDI), running joint lists, obtained only 14.5 percent, more than 5 percent less than the sum of their independent numbers in 1963. In terms of social reforms, the PSI's experience of government was also a delusion. The PSI played a major role in introducing a **divorce** law in 1970, but the Italian economy remained in mostly private hands. Worst of all, the PSI, hitherto incorruptible, began to taste the pleasures of patronage.

In 1972, the PSI obtained its worst electoral result ever, just 9.6 percent. This poor performance was repeated in 1976, although the party received a boost in 1978 when one of its historic leaders, **Alessandro Pertini**, became the first member of the PSI to become **president of the Republic**. The consequence of these electoral disasters was a generational change in the party's leadership. In July 1976, **Bettino Craxi** was elected leader. After an opportunistic and electorally unrewarding spell in opposition during the government of national solidarity (1976–1979), Craxi made the PSI the fulcrum of Italian politics in the 1980s. But with power came corruption. The PSI's top politicians were notoriously venal. When the bribery investigations began in 1992, the PSI was hit harder than any other party, and its electoral support withered. In March 1994, the PSI obtained just 2.2 percent of the vote. Later in 1994, the party split into four fragments (the "Italian Socialists," the "Laborists," the "Reformists," and a minuscule group of diehard Craxiani). *See also* AMATO, GIULIANO; BISSOLATI, LEONIDA; BOBBIO, NORBERTO; BRIGATE ROSSE; GENTILONI PACT; GIOLITTI, GIOVANNI; LOMBARDI, RICCARDO; MARCH ON ROME; MATTEOTTI, GIACOMO; OPENING TO THE LEFT; *PENTAPARTITO*.

PASOLINI, PIERPAOLO (1922–1975). Director, novelist, poet, and critic, Pierpaolo Pasolini was born and educated in **Bologna** and studied first art history and then (after an interlude in which he was drafted into the Italian army) modern literature. After graduating, Pasolini went to **Rome** and drifted into the underworld of prostitutes—both male and female—their procurers, and petty criminals that populate his films and stories. His first novel was banned for obscenity, a punishment that did not stop his book of poems, *Le ceneri di*

Gramsci (*Gramsci's Ashes*, 1957) from winning the prestigious Viareggio Prize. In 1959, he published a second novel about slum life, *Una vita violenta* (*A Violent Life*).

Pasolini's first feature film, *Accatone*, was issued in 1961. The film's naturalism—like his novels set in Rome's underworld—created an uproar in Italy but was rewarded with international critical acclaim. The following year, Pasolini was given a suspended prison sentence for blasphemy after the release of *RoGoPaG*, a collection of four shorts directed by **Roberto Rossellini**, Jean-Luc Godard, Pasolini, and Ugo Gregoretti. Paradoxically, his next major film, *Il Vangelo secondo Matteo* (*The Gospel According to St. Matthew*, 1964), is widely recognized as one of the finest biblical movies ever made; even the **Vatican** awarded it a prize. Pasolini, a Marxist and nonbeliever, strove to present a sober picture of the story of Christ (who was played by a Spanish architecture student) and to portray the spirituality of the Christian religion—a dimension he believed that Marxists neglected. He followed *Matteo* with the fablelike *Uccellacci e uccellini* (*The Hawks and Sparrows*, 1966). During the student uprisings of the late 1960s, he took an equivocal position, writing a famous poem called "*Vi odio figli di papà*" (literally, "I Hate You Daddy's Boys") that suggested the real working-class heroes were the policemen being assaulted by the upper-class revolutionaries.

Pasolini's subsequent films were for the most part concerned with explicit sexual themes. *Teorema* (*Theorem*, 1968) was prosecuted unsuccessfully for obscenity; he also made a brilliantly bawdy film version of Boccaccio's *Decamerone* (*The Decameron*, 1971). His last film, *Salò, o le centoventi giornate di Sodoma* (*Salò, or the 120 Days of Sodom*, 1975), was an adaption of De Sade set in the dying days of **Benito Mussolini**'s regime. The film displays Pasolini's fascination with cruelty and sexual violence, to which he fell victim. In 1975, he was murdered near Rome by a homosexual prostitute. *See also* CINEMA; LITERATURE; SESSANTOTTO, IL.

PAVESE, CESARE (1908–1950). One of the leading novelists associated with **neorealism**, Cesare Pavese was born in Cuneo (Piedmont). He took his degree in **literature** in 1930 and worked as a teacher of English while publishing critical essays on modern American writers such as Walt Whitman, Mark Twain, Sinclair Lewis, and, above all, Herman Melville, whose *Moby Dick* Pavese translated into Italian.

In 1936 (the year in which his first volume of poems appeared), Pavese was sentenced to a period of *confino* in a remote Calabrian village for passing on politically compromising letters to a communist militant with whom he was having an affair. As a known antifascist, Pavese was forced to live in hiding in the countryside during the last months of the war, and this experience—together with the political fervor engendered in him by his decision to join the **Partito Comunista Italiano**/Italian Communist Party (PCI)—led him to produce by 1950 a string of novels and stories that have become classics of contemporary Italian literature. *La Casa in collina* (*The House on the Hill*), *Il Compagno* (*The Comrade*), and *La Luna e i falò* (*The Moon and the Bonfires*) all appeared between 1947 and 1950, and they permanently established Pavese's reputation as one of the most acute writers in modern fiction. Of all the Italian neorealist writers, he is the one whose work seems most likely to stand the test of time, though some of his later work, notably *La Bella Estate* (*The Fine Summer*), a 1949 collection of three stories, showed that he was chafing under the restrictions of the neorealist genre.

Pavese committed suicide in 1950. The publication of his diaries in 1952 showed that he had long been struggling with a profound sense of personal anguish.

PEACE TREATY OF 1947. On 29 September 1943, an "instrument of surrender" was signed in Malta by General **Pietro Badoglio**, then prime minister of the Kingdom of Italy, and General Eisenhower for the Allies. It provided for the unconditional surrender of Italian air, sea, and land forces. Italy was to be occupied by Allied armies. All organizations of the **Partito Nazionale Fascista**/National Fascist Party (PNF) were to be immediately disbanded. All Italian laws that provided for discrimination on grounds of race, creed, or opinion were to be rescinded under the supervision of an Allied Control Commission.

King **Victor Emmanuel III** declared war on Germany in October 1943 and thus Italy became a "cobelligerent." Opinion on the left, certainly, expected cobelligerent status to entitle Italy to favored treatment in the final peace treaty. But the treaty signed in Paris on

10 February 1947, obliged Italy to cede the Italian border cities of Tenda and Briga to France after a plebiscite. Under pressure from the USSR, Italy had to cede **Fiume**, Zara, Pola, and most of Venezia Giulia to Yugoslavia. Even **Trieste** and its hinterland, fruit of the sacrifices made as allies of the Entente powers between 1915 and 1918, were to be turned over to the Allies as a free territory. Italy's colonial losses included some areas acquired not only before **World War II** and **Fascism**, but even before **World War I**. For example, the Dodecanese Islands were assigned to Greece, and Italy's African colonies—not only **Ethiopia** but Eritrea and Italian Somaliland—were turned over to the United Nations (UN). Finally, Italy was effectively disarmed and was to pay reparations to Albania, Ethiopia, Greece, Great Britain, the United States, the USSR, and Yugoslavia. The United States and Britain renounced their shares. The Soviet Union received $100 million; the others divided a total of $260 million among them. Italy was also debarred from joining the UN.

The terms of the peace treaties were regarded as extremely harsh in Italy and caused temporary political difficulty for the government of **Alcide De Gasperi**. On 26 September 1951, Britain, France, and the United States made a joint declaration of moral rehabilitation stating that Italy had shown that it was a fully fledged democracy and that there was therefore no justification for excluding it from the UN. At a meeting of the Atlantic Council in December 1951, this position was supported by 10 other signatories of the 1947 Paris Treaty, although the USSR and its allies remained opposed. Italy was finally admitted into the UN in December 1955 and took its seat the following year. *See also* SÜD TIROL VOLKSPARTEI (SVP).

PEANO, GIUSEPPE (1858–1932). The son of a peasant family from a small village near Cuneo in Piedmont, Giuseppe Peano was one of the most important mathematicians of his day. He began his university career in 1876 at **Turin**, where he would continue to work and teach for the rest of his career. In 1884, he edited and published a new edition of a textbook on calculus written by his professor, Angelo Genocchi, who, with a most unacademic modesty, declared in the preface that most of the revisions and innovations in the book were to be attributed to "that outstanding young man Dr. Giuseppe Peano."

In 1889, Peano published (in Latin) what have since become known as the Peano axioms. These are a landmark in the history of mathematical logic, a field of which Peano, along with Gottlob Frege and Bertrand Russell, can justly claim to be the founder. Russell met Peano at the International Conference of Philosophy in Paris in 1900 and described the encounter as a "turning point" in his life. Russell recounts that in the discussions at the conference, Peano "was always more precise than anybody else" and always "got the better of any argument on which he embarked." Russell and Alfred North Whitehead's great work *Principia Matematica* was hugely indebted to Peano's groundbreaking ideas. Peano was also responsible for other great discoveries, notably "space-filling" curves in 1890 and innovations in vector analysis and differential equations.

Peano devoted many years of his life to working on the huge *Formulario Matematico*, a giant textbook containing over 4,000 theorems and formulae, which finally appeared in 1908. The book was published in Interlingua, a language Peano had invented whose grammar was based upon a simplified form of Latin. This did little for the work's international appeal. Peano died of a heart attack in 1932.

PELLA, GIUSEPPE (1902–1981). Born in Vercelli in Piedmont, Giuseppe Pella's early political experience was as a *Podestà* (a Fascist equivalent of an appointed mayor). Pella came to the **Democrazia Cristiana/**Christian Democracy Party (DC) by way of **Azione Cattolica Italiana/**Catholic Action (ACI). As a cautious economist first elected to **Parliament** in 1946, he acquired policy experience by serving as chair of the Finance Committee, became deputy minister of finance, and, within a year, was minister of finance, serving also as minister of the treasury and budget. In this role, he implemented tight controls on public spending that were controversial both within the DC and without but stabilized the economy and lay the groundwork for the **economic miracle**. In August 1953, he became premier and also held the foreign affairs and budget portfolios. Pella was chairman of the parliamentary assembly of the European Coal and Steel Community (ECSC) from December 1954 to November 1956. Even after leaving these responsibilities, he served again in the cabinet of **Adone Zoli** (1957–1958) as vice premier in charge of foreign affairs. Subsequently, he served in governments headed by **Antonio Segni** (1959–1960) and **Amintore Fanfani** (1960–1962) at budget and finance. He died in **Rome** in 1981.

PELLOUX, LUIGI GIROLAMO (1839–1924). General Pelloux fought in all three of the wars that established Italian independence and reunification. In 1870, he commanded the artillery that breached the walls of **Rome**. His political career began in 1880, when he was elected to the Chamber of Deputies. A troublesome and ambitious minister of war under both **Antonio Starabba Di Rudinì** and **Giovanni Giolitti**, Pelloux was identified by King Humbert I in June 1898 as a strong leader who could restore calm after the bloody rioting of the previous months. In his initial statements to **Parliament**, Pelloux claimed that he would have no need of the restrictive laws against political organization and free speech proposed by his predecessor, Rudinì. In February 1899, however, Pelloux reneged on his word. His second government, formed in May 1899 with the center-right deputies led by **Sidney Sonnino**, struggled for several weeks to pass a harsh packet of repressive measures. The left, especially the **Partito Socialista Italiano/**Italian Socialist Party (PSI), responded with a filibuster—the first time this tactic had been used in the Italian Parliament. At the end of June 1899, Pelloux lost patience and had the law passed by royal decree. Humbert closed the Parliament until November. The next year, following a sentence by the High Court declaring the royal decree of June 1899 constitutionally invalid, Pelloux tried again to get parliamentary approval for the measures. He was not successful; parliamentary filibustering caused the government to withdraw the proposals.

Pelloux decided that there was no option but to go to the polls and have the electorate confirm or reject his policies. Elections were held at the beginning of June 1900. The PSI, Radicals, and Republicans together obtained almost 100 deputies, and the traditional left led by **Giuseppe Zanardelli** did well, too. Pelloux's majority had been considerably reduced, and on 18 June 1900, he resigned and returned to the armed forces, in command of the garrison in **Turin**. He played no further role in politics. He died in Bordighera (Liguria) in 1924.

PENTAPARTITO. This term was used to describe the five-party coalition of the **Democrazia Cristiana/**Christian Democracy Party (DC), the **Partito Socialista Italiano**/Italian Socialist Party (PSI), the **Partito Repubblicano Italiano**/Italian Republican Party (PRI), the **Partito Socialista Democratico Italiano**/Italian Social Democratic Party (PSDI), and the **Partito Liberale Italiano**/Italian Liberal Party (PLI) that governed Italy between June 1981 and April 1991, with two brief interludes. Between December 1982 and September 1983, the veteran DC statesman, **Amintore Fanfani**, presided over a government that did not contain the PRI; between April and July 1987, Fanfani also headed a short-lived DC-only minority government.

In all, there were nine separate governments that fitted the *pentapartito* model. The first two were formed by the PRI's **Giovanni Spadolini** (July 1981–December 1982). After the first Fanfani interlude, direction of the government passed to the leader of the PSI, **Bettino Craxi**, who was prime minister from August 1983 to April 1987. Between 1987 and 1991, the premiership passed back into the hands of the DC. Three senior DC politicians headed administrations in the last four years of the *pentapartito*: **Giovanni Goria** was in office from July 1987 to April 1988; **Ciriaco De Mita**, then secretary of the DC, was in power from April 1988 to August 1989; and **Giulio Andreotti**, who became premier for the sixth time after the June 1989 elections, governed until April 1991, when he attempted to reshuffle the cabinet to remove the PRI's hold on the ministry of post and telecommunications. The PRI left the government in a huff, and Andreotti reconstituted his government with representatives from the four remaining parties and with a heavy presence of ministers from the PSI.

This account of the numerous ministerial changes underlines the most important feature of party politics during the *pentapartito* decade: their extreme tendentiousness. The Craxi governments were sabotaged by the DC, which feared the PSI leader's emergence as a national figure; between July 1987 and June 1989, the PSI repaid the compliment with interest. The political instability of the *pentapartito* coincided with extraordinary misgovernment. The national debt expanded from approximately 60 percent of GNP in 1981 to about 100 percent in 1991; there were several years in which annual government spending exceeded tax revenues by as much as 12–14 percent of GDP. In **southern Italy**, the **mafia**'s influence grew sharply. Law and order all but broke down in regions such as Calabria and **Sicily**.

Worst of all, these years saw the cancer of endemic corruption metastasize within the Italian body politic. Apart from Spadolini and Fanfani (who in any case belonged to an earlier, cleaner generation of politicians), most of the principal figures of the *pentapartito* era were tarnished by the anticorruption and antimafia investigations of 1992–1994.

PERTINI, ALESSANDRO (1896–1990). "Sandro" Pertini was an icon of the Italian left and probably the most popular president of the first republic. Born in Savona (Liguria), he served during **World War I** as an officer in a machine-gun battalion. After 1918, Pertini joined the **Partito Socialista Italiano**/Italian Socialist Party (PSI), but, in 1922, he passed to the socialist reformists. He was an active antifascist. In May 1925, he was arrested while printing a pamphlet entitled *Sotto la dittatura barbara fascista* (*Under the Barbaric Fascist Dictatorship*), which earned him eight months' imprisonment. Amnestied, he was one of a group of youthful socialists who spirited **Filippo Turati** out of Italy (crossing from Savona in Liguria to Corsica in a motorboat) and then accompanied the veteran socialist leader to Paris. Pertini was sentenced in absentia to 10 years' imprisonment for this feat. Unable to return to Italy, he settled in Nice and operated a clandestine radio station. In 1928, he was arrested by the French police. His trial in January 1929 became a cause célèbre. Pertini used the trial as an opportunity to denounce the Fascist regime publicly and escaped with a suspended one-month prison sentence.

In 1929, Pertini, calling himself Luigi Roncaglia, returned to Italy intent on assassinating **Benito Mussolini**. Unluckily seen and recognized by a lawyer from Savona, he was arrested once more and sentenced to 10 years' imprisonment in November 1929. Subjected to solitary confinement, Pertini's health collapsed, and only an international campaign by antifascist exiles abroad succeeded in getting him transferred to an easier jail in Foggia (Apulia), where he was a fellow prisoner of **Antonio Gramsci**. Despite his precarious health, Pertini staunchly resisted attempts by his family to obtain a pardon for him. Indeed, in November 1933, he was given a further nine-year prison sentence for insulting a notoriously sadistic prison officer.

Pertini spent the period 1940–1943 in the prison camp for antifascist intellectuals on the Isle of Ventotene. Liberated in August 1943, he rushed to **Rome**, where he became a member of the central committee of the newly reconstituted PSI. He was given responsibility for organizing the party's military effort against the Nazis. He took a leading role in the street battles that followed Italy's surrender on 8 September 1943, but in October he was captured and condemned to death by the Nazis. A daring rescue by partisans in January 1944 saved his life. Pertini spent the rest of the war in permanent danger of death and torture as one of the principal leaders of the **Comitato di Liberazione Nazionale**-Alta Italia/Committee of National Liberation-Northern Italy (CLNAI), and, in March 1945, he was one of the organizers of the popular insurrection in **Milan**. He was awarded the gold medal for valor for his services to the **resistance**.

After the war, Pertini naturally became a leading figure in the PSI, even though his political line was only rarely in accord with the party leadership's. Pertini was elected to **Parliament** in 1953 and retained his seat in the Chamber of Deputies until 1978. From 1968 to 1976, he was president of the Chamber.

In 1978, Pertini was elected **president of the Republic**, with 832 votes out of a possible 995. As the historian Paul Ginsborg has remarked, Pertini's selection was an "extraordinarily felicitous choice." Pertini brought the presidency closer to the people by inviting thousands of schoolchildren to visit him in the presidential palace, he took the bold political step of going outside the **Democrazia Cristiana/ Christian Democracy Party (DC)** for the premiership, and he invoked the values of the resistance as a basis for a rebirth of Italy's stagnant democracy. Perhaps the most enduring image of Pertini's presidency occurred during the 1982 World Cup final between Italy and West Germany. Throwing protocol to the winds, Italy's first citizen celebrated Italy's winning goal with a patriotic joy that was published on the front pages of newspapers throughout the world. Pertini died in Rome in February 1990, aged nearly 94. His death was marked by widespread public mourning.

PIACENTINI, MARCELLO (1881–1960). The son of a Roman architect, Marcello Piacentini is the best-known exponent of architecture celebrating the Fascist revolution, what he called the "national road to architecture." Whether or not one approves of his politics, no one can dispute that Piacentini's buildings were striking. His monument to victory in **World War I** in German-speaking Bolzano is a physically massive reminder of the defeat that Austria had suffered. It remains intensely unpopular in Bolzano for this reason. His central administration building for **Rome**'s La Sapienza University is a huge edifice, with an imposing entrance flanked by monumental pillars.

In 1938, Piacentini was given the task of building EUR (Esposizione Universale di Roma), a new town on the outskirts of Rome that would celebrate the 20th anniversary of the fascist revolution. The project was only completed after the war, but it contains buildings that were the culmination of Piacentini's work. The Colosseo Quadrato, with its huge buildings, their flat facades all embedded with oppressively numerous rows of windows, is the concrete manifestation of the paintings of **Giorgio De Chirico**. EUR has an impact on the senses even today: fascist architecture recalls to us the gigantic ambitions (or delusions of grandeur) the regime had for the Italian people. Piacentini died in Rome in 1960.

PIANO, RENZO (1937–). Born in **Genoa** (Genova) to a family of builders, Renzo Piano is an architect with a worldwide reputation for innovation and striking design. He was educated at **Milan**'s Politecnico University. Piano became an internationally renowned figure in the 1970s after he collaborated with a British architect, Richard Rogers, to build the Centre Pompidou in Paris. Their radical design, with its hundreds of external pipes and innovative use of internal exhibition space, was decried by many but has since become a much-loved monument. Piano's studio has since put its name to blueprints for major projects round the world. Piano designed Kansai International Airport in Japan (1987–1990), planned the Potzdammerplatz in Berlin in the 1990s, and designed the Parco della musica in **Rome** (2002) and the Klee Center in Berne (2006). His dazzling design for a giant London skyscraper (310 meters or 1,016 feet), the Shard London Bridge, was approved in 2006. A giant glass knife piercing the sky, the Shard looks set to be one of the most-discussed buildings of recent times.

Piano was awarded the Pritzker Architecture Prize by President Bill Clinton in a White House ceremony in June 1998. The $100,000 prize, which is only made to the most distinguished practitioners of the architectural art, had only previously been awarded to one other

Italian, Aldo Rossi, in 1990. The jury praised the "rare melding of art, architecture and engineering" in Piano's work and compared his "intellectual curiosity" to that of Leonardo and Michelangelo. Piano has been a UNESCO goodwill ambassador since 1994.

PIANO SOLO. *See* SOLO PLAN.

PIANURA PADANA. The area drained by Italy's longest river, the Po, the Pianura Padana (the Po Plains) is Italy's industrial and commercial heartland. Its biggest manufacturing centers (**Turin, Milan, Bologna**, Brescia, Mestre, Varese) are among the busiest in Europe. Per capita income is extremely high—over € 26,000 on average, with a peak of nearly € 30,000 in Lombardy—and unemployment, which has rarely exceeded 4 percent in recent years, is far below the Italian national average. Per person productivity in manufacturing has been estimated to be higher than anywhere in the world except some parts of the United States. Apart from the giant **FIAT** car company, most of the industrial production of the region is concentrated in small- and medium-sized companies specializing in a vast range of niche products for export as well as domestic consumption. Ceramics, textiles, optical equipment, and food processing are just some of the major providers of employment in the region, which is the size of Denmark.

Politically the region has been traditionally divided between the "red zones," where the **Partito Comunista Italiano**/Italian Communist Party (PCI) held sway (Bologna, Parma, Turin), and the "white zones," dominated by the **Democrazia Cristiana**/Christian Democracy Party (DC) (Milan, Brescia, Verona, Vicenza, Padua). This division was memorably depicted in the short stories of **Giovanni Guareschi** in the immediate postwar period.

To a certain extent, this right-left division still holds. Lombardy and the western parts of Venetia have voted for the **Lega Nord/** Northern League (LN) and **Forza Italia** since 1993; Emilia-Romagna and, to a lesser extent, Turin and its surroundings, remain bastions of the **Democratici di Sinistra**/Democrats of the Left (DS). Despite being only the third party in the region, in 1996, the Northern League announced its intention to bring into being an independent republic called "Padania." This project is very unlikely to be realized, but it does show that some political figures think they may gain from appeals to self-conscious local pride in being both a political and an economic model for the rest of Italy. This is particularly true of Venetia, whose political leaders of all parties are determined to obtain greater autonomy from **Rome**.

The countryside is for the most part flat and uninteresting and is covered by thick fogs from November to April. Such cities as Verona (with its remarkable Roman amphitheater), Cremona (with its covered arcades and small workshops where craftsmen continue to construct violins using techniques not significantly different from those employed by Stradivarius), Vicenza (with its superb Palladian architecture), Ravenna (with its Roman mosaics), and Padua and Bologna (with their ancient universities) are of great artistic and historical interest. Most spectacular of all is **Venice**, for long the dominant political power in the region and still today a city of unparalleled beauty. The region's cooking, with Parma and Bologna as the undisputed gastronomic capitals, is internationally famous. *See also* ECONOMY.

PIRANDELLO, LUIGI (1867–1936). Italy's greatest 20th-century playwright, Luigi Pirandello was also a novelist of distinction. His political legacy, however, is less inspiring: Like **Giovanni Gentile** and **Gabriele D'Annunzio**, he yielded to the flattery of the Fascist state. Pirandello was born in Girgenti (modern-day Agrigento), **Sicily**, in 1867. He was educated in Bonn, Germany, where he was briefly the Italian language instructor at the university. He returned to Italy in 1897 to work as a teacher of Italian literature and language in **Rome**, a post he retained until 1922. His life in this period was vexed by the irrational behavior of his wife, who believed, apparently without grounds, that Pirandello was a persistent adulterer. This domestic anguish insinuated itself into his work; the protagonist of Pirandello's first novel, *L'esclusa* (*The Outcast*, 1901), is a woman who is unjustly accused of being an adulteress.

Pirandello's second novel, *Il fu Mattia Pascal* (*The Late Mattia Pascal*, 1904), was a study in alienation and irony. The protagonist, Mattia Pascal, a timid, perfectly ordinary middle-class man, argues furiously with his wife one day and leaves her. Then two events occur that make it possible for him to begin life afresh. First he wins the lottery and becomes financially independent. Then he is wrongly identified as the victim of a road accident. Liberated from all his past ties, he takes a new name, Adriano Meis. However, he soon finds that it is impossible to live in modern society without the "form" that is given to us by bureaucratic recognition. Adriano Meis cannot fully exist because nobody has an official document proving it. Mattia Pascal thus fakes Adriano Meis's suicide and attempts to return to his former life, but his wife has remarried. Nothing remains of his former life except his tomb. He has truly become "The late Mattia Pascal." The novel conveys a sense of human absurdity and estrangement with great poignancy.

Pirandello began writing for the theater in 1916, creating a cycle of somewhat traditional plays set in Sicily and spoken in **dialect**. The two plays that made his reputation, however, *Così è . . . se vi pare* (*That's How It Is . . . If You Think So*, 1917) and *Sei personaggi in cerca di un autore* (*Six Characters in Search of an Author*, 1921), were astonishingly original. As well as being formidably intellectual, they broke with the tradition of theatrical realism (the play as the presentation of a finished drama portraying "reality") and established a new dramatic custom: the play as an artifice for interpretation. There is no "truth" in Pirandello's plays, just contrasting and conflicting meanings explained at length by characters on an often-bare stage that compels the audience to concentrate on the dialogue and think about, not just accept, what is being said. Modern drama owes a great debt to Pirandello and his near contemporary, Berthold Brecht.

Pirandello was lauded by the Fascist state, greatly flattering his vanity. He signed Gentile's 1925 manifesto of Fascist intellectuals and, in 1929, agreed to become a member of the **Accademia d'Italia**. His identification with **Benito Mussolini**'s regime did not affect his growing international reputation, however. In 1934, he was awarded the Nobel Prize in **Literature**. He died in 1936 in **Rome**. By his express wish, there were no speeches or ceremonies at his funeral, and even his children were forbidden to accompany him to his grave.

POLICE. Italy has an abundance of police forces, administered by various public authorities. The Vigili Urbani (municipal traffic police) are appointed and paid locally. The interior ministry in Rome is in charge of the 82,000-strong public security police, whose subdivisions include the highway patrol (Polizia stradale) and railway police. Organized in 1946, their numbers included many former Fascist militia members and thus came to be seen as a holdover from the former regime. In the immediate postwar period, interior minister **Mario Scelba** relied on the public security police when he formed the so-called *celere* (riot squads) to break up leftist demonstrations and picket lines.

The Ministry of Agriculture administers the *Corpo forestale* or forestry corps. Under the control of the Treasury Ministry are the Guardie di Finanza (GDF), the gray-uniformed finance guards (more than 40,000 in number) whose responsibilities include border control, customs collection, antismuggling activity, and the collection of taxes. Like other Italian police (save the municipal police), the GdF are paramilitary and equipped with automatic rapid-fire weapons, light armored vehicles, and helicopters.

The senior and most respected force remains the *carabinieri*, part of the armed forces who serve as military police at army installations and as battle police in wartime. Accordingly, they are administered by the Ministry of Defense and are variously called *La Benemerita* (The Most Deserving) and *l'Arma Fedelissima* (The Most Faithful Service). The 20 *carabinieri* legions (one in each region) are subdivided into provincial groups and dispersed in 4,700 local stations, each of which is headed by a *maresciallo* (a noncommissioned officer). Each public prosecutor's office has a detachment of *carabinieri* to execute arrests, carry out searches, and conduct investigations. There are also specialist armored brigades, helicopter-borne forces, parachutists, frogmen, and the *Gruppo d'intervento speciale* (GIS), which has trained with Britain's and Germany's antiterrorist commandos.

Many *carabinieri* have been killed in the last two decades by the terrorists of the **Brigate Rosse**/Red Brigades (BR) or by the **mafia**. This may help explain why they are seen as a disciplined force at the service of the public rather than enforcers of particular political persuasions. In fact, commemorative plaques at sites of German or Fascist executions of partisans (e.g., Fiesole near Florence; Ardeatine caves outside Rome) reproduce accounts of individual *carabinieri* who volunteered to take the place of terrified civilians pleading for their lives. When *carabinieri* are ambushed and killed by criminal elements, it is not unusual for spontaneous offerings of flowers to mark the spot. *See also* SEGNI, ANTONIO; SOLO PLAN; TAMBRONI, FERNANDO.

POPULATION. Italy's official population in the census taken in 2001 was just under 57 million. Since 2001, **immigration** from the third world and Eastern Europe has increased rapidly, and the best estimate of Italy's population is currently about 58.5 million people, about 5 percent of whom are non-Italian natives. The Italian statistical agency, ISTAT, has calculated that the average age is just over 41 (but is increasing rapidly). Italians are among the longest-lived peoples in the world: Men live on average to 77 years of age, while women reach 83.

The birthrate, as in most advanced European countries, is low (about 1.3 children per woman of child-bearing age), though it has inched up from its low point in the mid-1990s and is now higher than several of Italy's European neighbors. One cause for the low birthrate is that Italians are marrying later. Despite much less traditional sexual mores and family structures than even 20 or 30 years ago, most babies are born in wedlock and baptized in church.

Italy's population (measured by inhabitants within the current borders, because Italy gained territory in 1866, 1871, and 1918 and lost territory in 1945) was about 22 million people at unification in 1861. It increased to 33 million in 1901 and to just under 40 million in 1921; in other words, it almost doubled in 60 years. This was despite the fact that migration, above all to the United States and to South America, hugely affected Italy's population growth after 1861. Between 1887, when the United States opened its borders, and 1900, 269,000 people a year left Italy for foreign shores. Such migration initially affected the North of the country more, but by the late 1880s hundreds of thousands of southerners were joining the exodus. After 1900, both the amount of migration and the relative share of southerners going abroad increased. Between 1910 and 1913, more than 600,000 Italians emigrated every year. Literally millions of Italians passed through Ellis Island or trod the streets of Buenos Aires.

Under **Fascism**, the Italian state used propaganda and material incentives to raise the birthrate, outlawed abortion and contraception, and made migration abroad much more difficult. The United States passed discriminatory immigration laws designed to reduce the numbers of Italians (among others) entering the country. Nevertheless, Italy's population grew only to 42.4 million in 1936. When the 1951 census was taken, after a second war in which hundreds of thousands of mostly young Italians had died, the population had risen to 47.5 million.

Like most other European countries, Italy enjoyed a "baby boom" in the prosperous years of the **economic miracle**. Italy added nine million people between 1951 and 1981, although thereafter population growth leveled off. This was despite the fact that Italy once again became a substantial net exporter of people after 1945. More than 2.6 million Italians emigrated between 1946 and 1960. The distribution of migrants was different after **World War II**, however. The most common destination, taking nearly 21 percent of all migrants in these years, was France, with Argentina a close second. Venezuela was a popular choice, while many Italians went to work as miners in Wales or Belgium. Millions of Italians also migrated within Italy, with cities such as **Turin** being transformed by the influx of job seekers from **southern Italy**.

Today, Italy's most populous regions are Lombardy, Sicily, and Campania. **Rome** is the largest city, with a population of about 2.5 million, although if one adds the surrounding metropolitan area **Milan** emerges as the biggest city, with a population of 4.3 million. Milan, Rome, and **Naples** apart, Italy has very few big cities. Population is spread out among a large number of provincial capitals with populations of over 100,000. *See also* IMMIGRATION; MINORITIES.

PRATOLINI, VASCO (1913–1991). Born in a working-class district on the "wrong" bank of the Arno River (the "Oltrarno"), Pratolini did not have the classical training of most Italian literary luminaries. He was self-taught by following his insatiable literary curiosity. By the time he was 19, he was part of the Fascist literary left, collaborating with the editors of a well-known Fascist weekly, *Il Bargello*. By 1938, his enthusiasm for the party's polemics against the traditionally privileged bourgeoisie seemed to be waning. In fact, he had begun another periodical, *Campo di marte*, which lasted for just one year (August 1938 to August 1939) before being closed by the minister of

352 PRESIDENT OF THE COUNCIL OF MINISTERS

culture because its **neorealism** and concern for social issues convinced some Fascists that the editors were leftists.

After **World War II**, Pratolini began a period of feverish writing. He published *Il Quartiere* (*The Neighborhood*, 1943), *Cronaca familiare* (*Family Chronicle*, 1947), and *Diario sentimentale* (*Sentimental Diary*, 1957), all representations of life in the Oltrarno. These early works were followed by a series of mature works, several of which were made into successful films. *L'eroe del nostro tempo* (*The Hero of Our Times*, 1949) and the three-part *Una storia italiana* (*An Italian Story*, 1955–1966) are probably the best-known of these books. Pratolini died in **Rome** in January 1991.

PRESIDENT OF THE COUNCIL OF MINISTERS. The Italian **Constitution** of 1948, drawn up by the **Constituent Assembly** elected in June 1946 was a political compromise based upon careful choices by its authors. One choice was to impede the reappearance of a "Man on Horseback." If executive powers had been concentrated in the hands of either **Palmiro Togliatti** or **Alcide De Gasperi**, the other would have perceived a threat. The postwar Italian republic was thus created on a parliamentary model, which is to say that the executive was chosen by and depends for its life on the support of the legislature. The president of the Council of Ministers has had much less control than, say, an English prime minister over the composition of his cabinet, although he (so far there have been no **women**) is often referred to as *primo ministro* or premier. Cabinets have normally been chosen from among the coalition partners' leaders, with account being taken of the intense rivalry among intraparty factions. The Constitution gives the president of the Council only the power to "coordinate" the activities of the government.

One consequence of the dominance of the political parties has been the ease with which parties excluded from a share of power and its perquisites can join forces to bring down a government without necessarily being able to agree on the composition of an alternative. In all, Italy had 55 presidents of the Council in the first 50 years of the republic, almost all of whom were drawn from the centrist factions of the **Democrazia Cristiana**/Christian Democracy Party (DC). The exceptions were **Giovanni Spadolini** (whose government lasted 17 months beginning in June 1981), **Bettino Craxi** (1983–1987), **Carlo**

Azeglio Ciampi (1993–1994), **Silvio Berlusconi** (May–December 1994), **Lamberto Dini** (1995–1996), and **Romano Prodi**, made president of the Council in May 1996. Ciampi and Dini were apolitical technocrats pressed into service by President **Oscar Luigi Scalfaro** because **Parliament** was unable to agree upon a nominee from the political parties. Dini's government, in particular, was unique in that it did not contain a single member of either branch of the legislature, only jurists, professors, economists, and military men brought in to head the main departments of state.

Enhancing the powers of the chief executive is a central theme in Italian politics today, even though it clearly reverses one of the fundamental institutional choices made in the **Constituent Assembly**. *See also* PRESIDENT OF THE REPUBLIC.

PRESIDENT OF THE REPUBLIC. Article 83 of the Italian **Constitution** assigns the task of electing the president to an electoral college composed of the two chambers of **Parliament** and representatives from Italy's regional governments. A two-thirds majority is necessary until the fourth round of balloting; thereafter, a simple majority is sufficient. The party leaders have the task of finding a nominee who will be supported by a broad coalition of electors—a task that is rendered all the more difficult by the fact that the ballot is secret and the influence of the party whips cannot be brought to bear. The negotiations often go on for weeks as the number of ballots grows without conclusion.

The Italian president, chosen for a seven-year term, is more institutionally powerful than a German president but much less powerful than the president of France or the United States. He is the titular head of the High Council of the Judiciary (the executive committee of the legal profession) and has the right to nominate five members of the Constitutional Court. He can nominate senators for life. Most important, he formally nominates the **president of the Council of Ministers** (who must be approved by Parliament) and decides whether or not to resolve a government crisis by dissolving Parliament and calling an election.

For most of the postwar period, these powers meant little beyond interviewing prospective presidents of the Council to encourage the parties to find a nominee acceptable to a majority of Parliament, but in recent years the president's role as a crisis manager has propelled him to center stage. President **Francesco Cossiga** took an important public role during the political crises of the early 1990s, and **Oscar Luigi Scalfaro** played a decisive role in the establishment of the governments of **Carlo Azeglio Ciampi** and, above all, of **Lamberto Dini** in the mid-1990s. As president, Ciampi acted as a brake on some of the more controversial policies proposed by **Silvio Berlusconi** between 2001 and 2006.

PRESS. The Italian press is characterized by two main features: its localism and its limited circulation. Italians read newspapers much less than northern Europeans do.

There are only three newspapers that can claim an authentic national circulation: *Corriere della Sera* (center-right in political orientation, although critical of the center-right's current leaders); *La Repubblica* (left, but not uncritically so); and *La Gazzetta dello Sport*, which dedicates acres of newsprint to the triple sporting obsessions of Italian males: football (**calcio**), cycling, and motor racing. These newspapers each sell over 500,000 copies per day. The other newspapers selling more than 300,000 or so copies a day throughout the country are all clearly associated with a particular city or region. *La Stampa*, a newspaper with clear, modern graphics, is owned by the **FIAT** group and has a readership drawn mainly from Piedmont and Liguria. *Il Giornale*, a hard-hitting right-wing newspaper owned by Paolo Berlusconi, **Silvio Berlusconi**'s brother, is principally sold in Milan and Lombardy. *Il Messaggero* is a **Rome** newspaper; *Il Mattino* is from **Naples** and **southern Italy**. One important newspaper that has a lower circulation, but which is highly influential, is *Il Sole 24 Ore*, the Italian equivalent of the *Financial Times*, which is the house organ of **Confindustria**, the industrialists' association.

Several political parties have daily newspapers. These no longer sell in large quantities, but they are in any case generously subsidized by the state. The largest and most famous of these is unquestionably *L'Unità*, the newspaper founded by **Antonio Gramsci**, which was the house organ of the **Partito Comunista Italiano**/Italian Communist party (PCI) and which now, in a somewhat more independent manner, performs the same role for the **Democratici di Sinistra**/Democrats of the Left (DS). Another political paper worth mentioning is *Il Foglio*, a broadsheet written by political insiders for other political insiders.

It should be said that the quality of most of these newspapers, if measured by the number of pages given over to cultural issues, long articles giving background on political or historical questions, and reviews of books or exhibitions, is extremely high. In fact, the intimidating nature of the principal Italian newspapers may explain why so few Italians actually read them. Only about 10 percent of Italians buy a newspaper every day; in Molise, a small southern region that has no big city nearby, this figure drops to around 5 percent. Purchase of newspapers has also been hit by the diffusion of the Internet, although the main Italian newspapers were quick to develop often excellent websites as an adjunct to their printed product. Nevertheless, the absence of a nationally distributed, middle-brow newspaper like Great Britain's *Daily Mail* is interesting. Even more interesting is the absence of a scandalistic, sex and soaps daily tabloid like Britain's *Sun* or Germany's *Bild*. Italians are certainly interested in this kind of stuff: The word *paparazzi*, after all, is Italian, and there are a number of best-selling weekly magazines (*Novella 2000*, *Gente*) that specialize in photo reportages of adulterous film stars and politicians with sagging bellies.

Two newspapers that deserve special attention here are *Corriere della Sera* and *La Repubblica*. The *Corriere* was founded in 1876 and was owned by the Crespi family until the 1970s. Under the editorial leadership of two outstanding personalities, Eugenio Torelli Viollier and **Luigi Albertini**, the paper grew into one of Europe's best-selling and most influential newspapers before **World War I**, boasting contributions from **Luigi Einaudi**, **Gabriele D'Annunzio**, and **Luigi Pirandello**, among others. The paper was antifascist under Albertini, but he was forced out in 1925, and the paper supported the regime from then on. It backed the Republic in 1946 and on the whole, in the words of its most famous postwar journalist, **Indro Montanelli**, "held its nose" and voted for the **Democrazia Cristiana**/Christian Democracy (DC). The current editor is Paolo Mieli, who is a well-regarded historian and essayist as well as a journalist.

La Repubblica is a much more recent paper. Founded in 1975 by Eugenio Scalfari, it has a semi-tabloid format but is daunting in content, with limited coverage of trivia (though generous sports coverage) and very little *cronaca nera* (accounts of court cases, crimes, road accidents, and so on). The paper is politically progressive and aimed at professionals. It was an immediate success and reached a daily sale of 800,000 copies at the end of the 1980s. During the political crisis of the early 1990s the paper was one of the most vocal critics of the political parties and their leaders, especially **Giulio Andreotti**. *Repubblica* has been a consistently innovative paper. For instance, it was the first to introduce a give-away glossy magazine (*Venerdì*) and also publishes a color supplement for **women**. *Repubblica* is part of the Espresso group of newspapers and journals. Its sister paper, the weekly news magazine *L'Espresso*, is an investigative news and comment magazine with a large circulation and strong anti-Berlusconi political views.

No survey of the press is complete without a brief discussion of Italy's intellectual press. In the early 20th century magazines such as *La Voce* and *Leonardo* were influential literary magazines. **Benedetto Croce**'s *La Critica* was one of the most important philosophical and political magazines in Europe. After **World War II**, there was a lively political and ideological debate in Italy in intellectual journals such as *Il Mulino*, *Il Ponte*, *Nuovi Argomenti*, and *Il Politecnico*. The same tradition carries on today in the bimonthly *Micromega*, which has a reputation among intellectuals and philosophers that extends well beyond Italy itself. *See also* MEDIA.

PRINETTI-BARRÈRE NOTES. On the heels of the June 1902 renewal of the Triple Alliance pledging Austrian, German, and Italian cooperation in the event of a general European war, Italy sought to ensure its own freedom of maneuver. Essentially, it did what the German Foreign Office had accomplished with "Reinsurance Treaties": leaving in one's own hands the final decision of whether or not to commit military forces to the side of an ally in the event of war.

In **Rome**, the French ambassador was Camille Barrère, to whom the Italian foreign minister, Giulio Prinetti (1851–1908), presented in 1902 a note assuring Barrère that should France be attacked, Italy would remain neutral. The same would occur even if, as a consequence of a direct attack, France felt herself "compelled, in defense of her honor or her security," to declare war. This meant that Italy might join in hostilities if, in Italy's view, France was attacking Germany without provocation. Reciprocal recognition of Italian claims in **Libya** and French claims in Morocco was also included.

Italy's agreements with Germany specified that in the event of a French attack on Germany, Italy should come to Germany's assistance. On the other hand, if Germany attacked France, Italy would remain "benevolently neutral." Only neutrality was pledged, just as Germany's secret "Reinsurance Treaties" had left in Germany's hands the question of which to choose in the event of an Austro-Russian conflict: assistance to Austria or "benevolent neutrality"— that is, only if France attacked Germany was Italy pledged to provide assistance.

Historians use a different measure in looking at Germany's diplomacy in this period from the one used when examining Italy's initiatives, however. Germany's protection of its freedom of maneuver is defined as an exercise of *Realpolitik*, while Italy's efforts are oddly alleged to reveal a basically duplicitous nature. These commitments were not made known beyond their principals until the 1920 publication in France of collections of Foreign Ministry documents.

PRODI, ROMANO (1939–). Romano Prodi was born in the province of Reggio Emilia (Emilia-Romagna) in August 1939. Like all but two of his eight brothers and sisters, he initially followed an academic career, becoming a professor of economics at the University of **Bologna**. In 1978, he became minister for industry in **Giulio Andreotti**'s short-lived fourth government.

In 1982, Prodi was asked to take over the chairmanship of the **Istituto per la Ricostruzione Industriale**/Institute for Industrial Reconstruction (IRI), the huge holding company that used to manage the Italian state's widespread industrial interests. When Prodi took over IRI, the company was sinking under the burden of its debts. By rationalizing the company's steel production in particular, Prodi was able to transform IRI into a profit-making concern by 1989, although his attempts to privatize substantial segments of IRI's activities were blocked by his political opponents. Prodi's career at IRI was linked to the continuance of **Ciriaco De Mita** as secretary of the **Democrazia Cristiana**/Christian Democracy Party (DC). When De Mita was ousted in 1989, Prodi soon lost his post.

Prodi—whom the Italian left had long regarded as the acceptable face of the DC—was spoken of as a potential premier during the government crises of April 1993 and January 1995. In February 1995, Prodi launched himself into politics, nominating himself as the candidate for the premiership of a broad coalition of center-left parties, including the **Partito Democratico della Sinistra/** Democratic Party of the Left (PDS) and **Partito Popolare Italiano/** Italian Popular Party (PPI). Led by Prodi, the **Olive Tree Coalition/**Ulivo scored a narrow victory in the general elections held on 21 April 1996. In mid-May 1996 Prodi became prime minister at the head of a government that contained 10 PDS ministers but that relied on the votes of the **Partito di Rifondazione Comunista/** Communist Refoundation Party (PRC) for a parliamentary majority. The main achievement of Prodi's government was qualifying to enter the euro, although the finance minister, **Carlo Azeglio Ciampi**, deserves much of the credit for this feat. Italy entered the euro system on schedule on 1 January 1999, despite the fact that its stock of public debt was greatly over the amount permitted by the 1992 Treaty on European Union (EU).

Prodi's reward was to be almost immediately overthrown by his parliamentary majority. The PRC, angry about the social costs of the austerity policies introduced by Prodi and Ciampi, brought his government down in October 1998. Prodi fell on his feet, however. He became president of the European Commission in 1999 and stayed in the job until 2004, overseeing the introduction of the euro in note form in 2002 and, even more important, the enlargement of the EU by 10 central European and Mediterranean countries in May 2004. Prodi returned to Italian politics after his spell in Brussels and was drafted by the squabbling parties of the center-left to lead them against **Silvio Berlusconi** in the April 2006 elections. Prodi established his authority by winning a U.S.-style primary for the leadership of his new coalition, the Unione/Union, in October 2005. In April 2006, he led the Union to a knife-edge victory in the general elections and became premier for the second time. *See also* D'ALEMA, MASSIMO; EUROPEAN INTEGRATION.

PROPAGANDA DUE (P2). A secretive masonic lodge, the P2 was described as "an association for criminal purposes" by President

Alessandro Pertini in October 1981. The existence of the lodge—which boasted over 900 members of Italy's political, business, military, and journalistic elite—was discovered in March 1981 by prosecutors investigating the illegal activities of two of its members, the financier Michele Sindona (poisoned in prison in 1987) and "God's banker," Roberto Calvi, who had made huge illegal payments to **Bettino Craxi**, leader of the **Partito Socialista Italiano**/Italian Socialist Party (PSI), shortly before being found hanging under Blackfriars Bridge in London in June 1982. The lodge's political objectives, as revealed by its grand master, the ex-Nazi collaborator Licio Gelli, were to infiltrate members into the highest ranks of the state and **media** (the TV entrepreneur **Silvio Berlusconi** was a member of the lodge) and to press for a presidential republic as a better bulwark against the danger thought to be posed by the **Partito Comunista Italiano**/Italian Communist Party (PCI).

The Italian **Parliament** outlawed the organization in December 1981 and established a Commission of Inquiry, whose May 1984 report confirmed that the P2 had indeed intended to manipulate Italy's democratic institutions. Only then did Pietro Longo, leader of the **Partito Socialista Democratico Italiano**/Italian Social Democratic Party (PSDI), as senior politician most directly involved in the scandal, resign from the government. During the inquiry it also became clear that Gelli had been closely connected with the Italian secret services and with right-wing terrorist groups, and with **Giulio Andreotti**, who was accused of being the godfather of the secretive association. No proof of this charge—which Andreotti indignantly denied—has ever been found. It does seem certain, however, that the P2 had friends in high places. Gelli was subsequently treated with extraordinary leniency by the authorities, and Italy's high court has since denied—in the face of all the evidence—that the P2 was a subversive organization.

PUCCINI, GIACOMO (1858–1924). Second only to **Giuseppe Verdi** in the annals of Italian opera, Giacomo Puccini was born in Lucca (Tuscany) to a family of musicians. He studied at the conservatory in **Milan** between 1880 and 1883, but his first publicly performed works did not achieve any great critical or popular success. His third and fourth scores, *Manon Lescaut* (1893) and *La Bohème* (1896), by contrast, won international acclaim and remain today two of the most frequently performed classical operas. His two subsequent works, *Tosca* (1900) and *Madame Butterfly* (1904), were initially greeted with skepticism by musical critics, but met with overwhelming enthusiasm from audiences.

After 1904, Puccini collaborated with some of the finest orchestras in the world, producing a series of comparatively minor works. At the time of his death in 1924 in Brussels, he was working on what is arguably his masterpiece, *Turandot*, which was finished by the composer Franco Alfano and presented at the Scala Theater in Milan in 1926. During the performance, the conductor, **Arturo Toscanini**, famously halted the music in the middle of the third act to tell an emotional audience "at this point, the maestro died." Less musically innovative than Verdi, Puccini's operas are nevertheless characterized by rich orchestration, a wonderful gift of melody, great dramatic intensity, and pervasive eroticism.

– Q –

QUADRUMVIRATE. The four men who led the **March on Rome** were designated field marshals of the Fascist revolution: **Italo Balbo**, **Emilio De Bono**, **Cesare Maria De Vecchi**, and **Michele Bianchi**, secretary general of the **Partito Nazionale Fascista**/National Fascist Party (PNF) until 1923. These four constituted the quadrumvirate. All were "Fascists of the first hour." Of the four, Italo Balbo was the only one toward whom **Benito Mussolini** showed a certain wariness. The only institutional function performed by the quadrumvirate was membership by right in the **Fascist Grand Council**. *See also* FASCISM; VICTOR EMMANUEL III.

QUALUNQUISMO. In Italian, *l'uomo qualunque* is "the man in the street" or "the common man." *Qualunquismo* in the vocabulary of Italian politics means promoting populist, intellectually discreditable policies by demagogic means. The term has its origin in the 1944 political party called the Fronte dell'Uomo Qualunque/The Common Man's Front (UQ). Its founder was a playwright and journalist called Guglielmo Giannini. Well financed by wealthy businessmen who had enjoyed close ties with the Fascist regime, Giannini's party fought the June 1946 election to the **Constituent Assembly** under the slogan (the translation sanitizes the mildly obscene original) "We've had our fill of people bossing us about" and polled 1.2 million votes. In local elections in November 1946, the party actually obtained more votes in **Rome** than the **Democrazia Cristiana/** Christian Democracy Party (DC). This was the high point of its success. In 1947, when the DC ended its joint government with the **Partito Socialista Italiano/**Italian Socialist Party (PSI) and the **Partito Comunista Italiano/**Italian Communist Party (PCI), the UQ lost its main reason for being. The party fought the 1948 elections in the company of the **Partito Liberale Italiano/**Italian Liberal Party (PLI) but then declined in significance, with many of its members joining the neofascist **Movimento Sociale Italiano/** Italian Social Movement (MSI) or the monarchists. Giannini died in **Rome** in 1960. In recent times, the politician most regularly accused of *qualunquismo* has been **Umberto Bossi**.

QUASIMODO, SALVATORE (1901–1968). Born in one of Italy's southernmost cities, Ragusa (**Sicily**), Quasimodo was brought up in a railwayman's family and was given a technical education. He attended the University of **Rome** (La Sapienza) in 1921, initially to study engineering, but soon gave up his studies, and eventually found work as a clerk. In 1930, his first collection of poems, *Acque e terre* (*Water and Earth*), appeared after he was introduced into literary circles by his brother-in-law, **Elio Vittorini**. Two further collections were published in the 1930s, and during the war he published two great collections of lyrics translated from ancient Greek. In 1941, he was appointed professor of Italian **literature** in **Milan**.

Quasimodo's prewar poetry had taken no particular social position, but the tragic experience of **World War II** convinced him that he needed to take a stand on social issues. His overall body of work (which included translations of modern classics such as e.e. cummings, Ezra Pound, and Pablo Neruda) was recognized in 1959 by the award of the Nobel Prize. Upon his death in 1968 in **Naples**, Quasimodo enjoyed an international reputation as a poet.

– R –

RACIAL LAWS. Fascist Italy was not overtly anti-Semitic until relatively late in the regime's history. In April 1933, **Benito Mussolini** publicly invited the chief rabbi of **Rome** to express his solidarity against the abuses of Jews' rights taking place in Germany. Not until September–October 1938—after joining the anti-Comintern Pact with Germany and Japan—did Italy approximate German racial legislation, making it illegal for Jews to be teachers at any level, work as journalists, join the **Partito Nazionale Fascista**/National Fascist Party (PNF), study in state schools, or hold any government positions. Italians of "Aryan race" were forbidden to marry Jews. Limited exemptions were granted for Jews who had served Italy with distinction (for instance by being wounded in battle, or having joined the PNF before 1922). These restrictions were the culmination of a series of previous initiatives in the field of racial policy: In April 1937, all sexual relations between Italians and Africans had been forbidden by law, and, in July 1938, a "Manifesto of Racial Scientists" was published in the *Giornale d'Italia* with the approval of the government. The Fascist authorities also sponsored an anti-Semitic magazine entitled *La Difesa della Razza* (*Defense of the Race*) from August 1938 onward. A moving picture of the plight of Italy's Jews after the publication of the racial laws is to be found in a famous novel by **Giorgio Bassani**, *Il giardino dei Finzi-Contini* (*The Garden of the Finzi-Continis*, 1956), made into a film directed by **Vittorio De Sica**.

Although these new restrictions severely wounded many Italian Jews and caused many prominent Italian Jews to leave the country, the legislation was not as ruthlessly enforced as in Germany. Moreover, compared with France and many other countries in Nazi-occupied Europe, non-Jewish Italians showed an unusual degree of solidarity with their Jewish fellow citizens. During the German occupation of Rome, the contributions of Christian Italians enabled the Jewish community to pay—indeed exceed—the huge ransom in gold demanded by the Nazis as a price for not herding Rome's Jews off to forced labor camps. Italian commanders and diplomats in Croatia, Greece, and southern France used bureaucratic cavils of every kind to block shipments of Jews. In November 1942, when Mussolini learned that Jews sent to Germany from Croatia were being gassed, he apparently ordered that the delaying tactics should be continued. Even after Nazi minister Von Ribbentrop visited Mussolini in February 1943 to deplore the failure of Italian officers to comply with an ally's requests on racial policy, obstruction continued. In all, about 80 percent of Italy's 50,000-strong prewar Jewish community managed to survive the Holocaust.

Some 10,000 Italian Jews were nevertheless deported to Auschwitz; of these, nearly 8,000 died. Their story is recounted in **Primo Levi**'s classic *Se Questo è un'uomo* (*If This Is a Man*, 1947). Explicit repudiation of the racial laws was one of the key policy changes introduced by **Gianfranco Fini**, the leader of the **Alleanza Nazionale**/National Alliance (AN), when he began the task of modernizing Italy's neofascist Right in the mid-1990s.

RADICAL PARTY. *See* PARTITO RADICALE (PR).

RATTAZZI, URBANO (1808–1873). A native of Alessandria (Piedmont), Rattazzi became a parliamentary deputy in 1848. In 1852, Rattazzi, leader of the relatively radical wing of the Parliament, made the political agreement known as the *connubio* (union) with **Camillo Benso di Cavour** and established himself as the second most important political figure in pre-**Risorgimento** Piedmont. The alliance between the two men dissolved on the eve of the war with Austria in 1859. Rattazzi, who was a favorite of King **Victor Emmanuel II**, became minister of the interior in the short-lived government formed by General **Alfonso Ferrero La Marmora** after the Treaty of Villafranca in July 1859, which had provoked Cavour's resignation. As minister of the interior Rattazzi initiated an important reform of local government that extended the Piedmontese form of provincial and communal administration to Lombardy. The same law, in slightly modified form, was extended throughout the peninsula after unification and established Italy as a centralized state whose lower levels of administration were conceded little autonomy.

In March 1862, Rattazzi formed his first cabinet, taking the offices of foreign and interior minister as well as the premiership. His government made the important decision to introduce a single Italian currency, which increased Italy's ability to borrow in the international markets, but fell afoul of public opinion in September 1862 when the government used troops to prevent **Giuseppe Garibaldi** from marching on **Rome**. Rattazzi's administration resigned in November 1862, but he returned to the premiership in April 1867. The most important act of his short-lived administration was a law in August 1867 that nationalized and auctioned off the land and property held by thousands of religious institutions all over Italy. Garibaldi's attempts to seize Rome in 1867, which ended in the disaster of Mentana, once more brought down Rattazzi's government. Caught between public opinion, which regarded him as too cautious on the Roman question, and France, which suspected him of aiding and abetting Garibaldi, Rattazzi dithered and lost the favor of the king. He died in Rome in 1873. Contemporary writers judged his political record harshly, but, in retrospect, it seems that circumstances, rather than ineptitude, were the chief cause of Rattazzi's ministerial failures.

RAUTI, GIUSEPPE UMBERTO (1926–). "Pino" Rauti has been the most vocal and uncompromising fascist leader in postwar Italy. As a youth he served in the armed forces of the **Republic of Salò**. Rauti has always remained faithful to the anticapitalist rhetoric of the Salò Republic; for him **Fascism** is a revolutionary ideology whose main goal should be the overthrow of the institutions of the bourgeois state. These radical sentiments were frowned upon by the leadership of the **Movimento Sociale Italiano**/Italian Social Movement (MSI) for much of the postwar period, and Rauti's relationship with Italy's neofascist party has thus always been a troubled one. Between 1956 and 1969, in fact, Rauti was not a member of the MSI, preferring to act as the theoretician of a neo-Nazi group with the ominous name Ordine Nuovo (New Order). Inspired by the political thought of the philosopher Julius Evola, the "New Order" group propagated a sub-Nietzscheian ideology deriding safe bourgeois weaklings and the utilitarian values of democratic civilization while exalting the superman, the hero, the aristocrat, and the warrior. Ordine Nuovo would prove to be the breeding ground for many of the neofascist terrorists who plagued Italy in the 1970s, but by then Rauti, finding some of his disciples too extreme, had returned to the MSI. The movement was officially dissolved by the courts in November 1973.

Rauti became a parliamentary deputy for the MSI in 1972. He swiftly became an influence among the party's most youthful members and diffused his belief in the necessity of a "Fascism of the left." His conviction that the fascist movement should take aim at the egoism, materialism, and superficiality of modern life, and abandon all thought of cooperating with the political parties of Italy's corrupt democracy, gradually won over a majority of the MSI's members. Rauti became secretary of the MSI at a heated party conference in Rimini in January 1990. "Fascism of the left," however, was not popular with the MSI's intensely conservative petty bourgeois electorate, and the party suffered the worst defeat of its history in the 1990 local elections, obtaining just 4 percent of the vote. After a further disaster in regional elections in **Sicily** in June 1991, Rauti was obliged to resign.

Despite the electoral success brought to the neofascist movement in Italy by his successor, **Gianfranco Fini**, Rauti has been unable to digest the transformation of the MSI into the **Alleanza Nazionale**/National Alliance (AN). At the Seventeenth and last Party Conference of the MSI at Fiuggi in January–February 1995, Rauti left the party rather than accept Fini's apparent abandonment of fascist ideology and objectives. He became the leader of a split-off party, the Fiamma tricolore (whose emblem was a flame burning in the three colors of the Italian flag), but this movement split too, and Rauti was left to form yet another movement of the far right, the Movimento Idea Sociale/Social Idea Movement. *See also* ALMIRANTE, GIORGIO; MOVIMENTO SOCIALE ITALIANO.

RED BRIGADES. *See* BRIGATE ROSSE (BR).

REFERENDUMS. Article 75 of the 1948 **Constitution** permits the electorate to repeal all or part of a law (or a decree that has the force of law) by popular referendum, though not to write new legislation, which is the explicit function of Parliament. Only international treaties, amnesties or pardons, and all fiscal and budget legislation cannot be abrogated in this way. A referendum can only be called if five regional governments or 500,000 legal adults petition for it. It must also be approved by the Constitutional Court and may not coincide with a general election. On three occasions (in

1972, 1976, and 1987), Italian governments engineered elections to postpone referendums on **divorce**, abortion, and nuclear power, though all three were eventually held. To pass, a majority of all eligible voters must vote, and a simple majority must back the wording of the referendum's sponsors. The first referendums were on the divisive social issues of divorce (12–13 May 1974) and abortion (17–18 May 1981). On both issues, there were a huge turnout (80 percent) and clear decisions in favor of the existing laws.

Since 1981 referendums have become a characteristic feature of the Italian political system; apart from Switzerland, no other country relies on popular plebiscites as much. Among other issues, referendums have been held on reinstating wage-indexing (1985), abolishing the nuclear power program (1987), and banning hunting and the use of pesticides (1990). Only the last of these failed to meet the 50-percent participation requirement. The culmination of this growing use of the referendum was the campaign for electoral reform led by **Mario Segni** between 1988 and 1993. The referendums of June 1991 (on preference voting) and April 1993 (on the repeal of proportional representation in elections to the Senate) were decisive affirmations of the people's will for radical change to the political system.

The triumph of the April 1993 referendum on electoral reform disguised some of the serious defects inherent in overuse of the referendum strategy. In both April 1993 and June 1995, voters were asked to make absurdly technical changes to the law on a vast range of subjects, as well as deciding major issues such as electoral reform and the privatization of the state broadcasting system. Referendum fatigue has also set in. Since 1995, no referendum has reached the 50 percent quota that makes its results legally binding. In June 2005, an attempt to repeal a highly controversial law restricting infertility treatment and artificial insemination attracted only 25 percent of the electorate to the polls. The reliance on the referendum has long been regarded as a sign of Italy's need for constitutional and political reform, but recent referendums seem to show that Italy's voters have lost faith even in this instrument. *See also* BONINO, EMMA; FANFANI, AMINTORE; PANNELLA, MARCO; PARTITO RADICALE (PR).

REGIONALISM. Articles 114–133 (Title V) of the 1948 **Constitution** set out the powers and limitations on Italy's regions, of which there are 20, subdivided into 103 provinces: Piedmont, Lombardy, Veneto, Liguria, Emilia-Romagna, Tuscany, Umbria, The Marches, Latium, Abruzzi, Molise, Campania, Puglia, Basilicata, and Calabria, **Sicily**, **Sardinia**, Trentino-Alto Adige, Friuli-Venezia Giulia, and the Valle d'Aosta. The last five are accorded semiautonomous status. Note that Sicily and Sardinia are islands; the other "special status" regions are border regions with large non-Italian-speaking **minorities**.

At the close of **World War II**, General de Gaulle's government in France sought to make good its territorial claims against Italy by occupying the Val d'Aosta and parts of Piedmont. Anglo-American counterpressure, including President Harry S. Truman's threat to halt aid to France, obliged de Gaulle to withdraw, whereupon the Italian government announced that the Valdostani would have some administrative autonomy and that public schools would be instituted in which French would be the language of instruction.

The **World War I** settlements had included Austria's cession of the provinces of Trento (predominantly Italian-speaking) and Bolzano (Süd Tirol or Alto Adige), which is predominantly German-speaking. **Benito Mussolini**'s government had sought to Italianize both Val d'Aosta and Alto Adige by the selective assignment of teachers and other civil servants, investment policy, and labor transfers. In 1939, Adolf Hitler and Mussolini agreed to allow the local German-speaking population in Alto Adige, which was to be recognized as "forever Italian," to choose, in a plebiscite, between being Italian or being German. Those choosing the latter option were to be transferred to the Third Reich. Others would accept Italianization. Of the nearly 267,000 voting, over 185,000 (nearly 70 percent) voted to go to Germany. The onset of World War II interrupted the transfer of such a large number of persons. When Italy surrendered to the Allies in 1943, many German speakers were still in Alto Adige, which Germany quickly annexed. When the region was returned to Italy, two-thirds of the region's population was—and remains—ethnically German. On 5 September, Prime Minister **Alcide De Gasperi**, who was himself from the Trentino, signed agreements with the Austrian government (the De Gasperi-Gruber Accord) guaranteeing the administrative, cultural, and economic autonomy of Alto Adige. Thus, two years before the Constitution created "special status," both Val d'Aosta and Trentino-Alto Adige had acquired that status.

Each of the 20 regions, according to the enabling legislation passed by the **Parliament**, is governed by a legislative body (the Regional Council), which elects from among its members both the executive *Giunta* (cabinet) and the region's president, who "represents the Region; promulgates regional laws and regulations; directs the administrative functions delegated by the State to the Region, in conformity with the instructions issued by the central government." The better to ensure that conformity, the Constitution also calls for a resident commissioner to reside in the regional capital, whose duty is to "supervise the administrative functions of the State and ensure their coordination with those exercised by the Region." That commissioner must countersign all regional legislative acts "within 30 days." These regional entities were brought into existence only in 1970, 22 years after the Constitution called for them. Earlier attempts to implement the devolution to the regions of the powers exercised by the central government ran afoul of what, for the dominant **Democrazia Cristiana**/Christian Democracy Party (DC), was an unacceptable reality: that such a reform would add to the power of the **Partito Comunista Italiano**/Italian Communist Party (PCI) in the "Red Belt" of central Italy.

It was not until 1977 that the strength of the left could be applied to the question of regional devolution. The regions were given a measure of financial autonomy, especially in health care and city planning. The great divergences found in the success with which the gains in regional autonomy are utilized to the advantage of the citizenry have been the subject of a major study, which has concluded that those regions with a strong tradition of civic order are quicker to organize, to utilize the funds provided by the state, and to monitor expenditures.

Since the 1990s, the political success of the **Lega Nord**/Northern League (LN) has put the whole question of greater regional powers onto the agenda. The center-left responded in 2000 by passing a somewhat half-hearted constitutional reform that reinforced the powers of the president of the region and allowed the regions to rewrite their own statutes and lay down the nature of their institutions and electoral laws for themselves. The regions are also being allowed to keep a greater share of sales tax revenues and become more self-financing. A state-regions coordination committee has also been introduced to improve policy making and to involve the regions at an earlier stage. These reforms were not enough for the Lega, which insisted during the 2001–2006 administration of the **Casa delle Libertà**/House of Freedoms upon a constitutional reform to give substantial powers over health care, the **police**, and **education** to the regions. The League also wanted the Senate to be turned into a chamber representing the regions. A major constitutional reform was eventually passed but was rejected by a resounding 61–39 percent majority in a **referendum** held in June 2006. *See also* ALPS; BATTISTI, CESARE; DIALECTS; IRREDENTISM; SÜD TIROL VOLKSPARTEI; TRIESTE.

REPUBBLICA SOCIALE ITALIANA/Italian Social Republic (RSI). *See* SALÒ, REPUBLIC OF.

REPUBLICAN PARTY. *See* PARTITO REPUBBLICANO ITALIANO (PRI).

RERUM NOVARUM. The *Rerum Novarum* was the key statement of the Catholic Church's social doctrine and its response to the rising challenge of socialism. It was promulgated by Pope Leo XIII on 15 May 1891. The attitude to social and economic questions of both the **Partito Popolare Italiano**/Italian Popular Party (PPI) and its successor, the **Democrazia Cristiana**/Christian Democracy (DC), has been based on this papal encyclical.

The *Rerum Novarum* starts from the premise that the masses endure "truly miserable conditions, unworthy of human dignity." The encyclical goes on, however, to insist that socialism "is unacceptable to the workers" since the purpose of work is the ownership of private property, which socialism seeks to abolish and which is anyway sanctioned by divine law. Socialism is also depicted as the enemy of the family. Socialism, in short, is "harmful for society itself." It breeds class hatred, and its statist ideology is unnatural.

The "right remedy" proposed by the *Rerum Novarum* is one in keeping with the teachings of Christ, of respect for the poor (though with the conviction that human inequality is part of the divine order of things), and the obligation to be charitable. More to the point, however, the encyclical envisages state action, "in perfect harmony with Catholic doctrine," to "take necessary steps to ensure the welfare of the workers" since this is both good Christian doctrine and the best way of ensuring that the workers do not "attempt other ways to salvation." Leo recommends **cooperatives** as an ideal form of private enterprise; paragraph 40 of the encyclical seems much less sure that **trade unions** are beneficial: Catholic workers, the *Rerum Novarum* says, must choose between enrolling in organizations "dangerous to religion" or founding their own associations to free themselves from the "unjust and intolerable repression" that unions represent. *See also* CATHOLICISM; GENTILONI PACT.

RESISTANCE. The collapse of **Benito Mussolini**'s regime and the subsequent German invasion of Italy led Italy's antifascist forces to organize partisan activity (sabotage, ambushes, and attacks on Fascist sympathizers) throughout occupied Italy. Initially, this activity was largely spontaneous, with the so-called GAP (gruppi armati patriottici) carrying out sporadic actions. During 1944, however, on the initiative of the **Comitati di Liberazione Nazionale**/National Liberation Committees (CLN), resistance became more systematic. The political parties organized their volunteers in separate brigades (the Garibaldi brigade for the communists and the Justice and Liberty brigade for the **Partito d'Azione**/Action Party [PdA]), and partisan activity was coordinated from June 1944 by an underground military command presided over by a regular army general, Raffaele Cadorna, and two men who would become key figures in postwar politics, **Luigi Longo** and **Ferruccio Parri**. In all some 300,000 Italians (including more than 30,000 **women**) are calculated to have taken part in partisan activity. Tens of thousands of them were killed: The accepted figure is approximately 45,000, including 4,000 women. The resistance proved able to inflict major damage on the German army's operations. In the spring of 1945 partisans liberated all the major cities of northern Italy before Allied troops could intervene. Partisans caught and killed Mussolini on 27 April 1945. Allied Commander General Harold Alexander ordered the demobilization of partisan bands on 2 May 1945.

The heroic actions of many partisan groups are a source of deep national pride for Italy. Many Italians regard the resistance as being the experience that enabled Italy to forge a genuine democracy after **World War II**. The scars of the struggle were deep, however. The Nazis and their Fascist accomplices committed more than 400 massacres of unarmed civilians during the German occupation. The worst such massacres were at the Ardeatine caves (March 1944) in **Rome**, where German soldiers shot 335 political prisoners as a reprisal for a partisan attack on German troops; at Saint Anna di Stazzema in Tuscany, where 560 civilians were killed in August 1944; and at Marzotto, near **Bologna**, in September 1944, where 1,836 men, women, and children were slaughtered as a reprisal for partisan raids.

The resistance was also a civil war. Many Italians continued to support the **Republic of Salò**, and the combat between the neofascist squads and the partisans was without quarter. After the end of the conflict, the hatreds and ideological tensions generated by the Nazi occupation spilled over into ruthless reprisal killings of former Fascists. Hundreds of such individuals, including many priests, were murdered in the immediate postwar months, and violence against suspected former Fascists, or even rival partisan groups, occurred until the end of the 1940s. The postwar massacres are a highly controversial subject in contemporary Italian historiography. *See also* BOBBIO, NORBERTO; FLORENCE; NEOREALISM; PERTINI, ALESSANDRO; ROSSELLINI, ROBERTO.

RETE, LA (The Network). A political movement of pronounced progressive sympathies, La Rete provided a political vehicle for the social and civic activism of many thousands of mostly young people who were already involved in voluntary, church, and local associations against scourges such as the **mafia**, unemployment, urban degradation, and political corruption.

La Rete was officially founded in January 1991. Its first leader— or, more accurately, "national coordinator"—was the former mayor of **Palermo**, **Leoluca Orlando**, who had left the **Democrazia Cristiana**/Christian Democracy Party (DC) the previous year after the party hierarchy insisted that he should govern in conjunction with the party's national allies and should abandon the heterogeneous local coalition of progressives supporting his administration. Palermo has ever since been the heart of La Rete's support, but the new movement took root in other cities where there were strong traditions of urban activism and Christian socialism, notably **Milan**, **Turin**, and the Trentino. From the very beginning, La Rete attempted to renounce all the traditional forms of party organization, allowing the maximum possible local autonomy for the small self-financed cells of citizens who constitute its membership.

In the 1992 general elections, La Rete obtained over 700,000 votes—2 percent of the electorate—despite the fact that it did not run candidates throughout the country, but only in areas where it had some semblance of local organization.

La Rete failed to fulfill its promise, however. Anxious not to be wiped out by a change in the **electoral laws**, it reneged on its earlier commitment to abolish the proportional system of parliamentary representation during the referendum on the question in April 1993. In the June 1993 local elections, the party headed broad leftist coalitions in Turin, Milan, and Catania. Despite the favorable circumstances (the elections were held shortly after **Giulio Andreotti** and other DC leaders were accused of links to the mafia), all three of its candidates lost, a defeat that was only partially remedied by Orlando's triumphant reelection—by a 75 percent plurality—as mayor of Palermo in a second round of local elections in November 1993.

La Rete fought the 1994 election as part of the progressive coalition headed by the **Partito Democratico della Sinistra**/Democratic Party of the Left (PDS). It was unexpectedly overtaken in **Sicily** by **Forza Italia** and did not advance beyond the 2 percent of the national vote it had obtained in 1992. In 1999, La Rete merged with the Democratici per Prodi, and most of its former activists are now to be found in **Democrazia e Libertà**/Democracy and Liberty (DL).

REVOLUTIONS OF 1848. Even by the turbulent standards of the "year of revolutions," Italy endured a period of exceptional upheaval in 1848–1849. Tension had been building throughout 1847. Poor harvests, the liberal reformism of Pius IX, and resentment at the heavy taxes levied by the Austrians (which gave rise to the so-called smokers' strike in Lombardy in January 1848) all contributed to a favorable climate of opinion for a revolt against absolutism. The catalyst for revolution was the successful revolt of the people of **Palermo** and **Naples** in January 1848, which compelled Ferdinand II to concede a constitutional monarchy, and then the French Revolution of February, which ignited public opinion in Berlin and Vienna, where Klemens von Metternich himself was deposed by a popular insurrection on 13 March.

The first stage of revolutionary activity in Italy was liberal and constitutionalist. As soon as news of the downfall of Metternich reached **Milan**, Lombardy and **Venice** rose in revolt against the Austrians in March 1848. During the "five glorious days" (18–23 March 1848), the Milanese drove the Austrians from the city. In Venice, the people seized power and hoisted the tricolor, declaring a republic. Insurrections broke out in **Bologna**, Parma, Piacenza, and other northern Italian cities. Against the wishes of some of their most influential leaders, the cities and republics of northern Italy voted to unify themselves with Piedmont-**Sardinia**, which declared war on Austria in March after already having adopted a liberal Constitution. Defeat at Custoza was followed by an armistice with the Austrians and the reoccupation of Milan by General Joseph Radetzky's forces.

The reoccupation of Milan only inflamed the peninsula further. The peoples of the Papal States, angered by Pius IX's tacit support for Austria, rose in revolt in **Rome** in November and imposed on the pope a government of pronounced liberal sympathies. On 24 November, Pius IX fled to Naples (where Ferdinand and the forces of reaction had bloodily regained control). The revolt in Rome, and similar uprisings in **Florence**, Livorno (Leghorn), and **Genoa**, were explicitly republican and democratic—even socialist—in tone. In Rome, the liberal government appointed by the pope lasted but a few days. On 21–22 January 1849, free elections by universal male suffrage were held, and on 9 February Rome became a republic. Church property was confiscated, public workshops and housing were provided, and certain taxes were abolished. **Giuseppe Mazzini** arrived in Rome in March 1849 and was swiftly given dictatorial power.

Papal authority was restored in Rome by the French army. Louis Napoleon, anxious to curry favor with French Catholics, sent an expeditionary force of 10,000 men to Italy in April 1849. Led by **Giuseppe Garibaldi**, the Romans mounted a spirited resistance, and it was only after reinforcements arrived from Naples and Spain, and a month of destructive bombardment, that the city surrendered to the French at the beginning of July 1849. Venice was the last bastion of revolution to fall: It eventually surrendered to General Radetzky after a bloody siege on 23 August 1849. *See also* PAPACY.

RICASOLI, BETTINO (1809–1880). A wealthy Tuscan landowner who delighted in experimenting with modern techniques in agriculture, Ricasoli took an equally earnest interest in promoting Italian unification. His first venture in this direction was the publication of a newspaper, *La Patria (The Motherland)*, in 1847. He was an active organizer of the Italian National Society in Tuscany and in 1859–1860 emerged as one of the leaders of the Florentine nationalists. **Florence** rose in support of the Kingdom of Piedmont-Sardinia in April 1859, and Ricasoli was appointed minister of the interior for Tuscany by the representative of the Sardinian throne, Count Carlo Boncompagni, who was voted dictatorial powers for the duration of the war.

After the peace of Villafranca in July 1859, Ricasoli took the lead in ensuring that ducal rule was not restored in Tuscany and guided the plebiscite in March 1860 by which Tuscany voted to join the Kingdom of Sardinia. His success in this endeavor made him a political figure of national standing, and when **Camillo Benso di Cavour** died unexpectedly in June 1861, **King Victor Emmanuel II** turned to the energetic and dignified Ricasoli as a replacement.

Ricasoli thus became prime minister on 12 June and reserved for himself the portfolios of foreign and interior minister. He soon won the nickname "the Iron Baron." His government initiated a policy of fierce repression in **southern Italy**, where disgruntled peasants were in revolt, and established a highly centralized form of local government in October 1861. In February 1862, Ricasoli lost the confidence of the king and was replaced by **Urbano Rattazzi**. He was out of power until June 1866, when he became prime minister on the day of the outbreak of war with Austria. Ricasoli's second premiership was dominated by the dismal performance of the Italian army and fleet, which were defeated at the battles of Custoza and Lissa, respectively, and by the decision to block **Giuseppe Garibaldi**'s advance in the Trentino for political reasons. Ricasoli also ordered the savage repression of a popular uprising against the monarchy in **Palermo** in September 1866. Hundreds of rebels were shot and thousands arrested, and much of **Sicily** was put under martial law until December.

In February 1867, Ricasoli's government was defeated in **Parliament** over the question of relations with the Church. The king asked Ricasoli to form a new government, but after elections in March 1867, he resigned once more and never again held high office. *See also* RISORGIMENTO.

RIFONDAZIONE COMUNISTA. *See* PARTITO DI RIFONDAZIONE COMUNISTA (PRC).

RISORGIMENTO. In Italian, the Risorgimento means the awakening of national sentiment that led to the creation of the modern Italian state. The decisive moment for Italian political unity was the wars of 1859–1861. Thanks to a felicitous combination of international and domestic factors and skillful diplomacy, Italy was substantially united under the rule of the House of Savoy. First, the international context was favorable for the reduction of Austrian power in Italy. Austria had isolated itself during the Crimean War by staying neutral and was facing France's challenge to its role as the power broker in Europe. Liberal England, moreover, wished to see the end of the anachronistic absolutist regime of the Bourbons in **southern Italy**. Within Italy, Piedmont-**Sardinia**, thanks to the modernizing efforts of **Camillo Benso di Cavour**, had emerged as a power of some weight capable of attracting the middle classes of Lombardy, Tuscany, and the rest of northern Italy to its cause. Liberal and nationalist ideas, moreover, were widespread by the end of the 1850s. The views of **Vincenzo Gioberti**, **Cesare Balbo**, and **Massimo D'Azeglio** had been read by every educated Italian, and republicans and democrats such as **Carlo Cattaneo** and **Giuseppe Mazzini** also had a substantial following, particularly in **central Italy**.

Cavour's unique diplomatic skills turned these favorable conditions into political action. First, he persuaded Napoleon III to ally France to Piedmont in July 1858 at Plombières by promising France Nice and the duchies of central Italy (the eventual status of Savoy was left open) in exchange for French assistance to liberate Lombardy and Venetia from Austrian rule. The four northern Italian regions so liberated were then to form a federation under the presidency of the Pope. Cavour then goaded Austria into declaring war in April 1859, allowing Piedmont-Sardinia to appear as the innocent

victim of an act of aggression by a larger power. As the bloody battles of Magenta and Solferino demonstrated, without French support
the Piedmontese army would never have been able to defeat the Austrians. Simultaneous insurrections in Tuscany, Modena, and Parma
in favor of unification with **Turin** were in large part organized by
Cavour's agents, thus nullifying the Plombières agreement by thwart-
ing Napoleon III's ambitions. The peace of Villafranca in July
1859—which granted Lombardy to Piedmont but insisted on the return of absolute rule in **central Italy**—was a tardy attempt
by Napoleon and the Austrians to close the Pandora's box opened by
their own ambition. The treaty provoked Cavour's resignation, but
by now the movement for unification with Piedmont in central Italy
was too strong to be blocked by anything short of a bloody war of repression. Cavour returned triumphantly to office in January 1860
and, in exchange for the cession of Savoy as well as Nice to France,
was allowed to incorporate all of north-central Italy into Piedmont-
Sardinia.

Mazzini and **Giuseppe Garibaldi** regarded Cavour's patient
diplomacy as too cautious, however. At the beginning of 1860, the
so-called Action Party was founded with the specific goal of liberating **Rome**, **Venice**, and **southern Italy** from absolutist and Papal
rule. In April 1860, Garibaldi and his "Thousand" redshirts sailed
from **Genoa** to **Palermo** to assist the Mazzinian uprising that had
broken out against Bourbon rule. With the assistance of the British
fleet, Garibaldi disembarked and swiftly established his personal dictatorship over **Sicily**. In August 1860, he crossed the Strait of
Messina at the head of an army of Sicilians and marched on **Naples**,
which he entered in September without encountering resistance. He
was joined by Mazzini and Cattaneo, who openly argued that the redshirts' conquests should herald a democratic and republican solution
to the unification of Italy.

Cavour, alarmed by this project, used the threat of a democratic
revolution in Italy to persuade France to give him a free hand in
southern Italy. Piedmontese troops invaded the Papal States and
blocked Garibaldi's road to **Rome**, and at Teano on 26 October 1860,
Garibaldi ceded his conquests in person to **Victor Emmanuel II**.
This decision was confirmed by regional plebiscites in February
1861. Only the wealthiest citizens were allowed to vote, and, partic-

ularly in the south, ballot fraud was widespread. Italy had completed its liberal revolution but had installed a regime that was ignorant of the needs of the southern peasantry and strongly identified with the interests of the northern upper classes. It is not fanciful to claim that many of Italy's subsequent problems stemmed from the political settlement of the process of unification. *See also* MONARCHY.

ROCCO, ALFREDO (1875–1935). Rocco, a legal scholar from **Naples** who had been one of the leading lights of the Italian nationalist movement, became one of the foremost ideologues of **Fascism**. In 1918, he began publishing *La Politica*, a review in which he articulated the classic precept of the supremacy of the state over the individual. Elected president of the Chamber of Deputies after the 1924 elections, he held that position throughout the crisis provoked by the murder of **Giacomo Matteotti** before, in January 1925, becoming minister of justice. In this post, his first duty was to introduce a law banning secretive associations such as the Freemasons. **Antonio Gramsci** made his only parliamentary speech in opposition, illustrating that the law gave the government the power to ban opposition associations of any kind. This measure was a prelude to Rocco's drastic measures dissolving all opposition parties, reintroducing the death penalty, and instituting special tribunals for political activity in October 1926.

In 1928, Rocco was responsible both for the new electoral law, with its plebiscitary character, and the law that precisely defined the role and functions of the **Fascist Grand Council** and transformed it from a party body to an organ of the state. Rocco capped his spell at the justice ministry by introducing new penal codes in 1930–1931. These included the Testo Unico di Pubblica Sicurezza (Consolidated Public Security Laws), still in force in postfascist Italy. Generally, they were intended to enshrine Rocco's fundamental principle of jurisprudence—the priority of collective institutions over individual rights and the primacy of the monolithic state above all other institutions of any kind. Rocco opposed the **Lateran pacts** in 1929 because he believed that they would weaken the power of the state.

Rocco also played a key role in the creation of **corporatism**. In 1926, he wrote the Labor Charter, which prohibited strikes and effectively closed down all trade unions except the fascist Confederazione Italiana

Sindacati Nazionali Lavoratori/Italian Confederation of National Workers' Unions (CISNAL). When the Ministry of Corporations was created in 1926, he was called on to head it since corporatism was the institutional core of the entire Fascist system. He also headed the subsequent (1930) Consiglio Nazionale delle Corporazioni (National Council of Corporations) to which all workers' syndicates were automatically attached. At the time of his death in 1935, he was rector of the University of **Rome**.

ROME (Roma). Probably no other city has been so central for the development of European civilization as Rome. The city's modern history has been characterized by its unique role as the dual capital of both world **Catholicism** and the secular Italian state. Between 1798, when the short-lived Roman republic was formed, and 1870, when Italian troops occupied the town and made the "eternal city" the capital of the new Italian state, Rome's status as the capital of the Papal States was a perennial source of internal and international tension. In 1849, a second Roman Republic fought heroically against French troops, who eventually restored the city to the pope; in 1861 and 1867, the French again ensured that papal authority over the city remained intact. Only when the French were defeated by Germany in 1870 was the Italian army able to enter Rome through Porta Pia. Memorialists recall that from the window sills along the entry route, Piedmontese flags with the heraldic symbol of the House of Savoy suddenly appeared in place of the theretofore ubiquitous white and gold of the papal banner. Cries of "Long Live the King!" and "Long Live Italy!" accompanied the fanfares of **Bersaglieri** bands. A provincial plebiscite held two weeks later resulted in 133,681 votes in favor of annexation and only 1,507 opposed. The probability of becoming the national capital had an immeasurable influence on that electoral outcome. Rome became the capital of Italy in 1871, and Pope Pius IX declared himself to be a prisoner in the **Vatican** and began a period of tension between the secular state and the Church that lasted until the 1929 signature of the **Lateran pacts**.

Rome's population expanded greatly after it became capital. Only 244,000 in 1870, it had reached 1.6 million by 1931 and over 2,000,000 by the early 1960s. Huge new suburbs were built, the most important of which, from the architectural point of view, is EUR (Esposizione

Universale di Roma), designed by the urbanist and architect **Marcello Piacentini** between 1938 and 1942 and constructed after the war.

Rome suffered much less than many other Italian cities during **World War II**. It fell to the Allies on 4 June 1944, and became the seat of the provisional government. This does not mean that the war was without its costs for the people of the city. On 23 March 1944, Roman partisans bombed a truckload of German guards, killing 32 soldiers. For each dead German, the outraged commander had 10 prisoners (starting with Jews) killed in the Ardeatine caves. Although the entrance to the caves was blown up and sealed after the massacre, witnesses were aware of what had been done, and the site was uncovered within a month. It is today the site of an annual commemoration ceremony. The German officer in charge, Erich Priebke, was extradited and placed on trial for war crimes in 1996.

Rome hosted the Olympics in 1960 and the final of the World Cup in 1990. In 2000, the Catholic Church held a rare Jubilee that brought millions of pilgrims to the city from all over the world. The relationship between the secular state and the Vatican remains a core concern even today. Rome is, however, the center of Italian political life (all the principal parties have their headquarters in Rome except for the **Lega Nord**/Northern League [LN]). In recent years, the city administration has made notable strides in protecting and valorizing Rome's unique architectural and artistic heritage, and the city, which not so long ago was a symbol of bureaucratic inefficiency and urban decline, is now enjoying something of a cultural and economic boom. Rome is the only **southern Italian** city able to match the wealthy towns of the North in terms of income per capita.

ROSI, FRANCESCO (1922–). Born in **Naples** a month after the **March on Rome**, Francesco Rosi is a film director whose work has combined a high degree of political commitment with a remarkable capacity to portray the full gamut of personal emotions in the characters of his films (Rosi has always invariably been his own scriptwriter). His first critical hit was *I magliari* (*The Confidence Tricksters*, 1959), which starred the Roman actor Alberto Sordi. His three finest works are widely held to be *Mani sulla città* (*Hands on the City*, 1963), *Cadaveri eccellenti* (*Illustrious Corpses*, 1976) and *Tre Fratelli* (*Three Brothers*, 1981). The first of these, which deals with the speculative building boom of the 1960s in Naples and its human and urban costs, caused a major political row when it appeared. The second is a cinematic rendition of **Leonardo Sciascia**'s novel of the same name; Rosi brilliantly shows the protagonist, Inspector Rogas, in his progress toward the truth about a series of political killings—a truth that we never discover because Rogas and the secretary of the "Revolutionary Party" are themselves assassinated in the last scene. As a parable for the many mysterious political killings endured by postwar Italy, the film (and the book) is unparalled. Rosi had earlier done a docudrama about the life (and mysterious death) of **Enrico Mattei**.

By contrast, *Tre Fratelli*, which deals with the issue of terrorism in the 1970s, is based on a simple device. Three brothers return home for the funeral of their peasant father. The eldest (Philippe Noiret) is a senior magistrate active in the fight against the **Brigate Rosse**/Red Brigades (BR) and is permanently at risk of being killed or wounded in his job; the second (Vittorio Mezzogiorno) is a deeply religious social worker, who dreams that Italy's woes can be cured by love; and the third (Michele Placido) is a factory worker and activist in **Lotta Continua**. The film explores the three brothers' attitudes toward Italy's problems via flashbacks, dreams, and intense political discussion and yet remains a deeply moving threnody to the Italian family. The film is also of great visual beauty. Rosi's last major feature film was *La Tregua* (*The Truce*, 1996), a rendition of **Primo Levi**'s book about his return from Auschwitz. *See also* CINEMA.

ROSSELLI, CARLO (1899–1937) and NELLO (1900–1937). Antifascist martyrs, the Rosselli brothers were two of the bravest and most intellectually sophisticated leaders of the struggle against **Benito Mussolini**. Born in **Rome** to a wealthy Jewish family from Tuscany, the brothers were brought up in **Florence**, which in the early 1920s was the scene of some of the worst acts of *squadrismo* in Italy. Greatly influenced by **Gaetano Salvemini** and **Piero Gobetti**, Carlo, when a professor of political economy at the University of **Genoa**, was among the organizers of a "cultural circle" for the propagation of democratic ideas and free thought, which was shut down in Florence by Fascist bullies in December 1924. Beaten—literally—but not bowed, the brothers, together with Salvemini, printed and distributed a subversive leaflet, *Non Mollare!* (*Don't Give Up!*) in 1925 and participated in the escape from Italy of Filippo Turati and Salvemini. Carlo was arrested and sentenced to five years' imprisonment on the island of Lipari in 1927, but he managed to escape in 1929. In 1930 he published, in Paris, his most important work, *Il Socialismo liberale* (*Liberal Socialism*), a book that was not only antifascist but critical of the authoritarian tendencies of Soviet communism and a plea for a form of socialism founded on liberal principles of human rights. *Socialismo liberale* was secretly distributed within Italy and made Carlo the undisputed leader of the clandestine organization known as **Giustizia e Libertà**. Carlo Rosselli, in fact, can be regarded as the principal influence on the young intellectuals who would later form the **Partito d'Azione**/Action Party (PdA) and occupy an important place in all the most important parties of the left and center after 1945.

Carlo did not restrict his antifascist activity to theorizing. In 1936, he organized a column of Italian antifascist volunteers and served in the **Spanish Civil War**. Struck down by illness, he returned to Paris, where he was joined by Nello, who in the meantime had become a prominent historian of the **Risorgimento** and had seen the inside of several Fascist jails. In June 1937, the two brothers were stabbed to death by a group of French hoodlums hired by the Fascists; it has since been established that Mussolini gave the order for the brothers' murder.

ROSSELLINI, ROBERTO (1906–1977). Regarded by many as Italy's greatest film director, Rossellini made his international reputation with a depiction of the **resistance** to the Nazi occupation, *Roma, città aperta* (*Open City*, 1945). Shot on location in war-torn Rome, using a jumble of film types and with a cast of largely unprofessional actors, the film tells the story of the unsuccessful attempt of an underground leader, Manfredi, to elude the Gestapo. Manfredi is helped by a defiant group of Roman workers and by a Catholic priest, Don Pietro. Both Manfredi and Don Pietro are captured and tortured. In the moving final scene, Don Pietro is shot by a firing squad. Yet the message of the film is one of hope. From a distance, the children from Don Pietro's church in the slums witness his brave death and walk down the hill from the place of execution to a city that will be theirs. The film is notable also for the performance of a brilliant actress, Anna Magnani, who plays the resourceful Pina, a pregnant slum woman who works, feeds a family, and aids the resistance with courage and good humor. The scene in which Pina is shot by the German soldiers who had arrested her lover is one of the most evocative images in the history of the **cinema**.

Rossellini continued to work in the neorealist idiom, producing the classic films *Paisà* (*Paisan*, 1947) and *Germania, anno zero* (*Germany, Year Zero*, 1947). But *Stromboli, terra di Dio* (*Stromboli*, 1949) was criticized both by neorealist critics, for its unsympathetic portrayal of the Stromboli peasants and for its unabashed religious content, and by the Church, which regarded the film as the product of sin (the film starred Ingrid Bergman, with whom Rossellini had an affair and whom he married after she divorced her Swedish husband).

Rossellini's break with **neorealism** came in 1953 when he directed *Viaggio in Italia* (*Journey to Italy*), a film about a prudish English couple whose relationship is threatened by the emotions they experience upon visiting **Naples**. The film's overt religious content and taxing longeurs were excoriated in Italy. In France, however, Rossellini's film, and all his subsequent work in the 1950s and 1960s, was greatly admired by both critics and filmmakers, especially Godard and Truffaut.

Rossellini returned to popular and critical favor in Italy only in 1959, with *Il generale della Rovere* (*General Della Rovere*, 1959). Starring **Vittorio De Sica**, this story about a confidence trickster hired by the German occupiers to discover the identity of a resistance leader, but who ultimately rejects his paymasters and dies a hero's death, won the Golden Lion at the **Venice** Film Festival and was a huge commercial success. In the 1960s, Rossellini was one of the first directors to experiment with the new medium of television. Between 1966 and 1973, he made a series of masterful historical dramas as well as a number of documentaries. When he died in 1977, he was regarded as one of the most original figures in the history of film.

RUBBIA, CARLO (1934–). A scientist from Gorizia, on the border with Slovenia, Carlo Rubbia won the Nobel Prize in Physics in 1984. A graduate of the elite Scuola Normale di Pisa (although he was unsuccessful in his original application and was admitted only after another student dropped out), Rubbia has done most of his scientific research abroad; indeed, he has been publicly very critical of the Italian state's support for young scientists. He began his work on the structure of "weak interactions" at Columbia University, and his main scientific research has been done at Harvard University, where he was professor between 1971 and 1988, and at the Conseil Européen pour la Recerche Nucléare/European Center for Nuclear Research (CERN) in Geneva (Switzerland).

As Rubbia's Nobel autobiography states, at CERN in the early 1980s he suggested "transforming an existing high energy accelerator into a colliding beam device in which a beam of protons and of antiprotons, their antimatter twins, [were] counter-rotating and colliding head on." The result of this insight was the discovery of W and Z particles. Rubbia and his collaborator, Simon van der Meer, shared the Nobel Prize just two years after these discoveries, one of the quickest-ever awards of the prize.

Rubbia was director-general of CERN from 1989 to 1993, and in 1994 he became director of the International Center for Theoretical Physics in **Trieste**, near his hometown of Gorizia. He was director of the Ente per le Nuove Tecnologie, l'Energia e l'Ambiente (ENEA), the Italian state entity for the development of new technologies and for environmental science, between 1999 and 2005. This appointment terminated in July 2005 when Rubbia made his most devastating critique to date of political interference in the management of Italian science.

RUGGIERO, RENATO (1930–). An internationally respected diplomat who has been an important figure in Italian **foreign policy** since the 1960s, Ruggiero was born in **Naples** in April 1930. He took a law degree and then passed into the diplomatic service, working in the Moscow embassy at the height of the "thaw" and in Washington during the Cuban missile crisis. Ruggiero became ambassador to Belgrade in 1966. In 1969, he became part of the permanent Italian mission at the European Community (EC) in Brussels, and in June 1970, when an Italian, **Franco Maria Malfatti**, was appointed President of the European Commission, Ruggiero became chief of Malfatti's cabinet. Malfatti did not last long in the job, but Ruggiero played a crucial role in many of the EC's key decisions in the 1970s. He was involved in the negotiations that led to British entry in the EC (in 1980, he was awarded an honorary baronetcy for his friendship to Britain) and served as director general for regional policy, one of the most important jobs in Brussels. In 1977, he became official spokesman for Roy Jenkins, the president of the European Commission.

Ruggiero returned to Rome in 1978 and occupied a series of senior roles in Italian diplomacy, including being diplomatic advisor to **Giulio Andreotti**. Between 1985 and 1987, he reached the peak of the foreign ministry hierarchy, becoming Secretary General of the Ministry for Foreign Affairs—in effect, he was Italy's chief diplomat. At this point in his career Ruggiero passed into politics, becoming minister for trade for four years (1987–1991). In 1995, he was elected director general of the newly constituted World Trade Organization (WTO), which he directed, with some aplomb, for four years. In June 2001, he was nominated foreign minister by **Silvio Berlusconi**, but Ruggiero, as the quintessential insider in international organizations, was visibly uneasy with the anti-Europeanist rhetoric of the **Lega Nord**/Northern League (LN) and with the dilettantism of much of the government. He resigned after only six months in the job in January 2002. Since 2002, Ruggiero has worked in international banking. *See also* EUROPEAN INTEGRATION.

RUMOR, MARIANO (1915–1990). Benjamin Disraeli's observation that becoming prime minister is much like climbing a greasy pole is well illustrated by Mariano Rumor. One of many Christian Democrats to serve as premier, he reached the pinnacle by devoted service to the party. A high school teacher who was active on the provincial **Comitato di Liberazione Nazionale**/National Liberation Committee (CLN) in his native Vicenza after 8 September 1943, he served his party at both the national and local levels. Elected to the **Constituent Assembly** in 1946 and subsequently to **Parliament** in every election until his death, Rumor was also vice secretary of the **Democrazia Cristiana**/Christian Democracy Party (DC) in 1950–1951 and again between 1954 and 1958.

His first ministerial appointment was as deputy secretary in the Ministry of Agriculture under **Alcide De Gasperi** (1951) and **Giuseppe Pella** in 1954. One of the leading lights of the centrist *doroteo* faction, he became a fixture in subsequent DC administrations until, in December 1968, he became **president of the Council of Ministers** in his own right, a post he retained until August 1970, heading three different coalitions. His period as prime minister was characterized by both intricate political maneuvering within the DC and growing social tensions and political violence in Italy. His government did, however, pass the enabling legislation that authorized the holding of **referendums** and instituted a regional layer of government.

Rumor returned to the premiership in July 1973, and his administration lasted, in two incarnations, until November 1974. In these years, public dissatisfaction with the DC's corruption and misrule came to a head. Rumor was subsequently implicated personally in the Lockheed bribery scandal (which forced President **Giovanni Leone** to resign before his term had expired) but was exonerated by Parliament in 1978. The following year, he was elected to the Italian Senate and was reelected in 1983 and 1987. He died in **Rome** in 1990. *See also* REGIONALISM; TAMBRONI, FERNANDO.

RUTELLI, FRANCESCO (1954–). Currently deputy prime minister and minister for cultural heritage in the government elected in April 2006 and headed by **Romano Prodi**, Francesco Rutelli is one of the most prominent figures in contemporary Italian politics. Despite his relative youth, he has had a turbulent and lengthy political career. He entered politics as a member of the **Partito Radicale**/Radical Party (PR) in the 1970s and made his name in the PR's battles to liberalize the **divorce** and abortion laws. In 1981, he became leader of the PR and was elected to the Chamber of Deputies in 1983. An ardent **environmentalist**, Rutelli passed to the Verdi (Greens) in the late 1980s and became national coordinator of the Federazione dei Verdi/Green Federation in 1992. In April 1993, he was nominated to be minister of the environment by **Carlo Azeglio Ciampi**, but he resigned, along with the ministers nominated by the **Partito Democratico della Sinistra**/Democratic Party of the Left (PDS), after just one day to protest the Chamber of Deputy's decision to deny a judicial request authorizing an investigation into the personal affairs of **Bettino Craxi**.

In December 1993, Rutelli became mayor of his native **Rome**, beating **Gianfranco Fini**, the national secretary of the **Movimento Sociale Italiano**/Italian Social Movement (MSI), in a run-off. Reelected in 1997, he was a success as mayor, winning plaudits for his exemplary organization of the Papal Jubilee in 2000, when millions of young Catholics descended upon Rome. Rutelli moved toward **Catholicism** in the 1990s, and this, together with his high public profile as mayor, caused the parties of the center-left to prefer him to **Giulio Amato** as their candidate for the prime ministership in the general elections of May 2001. Rutelli lost, but he performed well during the electoral campaign. Rutelli became leader of **Democrazia e Libertà**/Democracy and Liberty (DL) in 2002. Since then, he has been one of the most influential figures in Italian politics.

– S –

SAINT GERMAIN, TREATY OF. The Treaty of Saint Germain between the victorious Allies and Austria was signed on 10 September 1919. The former Austro-Hungarian empire was broken up, and new nations—Czechoslovakia, Hungary, and Yugoslavia—were created. Italy's territorial claims against Austria were one of the thorniest issues in the peace settlement, and the treaty left the Italian public feeling that Italy had been betrayed by its fellow powers. The secret **Treaty of London** (April 1915), which had secured Italian accession to the war on the side of the Entente, and a subsequent deal among the wartime premiers of France, Great Britain, and Italy in April 1917, had promised Italy large gains at the expense of Austria, control over much of the Dalmatian coastline (modern-day Croatia), the Dodecanese Islands, Smyrna in Asia Minor, and colonial compensation.

These exorbitant promises, made at a moment when the Entente powers were desperate to get Italy into the conflict, seemed excessively generous compensation for Italy's contribution once the war was over. Moreover, the United States had entered the war in 1917, and President Woodrow Wilson was determined to shape the postwar peace in accordance with the principle of self-determination of racial minorities. In particular, he was adamant that Italy would not acquire sovereignty over several hundred thousand Slavs in Dalmatia. Despite Italy's representative at Paris, Prime Minister **Vittorio Emanuele Orlando**, walking out of the peace conference in protest, Italy's expectations were cut back sharply. Wilson conceded Italy the

Brenner frontier (ensuring that hundreds of thousands of German nationals were incorporated into Italy) and allowed **Trieste** and Istria, but not Dalmatia, to become Italian territory. Italy also maintained de facto control over the Dodecanese Islands but had to renounce its territorial ambitions in Asia Minor. Cunningly, Britain and France took advantage of Italy's self-imposed exclusion from the conference table to ensure both that Italy was not given any of the former German or Turkish colonies as a "mandate" from the League of Nations and that it was not compensated with territorial gains in Africa.

In objective terms, Italy was not badly treated by the peace settlement. Italy's statesmen, however, had been convinced that the settlement would transform the Mediterranean into an "Italian lake" and that Italy would emerge as one of the indisputably great powers. The disillusionment was therefore enormous, with even moderates denouncing Italy's supposed betrayal at the hands of the other powers. Resentment at the peace settlement enabled **Gabriele D'Annunzio** to seize the town of **Fiume** (which had been given to Yugoslavia) on the Dalmatian coast and fanned the already smoldering flames of nationalism and **Fascism**.

SALANDRA, ANTONIO (1853–1931). Born in the province of Foggia in August 1853, Salandra, a conservative nationalist politician, is chiefly famous for having led Italy into **World War I**. As prime minister from March 1914 to June 1916, he negotiated the **Treaty of London** (April 1915), under the terms of which Italy would join the war on the side of Britain and France. These arrangements were not revealed to **Parliament**, whose members might well have opposed them, and their negotiation required Salandra, and his foreign minister **Sidney Sonnino**, to play a careful double game. With a logic not unlike **Benito Mussolini**'s in 1940, Salandra reckoned that the time had come for Italy to choose (what seemed at the time) the winning side. His subsequent reference to *sacro egoismo* was as ill-timed as it was candid.

Salandra's decision backfired, however. The Austrian army's successful *Strafexpedition*, a spring 1916 attack in the Trentino that exposed the Italian army on the Isonzo front near **Trieste** to the risk of being cut off and forced to surrender, brought Salandra down. Neutralist supporters of **Giovanni Giolitti**, who had never forgiven

388 • SALÒ, REPUBLIC OF

Salandra for his double dealing in 1915, joined forces with Salandra's critics in the prowar camp to bring down the "government of discord." Salandra was replaced by **Paolo Boselli**.

It was only after the war that Salandra again became a candidate for premier. Fascist street violence had forced **Luigi Facta** to recognize his impotence and resign in October 1922. Salandra hoped to head a government including the Fascists. Nationalist leaders recommended that Mussolini accept such an arrangement, but the Fascist leader held out for nothing less than forming his own government. Only after the publication of documents connecting Mussolini directly with the murder of **Giacomo Matteotti** did Salandra join the opposition, which by then was totally ineffective. Salandra died in Rome in December 1931. *See also* MARCH ON ROME.

SALÒ, REPUBLIC OF. Two weeks after Anglo-American forces landed in **Sicily** (10 July 1943), the **Fascist Grand Council** supported a document submitted by **Dino Grandi** urging the king to retake command of Italian forces and resume "that supreme initiative in making decisions which our institutions attribute to him." The vote was 19 in favor, 7 opposed, and 1 abstention. King **Victor Emanuel III** thereupon ordered **Benito Mussolini**'s arrest and transfer to a prison on the Gran Sasso Mountain in Abruzzo, where he was kept under close guard until he was freed by German glider-borne paratroopers in a daring raid on 12 September.

The king initially chose Marshal **Pietro Badoglio** to head what became a royal-military dictatorship still intent on continuing the war, at least while negotiations with the Allies could proceed. When Italy surrendered on 8 September 1943, the king, Badoglio, and the government fled south to Brindisi by way of Pescara, leaving the army without orders; this proved the final blow to the **monarchy**. Even before Mussolini's rescue from Gran Sasso, several Fascist leaders (**Roberto Farinacci**, Vittorio Mussolini, and Alessandro Pavolini) had announced from East Prussia the creation of a new Fascist government. By 23 September, an ailing Mussolini was installed by the Nazis at the head of a puppet regime at the town of Salò on Lake Garda. He immediately renamed the **Partito Nazionale Fascista**/National Fascist Party (PNF). It was now to be the Partito Repubblicano Fascista/Fascist Republican Party, infuriated with the monarchy and with those Fascists who had voted against Mussolini. A party congress held in nearby Verona 14–16 November 1943, established the new regime's fundamental principles in an 18-point program that announced the end of the monarchy and articulated an ideology that paid lip service at least to the necessity of limiting the power of private capitalism. In January 1944 several members of the Grand Council who had voted against Mussolini were convicted of treason and executed, including Mussolini's son-in-law, **Galeazzo Ciano**.

The true believers who stayed with Mussolini or were conscripted in the North were teamed with German units to function as "order maintainers" and as an antipartisan militia. Anxious to prove their mettle to their diffident German comrades-in-arms, they were responsible for savage acts of repression in Emilia-Romagna and other northern regions.

The Republic of Salò came to a end in the spring of 1945. As Allied forces advanced on both the Tyrrhenian and Adriatic fronts and German General Karl Wolff, in Switzerland, began negotiations with the Allies for the surrender of the German forces in Italy, Mussolini sought to escape to Switzerland, then Austria. Together with his mistress, Clara Petacci, he was apprehended—despite the German uniforms they wore to assist in their escape—and summarily executed by partisans on 28 April 1945.

Most of the Salò survivors returned to their homes and drifted, politically, into the **Movimento Sociale Italiano**/Italian Social Movement (MSI). The MSI's longtime leader, **Giorgio Almirante**, was himself an unashamed supporter of **Fascism**'s final phase. The savagery of the fascist militias left a scar on Italy's conscience, and it is only recently, with the emergence of **Gianfranco Fini**'s "fascism in a double-breasted suit," that the passions aroused by the memory of Salò have begun to subside. *See also* RESISTANCE.

SALVEMINI, GAETANO (1873–1957). Born in Molfetta, near Bari, Salvemini was a historian best known for his work on the French Revolution. He was also a prolific journalist and a liberal-socialist publicist of some importance. Salvemini managed to argue with both the political systems of prefascist Italy and **Fascism** itself.

Salvemini was particularly damning of *trasformismo*. Writing in the magazine *Unità*, of which he was a founder, Salvemini attacked

Giovanni Giolitti for being *il ministro della malavita* (the minister of the criminal underworld) in 1910. It was a view he disavowed only in 1945 in the introductory essay to a study of the Giolittian era.

Salvemini bitterly opposed the war in **Libya** in 1911–1912 and the whole idea that poverty-stricken Italy, unable even to settle its own southern question, should benefit from the absorption of even poorer territories in North Africa. Both an Anglophile and a Francophile, he favored entry into **World War I** on the side of these democratic states, especially after the attack on Belgium. When the question of a Yugoslavian state was raised, Salvemini was among the "renouncers," that is, those who thought that friendly relations with a new state replacing Austria would be beneficial, and therefore it was justifiable to renounce any claims to Dalmatia.

Salvemini became internationally known for his courageous criticism of Fascism. He was the chair of modern history at the University of **Florence** when **Benito Mussolini** came to power but resigned rather than sign the "loyalty oath" required of all state employees (including professors). Together with **Carlo and Nello Rosselli**, he founded in 1925 the antifascist publication *Non Mollare!* (*Don't Give Up!*). He was arrested in June 1925 and after an amnesty was forced to flee to Paris, where he lived as an exile. Salvemini was one of the founders of **Giustizia e Libertà**/Justice and Liberty (GL).

Salvemini subsequently moved to England and, in 1934, to the United States, where he accepted an appointment to Harvard's history department. Two of his books, *The Fascist Dictatorship in Italy* (1928) and especially *Under the Axe of Fascism* (1936), were decisive exposés of Mussolini's rule for a British and American audience. On his return to the University of Florence in 1948, he is said to have opened his first lecture with the words, "Stavo dicendo . . ." ("As I was saying . . ."). He died in Sorrento (**Naples**) in September 1957.

SARACCO, GIUSEPPE (1821–1907). Born in Bistagno, near Alessandria in Piedmont, Giuseppe Saracco had a distinguished political career that spanned the entire period from the **Risorgimento** to the Giolittian age. He entered the Piedmontese Parliament in 1849 and served as a minister on many occasions under all the leading figures of liberal Italy. In 1898, he became president of the Senate, of which he had been a member since 1865. As Christopher Seton-

Watson has written of him, Saracco "had twice accepted cabinet office from **Francesco Crispi** without damaging a reputation for integrity, common sense, and financial wisdom." After the policy of savage repression of the Milanese working class imposed by General **Luigi Girolamo Pelloux** caused a constitutional crisis, Saracco was asked to head a government of national reconciliation in June 1900. His government lasted just six months, though his tenure of office was spoiled by the assassination of King Humbert I in July. Saracco's government fortunately did not panic and did not resort to repressive measures. The prime minister's calm and good sense undoubtedly defused a situation that might have been explosive. Saracco was obstructing **Giovanni Giolitti**'s return to the power, however, and in February 1901 a heterogeneous group of conservatives, Giolittians, and socialists brought down his government. Saracco died in his native Piedmont in January 1907. *See also* MONARCHY.

SARAGAT, GIUSEPPE (1898–1988). Born and educated in **Turin**, Saragat served in **World War I** as an enlisted man (although a university graduate), becoming an officer in the artillery by battlefield promotion. In 1922 he joined the **Partito Socialista Italiano/**Italian Socialist Party (PSI). Together with **Pietro Nenni** and **Alessandro Pertini**, Saragat entered the executive committee in 1925 but soon left Italy to protest **Fascism**, fleeing first to Austria, then to France. He reentered Italy in 1943, was arrested, and escaped, then resumed secret activity in the Partito Socialista Italiano d'Unità Proletaria/ Italian Socialist Party of Proletarian Unity (PSIUP), eventually being elected to its executive committee.

Saragat feared, however, that unity on the left would mean subordination to the Communists. While expressing admiration for the organizational skills of the **Partito Comunista Italiano/**Italian Communist Party (PCI) militants, he deplored the "democratic centralism" that distanced the militants from policy choices made at the top. Where Communists win, "capitalism dies but Socialism is not born." Saragat wanted what **Alcide De Gasperi** apparently also sought: a reformist coalition with legal limits established by a constitutional framework. In January 1947, accordingly, a group of dissident socialists around Saragat met in **Rome**'s Palazzo Barberini to give birth to the Partito Socialista Lavoratori Italiano. The name was later changed to **Partito Socialista Democratico Italiano**/Italian Social Democratic Party (PSDI) after the **Constituent Assembly**, of which Saragat was the chairman, had completed its work.

Saragat served as vice premier in governments headed by **Mario Scelba** and **Antonio Segni** between 1954 and 1957. He also served as foreign minister in several Moro governments (1964–1968). In fact, the PSDI took part in **Democrazia Cristiana**/Christian Democracy Party (DC) coalitions so regularly that it was derisively called the "secular arm of the DC." The PSI, on the other hand, continued its "Unity of Action" pact with the PCI until 1956, when the Soviet crushing of the Hungarian uprising caused a break between Nenni and **Palmiro Togliatti** that was never healed. Nenni met secretly with Saragat to discuss reunification, but nothing came of the meeting until a decade had passed. In October 1966 the Partito Socialista Unificato/Unified Socialist party (PSU) came into existence but lasted only until the elections of 1968, in which the PSU lost over a quarter of its former electorate. The PSI and PSDI quickly returned to their former autonomy.

At the end of **Giovanni Gronchi**'s term as president of the republic, Antonio Segni and Saragat were the leading contenders to replace him. Saragat was supported by Communists, Socialists, Social Democrats, the **Partito Repubblicano Italiano**/Italian Republican Party (PRI), and, initially, the supporters of **Amintore Fanfani** in the DC. However, calls for party unity brought the *fanfaniani* back to the DC fold, with the result that Segni, supported by the entire DC, the monarchists, and the neofascists, was elected. When Antonio Segni resigned from the presidency because of failing health in December 1964, however, the ensuing stalemate between the DC candidates to replace him, **Giovanni Leone** and Fanfani, enabled the PCI to support Saragat as a (relatively) left candidate. On the 14th day of balloting, he became president.

His presidency was marred by a tacit tolerance of right-wing terrorism and judicial obfuscation. Thus, when Saragat sought a second term in 1971, only the **Partito Liberale Italiano**/Italian Liberal Party (PLI), the PRI, and his own PSDI supported his candidacy. After 20 ballots, the DC produced Giovanni Leone as a compromise candidate, and Saragat lost. As a matter of right, ex-President Saragat became a life senator; as a matter of courtesy, his party made him president of the Social Democrats for life.

SARDINIA (Sardegna). Like **Sicily**, Sardinia has a rich history that
has bred a strong independent cultural tradition. Unlike Sicily, whose
capital city of **Palermo** was once among the leading cultural centers
of Europe, no Sardinian tradition of grandeur exists. To be sure,
the island has been inhabited since neolithic times, and the Phoeni-
cian, Carthaginian, and Roman civilizations all left their traces on its
history.

With the decline of the Roman Empire, the islands of the Mediterranean were threatened by the rising power of the Arabs. To defend
itself, Sardinia was divided (around AD 900) into four states called
giudicati, forming the basis for the territorial boundaries of the
modern-day provinces of Cagliari (which is the largest city), Sassari,
Oristano, and Nuora. The *giudicati* became, in effect, small independent kingdoms, although they were also early examples of constitutional regimes insofar as an assembly of the people known as the
corona de logu decided major questions of national interest. The rule
of the *giudicati* came to an end in the late Middle Ages, after which
political power was exercised by Spanish dynasties. Sardinia remained Spanish until the early 18th century, and Sardinian culture
and its distinctive language has been greatly influenced by Spain's
long domination. In 1718, at the end of the War of the Spanish Succession, Sardinia was awarded to the House of Savoy, although it
continued to maintain its formal independence from the Savoy's other
domains until 1847, when Sardinia and Piedmont fused into a single
state with a single Parliament, legal system, and government. The
subsequent transformation of the Kingdom of Sardinia into the Kingdom of Italy did not lead to special favors. Like the rest of **southern
Italy** it remained a semifeudal backwater. As late as 1911, more than
half of adult Sardinians could not read or write. Few were conversant
in Italian; most spoke only *Sardu*, a language similar to Catalan.

In 1948, the island became one of five special regions that enjoy a
certain legal autonomy from Rome, particularly in questions of urban
planning. This autonomy has permitted the development of one of the
Mediterranean's most skillfully marketed tourist industries; **environmental** activists claim that it has also led to the "cementification" of
one of the most beautiful coastlines in the world. The Emerald Coast
was effectively colonized by the Aga Khan, drawing in his wake jet-
setters and yachtsmen tying up indescribably luxurious seaworthy

vessels. Such an influx of well-off individuals in the 1950s and 1960s (even today, Sardinia has managed to maintain an elite tourism) revived one of the island's most insidious traditions: banditry. As recently as the 1980s and 1990s, there were frequent cases of kidnapping for ransom, which occasionally led to tragic murders. In the mid-1960s a special unit of the Italian police was sent to Sardinia to hunt down the most notorious bandits, in hiding in some of the wildest terrain in Europe. Tourism remains, however, the mainstay of an economy that has suffered greatly since the late 1970s, when traditional industries such as sulfur and coal mining became obsolete. Sardinia's current gross regional product is, however, less than half the figure achieved by the richer regions of the country, and unemployment has reached 30 percent in the poorest parts of the island.

A few leading Sardinian families have provided many of republican Italy's leading politicians. President **Antonio Segni**, his son **Mario Segni**, **Francesco Cossiga**, and the Partito Comunista Italiano/Italian Communist Party/ (PCI) leader **Enrico Berlinguer** all hailed from these influential and interrelated families in the province of Sassari. This is not to mention **Antonio Gramsci**, certainly one of the leading theoreticians on the historical left. The DC-dominated postwar politics on the island, although the nationalist Partito Sardo d'Azione/Sardinian Action Party could count on an important minority vote. *See also* CASSA PER IL MEZZOGIORNO; DIALECTS; LAND REFORM; REGIONALISM.

SCALFARO, OSCAR LUIGI (1918–). Born in Novara (Piedmont), Scalfaro, who is a fervent Catholic, entered politics by way of his activism in **Azione Cattolica Italiana**/Catholic Action (ACI). In 1946, as a young public attorney, he was elected to the **Constituent Assembly** for the **Democrazia Cristiana**/Christian Democracy Party (DC). Never identified with any of the DC's factions or associated with the party's power brokers, Scalfaro took nearly 20 years to reach cabinet rank, although he was entrusted with several junior ministerial posts in the 1950s and early 1960s. Minister of transport between 1964 and 1968, and again in 1972, Scalfaro was also briefly education minister from 1972 to 1973.

An astute and knowledgeable parliamentarian, Scalfaro became deputy president of the Chamber of Deputies in 1976. He was called to ministerial office once more in 1983, when he became minister for the interior under **Bettino Craxi**. Scalfaro lasted all four years of Craxi's premiership, but by the late 1980s he had begun to speak out against the rising corruption and moral degeneracy of the Italian political system.

By 1992, Scalfaro was regarded as one of the "grand old men" (he was 74) of Italian politics. Elected to the presidency of the Chamber of Deputies following the elections of April 1992, his personal probity and uncompromising honesty became immense assets during the presidential election of May 1992. Initially, Scalfaro was not the candidate of any party, but in the mood of national revulsion at petty party politics caused by the **mafia**'s murder of the prosecutor **Giovanni Falcone**, Scalfaro emerged as a figure who might restore public opinion's shaken faith in the country's institutions.

It is generally agreed that Scalfaro performed exceptionally well as first citizen. Making shrewd use of his constitutional power to nominate the premier for **Parliament**'s approval, he played an active political role between 1992 and 1999 and filled the institutional vacuum caused by the collapse of the former party system. In particular, he was the architect of the nonpolitical 1995–1996 administration of **Lamberto Dini**, the technocratic competence of which arguably saved Italy from an international crisis of confidence. Despite his somewhat priestly manner and a fondness for high-flown rhetoric, Scalfaro's standing in public opinion remained high throughout his presidential mandate. He is a senator for life and is still politically active. Since leaving the presidency in 1999, he has been an outspoken critic of **Silvio Berlusconi**. *See also PENTAPARTITO*; PRESIDENT OF THE REPUBLIC.

SCELBA, MARIO (1901–1991). Born in the Sicilian province of Catania, Scelba was a militant in Catholic youth federations. For a time he was secretary to **Luigi Sturzo** and an early member of the **Partito Popolare Italiano**/Italian Popular Party (PPI), forerunner of the **Democrazia Cristiana**/Christian Democracy Party (DC). During the Fascist years he sought to keep a Catholic party alive. Indeed, at war's end he was one of five or six leaders of the new DC. After early ministerial service (with **Ferruccio Parri** in 1945 and, subsequently, with **Alcide De Gasperi**, 1945–1947), he became minister of the interior in De Gasperi's second government in 1947 and stayed at that post through successive governments until 1953. In 1954, he formed his own government, in which he was both **president of the Council** and minister of the interior; it lasted for 17 months.

Scelba is perhaps best remembered for this period as minister of the interior. In that capacity, he reorganized the **police,** purging from the ranks all ex-partisans who had joined the force. He also inspired the creation of the *celere*, antiriot police, used with telling effect on labor, left, or other demonstrators against government policies. Scelba joined **Amintore Fanfani**'s third government as minister of the interior (1960–1962). In 1968, he was elected to the Senate and was president of the European Parliament between 1969 and 1971. He died in **Rome** in October 1991.

SCHIAPARELLI, GIOVANNI VIRGILIO (1835–1910). Born at Savigliano in Lombardy, Schiaparelli was an eminent pioneer of astronomy who directed the Brera observatory in **Milan** from 1862. Learned in Arabic and Sanskrit (which gave him access to those civilizations' studies on the stars), he discovered an asteroid, 69 Hesperia, in April 1861, and geological features on the moon and Mercury are named after him.

Schiaparelli's lasting fame, however, derives from a mistaken observation and the mistaken translation into English of his description of this observation. In 1893, he published two papers on the subject of "life on Mars" in which he spoke of having identified *canali* on the planet's surface that were probably the "main means" by which water (and with it organic life) was diffused. The word *canali* was translated into English as "canals" instead of the correct "channels" or "grooves," and as a result many people sprang to the conclusion that there must be intelligent life on Mars. Schiaparelli's observations were subsequently shown to be optical illusions, but by then early science fiction writers had done their worst, and the notion of little green men was fixed in the popular imagination.

The Mars error should not detract from Schiaparelli's importance in the history of astronomy. Schiaparelli was awarded the Bruce medal in 1902, which has since become the highest honor for astronomy, and was awarded the gold medal of the British Royal Academy. He died in Milan in July 1910.

SCIASCIA, LEONARDO (1921–1989). Born near Agrigento in **Sicily**, Sciascia began his literary career in the 1950s, but it was in the early 1960s that he published the two works that have since received most attention outside Italy, *Zii siciliani* (*Sicilian Uncles*, 1960) and *Il giorno della civetta* (*The Day of the Owl*, 1961). The latter book, with its portrayal of the vain efforts of a northern Italian policeman to get to the bottom of a murder committed in a provincial Sicilian town, was made into a successful film by Damiano Damiani.

Sciascia was a prolific writer, but two books in particular warrant mention. *Il mare di colore vino* (*The Wine Dark Sea*, 1973) is an extraordinary collection of short stories that mix humor, black irony, and pathos as few contemporary writers have succeeded in doing; *Candido owero un sogno fatto in Sicilia* (*Candido, Or a Dream That Took Place in Sicily*, 1977), which portrays a guileless Sicilian whose personal idealism leads him into disillusioning experiences with the equally dishonest philosophies of **Catholicism** and communism, is a brilliant contemporary reworking of Voltaire's *Candide*.

Sciascia was essentially a moralist. Since the Italian political class is not distinguished by its integrity, Sciascia inevitably became involved in political polemic. He famously argued in the 1970s that he was for neither the terrorists of the **Brigate Rosse/**Red Brigades (BR) nor the Italian state, a moral equation that struck many as repulsive. He was a parliamentary deputy for the **Partito Radicale/**Radical Party (PR). In an interview-book toward the end of his life, he summarized the purpose of his own work as being that of using "Sicily as a metaphor" for the human condition. He died in **Palermo** in June 1989.

SECCHIA, PIETRO (1903–1973). Born in Vercelli near **Turin**, Pietro Secchia was a powerful figure in the **Partito Comunista Italiano/**Italian Communist Party (PCI) from the early 1930s until the mid-1950s and the leader of the party's Stalinist wing. A founding member of the PCI in 1921, Secchia became the leader of the Federazione Giovanile Comunista Italiana/Italian Communist Youth Federation (FGCI) and in 1928 a member of the party's central committee, with a place on the politburo. In this role, he cast the decisive vote, in January 1930, that led the PCI to approve underground activities against the Fascist regime and to construct a network of clandestine cells within Italy. In July 1930, the first head of the party's "internal center," Camilla Rovera, was arrested by the police. Secchia was named as her substitute. In April 1931, he himself was arrested in Turin and condemned to 18 years in prison.

Secchia was liberated in August 1943, when he immediately resumed his role as one of the PCI's most influential figures and took an active role in the **resistance** against the Nazis as the chief commissar of the PCI's partisan forces. At the Fifth Congress of the PCI in January 1946, Secchia was placed in charge of the vital task of forming the political consciousness of the rapidly growing membership. **Palmiro Togliatti** apart, Secchia was by now the most important figure in the PCI, a fact that was recognized by his appointment as deputy secretary at the Sixth Congress of the PCI in 1948. Working with fanatical dedication, Secchia built a party that boasted over two million members by the early 1950s but that was also dominated by an unblushing personality-cult of Josef Stalin and an uncritical belief in the superiority of the Soviet model. Secchia's influence decreased after Stalin's death in 1953 and after a scandal involving one of his most trusted assistants, who had absconded with secret party documents and a considerable sum of money in July 1954. In January 1955, Secchia was compelled to undergo "self-criticism" and was removed from his post as the PCI's chief organizer.

From 1955 to his death in 1973, Secchia opposed the PCI's gradual move away from Moscow under Togliatti and his successor, **Luigi Longo**. In 1965, he published a two-volume history of the "war of liberation" fought by the partisans in Italy between 1943 and 1945.

SEGNI, ANTONIO (1891–1972). Sardinian born, Segni studied law at Sassari University. He then was appointed to the law faculty at the University of Perugia, where he taught until 1925. While a student he had organized a section of **Azione Cattolica Italiana**/Catholic Action (ACI), the first in Sassari. A member of the National Council of the **Partito Popolare Italiano**/Italian People's Party (PPI), he was its candidate in the elections of 1924. With the advent of **Fascism**, he withdrew from political life altogether.

Segni's academic career next took him to Cagliari, then to Pavia, then back to Sassari, where he became rector of its university between 1946 and 1951, when he accepted a teaching assignment in **Rome**. He had resumed political life in 1942 by collaborating in the founding of the **Democrazia Cristiana**/Christian Democracy Party (DC), being made its head for Sardinia. He was chosen as a deputy to the **Constituent Assembly**, then to the first **Parliament** and to all subsequent Parliaments.

In the second government of **Ivanoe Bonomi** (January–June 1945), Segni was made deputy minister for agriculture and forests, a post he retained in the subsequent governments of **Ferruccio Parri** and **Alcide De Gasperi**. In July 1946, he became minister of that department, a post he retained until 1951. For the next three years, he was minister of **education**. In 1955, he was invited to form a government, which lasted until 1957. After an interval of serving under **Amintore Fanfani** (1958–1959), he was once again asked to form a government in 1959, in which he was also minister of interior. This government was succeeded by that of **Fernando Tambroni** (April–July 1960). In the subsequent government, Segni was foreign minister, until he was elected president of the Republic in May 1962. He resigned for reasons of health 30 months later, becoming automatically a life senator.

His resignation ended a stormy presidency. The **opening to the left**, for which he had no sympathy whatsoever, had induced the **Partito Socialista Italiano**/Italian Socialist Party (PSI) to break with the **Partito Comunista Italiano**/Italian Communist Party (PCI). The price exacted included reforms such as the nationalization of the electricity industry. Meanwhile widespread and successful industrial action had added to labor costs, thus fueling inflation. Worried about the trend of events, Segni conferred with military leaders and with the president of the Senate, who was known to favor an emergency government to put a stop to socialist-inspired reforms. Subsequent parliamentary and journalistic investigation alleged that a coup d'etat had been a real possibility. Segni was ultimately exonerated, but the episode left a sour taste for Italian democrats. Soon after this crisis Segni was struck with partial paralysis and resigned from the presidency. *See also* SOLO PLAN.

SEGNI, MARIO (1939–). Mario Segni, the son of President **Antonio Segni**, was born in the Sardinian city of Sassari in June 1939. Like his father, Segni followed a career as a law professor, before entering the Chamber of Deputies in 1976 as a standard bearer for the **Democrazia Cristiana**/Christian Democracy Party (DC).

By 1986, he had become convinced of the need for a reform of Italy's narrowly proportional system of electing its **Parliament**. In that year, Segni formed a pressure group dedicated to advocating the introduction of majoritarian principles of election to the Italian political system. This initiative was backed by nearly 200 members of Parliament from all the parties except the **Partito Comunista Italiano**/Italian Communist Party (PCI) and the neofascist **Movimento Sociale Italiano**/Italian Social Movement (MSI). In 1988, Segni also founded the Comitato per la Riforma Elettorale/Committee for Electoral Reform (COREL), which, as a starting point, pressed for the direct election of mayors in all urban centers.

The rigid opposition of the leadership of the DC and the **Partito Socialista Italiano**/Italian Socialist Party (PSI) to this proposal convinced Segni that it was necessary to resort to a **referendum**. In 1990 the COREL introduced three referendum proposals. The first eliminated the practice of multiple preference voting in elections to the Chamber of Deputies. The second sought to introduce the direct election of mayors in towns with more than 5,000 inhabitants. The third sought to introduce majoritarian principles in elections for three-quarters of the seats in the Senate, with one-quarter being assigned by proportional representation. In January 1991, the Constitutional Court allowed a referendum on the first of these proposals. On 9 June 1991, the referendum became the only one in postwar Italian history to be backed by a majority of all adults (not just of those voting)—a historic slap in the face for the party leaderships, which had opposed the referendum strenuously.

Once the June poll was over, Segni began campaigning for the two referendums denied by the Constitutional Court. In March 1993, the Italian Parliament enacted into law the scheme for the direct election of mayors; this law was first used in local elections in June 1993. In April 1993, Italians voted in a fresh referendum by a four to one margin to introduce a primarily majoritarian system of election for the Italian Senate. Immediately prior to the April poll, Segni left the DC.

Many believed that he would be able to parlay his success as the leader of the referendum campaigns into a position of national political leadership.

Since the April 1993 election, however, Segni has lost most of his luster. His "Segni Pact" did very badly in the March 1994 elections, winning no seats directly. Despite this fall from grace, Segni remains one of the most well-known figures in Italian politics.

SELLA, QUINTINO (1827–1884). Born in Biella (Piedmont) to a wealthy family of cloth manufacturers, Sella was a mathematician and geologist by training. Encouraged to take up politics by **Camillo Benso di Cavour**, he became finance minister in 1862 during **Urbano Rattazzi**'s premiership and held the position for most of the next 10 years. Personally austere, and a skilled administrator, he imposed a policy of rigid economy on Italy. In 1868, Sella was the architect of the deeply unpopular grist tax (*dazio sul macinato*), which, starting in January 1869, imposed a tax of two lire for every hundred kilograms of milled grain. This tax was deeply regressive (it removed 10 days' income from the pocket of the average agricultural laborer), and it provoked widespread riots that cost more than 200 lives. Sella won for himself the unenviable reputation as the "starver of the people." Nevertheless, if by the time of the "parliamentary revolution" in 1876 Italy's national accounts were in the black, much of the credit must be given to Sella and to his bitter rival but fellow fiscal conservative, **Marco Minghetti**.

Sella was a strong anticleric. As finance minister, he sold off the Catholic Church's assets in Italy at discount prices and joined the constitutional left in restricting the amount of independence allowed to the Church by the **guarantee laws** in 1871. Sella was a great lover of the mountains, and one of his most lasting achievements was to found the Italian Alpine Association in 1863. Despite his national standing as a politician, he did not disdain local office, and between 1870 and his death in 1884 he was president of the provincial council of Novara. *See also* ALPS; CATHOLICISM; LANZA, GIOVANNI.

SESSANTOTTO, IL. The year 1968 was turbulent throughout the industrialized world. In Italy, the student disturbances spread into the factories, provoking the "hot autumn" of 1969 and eventually the descent into outright terrorism in the 1970s. Italy's **universities** remained at a boiling point until the late 1970s; in 1977, there was another similar student uprising.

The causes of the first protests, which began in February 1967 with the occupation of university buildings in Pisa and **Turin**, are to be found in the changing nature of the Italian university and society. Newly rich, Italy was now for the first time beginning to produce large numbers of students with the income and inclination to pursue university studies. Such students arrived at university to find antiquated institutions teaching out-of-date curricula and with a privileged professoriate that was detached from the world the students knew. An inadequate university reform law (the "Gui law") did little to improve matters. Young people born in the aftermath of **World War II** were also in rebellion against the conservative values of traditional Italian society. Last, but not least, Italy's standing as the most faithful ally of the United States did not help. The suppression of democracy in Greece, the fear of a U.S.-backed coup in Italy, and the ongoing Vietnam War all combined to make revolutionary, especially Maoist, thought seem a useful interpretative tool.

But the point of revolutionary politics is not to interpret the world but to change it. By February 1968, literally dozens of university buildings had been occupied, well in advance of the more famous "events" of Paris in May–June 1968. On 1 March 1968, the so-called battle of Valle Giulia took place, in which radical students tried to "liberate" the faculty of architecture in **Rome** from the police, who had thrown out student occupiers the day before. About 4,000 students attacked the **police**, throwing stones and metal objects. The police responded with baton charges, tear gas, and indiscriminate beatings of the students they captured. All told, 150 policemen and nearly 500 students were injured; miraculously, nobody was killed. The "battle" inspired **Pierpaolo Pasolini** to write his famous poem "Vi odio figli di papà" ("I Hate You Daddy's Boys"), in which he openly sympathized with the young proletarian *carabinieri* under attack by their wealthier and politically more radical peers.

There were literally thousands of incidents in the next two to three years in the universities and the schools, especially the *licei* frequented by aspirant university students. Clashes between the far left groups and far right squads became commonplace in the early 1970s, and numerous activists were killed or badly beaten on both sides. The student movement spread into the factories. Movements, such as **Lotta Continua** and Avanguardia operaia (Workers' Avant-guard), actively tried to stoke a revolutionary situation; the **Partito Comunista Italiano**/Italian Communist Party (PCI), by contrast, inveighed against the groupuscles of the far left and sought moderation and dialogue.

Terrorism from both the left and the right found its roots in this milieu. As late as 1977 there were scenes of urban warfare in Italy. In March 1977 first Rome and then **Bologna** were the scene for clashes between the police and so-called autonomists, ultraradicals with no ties to the official political parties. In October of the same year, the murder of a radical, Walter Rossi, by neofascist thugs provoked a massive riot in Turin, during which a student worker not involved in the clashes was killed.

The events of 1968 and 1977 have resonance even today. Many *sessantottini* have become influential **media** figures, politicians, and intellectuals (by no means all are still on the left), and on the right the current leading members of **Alleanza Nazionale**/National Alliance (AN) preserve a fond recollection of their time as *picchiatori* ("hard fighters") whose earliest political experience was in street battles with the Marxist left. *See also* BRIGATE ROSSE (BR); NEGRI, ANTONIO; STRATEGIA DELLA TENSIONE.

SFORZA, CARLO (1872–1952). A career diplomat, Sforza played a crucial role in restoring Italy to the society of nations in the immediate post-1945 period. He began his career in 1896 and swiftly rose in the ministerial hierarchy to become ambassador to China between 1911 and 1915. **Francesco Saverio Nitti** gave him his first ministerial post, as undersecretary for foreign affairs in 1919, and in the same year he was appointed to the Senate. In 1920, in the last cabinet formed by **Giovanni Giolitti**, Sforza became foreign minister, and in this role negotiated the treaty of Rapallo with Yugoslavia that ended the diplomatically sensitive crisis over **Fiume**. In 1922 Sforza became ambassador to France. He was in Paris when **Benito Mussolini** took power in October 1922.

Unlike many Italian liberals, Sforza denounced **Fascism** immediately. Returning to Italy, he collaborated with the democratic forces that tried to organize opposition to the dictatorship after the murder of **Giacomo Matteotti** and wrote articles critical of the regime for the *Corriere della Sera*. In October 1926, his home was sacked by a Fascist squad in the wake of a failed attempt on Mussolini's life, and he was constrained to immigrate, first to Belgium and then to the United States. For the next 15 years, he was one of the dictatorship's most uncompromising public critics.

In July 1942, at a conference of antifascist exiles in Uruguay, Sforza unveiled an eight-point plan for a **Constituent Assembly** that would draw up a democratic republic in Italy after the fall of Fascism. This move presaged his return to Italy after the fall of Mussolini, when he became foreign minister in the government formed in Allied-held territory in October 1943 by **Pietro Badoglio**. Sforza held office in Badoglio's second, short-lived administration in April 1944 and then joined the Salerno-based government of **Ivanoe Bonomi**. When Bonomi resigned in November 1944, Sforza was nominated as his successor, but his republicanism caused the British to veto his election. He held no place of significance in the second Bonomi cabinet (December 1944 to June 1945) but was given the sensitive post of high commissioner for the punishment of the Fascists' crimes. He resigned from this post in January 1945.

In February 1947, Sforza returned to the ministry of foreign affairs, a post he continued to hold until 1951. Almost his first action as foreign minister was to request amendments to the treaty of peace signed by Italy on 10 February 1947. Sforza followed a strongly pro-American policy during his tenure as foreign minister. The culmination of his political and diplomatic career was Italy's accession to **North Atlantic Treaty Organization (NATO)** in 1949 and the active role he took in promoting European economic integration. Sforza died in **Rome** in 1952. *See also* FOREIGN POLICY.

SICILY (Sicilia). The largest island in the Mediterranean and Italy's largest region, Sicily is inhabited by slightly more than five million people. Its largest cities are **Palermo**, the regional capital, Catania, Messina, Syracuse (Siracusa), Enna, Agrigento, and Caltanisetta.

Throughout its history Sicily has been the victim of wave after wave of foreign invaders; the ancient Greeks, Carthaginians, Romans, Moors, Normans, French, and Spaniards (Sicilian wits add that the Italians are the last in the list) all occupied the island over the centuries and left their genetic and cultural imprints. Sicily has some of the most remarkable remnants of Greek civilization in the whole Mediterranean (the Greco-Roman Theater in Taormina, the Greek Theater in Syracuse, and the majestic Valley of the Temples near Agrigento all prove this assertion).

In economic terms Sicily is one of the poorest regions of Italy. The outskirts of the major towns are dominated by half-built projects, often without roofs, that were quickly flung up to house migrants from the countryside in the 1960s. Unemployment and drug abuse are rife, and foreign and mainland Italian investment is scared off by the ubiquitous intrusion of the **mafia**. Nevertheless, there are some success stories, particularly in the eastern part of the island. Messina and Syracuse, for instance, are bustling commercial cities.

Politically the island is one of Italy's five special autonomous regions. Its own elected assembly (whose members pay themselves generous salaries) and the regional government exercise considerable authority. For most of the postwar period, local government was firmly in the hands of the **Democrazia Cristiana**/Christian Democracy Party (DC), but the anticorruption and antimafia investigations of the 1990s ended this hegemony. In the elections of March 1994 **Forza Italia** emerged as the largest political force. Together with its allies in the **Unione dei Democratici Cristiani e Democratici di Centro**/Union of Christian Democrats and Democrats of the Center (UDC), Forza Italia remains the largest party today.

Sicily has made a remarkable contribution to contemporary Italian and world culture. The writers **Luigi Pirandello**, **Giovanni Verga**, **Leonardo Sciascia**, **Salvatore Quasimodo**, **Elio Vittorini**, and **Giuseppe Tomasi Di Lampedusa** were all Sicilians, as was the painter Renato Guttuso. The island is craggy, in places arid, but of spectacular natural beauty. The eastern part of the island is dominated by Mount Etna, a 3,510-meter (11,000-foot) active volcano whose frequent eruptions are a regular source of disturbance. *See also* CRISPI, FRANCESCO; FALCONE, GIOVANNI; ORLANDO, LEOLUCA; REGIONALISM.

SILONE, IGNAZIO (pseud. Ignazio Tranquillini, 1900–1978). Ignazio Silone was a native of the province of Aquila (the Abruzzi) who was orphaned by an earthquake in his early teens. After the death of his parents Silone was obliged to break off his studies. He became involved in the workers' movement and in the antiwar struggle. An ardent socialist, he was implacably opposed to the Fascists from the very beginning, and in the early 1920s worked for a **Trieste** newspaper, *Il Lavoratore*, that was a frequent target for Fascist squads.

After **Benito Mussolini** introduced the series of repressive measures outlawing all political dissent and organization in 1925–1926, Silone, who by now was a member of the **Partito Comunista Italiano**/Italian Communist Party (PCI), joined **Antonio Gramsci** in clandestine activities against the regime. He narrowly avoided arrest and incarceration, escaping to Switzerland with the police on his trail in 1928. His brother Romolo, who allegedly took part in an April 1928 bomb attack against **Victor Emmanuel III**, was less fortunate. He was tortured and died in a Fascist prison in 1932. As one of the most important exiled Italian communists, Silone took an active role in the Communist International, but this firsthand experience of the communists' doctrinaire subordination to Stalinism led him to break with the PCI in July 1931. Academic research has since established that during these years Silone was in fact a double agent of the Fascist police and under the pseudonym "Silvestri" was informing on the activities of the PCI. Silone eventually broke with both the Fascist police and Stalinism.

Silone's most important books were first published in Switzerland. *Fontamara* was published in 1933, first in German, then in more than 20 other languages. *Vino e pane* (*Bread and Wine*, 1936), his greatest novel, followed three years later. It tells the story of a communist intellectual, Pietro Spina, who disguises himself from the Fascists by pretending to be Don Paolo Spada, a priest. Living among the peasants in an out-of-the-way mountain village in the Abruzzi, Pietro comes to doubt that political solutions—particularly the narrow dogmatism of the Communist Party—can bring about an improvement in the lot of the ordinary people. By the end of the novel, he is in despair, but, in fact, his own humanity and decency have already been an example for the villagers. Like George Orwell, Silone's contemporary and friend, Silone came to the conclusion that common decency, not political blueprints, was the key to creating a better society. While in exile, Silone also wrote two important treatises on politics, *Fascismo, le sue origini e il suo sviluppo* (*Fascism: Its Origins and Development*, 1935) and *La scuola dei dittatori* (*The School for Dictators*, 1938).

After **World War II**, Silone played a major role in the formation of the anticommunist **Partito Socialista Democratico Italiano**/Italian Social Democratic Party (PSDI). His implacable and active postwar opposition to Stalinism may have cost him the place in Italian letters that he deserved. One of the most widely read and translated Italian authors in the 20th century, his works are scantily represented in Italian school textbooks and university courses even today. Silone died in Geneva in 1978. *See also CONFINO*; FASCISM; *SQUADRISMO*.

SOCIAL DEMOCRAT PARTY. *See* PARTITO SOCIALISTA DEMOCRATICO ITALIANO (PSDI).

SOCIALIST PARTY. *See* PARTITO SOCIALISTA ITALIANO.

SOLO PLAN. In July 1964, during lengthy negotiations over the formation of a new government, the then president, **Antonio Segni**, invited the head of the *Carabinieri*, General **Giovanni De Lorenzo**, to the presidential palace for formal talks. This seemingly innocuous event would later take on great significance.

In 1967, the news magazine *Europeo* published extracts from secret files that De Lorenzo had accumulated, in his former role as head of army intelligence, on the private lives of prominent politicians, including Segni's successor as president, **Giuseppe Saragat**. On 10 May 1967, another magazine, *Espresso*, broke the news of the so-called Piano Solo (Solo Plan), drawn up by De Lorenzo at the beginning of 1964. The Solo Plan foresaw the arrest and imprisonment of lists of persons who were regarded as subversive; the occupation of prefectures, television studios, telephone exchanges, and party headquarters; and unilateral action by the *Carabinieri* rather than joint action with other, less trustworthy branches of the armed forces.

On 26 June 1964, the day that the center-left coalition led by **Aldo Moro** collapsed, De Lorenzo apparently gave orders for detailed local contingency plans to be drawn up, although his orders were greeted with some perplexity, and little enthusiasm, by the policemen who would have had to carry them out. The **press** outcry led to a parliamentary investigation that found that De Lorenzo, who in the meantime had become head of the armed services, was merely engaging in defensive emergency planning for the eventuality of an institutional breakdown. Not surprisingly, this conclusion was not shared by the putative targets of the Solo Plan. How much Segni knew of De Lorenzo's schemes has never been clarified, and **Francesco Cossiga**, who acted as liaison between De Lorenzo and Segni, has never been trusted by Italian progressive opinion since. The military coups in Greece in 1967 and Chile in 1973 suggested that the left's fears were not entirely misplaced. De Lorenzo was elected to **Parliament** as a monarchist in 1968, and he later joined the neofascist **Movimento Sociale Italiano**/Italian Social Movement (MSI). He died in **Rome** in 1973. *See also* GLADIO; POLICE.

SONNINO, GIORGIO SIDNEY (1847–1922). The Tuscan-born Sonnino (his mother was Welsh) entered politics only in 1880, after beginning a successful diplomatic career. Shortly after becoming a parliamentary deputy, he was one of the leaders of the movement to introduce universal suffrage into the electoral reform of 1882. Sonnino's first ministerial job was as minister of finance from 1893 to 1896. He skillfully steered bank reforms through **Parliament** and all but balanced the budget despite the outlays caused by Italy's adventures in Africa.

In 1897, he published an article entitled *"Torniamo allo statuto"* ("Back to the Constitution"), which urged the crown to reclaim its right under the **Statuto Albertino** to name the executive independently of **Parliament**. Sonnino argued that Parliament was inept and corrupt and that its role should be merely consultative. These views were immensely influential, and they underlay the authoritarian attempts of the conservative governments of **Antonio Starabba Di Rudinì** and **Luigi Girolamo Pelloux** from 1898 to 1900 to combat social unrest and the nascent workers' movement by authorizing emergency measures with a royal decree rather than with a vote of Parliament.

Sonnino, in short, was the conservative counterpart of **Giovanni Giolitti**. Since the first decade of the 20th century was dominated by

Giolitti, Sonnino was only briefly prime minister in 1906 and again from December 1909 to March 1910. In October 1914, he became foreign minister and kept that role throughout **World War I**. He negotiated Italy's entrance into the war on the side of the Entente in 1915, winning the promise of substantial territorial gains in Dalmatia and the eastern Mediterranean from Great Britain and France. After the war, however, Britain and France did not support Italy's claims at the Paris peace conference, and the Italian government briefly walked out of the talks. The report on the **Caporetto** disaster by the Commission of Inquiry, published in 1919, roundly criticized him for not having sought a separate peace with Austria. Nominated to the Senate in 1920, Sonnino died in **Rome** in 1922. His diaries are one of the outstanding historical sources for the politics of this period. *See also* ORLANDO, VITTORIO EMANUELE.

SOUTHERN DEVELOPMENT FUND. *See* CASSA PER IL MEZ-ZOGIORNO.

SOUTHERN ITALY (Il Mezzogiorno). The Mezzogiorno comprises the regions of Apulia, Basilicata, Calabria, Campania, Latium (south of Rome), and Molise. Campania is Italy's second-largest region by **population**, with nearly 6,000,000 inhabitants; Molise is the second-smallest, with just 320,000 citizens. The largest city in southern Italy is **Naples**, which has a population of 1.5 million people as well as a huge metropolitan area, but Bari (330,000 inhabitants, plus over 1,000,000 in the metropolitan area), Salerno (146,000), Reggio Calabria (200,000), Taranto (200,000), and Brindisi (90,000) are all important cities. All these cities are ports. Southern Italy is largely mountainous in terrain, with many peaks reaching over 2,000 meters (6,600 feet), and there are very few centers of any size, except Matera and Potenza in Basilicata, away from the coast. The region is very arid and suffers from acute shortages of water in the summer.

The coast of the Mezzogiorno is famous for its natural beauty. The Gargano peninsula in Apulia, Tropea in Calabria, the Amalfi coast in Campania, and the islands of the Bay of Naples (Capri, Ischia, Procida) are renowned throughout the world, as is Vesuvius, the active volcano overlooking Naples. In ancient times the Mezzogiorno was colonized by the Greeks, and there are still important remains of

Greek culture and civilization to be found. The temples of Paestum (near Salerno) are some of the best-preserved remnants of ancient Greek architecture still standing, while the *Bronzi di Riace*, astonishingly lifelike bronze statues of Greek warriors, are to be found in Reggio Calabria. Of most historical interest are the Roman towns of Pompeii and Herculaneum, destroyed by Vesuvius in AD 79 and rediscovered in the 1730s and 1740s.

Southern Italy has suffered a troubled history within the Italian state. With unification in 1861, two economies, one that was already industrializing and the other preindustrial, were hammered together, with the Mezzogiorno being treated almost as a colony of the more developed north. During the 1860s and again in the 1890s, the Italian army was utilized to put down peasant revolts in the Mezzogiorno. Rural poverty in southern Italy caused an exodus in the 1890s and early 20th century. Millions of southern Italians migrated to the United States, South America, and northern Europe.

The *latifondi* system of land tenure gave rise to a more acutely hierarchical society than in northern Italy. Public **education** was also much slower to be developed than in the North. The North–South gap was neglected by the state until after **World War II** and still has not been fully eradicated: In 1980, Calabria had the same rate of illiteracy as Piedmont in 1880. The **Cassa per il Mezzogiorno** (Southern Development Fund) was created in 1950 to overcome these disparities. Yet in the first decade of its program, three million southerners left for either northern Italy or northern Europe in search of work.

Like **Sicily**, southern Italy is plagued with criminality. In Calabria, the local **mafia** equivalent is called the *'ndrangheta*; in Naples and Campania, it is called the *Camorra*. In Apulia, organized crime exists but on a lesser scale, although Bari has a major problem with drugs and microcriminality. Reggio Calabria and Naples, despite the efforts of local prosecutors and judges to eradicate crime, are two of the most violence-ravaged cities in Europe and, again as in Sicily, there is considerable evidence of political complicity with the gang bosses.

The root cause of criminality in southern Italy is the region's relative (and absolute) poverty. Notwithstanding the Italian state's efforts to bridge the gap between north and south, the difference in wealth between northern and southern Italy persists. Per capita income in Calabria is under €15,000; in Campania and Apulia, it is little more than this sum. This is €10,000 per year less than in **Central Italy** and about half of some of the wealthier provinces of the North (Bolzano, Milan, Bologna, Varese). Unemployment rates touch 30 percent in some cities of the South, and black market labor is a huge problem. Hundreds of thousands of people are exploited in the informal **economy**.

Politically the Mezzogiorno tends to the right. The **Alleanza Nazionale**/National Alliance (AN) has its stronghold in southern Latium and Apulia and regularly gets over 20 percent of the vote in these areas. However, Campania has repeatedly voted for the center-left in recent years; in 2005, Apulia surprised the nation by electing an openly gay communist, Niki Vendola, as its regional president. *See also* IMMIGRATION.

SOUTH TYROL PEOPLE'S PARTY. *See* SÜD TIROL VOLKSPARTEI (SVP).

SPADOLINI, GIOVANNI (1923–1994). The first prime minister of the Italian republic not to be a member of the **Democrazia Cristiana**/Christian Democracy Party (DC), Giovanni Spadolini was one of the few first-rank figures in recent Italian history whose reputation was enhanced by his years at the head of the principal institutions of the state. Spadolini was a latecomer to political life. Before 1972, when he was elected to the Senate on the **Partito Repubblicano Italiano**/Italian Republican Party (PRI) ticket, Spadolini had been a successful newspaperman for more than 20 years. Since 1968, in fact, he had been editor of Italy's most prestigious newspaper, *Corriere della Sera.*

Spadolini served as a minister twice in the 1970s. Between 1974 and 1976, he was minister for cultural heritage. In 1979 he became minister for **education**. In the same year, he replaced **Ugo La Malfa** as leader of the PRI, a position he retained until 1987. In June 1981, Spadolini headed the first government containing all five main noncommunist parties, the so-called ***pentapartito***. His premiership was dominated by financial-political scandals and by the **mafia**'s increasingly assertive and brutal role in **Sicily**, but Spadolini and the PRI emerged from this period in Italian history with their reputations enhanced. In the June 1983 elections, the PRI obtained more than 5 percent, its best showing since the war.

During the governments of **Bettino Craxi**, Spadolini was minister for defense (July 1983 to March 1987), although he briefly resigned in objection to Craxi's position during the *Achille Lauro* dispute in October 1985. Spadolini fervently supported Italy's membership in the **North Atlantic Treaty Organization (NATO)** and saw no utility in antagonizing Italy's most powerful ally. Spadolini was president of the Senate from 1987 to 1994, and in 1991 he was made a life senator. In April 1994, he was the center-left's candidate for the presidency of the Senate, but he lost by a single vote.

Spadolini was a hugely successful writer of popular history books and a leading scholar of the Giolittian period in Italian history. A noted bibliophile, his private library contained thousands of rare books. He died in August 1994.

SPANISH CIVIL WAR. With the absorption of **Ethiopia**, Italy had reason to be a "satisfied" power that could be expected to sustain the status quo. But at the same time, Fascist doctrine insisted that it was "unfascist" to be "satisfied." This division largely reflected the differences between "Fascists of the first hour" and the younger members of the party hierarchy. When Count **Galeazzo Ciano**, **Benito Mussolini**'s son-in-law, was suddenly elevated to be minister for foreign affairs in June 1936, an opportunity was presented to him to make his own mark. Pressed by the **Vatican**, which was in an uproar over the mistreatment and murder of priests by the revolutionary parties in Spain, Italy was soon drawn into the Spanish conflict. By October 1936, Italian ground troops were in Spain.

The first troops sent were a "Legion" of blackshirt militia under the command of General Carlo Roatta. Mostly *squadristi*, they found combat even against the relatively shabbily armed and poorly disciplined Republican forces little to their liking. After a stinging defeat at Guadalajara in March 1937, Mussolini made success in Spain a matter of national prestige. The blackshirts were stiffened by an infusion of regular Italian army troops. By 1937, their number exceeded 70,000.

The Spanish Civil War was also a watershed for the antifascist opposition. Many Italian partisans received their battlefield training on the rugged soil of Spain: **Luigi Longo**, **Pietro Nenni**, **Carlo Rosselli**, and at least 3,500 others all fought in Spain. At Guadalajara,

Italians fought Italians, and the Garibaldi Battalion of the International Brigades played an important role in the Republic's victory. The murder of the Rosselli brothers, Carlo and Nello, in Paris in 1937 was carried out in revenge for their activities in Spain.

By March 1939, when Madrid fell to Francisco Franco, Italy had expended, according to official figures, about 8,500 million lire and lost nearly 4,000 dead and 12,000 wounded to help Franco's cause. The Spanish war, coming on top of the involvement in Ethiopia, weakened Italy at the very moment that Mussolini was raising the rhetorical tone of his **foreign policy** ambitions. *See also SQUADRISMO.*

SPINELLI, ALTIERO (1907–1986). Born in **Rome**, Spinelli's early political activity was as a member of the Federazione Giovanile Comunista Italiana/Italian Communist Youth Federation (FGCI). He was arrested and sentenced by the special tribunal to 10 years' imprisonment and to *confino* for six more in 1927. On his release, he left the **Partito Comunista Italiano**/Italian Communist Party (PCI) because of the Stalinist purges. Together with **Ernesto Rossi**, his fellow prisoner on the isle of Ventotene, he wrote the *Manifesto for a Free United Europe* (1941) and led the Federalist movement, first from Paris, then from Switzerland, during the years before the **Resistance**, which he joined in **Milan**, where he also joined the **Partito d'Azione**/Action Party (PdA). Spinelli left its secretariat in 1946 to become secretary of the European Federalist Movement. In that capacity he worked closely with **Alcide De Gasperi**, Paul-Henri Spaak of Belgium, Konrad Adenauer of West Germany, and Jean Monnet of France toward the building of a more united Europe. He was particularly influential in 1952–1953, when he persuaded the Italian government to press for the possibility of the creation of a European Political Community as part of the treaty establishing a European Defense Community.

Spinelli directed the Italian Institute of International Affairs between 1967 and 1970, when he became a member of the European Commission, where he stayed until 1976. In that year he won a seat in the Chamber of Deputies as an independent on the PCI ticket, and he repeated that victory in 1979. Simultaneously, he served in the European Parliament, and was elected to that body in

1979. During his time as a member of the European Parliament he was the inspirer of the draft "Treaty on European Union," which the Parliament presented to the national governments in February 1984. Spinelli died in Rome in May 1986. *See also* EUROPEAN INTEGRATION.

SQUADRISMO. After World War I, formerly subservient farmhands and factory workers no longer deferred to property owners, who controlled political power on the local scene and enjoyed easy access, through prefects and parliamentarians alike, to national power as well. The victory in the 1919 elections of the **Partito Socialista Italiano**/Italian Socialist Party (PSI) frightened conservatives, who began to see the Fascists as effective instruments against the rise of unions trying to organize farm workers and factory workers alike. Financial support for the Fascist movement swelled as the Fascists went into action against socialists and workers.

Black-shirted, black-fez-wearing action squads (*squadre d'azione*) were equipped with small arms and blackjacks (*il santo manganello* or "holy club") and used vehicles often provided by sympathizers in army motor pools. When they were on an "expedition," they would converge upon their target and would beat union organizers, administer massive doses of castor oil with humiliating effect, pillage rival buildings, and create as much confusion on the left as possible. Police rarely appeared on the scene until the squads had left. Even less frequently did they make arrests. Local Fascists who led the action squads took the title *Ras*, which was derived from Ethiopian tribal chiefs. A brief list of outrages committed by the squads gives a clear idea of the lawlessness that prevailed in the last years of liberal Italy. In November 1920, nine socialists were killed, and more than 50 were wounded, when 500 armed Fascists burst into a meeting of the **Bologna** city council. In July 1921, 18 people died in a pitched battle between a Fascist squad and the townsfolk and **police** of Sarzana (Liguria). On 1 May 1922, clashes between the squads and socialists left dozens dead and wrecked rallies of the PSI all over Italy. The **March on Rome** in October 1922 would not have been possible had the squads not made Italy ungovernable in the preceding months.

Mussolini owed his accession to power to *squadrismo* and to the timidity of the politicians of liberal Italy, who were unwilling to meet illegal violence with the force of law. One of Mussolini's first acts as premier was to transform the squads into the Milizia Volontario di Sicurezza Nazionale/Voluntary Militia of National Security (MVSN). Flushed by this institutional legitimization, the squads continued their reign of terror throughout the first years of Mussolini's premiership and were only brought to heel after Mussolini had consolidated his regime. By 1932, the original *squadristi* who had participated in the March on Rome were styled the *Vecchia Guardia* (The Old Guard), thus emphasizing that their role was in the past and not in the future of **Fascism**. *See also* ARDITI; FASCISM; FARINACCI, ROBERTO; MATTEOTTI, GIACOMO; SPANISH CIVIL WAR.

SRAFFA, PIERO (1898–1983). An extremely influential economist who was a close friend of both John Maynard Keynes and Ludwig Wittgenstein, Sraffa was born in **Turin** to an academic family. After taking a degree in economics under the supervision of **Luigi Einaudi**, he worked as an academic in Italy. Sraffa was both a personal friend and political associate of **Antonio Gramsci**, and his position in the mid-1920s in Italy was by no means safe. Keynes accordingly arranged for him to be brought to England as a lecturer at Cambridge. Somewhat diffident in personality, Sraffa did not enjoy lecturing and, thanks to Keynes's intervention, subsequently became librarian of Kings College, Cambridge, and editor of the collected works of the 19th-century economist David Ricardo. It took Sraffa 20 years to complete his edition of Ricardo's works, but the final result, with his introductory essay on Ricardo's thought, was regarded as a definitive statement on Ricardo and on classical economics more generally.

Sraffa, who would have fared ill under modern academic requirements to "publish or perish," finally produced a short book of his own in 1960. *The Production of Commodities by Means of Commodities* opened up a wide-ranging debate in academic economics and ensured his reputation as one of the most original of all contemporary economists. Sraffa was also a shrewd practical economist. He invested in Japanese government bonds after the war and made a fortune.

Sraffa was an intellectual of acute sensibility and broad interests. He was well able to discuss philosophy with Ludwig Wittgenstein, who wrote in the introduction to *Philosophical Investigations*, one of the most important works of philosophy of the 20th century, that he was "indebted" to Sraffa's "stimulus" for "the most consequential ideas of this book." Sraffa was a fellow of Trinity College, Cambridge, and died in England in 1983.

STARACE, ACHILLE (1889–1945). The Pugliese Starace was decorated for bravery in **World War I** and was a "Fascist of the first hour." He was secretary of the **Partito Nazionale Fascista/**National Fascist Party (PNF) between 1931 and 1939, the longest tenure of any individual in this office. The position was a powerful one. The secretary nominated (and **Benito Mussolini** appointed) all secretaries of the PNF's provincial federations and had a seat on the party's National Directorate.

Starace remained faithful to the militantly antibourgeois program of San Sepolcro (the Milan Fascist meeting of 1919). In ever-stylish Italy, for example, he discouraged all forms of dress that underscored class distinctions as well as the frequenting of night clubs. He considered abolishing the class system in railway compartments and even talked of closing the stock exchange. Starace also invented much of the mock-Roman symbolism of the regime. At Starace's prompting, Mussolini even introduced the slogan *Usate l'italianissimo voi!*—a campaign to make Italians use the second person plural (*voi*) as the formal form of address, rather than the deferential and formal third person singular (*Lei*). Ever ready to ritualize **Fascism**, he became known as its choreographer, assuring that each public appearance of the Duce or of the party hierarchs was greeted with shouted slogans: *Saluto al Duce! Eja, eja, alala!* and other forms of pageantry.

Starace was eased out only when Mussolini hesitated about going to war before the completion of military preparations. A leading member of the war party, Starace had given the Duce estimates of public morale that were flatly contradicted by all other advisors. After 1941, Starace lost favor with Mussolini and was even imprisoned in a forced labor camp during the **Republic of Salò**. This fall from grace did not save him from the partisans, however. Starace was tried and shot in **Milan** on the same day as his former leader, and his body was exposed to the crowd in Piazza Loreto along with the other members of the PNF hierarchy.

STATUTO ALBERTINO (1848). The basis of constitutional government in Italy until the foundation of the First Republic in 1948, the Statuto Albertino (named after King **Charles Albert**) ended the absolute power of the House of Savoy. The statute was drawn up by a committee of liberal noblemen, including **Cesare Balbo** and **Camillo Benso di Cavour**, in order to head off popular discontent in Piedmont. In this respect it was very successful: The Piedmont-Sardinian throne escaped relatively unscathed in the so-called year of revolutions.

Most of the statute's 88 articles were concerned with delineating the relative powers of the sovereign and the **Parliament**. The king was made chief executive and nominal head of the judiciary and was given a legislative veto. He could appoint ministers, but the ministers themselves were subject to a vote of confidence from Parliament. The legislature itself was divided into two branches. The Senate was composed of life members appointed by the king; the Chamber of Deputies was elected by an electoral law that was not specified in the statute itself, but featured an extremely restrictive property qualification. Voters had to be at least 25 years of age, be literate, and pay at least 40 lire in taxes every year. Approximately 80,000 people—barely 2 percent of the population—met these conditions.

The statute guaranteed important civil rights. Equality before the law was established "for all subjects, whatever be their rank"; the freedoms of property, press, and person were sanctioned. **Catholicism** was stated to be the "sole religion of the State," but the principle of toleration for other faiths was established. At the end of March 1848, Charles Albert put legal flesh to these constitutional bones by signing a new **press** law that authorized any writings except those that offended against public decency or obstructed the "regular functioning of government." This formulation was ambiguous, but it was regarded as a step forward from the previous system of ecclesiastic and temporal censorship. Between March and June 1848, Jews were admitted to the same civil status as Catholics throughout the kingdom.

STRATEGIA DELLA TENSIONE, LA. The "strategy of tension" refers to the collective acts of terrorism perpetrated by right-wing groups in Italy between the late 1960s and early 1980s that had the

purpose of provoking a climate of fear among the conservative electorate and thus an unwillingness to contemplate political change—
although there is also a general consensus that the neofascist groups
hoped that terror might provoke a strong government with military
involvement. As the term suggests, it has been established by judicial
investigation that there is reason to believe that far-right groups con-
sciously plotted their actions and were not conducting random acts of
terror. Many investigators in Italy believe that the groups themselves
were backed, perhaps even armed, by the Italian secret services and
by the Central Intelligence Agency (CIA). The latter assertion has
never been proved, but the belief that the secret services were involved is strongly suggested by the evidence.

The strategy of tension can be said to have had its onset in December 1969, when a bomb blasted a bank in Piazza Fontana in **Milan**, killing 16 individuals and wounding nearly a hundred. Two other
bombs exploded in Rome on the same day. In the aftermath of the attack an anarchist, Giuseppe Pinelli, "fell" out of a window in the Milan police headquarters, where he was being interrogated by Luigi
Calabresi (who was himself murdered in 1972, allegedly by members
of **Lotta Continua**). A second anarchist, Pietro Valpreda, was subsequently arrested and charged with planting the bomb. He spent three
years under arrest without trial until the pressure of public opinion
forced his release. Responsibility for the massacre was eventually attributed, in 2001, to three members of the neofascist group Ordine
Nuovo: Delfo Zorzi, the movement's leader; Carlo Maria Maggi; and
Giancarlo Rognoni. In 2004, however, Zorzi, Maggi, and Rognoni
were acquitted by the Court of Appeal on grounds of insufficient evidence. This sentence was later confirmed by the Court of Cassation.
Nevertheless, these two courts *did* establish that Ordine Nuovo was
without doubt responsible for the massacre.

Piazza Fontana was only the first of a series of further bomb attacks. In May 1974, a bomb killed eight citizens in Brescia (Lombardy); in August of the same year the *Italicus* high-speed train was
blown up and derailed, causing the deaths of 12 passengers. In both
cases, nobody has ever been tried. The worst attack carried out during the strategy of tension occurred in August 1980, when two suit-
case bombs planted in **Bologna** station cost 85 lives. More than 200
people were injured. This attack was subsequently attributed, in No-

vember 1995, to two right-wing extremists, Valerio Fioravanti and Francesco Mambro, who have never ceased to proclaim their innocence. The same sentence condemned Licio Gelli, the head of the secret **Propaganda Due** (P2) masonic lodge, along with two officers of the secret services, for having misled the investigation. In June 2002, three more neofascists, including a secret services officer, were sentenced to prison terms for misleading the investigation.

The Bologna blast was not the end of terror bombings in Italy. In December 1984, another high-speed train was blown up in the same place as the *Italicus* attack: 17 passengers died and 250 were injured. In May and July 1993, at the height of the political crisis provoked by the **Mani pulite** investigations, bombs exploded in **Florence**, near the Uffizi galleries, in Milan, and in Rome. Ten died and dozens were wounded. These attacks have been attributed to the **mafia**, which in the same year killed judges **Giovanni Falcone** and Paolo Borsellino.

STRESA FRONT. The prime ministers of France and Great Britain (Pierre Étienne Flandin and Ramsay MacDonald) met **Benito Mussolini** at Stresa in Piedmont on 11–14 April 1935, to reaffirm the validity of the **Locarno Pact** and to show their unity in the face of the rising power of Hitlerite Germany, which had unilaterally renounced the disarmament clauses of the Versailles Treaty only two weeks before. Looming over the talks, which ended with a worthy communiqué expressing their mutual desire for peace, rejection of unilateral actions, and commitment to the League of Nations, was the question of **Ethiopia**, which the Fascist regime was determined to acquire. The Ethiopian government had denounced the regime before the League of Nations in January, and the Fascist press was conducting a heated propaganda campaign against the African state. The British subsequently proposed that Italy should gain a tract of the Ogaden desert in exchange for territorial concessions to Ethiopia in British Somaliland. Mussolini responded angrily to this meager offer, threatening a war that would mean the "cancellation of Ethiopia from the map." According to Mussolini's Australian biographer, R. J. B. Bosworth, the British minister responsible for the talks, Sir Anthony Eden, came away from **Rome** with the impression that Mussolini was a "complete gangster" and "the anti-Christ." *See also* HOARE-LAVAL PACT.

STURZO, LUIGI (1871–1959). Born in Caltagirone (**Sicily**), Luigi Sturzo was ordained in 1904. Convinced of the need for the Church to involve itself in the lives of the working class, and to provide a Catholic alternative to socialism, "Don" Sturzo (the Sicilian honorific is nearly always applied by Italians—even non-Sicilians—to refer to a priest) interpreted his calling to include social and political action. He held elected office in Caltagirone, wrote for the Catholic press, and was secretary of **Azione Cattolica Italiana/**Catholic Action (ACI) between 1915 and 1917. With the tacit support of the **Vatican**, which had previously blocked any attempt to found a political movement that was not under the Church's direct control, Don Sturzo launched the **Partito Popolare Italiano/**Italian People's Party (PPI) in January 1919. The new movement sought to offer the working class a moderate alternative to the corruption and ineptness of Italian liberalism and the revolutionary politics of the **Partito Socialista Italiano/**Italian Socialist Party (PSI). The message found plenty of listeners: In the elections of November 1919, the PPI obtained nearly 21 percent of the votes and over 100 seats in the Chamber of Deputies.

Don Sturzo early recognized the dangers for democracy presented by **Fascism**, but despite the frequent acts of intimidation against the PPI's local organizations and activists, the party as a whole was more afraid of the PSI. In October 1922, the party was passive in the face of the Fascist coup and decided, against Don Sturzo's will, to participate in the government formed by the Fascist leader.

Don Sturzo's critical attitude toward **Benito Mussolini** was too controversial for a Vatican that, since the election of Pope Pius XI in February 1922, had cultivated good relations with the Fascists. Prior to the parliamentary debate over the "**Acerbo** Law" on electoral reform in 1923, the Fascists threatened to wage war against the Church if the Vatican did not disown the "priest from Caltagirone." The Church replied to this open threat by inviting Don Sturzo to step down, which he did in July. He continued to remain a member of the PPI's national council. In 1924 the PPI, with Don Sturzo to the fore, endorsed the boycott of Parliament by the democratic parties after the murder of **Giacomo Matteotti**. In October 1925, the Vatican bowed to Fascist pressure and instructed Don Sturzo to leave for London.

He spent the next 20 years in foreign exile. During his time abroad, he wrote numerous books under the watchful eye of the Church authorities, and finally returned to Italy in 1946. He took only a consultative role in the political development of the **Democrazia Cristiana**/Christian Democracy Party (DC). In 1953, he was appointed senator for life of the Italian Republic. He died in **Rome** in 1959. *See also* CATHOLICISM; DE GASPERI, ALCIDE; PAPACY.

SÜD TIROL VOLKSPARTEI/South Tyrol People's Party (SVP). The official voice of the German-speaking majority in the province of Bolzano, the SVP was founded in May 1945 by Erich Ammon, the recognized leader of those German-speaking Italian citizens who had chosen not to take German citizenship or to immigrate to Germany during the war. After the collapse of Nazi Germany and the reconstitution of Austria, the new party's representatives played an important background role in the talks between Italy and Austria that led, in September 1946, to the signature of a crucial accord between **Alcide De Gasperi** and the Austrian chancellor, Karl Gruber. Under its terms, Italy, in exchange for a guarantee of its borders, made a commitment to allow citizens who had opted for citizenship of the Third Reich to regain their Italian nationality and promised to introduce measures that would permit the German-speaking minority to exercise considerable local autonomy.

The SVP's political activity since 1946 has mostly been concerned with securing and amplifying the guarantees of autonomy provided by the De Gasperi-Gruber accord. The 1948 decision to make Trentino Alto-Adige one of five special autonomous regions recognized by Italy's Constitution gave the two provinces of Trento and Bolzano substantial political autonomy while continuing subsidies from Rome. In 1964, after a period of prolonged international pressure from the Austrian government, the SVP persuaded Italy to grant a "packet" of measures ensuring greater attention to the rights of the German- and Romansch-speaking (*Ladini*) minorities in Bolzano, and in the early 1970s the party succeeded in making knowledge of German compulsory for anybody employed in the public services. This measure enormously embittered the tens of thousands of Italians living in Bolzano and allowed the neofascist **Movimento Sociale Italiano**/Italian Social Movement (MSI) to establish itself as the main opposition party. Despite the concessions to the German-speaking minority, Alto Adige was the theater for sporadic outbursts of terrorist activity in the 1970s by nationalists organized as *Ein Tirol* ("One Tyrol"). The SVP did not always condemn the activities of this organization.

The SVP has dominated general and local elections in the province of Bolzano throughout the postwar years. It survived the crash of its main ally in Rome—the **Democrazia Cristiana**/Christian Democracy Party (DC)—with aplomb. Bolzano's tranquility is only skin deep, however. Only the Italian taxpayers' largesse has prevented the growth of a movement in favor of rewriting the De Gasperi-Gruber accords to allow either outright independence or unification with Austria. *See also* ALPS; REGIONALISM.

SVEVO, ITALO (pseud. Ettore Schmitz, 1861–1928). Born in **Trieste**, Italo Svevo was a neglected genius who, by bitter irony, was killed in a road accident just as he was winning European-wide fame for his dense, intellectually challenging novels. Svevo worked in obscurity for most of his career. Financial problems forced him to skip a university education and to work as a bank clerk from 1880 until 1899 (when he became a partner in his father-in-law's business). He was accordingly self-educated, reading widely in German idealist philosophy and the French realists.

Svevo's first novel, *Una Vita* (*A Life*), was published in 1892 to general critical indifference. His second novel, *Senilità* (*Senility*, 1898), met the same fate. Yet both novels were remarkable and meticulously observed portrayals of ordinary middle-class individuals unable to escape their own deficiencies and the circumstances of their lives. After the critical disappointment of *Senilità*, Svevo was silent for over 20 years. In 1905, he met James Joyce, who was living in Trieste at that time. He became a close friend of the great Irish writer, and in 1925, after Joyce had achieved international renown, he was able to bring Svevo's masterpiece, *La coscienza di Zeno* (*The Conscience of Zeno*, 1923), to the attention of the leading literary critics of the day. After years of anonymity, Svevo was suddenly recognized as one of the most insightful contemporary novelists.

La coscienza di Zeno merited this extraordinary acclaim. The novel is the diary of Zeno Cosini, a middle-aged man who has been encouraged by his analyst to write down his memoirs as a way of curing himself of nicotine addiction. As the tale unfolds, it becomes obvious that Zeno's compulsive smoking is only a symptom of a deeper malaise, a manifestation of his profound alienation from the structures of modern life. Like Joyce and Marcel Proust, Svevo concentrates on the depiction of his central character's inner life, not, as in 19th-century fiction, upon the external events that constitute the story. Svevo's novel is today recognized as one of the classics of literary modernism and one of the most successful literary representations of Freudian theories of the unconscious. *See also* LITERATURE.

– T –

TAMBRONI, FERNANDO (1901–1963). Born in Ascoli Piceno, by the mid-1920s Tambroni was an ambitious young lawyer, a prominent activist in the Federazione Universitaria Cattolici Italiana/ Catholic University Graduates' Movement (FUCI), and a functionary of the **Partito Popolare Italiana**/Italian Popular Party (PPI). His detractors argue that the aftermath of his 1926 arrest for alleged anti-regime activity—which was cited in his 1963 obituary notice—revealed a certain opportunism. His arrest was presented as showing him to be antifascist, but no mention was made of his immediately joining the **Partito Nazionale Fascista**/National Fascist Party (PNF). Such expediency, while not unusual in itself, makes more comprehensible his brief but turbulent spell in 1960 as the head of a government with dramatic implications for the future.

Tambroni returned to the PPI in time to be elected to the Chamber of Deputies in 1946 and to take up a place in the **Democrazia Cristiana**/ Christian Democracy Party (DC). Service in several of **Alcide De Gasperi**'s governments (January 1950 to June 1953) and in governments headed by **Giuseppe Pella** and **Amintore Fanfani**, to whom he grew very close, led to service as minister of the interior under **Antonio Segni** (February 1959 to February 1960). When the **Partito Liberale Italiano**/Italian Liberal Party (PLI) withdrew its support from that government, the DC became dependent on the neofascist **Movimento Sociale Italiano**/Italian Social Movement (MSI) for a parliamentary majority. Segni consequently resigned. After several unsuccessful attempts

at forming another government, President **Giovanni Gronchi** turned
to Tambroni, asking him to form a government pledged to resign after completing the budgetary process. When Tambroni's government
won a vote of confidence in the Chamber of Deputies (8 April 1960)
through the support of four monarchists and the MSI, three cabinet
members and an undersecretary immediately resigned. President
Gronchi, with the backing of the executive committee of the DC, then
persuaded **Parliament** to give Tambroni a limited mandate to steer
the budget through both houses, then resign. Tambroni, however, had
other ambitions. He announced sweeping schemes for new investment as well as higher wages and subsidies for entire categories of
the workforce.

Emboldened by its entry into Italian political life, the hitherto ostracized MSI declared its intention to hold its annual convention in
Genoa in July 1960. Genoa was the city in which partisans had accepted the surrender of General Meinhold's 11,000 German troops in
1945 and had the port operating when Allied armies arrived. A neofascist convention there was seen as a calculated affront.

From **Sicily** to **Milan** spontaneous protests erupted. **Police** repression was of a ferocity not seen in a decade. By mid-July, 10 demonstrators had been killed. The political right extolled Tambroni for
restoring order, while moderate and left opinion deplored the rebirth
of the conditions that had preceded the advent of **Fascism**. Italy
seemed on the verge of civil war. On 19 July, Tambroni resigned. His
party had no alternative but to become what **Aldo Moro** cited Alcide
De Gasperi as having called a "center party moving to the left." From
1960 until 1994, the MSI was excluded from any part in national governments. Moro used the incident to persuade major DC constituencies that there was no alternative to the **opening to the left**, while
Tambroni sank into an obscurity from which he never recovered. He
died in **Rome** three years after his dramatic fall from grace.

TITTONI, TOMMASO (1855–1931). Elected to **Parliament** when he
was just over 30 years old, Tittoni was one of the leading conservatives in liberal Italy. He was nominated to the Senate in 1902 and the
following year became foreign minister in the second government of
Giovanni Giolitti. Prime minister for two weeks during a government crisis in 1905, Tittoni held the post of foreign minister, with one

brief interlude as ambassador to Great Britain, until 1910. As foreign minister at a complex and difficult moment in European history, Tittoni skillfully managed to keep Italy from definitively joining either of the two armed camps forming in Europe and to keep tensions with Austria from boiling over into war. Between 1910 and 1916, he was ambassador to Paris; in 1919, he became foreign minister under **Francesco Saverio Nitti**. Tittoni supported the advent of **Fascism**, and served as president of the Senate until 1929, whereupon he became president of the **Accademia d'Italia**/Italian Academy and a member of the **Fascist Grand Council**. He died in his native **Rome** in 1931.

TOGLIATTI, PALMIRO (1893–1964). Togliatti was born in **Genoa** of Piedmontese parents. In 1911, while entered in an academic scholarship competition, Togliatti met **Antonio Gramsci**, another of the competitors. (Gramsci finished sixth; Togliatti second.) While both were studying at the University of **Turin**, they joined the **Partito Socialista Italiano**/Italian Socialist Party (PSI). After acquiring his degree in law, Togliatti interrupted his studies for a second degree (in philosophy) to serve in **World War I**. After his discharge, he collaborated with Gramsci in the Torinese weekly newspaper, *Il grido del popolo* (*The People's Cry*). At the Livorno (Leghorn) PSI Congress (21 January 1921), he helped lead the creation of the **Partito Comunista Italiano**/Italian Communist Party (PCI), with 58,000 members at birth. At the next two PCI congresses, he was elected to the central committee and to its executive committee. After several short-term incarcerations (1923 and 1925), he was a major organizer of the clandestine congresses of the PCI held in Lyons, France (1926), and in Cologne, Germany (1931), as well as the Antiwar Congress held in Brussels, Belgium, at the time of the Italian invasion of **Ethiopia**. Between 1936 and 1939, during the **Spanish Civil War**, he served in the International Brigade. Subsequently Togliatti left Europe to serve as a member of the Comintern, eventually rising to be its vice secretary. He spent the war years in Moscow broadcasting as "Mario Correnti."

He returned to Italy in 1944 to preside at the party's Salerno Congress as the party's general secretary, a post to which he was reelected in 1947. The party proclaimed that it had but one goal: the defeat of the Nazi occupiers and their Fascist underlings. The PCI should join the government although it was Catholic, conservative, and headed by a royally appointed army officer whose career had been advanced by his service to **Fascism**. Liberation had a higher priority than revolution. This was the so-called *svolta di Salerno* (the Salerno about-turn).

The central role of the PCI in the resistance, other parties' compromises with the regime, and the prowess shown by the Red Army led Togliatti to think that a socialist revolution by electoral means was not only possible but likely. Once parliamentary democracy was restored, a coalition might unite all those workers, peasants, youths, and intellectuals who shared the vision of a progressive democracy. The presence of Allied armies on Italian soil was an additional argument against any premature insurrection to install a dictatorship of the proletariat. Togliatti himself served in the governments headed by **Pietro Badoglio** (April–June 1944), **Ivanoe Bonomi** (June 1944–June 1945), **Ferruccio Parri** (June–December 1945), and **Alcide De Gasperi** (December 1945–July 1946). In July 1948, he was the target of an unsuccessful assassination attempt in **Rome**. When an interlocutor suggested mobilizing ex-partisans and arming communist cells, Togliatti's astounded reaction allegedly was, "what do you want to do, start a revolution?"

Togliatti made two main contributions to postwar politics: the stabilization of political life in the early postfascist years and the conversion of the PCI from a vanguard party to a mass organization that added communist political culture to much of Italian society. Its demonstrated ability to create an alternative civic sense, with recreation centers for both members and nonmembers; its libraries open to all (even during the midday break when most libraries close); and even its annual fundraiser, *Feste dell'Unità*, made for a strong sense of solidarity.

However, these attributes were counterbalanced by several negative features. For one, the party—at least until the 1980s—was totally lacking in internal democracy. This may have been a necessary price to pay for avoiding the sorts of factionalism that tormented other Italian parties. Second, not only was it hierarchical but—especially after Stalin's death in 1953—it was given to virtual beatification of its saints, Gramsci and Togliatti himself. The PCI, despite many protestations about its difference from other Western communist parties, followed the Moscow line obediently in the immediate postwar period and acquiesced in the most outrageous acts of the Soviet dictatorship, notably the 1956 invasion and repression of Hungary.

Togliatti used the 20th Congress of the Communist Party of the USSR to proclaim his doctrine of polycentrism, that is, each communist party taking its own road to socialism. He had already opposed the excommunication of parties from the Comintern for not accepting Soviet instruction. Togliatti's death at Yalta in the summer of 1964 ended the career of a supremely adaptable leader. *See also* BERLINGER, ENRICO; LONGO, LUIGI.

TOSCANINI, ARTURO (1867–1957). One of the greatest orchestral conductors of modern times, Toscanini was born in Parma, where he studied at the conservatory. After a distinguished early career as a musician and conductor, he became the first director of **Milan**'s La Scala Theater in 1898. Much of his subsequent career was spent in the United States as the director of New York's finest orchestras. Between 1937 and 1954, he was the director of the NBC symphony orchestra, which was dissolved upon his retirement in 1954. Famously choleric with wayward musicians, Toscanini preached and practiced a policy of strict fidelity to the original musical scores. His repertoire included Verdi, Puccini, Wagner, Beethoven, and Brahms, but few post-1918 works. Toscanini's relationship with the Fascist regime was a mixed one. He actually ran as a candidate for the **Partito Nazionale Fascista**/National Fascist Party (PNF) in the 1919 elections, but quickly lost sympathy with the regime. In May 1931, he refused to play the Fascist hymn *Giovinezza* as the prelude to a concert in **Bologna** and was brutally beaten by the blackshirts. Toscanini immigrated to the United States following this episode and only returned in 1956. He died the following year.

TOTÒ (ANTONIO CLEMENTE DE CURTIS, 1898–1967). Born in **Naples** (where else?), Totò (stage name) was the greatest Italian comedian of the 20th century. The illegitimate son of the Marquis Giuseppe de Curtis and Anna Clemente, Totò was a poet, wit, and actor in more than 100 films, most of them cheap and simple comedies. He began his career in *avanspettacolo* (quick sketch comedy, like vaudeville) but moved into stage comedy in the late 1920s and to films in 1937, with the movie *Fermo con le mani* (*Keep Your Hands Still!*). At the height of his fame, in the 1950s, he was ubiquitous. In one four-year period (1953–1956), he managed to star in 21 separate films. His costars included a young Sofia Loren (in *Tempi Nostri*, 1954) and Marcello Mastroianni (in *I soliti ignoti*, 1958), and he was directed by **Vittorio De Sica, Alessandro Blasetti**, and Mario Monicelli, among others. He gave an inspired performance in a serious role in **Pierpaolo Pasolini**'s *Uccellacci e Uccellini* (*Hawks and Sparrows*, 1966).

Totò continued making films until he died, although he himself was convinced that only a handful of his films would survive. His catchphrases became part of everyday colloquial language, as did his dry, Groucho-like humor ("he was so unpleasant a man that when he died his relatives called for an encore"). Totò once said that you could always recognize a Neapolitan by his ability to live without a single lira, but he was himself generous in using his money to help young actors. In his movies, but also in life, he enjoyed guying the aristocracy. In 1946, he changed his name by deed poll to a parody of an aristocratic name, replete with the most fantastic titles. He died in **Rome** in April 1967. *See also* CINEMA.

TRADE UNIONS. The prefascist trade unions, whether of Catholic or Marxist inspiration, were equally the targets of systematic violence at the hands of Fascist action squads, then of outright prohibition. During the **resistance,** however, the **Comitati di Liberazione Nazionale**/National Liberation Committees (CLN) drew many of their leaders together. The collaborative spirit that informed the resistance moved its component parties to work together in reconstituting the Confederazione Generale Italiana del Lavoro/Italian General Confederation of Labor (CGIL) in 1944. Giuseppe di Vittorio, of the **Partito Comunista Italiano**/Italian Communist Party (PCI), was its first postwar president. In the early reconstruction years the union made continual concessions, eager to avoid antagonizing the dominant **Democrazia Cristiana**/Christian Democracy Party (DC). By late 1946, factory committees had been effectively emasculated, thus silencing for a time the workers' voice on the shop floor.

After the 1948 elections and the onset of the Cold War, nothing could prevent Catholic members from leaving the CGIL and forming their own Confederazione Italiana Sindacati Lavoratori/Italian Confederation of Workers' Unions (CISL). They were soon followed by the Social Democrats and Republicans, who had formed the Unione Italiana del Lavoro/Italian Union of Labor (UIL). The CGIL, from being a three-party union, became a "transmission belt" for the PCI. This led to a persistent employers' offensive, generously backed by the U.S. embassy and the American Federation of Labor (AFL), so that by 1955, the influence of the CGIL had noticeably decreased. It was not until July 1972 that a broad CGIL-CISL-UIL federation was reformed. The components cooperated but retained their independence.

In the late 1960s many young Italian workers, especially migrants from the South, inspired by what they saw happening in France, concluded that the moment had come for a New Left. Disruptive and often violent, it led to immediate results. Union leaders demanded total autonomy from political parties, the better to respond to this uncompromising spirit. Thereafter the unions began to recover some of their lost standing among workers. At the end of the "hot autumn" of 1969, concessions included the right to convene shop-floor assemblies for up to 10 hours annually at employer expense, the 40-hour week, and the beginnings of wage-leveling. In 1970 and 1971 the unions began to reintroduce elected factory councils. Union training schools offered courses on trade union history and political theory. In 1973, the metalworkers' contract entitled them to up to 150 hours paid time off every three years for instruction in public institutions in pursuit of higher qualifications. Feminist collectives became widespread by the use of this provision.

The greatest gain obtained by the unions, however, was unquestionably the *scala mobile* ("moving staircase"), automatic wage indexing for all categories of workers. This technique of protecting wages from inflation was extended from industrial workers to the rest of the economy in 1975, but it proved to be a heavy burden for Italian business. It was overturned by negotiations between the government of **Giuliano Amato** and the unions in July 1992.

Union power peaked in the late 1970s. In 1980, **FIAT** pointed to a declining market share to explain a chain of dismissals. The reaction was a union call for a total shutdown. After 34 days, in a spontaneous counterstrike, up to 40,000 foremen, white-collar workers, and line workers who wanted to return to work paraded through the streets of **Turin**. A turning point was reached when the union capitulated. Italy remains one of the most highly unionized countries in the world.

General strikes occur regularly, and certain industries, notably the railways, are prone to industrial action. *See also* COBAS; CORPO-RATISM; FASCISM; LOTTA CONTINUA; *SQUADRISMO*.

TRASFORMISMO. A key term in Italian politics, *trasformismo* was born in 1882, when **Agostino Depretis**, anxious to widen his parliamentary majority and to lessen his dependence on the parliamentary left, invited members of the parliamentary right to "transform themselves" into centrists and join with him in carrying out a specific program of common policies while sharing in the good things of government. Led by **Marco Minghetti**, a substantial group of former rightists did in fact reinforce Depretis's cabinet in 1883. **Giovanni Giolitti** was a flawed master of the same technique. His decision to open the doors of parliamentary respectability to the Fascists in the 1921 election campaign illustrates the dangers of this brand of accommodating, inclusive politics. A more recent example is the **opening to the left** in the 1960s, when the **Democrazia Cristiana/** Christian Democracy Party (DC) successfully persuaded the **Partito Socialista Italiano/**Italian Socialist Party (PSI) to join its majority. The word *trasformismo* is thus commonly used to describe the practice of ruling politicians to seek a stable majority by patronage rather than by ideological solidarity.

TREVES, CLAUDIO (1869–1933). Born in **Turin** to an affluent family, Treves studied jurisprudence at the University of Turin and became a leading deputy of the **Partito Socialista Italiano/**Italian Socialist Party (PSI). Together with **Leonida Bissolati**, he bent his efforts to persuading his constituents to accept reform as preferable to revolution. For Bissolati, this could even mean agreeing to join bourgeois governments, though Treves's view was that this was taking reform too far. Yet when the PSI supported a more intransigent position than his, Treves began publishing *Critica Sociale* (*Social Criticism*), which came close to justifying the war in **Libya**, contrary to the party's position. He seemed unable to choose between violent revolution (which he rejected) and sharing power with the bourgeoisie (which he also rejected).

Even in the Socialist Party's internal affairs the importance attached to doctrinal purity was often self-defeating. Turati and Treves, for example, who were on the left wing of the reformists, were the right wing of the official party once it was in the hands of intransigents. Convinced that the maximalists' policies were bound to fail, the reformists refused to accept places offered them on the party's executive committee. These maneuvers, not surprisingly, left the party divided between equally unyielding reformists and revolutionaries and quite unable to respond effectively to changing circumstances. They nevertheless refused to cooperate with the **Partito Popolare Italiano**/Italian People's Party (PPI) to impede the seizure of power by the Fascists. Events were to prove that time was not on their side.

At the 1919 Socialist Congress, Treves and the other moderates were outvoted by four to one. Even after the most radical wing of the PSI split from the party at Livorno (Leghorn) in January 1921 to form the Partito Comunista d'Italia, Treves and Turati remained in a minority, and they were eventually expelled in October 1922. They formed the Partito Socialista Unitario/Unitary Socialist Party (PSU) and decided—too late—to cooperate with the Catholic Party to oppose **Fascism**. In November 1926, Treves, together with **Giuseppe Saragat** and **Ferruccio Parri**, fled to Paris, where Treves edited *La Libertà* (*Liberty*). By the mid-1920s, most reform socialists were to be found in Paris. Treves died there in 1933.

TRIESTE. The largest city in Italy's northeast, with some 300,000 inhabitants, Trieste marks the border with the republic of Slovenia and is one of the most important ports on the Adriatic. While its history goes back to pre-Roman times, it was under the dominion of the Habsburgs from 1382 to 1918. The foundation of the city's commercial wealth goes back to 1719, when it became a free port. Briefly occupied by the French during the Napoleonic wars, it was restored to Austria in 1813 and became an autonomous province within the Austrian Empire in 1850. The population was nevertheless mostly Italian speaking, and after the **Risorgimento**, nationalist sympathies began to spread. The 1882 hanging by the Austrians of Guglielmo Oberdan, an irredentist, only inflamed pro-Italian feeling. During **World War I**, Trieste was the prize for which Italian troops fought 11 battles on the Isonzo River, which empties into the Adriatic near the city. Italian troops entered the city in November 1918. Trieste, along with the Istrian Peninsula, became Italian by the Treaty of **Saint Germain** in

June 1919. Half a million Slovenes were thereby placed under Italian rule.

In 1945, after two years of Nazi occupation, Istria and Trieste were captured by Yugoslav partisans, who carried out a ruthless policy of "ethnic cleansing" at the expense of the Italian-speaking community. Thousands were murdered, and tens of thousands more fled to Italy. In June 1945, the former province of Trieste was divided into a small "zone A," which was administered by the British and Americans and included the city, and a much larger "zone B," left in the hands of the Yugoslav government. The peace treaty of February 1947 defined the city itself as a free territory. Italy reoccupied "zone A" in 1953, and in 1954 the Yugoslav government recognized Italian sovereignty over the city. The present border was fixed by the Treaty of Osimo in November 1975.

The loss of its hinterland in Istria after 1945 explains why, at 220 square kilometers (85 square miles), Trieste is by far the smallest Italian province. Trieste is anomalous in other ways. Its long domination by Austria has ensured that the city's architecture has little in common with the rest of Italy and much in common with mid-European cities, such as Prague or Vienna. Trieste is also the windiest city in Italy. The so-called *bora* can blow for weeks on end; special railings are in place along the most exposed streets to protect citizens from being blown off their feet. *See also FOIBE*; IRREDENTISMO; MAGRIS, CLAUDIO.

TRIPLE ALLIANCE. A secret treaty signed by Germany, Austria-Hungary, and Italy on 20 May 1882, the Triple Alliance bound the signatories to offer mutual assistance in the event that any one of them should be attacked by two or more powers—Russia and France being perceived as the main dangers. It was to be renewed at five-year intervals and was in effect until 1915. The alliance was motivated by Otto von Bismarck's desire to isolate France and by Austria-Hungary's desire to obtain backing against Russia for its adventures in the Balkans. For Italy, allying with its historic enemy, Austria, represented a sea change in **foreign policy** and signaled that the cabinet of **Agostino Depretis** did not intend to listen to the nationalists, who since the mid-1870s, had been pressing the Italian government to put the liberation of the Trentino and **Trieste**—the two largest provinces still under Austrian domination—at the core of its foreign policy.

Foreign Minister Felice Nicolis di Robilant, the architect of the new policy, was motivated by Italy's need for diplomatic support against France, which was blocking its attempts to expand into Tunisia and to build a North African empire. French support for the pope was feared as well. While the alliance offered none of the guarantees of Italy's position in **Rome** sought by Italy, it did provide assurances against an attack by France.

The threat posed by this alliance prompted France to ally itself with Russia in 1894 and to enter an *entente cordiale* with Great Britain in 1904, thus dividing Europe into two counterposed blocs of powers. Many historians believe that the origins of **World War I** are to be found in the frictions between the powers that this situation inevitably provoked. In 1915, however, Italy entered the war on the side of Britain and France, rather than Austria-Hungary and Germany. *See also* LONDON, TREATY OF.

TURATI, FILIPPO (1857–1932). Turati was the most prominent reformist voice in the early days of the Italian socialist movement. From 1891 onward, he was editor of the review *Critica sociale*. In 1892, he was the author, together with his companion, the former Russian revolutionary Anna Kuliscioff, of the newly formed **Partito Socialista Italiano**/Italian Socialist Party's (PSI) political program. He became a parliamentary deputy in 1896, a role that did not save him from arrest and imprisonment in 1898 during the indiscriminate repression of the socialist movement ordered by the government of **Antonio Starabba di Rudinì** in that year.

Despite the Italian state's heavy-handed treatment of the workers' movement, Turati was no revolutionary. In November 1900 — at his behest — the PSI committed itself to a gradual transformation of Italian society via parliamentary institutions and gave parliamentary backing to the liberal government headed by **Giuseppe Zanardelli** in 1901. Although this approach was criticized by many in the PSI, it remained the primary strand of thinking within the PSI until the 1912 party conference. In that year, the so-called maximalists, led by **Benito Mussolini**, became the majority voice in the party, while the reformists of the right, who wished to turn the PSI into a labor party on the British model, were expelled. Turati, who subscribed to neither group, was left in the middle.

Turati bitterly opposed Italy's entry into **World War I**. He foresaw that the war would heighten Italy's class divisions and block the economic modernization that was a precondition for a peaceful transition to socialism. After the disaster of **Caporetto** in 1917, however—to the disgust of many in the PSI—he did support the defense of Italian territory.

The PSI entered the Third International created by the Bolsheviks in 1919, and one of V. I. Lenin's explicit conditions for the party's continued membership was the expulsion of Turati and his fellow moderates. Many even of the maximalists balked at this demand, but by 1922 Turati's studied moderation and defense of parliamentary institutions were in any case anathema to the PSI's militants. On 1 October 1922, Turati was expelled by the narrow margin of 32,000 votes to 29,000. Undeterred, he organized a new leftist party, the Partito Socialista Unitario/Unitary Socialist party (PSU), which attracted many of the bravest young socialists in Italy. Following the murder of his friend and comrade **Giacomo Matteotti** by the Fascists, Turati joined with **Alcide De Gasperi** and **Giovanni Amendola** in boycotting **Parliament**. The failure of the boycott left Turati in personal danger, and he escaped to Paris, where he continued the resistance to **Fascism** and sought to reunify the PSI into a single antifascist force. He died in exile. *See also* AVENTINE SECESSION; BISSOLATI, LEONIDA.

TURIN (Torino). Located in the northwest corner of Italy near the French border, Turin is the fourth-largest city in Italy, with a current population of around 900,000. Like **Milan**, Turin can trace its history to Roman times, but its modern history began in 1718, when it became the capital of the kingdom of **Sardinia**. During the Napoleonic wars the city was a constant battleground. In 1798, it fell to the French. Austro-Russian forces fighting in Italy reconquered it in 1799, and the French retook the city in 1800. It remained in French hands until 1815, when the **Congress of Vienna** restored the Sardinian throne. In 1821, the city rose in revolt and demanded the granting of a constitutional **monarchy**; only the intervention of Austria restored absolute rule. After the **Risorgimento** in 1859–1861, Turin was the seat of the kingdom of Italy until 1865, when the capital was transferred first to **Florence** and then, in 1870, to **Rome**. The decision to move the capital provoked massive popular demonstrations in Turin in September 1864 that left 50 dead.

At the end of the 19th century, Turin was **Milan**'s only rival for the title of Italy's industrial capital. **FIAT**—still the city's largest employer—began operations in 1899 and was soon giving work to tens of thousands of workers at its Mirafiori plant. The city's workers gallantly resisted the Nazis during the German occupation in the latter stages of the war. During the 1950s and 1960s, the city became home to hundreds of thousands of southern Italian migrants, who were housed in hastily built projects on the city's outskirts. Turin naturally became one of Italy's most highly unionized cities, and the city has frequently been the scene of street clashes between the authorities and striking workers, most particularly during the "hot autumn" of 1969. Apart from FIAT, Turin is chiefly famous outside of Italy for being the home of the Juventus soccer club and for hosting the 2006 Winter Olympics.

The city's 15th-century cathedral houses the "shroud of Turin," a cloth that appears to have an imprinted image of Christ, popularly believed to be the sheet in which Jesus was wrapped when he was taken down from the Cross. Carbon dating has confirmed that the shroud dates back to well before the Middle Ages. In 1997, the shroud miraculously escaped destruction in a major fire that left lasting damage to the cathedral. *See also* CALCIO; NAPOLEONIC ITALY; TRADE UNIONS, ECONOMY.

– U –

ULIVO. *See* OLIVE TREE COALITION.

UNGARETTI, GIUSEPPE (1888–1970). A personal, autobiographical poet, Giuseppe Ungaretti was born in Egypt and schooled in France, where he attended the Sorbonne and imbibed the philosophy of Henri Bergson at its source. He arrived in Italy in 1914, where he began to publish poetry in the Florentine review *Lacerba*. Loudly prowar, Ungaretti fought in **World War I** as a common soldier, and his war poetry, gathered in the collection *L'Allegria* (*Joy*, 1917), is the greatest poetic testimony of the war on the Italian front. The

436 • UNIONE DEI DEMOCRATICI CRISTIANI E DEMOCRATICI DI CENTRO

experience of combat transformed his jingoism into a more reflective understanding of the horrors that war inevitably brings. In the poem "San Martino del Carso," he superbly conveyed the anguish he felt on seeing a village that had been battered by artillery: "Of these houses/Nothing remains/But a few/Broken Walls/Of the many/Who wrote me/None now are here/But in my heart/No cross is missing/My heart/Is the most shattered village of all."

Ungaretti's second major collection, *Sentimento del tempo* (*The Sentiment of the Time*, 1933), saw the poet experimenting with religious themes and with more traditional metrical structures, as he attempted to recapture the "song" of classical Italian poetry. Between 1936 and 1942, Ungaretti lived in Brazil, where he taught Italian culture in São Paulo. His stay was marked by the tragic death of his son, Antonietto, whom he later remembered in the lyrics that constituted half of his 1947 collection, *Il dolore* (*Grief*). The remainder of the poems were dedicated to "occupied **Rome**," and many critics regard them as his finest work. Ungaretti's collected works were published in 1970, shortly before his death. *See also* LITERATURE.

UNIONE DEI DEMOCRATICI CRISTIANI E DEMOCRATICI DI CENTRO/Union of Christian Democrats and Democrats of the Center (UDC). The UDC is the third-largest party in the center-right **Casa delle Libertà**/House of Freedoms (CDL). Formed in December 2002, the party united within its ranks three political forces of Christian democratic principles and ideology: the Cristiani Democratici Uniti/Christian Democratic Union (CDU), whose leader was **Rocco Buttiglione**; the Centro Cristiano Democratico/Christian Democratic Center (CCD), whose chief figure was **Pierferdinando Casini**; and Democrazia Europea/European Democracy (DE), a political movement inspired by the Catholic trade unionist Sergio D'Antoni and supported by **Giulio Andreotti**. D'Antoni left the party within two years, however, to join **Romano Prodi** in the opposite center-left coalition. The new party's leader was a well-known Catholic intellectual called Marco Follini; Buttiglione was party president. Follini's relationship with **Silvio Berlusconi** and with other members of Berlusconi's government such as the **Lega Nord**/Northern League (LN) was very tense. Follini frequently attacked the government, especially over the LN's plans to revise the **Constitution**. Follini eventually joined the government as deputy prime minister in December 2004, but lasted in the job only until April 2005. He also resigned from the party secretaryship in October 2005, being replaced by Lorenzo Cesa.

Despite these dissensions within the party and with its allies, the UDC has consolidated its political presence since 2002. In April 2006 the party, which boasts the distinctive shield and cross emblem of the former **Democrazia Cristiana**/Christian Democracy party (DC), took almost 2.6 million votes in elections for the Chamber of Deputies (39 seats) and 2.3 million in the Senate elections (21 seats), nearly double the number of the CCD and CDU combined in 2001. In both chambers, the UDC took almost 7 percent of the vote. Many of the UDC's votes came from disillusioned supporters of **Forza Italia**, but it is also clear that the party retained many of the votes cast for D'Antoni's DE in the previous 2001 elections. The UDC is helped by the leadership of Casini, who is one of the most charismatic, and one of the few young, leaders in Italian politics today.

UNIVERSITIES. Bologna University was founded in 1088 and is usually regarded as the oldest university in the world. Several other Italian universities, notably **Naples** and Padua, date back to the 13th century.

The modern history of the Italian university dates from 1859, when the Casati educational law laid down the fundamental characteristics of a modern university. Universities were charged with a double goal of preparing youth (which until after **World War II** mostly meant men) for technically skilled work in the public sphere and private professions, and with "maintaining and nurturing" scientific and literary culture. There were to be five faculties: theology, law, medicine, natural sciences, and arts and letters. With the exception of reforms introduced by the philosopher **Giovanni Gentile** in his 1923 educational act, this structure remained the basis of Italian higher education until the 1960s, although new faculties, such as engineering, were added, and the number of students gradually rose.

Nevertheless, in the mid-1960s, Italian universities were hierarchical, elitist institutions lacking modern facilities such as study rooms, sports halls, dormitories, and scholarships. The curriculum was outdated and was taught by learned but distant professors whose hostility to innovation was legendary. When the prosperous baby boom generation began to reach the university system in the mid-1960s, the by-now crowded universities proved unable to adapt and entered into the most prolonged crisis of higher education (from 1966 to 1978) anywhere in the advanced industrial world.

In 1980, when the wave of protest had finally ebbed, a major reform of the universities was introduced. The PhD was finally introduced, the professoriate was split into three categories (researcher, associate professor, and full professor), and departments were introduced and given the task of conducting research. A ministry for research and the universities was set up in 1987. Universities nevertheless remained highly centralized, with promotion taking place through national public examinations and with curricular development being tightly controlled by the ministry. Despite some attempts to provide more autonomy in these areas, Italian universities remain among the most state-controlled in the world.

In 1999 the traditional four-year, master's-equivalent degree, or *laurea*, was abolished and replaced with a new system of a three-year diploma followed by a two-year "specialist" degree. The aim of the reform was to increase the number of people graduating with at least three years' college in their early or midtwenties (completion rates had been among the worst in Europe), but in this respect it has failed. The reform has been botched, completion rates have not significantly increased, and serious questions have been raised about the quality of the new degrees, with many people asserting that they have turned the university into an *esamificio* (exam mill).

Italy's universities are today in an authentic crisis. The country spends less on research and higher **education** than almost any other industrial country and spends the money badly; there is a brain drain of frightening proportions as young researchers flee to the United States, Great Britain, northern Europe, and other more progressive systems; and professors are underpaid and too often unproductive. Teaching is old-fashioned and often neglected by the senior professors. Yet reform seems distant, and some obvious changes, such as increasing fees, would arouse passionate opposition among both faculty and students.

A measure of Italy's backwardness is to be found in the international rankings published by the Shanghai Jiao Tong University. Only *one* Italian university made the top 100 in 2006 (La Sapienza in

Rome), and it was last among this elite group. Only five others made the top 200. European universities fared poorly by comparison with American institutions in this ranking, but Britain, the Netherlands, the Scandinavian countries, Germany, Switzerland, and Belgium all scored better (in some cases, far better) than Italy. *See also* SES-SANTOTTO, IL.

UOMO QUALUNQUE. *See QUALUNQUISMO.*

– V –

VATICAN. An independent city-state of 0.44 square kilometers (0.17 square miles), the Vatican consists of Saint Peter's cathedral (so named because it was built by Emperor Constantine in the fourth century AD on what legend reputed to be the tomb of the apostle Peter), its surrounding palaces (which include the pope's private quarters and the Vatican library), and a substantial walled park behind Saint Peter's. The city has fewer than 1,000 residents, of whom approximately 400 carry the Vatican passport. The pope's territorial authority also extends over a handful of important buildings elsewhere in **Rome**, including the cathedral.

The pope rules as absolute monarch over the tiny city-state, which has its own railway station and its own newspaper (the *Osservatore Romano*, the official organ of the Vatican). A regiment of (volunteer) Swiss guards, in colorful costumes designed by Raphael, maintains a symbolic defense of the tiny state. The Vatican maintains an observer at the United Nations but is not a member. Nevertheless, since the signing of the **Lateran pacts** in 1929, it has been recognized as a sovereign state. The Vatican is full of priceless works of art by the great Renaissance masters. The recently restored frescoes painted by Michelangelo on the ceilings of the Sistine chapel continue to draw awed art lovers from around the world. *See also* CATHOLICISM; GUARANTEE LAWS; PAPACY.

VELTRONI, WALTER (1955–). While still in a Roman secondary school, Veltroni joined the Federazione Giovanile Comunista Italiana/Italian Communist Youth Federation (FGCI) and was soon elected secretary of his cell. In 1975, he was elected provincial secretary and a member of the national executive of the FGCI. The next year (he was just 21), he was elected to the city council of **Rome** and within another year was put in charge of propaganda for the Roman federation of the **Partito Comunista Italiano**/Italian Communist Party (PCI). By 1980, he was second in charge of propaganda and relations with the **press** of the national party.

Veltroni was elected to the Chamber of Deputies in 1987 and was reelected in 1992 and in 1996 as a member of the **Partito Democratico della Sinistra**/Democratic Party of the Left (PDS). He served as deputy prime minister and as minister for culture in the government of **Romano Prodi** (1996–1998). In the latter capacity, he is largely credited with overseeing—even with monthly personal visits—the final stages of restoration of the Borghese Art Museum, a 17th-century villa that has been the property of the Italian state since 1902. It includes paintings by Caravaggio, Titian, and Raphael as well as sculptures by **Antonio Canova** and Bernini. The villa's reopening to the public in summer 1997 was regarded as a turning point in Italy's notoriously neglectful approach to its cultural heritage.

Veltroni became mayor of Rome in 2002. He is associated with the idea of transforming the **Olive Tree Coalition**/Ulivo into a single "Democratic Party" on the U.S. model. Veltroni, in fact, is a student of the Democratic Party and has written several books and essays on the Kennedy family. Should the Democratic Party idea take off, Veltroni would be a serious candidate for its leadership. *See also* DEMOCRATICI DI SINISTRA (DS).

VENICE (Venezia). One of the most famous and visited cities in the world, Venice was long one of Europe's most powerful independent states, *La Serenissima Repubblica* (The Most Serene Republic). The doges of Venice (chosen by a popular assembly until AD 1172 and by a Grand Council of noblemen thereafter) dominated the eastern Mediterranean and trade between Europe and the East until the 18th century, when Venice's centuries-long struggle against the power of the Ottoman Turks was brought to an end by the Peace of Passerowitz, in which the Venetians lost all their colonies except for settlements along the Dalmatian coastline.

The city's modern history began in 1797, when a century of economic decline ended in a popular revolt against the aristocracy and the institution of a short-lived democracy. Briefly under Austrian rule, Venice became part of Bonaparte's Kingdom of Italy, but at the Congress of Vienna it was restored to Austria. In 1848, under the leadership of **Daniele Manin**, the city established a republic that held out against the Austrians until August 1849. It subsequently remained under Austrian rule until 1866 when, after a plebiscite, it passed into Italian hands.

With the possible exceptions of **Florence** and Saint Petersburg, it is probably fair to say that no city in the world has so large a share of the world's artistic and cultural heritage as Venice. Its long dominant position and its commercial wealth made the city a mecca for artists during the Renaissance and after. Bellini, Giorgione, Tiziano, Tintoretto, Veronese, Tiepolo, and Canaletto are all "Venetian" artists.

The modern city has 70,000 inhabitants, down from 150,000 just a few decades ago. On the other side of the lagoon is the large industrial satellite-city of Mestre, with nearly 400,000 citizens. Tens of millions of tourists every year take a gondola down the Grand Canal or visit Saint Mark's Square. Tourism, while an immense source of income for the local economy, has inflicted substantial **environmental** costs, and on some days during the high season the city has to block the road link from Mestre to prevent overcrowding. Venice is currently sinking into its lagoon at a dangerous rate, and the city council, the Italian government, and UNESCO are studying various projects to stop the slide. *See also* NAPOLEONIC ITALY.

VERDI (Greens). *See* ENVIRONMENTALISM.

VERDI, GIUSEPPE (1813–1901). Born near Parma, Verdi's early musical and private life was characterized by setbacks. His attempt to enter the conservatory at **Milan** in 1832 was rebuffed on the grounds of his excessive age and insufficient piano technique. Between 1838 and 1840, he had to endure the tragedy of losing his wife and children to illness. Only in 1842, when he composed *Nabucco*, did his luck begin to turn. In the next 15 years he wrote nearly 20 operas, including *Rigoletto* (1851) and *La Traviata* (1853). By now internationally famous, he began writing and presenting operas all over the

world: *Aida* (1871), perhaps his most famous work, was first produced in Cairo with the pyramids as a backdrop. Verdi was a patriot
and a supporter of the unification of Italy and was elected to the first
Italian Parliament in 1861. During the 1850s, audiences who wanted
to show their support for Italian nationalism would hang banners in
the theater reading "Viva V.E.R.D.I." As well as showing their affection for a great composer, the letters stood for "Vittorio Emanuele Re
d'Italia."

After *Aida*, Verdi's production became less intense. In 1874, he
composed the requiem mass for the novelist **Alessandro Manzoni**.
His last two great works were both based on Shakespeare's plays:
Otello (1877) and *Falstaff* (1893). Musically less challenging than his
great German contemporary, Wagner, Verdi's operas have nevertheless lost none of their appeal for audiences all over the world. In Italy,
he remains a popular composer in the widest sense of the word, and
new productions of *Rigoletto* or *La Traviata* are whistled off the stage
if they do not meet the public's demanding standards for singing and
orchestration.

VERGA, GIOVANNI (1840–1922). The greatest exponent of *verismo*
(naturalism) in Italian **literature**, Giovanni Verga's exceptional powers of realistic description have led to comparisons with such writers
as Emile Zola and D. H. Lawrence. Verga was born in Catania, **Sicily**,
but spent much of his life in **Florence** and **Milan**. Between 1866 and
1881, Verga produced several novels and plays, but with *I
Malavoglia* (*The House of the Medlar Tree*, 1881) he established
himself as a writer of international repute. *I Malavoglia* is the story
of a family of Sicilian fishermen who tempt fate by foolishly specu-
lating on a cargo of lupins. This act of vainglory is the harbinger of a
series of disasters that lead the family into misery and dishonor.
Verga's theme, in short, is the pessimistic one of determinism: the in-
ability of human beings to escape the circumstances of their birth.
The book inspired **Luchino Visconti**'s classic neorealist film *La
terra trema* (*The Earth Trembles*, 1948).

In 1886, Verga published a second novel with a similarly fatalistic
theme, *Mastro Don Gesualdo*, which is the story of a man who is determined to acquire possessions at all costs. He succeeds, but at the
end of the novel, despite his daughter's brilliant marriage, he dies

without the family love and affection, which, Verga seems to imply, alone give meaning to life. In the mid-1890s, Verga returned to Catania and worked half-heartedly at a third book, this time set in high society, portraying "the defeated," but never finished it. Nominated to the Senate in 1920, he died in his ancestral home in Catania in 1922.

VICTOR EMMANUEL I/Vittorio Emanuele I (1759–1824). *See* MONARCHY; VIENNA, CONGRESS OF.

VICTOR EMMANUEL II/Vittorio Emanuele II (1820–1878). Born in **Turin** on 19 March 1820, this last king of Sardinia and first king of a united Italy grew up in Tuscany and Piedmont. He was the son of **Charles Albert** and Maria Teresa of Tuscany. As a young man, he married Maria Adelaide, daughter of the Austrian viceroy in Lombardy-Venetia. Despite his lack of command experience, he led a division in the War of Independence of 1848–1849. Defeat at Novara led his father to abdicate and brought young Victor Emmanuel to the throne. In that position, he negotiated an armistice with General Radetzky.

He revealed his absolutist inclinations by twice dissolving **Parliament** when its majority objected to the resultant treaty. The king twice called for new elections until the majority that he preferred was realized. Parliament approved the treaty with Austria in 1850. The king further circumvented the parliament by making a secret arrangement with France for the dispatch of Piedmontese troops to the Crimea in 1854, just as he was later to make a secret alliance with France in the event of war with Prussia. After **Giuseppe Garibaldi** had ceded **southern Italy** to Piedmont (18 March 1861), his influence with the new king of Italy grew, to the intense chagrin of **Camillo Benso di Cavour**. In fact, Victor Emmanuel retained secret contacts with both **Giuseppe Mazzini** and Garibaldi throughout his reign. When **Rome** was absorbed, the Piedmontese king of united Italy began to be called "Father of his Country." His dynastic policy often put him at odds with his government, his claims to uphold the **Statuto Albertino** notwithstanding. His maneuvering brought down the governments of both **Bettino Ricasoli** and **Marco Minghetti**. One of his sons, Amadeo, was king of Spain from 1870 to 1873.

His wife, having produced eight children (three of whom died in childhood), passed away in 1855. He remarried morganatically. His new wife was Rosa Vercellana Guerrieri, whom he gave the title of Countess of Mirafiore e Fontanafredda.

Victor Emmanuel laid the groundwork for the **Triple Alliance** by visiting both Berlin and Vienna in 1873. He died in Rome in 1878, aged 58, and was succeeded by his son, Humbert I (Umberto I). *See also* MONARCHY; REVOLUTIONS OF 1848; RISORGIMENTO; TURIN; VICTOR EMMANUEL III.

VICTOR EMMANUEL III/Vittorio Emanuele III (1869–1947). Born in **Naples** in November 1869, Victor Emmanuel III was the son of Humbert I and Margherita di Savoia (Margaret of Savoy). Despite his minimal stature (he was barely five feet tall), his education was military. By 1897, not yet 30 but already a general, he commanded an army corps. Additional studies included law, history, and political subjects. In 1896, he married Elena of Montenegro. When an anarchist assassinated his father (in July 1900 in Monza), Victor Emmanuel succeeded to the throne.

The centrality of the governments of the right ended with **Giuseppe Zanardelli** and his successor, **Giovanni Giolitti**, with whom the king fell out, in 1914, over the intervention issue. Neutralist Giolitti was not in tune with Victor Emmanuel's interventionist spirit; the king preferred **Antonio Salandra** as prime minister but accepted the constitutional limitations on his powers of initiative.

When Italy emerged from **World War I** impoverished and torn, Victor Emmanuel III came to see **Fascism** as a tool to be used in forestalling the rise of Bolshevism. Apparently convinced that he could avoid civil war and could tame **Benito Mussolini**, the king failed to act or to use the army against Fascism's political terrorism or the **March on Rome**. By 1925, legal opposition had been eliminated and the **Partito Nazionale Fascista**/National Fascist Party (PNF) was the only legal political party. Ceremonial powers were all that was left to the monarch, especially after the title **president of the Council of Ministers** was changed by law (24 December 1925) to make Mussolini head of the government. This pill was eventually sweetened by the conferring on the king of the titles of Emperor of Italian East Africa (1936) and King of **Albania** (1939). The king's acceptance of a subservient role vis-à-vis Mussolini prevented the officers' corps of the army, always loyal to the throne, from opposing what was, after all, the legitimate Italian government. Resentment ran deep among officers raised in Piedmontese traditions, especially when Mussolini gave status equal to the Royal Army to the blackshirts of the militia, made up largely of former *squadristi* and street fighters.

A full three years after Italy's invasion of France in 1940, humiliating defeats in North Africa and the USSR, together with the imminence of Allied landings in Italy itself, combined to convince the king to save what he could. On 25 July 1943, he sought to preserve the monarchical institution by having Mussolini arrested and by putting Marshal **Pietro Badoglio** in charge of the government. After 40 days, on 8 September, the marshal announced an armistice with the Allies and Victor Emmanuel, together with his court and Badoglio, fled Rome to travel south to areas already under Allied occupation, leaving the Italian army without orders in the face of the inevitable German drive to occupy immediately all of Italy as far south as **Naples** and to suppress Italian forces everywhere. Those who resisted were quickly overrun. Many simply shed their uniforms and headed home.

Victor Emmanuel declared war on Germany in October 1943, thus making Italy a "cobelligerent." The postwar climate of hostility to all identifiable supporters of Fascism, his flight from Rome, and his failure to act against Fascism in any way before 1943 ensured that Victor Emmanuel could no longer plausibly stay on the throne in the postwar period. He abdicated in favor of his son, Humbert II, on 9 May 1946, and went into exile in Alexandria, Egypt, where he died on 28 December 1947. The abdication did not suffice to preserve the **monarchy**, however. On 2 June 1946, the Italians voted narrowly to establish a republic. The Savoy dynasty's role in Italy was ended by popular will and its own collusion with the Fascist state. *See also* CONSTITUENT ASSEMBLY, ETHIOPIA; FACTA, LUIGI; FASCIST GRAND COUNCIL; PEACE TREATY OF 1947.

VIENNA, CONGRESS OF. So far as Italy was concerned, the Congress of Vienna (November 1814 to June 1815) represented an attempt by the great powers, especially Austria, to restore absolutism in the Italian peninsula. The Trentino, South Tyrol, and Venezia Giulia were all reabsorbed into the Austrian empire; Lombardy-Venetia became an Austrian colony ruled, from January 1816, by an Austrian viceroy applying Austrian law. The Duchies of Modena, Parma, and Lucca, and the Grand Duchy of Tuscany, were allowed nominal independence but were ruled by individuals related by ties of marriage to the Austrian court. Elsewhere in Italy, absolutism was reinforced by the restoration of the pre-Napoleonic order. The Papal States, comprising the modern regions of Emilia-Romagna, the Marche, Umbria, and Latium, were re-created, and, in **southern Italy**, Klemens von Metternich insisted upon the return of the Bourbon Ferdinand IV of **Naples**, whose authority was also extended over **Sicily**, thereby creating in December 1816 the Kingdom of the Two Sicilies. The only part of Italy where Austria's writ did not run was thus the Kingdom of Piedmont-Sardinia, but this, too, was an absolute **monarchy**, ruled over by King Victor Emmanuel I.

The return of absolutism did not go unchallenged. In July 1820, the people of Naples, led by a large part of the armed forces, rebelled and imposed on Ferdinand a constitutional monarchy modeled on the Spanish Constitution of 1812. Seizing the opportunity to declare independence, the city of **Palermo** also rose in revolt, and a bloody civil war began in Sicily between supporters and opponents of unification with Naples. At the conference of Troppau in October 1820, the Holy Alliance powers (Austria, Russia, and Prussia) warned that they would intervene to protect the principle of absolute monarchy, and in March 1821 Austrian troops restored Ferdinand to power. Violent repression of the *carboneria*, intricately organized sects of liberal revolutionaries, followed.

The revolts in southern Italy were a prelude to similar unrest in Piedmont-Sardinia. On 10 March 1821, the *carbonari* seized **Turin**, proclaimed a constitutional monarchy, and declared Victor Emmanuel I the king of all Italy—thereby effectively declaring war on Austria. Rather than concede a constitutional monarchy, Victor Emmanuel handed power to Prince **Charles Albert** who, as regent, agreed to the constitutional monarchy but refused to make war on Austria. On 23 March, reneging on his word, Charles Albert fled to join the loyalist forces of Victor Emmanuel's brother, Charles Felice, who with massive Austrian support crushed the constitutionalists at the battle of Novara at the beginning of April. On 19 April 1821, Victor Emmanuel abdicated, allowing Charles Felice to ascend to the throne. The restoration of absolutism in Italy was confirmed by the Congress of Verona (October–December 1822).

VISCONTI, LUCHINO (1906–1976). The scion of one of Italy's oldest and most aristocratic families, Visconti entered the **cinema** relatively late and was nearly 30 when a chance social contact enabled him to work with the great French director Jean Renoir. Visconti's first film, *Ossessione* (*Obsession*, 1942), was based on the American novel *The Postman Always Rings Twice* and aroused an uproar in Italy because of its frank sexuality. Visconti had to make a personal appeal to **Benito Mussolini** to get the film past the censors. Fortunately the dictator allowed this first masterpiece of **neorealism** to appear with only limited cuts. Visconti was later arrested by the authorities and charged with aiding the **resistance**. For some time he was at grave risk of execution. In 1947 Visconti made his second great film, *La terra trema* (*The Earth Trembles*), which was based on **Giovanni Verga**'s novel *I malavoglia*. Set in the Sicilian fishing village of Aci Trezza, the film manages both to show the hardship and agony of the villagers' lives and to include scenes of ravishing poetic beauty. Visconti used no professional actors in the film, and the film had to be subtitled in Italian for non-Sicilian viewers.

Visconti produced two masterpieces in the 1950s. *Senso* (*Feeling*, 1954) was his first foray into the use of color, but its visual opulence and subject matter (the film is a love story set during the **Risorgimento**) were regarded with suspicion by the neorealists. *Rocco e i suoi fratelli* (*Rocco and his Brothers*, 1960), by contrast, marked a return to the naturalism of his earlier films and was a major critical and box office success. From 1960 onward, however, Visconti turned more toward the big-budget, visually enchanting style of *Senso*. Turning his back on neorealism and Italy's Marxist critical establishment, Visconti chose to adapt Di Lampedusa's novel *Il Gattopardo* (*The Leopard*, 1963), even though the book had been derided as reactionary when it first appeared in the late 1950s. The film won the Palme d'Or at Cannes. Visconti's last major film was *Morte a Venezia* (*Death in* **Venice**, 1971). The depiction of the decadent beauty of Venice is the most successful aspect of the film; the psychological trauma undergone by Aschenbach, the protagonist, is portrayed somewhat ponderously. In addition to his film career, Visconti was

Italy's preeminent opera and theater director. He died in **Rome** in 1976.

VISCONTI-VENOSTA, EMILIO (1829–1914). One of liberal Italy's most adept diplomats and statesmen, Emilio Visconti-Venosta was the scion of a prominent Milanese family. In his youth, he was a follower of **Giuseppe Mazzini**, but by 1861, when he entered **Parliament**, he had become fully reconciled to constitutional liberalism. Visconti-Venosta was foreign minister almost continuously from 1863 to 1876; during this period, he promoted the policy of close relations with Germany that enabled Italy to complete the process of unification begun in 1860–1861 and played a major role in resolving the crisis of relations with the **Vatican** after the occupation of **Rome** in 1870 by promoting the so-called **guarantee laws**. The rise of **Agostino Depretis** and **Francesco Crispi** signaled the end of his career for 20 years.

Finally, in 1896, after the Italian defeat at the battle of Adowa brought a rude awakening from Crispi's imperialistic dreams, **Antonio Starabba Di Rudinì** called Visconti-Venosta back to office. The veteran diplomat subtly steered Italy away from its alliance with Austria and Germany, improving relations with France and maintaining good relations with Great Britain even as Germany began to challenge British dominance. Unlike Crispi, Visconti-Venosta was a realist who was aware that diplomacy, not force of arms, was the key to a successful **foreign policy** for Italy. He relinquished his office in 1901, but played an important role as mediator between France and Germany at the Algeciras Conference in 1906. He died in **Rome** in 1914.

VITTORINI, ELIO (1908–1966). Born in 1908 in Syracuse (**Sicily**), Vittorini was one of the most influential editors and writers of postwar Italy. His first steps into the literary world came during the late 1920s, when he began to collaborate with *Solaria*, the Florentine literary periodical edited by **Eugenio Montale**. In 1933, *Solaria* began publishing his first novel, *Il garofano rosso* (*The Red Carnation*), in installments, but the censor, disliking this study of a youth whose adolescent rebelliousness finds an outlet in the violence and camaraderie of the Fascist movement, suspended publication. In the late

1930s, Vittorini translated American realists, such as John Steinbeck and Ernest Hemingway. Their influence can be seen in his two most important novels, *Conversazione in Sicilia* (*Conversations in Sicily*, 1942) and *Uomini e no* (*Men and Others*, 1945), which was based on his experiences as a wartime partisan in **Milan**.

In 1945, Vittorini became a member of the **Partito Comunista Italiano**/Italian Communist Party (PCI) and founded *Il Politecnico*, the theoretical journal of the **neorealist** movement in the arts. The review closed in 1947 after Vittorini clashed with **Palmiro Togliatti**, the secretary of the PCI, who accused Vittorini of privileging literary culture over political commitment. Vittorini replied that the PCI should not expect writers to merely "blow the revolution's flute." To preserve his independence, Vittorini left the PCI in 1951.

In 1950, he became an editor for the *Turin* publisher, Einaudi, responsible for discovering and nurturing new writers of talent. Vittorini's political and literary preferences were not always helpful in this role. In 1957, he rejected **Giuseppe Tomasi Di Lampedusa**'s remarkable novel *Il Gattopardo* (*The Leopard*), on the grounds that it was reactionary in sentiment and over-literary in language and style. After the mid-1950s, Vittorini published no more novels. He was joint editor, however, with **Italo Calvino**, of the avant-garde journal *Menabò* from 1960 onward. He died in Milan in 1966. *See also* LITERATURE.

VOLTA, ALESSANDRO (1745–1827). Born in Como (Lombardy), Alessandro Volta was the first man to invent a battery capable of storing electricity. Volta was professor of physics at the University of Pavia from 1779 to 1804 and was ennobled by Napoleon for his discoveries.

Volta was responsible for a string of crucial scientific breakthroughs. In 1776, he discovered the properties of what was then called swamp gas but is today known as methane. In 1799, he invented the "voltaic pile," or battery. Volta's pile consisted of a number of discs of zinc and silver separated by pieces of brine-soaked cloth and arranged in a vertical column. The electric current ran for several hours from the wire joining the upper zinc disc to the silver disc below. For the first time, it was shown to be possible to have an unbroken current of electricity in a circuit. Volta communicated his success in a March 1800 letter to Joseph Banks, the president of the British Royal Society, and an article on his discovery was published in the Royal Society's *Philosophical Transactions* in September 1800. Worldwide fame rapidly followed. In 1881, Volta's research legacy in the field of electricity was honored by the decision to name the unit of measurement of electric potential the "volt" in his honor.

Volta died in his native Como in 1827. For many years, he was depicted on the 10,000 lire note.

– W –

WOMEN. The history of women in contemporary Italy can be defined as the glacial acquisition of basic political and economic rights. Even more than most Western nations, Italy has been highly resistant to giving women formal legal and political equality. Until 1874, women were all but excluded from advanced education, and it was not until after 1900 that women began to frequent *licei* and university faculties in any numbers. There were only 250 female university students in the whole country in 1900, and no woman obtained a degree in engineering until 1908 (Emma Strada). Professional *albe* (guilds) were no more willing to admit women. The first female lawyer called to the bar was Teresa Labriola, in 1912.

The cause of votes for women was promoted by a national suffragettes' committee but met a good deal of unexpected opposition from the **Partito Socialista Italiano**/Italian Socialist party (PSI), whose leaders feared that women would vote for conservatives. In 1912, however, **Filippo Turati**, perhaps pushed by his formidable companion Anna Kuliscioff, was one of several prominent socialists who argued for the inclusion of women's suffrage in the **electoral law** of that year (the conservative **Sidney Sonnino** also supported the proposal). **Giovanni Giolitti** described the idea as a "leap in the dark." Women continued to rank alongside certified idiots, bankrupts, and imprisoned criminals in not possessing the suffrage.

Women would in fact vote for the first time in free national elections only in June 1946. A law extending the vote to women was passed in September 1919, but **Parliament** was dissolved before the law was approved by the Senate. When **Fascism** took power in October 1922, women were given the vote in local and provincial elections, subject to certain restrictions, but such elections were abolished after 1926 in any case. The vital and courageous role played by many women in the **resistance** was a crucial factor in winning them the vote.

Fascism was in general a nightmare for women, who were portrayed in the regime's ideology and propaganda as breeding machines. One of the best-known Fascist slogans was "maternity means to a woman what war means to a man," and failure to have large families was regarded as treachery toward the Italian "race." Birth control was rigorously forbidden. Women were forbidden to take many jobs (they could not be teachers of **literature** or philosophy at a *liceo*, for instance), and their wages were fixed at lower rates than men doing the same job. The aim of these policies was to drive women out of the labor market and back to the home.

The modern women's rights movement was born in the 1960s and early 1970s. In part, it was a reaction against anachronistic restrictions on **divorce**, contraception, and, to a lesser extent, abortion, but it was also a rejection of the sexism of the revolutionary and radical groups of the left. **Lotta Continua** for instance, was a notoriously sexist organization. Led by the **Partito Radicale**/Radical Party (PR) and the Movimento di Liberazione della Donna/Women's Liberation Movement (MLD), women campaigned for the free distribution of contraceptives, the legalization of abortion, and the creation of nursery schools and other social services that were in short supply. **Emma Bonino** is just one leading contemporary politician whose career began in the 1970s feminist movement.

Women in Italy today are more equal with men than ever before. It remains true, however, that the level of female participation in the workforce is the lowest in Europe, and there are remarkably few women deputies or senators even today. In 2005, an attempt by the **Forza Italia** minister for equal opportunities, Stefania Prestagiacomo, to introduce *quote rose* ("pink quotas") to ensure that a guaranteed proportion of parliamentary candidates were women, was defeated—by some ridiculed—in Parliament. *See also* CONSTITUTION; DELEDDA, GRAZIA; GARIBALDI, ANITA; IOTTI, LEONILDE; LEVI-MONTALCINI, RITA; MONTESSORI, MARIA; MORANTE, ELSA.

452 • WORLD WAR I

WORLD WAR I (1915–1918). Italy's decision to participate in the war that broke out in August 1914 was a matter of acute calculation of the country's best interests. When war broke out, Italy was joined in the **Triple Alliance** with Germany and Austria. Seen by the Italian government as purely defensive, the treaty promised Italy's assistance to Germany and Austria should either be the victim of an attack. As Austria's displeasure mounted concerning Serbian aggrandizement at Turkey's expense in the Balkan Wars, Italy made clear that the Triple Alliance would never be a license for Austria to engage in aggressive war against the Serbs. Thus, when the assassination of Archduke Francis Ferdinand led to Austria's ultimatum to Serbia, Italy—claiming that the Triple Alliance's conditions had not been met—declared its neutrality, while Serbia's and Austria's allies mobilized for what each thought would be a swift war resolving outstanding problems of national aspirations, imperial ambition, and the settling of scores.

It soon became clear that the most an Austrian victory might yield to Italy would be concessions in Africa (perhaps Tunisia, French since 1830). But a French victory over Austria and Germany could mean that territories such as the Trentino might become Italian. Neutrality, the policy favored by **Giovanni Giolitti**, might favor either Austria or Serbia at war's end but certainly not Italy. The decisive factor was the desire to establish Italian credentials as a power and to take part in establishing the postwar equilibrium. Thus, the **Treaty of London** of April 1915 formalized Italian entry into the war as an ally of France and Britain. It was accepted by the Italian Parliament only after **Gabriele D'Annunzio** and other nationalists had manipulated crowds in the public squares of Italy to rout opposition opinion that, in fact, held the majority in **Parliament**.

War fever, however, was followed by bloody reality. Hostilities in some of Europe's highest mountains could not have begun at a worse time. Russian forces had suffered defeats that obliged them to withdraw from (Austrian) Galicia, thus freeing Vienna to reinforce its positions in the **Alps** and in Friuli. In 1916, the Austrian *Strafexpedition* in the Trentino caused the government of **Antonio Salandra** to fall. By the summer of 1917, 11 bloody but indecisive battles at the Isonzo River had been fought on a 96-kilometer (60-mile) front and had advanced Italian forces barely 16 kilometers (10 miles) toward **Trieste**. When the Austrians learned of a massive Italian offensive being planned by General **Luigi Cadorna** for the spring of 1918, they sought, and received, assistance from their German ally in the form of experienced troops and officers. The 12th battle of the Isonzo, begun in October 1917, ended at **Caporetto**, where the Italian line broke.

Rumors of a rout became self-fulfilling. It was only at the Piave River that the line finally held. British and French reinforcements soon arrived and enabled the Italian army to counterattack with a vengeance, driving Austria to ask for an armistice after a stunning defeat at Vittorio Veneto in October 1918, at which the Italians took more than 400,000 prisoners. The armistice came on 3 November 1918, eight days before the armistice on the Western Front. In all, Italy lost 650,000 killed or missing during the war, less than the terrible sacrifices made by France and Germany, but comparable with Great Britain. Half a million men were permanently disabled.

The war also reduced respect for Parliament and for the liberals who controlled it. The growing gap between the wealthy and the poor heightened social tension. Moreover, many returning veterans found that even the newer engineering and metallurgical industries, made rich by the conflict, now faced shrinking markets and needed no new workers. Thus, not only were social divisions sharper than they remembered, but the consequent bitter tensions did not stand comparison with the comradeship of the military life. All of these factors contributed to the rise of **Fascism**. *See also* BOSELLI, PAOLO; DIAZ, ARMANDO; FIAT; ORLANDO, VITTORIO EMANUELE; SAINT GERMAIN, TREATY OF; SONNINO, SIDNEY.

WORLD WAR II (1940–1945). Italy entered the war on 10 June 1940, by launching a surprise attack on France. Within a month, Italian forces attacked France's British ally in the Sudan and Kenya from garrisons in **Ethiopia**. By mid-August 1940, British Somaliland had been occupied, and Egypt was being threatened by the Italian army in **Libya**.

These early successes were the only ones Italy would enjoy, however. Despite spending a huge portion of its national income on the military (in 1940 it was spending 85 percent as much as the British even though its national income per capita was only one-quarter as much), Italy did not possess the technological means, the industrial power, or the skilled personnel to conduct a modern war. Italian tanks were badly designed and short of cannon power, aircraft and artillery were almost as inadequate, and communications technology was antiquated. The tide of battle soon turned. In January 1941, South African and Indian forces carried the war to the Italians in Libya, Ethiopia, and the occupied British territories. By April 1941, deposed emperor Haile Selassie had been returned to Addis Ababa by British-led forces. Fighting in North Africa continued throughout 1941 as tens of thousands of Italians, severely demoralized by incompetent leadership and inadequate supplies, were taken prisoner at a cost of hundreds of British casualties.

Even more humiliating was the fate of the Italian army in its Greek campaign, begun in October 1940. By the end of November, Italian frontal attacks had worn down the troops to such a point that—despite reinforcements—Greek counteroffensives had pushed Italian troops back into **Albania**. In order to prevent the total humiliation of his Italian ally, Adolf Hitler ordered the *Wehrmacht* to invade Greece (where it accomplished in two weeks what had eluded the Italians for six months). In April 1941, the Greeks agreed to surrender to Germany but not to Italy. Only **Benito Mussolini**'s personal appeal persuaded Hitler to include Italy in the April 1941 armistice proceedings. Italians provided the main occupation forces in Greece until September 1943.

Further huge losses in men and matériel came in 1942. The substantial Italian army on the Eastern front was slaughtered at Stalingrad, and at El Alamein in October 1942, Italian and German troops were crushed by British and Australian forces. The **Axis** army was driven back into Tunisia, where Italian soldiers fought heroically against the Americans at the bloody battle of Mareth in February 1943. By mid-1943, more than 300,000 Italians had fallen in combat or had been taken prisoner. In July 1943, the Allies invaded **Sicily**, provoking the downfall of Mussolini and his replacement by Marshall **Pietro Badoglio**. Italy stayed in the war until 8 September 1943, while secretly negotiating with the Allies for "cobelligerent" status if it changed sides. The delay enabled the Germans to move 16 divisions into Italy and ensured that the subsequent Allied campaign in the peninsula would be bloody and prolonged.

Italy surrendered on 8 September and the king and Badoglio fled to British-occupied Brindisi. Bereft of orders, the Italian army collapsed in the face of the Germans: Tens of thousands of soldiers either took to the hills or were rounded up and sent to labor camps in

Germany. Where Italian troops fought, they were treated with brutality by the Germans. The *Acqui* division garrisoning the island of Cephalonia in Greece resisted the Germans for a week, losing over a thousand dead. When they finally surrendered, the Germans massacred 4,750 men in cold blood.

From September 1943 onward, central Italy was a battleground as Allied troops slogged their way up Italy against skillful and tenacious German resistance. The battles of Monte Cassino (January–May 1944) and Anzio cost the Allies tens of thousands of casualties. Rome fell in June 1944. During the winter of 1944, the Allies became bogged down in the difficult terrain of the Apennines, which enabled the Germans to turn their efforts to eliminating partisan activity in their rear. Massacres, such as the one at Marzotto near **Bologna** (October 1944), where nearly 2,000 innocent civilians were killed, were among the worst acts of "reprisal" conducted by the Nazis anywhere in Europe.

Northern Italy was the setting for a civil war after September 1943. Troops loyal to Mussolini's **Republic of Salò**, with the help of German troops, waged a war of terror against the partisan bands controlled by the **Committees of National Liberation**. By the spring of 1944, more than 100,000 partisans were in the field. The partisans had de facto control of large swathes of territory and were coordinated militarily by a command headed by General Raffaele Cadorna and two political deputies, the communist **Luigi Longo** and **Ferruccio Parri** of the **Partito d'Azione**/Action Party (PdA). When German resistance finally crumbled in the spring of 1945, the partisans themselves liberated the major cities of the North and dealt out rough justice to Fascist officials and collaborators. Mussolini himself was caught and executed by the partisans on 28 April 1945. *See also* COMITATI DI LIBERAZIONE NAZIONALE; FASCISM; FASCIST GRAND COUNCIL; PARALLEL WAR; RESISTANCE.

– Y –

YOUTH MOVEMENTS, FASCIST. The organization of youth by age groups began with the paramilitary *Balilla* (Organizzazione Nazionale Balilla, ONB)—organized in January 1926—for 8- to 14-year-olds. At 14, one enrolled in the *Avanguardisti* (for those between

14 and 19) and, finally, in Fascist University Youth (Gioventù Universitaria Fascista), which aimed at continuing the inculcation of military values in young Italians (18- to 29-year-old male and female university students). This system was proclaimed by nationalists as ensuring that in any future war, a race of warriors would meet the enemy with "eight million bayonets." (A favorite comment on this Mussolinian boast was that the enemy, unfortunately, was equipped with tanks.) Similarly, young females were brought into the Piccole Italiane (Little Italians) group to acquire and perfect the skills needed to be the mothers of tomorrow's warriors, the true heirs of Roman military prowess. It also served as a sporting, athletic, and disciplinary body. Giovani Italiane/Female Italian Youth drew Italian adolescent females (ages 14–18). Once adulthood approached, it was expected that all these young people, male and female alike, would move into membership in the **Partito Nazionale Fascista**/National Fascist Party (PNF).

One of the functions of senior members of these organizations was to take a supervisory part in the summer camps, which were widely admired abroad. These camps exposed urban children to fresh air, exercise, and sunshine at seaside and mountain resorts established for them. Special trains were laid on for the participants, and camping kits were distributed while they were taught patriotic and party songs. Healthy bodies and high spirits, it was assumed, make better soldiers. *See also* FASCISM.

– Z –

ZANARDELLI, GIUSEPPE (1826–1903). Born in Brescia, as a young man Giuseppe Zanardelli was an active participant in the nationalist struggle. In 1848, and again in 1859, he led the citizens of Brescia in insurrections against Austrian rule. He entered **Parliament** in 1860 as a member of the constitutional left. After **Agostino Depretis**'s accession to power in 1876, he became minister for public works, then minister of the interior. In this role, he was responsible for the first liberalization of the **electoral law** in 1880. Between 1881 and 1883 and 1887 and 1891, he was minister of justice under both Depretis and **Francesco Crispi**. During the second of these spells in office, he successfully introduced a new penal code which among other provisions abolished the death penalty.

Zanardelli's progressive sympathies caused him to look upon the *trasformismo* of Depretis with a less than charitable eye. From December 1897, Zanardelli did, however, participate in the second government of **Antonio Starabba di Rudinì** and was one of the architects of the panicky repression of the socialist and Catholic movements in May 1898. Following the accession to power of **Luigi Girolamo Pelloux**, however, Zanardelli performed an enviable feat of political acrobatics and aligned himself with **Giovanni Giolitti** and the socialists against the Right. In addition to his occasional ministerial duties, Zanardelli held the post of president of the Chamber of Deputies for much of the decade.

Zanardelli became prime minister in 1901, in the aftermath of the assassination of King Humbert I. His government, which was dominated by his political heir, Giovanni Giolitti, was the most liberal administration Italy had experienced since 1861. While prime minister Zanardelli unsuccessfully tried to introduce a **divorce** law. He held the post until his death in 1903.

ZOLI, ADONE (1887–1960). Born in Cesena in the province of Forlì (Emilia-Romagna), Adone Zoli was a close collaborator of **Luigi Sturzo** after the foundation of the **Partito Popolare Italiano/**Italian People's Party (PPI) in 1919. He took an active role in the Tuscan **Comitati di Liberazione Nazionale/**National Liberation Committees (CLN) during the **resistance**, from which position he moved to being vice mayor of **Florence** and a member of the national council of the **Democrazia Cristiana/**Christian Democracy Party (DC). He was elected to the Senate in 1948 and reconfirmed in the elections of 1953 and in 1958. He was briefly vice president of the Senate, before becoming minister of justice in 1951. Zoli also served as finance minister and as minister for the budget between 1955 and 1957. He briefly headed a DC-only cabinet, between May 1957 and June 1958. Politically close to **Amintore Fanfani**, Zoli's government nevertheless represented all strains of opinion within the DC. He died in **Rome** in February 1960.

Appendix

Table 1. Royal Heads of State

The Kingdom of the Two Sicilies	
Ferdinand I of Bourbon	1815–1825
Francis I of Bourbon	1825–1830
Ferdinand II of Bourbon	1830–1859
Francis II of Bourbon	1859–1860
Kingdom of Sardinia	
Victor Emmanuel I	1814–1821
Charles Felice	1821–1831
Charles Albert	1831–1849
Victor Emmanuel II	1849–1861
Kingdom of Italy	
Victor Emmanuel II	1861–1878
Humbert I	1878–1900
Victor Emmanuel III	1900–1946
Humbert II	May–June 1946

Il Giornale, Diario d'Italia, 1994.

Table 2.   Heads of Government, 1861–1945

Cavour	March–June 1861
Ricasoli I	June 1861–March 1862
Rattazzi I	March–December 1862
Farini	December 1862–March 1863
Minghetti I	March 1863–September 1864
Lamarmora I	September 1864–December 1865
Lamarmora II	December 1865–June 1866
Ricasoli II	June 1866–April 1867
Rattazzi II	April–October 1867
Menabrea I	October 1867–January 1868
Menabrea II	January 1868–May 1869
Menabrea III	May–December 1869
Lanza	December 1869–July 1873
Minghetti II	July 1873–March 1876
Depretis I	March 1876–December 1877
Depretis II	December 1877–March 1878
Cairoli I	March–December 1878
Depretis III	December 1878–July 1879
Cairoli II	July–November 1879
Cairoli III	November 1879–May 1881
Depretis IV	May 1881–May 1883
Depretis V	May 1883–March 1884
Depretis VI	March 1884–June 1885
Depretis VII	June 1885–April 1887
Depretis VIII	April–July 1887
Crispi I	July 1887–March 1889
Crispi II	March 1889–February 1891
Di Rudini I	February 1891–May 1892
Giolitti I	May 1892–December 1893
Crispi III	December 1893–March 1896
Di Rudini II	March–July 1896
Di Rudini III	July 1896–December 1897
Di Rudini IV	December 1897–June 1898

Table 2. (*continued*)

Di Rudini V	June 1898
Pelloux I	June 1898–May 1899
Pelloux II	May 1899–June 1900
Saracco	June 1900–February 1901
Zanardelli	February 1901–November 1903
Giolitti II	November 1903–March 1905
Fortis I	March–December 1905
Fortis II	December 1905–February 1906
Sonnino I	February–May 1906
Giolitti III	May 1906–December 1909
Sonnino II	December 1909–March 1910
Luzzatti	March 1910–March 1911
Giolitti IV	March 1911–March 1914
Salandra I	March–November 1914
Salandra II	November 1914–June 1916
Boselli	June 1916–October 1917
Orlando	October 1917–June 1919
Nitti I	June 1919–May 1920
Nitti II	May–June 1920
Giolitti V	June 1920–July 1921
Bonomi I	July 1921–February 1922
Facta I	February–August 1922
Facta II	August–October 1922
Mussolini	October 1922–July 1943
Badoglio I	July 1943–April 1944
Badoglio II	April–June 1944
Bonomi II	June–December 1944
Bonomi III	December 1944–June 1945

Source: *Diario d'Italia*. 1994. *Il Giornale*.

Table 3. Elections to the Chamber of Deputies, 1861–1924

Year	Number of Votes Cast	Percent Voting	Largest Party	Percent
1861	239,746	57.1	Moderate Right	47.6
1865	271,522	54.4	Moderate Right	42.0
1867	258,119	52.0	Moderate Right	44.2
1870	240,731	45.4	Moderate Right	47.2
1874	319,493	55.8	Moderate Right	44.7
1876	358,899	59.2	Constitutional Left	62.6
1880	369,953	59.2	Constitutional Left	55.1
1882	1,222,555	60.6	Constitutional Left	58.3
1886	1,406,658	58.2	Constitutional Left	52.2
1890	1,479,475	53.7	Constitutional Left	51.8
1892	1,643,417	56.1	Constitutional Left	53.6
1895	1,257,888	59.3	Constitutional Left	48.2
1897	1,242,657	58.6	Constitutional Left	40.6
1900	1,310,480	58.3	Constitutional Left	43.7
1904	1,593,886	62.7	Constitutional Left	45.7
1909	1,903,687	65.0	Constitutional Left	43.1
1913*	5,100,615	59.0	Constitutional Left	33.3
1919	5,793,507	56.6	PSI	32.3
1921	6,701,496	58.4	PSI	24.7
1924**	7,614,451	63.1	PNF	65.0

Notes
Percentage figures have been rounded to the nearest tenth.
*1913 was the first year with universal male suffrage.
**The 1924 election was conditioned by Fascist violence.
Source: S. Piretti, Le elezioni politiche in Italia dal 1848 a oggi (Bari: Laterza, 1995).

Table 4. Presidents of the Republic, 1946–2006

Enrico Di Nicola	1946–1948
Luigi Einaudi	1948–1955
Giovanni Gronchi	1955–1962
Antonio Segni	1962–1964
Giuseppe Saragat	1964–1971
Giovanni Leone	1971–1978
Alessandro Pertini	1978–1985
Francesco Cossiga	1985–1992
Oscar Luigi Scalfaro	1992–1999
Carlo Azeglio Ciampi	1999–2006
Giorgio Napolitano	2006–

Table 5. Italian Cabinets and Prime Ministers since 1945

Premier	Composition	Tenure
Parri	DC-PCI-PSIUP-PLI-**PdA**	June–November 1945
DeGasperi I	**DC**-PCI-PSIUP-PLI-PdA	December 1945–July 1946
De Gasperi II	**DC**-PCI-PSI-PRI	July 1946–January 1947
De Gasperi III	**DC**-PCI-PSI	February–May 1947
De Gasperi IV	**DC**-PSLI-PRI-PLI	May 1947–May 1948
De Gasperi V	**DC**-PSLI-PRI-PLI	May 1948–January 1950
De Gasperi VI	**DC**-PSLI-PRI	January 1950–July 1951
De Gasperi VII	**DC**-PRI	July 1951–June 1953
De Gasperi VIII	**DC**	July 1953
Pella	**DC**	August 1953–January 1954
Fanfani I	**DC**	January 1954
Scelba	**DC**-PSDI-PLI	February 1954–June 1955
Segni I	**DC**-PSDI-PLI	July 1955–May 1957
Zoli	**DC**	May–June 1957
Fanfani II	**DC**-PSDI	July 1958–January 1959
Segni II	**DC**	February 1959–February 1960
Tambroni	**DC**	March–July 1960
FanfaniIII	**DC**	July 1960–February 1962
Fanfani IV	**DC**-PSDI-PRI	February 1962–May 1963
Leone I	**DC**	June–November 1963
Moro I	**DC**-PSI-PSDI-PRI	December 1963–June 1964
Moro II	**DC**-PSI-PSDI-PRI	July 1964–January 1966
Moro III	**DC**-PSI-PSDI-PRI	February 1966–June 1968
Leone II	**DC**	June–November 1968
Rumor I	**DC**-PSU-PRI	December 1968–July 1969
Rumor II	**DC**	August 1969–February 1970
Rumor III	**DC**-PSI-PSDI-PRI	March–July 1970
Colombo	**DC**-PSI-PSDI-PRI	August 1970–January 1972
Andreotti I	**DC**	February 1972
Andreotti II	**DC**-PSDI-PLI	June 1972–June 1973
Rumor IV	**DC**-PSI-PSDI-PRI	July 1973–March 1974
Rumor V	**DC**-PSI-PSDI	March–October 1974
Moro IV	**DC**-PRI	November 1974–January 1976
Moro V	**DC**	February–April 1976
Andreotti III	**DC**	July 1976–January 1978
Andreotti IV	**DC**	March 1978–January 1979

(*continued*)

Table 5. (*continued*)

Andreotti V	**DC**-PRI-PSDI	March–August 1979
Cossiga I	**DC**-PSDI-PLI	August1979–March 1980
Cossiga II	**DC**-PSI-PRI	April–September 1980
Forlani	**DC**-PSI-PSDI-PRI	October 1980–May 1981
Spadolini I	DC-**PRI**-PSI-PSDI-PLI	June 1981–August 1982
Spadolini II	DC-**PRI**-PSI-PSDI-PLI	August–November 1982
Fanfani V	**DC**-PSI-PSDI-PLI	December 1982–April 1983
Craxi I	DC-**PSI**-PSDI-PRI-PLI	August 1983–June 1986
Craxi II	DC-**PSI**-PSDI-PRI-PLI	August 1986–March 1987
Fanfani VI	**DC**	April–July 1987
Goria	**DC**-PSI-PSDI-PRI-PLI	July 1987–March 1988
De Mita	**DC**-PSI-PSDI-PRI-PLI	April 1988–May 1989
Andreotti VI	**DC**-PSI-PSDI-PRI-PLI	July 1989–March 1991
Andreotti VII	**DC**-PSI-PSDI-PLI	April 1991–April 1992
Amato	**DC**-PSI-PSDI-PLI	July 1992–April 1993
Ciampi	Government formed without negotiations with the parties	April 1993–January 1994
Berlusconi I	**FI**-LN-AN-CCD-UC	May–December 1994
Dini	Government of nonparty experts	January 1995–February 1996
Prodi	**Ulivo**	May 1996–October 1998
D'Alema I	**Ulivo**-PdCI-UDEUR	October 1998–December 1999
D'Alema II	**DS**-PPI-PdCI-UDEUR RI-Others	December 1999–April 2000
Amato II	**DS**-PPI-PdCI-UDEUR RI-Others	April 2000–June 2001
Berlusconi II	**FI**-LN-UDC-AN	June 2001–April 2005
Berlusconi III	**FI**-LN-UDC-AN	April 2005–May 2006
Prodi II	**Ulivo**-PRC-Greens-PdCI	May 2006–

Note: The prime minister's party is indicated by boldface type.

Table 6. Elections to the Chamber of Deputies, 1946–1992: Share of Vote Obtained by Main Political Parties

Year			Party			
DC	PCI	PSI	MSI	PSDI	PRI	PLI
1946	35.2	18.9	20.7	—	—	4.4	6.8[a]
1948	48.5	—	31.0[b]	2.0	7.1	2.5	3.8
1953	40.1	22.6	12.7	5.8	4.5	3.0	1.6
1958	42.3	22.7	14.2	4.8	4.6	1.4	3.5
1963	38.3	25.3	13.8	5.1	6.1	1.4	7.0
1968	39.1	26.9	14.5	4.5	*c	2.0	5.8
1972	38.7	27.1	9.6	8.7	5.1	2.9	3.9
1976	38.7	34.4	9.6	6.1	3.4	3.1	1.3
1979	38.3	30.4	9.8	5.3	3.8	3.0	1.9
1983	32.4	30.8	11.4	8.8	4.1	5.1	2.9
1987	34.3	26.6	14.3	5.9	2.9	3.7	2.1
1992	29.7	21.7[d]	13.6	6.5	2.6	4.7	2.8

Notes

[a](1946). "Liberal" opinion represented by the Unione Democratica Nazionale (UDN).

[b](1948). PCI and PSI presented a joint list.

[c](1968). PSI and PSDI presented a joint list under the name Partito Socialista Unitario (PSU).

[d](1992). PCI vote obtained by adding the share of the vote obtained by the PDS (16.1%) and PRC (5.6%).

Source: S. Piretti, *Le elezioni politiche in Italia dal 1848 a oggi* (Bari: Laterza, 1995).

Table 7. Elections to the Senate, 1948–1992: Share of Vote Obtained by Main Political Parties

Year			Party			
DC	PCI	PSI	MSI	PSDI	PRI	PLI
1948	48.1	—	30.8	0.7	4.2	2.6	5.4
1953	39.9	20.2	11.9	62.1	4.3	1.1	2.8
1958	41.2	21.8	14.1	4.4	4.4	1.4	3.9
1963	38.3	25.3	13.8	5.3	6.3	0.8	7.4
1968	38.3	30.0	15.2	4.8	—	2.2	6.8
1972	38.1	28.1	10.7	9.1	5.4	3.0	4.4
1976	38.9	33.8	10.2	6.6	3.1	2.7	1.4
1979	38.3	31.5	10.4	5.7	4.2	3.4	2.2
1983	32.4	30.8	11.4	7.3	3.8	4.7	2.7
1987	33.6	28.3	10.9	6.5	2.4	3.9	2.2
1992	27.3	23.6	13.6	6.5	2.6	4.7	2.8

Source: S. Piretti, *Le elezioni politiche in Italia dal 1848 a oggi*. Bari: Laterza1995.

Table 8.   Elections to the Chamber of Deputies, 1994–2006: Share of Vote Obtained by Main Political Parties

	Year								Party
	FI	DS[a]	AN	PPI	LN	PRC	UDC[b]	DL[c]	ULIVO[d]
1994	21.0	20.4	13.5	11.1	8.4	6.0	—	—	—
1996	20.6	21.1	15.7	6.8	10.1	8.6	5.8	—	—
2001	29.5	16.6	12.0	—	3.9	5.0	3.2	14.5	—
2006	23.7	—	12.3	—	4.6	5.8	6.8	—	31.3

[a]In 1994 and 1996, PDS.
[b]In 1996 and 2001, sum of vote obtained by CCD-CDU.
[c]DL formed by PPI plus Dini and Prodi's personal parties.
[d]In 2006 elections, DS and DL present a single list as the Ulivo.

Table 9.   Italian Resident Population by Census Return, 1861–2001 (in Thousands)

Year	Male	Female	Total
1861	13,399	12,939	26,328
1871	14,316	13,835	28,151
1881	15,134	14,657	29,791
1901	16,990	16,788	33,778
1911	18,608	18,313	36,921
1921	18,814	19,042	37,856
1931	20,181	20,862	41,043
1936	20,826	21,573	42,339
1951	23,259	24,257	47,516
1961	24,784	25,840	50,624
1971	26,476	27,661	54,137
1981	27,506	29,051	56,557
1991	27,577	29,220	56,778
2001	27,587	29,409	56,996

*Average annual increment.
Figures are rounded to the nearest thousand.
Source: ISTAT, http://www.istat.it

Table 10.   Distribution of Working Population by Sector, 1861–1991

Year	Agriculture	Industry	Services	Percent Working
1861	69.7	18.1	12.2	59.0
1871	67.5	19.2	13.3	56.6
1881	65.4	20.2	14.4	54.0
1901	61.7	22.3	16.0	49.4
1911	58.4	23.7	17.9	47.4
1921	55.7	24.8	19.5	46.1
1931	51.7	26.3	22.0	44.4
1936	49.4	27.3	23.3	43.8
1951	42.2	32.1	25.7	41.2
1961	29.1	40.6	30.3	38.7
1971	17.2	44.4	38.4	34.8
1981	12.8	36.3	50.9	36.6
1991	08.4	32.0	59.6	42.0
2004	04.4	30.7	64.9	38.3

Source: Diario d'Italia, 1994. Il Giornale. For 2004: ISTAT, http://www.istat.it

Table 11.   Italian GNP at Constant 1938 Figures, 1861–1951

Year	GNP (billion lire)	Income per Capita* (lire)
1861	49.7	1,845
1871	54.6	1,897
1881	55.5	1,877
1891	63.0	1,906
1901	74.9	2,259
1911	95.0	2,455
1921	100.0	2,884
1931	125.0	3,029
1941	161.0	3,022
1951	186.0	3,479

*Per capita income calculated as a 10-year average, except for 1941 and 1951.
1941–1951 average per capita income 2,655 lire.
Value of 1938 lira: £1 sterling = approximately 90 lire; $1 U.S. = approximately 20 lire.
Source: Diario d'Italia, 1994. Il Giornale. 1994.

Table 12.   Annual Economic Growth, 1952–1974: The Economic Miracle

Year	Real GNP Growth (%)
1952	4.4
1953	7.5
1954	3.6
1955	6.7
1956	4 7
1957	5.3
1958	4.8
1959	6.5
1960	6.3
1961	8.2
1962	6.2
1963	5.6
1964	2.6
1965	3.2
1966	5.8
1967	7.0
1968	6.3
1969	5 7
1970	5.0
1971	1.6
1972	3.1
1973	6.9
1974	3.9

Source: ISTAT, http://www.istat.it

Table 13. Per Capita Income, EU Member States

Country	Income*
Luxembourg	61,610
Ireland	32,930
Austria	31,800
Denmark	31,770
Belgium	31,530
Great Britain	31,430
Netherlands	31,360
Sweden	29,880
Finland	29,800
France	29,460
Germany	28,170
Italy	28,120
Spain	24,750
Greece	22,230
Cyprus	22,230
Slovenia	20,830
Portugal	19,240
Malta	18,590
Czech Republic	18,420
Hungary	15,800
Slovakia	14,480
Estonia	13,630
Poland	12,730
Lithuania	12,690
Latria	11,820
Romania	08,330
Bulgaria	07,720

*U.S. dollars at PPP using 2004 official statistics for population and GNP.
Source: World Bank Development Indicators, July 2006.

Bibliography

The literature of Italian studies in English is a patchy one. Some subjects—the mafia being a predictable example—have been treated in great detail and have inspired a very large number of outstanding monographs. More generally, the social history of Italy's rural, peasant communities and studies of the folkways of southern Italy have provided a rich source of material for scholars and writers. Italy's economic history is more sketchily treated, but there are several outstanding general histories, the most recent of which is Vera Zamagni's *Economic History of Italy* (1993). Political and intellectual history, by contrast, is—the Fascist interlude apart—full of gaps. Only a handful of Italian statesmen have been the subject of full-length biographies in any period (including Fascism, where Mussolini has hogged the attention), and Italy's most representative writers, philosophers, and political thinkers simply have not been accorded as much attention as—for instance—their French and German peers. This relative neglect of Italian political and intellectual life has three major contributory causes. First, Italian is not as widely read as French or German in Britain and the United States; second, Italian politics and culture is (wrongly) considered to be less important, or less influential; third, Italy's fascinating social culture, and the modern preference for sociological history over narrative history on political subjects, seems to have taken precedence. It cannot be denied, however, that the fact that there exists no English-language biography of (and this is an abbreviated list) Agostino Depretis, Alcide De Gasperi, Palmiro Togliatti, Aldo Moro, Enrico Berlinguer, and Giulio Andreotti represents a serious shortcoming for anybody anxious to expand his or her knowledge of the country's history.

Intellectuals and writers have been similarly neglected: Vilfredo Pareto, Gaetano Mosca, Antonio Labriola, Benedetto Croce, Giovanni Gentile, and Gaetano Salvemini are social thinkers of the first rank, and although interest in Croce has recently revived, it cannot be said that any of these remarkably influential figures have received their due. Only Antonio Gramsci has been canonized by English-language writers, and in his case the problem is almost the abundance of studies on the former communist leader's life and thought. In other aspects of cultural life—the cinema, art, architecture, and even literature—Italy emerges very satisfactorily. The body of literature describing Italy's towns, regions, and cuisine, of course, can only be described as monumental, and this bibliography has merely hinted at its size.

The bibliography follows the standard procedure for general texts on Italy by arranging the material by historical period, after a brief section listing books that give Italian political, economic, and social history the broad-brush treatment. These periods are the Risorgimento (i.e., from 1815 to approximately 1861); liberal Italy (1861–1922); Fascist and wartime Italy (1922–1946); and Republican Italy (1946–). Each section is divided into subsections separating general works on each period from specific texts in politics, society, and economics. The final section, on Republican Italy, has been enriched with two further subsections dealing with the literature on the mafia phenomenon and on the crisis of the Italian state between 1992 and 1995, which has generated a substantial literature in English and a vast one in Italian. Rounding off the bibliography are sections on intellectual and cultural history, Italy's regions and cities, and guidebooks. With few exceptions, the bibliography concentrates on relatively recent texts (1970 or later, with exceptions in outstanding cases). There are two recent bibliographies in English that deal with Italian subjects: Martin J. Bull *Contemporary Italy. A Research Guide* (1996), and F. J. Coppa and M. Roberts, *Modern Italian History: An Annotated Bibliography* (1990).

An important point about the bibliography is the number of texts in Italian. For the reasons given above, it is almost impossible to comprehend the country's political history in particular unless one reads the original language. Books in Italian therefore accompany every section of the bibliography, and political subjects are given special prominence. It should be noted in passing that political historians and contemporary writers on politics in Italy are of an extremely high standard and naturally deal with many issues in a detail that English language writers cannot match. Italian history is often partisan history, with liberals, communists, and Catholics still struggling to capture the country's past, but it is difficult to see why this should be regarded as a defect when it imparts such vitality to the scholarly debate.

Despite the fact that so much of the best writing on modern Italian history has never been translated, and despite the gaps that exist in the English-language bibliography, it remains true that Italy's political, economic, and social history has inspired some very fine and readable scholarship by English-language authors. A reader wishing to become acquainted with Italy's modern history should certainly start with Christopher Duggan's *A Concise History of Italy* (1994), or Denis Mack Smith's *Italy: A Modern History* (1997, 2nd ed.), both of which are splendid introductory texts. Martin Clark's *Modern Italy 1871–1995* (1995) is an undoubted achievement, though he downplays the role of politics excessively. Mack Smith's *The Making of Italy 1796–1866* (1986), and his biographies of Camillo Benso di Cavour, Giuseppe Mazzini, and Giuseppe Garibaldi, are very readable introductions to the Risorgimento. Harry Hearder's *Italy in the Age of the Risorgimento* (1983) is also a fine book. Liberal Italy's politics are treated in magisterial fashion by Christopher Seton-Watson's *Italy from Liberalism to Fascism 1870–1925* (1967). Benedetto Croce's *A History of Italy 1870–1915* (1929) is both a classic of historical writing and a revealing insight into Italian liberalism.

Fascism has inspired numerous important books in English. To name just three, R. J. B. Bosworth's *Mussolini* (2002) is a highly critical and well-researched account of the dictator's life. His *Mussolini's Italy: Life Under the Dictatorship 1915–1945* (2005) is an outstanding discussion of the social history of the Fascist period. Adrian Lyttleton's *The Seizure of Power. Fascism in Italy 1919–1929* (1973) is the definitive text in either language of the regime's birth and early years in power. The doyen of historians of Fascism, however, is Renzo De Felice, whose seven-volume study of Mussolini's life and times is regrettably only available in Italian. His 1977 *Interpretations of Fascism*, however, in an excellent translation by Brenda Huff Everett, provides a more than adequate introduction to his work. De Felice is just one of several outstanding Italian historians (others are Giorgio Candeloro, Federico Chabod, Arturo Jemolo, and Rosario Romeo) whose work is a delight for anyone with a basic knowledge or better of the Italian language. Paul Ginsborg's *A History of Contemporary Italy: Society and Politics, 1943–1988* (1990) is probably the best available introduction in English to postwar Italy.

A remarkable piece of social anthropology that deserves mention is David I. Kertzer's *Comrades and Christians* (1980), which describes the competing strategies used by the Church and the Communist Party to win the attention of the working class in Bologna and leaves an indelible picture of what life in the popular quarters of 1970s Bologna was like. The phenomenon of the mafia is skillfully dissected in Pino Arlacchi's *Mafia Business: The Mafia Ethic and the Spirit of Capitalism* (1988). More recently, Robert Putnam's *Making Democracy Work: Civic Traditions in Modern Italy* (1993) uses detailed historical research into the communes of northern and southern Italy to make a broad case for the importance of civic associations for the well-being of democratic government; both the method and the conclusions of the book have aroused spirited controversy.

Relatively few journal articles have been mentioned in the bibliography, which makes this an appropriate place to list some of the journals that most closely occupy themselves with Italy. Of the major scholarly reviews, the *Journal of Modern History* and the *Journal of Contemporary History* have both given considerable space in recent times to Italian subjects, especially Fascism. The *European History Quarterly* and *Contemporary European History* are other academic journals in which articles on Italian history have appeared regularly. *West European Politics* has dedicated a couple of monographic issues to Italy in recent years and frequently publishes articles on Italian politics. The *Journal of Modern Italian Studies*, which is published by Routledge three times a year, and *Modern Italy*, the journal of the Association for the Study of Modern Italy, contain articles and reviews that are essential sources for Italianists. The journal of the Society for Italian Studies, *Italian Studies*, provides articles on cultural, literary, and intellectual subjects, as does *Italian Culture*, the journal of the American Association for Italian Studies. Literary and cultural subjects can also be found in the *Italian Quarterly* and *Italica*.

Italy has a flourishing intellectual culture. *Passato e presente*, *Storia contemporanea*, *Rivista storica italiana*, *Contemporanea*, *Nord e Sud*, *Quaderni storici*, *Clio*, *Società e storia*, and *Ricerche di Storia Politica* are all excellent historical and cultural journals. Contemporary political issues are discussed in the lively bimonthly *Il Mulino*, and such publications as *Il Ponte*, *MicroMega*, and *Reset* testify to the vitality of Italian political debate. The news magazines *Panorama* and *Espresso* offer dozens of pages every week giving "insider" accounts of Italian politics, publishing leaked documents, and analyzing the economy. A section on the periodical press, giving website links, has been added to this edition.

A vital source for contemporary events is the annual Italian Politics series, published in Italy by Il Mulino of Bologna since 1986, and in English by Pinter publishers until 1993, Westview Press until 1999, and Berghahn since then. Each edition consists of 9 to 12 essays by established experts on significant developments in the political, economic, and institutional life of Italy in the previous year. The annual reports published by ISTAT, the Italian government statistical agency, are very useful for current social and economic trends.

Researchers wishing to do archive work in Italy will find that there is a huge number of foundations and collections of papers, most of which possess a website and some of which have arranged for the online consultation of documents. Almost every town has a *Museo storico* that stores documents of local (but often national) interest. The last section of this bibliography contains a number of links to websites useful for researchers on modern and contemporary Italy or for individuals trying to find out basic facts about Italy's government and economy.

CONTENTS

A. GENERAL WORKS

Absolom, Roger. *Italy since 1880: A Nation in the Balance?* London: Longman, 1995.

Baranski, Z., and R. J. West, eds. *The Cambridge Companion to Modern Italian Culture*. Cambridge: Cambridge University Press, 2001.

Barbagli, A. *Sotto lo stesso tetto: mutamenti di famiglia in Italia dal XVal XX secolo*. Bologna: II Mulino, 1988.

Barbagli, M. *Educating for Unemployment: Politics, Labor Markets and the School System 1859–1973*. New York: Columbia University Press, 1982.

Barbaro, I. *Storia del sindacalismo italiano*. 3 vols. Florence: La nuova Italia, 1973.

Bell, Rudolph M. *Fate and Honor, Family and Village: Demographic and Cultural Change in Rural Italy Since 1800*. Chicago: University of Chicago Press, 1981.

Bevilacqua, P. *Breve storia dell'Italia meridionale dall'Ottocento a oggi*. Rome: Donzelli, 1993.

———. *Storia dell'agricoltura italiana in eta contemporanea*. 3 vols. Venice: Marsilio, 1989–1991.

Bosworth, R. J. B., and Sergio Romeno, eds. *La politica estera italiana 1860–1985*. Bologna: Il Mulino, 1991.

Bull, Martin J. *Contemporary Italy: A Research Guide*. Westport, Conn.: Greenwood Press, 1996.

Candeloro, Giorgio. *Storia dell'Italia moderna*. 12 vols. Milan: Feltrinelli, 1970–1986.

Cannistraro, P. *Historical Dictionary of Fascist Italy*. Westport, Conn.: Greenwood Press, 1982.

Cappelletti, Mauro, J. Merryman, and J. M. Perillo. *The Italian Legal System: An Introduction*. Stanford, Calif.: Stanford University Press, 1967.

Castronovo, Valerio. *Storia economica d'Italia. Dall'Ottocento ai nostri giorni*. Turin: Einaudi, 1995.

Castronovo, Valerio, and Nicola Tranfaglia. *Storia della stampa italiana. La stampa italiana dall'unità al fascismo*. Bari: Laterza, 1970.

Clark, Martin. *Modern Italy 1871–1995*. London: Longman, 1995.

Clough, Shepard, and Salvatore Saladino. *A History of Modern Italy*. New York: Columbia University Press, 1968.

Cohen, John, and Giovanni Federico. *The Growth of the Italian Economy, 1820–1960*. Cambridge: Cambridge University Press, 2001.

Coppa, F. J., ed. *Dictionary of Modern Italian History*. Westport, Conn.: Greenwood Press, 1985.

Coppa, F. J., and M. Roberts. *Modern Italian History: An Annotated Bibliography*. Westport, Conn.: Greenwood Press, 1990.

Cotta, Maurizio. "Italy." In *Parliaments in the Modern World*, edited by Gary W. Copeland and Samuel C. Patterson. Ann Arbor: University of Michigan Press, 1994.

Cotula, Franco, Marcello de Cecco, and Gianni Toniolo, eds. *La Banca d'Italia. Sintesi della ricerca storica 1893–1960*. Rome: Laterza, 2003.

De Bernardi, Alberto, and Luigi Canapini. *Storia d'Italia, 1860–1995*. Milan: Mondatori, 1996.

De Felice, Renzo, ed. *Storia d'Italia dall'unità alla repubblica*. 7 vols. Naples: Edizioni scientifiche italiane, 1976–1983.

Dickie, John, and J. Foot, eds. *Disastro! Disasters in Italy since 1860: Culture, Politics, Society*. London: Palgrave, 2002.

Di Giorgio, M. *Le italiane dall'unita a oggi*. Bari: Laterza, 1992.

Di Rosa, G. *Storia del movimento cattolico in Italia*. 2 vols. Bari: Laterza, 1966.

Di Scala, Spencer M. *Italy from Revolution to Republic: 1700 to the Present*. Boulder, Colo: Westview Press, 1995.

Domenico, Roy Palmer. *Remaking Italy in the Twentieth Century*. Lanham, Md.: Rowman & Littlefield, 2002.

Donovan, Mark, ed. *Italy*. 2 vols. Dartmouth, U.K.: Ashgate, 1998.

Duggan, Christopher. *A Concise History of Italy*. Cambridge: Cambridge University Press, 1994.

Evans, David. *Years of Liberalism and Fascism: Italy 1870–1945*. London: Hodder & Stoughton Educational, 2003.

Galasso, Giuseppe. *Storia d'Italia*. Vols. 20–23. Turin: UTET, 1979.

Ghisberti, Alberto. *Storia costituzionale d'Italia 1849–1948*. Bari: Laterza, 1967.

Giovarmi, Federico. "Italy, 1860–1940: A Little Known Success Story." *Economic History Review*. 59, no. 4 (Winter 1996): 764–786.

Holmes, G. ed. *An Illustrated History of Italy*. Oxford: Oxford University Press, 2001.

Isnenghi, Mario. *Le guerre degli italiani: Parole, immagini, ricordi, 1848–1945*. Bologna: Il Mulino, 2005.

———. *L'Italia in piazza. I luoghi della vita pubblica dal 1848 ai giorni nostri*. Bologna: Il Mulino, 2004.

Jemolo, Arturo. *Church and State in Italy 1850–1950*. Oxford: Blackwell, 1960.

Kertzer, David I., and Richard P. Saller, eds. *The Family in Italy from Antiquity to the Present*. New Haven, Conn.: Yale University Press, 1991.

Livi-Bacci, M. *A History of Italian Fertility during the Last Two Centuries*. Princeton, N.J.: Princeton University Press, 1977.

Mack Smith, Denis. *Modern Italy: A Political History*. New Haven, Conn.: Yale University Press, 1997.

Mammarella, Giuseppe, and Paolo Cacace, *La politica estera dell'Italia: Dallo stato unitario ai giorni nostri*. Rome: Laterza, 2006.

Moliterno, G. ed. *Encyclopaedia of Contemporary Italian Culture*. London: Routledge, 2000.

Murialdi, Paolo. *Storia del giornalismo italiano: Dalle gazzette a internet*. Bologna: Il Mulino, 2006.

Piretti, Maria Serena. *Le elezioni politiche in Italia dal 1848 a oggi*. Bari: Laterza, 1995.

Procacci, Giuliano. *History of the Italian People*. Translated by Anthony Paul. Hammondsworth, U.K.: Penguin Books, 1973.

Putnam, Robert, and Robert Leonardi. *Making Democracy Work: Civic Traditions in Modern Italy*. Princeton, N.J.: Princeton University Press, 1993.

Redford, Bruce. *Venice and the Grand Tour*. New Haven, Conn.: Yale University Press, 1996.

Romeno, R., ed. *Storia dell'economia italiana*. Turin: Einaudi, 1990–1991.

Romeo, Rosario. *Breve storia della grande industria in Italia*. Milan: II Saggiatore, 1991.

Sabbatucci, Giovanni, and Vittorio Vidotti, eds. *Storia d'Italia*. 6 vols. Rome: Laterza, 1994–1999.

Sereni, Emilio. *History of the Italian Agricultural Landscape*. Princeton, N.J.: Princeton University Press, 1997.

Sorcinelli, P. *Eros: Storie e fantasie degli italiani dal 800 a oggi*. Bari: Laterza, 1993.

Tannenbaum, E. R., and E. P. Noether, eds. *Modern Italy: A Topical History since 1861*. New York: New York University Press, 1974.

Webster, Richard Allen. *Christian Democracy in Italy, 1860–1960*. London: Hollis & Carter, 1961.

Woolf, Stuart J. *A History of Italy, 1700–1860. The Social Constraints of Political Change*. New York: Methuen, 1979.

Zamagni, Vera. *The Economic History of Italy 1860–1990*. Oxford: Clarendon Press, 1993.

B. ITALY 1815–1861: THE RISORGIMENTO

1. General Histories

Beales, Derek, and Eugenio F. Biagini. *The Risorgimento and the Unification of Italy*. London: Longman, 2002.

Berkeley, G. F. H. *Italy in the Making*. Reprint. 3 vols. Cambridge: Cambridge University Press, 1968.

Davis, John A., and Paul Ginsborg, eds. *Society and Politics in the Age of the Risorgimento: Essays in Honour of Denis Mack Smith*. Cambridge: Cambridge University Press, 2002.

Gobetti, Piero. *Risorgimento senza eroi*. Torino: Einaudi, 1976.

Gramsci, Antonio. *Il Risorgimento*. Turin: Einaudi, 1955.

Hearder, Harry. *Italy in the Age of the Risorgimento 1790–1870*. London: Longman, 1983.

Laven, David. *Restoration and Risorgimento: Italy 1796–1870*. Oxford: Oxford University Press, 2007.

Mack Smith, Denis. *The Making of Italy 1796–1866*. London: Macmillan, 1986.

Omodeo, Adolfo. *L'eta del risorgimento italiano*. Naples: Edizioni scientifiche italiane, 1960.

Riall, Lucy. *The Italian Risorgimento: State, Society and National Unification.* New York: Routledge, 1994.

Romeo, Rosario. *Dal Piemonte sabauda all'Italia liberale.* Torino: Einaudi, 1961.

——. *Risorgimento e capitalismo.* Bari: Laterza, 1963.

Rosselli, Nello. *Saggi sul Risorgimento.* Turin: Einaudi, 1980.

Salvatorelli, Luigi. *Pensiero e azione del Risorgimento.* Torino: Einaudi, 1974.

Salvemini, Gaetano. *Scritti sul Risorgimento.* Milan: Feltrinelli, 1961.

Scirocco, Alfonso. *L'Italia del Risorgimento.* Bologna: Il Mulino, 1990.

2. Studies in Biography, Politics, Economics, and Society

Acton, Harold. *The Last Bourbons of Naples (1825–1861).* London: Methuen, 1961.

Broers, Michael. "The Police and the Padroni: Italian Notabili, French Gendarmes and the Origins of the Centralized State in Napoleonic Italy." *European History Quarterly.* 26, no. 2 (July 1996): 331–354.

Budden, Julian. *Verdi.* New York: Random House, 1987.

Coppa, Frank J. *Camillo Di Cavour.* New York: Twayne, 1973.

——. *The Origins of the Italian Wars of Independence.* White Plains, N.Y.: Longman, 1992.

Davis, John A. *Conflict and Control: Law and Order in Nineteenth Century Italy.* Basingstoke, U.K.: Macmillan, 1988.

Eisenstein, Elizabeth. *The First Professional Revolutionary: Filippo Michele Buonarotti.* Cambridge: Cambridge University Press, 1959.

Finley, Milton. *The Most Monstrous of Wars: The Napoleonic Guerilla War in Southern Italy.* Columbia: University of South Carolina Press, 1994.

Ginsborg, Paul. *Daniele Manin and the Venetian Revolution of 1848–1849.* Cambridge: Cambridge University Press, 1979.

Hearder, Harry. *Cavour.* New York: Longman, 1994.

Hibbert, Christopher. *Garibaldi and His Enemies: The Clash of Arms and Personalities in the Making of Italy.* London: Penguin Books, 1987.

Hughes, Steven C. *Crime, Disorder and the Risorgimento: The Politics of Policing in Bologna.* Cambridge: Cambridge University Press, 1994.

Kertzer, David I. *Family, Political Economy and Demographic Change: The Transformation of Life in Casalecchio, Italy, 1861–1921.* Madison: University of Wisconsin Press, 1989.

King, Bolton. *The Life of Mazzini.* New York: Dutton, 1911.

Lepre, A. *La rivoluzione napoletana del 1820–1821.* Rome: Edizioni Riuniti, 1967.

Lovett, C. M. *Carlo Cattaneo and the Politics of the Risorgimento, 1820–1860.* The Hague: Martin Nijhoff, 1972.

——. *The Democratic Movement in Italy, 1830–1876.* Cambridge, Mass.: Harvard University Press, 1982.

Mack Smith, Denis. *Cavour*. London: Weidenfeld and Nicholson, 1985.
——. *Cavour and Garibaldi: A Study in Political Conflict*. Cambridge: Cambridge University Press, 1985.
——. *Garibaldi*. London: Hutchinson, 1982.
——. *Mazzini*. New Haven, Conn: Yale University Press, 1994.
Pick, Daniel. *Rome or Death: The Obsessions of Giuseppe Garibaldi*. London: Cape, 2005.
Reinerman, Alan J. "Metternich, Alexander I and the Russian Challenge in Italy." *Journal of Modern History* 46, no. 2 (June 1974): 20–38.
Ridley, Jasper. *Garibaldi*. London: Constable, 1974.
Roberts, William. *Prophet in Exile: Joseph Mazzini in England, 1837–1868*. New York: Peter Lang, 1989.
Robertson, Priscilla. *Revolutions of 1848: A Social History*. Princeton, N.J.: Princeton University Press, 1971.
Romani, G. T. *The Neapolitan Revolution of 1820–1821*. Evanston: University of Illinois Press, 1950.
Romeo, Rosario. *Cavour*. 3 vols. Bari: Laterza, 1984.
Sarti, Roland. *Mazzini: A Life for the Religion of Politics*. Westport, Conn.: Greenwood Press, 1997.
Schneid, Frederick. *Napoleon's Italian Campaigns, 1805–1815*. Westport, Conn.: Praeger, 2002.
Spadolini, Giovanni. *Cattolicismo e risorgimento*. Florence: Le Monnier, 1986.
Taylor, A. J. P. *The Italian Problem in European Diplomacy*. Manchester, U.K.: University of Manchester Press, 1934.
Trevelyan, G. M. *Garibaldi and the Thousand*. London: Longman, 1909.
Villani, P. *L'Italia napoleonica*. Naples: Guida, 1978.

C. LIBERAL ITALY

1. General Histories

Aquarone, Alberto. *L'Italia Giolittiana*. 2 vols. Bologna: II Mulino, 1981–1988.
Arfe, G. *Storia del socialismo italiano 1892–1926*. Turin: Einaudi, 1965.
Bosworth, R. J. B. *Italy, The Least of the Great Powers: Italian Foreign Policy before the First World War*. New York: Cambridge University Press, 1979.
Cafagna, Luciano. "Italy 1830–1914." In *The Fontana Economic History of Europe*, edited by Carlo Cipolla. London: Fontana, 1973.
Carocci, Giampiero. *Giolitti e l'èta giolittiana*. Turin: Einaudi, 1974.
Chabod, Federico. *Storia della politica estera italiana dal 1870 al 1896*. Bari: Laterza, 1971.
Coppa, Frank J., ed. *Studies in Modern Italian History: From the Risorgimento to the Republic*. New York: Lang, 1986.

Croce, Benedetto. *A History of Italy 1871–1915*. Oxford: Oxford University Press, 1929.

——. *Storia d'Italia, 1871–1915*. Bari: Laterza, 1928.

Gentile, Emilio. *L'Italia giolittiana*. Rome: Laterza, 2003.

Lowe, C. J., and F. Marzari. *Italian Foreign Policy 1870–1940*. London: Routledge and Kegan Paul, 1975.

Mack Smith, Denis. *Italy and Its Monarchy*. New Haven, Conn.: Yale University Press, 1990.

Mafai, Miriam. *Pane Nero*. Milan: Arnaldo Mondatori, 1987.

Romanelli, Raffaele. *L'Italia Liberale*. Bologna: Il Mulino, 1990.

Sabbatucci, Giovanni, and V. Vidotto, eds. *Storia d'Italia, vol. 2. Il nuovo stato e la societa civile (1861–1887)*. Bari: Laterza, 1995.

Salomone, A. William. *Italy in the Giolittian Era. Italian Democracy in the Making 1900–1914*. Philadelphia: University of Pennsylvania Press, 1960.

Seton-Watson, Christopher. *Italy from Liberalism to Fascism 1870–1925*. London: Methuen, 1967.

Toniolo, Gianni. *An Economic History of Liberal Italy, 1850–1918*. London: Routledge, 1990.

Volpe, Gioacchino. *L'Italia moderna, 1815–1915*. Florence: Sansoni, 1958.

2. Studies in Biography, Politics, Economics, and Society

Agocs, Sandor. *The Troubled Origins of the Italian Catholic Movement*. Detroit: Wayne State University Press, 1988.

Ashley, Susan A. *Making Liberalism Work: The Italian Experience, 1860–1914*. New York: Praeger, 2003.

Ballini, Pierluigi. *Le elezioni nella storia d'Italia dall'unita al fascismo*. Bologna: Il Mulino, 1988.

Barbagallo, Francesco. *Francesco S. Nitti*. Turin: UTET, 1984.

Bell, Donald Howard, ed. *Sesto San Giovanni: Workers, Culture and Politics in an Italian Town, 1880–1922*. New Brunswick, N.J.: Rutgers University Press, 1986.

Berghaus, Gunter. *Futurism and Politics: Between Anarchist Rebellion and Fascist Reaction*. Oxford: Berghahn Books, 1996.

Bosworth, R. J .B. *Italy and the Approach of the First World War*. New York: St. Martin's Press.

Bütler, Hugo. *Gaetano Salvemini und die Italienische Politik vor dem Ersten Weltkrieg*. Tübingen: Niemeyer, 1978.

Candeloro, Giorgio. *Il movimento cattolico in Italia*. Rome: Editori Riuniti, 1972.

Capone, A. *Destra e sinistra da Cavour a Crispi*. Turin: UTET, 1981.

Cardini, Antonio. *Stato liberale e protezionismo in Italia, 1890–1900*. Bologna: Il Mulino, 1981.

Cardoza, Anthony, *Aristocrats in Bourgeois Italy: The Piemontese Nobility, 1861–1930*. Cambridge: Cambridge University Press, 2002.

Carocci, Giampiero. *Agostino Depretis e la politica interna italiana dal 1876 al 1887*. Turin: Einaudi, 1956.

———. *Il trasformismo dall'unita ad oggi*. Milan: Unicopli, 1992.

Caroli, Betty Boyd. *Italian Repatriation from the United States, 1890–1914*. New York: Center for Migration Studies, 1973.

Casalegno, Carlo. *La regina Margherita*. Bologna: Il Mulino, 2001.

Coppa, Frank J. *Economics and Politics in the Giolittian Age: Planning, Protection and Politics in Liberal Italy*. Washington, D.C.: Catholic University Press, 1971.

———. *Pope Pius IX: Crusader in a Secular Age*. Boston: Twayne Publishers, 1979.

Cordova, Ferdinando. *Massoneria e politica in Italia, 1892–1908*. Bari: Laterza, 1985.

Corner, Paul R. *Contadini e industrializzazione: Societa rurale e impresa in Italia dal 1840 al 1940*. Bari: Laterza, 1993.

De Grand, Alexander. *The Hunchback's Tailor: Giovanni Giolitti and Liberal Italy from the Challenge of Mass Politics to the Rise of Fascism*. Westport, Conn: Praeger, 2000.

De Nicolò, Marco. *Trasformismo, autoritarismo, meridionalismo: il ministro dell'interno Giovanni Nicotera*. Bologna: Il Mulino, 2001.

Di Iorio, Anthony. *Italy, Austria-Hungary and the Balkans 1904–1914*. Urbana: University of Illinois Press, 1980.

Di Scala, Spencer. *Dilemmas of Italian Socialism: The Politics of Filippo Turati*. Amherst: University of Massachusetts Press, 1980.

Duggan, Christopher. *Francesco Crispi: From Nation to Nationalism*. Oxford: Oxford University Press, 2002.

Forsyth, D. J. *The Crisis of Liberal Italy 1914–1922*. Cambridge: Cambridge University Press, 1993.

Galante Garrone, Alessandro. *I radicali in Italia 1849–1925*. Milan: Garzanti, 1973.

Galasso, Giuseppe. *La democrazia da Cattaneo a Rosselli*. Florence: Le Monnier, 1982.

Gentile, Emilio. *Il mito dello stato nuovo: dal radicalismo nazionale al fascismo*. Roma: Laterza, 1999.

Gerschenkron, A. *Economic Backwardness in Historical Perspective*. Cambridge, Mass.: Harvard University Press, 1962.

Gibson, Mary. *Prostitution and the State in Italy 1860–1915*. New Brunswick, N.J.: Rutgers University Press, 1986.

Giolitti, Giovanni. *Memoirs of My Life*. London: Chapman & Dodd, 1923.

Gonzales, Manuel G. *Andrea Costa and the Rise of Socialism in the Romagna*. Washington, D.C.: University Press of America, 1980.

Gooch, J. *Army, State and Society in Italy, 1870–1915*. Basingstoke, U.K.: Macmillan, 1989.

Hess, Robert L. *Italian Colonialism in Somalia*. Chicago: Chicago University Press, 1966.

Isnenghi, Mario and Giorgio Rochat. *La Grande Guerra 1914–1918*. Milan: La Nuova Italia, 2000.

Jensen, R. B. *Liberty and Order: The Theory and Practice of Italian Public Security Policy, 1848 to the Crisis of the 1890s.* London: Garland, 1991.

Kertzer, David I. *Family Life in Central Italy 1880–1910: Sharecropping, Wage Labor and Coresidence.* New Brunswick, N.J.: Rutgers University Press, 1984.

——. *Sacrificed for Honor: Italian Infant Abandonment and the Politics of Reproduction.* Boston: Beacon Press, 1993.

Ledeen, Michael A. *The First Duce: D'Annunzio at Fiume.* Baltimore, Md.: Johns Hopkins University Press, 1977.

Luzzatto, G. *L'economia italiana dal 1861 al 1894.* Turin: Einaudi, 1968.

Lyttleton, Adrian. *The Language of Political Conflict in Pre-Fascist Italy.* Occasional Paper No. 54. Bologna: Johns Hopkins University Research Institute, 1988.

Maloney, John M. *The Emergence of Political Catholicism in Italy: Partito Popolare 1919–1926.* Totowa, N.J.: Rowman & Littlefield, 1977.

Miller, J. E. *From Elite to Mass Politics: Italian Socialism in the Giolittian Era, 1900–1914.* Kent, Ohio: Kent University Press, 1990.

Mola, A. A. *Giolitti. Lo statista della nuova Italia.* Milan: Mondatori, 2003.

——. *L'imperialismo italiano: La politica estera dall'unita al fascismo.* Rome: Editori Riuniti, 1980.

Morris, Jonathon. *The Political Economy of Shopkeeping in Milan, 1885–1922.* Cambridge: Cambridge University Press, 1993.

Negri, Guglielmo, ed. *Giolitti e la nascita della banca d'Italia nel 1893.* Bari: Laterza, 1989.

Perfeti, F. *Il movimento nazionalista in Italia 1903–1914.* Rome: Bonacci, 1984.

Pernicone, Nunzio. *Italian Anarchism, 1864–1892.* Princeton, N.J.: Princeton University Press, 1993.

Petricioli, Marta. *L'Italia in Asia minore: equilibrio mediterraneo e ambizioni imperialiste alla vigilia della prima guerra mondiale.* Florence: Sansoni, 1983.

Polsi, Alessandro. *Alle origini del capitalismo italiano: Stato, banche e banchieri dopo l'unita.* Turin: Einaudi, 1993.

Randeraand, Nico. *Authority in Search of Liberty: The Prefects of Central Italy.* Amsterdam: Thesis Press, 1993.

Renzi, William A. *In the Shadow of the Sword: Italy's Neutrality and Entrance into the Great War 1914–1915.* New York: Peter Lang, 1987.

Ricolfi, M. *Il Psi e la nascita del partito di massa 1892–1922.* Bari: Laterza, 1992.

Romeno, Sergio. *Crispi: Progetto per una dittatura.* Milan: Bompiani, 1973.

Snowden, Frank M. *Naples in the Time of the Cholera, 1884–1911.* Cambridge: Cambridge University Press, 1996.

——. *Violence and the Great Estates in the South of Italy: Apulia 1900–1922.* Cambridge: Cambridge University Press, 1986.

Spadolini, Giovanni. *Giolitti e i cattolici 1901–1914.* Firenze: Le Monnier, 1991.

——. *L'opposizione cattolica da Porta Pia al 1898.* Florence: Vallechi, 1954.

Valeri, Nino. *Giovanni Giolitti.* Turin: Einaudi, 1972.

Webster, Richard A. *Industrial Imperialism in Italy 1908–1915*. Berkeley: California University Press, 1975.
Whittam, John. *The Politics of the Italian Army, 1861–1918*. Hamden, Conn.: Archon Books, 1977.

D. FASCISM

1. General Histories and Theoretical Works

Aquarone, Alberto. *L'organizzazione dello stato totalitario*. Turin: Einaudi, 1965.
Blinkhorn, Martin, *Mussolini and Fascist Italy*. London: Routledge, 1998.
Bosworth, R. J. B. *The Italian Dictatorship: Problems and Perspectives in the Interpretation of Mussolini and Fascism*. London: Arnold, 1998.
———. *Mussolini's Italy: Life under the Dictatorship 1915–1945*. London: Allen Lane, 2005.
Bosworth, R. J. B., and Patrizia Dogliani, eds. *Italian Fascism: History, Memory and Representation*. Basingstoke, U.K.: Macmillan, 1999.
Cannistraro, Philip V. *Historical Dictionary of Fascist Italy*. Westport, Conn.: Greenwood Press, 1982.
Cassels, Alan. *Fascism*. New York: Thomas Crowell, 1975.
Chabod, Federico. *Fascismo e antifascismo, 1918–1948*. 2 vols. Milan: Feltrinelli, 1962.
———. *A History of Italian Fascism*. London: Weidenfeld and Nicholson, 1963.
———. *L'Italia contemporanea 1918–1948*. Turin: Einaudi, 1961.
Collier, R. B., and D. Collier. "Inducements v. Constraints: Disaggregating Fascism." *American Political Science Review* 73 (1979): 967–986.
De Bernardi, Alberto. *Una dittatura moderna: Il fascismo come problema storico*. Milan: Mondatori, 2001.
De Felice, Renzo. *Fascism: An Informal Introduction to Its Theory and Practice*. New Brunswick, N.J.: Transaction Books, 1976.
———. *Interpretations of Fascism*. Translated by Brenda Huff Everett. Cambridge, Mass.: Harvard University Press, 1977.
———. *Mussolini*. 7 vols. Turin: Einaudi. Vol. 1, *Mussolini il rivoluzionario*, 1965. Vol. 2, *Mussolini il fascista. La conquista del potere 1921–1925*, 1966. Vol. 3, *Mussolini il fascista. L'organizzazione dello stato fascista 1925–1929*, 1969. Vol. 4, *Mussolini il duce I. Gli anni di consenso 1929–1936*, 1974. Vol. 5, *Mussolini il duce II. Lo stato totalitario*, 1981. Vol. 6, *Mussolini l'alleato I: 1940–1943*, 1990: Pt. 1, *Dalla Guerra "breve" alla guerra lunga*; Pt. 2, *Crisi e agonia del regime*. Vol. 7, *Mussolini l'alleato II. La Guerra civile 1943–1945*, 1997.
De Grand, Alexander. *Fascist Italy and Nazi Germany: The "Fascist" Style of Rule*. London: Routledge, 2004.

———. *Italian Fascism: Its Origin and Development*. Lincoln: University of Nebraska Press, 2000.

De Grazia, Victoria, and Sergio Luzzatti, eds. *Dizionario del fascismo*. Turin: Einaudi, 2003.

Diggins, John P. *Mussolini and Fascism*. Princeton, N.J.: Princeton University Press, 1972.

"Fascist Italy." *Fortune Magazine* July 1934.

Finer, Herman. *Mussolini's Italy*. New York: Grosset and Dunlap, 1935.

Forgacs, David, ed. *Rethinking Italian Fascism: Capitalism, Populism and Culture*. London: Lawrence and Wishart, 1986.

Galli, Giorgio. *Il Fascismo: Dallo squadrismo a Dongo*. Verona: Teti Editore, 1995.

Gentile, Emilio. *The Struggle for Modernity: Nationalism, Futurism and Fascism*. Westport, Conn: Praeger, 2003.

Goglia, L., R. Moro, and L. Nuti. *Guerra e pace nell'Italia del Novecento: Politica estera, cultura politica e correnti dell'opinione pubblica*. Bologna: Il Mulino, 2006.

Gregor, A. James. *Italian Fascism and Developmental Dictatorship*. Princeton, NJ: Princeton University Press, 1979.

Lupo, Salvatore. *Il fascismo: La politica in un regime totalitario*. Rome: Donzelli, 2005.

Lyttelton, Adrian, ed. *Liberal and Fascist Italy, 1900–1945*. Oxford: Oxford University Press, 2002.

Milza, P., and S. Berstein. *Le fascisme italien 1919–1945*. Paris: Editions du Seuil, 1980.

Morgan, Philip. *Italian Fascism 1915–1945*. New York: St. Martin's Press, 2004.

Payne, Stanley G. *A History of Fascism, 1914–1945*. Madison: University of Wisconsin Press, 1996.

Petri, Rolf. *Storia economica d'Italia: Dalla grande guerra al miracolo economico, 1918–1963*. Bologna: Il Mulino, 2003.

Pugliese, Stanislao G., ed. *Italian Fascism and Antifascism: A Critical Anthology*. Manchester, U.K.: Manchester University Press, 2001.

Salvatorelli, Luigi, and Giovanni Mira. *Storia d'Italia nel periodo fascista*. Turin: Einaudi, 1964.

Salvemini, Gaetano. *The Fascist Dictatorship in Italy*. New York: Henry Holt, 1927.

———. *The Origins of Fascism in Italy*. New York: Harper & Row, 1973.

———. *Under the Axe of Fascism*. New York: Viking Press, 1936.

Tannenbaum, Edward R. *The Fascist Experience: Italian Society and Culture, 1922–1945*. New York: Basic Books, 1972.

Tasca, Angelo. *Nascita e avvento di fascismo*. Florence: La Nuova Italia, 1950.

Toniolo, G. *L'economia dell'Italia fascista*. Rome: Laterza, 1980.

Veneruso, Danilo. *L'Italia fascista*. Bologna: II Mulino, 1990.

Whittam, John. *Fascist Italy*. Manchester, U.K.: Manchester University Press, 1995.

Wiskemann, Elizabeth. *Fascism in Italy: Its Development and Influence*. London: Macmillan, 1969.

2. Studies in Biography, Politics, Economics, and Society

Adamson, Walter L. *Avante-garde Florence: From Modernism to Fascism*. Cambridge, Mass.: Harvard University Press, 1993.

Adler, Franklin Hugh. *Italian Industrialists from Liberalism to Fascism: The Political Development of the Industrial Bourgeoisie, 1906–1934*. New York: Cambridge University Press, 1995.

Aga Rossi, Elena. *Una nazione allo sbando: L'armistizio italiano del settembre 1943*. Bologna: Il Mulino, 2006.

Amendola, Giovanni. *La democrazia contro il fascismo 1922–1924*. Milan: R. Ricciardi, 1960.

Baer, George W. *Test Case: Italy, Ethiopia and the League of Nations*. Stanford, Calif: Hoover Institution, 1976.

Belardelli, Giovanni. *Il ventennio degli intellettuali: cultura, politica, ideologia nell'Italia fascista*. Rome: Laterza, 2005.

Ben-Ghiat, Ruth. *Fascist Modernities: Italy 1922–1945*. Berkeley: University of California Press, 2001.

Ben-Ghiat, Ruth, and Mia Fuller, eds. *Italian Colonialism*. Basingstoke, U.K.: Palgrave Macmillan, 2005.

Berezin, Mabel. *Making the Fascist Self: The Political Culture of Interwar Italy*. Ithaca, N.Y.: Cornell University Press, 1997.

Bessel, Richard, ed. *Fascist Italy and Nazi Germany*. Cambridge: Cambridge University Press, 1996.

Betti, Carmen. *L'opera nazionale Balilla e l'educazione fascista*. Florence: Nuova Italia, 1984.

Bocca, Giorgio. *La repubblica di Mussolini*. Rome: Laterza, 1977.

———. *Storia dell'Italia partigiana*. Rome: Laterza, 1966.

Bosworth, R. J. B. *Mussolini*. London: Arnold, 2002.

Campi, Alessandro. *Mussolini*. Bologna: Il Mulino, 2001.

Carracciolo, Alberto, ed. *La Banca d'Italia tra l'autarchia e la guerra, 1936–1945*. Rome: Laterza, 1992.

Caretti, Stefano. *Il delitto Matteotti: Storia e memoria*. Manduria (Taranto): P. Lacaita, 2004.

Ciano, Galeazzo. *Diario, 1937–1943*. 3 vols. Milan: Rizzoli, 1950.

Colarizi, Simona. *L'Italia antifascista dal 1922 al 1940*. Rome: Laterza, 1976.

Cordoza, Anthony L. *Agrarian Elites and Italian Fascism: The Province of Bologna 1901–1926*. Princeton, N.J.: Princeton University Press, 1983.

Corner, Paul. *Fascism in Ferrara*. New York: Oxford University Press, 1975.

Coverdale, J. F. *Italian Intervention in the Spanish Civil War*. Princeton, N.J.: Princeton University Press. 1975.

Deakin, F. W. *The Brutal Friendship: Mussolini, Hitler and the Fall of Italian Fascism*. London: Weidenfeld and Nicholson, 1962.

———. *The Last Days of Mussolini*. London: Harmondsworth, 1966.

De Felice, Renzo. *D'Annunzio politico 1918–1938*. Rome: Laterza, 1978.

——. *Intellettuali di fronte al fascismo*. Rome: Bonacci, 1985.

De Grand, Alexander. *Bottai e la cultura fascista*. Rome: Laterza, 1978.

——. "Curzio Malaparte: The Illusion of a Fascist Revolution." *Journal of Contemporary History* 7, no. 1 (1972): 73–89.

——. *The Italian Nationalist Association and the Rise of Fascism in Italy*. Lincoln: University of Nebraska Press, 1978.

De Grazia, Victoria. *The Culture of Consent: The Mass Organization of Leisure in Fascist Italy*. New York: Cambridge University Press, 1981.

——. *How Fascism Ruled Women: Italy 1922–1945*. Berkeley: University of California Press, 1992.

Del Boca, A. *Gli italiani in Africa orientale*. 4 vols. Rome: Laterza, 1976–1984.

——. *Gli italiani in Libia*. 2 vols. Rome: Laterza, 1986–1988.

——. *L'impero africano del fascismo nelle fotografie dell'Istituto Luce*. Rome: Editori Riuniti, 2002.

Delzell, Charles. *Mussolini's Enemies: The Italian Anti-Fascist Resistance*. Princeton, N.J.: Princeton University Press, 1961.

Ecksteins, Modris. *Rites of Spring: The Great War and the Birth of the Modern Age*. New York: Anchor Books, 1989.

Ellwood, David. *Italy 1943–1945*. Leicester, U.K.: Leicester University Press, 1985.

Fabbre, Giorgio. *Mussolini razzista. Dal socialismo al fascismo: la formazione di un antisemita*. Milan: Garzanti, 2005.

Fernando Rizi, Fabio. *Benedetto Croce and Italian Fascism*. Toronto: University of Toronto Press, 2003.

Fracassi, Claudio. *Matteotti e Mussolini. Il delitto del lungotevere*. Milan: Mursia, 2004.

Fraddosio, Maria. "The Fallen Hero: The Myth of Mussolini and Fascist Women in the Italian Social Republic (1943–1945)." *Journal of Contemporary History* 31, no. 1 (1966): 99–124.

Franzinelli, Mimmo. *I tentacoli dell'OVRA: Agenti, collaboratori e vittime della polizia fascista*. Turin: Bollati Boringhieri, 1999.

Gentile, Emilio. *Fascismo e antifascismo: I partiti italiani tra le due guerre*. Florence: Le Monnier, 2000.

——. "From the Cultural Revolt of the Giolittian Era to the Ideology of Fascism." In *Studies in Modern Italian History*, edited by Frank J. Coppa, 103–119. New York: Peter Lang, 1986.

——. *Il culto del littorio: La sacralizzazione della politica nell'Italia fascista*. Rome: Laterza, 1995.

——. *La via italiana al totalitarismo*. Rome: Nuova Italia scientifiche, 1995.

——. *Le origini dell'ideologia fascista (1918–1925)*. Bologna: Il Mulino, 1996.

——. *Storia del partito fascista 1919–1922: Movimento e milizia*. Rome: Laterza. 1989.

Gillette, Aaron. *Racial Theories in Fascist Italy*. London: Routledge, 2002.

Giovagnoli, Agostino. *La cultura democristiana tra chiesa cattolica e identità italiana 1919–1941*. Rome: Laterza, 1991.

Gori, Gigliola. *Italian Fascism and the Female Body: Sport, Submissive Women and Strong Mothers*. London: Routledge, 2004.

Gregor, A. James. *The Fascist Persuasion in Radical Politics*. Princeton, N.J.: Princeton University Press, 1974.

———. *Interpretations of Fascism*. New Brunswick, N.J.: Transaction Publishers, 1997.

———. *Italian Fascism and Developmental Dictatorship*. Princeton, N.J.: Princeton University Press, 1979.

———. *Mussolini's Intellectuals: Fascist Social and Political Thought*. Princeton N.J.: Princeton University Press, 2005.

———. *Young Mussolini and the Intellectual Origins of Fascism*. Berkeley: University of California Press, 1979.

Griffin, Roger. *The Nature of Fascism*. London: Routledge Press, 1993.

Hamilton, Alexander. *The Appeal of Fascism*. London: Blond, 1971.

Hardie, Frank. *The Abyssinian Crisis*. Hamden, Conn.: Archon, 1974.

Hertner, Peter, and Giorgio Mori, eds. *La transizione dell'economia di guerra all'economia di pace in Italia e Germania dopo la prima guerra mondiale*. Bologna: Il Mulino/Istituto Italo-Germanico (Trento), 1983.

Hibbert, Christopher. *Duce*. Boston: Little, Brown, 1962.

Ipsen, Carl. *Dictating Demography: The Problem of Population in Fascist Italy*. Cambridge: Cambridge University Press, 1996.

Kallis, Aristotle. *Fascist Ideology: Territory and Expansionism in Italy and Germany*. New York: Routledge, 2000.

Katz, Robert. *Fatal Silence: The Pope, the Resistance and the German Occupation of Rome*. London: Cassell, 2004.

Kelikian, Alice A. *Town and Country under Fascism: The Transformation of Brescia 1915–1926*. New York: Oxford University Press, 1986.

Kent, Peter. *The Pope and the Duce: The International Impact of the Lateran Accords*. New York: St. Martin's Press, 1981.

Killinger, Charles L. *Gaetano Salvemini: A Biography*. Westport, Conn: Praeger, 2002.

Knox, McGregor. *Common Destiny: Dictatorship, Foreign Policy and War in Fascist Italy and Nazi Germany*. Cambridge: Cambridge University Press, 2000.

———. *Hitler's Italian Allies: Royal Armed Forces, Fascist Regime and the War of 1940–1943*. New York: Cambridge University Press, 2000.

———. *Mussolini Unleashed, 1939–1941: Politics and Strategy in Fascist Italy's Last War*. Cambridge: Cambridge University Press, 1982.

Koon, Tracey H. *Believe, Obey, Fight: Political Socialization of Youth in Fascist Italy*. Chapel Hill: University of North Carolina Press, 1985.

La Rovere, Luca. *Storia dei GUF: Organizzazione, politica e miti della gioventù universitaria fascista*. Turin: Bollati Boringhieri, 2003.

Landy, Marcia. *Fascism in Film: The Italian Commercial Cinema, 1931–1943*. Princeton, N.J.: Princeton University Press, 1986.

Lepre, Aurelio. *Mussolini*. Rome: Laterza, 1998.

Lyttleton, Adrian. *The Seizure of Power: Fascism in Italy 1919–1929*. London: Weidenfeld and Nicholson, 1973.

MacGregor-Hastie, Roy. 1963. *The Day of the Lion: The Life and Death of Fascist Italy*. New York: Coward-McCann.

Mack Smith, Denis. *Mussolini*. New York: Alfred A. Knopf, 1982.

———. *Mussolini's Roman Empire*. New York: Viking, 1976.

Mallett, Robert. *The Italian Navy and Fascist Expansionism, 1935–1940*. London: Frank Cass, 1998.

———. *Mussolini and the Origins of the Second World War, 1933–1940*. New York: Palgrave Macmillan, 2003.

Marchesini, Daniele. *Carnera*. Bologna: Il Mulino, 2006.

McClaren, Brian. *Architecture and Tourism in Colonial Libya: An Ambivalent Modernism*. Seattle: University of Washington Press, 2006.

Melograni, Piero. *Gli industriali e Mussolini*. Milan: Longanesi, 1972.

Michaelis, Meir. *Mussolini and the Jews: German-Italian Relations and the Jewish Question in Italy 1922–1943*. Oxford: Clarendon Press, 1978.

Milza, Pierre. *Le fascisme italien et la presse française, 1920–1940*. Bruxelles: Editions Complexe, 1987.

———. *Mussolini*. Paris: Fayard, 1999.

Mockler, Anthony. *Haile Selassie's War: The Italian-Ethiopian Campaign 1935–1941*. New York: Random House, 1985.

Modernism/Modernity. Vol. 1, no. 3 (September 1994). Special issue devoted to Marinetti and the Italian Futurists.

Moseley, Ray. *Mussolini's Shadow: The Double Life of Count Galeazzo Ciano*. New Haven, Conn: Yale University Press, 1999.

Moss, M. E. *Mussolini's Fascist Philosopher: Giovanni Gentile Reconsidered*. New York: Peter Lang, 2004.

Neri Serneri, Simone. *Classe, partito, nazione: alle origini della democrazia italiana, 1919–1948*. Manduria (Taranto): P. Lacaita, 1995.

Nolte, Ernst. *La crisi dei regimi liberali e i movimenti fascisti*. Bologna: II Mulino, 1970.

Ostenc, Michel. *Intellectuels italiens et fascisme (1915–1929)*. Paris: Payot, 1983.

Padiglione, Gustavo. *L'harem del duce*. Milan: Mursia, 2006.

Painter, Borden W. *Mussolini's Rome: Rebuilding the Eternal City*. Basingstoke, U.K.: Palgrave Macmillan, 2005.

Passerini, Luisa. *Fascism in Popular Memory: The Cultural Experience of the Turin Working Class*. New York: Cambridge University Press, 1987.

Peli, Santo. *La resistenza in Italia. Storia e critica*. Turin: Einaudi, 2004.

Pollard, John F. *The Vatican and Italian Fascism 1929–1932: A Study in Conflict*. New York: Cambridge University Press, 1985.

Pugliese, Stanislao. *Carlo Rosselli: Socialist Heretic and Antifascist Exile*. Cambridge, Mass.: Harvard University Press, 1999.

Quartermaine, Luisa. *Mussolini's Last Republic: Propaganda and Politics in the Italian Social Republic 1943–1945*. Exeter, U.K.: Elm Bank Publications, 2000.

Rhodes, Anthony. *The Vatican in the Age of the Dictators*. London: Hodder and Stoughton, 1973.

Roberts, David D. *The Syndicalist Tradition and Italian Fascism*. Chapel Hill: University of North Carolina Press, 1979.

Robertson, E. M. *Mussolini as Empire-builder: Europe and Africa 1932–1936*. London: Macmillan, 1977.

Rosselli, Aldo. *La famiglia Rosselli: Una tragedia italiana*. Milan: Bompiani, 1983.

Sarfati, Michele. *Gli ebrei nell'Italia fascista: Vicende, identità, persecuzioni*. Turin: Einaudi, 2000.

——. *Mussolini contro gli ebrei: cronaca dell'elaborazione delle leggi razziali del 1938*. Turin: Zamorani, 1994.

Sarti, Roland. *Fascism and the Industrial Leadership in Italy 1919–1940: A Study in the Expansion of Private Power under Fascism*. Berkeley: University of California Press, 1971.

Schmitz, David F. *The United States and Fascist Italy, 1922–1940*. Chapel Hill: University of North Carolina Press, 1988.

Schneider, Gabriele. *Mussolini in Afrika: Die Faschistiche Rassenpolitik in den Italienischen Kolonien 1936–1941*. Köln: SH-Verlag, 2000.

Scoppola, Pietro. *La Chiesa e il fascismo*. Rome: Laterza, 1971.

Segre, Claudio. *Fourth Shore: The Italian Colonization of Libya*. Chicago: University of Chicago Press, 1974.

——. *Italo Balbo: A Fascist Life*. Berkeley: University of California Press, 1987.

Snowden, F. M. *The Fascist Revolution in Tuscany, 1919–1922*. Cambridge: Cambridge University Press, 1989.

Spackman, Barbara. *Fascist Virilities, Rhetoric, Ideology and Social Fantasy*. Minneapolis: University of Minnesota Press, 1996.

Sternhall, Zeev. *The Birth of Fascist Ideology*. Princeton, N.J.: Princeton University Press, 1994.

Stille, Alexander. *Benevolence and Betrayal: Five Italian Jewish Families under Fascism*. New York: Summit Books, 1991.

Thompson, Doug. *State Control in Fascist Italy: Culture and Conformity, 1925–1943*. Manchester, U.K.: Manchester University Press, 1991.

Toscano, Mario. *The Origins of the Pact of Steel*. Baltimore, Md.: Johns Hopkins University Press, 1968.

Vivarelli, Roberto. *Il fallimento del liberalismo: studi sulle origini del fascismo*. Bologna: Il Mulino, 1981.

Wanroji, Bruno. "The Rise and Fall of Italian Fascism as a Generational Revolt." *Journal of Contemporary History* 22, no. 3. (1987): 401–418.

Wilhelm, Maria De Blasio. *The Other Italy: Italian Resistance in World War Two*. New York: Norton, 1988.

Willson, Perry. *Peasant Women and Politics in Fascist Italy: The Massaie Rurali*. London: Routledge, 2002.

Wilson, Perry R. *The Clockwork Factory: Women and Work in Fascist Italy*. Oxford: Clarendon Press, 1993.

Wiskemann, Elizabeth. *The Rome-Berlin Axis*. London: Fontana, 1966.

Woller, Hans. *I conti con il fascismo: L'epurazione in Italia, 1943–1948*. Bologna: Il Mulino, 1997.

Zapponi, Niccolò, ed. *Il fascismo nella caricatura*. Rome: Laterza, 1981.

E. POSTWAR ITALY

1. General Works

Allum, Percy. *Italy: Republic without Government?* London: Weidenfeld and Nicholson, 1973.

Barbagallo, Francesco, ed. *Storia dell'Italia repubblicana*. 3 vols. Turin: Einaudi, 1994–1997.

Bull, Martin J., and James L. Newell. *Italian Politics*. Cambridge: Polity Press, 2005.

Colarizi, Simona. *Storia dei partiti nell'Italia repubblicana*. Rome: Laterza, 1996.

Duggan, Christopher, and Christopher Wagstaff. *Italy in the Cold War*. Washington, D.C.: Berg Publishers, 1995.

Farneti, Piero. *The Italian Political System, 1945–1980*. London: Pinter, 1985.

Foot, John. *Modern Italy*. Basingstoke, U.K.: Palgrave Macmillan, 2003.

Galli della Loggia, Ernesto. *La morte della patria: La crisi dell'idea di nazione tra Resistenza antifascista e Repubblica*. Bologna: Il Mulino, 1999.

Gambino, Antonio. *Storia del dopoguerra: Dalla liberazione al potere DC*. Bari: Laterza, 1978.

Ginsborg, Paul. *A History of Contemporary Italy: Society and Politics 1943–1988*. London: Penguin, 1990.

——. *Italy and Its Discontents: Family, Civil Society, State, 1980–2001*. New York: Palgrave Macmillan, 2003.

Hughes, H. Stuart. *The United States and Italy*. Cambridge, Mass.: Harvard University Press, 1965.

Kogan, Norman. *A Political History of Post-War Italy*. New York: Praeger, 1983.

La Palombara, Joseph. *Democracy, Italian Style*. New Haven, Conn.: Yale University Press, 1987.

Lanaro, Silvio. *Storia dell'Italia repubblicana: Dalla fine della guerra agli anni novanta*. Venice: Marsilio, 1992.

Lepre, Aurelio. *Storia della prima Repubblica: L'Italia dal 1945 al 1992*. Bologna: Il Mulino, 1999.

Mammarella, Giuseppe. *L'Italia contemporanea*. Bologna: Il Mulino, 1993.

McCarthy, Patrick, ed. *Italy since 1945*. Oxford: Oxford University Press, 2000.

Pasquino, Gianfranco, ed. *Il sistema politico italiano*. Bari: Laterza, 1985.

———. *La politica italiana. Dizionario critico 1945–95*. Rome: Laterza, 1995.

Riscossa, S. "Italy 1920–1970." In *The Fontana Economic History of Europe*, edited by Carlo Cipolla. Vol. 6. London: Fontana, 1973.

Salvati, Michele. *L'economia italiana dal dopoguerra a oggi*. Milan: Garzanti, 1986.

Sassoon, Donald. *Contemporary Italy*. London: Longman, 1997.

Scoppola, Pietro. *La repubblica dei partiti: Profilo storico della democrazia in Italia 1945–1990*. Bologna: Il Mulino, 1991.

Spotts, F., and T. Weiser, *Italy: A Difficult Democracy*. Cambridge: Cambridge University Press, 1986.

Vassallo, Salvatore. *Il governo di partito in Italia 1943–1993*. Bologna: II Mulino, 1994.

Vespa, Bruno. *Storia d'Italia da Mussolini a Berlusconi*. Milan: Mondatori, 2004.

Willan, Philip. *Puppet Masters: The Political Use of Terror in Italy*. London: Constable, 1991.

Woolf, Stuart J. *The Rebirth of Italy, 1943–1950*. London: Longman, 1972.

2. Politics and Institutions

Agosti, A., L. Passerini, and N. Tranfaglia, eds. 1991. *La Cultura e i luoghi del 68*. Milan: Franco Angeli.

Alberoni, Francesco. *Italia in trasformazione*. Bologna: Il Mulino, 1976.

Allum, Percy. *Politics and Society in Post-war Naples*. Cambridge: Cambridge University Press, 1973.

Amato, Giuliano. 1980. *Una repubblica da riformare*. Bologna: Il Mulino.

Baget-Bozzo, G. *Il partito cristiano al potere: La DC di De Gasperi e di Dossetti 1945–1954*. Florence: Vallecchi, 1974.

———. *Il partito cristiano e l'apertura a sinistra: La DC di Fanfani e di Moro 1954–1962*. Florence: Vallecchi, 1977.

Baldassare, A., and C. Mezzanotte. *Gli uomini del Quirinale: Da Di Nicola a Pertini*. Bari: Laterza, 1985.

Bardi, Luciano, and Martin Rhodes, eds. *Italian Politics: Mapping the Future*. Boulder, Colo.: Westview Press, 1998.

Bellucci, Paolo, and Martin Bull, eds. *Italian Politics: The Return of Berlusconi*. Oxford: Berghahn, 2002.

Blondel, Jean, and Paolo Segatti, eds. *Italian Politics: The Second Berlusconi Government*. Oxford: Berghahn, 2003.

Caciagli, Mario, and David Kertzer, eds. *Italian Politics: The Stalled Transition*. Boulder, Colo.: Westview Press, 1996.

Caciagli, Mario, and Alan Zuckerman, eds. *Italian Politics: Emerging Themes and Institutional Responses*. Oxford: Berghahn, 2001.

Capano, G., and E. Gualmini. *La pubblica amministrazione in Italia*. Bologna: Il Mulino, 2006.

Carli, Guido. *Cinquant'anni di vita italiana*. Rome: Laterza, 1993.

Chimenti, Anna. *Storia dei referendum*. Bari: Laterza, 1993.

Collin, Richard. *The De Lorenzo Gambit: The Italian Coup Manqué of 1964*. Beverley Hills, Calif.: Sage, 1977.

Della Porta, Donatella. *Social Movements, Political Violence and the State: A Comparative Analysis of Italy and Germany*. Cambridge: Cambridge University Press, 1995.

Della Porta, Donatella, and Maurizio Rossi. *Cifre crudeli: bilancio dei terrorismi italiani*. Bologna: Istituto Carlo Cattaneo, 1984.

Della Sala, Vincent, and Sergio Fabbrini, eds. *Italian Politics: Italy between Europeanization and Domestic Politics*. Oxford: Berghahn, 2004.

De Luna, Giovanni. *Storia del partito d'Azione*. Milan: Feltrinelli, 1982.

De Lutiis, G. *Storia dei servizi segreti in Italia*. Rome: Editori Riuniti, 1991.

De Micheli, C., and L. Verzichelli. *Il Parlamento*. Bologna: Il Mulino, 2004.

Diani, Mario. *Green Networks: A Structural Analysis of the Italian Environmental Movement*. Edinburgh: Edinburgh University Press, 1995.

Di Loreto, P. *La difficile transizione: Dalla fine del centrismo al centro-sinistra 1953–1960*. Bologna: Il Mulino, 1993.

Di Palma, Giuseppe. *Political Syncretism in Italy: Historical Coalition Strategies and the Present Crisis*. Berkeley: University of California Press, 1978.

——. *Surviving without Governing: The Italian Parties in Parliament*. Berkeley: University of California Press, 1977.

Di Scala, Spencer. *Renewing Italian Socialism: Nenni to Craxi*. New York: Oxford University Press, 1988.

Drake, Richard. *Apostles and Agitators: Italy's Marxist Revolutionary Tradition*. Cambridge, Mass.: Harvard University Press, 2003.

——. *The Revolutionary Mystique and Terrorism in Contemporary Italy*. Bloomington: Indiana University Press, 1989.

Duroselle, J-B. *Le conflit de Trieste, 1943–1954*. Bruxelles: Université Libre, 1966.

Evans, Robert H. *Life and Politics in a Venetian Village*. Notre Dame, Ind.: Notre Dame University Press, 1976.

Feiler, Michael. "South Tyrol: Model for the Resolution of Minority Conflicts?" *Aussenpolitik* 47, no. 3 (1996): 287–299.

Ferrajoli, Luigi. "Democracy and the Constitution in Italy." *Political Studies* 44, no. 3 (1996): 457–472.

Ferraresi, Franco. *Threats to Democracy: The Radical Right in Italy after the War*. Princeton, N.J.: Princeton University Press, 1996.

——, ed. *La Destra radicale*. Milan: Garzanti, 1984.

Formigoni, Guido. *La Democrazia cristiana e l'alleanza occidentale: 1943–1953*. Bologna: Il Mulino, 1996.

Frankel, P. *Mattei: Oil and Power Politics*. London: Faber & Faber, 1966.

Friedman, Alan. *Giovanni Agnelli and the Network of Italian Power*. London: Harrap, 1988.

Galli, Giorgio. *Fanfani*. Milan: Feltrinelli, 1975.

———. *Il bipartitismo imperfetto: Comunisti e democristiani in Italia*. Bologna: Il Mulino, 1966.

———. *L'Italia sotterranea: Storia, politica e scandali*. Bari: Laterza, 1983.

———. *Storia del partito armato, 1968–1982*. Milan: Rizzoli, 1986.

Galli, Giorgio, and Alfonso Prandi. *Patterns of Political Participation in Italy*. New Haven, Conn: Yale University Press, 1970.

Gilbert, Mark, and Gianfranco Pasquino, eds. *Italian Politics: The Faltering Transition*. Oxford: Berghahn, 2000.

Giovagnoli, Agostino. *Il partito italiano: La Democrazia cristiana dal 1942 al 1994*. Rome: Laterza, 1996.

Graziano, Luigi, and Sidney Tarrow. *La crisi italiana*. 2 vols. Turin: Einaudi, 1979.

Guamieri, Carlo. *La giustizia in Italia*. Bologna: Il Mulino, 2001.

———. *Magistratura e politica in Italia*. Bologna: Il Mulino, 1993.

Harper, John L. *America and the Reconstruction of Italy, 1945–1948*. Cambridge: Cambridge University Press, 1986.

Hine, David. *Governing Italy: The Politics of Balanced Pluralism*. Oxford: Clarendon Press, 1993.

Hine, David, and Salvatore Vassallo, eds. *Italian Politics: The Return of Politics*. Oxford: Berghahn, 2000.

Ignazi, Piero. *Il Polo escluso: Profilo del Movimento sociale italiano*. Bologna. Il Mulino, 1989.

Lange, Peter, and Sidney Tarrow. *Italy in Transition: Conflict and Consensus*. London: Cass, 1980.

Lange, Peter, and M. Vannicelli. *Unions, Change and Crisis: French and Italian Union Strategy and the Political Economy, 1945–1980*. London: Allen and Unwin, 1982.

Leonardi, Robert, and Douglas A. Wertman. *Italian Christian Democracy: The Politics of Dominance*. Basingstoke, U.K.: Macmillan, 1989.

Levy, Carl, ed. *Regionalism, History, Identity and Politics*. Oxford: Berg, 1996.

Lorenzini, Sara. *L'Italia e il trattato di pace del 1947*. Bologna: Il Mulino, 2007.

Lumley, Robert. *Italian Journalism: A Critical Anthology*. Manchester, U.K.: Manchester University Press, 1996.

———. *States of Emergency: Cultures of Revolt in Italy 1968–1978*. London: Verso, 1990.

Mershon, Carol. *The Costs of Coalition*. Stanford, Calif.: Stanford University Press, 2002.

Miller, J. E. *Politics in a Museum: Governing Postwar Florence*. Westport, Conn.: Praeger, 2002.

———. *The United States and Italy. The Politics of Diplomacy and Stabilization*. Chapel Hill: University of North Carolina Press, 1986.

Montanelli, Indro. *L'Italia degli anni di piombo*. Milan: Biblioteca universale Rizzoli, 2001.

Negri, Toni. *Books for Burning: Between Civil War and Democracy in 1970s Italy*. London: Verso, 2005.

Newell, James L. *Parties and Democracy in Italy*. Aldershot, U.K.: Ashgate, 2000.

Nilsson, K. Robert. "The EUR Accords and the Historic Compromise: Italian Labor and Eurocommunism." *Polity* 14, no. 3 (Fall 1981): 29–50.

———. "The Italian Socialist Party." In *Italy at the Polls: 1983*, edited by Howard Penniman. Durham, N.C.: Duke University Press for the American Enterprise Institute, 1987.

Onida, Valerio. *La Costituzione*. Bologna: Il Mulino, 2004.

Panebianco, Angelo. "The Italian Radicals: New Wine in an Old Bottle." In *When Parties Fail*, edited by Kenneth Lawson and Peter Merkl. Princeton, N.J.: Princeton University Press, 1988.

Pasquino, Gianfranco. *La repubblica dei cittadini ombra*. Milan: Garzanti, 1991.

Pastorelli, P. *La politica estera italiana nel dopoguerra*. Bologna: Il Mulino, 1986.

Piattoni, Simona. *Il clientelismo: L'Italia in prospettiva comparata*. Rome: Carocci, 2005.

Pizzinelli, Corrado. *Scelba*. Milan: Longanesi, 1982.

Poggiolini, Ilaria. *Diplomazia della transizione: Gli alleati e il problema del trattato di pace italiano, 1945–1947*. Florence: Ponte alle Grazie, 1990.

Politica in Italia: I fatti dell'anno e le interpretazioni. Bologna: Il Mulino/Istituto Cattaneo. Vol. 1, edited by P. Corbetta and R. Leonardi, 1986. Vol. 2, edited by P. Corbetta and R. Leonardi, 1987. Vol. 3, edited by P. Corbetta and R. Leonardi, 1988. Vol. 4, edited by R. Catanzaro and R. Y. Nannetti, 1989. Vol. 5, edited by R. Catanzaro and F. Sabetti, 1990. Vol. 6, edited by F. Anderlini and R. Leonardi, 1991. Vol. 7, edited by S. Hellman and G. Pasquino, 1992. Vol. 8, edited by S. Hellman and G. Pasquino, 1993. Vol. 9, edited by C. Mershon and G. Pasquino, 1994. Vol. 10, edited. by P. Ignazi and R. S. Katz, 1995. Vol. 11, edited by M. Caciagli and D.I. Kertzer, 1996. Vol. 12, edited by R. D'Alimonte and D. Nelken, 1997. Vol. 13, edited by L. Bardi and M. Rhodes, 1998. Vol. 14, edited by D. Hine and S. Vassallo, 1999. Vol. 15, edited by M. Gilbert and G. Pasquino, 2000. Vol. 16, edited by M. Caciagli and A. Zuckerman, 2001. Vol. 17, edited by P. Bellucci and M. Bull, 2002. Vol. 18, edited by J. Blondel and P. Segatti, 2003. Vol. 19, edited by V. Della Sala and S. Fabbrini, 2004. Vol. 20, edited by C. Guarnieri and J. L. Newell, 2005. Vol. 21, edited by G. Aymot and L. Verzichelli, 2006.

Pombeni, Paolo. *La Costituente: Un problema storico-politico*. Bologna: Il Mulino, 1995.

Portelli, A. *The Battle of Valle Giulia: Oral History and the Art of Dialogue*. Madison: Wisconsin University Press, 1997.

Preda, Daniela. *Alcide De Gasperi, Federalista europeo*. Bologna: Il Mulino, 2004.

Pridham, G. *Political Parties and Coalition Behavior in Italy*. London: Routledge, 1988.

Putnam, Robert D. *The Beliefs of Politicians: Ideology, Conflict and Democracy in Britain and Italy*. New Haven, Conn: Yale University Press, 1973.

Rusconi, G. E., and H. Woller, eds. *Italia e Germania 1945–2000: La costruzione dell'Europa*. Bologna: Il Mulino, 2005.

Sabbatucci, Giovanni. *Il riformismo impossible: storia del socialismo italiano*. Bari: Laterza, 1991.

Sabetti, Filippo. *The Search for Good Government: Understanding the Paradox of Italian Democracy*. Montreal: McGill-Queen's University Press, 2000.

Sartori, Giovanni. *Teoria dei partiti e caso italiano*. Milan: SugarCo, 1982.

Scoppola, Pietro. *La proposta politica di De Gasperi*. Bologna: Il Mulino, 1977.

Seton-Watson, Christopher. "Italy's Imperial Hangover." *Journal of Contemporary History* 15, no. 1 (January 1980): 169–179.

Setta, Sandro. *L'Uomo Qualunque, 1944–1948*. Bari: Laterza, 1995.

Spini, Valdo. "The New Left in Italy." *Journal of Contemporary History* 7, no. 1 (January 1972): 51–72.

Tarrow, Sidney. *Between Center and Periphery: Grassroots Politicians in Italy and France*. New Haven, Conn.: Yale University Press, 1977.

———. *Democracy and Disorder: Protest and Politics in Italy, 1965–1975*. Oxford: Clarendon Press, 1989.

Tupini, G. De Gasperi. *Una testimonianza*. Bologna: Il Mulino, 1992.

Valdevit, G. *La questione di Trieste 1941–1954*. Milan: Angeli.

Valiani, Leo. *L'Italia di De Gasperi 1945–1954*. Florence: Le Monnier, 1982.

3. Studies in Society, Economics, and Culture

Acquaviva, S. S., and M. Santuccio. *Social Structure in Italy*. London: Martin Robertson, 1976.

Adler Hellman, Judy. *Journeys among Women: Feminism in Five Italian Cities*. Oxford: Oxford University Press, 1987.

Andall, Jacqui. *Gender, Migration and Domestic Service: The Politics of Black Women in Italy*. Aldershot, U.K.: Ashgate, 2000.

Angotti, T. *Housing in Italy: Urban Development and Political Change*. New York: Praeger, 1977.

Aymot, Grant. *Business, the State and Economic Policy: The Case of Italy*. London: Routledge, 2004.

Bagnasco, Arnaldo. *Tre Italie: La problematica territoriale dello sviluppo italiano*. Bologna: Il Mulino, 1977.

Bairetti, Piero. *Vittorio Valletti*. Turin: UTET, 1983.

Baldassari, Mario, ed. *Industrial Policy in Italy, 1945–1990*. London: Macmillan, 1993.

Baldassari, Mario, and Franco Modigliani, eds. *The Italian Economy: What Next?* London: Macmillan, 1995.

Banfield, Edward C. *The Moral Basis of a Backward Society*. Glencoe, Ill: The Free Press, 1958.

Barbagli, M. *Provando e riprovando: Matrimonio, famiglia e divorzio in Italia e in altri paesi occidentali*. Bologna: Il Mulino, 1991.

Barkan, Joanne. *Visions of Emancipation: The Italian Workers' Movement since 1945*. New York: Praeger, 1984.

Bedani, Gino. *Politics and Ideology in the Italian Workers' Movement: Union Development and the Changing Role of the Catholic and Communist Subcultures in Postwar Italy*. Oxford: Berg, 1995.

Birnbaum, Lucia Chiavola. *Liberazione della donna: Feminism in Italy*. Middletown, Conn.: Wesleyan University Press, 1986.

Bull, Anna Cento. *Social Identities and Political Cultures in Italy: Catholic, Communist and Leghist Communities between Civicness and Localism*. Oxford: Berghahn, 2001.

Bull, Anna Cento, and Adalgisa Giorgio. *Culture and Society in Southern Italy: Past and Present*. Supplement to *The Italianist* 14 (1994).

Carnevali, Francesca. 1996. "Between Markets and Networks: Regional Banks in Italy." *Business History* 38 (July 1996): 84–100.

Castronovo, Valerio. *Giovanni Agnelli: Il fondatore*. Turin: UTET, 2003.

———. *Le paure degli italiani*. Milan: Rizzoli, 2004.

Chubb, Judith. *Patronage, Power and Poverty in Southern Italy: A Tale of Two Cities*. Cambridge: Cambridge University Press, 1982.

Colombo, Asher, and Giuseppe Sciortino. *Gli immigrati in Italia*. Bologna: Il Mulino, 2004.

Dolci, Danilo. *Poverty in Sicily*. Translated by P. D. Cummins. Hammondsworth, U.K.: Penguin Books, 1966.

Esposito, Nicholas J. *Italian Family Structure*. New York: Peter Lang, 1989.

Ferrara, Maurizio, and Elisabetta Gualmini. *Rescued by Europe? Social and Labour Market Reforms in Italy from Maastricht to Berlusconi*. Amsterdam: Amsterdam University Press, 2004.

Garelli, F. *Religione e Chiesa in Italia*. Bologna: Il Mulino, 1991.

Giavazzi, Francesco, and Luigi Spaventa, eds. *High Public Debt: The Italian Experience*. Cambridge: Cambridge University Press, 1988.

Golden, M. *Labor Divided: Austerity and Working Class Politics in Contemporary Italy*. Ithaca, N.Y.: Cornell University Press, 1988.

King, R. L. *The Industrial Geography of Italy*. Beckenham, U.K.: Croom Helm, 1985.

———. *Land Reform: The Italian Experience*. London: Butterworth, 1973.

Lerner, Gad. *Operai: Viaggio all'interno di una classe che non c'e più*. Milan: Feltrinelli, 1988.

Locke, Richard. *Remaking the Italian Economy*. Ithaca, N.Y.: Cornell University Press, 1995.

Mafei, Miriam. *Il sorpasso: Gli straordinari anni del miracolo economico, 1958–1963*. Milan: Mondatori, 1997.

Padoa-Schioppa Kostoris, Fiorella. *Italy: The Sheltered Economy*. Oxford: Clarendon Press, 1993.

Podbielski, Gisele. *Twenty-Five Years of Special Action for the Development of Southern Italy*. Rome: SVIMEZ, 1978.

Revelli, Mario. *Lavorare in FIAT*. Milan: Garzanti, 1989.

Sabetti, Filippo. *Political Authority in a Sicilian Village*. New Brunswick, N.J.: Rutgers University Press, 1984.

Sarti, Roland. *Long Live the Strong: A History of Rural Society in the Apennine Mountains*. Amherst: University of Massachusetts Press, 1985.

Schneider, Jane, and P. Schneider. *Culture and Political Economy in Western Sicily*. New York: Academic Press, 1976.

Schneider, Jane, ed. *Italy's Southern Question: Orientalism in One Country?* Oxford: Berg, 1998.

Silei, Gianni. *Lo stato sociale in Italia: Storia e documenti*. Manduria (Taranto): P. Lacaita, 2004.

Soldani, S., and G. Turi. *Fare gli italiani: Scuola e cultura nell'Italia contemporanea*. 2 vols. Bologna: Il Mulino, 1994.

Sylos Labini, P. *Le classi sociali negli anni 80*. Bari: Laterza, 1982.

4. Communism and Intellectual Politics

Ajello, Nello. *Intellettuali e il PCI 1944–1958*. Bari: Laterza, 1979.

Amyot, Grant. *The Italian Communist Party: The Crisis of the Popular Front Strategy*. London: Croom Helm, 1981.

Blackmer, Donald, and Sidney Tarrow, eds. *Communism in Italy and France*. Princeton, N.J.: Princeton University Press, 1977.

Bobbio, Norberto. *Ideological Profile of Twentieth-Century Italy*. Translated by L. Cochrane. Princeton, N.J.: Princeton University Press, 1995.

Cafagna, Luciano. *La Grande Slavina*. Venice: Marsilio, 1993.

Clark, Martin. *Antonio Gramsci and the Revolution That Failed*. New Haven, Conn.: Yale University Press, 1977.

Claudin, Fernando. *Eurocommunism and Socialism*. London: New Left Books, 1978.

D'Alema, Massimo. *Dialogo su Berlinguer*. Florence: Giunti, 1994.

Evans, Robert H. *Coexistence: Communism and Its Practice in Bologna 1945–1965*. Notre Dame, Ind.: Notre Dame University Press, 1967.

Fiori, Giuseppe. *Vita di Enrico Berlinguer*. Rome: Laterza, 2004.

Fouskas, Vassilis. *Italy, Europe, the Left: The Transformation of Italian Communism and the European Imperative*. Aldershot, U.K.: Ashgate, 1998.

Gundle, Stephen. *Between Hollywood and Moscow: The Italian Communists and the Challenge of Mass Culture*. Durham, N.C.: Duke University Press.

———. *Communism and Cultural Change in Post-war Italy*. Cambridge: Cambridge University Press, 1984.

Hellman, Stephen. *Italian Communism in Transition: The Rise and Fall of the Historic Compromise in Turin 1975–1980*. New York: Oxford University Press, 1988.

Hobsbawm, Eric. *The Italian Road to Socialism: An Interview with Giorgio Naplestano*. Westport, Conn.: Lawrence Hill, 1977.

Ignazi, Piero. *Dal PCI al PDS*. Bologna: Il Mulino, 1992.

Joll, James. *Antonio Gramsci*. New York: Viking, 1977.

Kertzer, David I. *Comrades and Christians: Religion and Political Struggle in Communist Italy*. Cambridge: Cambridge University Press, 1980.

———. *Politics and Symbols: The Italian Communist Party and the Fall of Communism*. New Haven, Conn.: Yale University Press, 1996.

Mafei, Miriam. *Dimenticare Berlinguer*. Rome: Donzelli, 1995.

Moss, David. *The Politics of Left-Wing Violence in Italy, 1969–1985*. Basingstoke, U.K.: Macmillan, 1989.

Naplestano, Giorgio. *In mezzo al guado*. Rome: Editori Riuniti, 1979.

Ranney, Austin, and Giovanni Sartori, eds. *Eurocommunism: The Italian Case*. Washington, D.C.: American Enterprise Institute, 1977.

Ruscoe, James. *On the Threshold of Government: The Italian Communist Party, 1976–1981*. New York: St. Martin's Press, 1982.

Sassoon, Donald. *The Strategy of the Italian Communist Party: From the Resistance to the Historic Compromise*. London: Pinter, 1981.

Serfaty, Simon, and Lawrence Gray, eds. *The Italian Communist Party: Yesterday, Today, Tomorrow*. Westport, Conn.: Greenwood Press, 1980.

Shore, Chris. *Italian Communism: The Escape from Leninism: An Anthropological Perspective*. London: Pluto, 1990.

Spriano, Paolo. *Storia del partito comunista*. 6 vols. Turin: Einaudi, 1975.

Tarrow, Sidney. *Peasant Communism in Southern Italy*. New Haven, Conn.: Yale University Press, 1967.

Urban, George, ed. *Eurocommunism: Its Roots and Future in Italy and Elsewhere*. London: Temple Smith, 1978.

Urban, Joan Barth. *Moscow and the Italian Communist Party: From Togliatti to Berlinguer*. London: Tauris, 1986.

Vacca, Giuseppe. *Tra compromesso e solidarità. La politica del PCI negli anni 70*. Rome: Editori Riuniti, 1987.

Weinberg, Leonard. *The Transformation of Italian Communism*. New Brunswick, N.J.: Transaction, 1995.

5. Party Politics since the 1990s

Andrews, Geoff. *Not a Normal Country: Italy after Berlusconi*. London: Pluto, 2005.

Bardi, Luciano. "Anti-party Sentiment and Party System Change in Italy." *European Journal of Political Research* 29, no. 3 (April 1996): 345–363.

Bocca, Giorgio. *La Disunità d'Italia*. Milan: Garzanti, 1990.

Bossi, Umberto. *Vento dal Nord*. Milan: Sperling and Kupfer, 1992.

Bufacchi, Vittorio, and Simon Burgess. *Italy since 1989: Events and Interpretations*. London: Palgrave, 2001.

Bull, Anna Cento, and Mark Gilbert. *The Lega Nord and the Northern Question in Italian Politics*. Basingstoke, U.K.: Palgrave Macmillan, 2001.

Bull, Martin, and Martin Rhodes, eds. *Crisis and Transition in Italian Politics*. London: Frank Cass, 1997.

Burnett, Stanton H. *The Italian Guillotine: Operation Clean Hands and the Overthrow of Italy's First Republic*. Lanham, Md.: Rowman & Littlefield, 1998.

Campi, Alessandro. "What Is Italy's National Alliance?" *Telos* no. 105 (Fall 1995): 122–132.

Cotta, Maurizio, and Pierangelo Isernia. *Il gigante dai piedi di argilla: La crisi del regime partitocratrico in Italia*. Bologna: Il Mulino, 1996.

Diamanti, Ilvo. *La Lega: Geografia, storia e sociologia di un nuovo soggetto politico*. Rome: Donzelli, 1993.

Di Nicola, Primo. *Mario Segni*. Milan: Sperling and Kupfer, 1993.

Fabbrini, Sergio. *Tra pressioni e veto. Il cambiamento politico in Italia*. Rome: Laterza, 2000.

Gilbert, Mark. *The Italian Revolution: The End of Politics, Italian Style*. Boulder, Colo.: Westview Press, 1995.

Ginsborg, Paul. *Silvio Berlusconi: Television, Power and Patrimony*. London: Verso, 2005.

Guarino, Mario. *Fratello P2 1816: l'epopea piduista di Silvio Berlusconi*. Milan: Kaos, 2001.

Gundle, Stephen, and Simon Parker, eds. *The New Italian Republic: From the Fall of the Berlin Wall to Berlusconi*. London: Routledge, 1995.

Guzzini, Stefano. "The Long Night of the First Republic: Years of Clientelistic Implosion in Italy." *Review of International Political Economy* 2, no.1 (Winter 1995): 27–61.

Ignazi, Piero. *Postfascisti?* Bologna: Il Mulino, 1995.

Katz, Robert S. "Electoral Reform and the Transformation of Party Politics in Italy." *Party Politics* 2, no. 1 (January 1996): 31–53.

Lane, David. *Berlusconi's Shadow: Crime, Justice and the Pursuit of Power*. London: Allen Lane, 2004.

Magri, Lucio. "The Resistible Rise of the Italian Right." *New Left Review* no. 214 (December 1995): 125–133.

Mannheimer, Renato, ed. *La Lega Lombarda*. Milan: Feltrinelli, 1991.

McCarthy, Patrick. *The Crisis of the Italian State: From the Origins of the Cold War to the Fall of Berlusconi*. New York: St. Martin's Press, 1995.

McCarthy, Patrick, and Gianfranco Pasquino, eds. *The End of Post-war Politics in Italy: The Landmark Elections of 1992*. Boulder, Colo.: Westview Press, 1993.

Newell, James L. *The Italian General Election of 2001: Berlusconi's Victory*. Manchester, U.K.: Manchester University Press, 2002.

Newell, James L., and Martin J. Bull. "The Italian Election of 1996: The Italian Left on Top or on Tap." *Parliamentary Affairs* 49, no. 4 (October 1996): 616–647.

Pasquino, Gianfranco, and Carol Mershon, eds. *Italian Politics. Ending the First Republic.* Boulder, Colo.: Westview Press, 1994.

Ruggeri, Giovanni, and Paolo Guarini. *Berlusconi: Inchiesta sul Signor TV.* Milan: Kaos edizioni, 1994.

Salvadori, Massimo L. *Storia d'Italia e crisi di regime.* Bologna: Il Mulino, 1996.

Seisselberg, Jorg. "Forza Italia: A Media-Mediated Personalità Party." *West European Politics.* 19, no. 4 (October 1996): 715–743.

Tambini, Damien. *Nationalism in Italian Politics: The Stories of the Northern League, 1980–2000.* London: Routledge, 2001.

Travaglio, Marco, and Elio Veltri. *L'odore dei soldi.* Rome: Editori Riuniti, 2001.

Wallisch, Stefan. *Aufsteig und Fall der Telekratie.* Vienna: Böhlau, 1997.

6. The Mafia and Criminality

Arlacchi, Pino. *Mafia Business: The Mafia Ethic and the Spirit of Capitalism.* Oxford: Oxford University Press, 1988.

———. *Mafia, Peasants and Great Estates: Society in Traditional Calabria.* Cambridge: Cambridge University Press, 1993.

Behan, Tom. *The Camorra.* London: Routledge, 1996.

Blok, Anton. *The Mafia of a Sicilian Village, 1860–1960.* Oxford: Blackwell, 1974.

Canosa, Romeno. *Storia della criminalità in Italia dal 1946 a oggi.* Milan: Feltrinelli, 1995.

Catanzaro, Raimondo. *Men of Honor: A Social History of the Mafia.* New York: Free Press, 1988.

Cazzola, F. *L'Italia del pizzo.* Turin: Einaudi, 1992.

Chandler, B. J. *King of the Mountains: The Life and Death of Giuliano the Bandit.* Dekalb: Northern Illinois University Press, 1988.

Ciconte, Enzo. *'Ndrangheta dall'unita a oggi.* Rome: Laterza, 1992.

Dalla Chiesa, Nando. *Storia di boss, ministri, tribunali, giornali, intellettuali, cittadini.* Turin: Einaudi, 1990.

Della Porta, Donatella. *Lo scambio occulto.* Bologna: Il Mulino, 1992.

Dickie, John. *Cosa Nostra: A History of the Sicilian Mafia.* London: Coronet, 2004.

Duggan, Christopher. *Fascism and the Mafia.* New Haven, Conn: Yale University Press, 1989.

Falcone, Giovanni, and M. Padovano. *Cose di Cosa Nostra.* Milan: Rizzoli, 1991.

Farrell, Joseph, ed. *Understanding the Mafia.* Manchester, U.K.: Manchester University Press, 1997.

Gambetta, Diego. *The Sicilian Mafia.* Cambridge, Mass.: Harvard University Press, 1996.

Jamieson, Alison. *The Antimafia: Italy's Fight against Organized Crime.* London: Macmillan, 2000.

Lewis, Norman. *The Honored Society: The Sicilian Mafia Observed*. London: Eland, 2003.

Longrigg, Clare. *Mafia Women*. London: Chatto & Windus, 1997.

Lupo, Salvatore. *Storia della mafia dalle origini ai giorni nostri*. Rome: Donzelli, 1993.

Orlando, Leoluca. *Fighting the Mafia and Renewing Sicilian Culture*. San Francisco: Encounter Books, 2001.

Pantaleone, Michele. *The Mafia and Politics*. London: Chatto and Windus, 1966.

——. *Mafia e antimafia*. Naples: Pironti, 1992.

Sales, Isaia. *La Camorra, le camorre*. Rome: Editori Riuniti, 1988.

Schneider, Jane. *Reversibile Destiny: Mafia, Antimafia and the Struggle for Palermo*. Berkeley: University of California Press.

Siebert, Renate. *Secrets of Life and Death: Women and the Mafia*. London: Verso, 1996.

Sterling, Claire. *Octopus. The Long Reach of the International Sicilian Mafia*. New York: Norton, 1990.

Stille, Alexander. *Excellent Cadavers*. New York: Pantheon, 1995.

Tranfaglia, Nicola, ed. *Mafa, politica e affari 1943–1991*. Rome: Laterza, 1992.

Walston, James. *The Mafa and Clientelism: Roads to Rome in Post-War Calabria*. London: Routledge, 1988.

F. ARTS AND CULTURE

Amoia, Alba. *Twentieth Century Italian Women Writers*. Illinois University Press, 1996.

Angier, Carole. *Primo Levi: The Double Bond*. London: Penguin, 2002.

Arrowsmith, William. *Antonioni: The Poet of Images*. Oxford: Oxford University Press, 1995.

Baranski, Zymunt G., and Pertile, Lino, eds. *The New Italian Novel*. New York: Columbia University Press, 1994.

Baranski, Z. G., and R. Lumley, eds. *Culture and Conflict in Post-War Italy: Essays on Mass and Popular Culture*. Basingstoke, U.K.: Macmillan, 1990.

Bondanella, Peter. *The Cambridge Companion to the Italian Novel*. Cambridge: Cambridge University Press, 2003.

——. *The Cinema of Federico Fellini*. Princeton, N.J.: Princeton University Press, 1992.

——. *The Films of Roberto Rossellini*. Cambridge: Cambridge University Press, 1993.

——. *Italian Cinema: From Neorealism to the Present*. Woodland Hills, Calif.: Continuum, 2001.

Brand, Peter, and Lino Pertile, eds. *The Cambridge History of Italian Literature*. Cambridge: Cambridge University Press, 1999.

Braun, Emily, ed. *Italian Art in the Twentieth Century. Painting and Sculpture, 1900–1988*. New York: Te Neues, 1995.

Bruno, Giuliana, and Nadotti, Maria, eds. *Off-screen: Women and Film in Italy*. New York: Routledge, 1988.

Buss, Robin. *Italian Films*. New York: Holmes and Meier, 1989.

Cannon, JoAnn. *Postmodern Italian Fiction: The Crisis of Reason in Calvino, Eco, Sciascia, Malerba*. Cranbury, N.J.: Fairleigh Dickinson University Press, 1989.

Cottino-Jones, Marga. *A Student's Guide to Italian Film*. Dubuque, Iowa: Kendall-Hunt, 1995.

Doorden, Dennis P. *Building Modern Italy: Italian Architecture, 1914–1936*. Princeton N.J.: Princeton Architectural Press, 1988.

Fearn, Raymond. *Italian Opera since 1945*. London: Harwood Academic, 1998.

Gordon, Robert. *Introduction to Twentieth Century Italian Literature: A Difficult Modernity*. London: Duckworth.

Goy, Richard. *The Buildings of Venice*. San Francisco: Chronicle Books, 1994.

Haller, Hermann W. *The Hidden Italy: A Bilingual Edition of Italian Dialect Poetry*. Detroit: Wayne State University Press, 1986.

Hainsworth, Peter, and David Robey. *The Oxford Companion to Italian Literature*. Oxford: Oxford University Press, 2002.

Hay, James. *Popular Film Culture in Fascist Italy*. Bloomington: Indiana University Press, 1987.

Hewitt, Andrew. *Fascist Modernism: Aesthetics, Politics and the Avantgarde*. Stanford, Calif.: Stanford University Press, 1993.

House, Jane, and Artisani, Antonio, eds. *Twentieth Century Italian Drama: An Anthology: The First Fifty Years*. New York: Columbia University Press, 1995.

Lumley, Robert, ed. *Italian Cityscapes: Culture and Urban Change in Contemporary Italy*. Exeter, U.K.: University of Exeter Press, 2004.

Mangan. J. A., ed. *Superman Supreme: Fascist Body as Political Icon*. London: Frank Cass, 2000.

Nowell-Smith, Geoffrey, ed. *The Companion to the Italian Cinema*. London: British Film Institute, 1996.

Oppenheimer, Michael. *The Monuments of Italy*. 7 vols. London: I.B. Tauris, 2002.

Pinto, Sandra, ed. *A History of Italian Art in the Twentieth Century*. London: Thames & Hudson, 2002.

Riva, Massimo, ed. *Italian Tales*. New Haven, Conn.: Yale University Press, 2004.

Soby, James T., and Alfred H. Barr Jr. *Twentieth Century Italian Art*. Stratford, N.H.: Ayer, 1972.

Stewart, John. *Italian Film: A Who's Who*. London: McFarland, 1994.

Stone, Marla Susan. *The Patron State: Culture and Politics in Fascist Italy*. Princeton N.J.: Princeton University Press, 1998.

Wilkins, Ernest. *A History of Italian Literature*. Cambridge, Mass.: Harvard University Press, 1974.

G. PRINCIPAL PERIODICALS

(websites accessed October 19–21, 2006)
Adige: http://www.ladige.it
Ciak: http://www.mondadori.it/ame/it/gruppo/testate/ck.html
Corriere della Sera: http://www.corriere.it/
Espresso: http://espresso.repubblica.it/
Focus: http://www.mondadori.it/ame/it/gruppo/testate/fo.html
Foglio: http://www.ilfoglio.it/
Gazzetta del Sud: http://www.gazzettadelsud.it/
Gazzetta dello Sport: http://www.gazzetta.it/
Gazzettino: http://gazzettino.quinordest.it/
Giornale: http://www.ilgiornale.it/
Giorno: http://ilgiorno.quotidiano.net/
Mattino: http://ilmattino.caltanet.it/mattino/page_view.php
Messaggero: http://www.ilmessaggero.it/
Mondo: http://www.ilmondo.rcs.it/
Mulino: http://www.mulino.it/ilmulino/index.html
Nazione: http.//lanazione.quotidiano.net/
Padania: http://www.lapadania.com/
Panorama: http://www.panorama.it/home/index.html
Piccolo di Trieste: http://www.ilpiccolo.quotidianiespresso.it/
Repubblica: http://www.repubblica.it/
Resto del Carlino: http://ilrestodelcarlino.quotidiano.net/
Secolo XIX: http://www.ilsecoloxix.it/
Sole 24 Ore: http://www.ilsole24ore.com/
Stampa: http://www.lastampa.it/
Tempo: http://www.iltempo.it/
Unità: http://www.unita.it/

H. ITALY AND THE ITALIANS

Bareggi, Cristina, ed. *The Concise Oxford-Paravia Italian Dictionary*. Oxford: Oxford University Press, 2003.
Carluccio, Antonio. *An Invitation to Italian Cooking*. London: Headline Book, 2005.
Claridge, Amanda, et al. *Rome*. Oxford Archeological Guides. Oxford: Oxford Paperbacks, 1998.
Da Mosto, Francesco. *Francesco's Italy*. London: BBC, 2006.
Dunford, Martin, et al. *The Rough Guide to Italy*. London: Rough Guides, 2005.

Ellmer, Bruno H. *Classical and Contemporary Italian Cooking for Professionals*. New York: Van Nostrand Reinhold, 1990.

Eyewitness Travel Guides. *Italy*. London: Dorling Kindersley Publishers, 2006.

Facaros, Dana, and M. Pauls. *The Bay of Naples, Amalfi Coast and Southern Italy*. 2nd ed. Guilford, Conn.: Globe Pequot, 1996.

Hoffman, Paul. *The Sunny Side of the Alps and Year-round delights in South Tyrol and the Dolomites*. New York: Henry Holt, 1995.

Jones, Tobias. *The Dark Heart of Italy: Travels through Time and Space across Italy*. London: Faber & Faber, 2003.

McIntosh, Colin. *Oxford Italian Grammar and Verbs*. Oxford: Oxford University Press, 2002.

Morris, Jan. *Trieste and the Meaning of Nowhere*. London: Faber & Faber, 2002.

———. *Venice*. London: Faber & Faber, 1993.

Neale, C. Gordon. *Buying a House in Italy*. London: Vacation—Work, 2005.

Parks, Tim. *Italian Neighbours: An Englishman in Verona*. New York: Vintage, 2001.

Pavone, Ornella, ed. *Bed & Breakfast in Italy*. Milan: Touring Club Italiano, 2002.

Richards, Charles. *The New Italians*. London: Penguin, 1995.

Severgnini, Beppe. *La Bella Figura: A Field Guide to the Italian Mind*. New York: Broadway Books, 2006.

Shah, Michele. *Wines of Italy*. London: Michael Beazley, 2006.

Ward, Travis Neighbour, and Monica Larner. *Living, Studying and Working in Italy: Everything You Need to Know to Live the Dolce Vita*. New York: Owl Books, 2003.

I. USEFUL WEBSITES

Agnelli Foundation: http://www.fga.it/
Bank of Italy: http://www.bancaditalia.it/
CGIL: http://www.cgil.it/
Christian Democracy: http://www.sturzo.it/
Confindustria: http://www.confindustria.it/
Democratici di Sinistra: http://www.dsonline.it/partito/index.asp
Film: http://www.luce.it/istitutoluce/index.htm
Forza Italia: http://www.forza-italia.it/index3.htm
Government: http://www.governo.it/
Istituto Affari internazionali: http://www.iai.it/
Istituto Gramsci: http://www.gramsci.it/
Ministry for Foreign Affairs: http://www.esteri.it/ita/index.asp
Ministry for Universities and Research: http://www.miur.it/
National Archives: http://www.archivi.beniculturali.it/ACS/index.html
National Association of Partisans: http://www.resistenzaitaliana.it/

National Council for Research: http://www.cnr.it/sitocnr/home.html
National Statistical Agency: http://www.istat.it/
Parliament: http://www.parlamento.it/
Risorgimento: http://www.risorgimento.it/risorgimento/home_istituto.htm
Soccer: http://www.lega-calcio.it/
Television: http://www.rai.it/
U.S. Embassy: http://rome.usembassy.gov/english/

About the Authors

Mark F. Gilbert was born in Chesterfield, UK, in September 1961. He was educated at University College, Durham, and the University of Wales, College of Swansea, where he took his Ph.D. in December 1990. After teaching for Dickinson College's European Studies program in Bologna, Italy, he was assistant professor of political science at Dickinson College's home campus in Carlisle, Pennsylvania, between 1993 and 1996. Between September 1997 and June 2002, he was lecturer in Italian studies in the Department of European Studies and Modern Languages at the University of Bath, England. Since June 2002, he has been associate professor of contemporary European history at the University of Trento in Italy, as well as adjunct professor at the Johns Hopkins School for Advanced International Studies in Bologna and visiting research fellow of the Department of History, Birkbeck College, University of London. He became a fellow of the Royal Historical Society in June 2005. Mark Gilbert is the author of *The Italian Revolution: The End of Politics, Italian Style?* (Westview, 1995), and, with Anna Cento Bull, has also published *The Lega Nord and the Northern Question in Italian Politics* (Palgrave, 2001).

K. Robert Nilsson was born in Kearny, New Jersey, in 1927. After service in the U.S. Army Air Corps (1945–1947), he received his B.A. from Temple University and an M.A. in international relations from the Johns Hopkins University School of Advanced International Studies (including a year at the Bologna Center of SAIS that inspired an abiding interest in that country). While studying for his Ph.D. at Columbia University, he was enabled by a Fulbright grant to return to Bologna for dissertation research. In 1962, he began teaching European political systems, international relations, and the politics of modernization at Dickinson College in Carlisle, Pennsylvania. In 1965, he was asked by the college to establish a Center for International Studies in Bologna, which, in 2000, was posthumously renamed the K. Robert Nilsson Center for European Studies. As a student, as center director/professor, and on several sabbaticals, he spent over a dozen years living in Italy.

For a time he was chairman of the Italy Seminar at the Foreign Service Institute of the Department of State and was editor of the newsletter of the Conference Group on Italian Politics and Society. He wrote on international questions in general and Italian issues in particular in publications in the United States and Italy and was a member of the monthly University Seminar on Modern Italy at Columbia University. His retirement was spent in Carlisle, Pennsylvania, with frequent returns to Europe.